The
Promulgation
of *Universal*
Peace

The Promulgation of Universal Peace

Talks Delivered by
'Abdu'l-Bahá during
His Visit to the United States
and Canada in 1912

Compiled by Howard MacNutt

Bahá'í
PUBLISHING

Wilmette, Illinois

Library of Congress Cataloging in Publication Data
Abdu'l-Bahá, 1844–1921.
  [Speeches. English. Selections]
  The promulgation of universal peace : talks delivered by 'Abdu'l-Bahá during
his visit to the United States and Canada in 1912 / by 'Abdu'l-Bahá ; compiled by
Howard MacNutt.
    p. cm.
  Includes index.
  ISBN 978-1-931847-98-8 (alk. paper)
  1. Bahai Faith. I. MacNutt, Howard. II. Title.
  BP363.A3 2012
  297.9'3824—dc23
                                  2012001969

The Promulgation of Universal Peace was first published in two volumes, one
appearing in 1922, the second in 1925 (though pages 233 through 336 were
set in type and plated in 1922). In 1939 flat sheets of the two volumes were
bound as one volume, which retained the original introduction in English
and Persian. In 1943 the two volumes were reprinted as one volume without
the Persian introduction. The 1982 edition incorporated the original English
introduction and a new foreword. The 2007 edition includes paragraph
numbers and a talk given by 'Abdu'l-Bahá in Montreal, in Coronation Hall,
on September 3, 1912.

Cover design by Andrew Johnson
Book design by Patrick Falso

Contents

Contents

Contents

Contents

Contents

Contents

Contents

The
Promulgation
of Universal
Peace

This special centenary edition of
The Promulgation of Universal Peace is being published
in honor of the 100th anniversary
of the talks given by 'Abdu'l-Bahá in North America
in 1912.

Foreword to 1982 Edition

It is with great pleasure and a sense of the appropriateness of the time that we publish this new edition of *The Promulgation of Universal Peace,* for this year, 1982, marks the seventieth anniversary of the historic visit of 'Abdu'l-Bahá, son of Bahá'u'lláh, the Prophet-Founder of the Bahá'í Faith, to the American continent—an event that was to have a profound impact both on the young Faith's evolution throughout the world and on the lives of countless individuals. In 1908 the Young Turks Revolution had overthrown the tyrannical regime of the Ottoman Sulṭán 'Abdu'l-Ḥamíd. One of the first actions of the new leadership released all former political and religious prisoners, one of whom was 'Abdu'l-Bahá, Who had shared with His father forty years of persecution and exile, as well as sixteen additional years after His father's death.

Freed from the straitened and often dire circumstances under which He had conducted the Bahá'í Faith's affairs throughout the early years of His ministry as His father's appointed successor, 'Abdu'l-Bahá at once began to contemplate a sojourn to the West. Such a trip would serve both to strengthen the faith of the isolated groups of Bahá'ís throughout the European and North American continents and to garner publicity for the Faith. Thus 'Abdu'l-Bahá first traveled from the Holy Land to Egypt, then to Europe in 1911, returning to Egypt again for the winter. On 25 March 1912 He sailed from Alexandria—His destination: New York, and a journey that ultimately would take Him across the entire North American continent, with stops in many of the major cities of the United States.

For nine months, 239 days in all, 'Abdu'l-Bahá traveled constantly, up and down the Eastern seaboard from Maine to Washington, D.C., into the Chicago heartland, and back again, stopping in such cities as Philadelphia, Pittsburgh, and Cleveland, finally traversing the continent via Montreal, Minneapolis, St. Paul, and Denver to the west coast, after which He returned to New York, pausing for extended periods in some of the cities He had already visited. When 'Abdu'l-Bahá sailed from New York on 5 December 1912 He had completed one of the most strenuous teaching journeys in all recorded religious history, the more remarkable because it was accomplished by a man of sixty-eight Whose health was broken by long years of deprivation and imprisonment. He left behind Him a band of believers whom, though scattered and separated by long distances, His patient and persistent efforts had welded into a nascent Bahá'í community.

The Promulgation of Universal Peace is a compilation of many of the talks 'Abdu'l-Bahá gave during His visit to the United States and Canada, talks that expounded the principles of the Bahá'í Faith as promulgated by Bahá'u'lláh. Time and time again, to all who came to listen, Bahá'ís and non-Bahá'ís alike, He spoke of the equality of men and women, the harmony of science and religion, the need for universal education and universal language, the independent investigation of truth, the oneness of God, the oneness and continuity of the Prophets of God, the oneness of mankind, and the elimination of prejudices of all kinds—all essential for the universal peace that Bahá'u'lláh came to bring, and that gives the book its theme and title.

Though *The Promulgation of Universal Peace* is a compilation of talks and, therefore, not strictly speaking a work by 'Abdu'l-Bahá, yet it has a unique "style" of its own and a unique place in His collected writings and talks. His *Will and Testament,* written in three sections, provides the authority for the Administrative Order of the Bahá'í Faith and ensures its integrity and unity.

The Secret of Divine Civilization is a treatise on the general state of modern civilization. *A Traveler's Narrative* chronicles the early history of the Bábí and Bahá'í Faiths. *Memorials of the Faithful* contains 'Abdu'l-Bahá's remembrances of seventy-nine early Bahá'ís, all bound by their love for Bahá'u'lláh. *Some Answered Questions* is perhaps closest in format to *The Promulgation of Universal Peace*—a series of discourses on a variety of topics. But *Some Answered Questions* was shaped by questions put to 'Abdu'l-Bahá. In *The Promulgation of Universal Peace* 'Abdu'l-Bahá, for the most part, chose the topics—chose them with care and determination, sometimes even with deliberate repetition. For He had come to the West, not as a tourist, but as an emissary, as it were, of His father. Upon His arrival in New York He stated that "It is my purpose to set forth in America the fundamental principles of the revelation and teachings of Bahá'u'lláh."

And that is exactly what He did. This new edition of *The Promulgation of Universal Peace* enables us once again, seventy years after the talks were first given, to sit in the front row and listen as 'Abdu'l-Bahá patiently explains facet after facet of the Bahá'í Faith, showing how each can help bring hope and peace and balm to our troubled world, until we have the courage, as He said we must, "to give these principles unfoldment and application in the minds, hearts, and lives of the people."

Introduction to 1922 Edition

Two years before the crash of world war shook the continents and upheaved oceans 'Abdu'l-Bahá 'Abbás visited the United States of America, proclaiming the Glad Tidings of Universal Peace and the oneness of the world of humanity. In His message He reviewed social, religious and political conditions of the nations, foretold clearly the impending clash and conflict of militarism, summoning mankind to the standard of divine guidance upraised in this cycle of the cycles by the manifestation and teachings of Bahá'u'lláh. His visit, extending from April to December 1912, covered an itinerary across the continent and return, involving an extraordinary and incredible expenditure of energy on the part of One Who at the threshold of threescore years and ten had spent practically His whole lifetime in exile and imprisonment for the Cause of God.

This treasury of His words is a compilation of informal talks and extemporary discourses delivered in Persian and Arabic, interpreted by proficient linguists who accompanied Him, and taken stenographically in both Oriental and Occidental tongue.

Upon the day of His arrival in New York He said, "It is my purpose to set forth in America the fundamental principles of the revelation and teachings of Bahá'u'lláh. It will then become the duty of the Bahá'ís of this country to give these principles unfoldment and application in the minds, hearts and lives of the people." 'Abdu'l-Bahá's words, therefore, will be found characterized by a broad, clear simplicity and practical basis, marked by an absence of metaphysical flights, philosophical speculation and mere rhetorical eloquence, always reflecting the pure beauty of the Word of God, that primal, essential, eternal foundation upon which rest religion, science and all human advancement.

Everywhere in His journeying throughout the United States 'Abdu'l-Bahá was received and welcomed in a spirit of love and reverence. Temples and churches of all denominations, synagogues, peace societies, religious and educational institutions, colleges, women's clubs, metaphysical groups and new-thought centers opened their doors, pulpits and platforms willingly and without reservation to His message. He attended peace conferences at Lake Mohonk, visited the open forum at Green Acre on the Piscataqua, addressed large gatherings at Columbia and Leland Stanford Universities, spoke before scientific associations, socialistic bodies, ethical cults, welfare and charitable organizations, attended receptions and banquets in the mansions of the rich, visited the poor and lowly in their humble homes, carried the light of hope and uplift to darkened souls in Bowery Mission—in brief, proclaimed His message and teachings universally to every degree and capacity of humankind, with such pure and sincere motive that all heard Him gladly and without prejudice or antagonism. Furthermore, His beneficent activity in the Cause of God and loving service to mankind was without money and without price, for 'Abdu'l-Bahá in no instance accepted remuneration, a most unusual precedent and a wholesome variation from the money-getting methods of other visitors from the Orient. On the contrary, it was His custom to make liberal donations to needy churches and religious bodies, often assisting by generous gift and contribution societies and associations devoted to universal principles and ideals. Standing in the doorway of Bowery Mission one night He distributed two hundred dollars in silver to a long line of poor, disconsolate men, speaking words of uplift and encouragement as they passed before Him. Under all circumstances 'Abdu'l-Bahá refused to accept money for Himself or the Cause He represented. When the Bahá'ís of this country received word of His intended visit, the sum of eighteen thousand dollars was subscribed towards the expense of His journey. He was notified of this action, and a part of the money forwarded to Him by cable. He cabled in answer that the funds contributed by His friends could not be accepted, returned the money and instructed them to give their offering to the poor.

Briefly, the visit of 'Abdu'l-Bahá to the United States was unique and characteristic of His high, holy mission, reflecting an unmistakable altruism of purpose and purity of motive. Philosophers, scientists, agnostics, materialists, professors, diplomats and officials were found in His audiences intently listening, sincerely questioning His presentation of the exalted principles and perfect ideals of the Bahá'í revelation in their application to the education, uplift and unification of mankind. Everywhere in editorial comment and publication of news concerning Him the daily press was reverent and respectful in its tone and statement, instinctively recognizing His high purpose and the manifest virtue of His teachings to the world.

An understanding of the mission and significance of this radiant herald of the New Day would not be complete without vision of the cumulative chain of religious history which extends backward from the time of 'Abdu'l-Bahá's appearance here to a period practically contemporary with the birth of American Independence in 1776. This is of especial importance, too, in the light of the fact that when Bahá'u'lláh sent epistles to the kings and rulers of the earth in 1868 He addressed one to the republic of the United States, in which He said, "O concourse of rulers! . . . Bind ye the broken with the hands of justice, and crush the oppressor who flourisheth with the rod of the commandments of your Lord, the Ordainer, the All-Wise."* A very brief summary will be sufficient to show this spiritual sequence and historical progression of which 'Abdu'l-Bahá is the apex and consummation.

The earliest dawning rays of the effulgent Sun of Truth, the Word of God which shone forth from the heaven of divine will upon the horizon of the human world in this luminous cycle, were reflected in the pure mirrors of sanctity Shaykh Aḥmad-i-Aḥsá'í and Ḥájí Siyyid Kázim-i-Rashtí. As stars of morning precede the coming of the mighty luminary of day, these brilliant souls arose successively in Persia toward the close of the eighteenth century, piercing the somber shadows of night and proclaiming the splendor of the approaching manifestation. This mission completed, the lamps of their physical existence were extinguished in 1826 and 1844 respectively.

On 23 May 1844 Mírzá 'Alí-Muḥammad, the Báb, suddenly enkindled the world by declaring in Shíráz, Persia, that the Day of God was at hand. For six years as Herald and Forerunner this winsome messenger of the kingdom sounded His heavenly call, until in 1850 the flaming tongue and pen of His eloquence were stilled in the throes of a glorious martyrdom.

Then the heaven of religion overspread with the brilliant radiance of Bahá'u'lláh, the Glory of God, the manifest Word and Sun of Reality which poured its bounty upon the world of mankind forty years, extending to the time of its occultation [i.e., Bahá'u'lláh's passing] in 1892. Throughout these years this glorious being was subjected to continuous exile, imprisonment and oppression by earthly rulers, until after infinite hardships and suffering He as-

---

* The Tablet was actually addressed by Bahá'u'lláh to the "Rulers of America and the Presidents of the Republics therein." (See Bahá'u'lláh, *The Proclamation of Bahá'u'lláh to the Kings and Leaders of the World* [Haifa: Bahá'í World Centre, 1967], p. 63).

cended from these abject conditions and surroundings of religious and political tyranny to His abode in the supreme world.

But the equation of divine purpose was not yet complete. The coming of Bahá'u'lláh had fulfilled the prophetic promises of the sacred books of the Jews, Christians, Muslims, Zoroastrians, Hindus, Buddhists and others. Like mighty rivers restricted to their own watersheds these separate systems of religious belief and worship, incapable of mingling in their courses, had found their destined union and confluence in the infinite ocean of Bahá'u'lláh's utterance. Furthermore, the supreme and ultimate product of divine revelation, the apotheosis of prophecy and the universal outcome in which all the heavenly religions would consummate was that quintessence of the cycles, that "Mystery of God," a perfected "Servant" in whom the divine and human wills had found complete blending. This sanctified personage was to appear in the great Day of God, that Day of universal splendor when "the glory of the Lord shall be revealed, and all flesh shall see it together."

In the latter half of the nineteenth century the nations and peoples of the world had become so closely associated and wrought together in their physical existence, so interwoven and interdependent in the necessities and requirements of life, that the problems and politics of one government now affected and influenced the conditions of them all. The world had become one vast human family wherein interests were intimately related, responsibilities mutual and problems universal. Therefore, the Word of God revealed by Bahá'u'lláh was universal in its provision and remedy for the conditions of mankind—conditions which, although they were direct outcomes of human will and making, had been eternally foreseen by the omniscient eye and spoken by the tongues of prophets as recorded in all the holy books. Great numbers of brilliant souls throughout the east had accepted and followed this manifest standard of unity and reconciliation. In religious heredity, training and belief they had been diverse, hostile and irreconcilable, but under the benign, penetrating influence of the Holy Spirit of the Word made flesh in Bahá'u'lláh, they attained the blessed station of oneness and love in the heaven of the kingdom.

To strengthen, safeguard and increase this unity and love Bahá'u'lláh appointed a successor to Whom all should turn for guidance and illumination after His own departure, naming in the Book of the Covenant written by His own blessed hand His eldest son, the Greatest Branch, 'Abdu'l-Bahá, Center of the Covenant in Whom Bahá'ís throughout the world recognize the authority of perfect servitude at the threshold of the manifest Word. This is the essence of His title, entity and being, 'Abdu'l-Bahá, Servant of Bahá.

The great wisdom of this appointment is shown in many ways. It is particularly evident when we realize that from His earliest childhood 'Abdu'l-Bahá had been inseparably associated with Bahá'u'lláh. Born in Ṭihrán 23 May 1844, the day and date of the Báb's declaration, His very birth foretokened the significance of His life and being in the divine processes and consummations of this luminous cycle. At the age of eight years He was one of the little band of exiles who crossed the Persian border into 'Iráq, sharing vicissitudes and suffering with heroic strength and subjected with the rest to continuous imprisonments in various cities until they reached the prison-fortress of 'Akká in Syria [now Israel], 31 August 1868. Throughout this long and faithful vigil of devotion to Bahá'u'lláh and loyalty to the Cause of God, the record of 'Abdu'l-Bahá's life is pure and spotless, wonderful in its exaltation and effulgent with the beauty of holiness. When the tyrannous regime of Sulṭán 'Abdu'l-Ḥamíd ended, the gates of 'Akká were thrown open and 'Abdu'l-Bahá came forth free upon the fortieth anniversary of His entrance into that neglected and unspeakable place. This was 31 August 1908. In 1911, two years after His release from a living martyrdom of fifty-six years and at the age of sixty-seven, He visited Europe, returning to Egypt from whence in 1912 He sailed for America as stated.

Thus far the evidences of divine forces and influences surrounding the life of 'Abdu'l-Bahá should be sufficient to impress and convince any thoughtful soul that we are viewing an unusual and majestic personality, a world-commanding figure Who has appeared for the uplift, unification and peace of mankind. Dark indeed are the world horizons unless we behold the shining beauty of this Sun of Reality. The human world, plunging deeper and deeper with ever-increasing momentum into seas of materialism, is crying out in its crucial need and stress for help and remedy, for a new creative spirit of life and regeneration, a power and healing direct from God. And just at this time 'Abdu'l-Bahá, messenger of Universal Peace and the oneness of the world of humanity, is sounding His call of salvation to the nations of the earth in heavenly words fortified by an impelling dynamic spiritual power and surcharged with the pure breaths of the Holy Spirit. . . .

'Abdu'l-Bahá's station of servitude in the divine Cause is . . . worldwide and universal, beyond the limitation of race, denomination, creed or nationality, a station supreme in its loftiness, perfect in its humility—Servant of the servants of God. Significant indeed is His visit to the shores of the western world; pregnant indeed are His words to the highly organized material civilizations of the Occident; potent indeed is His message of peace and unity of mankind, cementing the east and the west in spiritual solidarity, blending the world that is old and the world that is new under the beneficent laws of the heavenly kingdom.

In obedience to the direct command of 'Abdu'l-Bahá, this introduction has been written by a humble follower of His light and a devoted lover of His beauty. May the Glory of God illumine this heart and guide this pen to do His will in this most great responsibility.

HOWARD MACNUTT

Extracts from Tablets

To his honor Mr. Howard MacNutt, Brooklyn, New York, U.S.A.

O thou old friend!

. . . Thy intention to print and publish the discourses of 'Abdu'l-Bahá which thou hast compiled is indeed very advisable. This service shall cause thee to acquire an effulgent face in the Abhá kingdom and shall make thee the object of praise and gratitude of the friends in the East as well as the West. But this is to be undertaken with the utmost carefulness so that the exact text may be reproduced and that all errors and deviations committed by previous interpreters shall be excluded.

ABDUL BAHA ABBAS

(Haifa, Palestine, 13 April 1919)

To his honor Mr. Albert R. Windust, Chicago, Illinois, U.S.A.

O thou servant of His Holiness Baha'Ullah!

. . . Name the book which Mr. MacNutt is compiling "The Promulgation of Universal Peace." As to its Introduction, it should be written by Mr. MacNutt himself when in heart he is turning toward the Abhá kingdom so that he may leave a permanent trace behind him. Send a copy of it to the Holy Land.

ABDUL BAHA ABBAS

(Bahjí, 'Akká, Palestine, 20 July 1919)

The
Promulgation
of Universal
Peace

Talks 'Abdu'l-Bahá Delivered in New York and Brooklyn

11 April 1912

Talk at Home of Mr. and Mrs. Edward B. Kinney
780 West End Avenue, New York

NOTES BY HOOPER HARRIS

HOW are you? Welcome! Welcome! 1

After arriving today, although weary with travel, I had the 2
utmost longing and yearning to see you and could not resist
this meeting. Now that I have met you, all my weariness has
vanished, for your meeting is the cause of spiritual happiness.

I was in Egypt and was not feeling well, but I wished to come 3
to you in America. My friends said, "This is a long journey; the
sea is wide; you should remain here." But the more they advised
and insisted, the greater became my longing to take this trip, and
now I have come to America to meet the friends of God. This
long voyage will prove how great is my love for you. There were
many troubles and vicissitudes, but, in the thought of meeting
you, all these things vanished and were forgotten.

I am greatly pleased with the city of New York. Its harbor 4
entrance, its piers, buildings and broad avenues are magnificent
and beautiful. Truly, it is a wonderful city. As New York has
made such progress in material civilization, I hope that it may
also advance spiritually in the Kingdom and Covenant of God
so that the friends here may become the cause of the illumination of America, that this city may become the city of love and
that the fragrances of God may be spread from this place to all
parts of the world. I have come for this. I pray that you may be

manifestations of the love of Bahá'u'lláh, that each one of you may become like a clear lamp of crystal from which the rays of the bounties of the Blessed Perfection may shine forth to all nations and peoples. This is my highest aspiration.

5   It was a long, long trip. The more we traveled, the greater seemed the expanse of the sea. The weather was brilliant and fine throughout; there was no storm and no end to the sea.

6   I am very happy to meet you all here today. Praise be to God that your faces are shining with the love of Bahá'u'lláh. To behold them is the cause of great spiritual happiness. We have arranged to meet you every day at the homes of the friends.

7   In the East people were asking me, "Why do you undertake this long voyage? Your body cannot endure such hardships of travel." When it is necessary, my body can endure everything. It has withstood forty years of imprisonment and can still undergo the utmost trials.

8   I will see you again. Now I will greet each one of you personally. It is my hope that you will all be happy and that we may meet again and again.

2

12 April 1912

Talk at Home of Mr. and Mrs. Howard MacNutt
935 Eastern Parkway, Brooklyn, New York

NOTES BY HOWARD MACNUTT

1   THIS is a most happy visit. I have crossed the sea from the land of the Orient for the joy of meeting the friends of God. Although I am weary after my long journey, the light of the spirit

shining in your faces brings me rest and reward. In this meeting the divine susceptibilities are radiant. This is a spiritual house, the home of the spirit. There is no discord here; all is love and unity. When souls are gathered together in this way, the divine bestowals descend. The purpose of the creation of man is the attainment of the supreme virtues of humanity through descent of the heavenly bestowals. The purpose of man's creation is, therefore, unity and harmony, not discord and separateness. If the atoms which compose the kingdom of the minerals were without affinity for each other, the earth would never have been formed, the universe could not have been created. Because they have affinity for each other, the power of life is able to manifest itself, and the organisms of the phenomenal world become possible. When this attraction or atomic affinity is destroyed, the power of life ceases to manifest; death and nonexistence result.

It is so, likewise, in the spiritual world. That world is the 2 Kingdom of complete attraction and affinity. It is the Kingdom of the One Divine Spirit, the Kingdom of God. Therefore, the affinity and love manifest in this meeting, the divine susceptibilities witnessed here are not of this world but of the world of the Kingdom. When the souls become separated and selfish, the divine bounties do not descend, and the lights of the Supreme Concourse are no longer reflected even though the bodies meet together. A mirror with its back turned to the sun has no power to reflect the sun's effulgence. Praise be to God! The purpose of this assembly is love and unity.

The divine Prophets came to establish the unity of the King- 3 dom in human hearts. All of them proclaimed the glad tidings of the divine bestowals to the world of mankind. All brought the same message of divine love to the world. Jesus Christ gave His life upon the cross for the unity of mankind. Those who believed in Him likewise sacrificed life, honor, possessions, family, everything, that this human world might be released from

5

the hell of discord, enmity and strife. His foundation was the oneness of humanity. Only a few were attracted to Him. They were not the kings and rulers of His time. They were not rich and important people. Some of them were catchers of fish. Most of them were ignorant men, not trained in the knowledge of this world. One of the greatest of them, Peter, could not remember the days of the week. All of them were men of the least consequence in the eyes of the world. But their hearts were pure and attracted by the fires of the Divine Spirit manifested in Christ. With this small army Christ conquered the world of the East and the West. Kings and nations rose against Him. Philosophers and the greatest men of learning assailed and blasphemed His Cause. All were defeated and overcome, their tongues silenced, their lamps extinguished, their hatred quenched; no trace of them now remains. They have become as nonexistent, while His Kingdom is triumphant and eternal.

4   The brilliant star of His Cause has ascended to the zenith, while night has enveloped and eclipsed His enemies. His name, beloved and adored by a few disciples, now commands the reverence of kings and nations of the world. His power is eternal; His sovereignty will continue forever, while those who opposed Him are sleeping in the dust, their very names unknown, forgotten. The little army of disciples has become a mighty cohort of millions. The Heavenly Host, the Supreme Concourse are His legions; the Word of God is His sword; the power of God is His victory.

5   Jesus Christ knew this would come to pass and was content to suffer. His abasement was His glorification; His crown of thorns, a heavenly diadem. When they pressed it upon His blessed head and spat in His beautiful face, they laid the foundation of His everlasting Kingdom. He still reigns, while they and their names have become lost and unknown. He is eternal and glorious;

they are nonexistent. They sought to destroy Him, but they destroyed themselves and increased the intensity of His flame by the winds of their opposition.

Through His death and teachings we have entered into His Kingdom. His essential teaching was the unity of mankind and the attainment of supreme human virtues through love. He came to establish the Kingdom of peace and everlasting life. Can you find in His words any justification for discord and enmity? The purpose of His life and the glory of His death were to set mankind free from the sins of strife, war and bloodshed. The great nations of the world boast that their laws and civilization are based upon the religion of Christ. Why then do they make war upon each other? The Kingdom of Christ cannot be upheld by destroying and disobeying it. The banners of His armies cannot lead the forces of Satan. Consider the sad picture of Italy carrying war into Tripoli. If you should announce that Italy was a barbarous nation and not Christian, this would be vehemently denied. But would Christ sanction what they are doing in Tripoli? Is this destruction of human life obedience to His laws and teachings? Where does He command it? Where does He consent to it? He was killed by His enemies; He did not kill. He even loved and prayed for those who hung Him on the cross. Therefore, these wars and cruelties, this bloodshed and sorrow are Antichrist, not Christ. These are the forces of death and Satan, not the hosts of the Supreme Concourse of heaven.

No less bitter is the conflict between sects and denominations. Christ was a divine Center of unity and love. Whenever discord prevails instead of unity, wherever hatred and antagonism take the place of love and spiritual fellowship, Antichrist reigns instead of Christ. Who is right in these controversies and hatreds between the sects? Did Christ command them to love or to hate each other? He loved even His enemies and prayed in the hour

7

of His crucifixion for those who killed Him. Therefore, to be a Christian is not merely to bear the name of Christ and say, "I belong to a Christian government." To be a real Christian is to be a servant in His Cause and Kingdom, to go forth under His banner of peace and love toward all mankind, to be self-sacrificing and obedient, to become quickened by the breaths of the Holy Spirit, to be mirrors reflecting the radiance of the divinity of Christ, to be fruitful trees in the garden of His planting, to refresh the world by the water of life of His teachings—in all things to be like Him and filled with the spirit of His love.

8   Praise be to God! The light of unity and love is shining in these faces. These spiritual susceptibilities are the real fruits of heaven. The Báb and Bahá'u'lláh over sixty years ago proclaimed the glad tidings of universal peace. The Báb was martyred in the Cause of God. Bahá'u'lláh suffered forty years as a prisoner and exile in order that the Kingdom of love might be established in the East and West. He has made it possible for us to meet here in love and unity. Because He suffered imprisonment, we are free to proclaim the oneness of the world of humanity for which He stood so long and faithfully. He was chained in dungeons, He was without food, His companions were thieves and criminals, He was subjected to every kind of abuse and infliction, but throughout it all He never ceased to proclaim the reality of the Word of God and the oneness of humanity. We have been brought together here by the power of His Word—you from America, I from Persia—all in love and unity of spirit. Was this possible in former centuries? If it is possible now after fifty years of sacrifice and teaching, what shall we expect in the wonderful centuries coming?

9   Therefore, let your faces be more radiant with hope and heavenly determination to serve the Cause of God, to spread the pure fragrances of the divine rose garden of unity, to awaken

spiritual susceptibilities in the hearts of mankind, to kindle anew the spirit of humanity with divine fires and to reflect the glory of heaven to this gloomy world of materialism. When you possess these divine susceptibilities, you will be able to awaken and develop them in others. We cannot give of our wealth to the poor unless we possess it. How can the poor give to the poor? How can the soul that is deprived of the heavenly bounties develop in other souls capacity to receive those bounties?

Array yourselves in the perfection of divine virtues. I hope 10 you may be quickened and vivified by the breaths of the Holy Spirit. Then shall ye indeed become the angels of heaven whom Christ promised would appear in this Day to gather the harvest of divine planting. This is my hope. This is my prayer for you.

3

12 April 1912

Talk at Studio of Miss Phillips
39 West Sixty-seventh Street, New York

NOTES BY JOHN G. GRUNDY

I GIVE you greeting in love and unity. The affairs of this world 1 are to be accounted as nothing compared to the joy and heavenly happiness of meeting the friends of God. It is to experience this great joy and blessing that I have come here although weary from my long voyage upon the sea. Tonight I am in the greatest happiness, looking upon this concourse of God. Your meeting here is surely an evidence that you are upholding the Cause of God, that you are aiding and assisting in establishing the Kingdom of God. Therefore, the culmination of my happiness is to look upon your faces and realize that you have been brought together by the power of the Blessed Perfection, Bahá'u'lláh. In this meeting you are upholding His standard and assisting His Cause. Therefore, I behold in you the making of a goodly tree upon which divine fruits will appear to give sustenance to the world of humanity.

2   With hearts set aglow by the fire of the love of God and spirits refreshed by the food of the heavenly spirit you must go forth as the disciples nineteen hundred years ago, quickening the hearts of men by the call of glad tidings, the light of God in your faces, severed from everything save God. Therefore, order your lives in accordance with the first principle of the divine teaching, which is love. Service to humanity is service to God. Let the love and light of the Kingdom radiate through you until all who look upon you shall be illumined by its reflection. Be as stars, brilliant and sparkling in the loftiness of their heavenly station. Do you appreciate the Day in which you live?

3   This is the century of the Blessed Perfection!

4   This is the cycle of the light of His beauty!

5   This is the consummate day of all the Prophets!

6   These are the days of seed sowing. These are the days of tree planting. The bountiful bestowals of God are successive. He who sows a seed in this day will behold his reward in the fruits and harvest of the heavenly Kingdom. This timely seed, when planted in the hearts of the beloved of God, will be watered by showers of divine mercy and warmed by the sunshine of divine love. Its fruitage and flower shall be the solidarity of mankind, the perfection of justice and the praiseworthy attributes of heaven manifest in humanity. All who sow such a seed and plant such a tree according to the teachings of Bahá'u'lláh shall surely witness this divine outcome in the degrees of its perfection and will attain unto the good pleasure of the Merciful One.

Today the nations of the world are self-engaged, occupied 7 with mortal and transitory accomplishments, consumed by the fires of passion and self. Self is dominant; enmity and animosity prevail. Nations and peoples are thinking only of their worldly interests and outcomes. The clash of war and din of strife are heard among them. But the friends of the Blessed Perfection have no thoughts save the thoughts of heaven and the love of God. Therefore, you must without delay employ your powers in spreading the effulgent glow of the love of God and so order your lives that you may be known and seen as examples of its radiance. You must deal with all in loving-kindness in order that this precious seed entrusted to your planting may continue to grow and bring forth its perfect fruit. The love and mercy of God will accomplish this through you if you have love in your own heart.

The doors of the Kingdom are opened. The lights of the Sun 8 of Truth are shining. The clouds of divine mercy are raining down their priceless jewels. The zephyrs of a new and divine springtime are wafting their fragrant breaths from the invisible world. Know ye then the value of these days.

Awake ye to the realization of this heavenly opportunity. 9 Strive with all the power of your souls, your deeds, actions and words to assist the spread of these glad tidings and the descent of this merciful bounty. You are the reality and expression of your deeds and actions. If you abide by the precepts and teachings of the Blessed Perfection, the heavenly world and ancient Kingdom will be yours—eternal happiness, love and everlasting life. The divine bounties are flowing. Each one of you has been given the opportunity of becoming a tree yielding abundant fruits. This is the springtime of Bahá'u'lláh. The verdure and foliage of spiritual growth are appearing in great abundance in the gardens of human hearts. Know ye the value of these passing days and vanishing nights. Strive to attain a station of absolute love one toward another. By the absence of love, enmity increases. By the exercise of love, love strengthens and enmities dwindle away.

10   Consider me—in the years of my advanced age, burdened with physical infirmities—crossing the wide ocean to look upon your faces. It is my hope that through the life of the spirit you may all become as one soul, as one tree adorning the rose garden of the Kingdom. It is my hope that the endless treasures of the bestowals of God may be yours here and hereafter. It is my prayer that the Supreme Concourse may be illumined by your brilliant lights shining forever in the heavens of eternal glory.

4

13 April 1912

Talk at Home of Mr. and Mrs. Alexander Morten
141 East Twenty-first Street, New York

NOTES BY ESTHER FOSTER

1   PRAISE be to God! This is a radiant gathering. The faces are brilliant with the light of God. The hearts are attracted to the Kingdom of Bahá. I beg of God that day by day your faces may become brighter; day by day you may draw nearer to God; day by day you may take a greater portion from the outpourings of the Holy Spirit so that you may become encircled by the bounties of heaven.

2   The spiritual world is like unto the phenomenal world. They are the exact counterpart of each other. Whatever objects appear in this world of existence are the outer pictures of the world of heaven. When we look upon the phenomenal world, we perceive

that it is divided into four seasons; one is the season of spring, another the season of summer, another autumn and then these three seasons are followed by winter. When the season of spring appears in the arena of existence, the whole world is rejuvenated and finds new life. The soul-refreshing breeze is wafted from every direction; the soul-quickening bounty is everywhere; the cloud of mercy showers down its rain, and the sun shines upon everything. Day by day we perceive that the signs of vegetation are all about us. Wonderful flowers, hyacinths and roses perfume the nostrils. The trees are full of leaves and blossoms, and the blossoms are followed by fruit. The spring and summer are followed by autumn and winter. The flowers wither and are no more; the leaves turn gray and life has gone. Then comes another springtime; the former springtime is renewed; again a new life stirs within everything.

The appearances of the Manifestations of God are the divine springtime. When Christ appeared in this world, it was like the vernal bounty; the outpouring descended; the effulgences of the Merciful encircled all things; the human world found new life. Even the physical world partook of it. The divine perfections were upraised; souls were trained in the school of heaven so that all grades of human existence received life and light. Then by degrees these fragrances of heaven were discontinued; the season of winter came upon the world; the beauties of spring vanished; the excellences and perfections passed away; the lights and quickening were no longer evident; the phenomenal world and its materialities conquered everything; the spiritualities of life were lost; the world of existence became like unto a lifeless body; there was no trace of the spring left. 3

Bahá'u'lláh has come into this world. He has renewed that springtime. The same fragrances are wafting; the same heat of the Sun is giving life; the same cloud is pouring its rain, and with our own eyes we see that the world of existence is advancing and progressing. The human world has found new life. 4

5   I hope that each and all of you may become like unto verdant and green trees so that through the breezes of the divine spring, the outpouring of heaven, the heat of the Sun of Truth, you may become eternally refreshed; that you may bear blossoms and become fruitful; that you may not be as fruitless trees. Fruitless trees do not bring forth fruits or flowers. I hope that all of you may become friends of the paradise of Abhá, appearing with the utmost freshness and spiritual beauty. I pray in your behalf and beg of God confirmation and assistance.

5

14 April 1912

Talk at Church of the Ascension
Fifth Avenue and Tenth Street, New York

NOTES BY AḤMAD SOHRÁB AND HOWARD MACNUTT

1   IN his scriptural lesson this morning the revered doctor read a verse from the Epistle of St. Paul to the Corinthians, "For now we see through a glass, darkly; but then face to face."

2   The light of truth has heretofore been seen dimly through variegated glasses, but now the splendors of Divinity shall be visible through the translucent mirrors of pure hearts and spirits. The light of truth is the divine teaching, heavenly instruction, merciful principles and spiritual civilization. Since my arrival in this country I find that material civilization has progressed greatly, that commerce has attained the utmost degree of expansion; arts, agriculture and all details of material civilization have reached the highest stage of perfection, but spiritual civiliza-

tion has been left behind. Material civilization is like unto the lamp, while spiritual civilization is the light in that lamp. If the material and spiritual civilization become united, then we will have the light and the lamp together, and the outcome will be perfect. For material civilization is like unto a beautiful body, and spiritual civilization is like unto the spirit of life. If that wondrous spirit of life enters this beautiful body, the body will become a channel for the distribution and development of the perfections of humanity.

Jesus Christ came to teach the people of the world this heavenly 3
civilization and not material civilization. He breathed the breath of the Holy Spirit into the body of the world and established an illumined civilization. Among the principles of divine civilization He came to proclaim is the Most Great Peace of mankind. Among His principles of spiritual civilization is the oneness of the kingdom of humanity. Among the principles of heavenly civilization He brought is the virtue of the human world. Among the principles of celestial civilization He announced is the improvement and betterment of human morals.

Today the world of humanity is in need of international 4
unity and conciliation. To establish these great fundamental principles a propelling power is needed. It is self-evident that the unity of the human world and the Most Great Peace cannot be accomplished through material means. They cannot be established through political power, for the political interests of nations are various and the policies of peoples are divergent and conflicting. They cannot be founded through racial or patriotic power, for these are human powers, selfish and weak. The very nature of racial differences and patriotic prejudices prevents the realization of this unity and agreement. There-fore, it is evidenced that the promotion of the oneness of the kingdom of humanity, which is the essence of the teachings

of all the Manifestations of God, is impossible except through the divine power and breaths of the Holy Spirit. Other powers are too weak and are incapable of accomplishing this.

5   For man two wings are necessary. One wing is physical power and material civilization; the other is spiritual power and divine civilization. With one wing only, flight is impossible. Two wings are essential. Therefore, no matter how much material civilization advances, it cannot attain to perfection except through the uplift of spiritual civilization.

6   All the Prophets have come to promote divine bestowals, to found the spiritual civilization and teach the principles of morality. Therefore, we must strive with all our powers so that spiritual influences may gain the victory. For material forces have attacked mankind. The world of humanity is submerged in a sea of materialism. The rays of the Sun of Reality are seen but dimly and darkly through opaque glasses. The penetrative power of the divine bounty is not fully manifest.

7   In Persia among the various religions and sects there were intense differences. Bahá'u'lláh appeared in that country and founded the spiritual civilization. He established affiliation among the various peoples, promoted the oneness of the human world and unfurled the banner of the Most Great Peace. He wrote special Epistles covering these facts to all the kings and rulers of nations. Sixty years ago He conveyed His message to the leaders of the political world and to high dignitaries of the spiritual world. Therefore, spiritual civilization is progressing in the Orient, and oneness of humanity and peace among the nations is being accomplished step by step. Now I find a strong movement for universal peace emanating from America. It is my hope that this standard of the oneness of the world of humanity may be upraised with the utmost solidity so that the Orient and Occident may become perfectly reconciled and

attain complete intercommunication, the hearts of the East and West become united and attracted, real union become unveiled, the light of guidance shine, divine effulgences be seen day by day so that the world of humanity may find complete tranquillity, the eternal happiness of man become evident and the hearts of the people of the world be as mirrors in which the rays of the Sun of Reality may be reflected. Consequently, it is my request that you should strive so that the light of reality may shine and the everlasting felicity of the world of man become apparent.

I will pray for you so you may attain this everlasting happiness. When I arrived in this city, I was made very happy, for I perceived that the people here have capacity for divine bestowals and have worthiness for the civilization of heaven. I pray that you may attain to all merciful bounties.

8

O Almighty! O God! O Thou compassionate One! This servant of Thine has hastened to the regions of the West from the uttermost parts of the East that, perchance, these nostrils may be perfumed by the fragrances of Thy bestowals; that the breeze of the rose garden of guidance may blow over these cities; that the people may attain to the capacity of receiving Thy favors; that the hearts may be rejoiced through Thy glad tidings; that the eyes may behold the light of reality; that the ears may hearken to the call of the Kingdom. O Almighty! Illumine the hearts. O kind God! Make the souls the envy of the rose garden and the meadow. O incomparable Beloved! Waft the fragrance of Thy bounty. Radiate the lights of compassion so that the hearts may be cleansed and purified and that they may take a share and portion from Thy confirmations. Verily, this congregation is seeking Thy path, searching for Thy mystery, beholding Thy face and desiring to be characterized with Thine attributes.

9

10   O Almighty! Confer Thou infinite bounties. Bestow Thine inexhaustible treasury so that these impotent ones may become powerful.

11   Verily, Thou art the Kind. Thou art the Generous. Thou art the Omniscient, the Omnipotent.

6

14 April 1912

*Talk at Union Meeting of Advanced Thought Centers
Carnegie Lyceum
West Fifty-seventh Street, New York*

NOTES BY MOUNTFORT MILLS AND HOWARD MACNUTT

1   I HAVE come from distant lands to visit the meetings and assemblies of this country. In every meeting I find people gathered, loving each other; therefore, I am greatly pleased. The bond of union is evidenced in this assembly today, where the power of God has brought together in faith, agreement and concord those who are engaged in furthering the development of the human world. It is my hope that all mankind may become similarly united in the bond and agreement of love. Unity is the expression of the loving power of God and reflects the reality of Divinity. It is resplendent in this Day through the bestowals of light upon humanity.

2   Throughout the universe the divine power is effulgent in endless images and pictures. The world of creation, the world of humanity may be likened to the earth itself and the divine power to the sun. This Sun has shone upon all mankind. In the

endless variety of its reflections the divine Will is manifested. Consider how all are recipients of the bounty of the same Sun. At most the difference between them is that of degree, for the effulgence is one effulgence, the one light emanating from the Sun. This will express the oneness of the world of humanity. The body politic, or the social unity of the human world, may be likened to an ocean, and each member, each individual, a wave upon that same ocean.

The light of the sun becomes apparent in each object accord-   3 ing to the capacity of that object. The difference is simply one of degree and receptivity. The stone would be a recipient only to a limited extent; another created thing might be as a mirror wherein the sun is fully reflected; but the same light shines upon both.

The most important thing is to polish the mirrors of hearts   4 in order that they may become illumined and receptive of the divine light. One heart may possess the capacity of the polished mirror; another, be covered and obscured by the dust and dross of this world. Although the same Sun is shining upon both, in the mirror which is polished, pure and sanctified you may behold the Sun in all its fullness, glory and power, revealing its majesty and effulgence; but in the mirror which is rusted and obscured there is no capacity for reflection, although so far as the Sun itself is concerned it is shining thereon and is neither lessened nor deprived. Therefore, our duty lies in seeking to polish the mirrors of our hearts in order that we shall become reflectors of that light and recipients of the divine bounties which may be fully revealed through them.

This means the oneness of the world of humanity. That is to   5 say, when this human body politic reaches a state of absolute unity, the effulgence of the eternal Sun will make its fullest light and heat manifest. Therefore, we must not make distinctions between individual members of the human family. We must not consider any soul as barren or deprived. Our duty lies in educating souls so that the Sun of the bestowals of God shall become resplendent in them, and this is possible through the power of the oneness of humanity. The more love is expressed among mankind and the stronger the power of unity, the greater will be this reflection and revelation, for the greatest bestowal of God is love. Love is the source of all the bestowals of God. Until love takes possession of the heart, no other divine bounty can be revealed in it.

6   All the Prophets have striven to make love manifest in the hearts of men. Jesus Christ sought to create this love in the hearts. He suffered all difficulties and ordeals that perchance the human heart might become the fountain source of love. Therefore, we must strive with all our heart and soul that this love may take possession of us so that all humanity—whether it be in the East or in the West—may be connected through the bond of this divine affection; for we are all the waves of one sea; we have come into being through the same bestowal and are recipients from the same center. The lights of earth are all acceptable, but the center of effulgence is the sun, and we must direct our gaze to the sun. God is the Supreme Center. The more we turn toward this Center of Light, the greater will be our capacity.

7   In the Orient there were great differences among races and peoples. They hated each other, and there was no association among them. Various and divergent sects were hostile, irreconcilable. The different races were in constant war and conflict. About sixty years ago Bahá'u'lláh appeared upon the eastern horizon. He caused love and unity to become manifest among these antagonistic peoples. He united them with the bond of love; their former hatred and animosity passed away; love and

unity reigned instead. It was a dark world; it became radiant. A new springtime appeared through Him, for the Sun of Truth had risen again. In the fields and meadows of human hearts variegated flowers of inner significance were blooming, and the good fruits of the Kingdom of God became manifest.

I have come here with this mission: that through your endeavors, through your heavenly morals, through your devoted efforts a perfect bond of unity and love may be established between the East and the West so that the bestowals of God may descend upon all and that all may be seen to be the parts of the same tree—the great tree of the human family. For mankind may be likened to the branches, leaves, blossoms and fruit of that tree.   8

The favors of God are unending, limitless. Infinite bounties have encompassed the world. We must emulate the bounties of God, and just as each one of them—the bounty of life, for instance—surrounds and encompasses all, so likewise must we be connected and blended together until each part shall become the expression of the whole.   9

Consider: We plant a seed. A complete and perfect tree appears from it, and from each seed of this tree another tree can be produced. Therefore, the part is expressive of the whole, for this seed was a part of the tree, but therein potentially was the whole tree. So each one of us may become expressive or representative of all the bounties of life to mankind. This is the unity of the world of humanity. This is the bestowal of God. This is the felicity of the human world, and this is the manifestation of the divine favor.   10

7

15 April 1912

Talk at Home of Mountfort Mills
327 West End Avenue, New York

<small>COMPILED FROM STENOGRAPHIC NOTES BY HOWARD MACNUTT</small>

1   A FEW days ago I arrived in New York, coming direct from Alexandria. On a former trip I traveled to Europe, visiting Paris and London. Paris is most beautiful in outward appearance. The evidences of material civilization there are very great, but the spiritual civilization is far behind. I found the people of that city submerged and drowning in a sea of materialism. Their conversations and discussions were limited to natural and physical phenomena, without mention of God. I was greatly astonished. Most of the scholars, professors and learned men proved to be materialists. I said to them, "I am surprised and astonished that men of such perceptive caliber and evident knowledge should still be captives of nature, not recognizing the self-evident Reality."

2   The phenomenal world is entirely subject to the rule and control of natural law. These myriad suns, satellites and heavenly bodies throughout endless space are all captives of nature. They cannot transgress in a single point or particular the fixed laws which govern the physical universe. The sun in its immensity, the ocean in its vastness are incapable of violating these universal laws. All phenomenal beings—the plants in their kingdom, even the animals with their intelligence—are nature's subjects and captives. All live within the bounds of natural law, and nature is the ruler of all except man. Man is not the captive of nature, for although according to natural law he is a being of the earth, yet

22

he guides ships over the ocean, flies through the air in airplanes, descends in submarines; therefore, he has overcome natural law and made it subservient to his wishes. For instance, he imprisons in an incandescent lamp the illimitable natural energy called electricity—a material force which can cleave mountains—and bids it give him light. He takes the human voice and confines it in the phonograph for his benefit and amusement. According to his natural power man should be able to communicate a limited distance, but by overcoming the restrictions of nature he can annihilate space and send telephone messages thousands of miles. All the sciences, arts and discoveries were mysteries of nature, and according to natural law these mysteries should remain latent, hidden; but man has proceeded to break this law, free himself from this rule and bring them forth into the realm of the visible. Therefore, he is the ruler and commander of nature. Man has intelligence; nature has not. Man has volition; nature has none. Man has memory; nature is without it. Man has the reasoning faculty; nature is deprived. Man has the perceptive faculty; nature cannot perceive. It is therefore proved and evident that man is nobler than nature.

If we accept the supposition that man is but a part of nature, 3 we are confronted by an illogical statement, for this is equivalent to claiming that a part may be endowed with qualities which are absent in the whole. For man who is a part of nature has perception, intelligence, memory, conscious reflection and susceptibility, while nature itself is quite bereft of them. How is it possible for the part to be possessed of qualities or faculties which are absent in the whole? The truth is that God has given to man certain powers which are supernatural. How then can man be considered a captive of nature? Is he not dominating and controlling nature to his own uses more and more? Is he not the very divinity of nature? Shall we say nature is blind, nature is not perceptive, nature is without volition and not alive, and

23

then relegate man to nature and its limitations? How can we answer this question? How will the materialists and scholastic atheists prove and support such a supposition? As a matter of fact, they themselves make natural laws subservient to their own wish and purpose. The proof is complete that in man there is a power beyond the limitations of nature, and that power is the bestowal of God.

4   In New York I find the people more endowed with spiritual susceptibilities. They are not mere captives of nature's control; they are rising out of the bonds and burden of captivity. For this reason I am very happy and hopeful that, God willing, in this populous country, in this vast continent of the West, the virtues of the world of humanity shall become resplendent; that the oneness of human world-power, the love of God, may enkindle the hearts, and that international peace may hoist its standards, influencing all other regions and countries from here. This is my hope.

8

16 April 1912

Talk at Hotel Ansonia to Bahá'í Friends of New Jersey
Broadway and Seventy-third Street, New York

NOTES BY AHMAD SOHRÁB

1   SOULS from the East and West have been brought together here through the power of the Holy Spirit. Such a gathering as this would be impossible through material means. A meeting of this kind has never been established in New York, for here tonight we find people from remote regions of the earth, associated

with the people of America in the utmost love and spiritual unity. This is only possible through the power of God. Christ appeared in this world nineteen hundred years ago to establish ties of unity and bonds of love between the various nations and different communities. He cemented together the sciences of Rome and the splendors of the civilization of Greece. He also accomplished affiliation between the Assyrian kingdom and the power of Egypt. The blending of these nations in unity, love and agreement had been impossible, but Christ through divine power established this condition among the children of men.

A much greater difficulty confronts us today when we en- 2 deavor to establish unity between the Orient and the Occident. Bahá'u'lláh through the power of heaven has brought the East and the West together. Erelong we shall know that they have been cemented by the power of God. The oneness of the kingdom of humanity will supplant the banner of conquest, and all communities of the earth will gather under its protection. No nation with separate and restricted boundaries—such as Persia, for instance—will exist. The United States of America will be known only as a name. Germany, France, England, Turkey, Arabia—all these various nations will be welded together in unity. When the people of the future are asked, "To which nationality do you belong?" the answer will be, "To the nationality of humanity. I am living under the shadow of Bahá'u'lláh. I am the servant of Bahá'u'lláh. I belong to the army of the Most Great Peace." The people of the future will not say, "I belong to the nation of England, France or Persia"; for all of them will be citizens of a universal nationality—the one family, the one country, the one world of humanity—and then these wars, hatreds and strifes will pass away.

Bahá'u'lláh appeared in a country which was the center of 3 prejudice. In that country were many different communities, religions, sects and denominations. All the animosities of past centuries existed among them. They were ready to kill each other. They considered the killing of others who did not agree with them in religious belief an act of worship. Bahá'u'lláh established such unity and agreement between these various communities that the greatest love and amity are now witnessed among them.

4   Today the Bahá'ís of the East are longing with deep desire to see you face to face. Their highest hope and fondest wish is that the day may come when they will be gathered together in an assembly with you. Consider well the power that accomplished this wonderful transformation.

5   The body of the human world is sick. Its remedy and healing will be the oneness of the kingdom of humanity. Its life is the Most Great Peace. Its illumination and quickening is love. Its happiness is the attainment of spiritual perfections. It is my wish and hope that in the bounties and favors of the Blessed Perfection we may find a new life, acquire a new power and attain to a wonderful and supreme source of energy so that the Most Great Peace of divine intention shall be established upon the foundations of the unity of the world of men with God. May the love of God be spread from this city, from this meeting to all the surrounding countries. Nay, may America become the distributing center of spiritual enlightenment, and all the world receive this heavenly blessing! For America has developed powers and capacities greater and more wonderful than other nations. While it is true that its people have attained a marvelous material civilization, I hope that spiritual forces may animate this great body and a corresponding spiritual civilization be established. May the inhabitants of this country become like angels of heaven with faces turned continually toward God. May all of them become the servants of the Omnipotent One. May they rise from present material attainments to such a height that heavenly illumination may stream from this center to all the peoples of the world.

The divine Jerusalem has come down from heaven. The bride   6
of Zion has appeared. The voice of the Kingdom of God has
been raised. May you attain supreme capacity and magnetic
attraction in this realm of might and power—manifesting new
energy and wonderful accomplishment, for God is your Assister
and Helper. The breath of the Holy Spirit is your comforter, and
the angels of heaven surround you. I desire this power for you.
Rest assured that these bounties now overshadow you.

9

17 April 1912

Talk at Hotel Ansonia
Broadway and Seventy-third Street, New York

NOTES BY HOWARD MACNUTT

DURING my visit to London and Paris last year I had many   1
talks with the materialistic philosophers of Europe. The basis
of all their conclusions is that the acquisition of knowledge
of phenomena is according to a fixed, invariable law—a law
mathematically exact in its operation through the senses. For
instance, the eye sees a chair; therefore, there is no doubt of the
chair's existence. The eye looks up into the heavens and beholds
the sun; I see flowers upon this table; I smell their fragrance; I
hear sounds outside, etc. This, they say, is a fixed mathematical
law of perception and deduction, the operation of which admits
of no doubt whatever; for inasmuch as the universe is subject
to our sensing, the proof is self-evident that our knowledge of
it must be gained through the avenues of the senses. That is to
say, the materialists announce that the criterion and standard

of human knowledge is sense perception. Among the Greeks and Romans the criterion of knowledge was reason—that whatever is provable and acceptable by reason must necessarily be admitted as true. A third standard or criterion is the opinion held by theologians that traditions or prophetic statement and interpretations constitute the basis of human knowing. There is still another, a fourth criterion, upheld by religionists and metaphysicians who say that the source and channel of all human penetration into the unknown is through inspiration. Briefly then, these four criteria according to the declarations of men are: first, sense perception; second, reason; third, traditions; fourth, inspiration.

2   In Europe I told the philosophers and scientists of materialism that the criterion of the senses is not reliable. For instance, consider a mirror and the images reflected in it. These images have no actual corporeal existence. Yet if you had never seen a mirror, you would firmly insist and believe that they were real. The eye sees a mirage upon the desert as a lake of water, but there is no reality in it. As we stand upon the deck of a steamer, the shore appears to be moving, yet we know the land is stationary and we are moving. The earth was believed to be fixed and the sun revolving about it, but although this appears to be so, the reverse is now known to be true. A whirling torch makes a circle of fire appear before the eye, yet we realize there is but one point of light. We behold a shadow moving upon the ground, but it has no material existence, no substance. In deserts the atmospheric effects are particularly productive of illusions which deceive the eye. Once I saw a mirage in which a whole caravan appeared traveling upward into the sky. In the far North other deceptive phenomena appear and baffle human vision. Sometimes three or four suns, called by scientists mock suns, will be shining at the same time, whereas we know that

the great solar orb is one and that it remains fixed and single. In brief, the senses are continually deceived, and we are unable to separate that which is reality from that which is not.

As to the second criterion—reason—this likewise is unreli- 3 able and not to be depended upon. This human world is an ocean of varying opinions. If reason is the perfect standard and criterion of knowledge, why are opinions at variance and why do philosophers disagree so completely with each other? This is a clear proof that human reason is not to be relied upon as an infallible criterion. For instance, great discoveries and announcements of former centuries are continually upset and discarded by the wise men of today. Mathematicians, astronomers, chemical scientists continually disprove and reject the conclusions of the ancients; nothing is fixed, nothing final; everything is continually changing because human reason is progressing along new roads of investigation and arriving at new conclusions every day. In the future much that is announced and accepted as true now will be rejected and disproved. And so it will continue ad infinitum.

When we consider the third criterion—traditions—upheld 4 by theologians as the avenue and standard of knowledge, we find this source equally unreliable and unworthy of dependence. For religious traditions are the report and record of understanding and interpretation of the Book. By what means has this understanding, this interpretation been reached? By the analysis of human reason. When we read the Book of God, the faculty of comprehension by which we form conclusions is reason. Reason is mind. If we are not endowed with perfect reason, how can we comprehend the meanings of the Word of God? Therefore, human reason, as already pointed out, is by its very nature finite and faulty in conclusions. It cannot surround the Reality Itself, the Infinite Word. Inasmuch as the source of traditions and interpretations is human reason, and human reason is faulty, how can we depend upon its findings for real knowledge?

5   The fourth criterion I have named is inspiration through which it is claimed the reality of knowledge is attainable. What is inspiration? It is the influx of the human heart. But what are satanic promptings which afflict mankind? They are the influx of the heart also. How shall we differentiate between them? The question arises: How shall we know whether we are following inspiration from God or satanic promptings of the human soul? Briefly, the point is that in the human material world of phenomena these four are the only existing criteria or avenues of knowledge, and all of them are faulty and unreliable. What then remains? How shall we attain the reality of knowledge? By the breaths and promptings of the Holy Spirit, which is light and knowledge itself. Through it the human mind is quickened and fortified into true conclusions and perfect knowledge. This is conclusive argument showing that all available human criteria are erroneous and defective, but the divine standard of knowledge is infallible. Therefore, man is not justified in saying, "I know because I perceive through my senses," or "I know because it is proved through my faculty of reason," or "I know because it is according to tradition and interpretation of the Holy Book," or "I know because I am inspired." All human standards of judgment are faulty, finite.

10

17 April 1912

Talk at Home of Mr. and Mrs. Edward B. Kinney
780 West End Avenue, New York

NOTES BY JOHN G. GRUNDY

IN the Holy Books it is recorded that when the Sun of Truth   1
dawns, it will appear in the East, and its light will be reflected in
the West. Already its dawning has taken place in the East, and
its signs are appearing in the West. Its illumination shall spread
rapidly and widely in the Occident. The Sun of Truth has risen
in Persia, and its effulgence is now manifest here in America.
This is the greatest proof of its appearance in the horizon of
the world, as recorded in the heavenly Books. Praise be to God!
That which is prophesied in the Holy Books has been fulfilled.

On Sunday last at Carnegie Hall the revered soul who intro-   2
duced 'Abdu'l-Bahá gave voice to the statement that according
to tradition demons would appear from the land of the sunrise,
but now we find angels appearing instead. At the time this
statement was made a reply was not possible, but today we will
speak of it. The great spiritual lights have always appeared in
the East. The Blessed Perfection, Bahá'u'lláh, appeared in the
East. Jesus Christ dawned upon the horizon of the East. Moses,
Aaron, Joseph and all the Israelitish prophets such as Jeremiah,
Ezekiel, Isaiah and others appeared from the Orient. The lights
of Muḥammad and the Báb shone from the East. The eastern
horizon has been flooded with the effulgence of these great
lights, and only from the East have they risen to shine upon the
West. Now—praise be to God!—you are living in the dawn of

a cycle when the Sun of Truth is again shining forth from the East, illumining all regions.

3   The world has become a new world. The darkness of night which has enveloped humanity is passing. A new day has dawned. Divine susceptibilities and heavenly capacities are developing in human souls under the training of the Sun of Truth. The capacities of souls are different. Their conditions are various. For example, certain minerals come from the stony regions of the earth. All are minerals, all are produced by the same sun, but one remains a stone while another develops the capacity of a glittering gem or jewel. From one plot of land tulips and hyacinths grow; from another, thorns and thistles. Each plot receives the bounty of the sunshine, but the capacity to receive it is not the same. Therefore, it is requisite that we must develop capacity and divine susceptibility in order that the merciful bounty of the Sun of Truth intended for this age and time in which we are living may reflect from us as light from pure crystals.

4   The bounties of the Blessed Perfection are infinite. We must endeavor to increase our capacity daily, to strengthen and enlarge our capabilities for receiving them, to become as perfect mirrors. The more polished and clean the mirror, the more effulgent is its reflection of the lights of the Sun of Truth. Be like a well-cultivated garden wherein the roses and variegated flowers of heaven are growing in fragrance and beauty. It is my hope that your hearts may become as ready ground, carefully tilled and prepared, upon which the divine showers of the bounties of the Blessed Perfection may descend and the zephyrs of this divine springtime may blow with quickening breath. Then will the garden of your hearts bring forth its flowers of delightful fragrance to refresh the nostril of the heavenly Gardener. Let your hearts reflect the glories of the Sun of Truth in their many colors to gladden the eye of the divine Cultivator Who has nourished

them. Day by day become more closely attracted in order that the love of God may illumine all those with whom you come in contact. Be as one spirit, one soul, leaves of one tree, flowers of one garden, waves of one ocean.

As difference in degree of capacity exists among human souls, as difference in capability is found, therefore, individualities will differ one from another. But in reality this is a reason for unity and not for discord and enmity. If the flowers of a garden were all of one color, the effect would be monotonous to the eye; but if the colors are variegated, it is most pleasing and wonderful. The difference in adornment of color and capacity of reflection among the flowers gives the garden its beauty and charm. Therefore, although we are of different individualities, different in ideas and of various fragrances, let us strive like flowers of the same divine garden to live together in harmony. Even though each soul has its own individual perfume and color, all are reflecting the same light, all contributing fragrance to the same breeze which blows through the garden, all continuing to grow in complete harmony and accord. Become as waves of one sea, trees of one forest, growing in the utmost love, agreement and unity.

If you attain to such a capacity of love and unity, the Blessed Perfection will shower infinite graces of the spiritual Kingdom upon you, guide, protect and preserve you under the shadow of His Word, increase your happiness in this world and uphold you through all difficulties. Therefore, it is my hope that day by day you will become more and more effulgent in the horizon of heaven, advance nearer and nearer toward the Kingdom of Abhá, attain greater and greater bounties of the Blessed Perfection. I am joyful, for I perceive the evidences of great love among you. I go to Chicago, and when I return I hope that love will have become infinite. Then will it be an eternal joy to me and the friends in the Orient.

11

18 April 1912

Talk at Home of Mr. and Mrs. Marshall L. Emery
273 West Ninetieth Street, New York

NOTES BY MISS DIXON

1   TONIGHT I wish to tell you something of the history of the Bahá'í Revelation.

2   The Blessed Perfection, Bahá'u'lláh, belonged to the nobility of Persia. From earliest childhood He was distinguished among His relatives and friends. They said, "This child has extraordinary power." In wisdom, intelligence and as a source of new knowledge, He was advanced beyond His age and superior to His surroundings. All who knew Him were astonished at His precocity. It was usual for them to say, "Such a child will not live," for it is commonly believed that precocious children do not reach maturity. During the period of youth the Blessed Perfection did not enter school. He was not willing to be taught. This fact is well established among the Persians of Ṭihrán. Nevertheless, He was capable of solving the difficult problems of all who came to Him. In whatever meeting, scientific assembly or theological discussion He was found, He became the authority of explanation upon intricate and abstruse questions presented.

3   Until His father passed away, Bahá'u'lláh did not seek position or political station notwithstanding His connection with the government. This occasioned surprise and comment. It was frequently said, "How is it that a young man of such keen intelligence and subtle perception does not seek lucrative appointments? As a matter of fact, every position is open to him." This is an historical statement fully attested by the people of Persia.

He was most generous, giving abundantly to the poor. None 4
who came to Him were turned away. The doors of His house
were open to all. He always had many guests. This unbounded
generosity was conducive to greater astonishment from the fact
that He sought neither position nor prominence. In comment-
ing upon this His friends said He would become impoverished,
for His expenses were many and His wealth becoming more and
more limited. "Why is he not thinking of his own affairs?" they
inquired of each other; but some who were wise declared, "This
personage is connected with another world; he has something
sublime within him that is not evident now; the day is coming
when it will be manifested." In truth, the Blessed Perfection was
a refuge for every weak one, a shelter for every fearing one, kind
to every indigent one, lenient and loving to all creatures.

He became well-known in regard to these qualities before the 5
Báb appeared. Then Bahá'u'lláh declared the Báb's mission to
be true and promulgated His teachings. The Báb announced
that the greater Manifestation would take place after Him and
called the Promised One "Him Whom God shall make manifest," saying that nine years later the reality of His own mission
would become apparent. In His writings He stated that in the
ninth year this expected One would be known; in the ninth
year they would attain to all glory and felicity; in the ninth
year they would advance rapidly. Between Bahá'u'lláh and the
Báb there was communication privately. The Báb wrote a letter
containing three hundred and sixty derivatives of the root Bahá.
The Báb was martyred in Tabríz; and Bahá'u'lláh, exiled into
'Iráq in 1852, announced Himself in Baghdád. For the Persian
government had decided that as long as He remained in Persia
the peace of the country would be disturbed; therefore, He was
exiled in the expectation that Persia would become quiet. His
banishment, however, produced the opposite effect. New tumult
arose, and the mention of His greatness and influence spread

everywhere throughout the country. The proclamation of His manifestation and mission was made in Baghdád. He called His friends together there and spoke to them of God.

6   At one point He left the city and went alone into the mountains of Kurdistán, where He made His abode in caves and grottoes. A part of this time He lived in the city of Sulaymáníyyih. Two years passed during which neither His friends nor family knew just where He was.

7   Although Bahá'u'lláh was solitary, secluded and unknown in His retirement, the report spread throughout Kurdistán that this was a most remarkable and learned Personage, gifted with a wonderful power of attraction. In a short time Kurdistán was magnetized with His love. During this period Bahá'u'lláh lived in poverty. His garments were those of the poor and needy. His food was that of the indigent and lowly. An atmosphere of majesty haloed Him as the sun at midday. Everywhere He was greatly revered and beloved.

8   After two years He returned to Baghdád. Friends He had known in Sulaymáníyyih came to visit Him. They found Him in His accustomed environment of ease and affluence and were astonished at the appointments of One Who had lived in seclusion under such frugal conditions in Kurdistán.

9   The Persian government believed the banishment of the Blessed Perfection from Persia would be the extermination of His Cause in that country. These rulers now realized that it spread more rapidly. His prestige increased; His teachings became more widely circulated. The chiefs of Persia then used their influence to have Bahá'u'lláh exiled from Baghdád. He was summoned to Constantinople by the Turkish authorities. While in Constantinople He ignored every restriction, especially the hostility of ministers of state and clergy. The official representatives of Persia again brought their influence to bear upon the Turkish

authorities and succeeded in having Bahá'u'lláh banished from Constantinople to Adrianople, the object being to keep Him as far away as possible from Persia and render His communication with that country more difficult. Nevertheless, the Cause still spread and strengthened.

Finally, they consulted together and said, "We have banished Bahá'u'lláh from place to place, but each time he is exiled his cause is more widely extended, his proclamation increases in power, and day by day his lamp is becoming brighter. This is due to the fact that we have exiled him to large cities and populous centers. Therefore, we will send him to a penal colony as a prisoner so that all may know he is the associate of murderers, robbers and criminals; in a short time he and his followers will perish." The Sulṭán of Turkey then banished Him to the prison of 'Akká in Syria. 10

When Bahá'u'lláh arrived at 'Akká, through the power of God He was able to hoist His banner. His light at first had been a star; now it became a mighty sun, and the illumination of His Cause expanded from the East to the West. Inside prison walls He wrote Epistles to all the kings and rulers of nations, summoning them to arbitration and universal peace. Some of the kings received His words with disdain and contempt. One of these was the Sulṭán of the Ottoman kingdom. Napoleon III of France did not reply. A second Epistle was addressed to him. It stated, "I have written you an Epistle before this, summoning you to the Cause of God, but you are of the heedless. You have proclaimed that you were the defender of the oppressed; now it hath become evident that you are not. Nor are you kind to your own suffering and oppressed people. Your actions are contrary to your own interests, and your kingly pride must fall. Because of your arrogance God shortly will destroy your sovereignty. France will flee away from you, and you will be overwhelmed 11 by a great conquest. There will be lamentation and mourning, women bemoaning the loss of their sons." This arraignment of Napoleon III was published and spread.

12   Read it and consider: one prisoner, single and solitary, without assistant or defender, a foreigner and stranger imprisoned in the fortress of 'Akká, writing such letters to the Emperor of France and Sulṭán of Turkey. Reflect upon this: how Bahá'u'lláh upraised the standard of His Cause in prison. Refer to history. It is without parallel. No such thing has happened before that time nor since—a prisoner and an exile advancing His Cause and spreading His teachings broadcast so that eventually He became powerful enough to conquer the very king who banished Him.

13   His Cause spread more and more. The Blessed Perfection was a prisoner twenty-five years. During all this time He was subjected to the indignities and revilement of the people. He was persecuted, mocked and put in chains. In Persia His properties were pillaged and His possessions confiscated. First, there was banishment from Persia to Baghdád, then to Constantinople, then to Adrianople, finally from Rumelia to the prison fortress of 'Akká.

14   During His lifetime He was intensely active. His energy was unlimited. Scarcely one night was passed in restful sleep. He bore these ordeals, suffered these calamities and difficulties in order that a manifestation of selflessness and service might become apparent in the world of humanity; that the Most Great Peace should become a reality; that human souls might appear as the angels of heaven; that heavenly miracles would be wrought among men; that human faith should be strengthened and perfected; that the precious, priceless bestowal of God—the human mind—might be developed to its fullest capacity in the temple of the body; and that man might become the reflection and likeness of God, even as it hath been revealed in the Bible, "Let us make man in our image."

Briefly, the Blessed Perfection bore all these ordeals and 15
calamities in order that our hearts might become enkindled
and radiant, our spirits be glorified, our faults become virtues,
our ignorance be transformed into knowledge; in order that we
might attain the real fruits of humanity and acquire heavenly
graces; in order that, although pilgrims upon earth, we should
travel the road of the heavenly Kingdom, and, although needy
and poor, we might receive the treasures of eternal life. For this
has He borne these difficulties and sorrows.

Trust all to God. The lights of God are resplendent. The 16
blessed Epistles are spreading. The blessed teachings are promulgated throughout the East and West. Soon you will see that
the heavenly Words have established the oneness of the world
of humanity. The banner of the Most Great Peace has been
unfurled, and the great community is appearing.

12

19 April 1912

Talk at Earl Hall
Columbia University, New York

<small>FROM STENOGRAPHIC NOTES</small>

IF we look with a perceiving eye upon the world of creation, 1
we find that all existing things may be classified as follows:
first, mineral—that is to say, matter or substance appearing in
various forms of composition; second, vegetable—possessing
the virtues of the mineral plus the power of augmentation or
growth, indicating a degree higher and more specialized than the
mineral; third, animal—possessing the attributes of the min-

eral and vegetable plus the power of sense perception; fourth, human—the highest specialized organism of visible creation, embodying the qualities of the mineral, vegetable and animal plus an ideal endowment absolutely absent in the lower kingdoms—the power of intellectual investigation into the mysteries of outer phenomena. The outcome of this intellectual endowment is science, which is especially characteristic of man. This scientific power investigates and apprehends created objects and the laws surrounding them. It is the discoverer of the hidden and mysterious secrets of the material universe and is peculiar to man alone. The most noble and praiseworthy accomplishment of man, therefore, is scientific knowledge and attainment.

2   Science may be likened to a mirror wherein the images of the mysteries of outer phenomena are reflected. It brings forth and exhibits to us in the arena of knowledge all the product of the past. It links together past and present. The philosophical conclusions of bygone centuries, the teachings of the Prophets and wisdom of former sages are crystallized and reproduced in the scientific advancement of today. Science is the discoverer of the past. From its premises of past and present we deduce conclusions as to the future. Science is the governor of nature and its mysteries, the one agency by which man explores the institutions of material creation. All created things are captives of nature and subject to its laws. They cannot transgress the control of these laws in one detail or particular. The infinite starry worlds and heavenly bodies are nature's obedient subjects. The earth and its myriad organisms, all minerals, plants and animals are thralls of its dominion. But man through the exercise of his scientific, intellectual power can rise out of this condition, can modify, change and control nature according to his own wishes and uses. Science, so to speak, is the breaker of the laws of nature.

3   Consider, for example, that man according to natural law should dwell upon the surface of the earth. By overcoming this

law and restriction, however, he sails in ships over the ocean, mounts to the zenith in airplanes and sinks to the depths of the sea in submarines. This is against the fiat of nature and a violation of her sovereignty and dominion. Nature's laws and methods, the hidden secrets and mysteries of the universe, human inventions and discoveries, all our scientific acquisitions should naturally remain concealed and unknown, but man through his intellectual acumen searches them out of the plane of the invisible, draws them into the plane of the visible, exposes and explains them. For instance, one of the mysteries of nature is electricity. According to nature this force, this energy, should remain latent and hidden, but man scientifically breaks through the very laws of nature, arrests it and even imprisons it for his use.

In brief, man through the possession of this ideal endowment of scientific investigation is the most noble product of creation, the governor of nature. He takes the sword from nature's hand and uses it upon nature's head. According to natural law night is a period of darkness and obscurity, but man by utilizing the power of electricity, by wielding this electric sword overcomes the darkness and dispels the gloom. Man is superior to nature and makes nature do his bidding. Man is a sensitive being; nature is without sensation. Man has memory and reason; nature lacks them. Man is nobler than nature. There are powers within him of which nature is devoid. It may be claimed that these powers are from nature itself and that man is a part of nature. In answer to this statement we will say that if nature is the whole and man is a part of that whole, how could it be possible for a part to possess qualities and virtues which are absent in the whole? Undoubtedly the part must be endowed with the same qualities and properties as the whole. For example, the hair is a part of the human anatomy. It cannot contain elements which are not found in other parts of the body, for in all cases the component

4

elements of the body are the same. Therefore, it is manifest and evident that man, although in body a part of nature, nevertheless in spirit possesses a power transcending nature; for if he were simply a part of nature and limited to material laws, he could possess only the things which nature embodies. God has conferred upon and added to man a distinctive power—the faculty of intellectual investigation into the secrets of creation, the acquisition of higher knowledge—the greatest virtue of which is scientific enlightenment.

5   This endowment is the most praiseworthy power of man, for through its employment and exercise the betterment of the human race is accomplished, the development of the virtues of mankind is made possible and the spirit and mysteries of God become manifest. Therefore, I am greatly pleased with my visit to this university. Praise be to God that this country abounds in such institutions of learning where the knowledge of sciences and arts may readily be acquired.

6   As material and physical sciences are taught here and are constantly unfolding in wider vistas of attainment, I am hopeful that spiritual development may also follow and keep pace with these outer advantages. As material knowledge is illuminating those within the walls of this great temple of learning, so also may the light of the spirit, the inner and divine light of the real philosophy glorify this institution. The most important principle of divine philosophy is the oneness of the world of humanity, the unity of mankind, the bond conjoining East and West, the tie of love which blends human hearts.

7   Therefore, it is our duty to put forth our greatest efforts and summon all our energies in order that the bonds of unity and accord may be established among mankind. For thousands of years we have had bloodshed and strife. It is enough; it is sufficient. Now is the time to associate together in love and harmony. For thousands of years we have tried the sword and warfare; let

mankind for a time at least live in peace. Review history and consider how much savagery, how much bloodshed and battle the world has witnessed. It has been either religious warfare, political warfare or some other clash of human interests. The world of humanity has never enjoyed the blessing of universal peace. Year by year the implements of warfare have been increased and perfected. Consider the wars of past centuries; only ten, fifteen or twenty thousand at the most were killed, but now it is possible to kill one hundred thousand in a single day. In ancient times warfare was carried on with the sword; today it is the smokeless gun. Formerly, battleships were sailing vessels; today they are dreadnoughts. Consider the increase and improvement in the weapons of war. God has created us all human, and all countries of the world are parts of the same globe. We are all His servants. He is kind and just to all. Why should we be unkind and unjust to each other? He provides for all. Why should we deprive one another? He protects and preserves all. Why should we kill our fellow creatures? If this warfare and strife be for the sake of religion, it is evident that it violates the spirit and basis of all religion. All the divine Manifestations have proclaimed the oneness of God and the unity of mankind. They have taught that men should love and mutually help each other in order that they might progress. Now if this conception of religion be true, its essential principle is the oneness of humanity. The fundamental truth of the Manifestations is peace. This underlies all religion, all justice. The divine purpose is that men should live in unity, concord and agreement and should love one another. Consider the virtues of the human world and realize that the oneness of humanity is the primary foundation of them all. Read the Gospel and the other Holy Books. You will find their fundamentals are one and the same. Therefore, unity is the essential truth of religion and, when so understood, embraces all the virtues of the human world. Praise be to God! This knowledge has been spread, eyes have been opened, and ears have become attentive. Therefore, we must endeavor to promulgate and practice the religion of God which has been founded by all the Prophets. And the religion of God is absolute love and unity.

13

19 April 1912

Talk at Bowery Mission
227 Bowery, New York

FROM STENOGRAPHIC NOTES

1   TONIGHT I am very happy, for I have come here to meet my friends. I consider you my relatives, my companions; and I am your comrade.

2   You must be thankful to God that you are poor, for Jesus Christ has said, "Blessed are the poor." He never said, "Blessed are the rich." He said, too, that the Kingdom is for the poor and that it is easier for a camel to enter a needle's eye than for a rich man to enter God's Kingdom. Therefore, you must be thankful to God that although in this world you are indigent, yet the treasures of God are within your reach; and although in the material realm you are poor, yet in the Kingdom of God you are precious. Jesus Himself was poor. He did not belong to the rich. He passed His time in the desert, traveling among the poor, and lived upon the herbs of the field. He had no place to lay His head, no home. He was exposed in the open to heat, cold and frost—to inclement weather of all kinds—yet He chose this rather than riches. If riches were considered a glory, the

Prophet Moses would have chosen them; Jesus would have been a rich man. When Jesus Christ appeared, it was the poor who first accepted Him, not the rich. Therefore, you are the disciples of Jesus Christ; you are His comrades, for He outwardly was poor, not rich. Even this earth's happiness does not depend upon wealth. You will find many of the wealthy exposed to dangers and troubled by difficulties, and in their last moments upon the bed of death there remains the regret that they must be separated from that to which their hearts are so attached. They come into this world naked, and they must go from it naked. All they possess they must leave behind and pass away solitary, alone. Often at the time of death their souls are filled with remorse; and worst of all, their hope in the mercy of God is less than ours. Praise be to God! Our hope is in the mercy of God, and there is no doubt that the divine compassion is bestowed upon the poor. Jesus Christ said so; Bahá'u'lláh said so. While Bahá'u'lláh was in Baghdád, still in possession of great wealth, He left all He had and went alone from the city, living two years among the poor. They were His comrades. He ate with them, slept with them and gloried in being one of them. He chose for one of His names the title of The Poor One and often in His Writings refers to Himself as *Darvísh*, which in Persian means poor; and of this title He was very proud. He admonished all that we must be the servants of the poor, helpers of the poor, remember the sorrows of the poor, associate with them; for thereby we may inherit the Kingdom of heaven. God has not said that there are mansions prepared for us if we pass our time associating with the rich, but He has said there are many mansions prepared for the servants of the poor, for the poor are very dear to God. The mercies and bounties of God are with them. The rich are mostly negligent, inattentive, steeped in worldliness, depending upon their means, whereas the poor are dependent upon God, and

45

their reliance is upon Him, not upon themselves. Therefore, the poor are nearer the threshold of God and His throne.

3   Jesus was a poor man. One night when He was out in the fields, the rain began to fall. He had no place to go for shelter so He lifted His eyes toward heaven, saying, "O Father! For the birds of the air Thou hast created nests, for the sheep a fold, for the animals dens, for the fish places of refuge, but for Me Thou hast provided no shelter. There is no place where I may lay My head. My bed consists of the cold ground; My lamps at night are the stars, and My food is the grass of the field. Yet who upon earth is richer than I? For the greatest blessing Thou hast not given to the rich and mighty but unto Me, for Thou hast given Me the poor. To me Thou hast granted this blessing. They are Mine. Therefore am I the richest man on earth."

4   So, my comrades, you are following in the footsteps of Jesus Christ. Your lives are similar to His life; your attitude is like unto His; you resemble Him more than the rich do. Therefore, we will thank God that we have been so blessed with real riches. And in conclusion, I ask you to accept 'Abdu'l-Bahá as your servant.

5   *At the end of this meeting, 'Abdu'l-Bahá stood at the Bowery entrance to the Mission hall, shaking hands with four or five hundred men and placing within each palm a piece of silver.*

Talks 'Abdu'l-Bahá Delivered in Washington, D.C.

20 April 1912

Talk at Orient-Occident-Unity Conference
Public Library Hall, Washington, D.C.

NOTES BY JOSEPH H. HANNEN

TONIGHT I am most happy in presenting myself before an audience such as this. I am an Oriental and have come into the West to meet the people of the Occident. Praise be to God! Upon the faces of those assembled here I perceive the light of God. This I consider an evidence of the possibility of uniting the East and the West, of establishing a perfect bond between Persia and America—one of the objects of this conference. For the Persians there is no government better fitted to contribute to the development of their natural resources and the helping of their national needs in a reciprocal alliance than the United States of America, and for the Americans there could be no better industrial outlet and market than the virgin commercial soil of Persia. The mineral wealth of Persia is still latent and untouched. It is my hope that the great American democracy may be instrumental in developing these hidden resources and that a bond of perfect amity and unity may be established between the American republic and the government of Persia. May this bond—whether material or spiritual—be well cemented. May the material civilization of America find complete efficacy and establishment in Persia, and may the spiritual civilization of Persia find acceptance and response in America.

1

2   Some of the creatures of existence can live solitary and alone. A tree, for instance, may live without the assistance and cooperation of other trees. Some animals are isolated and lead a separate existence away from their kind. But this is impossible for man. In his life and being cooperation and association are essential. Through association and meeting we find happiness and development, individual and collective.

3   For instance, when there is intercourse and cooperation between two villages, the advancement of each will be assured. Likewise, if intercommunication is established between two cities, both will benefit and progress. And if a reciprocal basis of agreement be reached between two countries, their individual and mutual interests will find great development. Therefore, in the unity of this radiant assemblage I behold the link between Orient and Occident. Such unity is the means and instrument of cooperation between the various countries of the East and West. It is evident, then, that the outcomes from this basis of agreement and accord are numberless and unlimited. Surely there will be great harvests of results forthcoming for Persia and America. In Persia advanced material civilization will be established and the doors thrown open wide to American commerce.

4   Above and beyond all this, a great love and fountain of affection shall bind and blend these two remote peoples, for Bahá'u'lláh has proclaimed to the world the solidarity of nations and the oneness of humanity. Addressing all mankind He has said, "Ye are all leaves of one tree and the drops of one sea." The world of humanity has been expressed by Him as a unit—as one family. It is, therefore, hoped that the American and Persian nations may be conjoined and united in reciprocal love. May they become one race endowed with the same susceptibilities. May these bonds of amity and accord be firmly established.

5   Bahá'u'lláh passed forty years of His life in prison and exile in order that He might upraise the banner of the oneness of the

world of men. For this He bore all these ordeals and difficulties. He was under the dominion of 'Abdu'l-Ḥamíd. I, too, was in the prison of 'Abdu'l-Ḥamíd until the Committee of Union and Progress hoisted the standard of liberty and my fetters were removed. They exhibited great kindness and love toward me. I was made free and thereby enabled to come to this country. Were it not for the action of this Committee, I should not be with you here tonight. Therefore, you must all ask assistance and confirmation in behalf of this Committee through which the liberty of Turkey was proclaimed.

Briefly, I have traveled this long distance, crossed the Atlantic Ocean to this western continent in the desire and hope that the strongest bond of unity may be established between America and Persia. I know this to be your wish and purpose also and am sure of your cooperation. We shall, therefore, offer supplication in the divine threshold that a great love may take possession of the hearts of men and unite the nations of the world. We will pray that the ensign of international peace may be uplifted and that the oneness of the world of humanity may be realized and accomplished. All this is made possible and practicable through your efforts. May this American democracy be the first nation to establish the foundation of international agreement. May it be the first nation to proclaim the universality of mankind. May it be the first to upraise the standard of the Most Great Peace, and through this nation of democracy may these philanthropic intentions and institutions be spread broadcast throughout the world. Truly, this is a great and revered nation. Here liberty has reached its highest degree. The intentions of its people are most praiseworthy. They are, indeed, worthy of being the first to build the Tabernacle of the Most Great Peace and proclaim the oneness of mankind. I will supplicate God for assistance and confirmation in your behalf.

2

21 April 1912

Talk at Studio Hall
1219 Connecticut Avenue, Washington, D.C.

NOTES BY JOSEPH H. HANNEN

1   I HAVE come here to visit you. With the greatest longing I have wished to see you. Realizing it was only with great difficulty that you could come to me and that very few could make the trip, I decided to come to you so that all might have the pleasure of meeting. Praise be to God! I am here, and I am looking into your faces—faces radiant with inner beauty, hearts attracted to the Kingdom of Abhá, spirits exhilarated through the glad tidings of God. Therefore, I have experienced the greatest possible happiness. And surely this happiness must be mutual, for the hearts are connected with each other and are filled with the same vibration. The flame and the light of love are reflected in all. Spiritual susceptibilities and heart longings fill every heart. If we should offer a hundred thousand thanksgivings every moment to the threshold of God for this love which has blended the Orient and Occident, we would fail to express our gratitude sufficiently. If all the powers of earth should seek to bring about this love between East and West, they would prove incapable. If they wished to establish this unity, it would prove impossible. But Bahá'u'lláh has accomplished both through the power of the Holy Spirit, and this bond of unity through love is indissoluble. It shall continue unto time everlasting, and day by day its power shall increase. Erelong it shall enchain the world, and eventually the hearts of all the nations of the world will be brought together by its constraining clasp. The world of humanity shall become

the manifestation of the lights of Divinity, and the bestowals of God shall surround all. From the standpoints of both material and spiritual civilization extraordinary progress and development will be witnessed. In this present cycle there will be an evolution in civilization unparalleled in the history of the world. The world of humanity has, heretofore, been in the stage of infancy; now it is approaching maturity. Just as the individual human organism, having attained the period of maturity, reaches its fullest degree of physical strength and ripened intellectual faculties so that in one year of this ripened period there is witnessed an unprecedented measure of development, likewise the world of humanity in this cycle of its completeness and consummation will realize an immeasurable upward progress, and that power of accomplishment whereof each individual human reality is the depository of God—that outworking Universal Spirit—like the intellectual faculty, will reveal itself in infinite degrees of perfection.

Therefore, thank ye God that ye have come into the plane 2 of existence in this radiant century wherein the bestowals of God are appearing from all directions, when the doors of the Kingdom have been opened unto you, the call of God is being raised, and the virtues of the human world are in the process of unfoldment. The day has come when all darkness is to be dispelled, and the Sun of Truth shall shine forth radiantly. This time of the world may be likened to the equinoctial in the annual cycle. For, verily, this is the spring season of God. In the Holy Books a promise is given that the springtime of God shall make itself manifest; Jerusalem, the Holy City, shall descend from heaven; Zion shall leap forth and dance; and the Holy Land shall be submerged in the ocean of divine effulgence.

At the time of the vernal equinox in the material world a 3 wonderful vibrant energy and new life-quickening is observed everywhere in the vegetable kingdom; the animal and human kingdoms are resuscitated and move forward with a new impulse. The whole world is born anew, resurrected. Gentle zephyrs are set in motion, wafting and fragrant; flowers bloom; the trees are in blossom, the air temperate and delightful; how pleasant and beautiful become the mountains, fields and meadows. Likewise, the spiritual bounty and springtime of God quicken the world of humanity with a new animus and vivification. All the virtues which have been deposited and potential in human hearts are being revealed from that Reality as flowers and blossoms from divine gardens. It is a day of joy, a time of happiness, a period of spiritual growth. I beg of God that this divine spiritual civilization may have the fullest impression and effect upon you. May you become as growing plants. May the trees of your hearts bring forth new leaves and variegated blossoms. May ideal fruits appear from them in order that the world of humanity, which has grown and developed in material civilization, may be quickened in the bringing forth of spiritual ideals. Just as human intellects have revealed the secrets of matter and have brought forth from the realm of the invisible the mysteries of nature, may minds and spirits, likewise, come into the knowledge of the verities of God, and the realities of the Kingdom be made manifest in human hearts. Then the world will be the paradise of Abhá, the standard of the Most Great Peace will be borne aloft, and the oneness of the world of humanity in all its beauty, glory and significance will become apparent. And now in your presence I wish to pray in your behalf. Let your hearts be attentive and directed to the Kingdom of Abhá.

Prayer in Persian   4
It is my hope that the supplication I have offered to the Kingdom of Abhá in your behalf may soon be answered and that its
results and effects may become manifest in your hearts and lives.

3

21 April 1912

Talk at Universalist Church
Thirteenth and L Streets, Washington, D.C.

NOTES BY JOSEPH H. HANNEN

THE doctrines and creed of this church, so capably expressed   1
by its revered minister, are truly commendable, sanctified and
worthy of praise and glorification, for these precepts are opposed
to the deep-rooted religious prejudices of the day. It is evident
that prejudices arising from adherence to religious forms and
imitation of ancestral beliefs have hindered the progress of humanity thousands of years. How many wars and battles have
been fought, how much division, discord and hatred have been
caused by this form of prejudice! But inasmuch as this century
is a century of the revelation of reality—praise be to God!—
the thoughts of men are being directed toward the welfare and
unity of humanity. Daily the mirage of imitations is passing
away, and the ocean of truth is surging more tumultuously. All
the existing nations had a divine foundation of truth or reality
originally, which was intended to be conducive to the unity and
accord of mankind, but the light of that reality gradually became
obscured. The darkness of superstitions and imitations came

and took its place, binding the world of humanity in the chains and fetters of ignorance. Enmity arose among men, increasing to such an extent that nation strove against nation in hatred and violence. War has been a religious and political human heritage.

2   Now it is enough! We must investigate reality. We must put away these superstitions. It is a self-evident truth that all humanity is the creation of God. All are His servants and under His protection. All are recipients of His bestowals. God is kind to all His servants. At most it is this: that some are ignorant; they must be educated in order that they may become intelligent. Some are immature as children; they must be aided and assisted in order that they may become mature. Some are sick and ailing; they must be healed. But the suffering patient must not be tested by false treatment. The child must not be warped and hindered in its development. The ignorant must not be restricted by censure and criticism. We must look for the real, true remedy.

3   All the Prophets of God, including Jesus Christ, appeared in the world for the education of humanity, to develop immature souls into maturity, to transform the ignorant of mankind into the knowing, thereby establishing love and unity through divine education and training. The Prophets have not come to cause discord and enmity. For God has wished all good for His servants, and he who wishes the servants of God evil is against God; he has not obeyed the will and emulated the example of God; he has followed Satanic leadings and footprints. The attributes of God are love and mercy; the attribute of Satan is hate. Therefore, he who is merciful and kind to his fellowmen is manifesting the divine attribute, and he who is hating and hostile toward a fellow creature is satanic. God is absolute love, even as Jesus Christ has declared, and Satan is utter hatred. Wherever love is witnessed, know that there is a manifestation of God's mercy; whenever you meet hatred and enmity, know

that these are the evidences and attributes of Satan. The Prophets have appeared in this world with the mission that human souls may become the expressions of the Merciful, that they may be educated and developed, attain to love and amity and establish peace and agreement.

In the world of existence the animal is a captive of nature. 4 Its actions are according to the exigencies and requirements of nature. It has no consideration or consciousness of good and evil. It simply follows its natural instinct and inclination. The Prophets of God have come to show man the way of righteousness in order that he may not follow his own natural impulse but govern his action by the light of Their precept and example. According to Their teachings he should do that which is found to be praiseworthy by the standard of reason and judgment of intellect, even though it be opposed to his natural human inclination; and he should not do that which is found to be unworthy by that same standard, even though it be in the direction of his natural impulse and desire. Therefore, man must follow and manifest the attributes of the Merciful.

The imperfect members of society, the weak souls in humanity, follow their natural trend. Their lives and actions are in accord with their natural propensities; they are captives of physical susceptibilities; they are not in touch or in tune with the spiritual bounties. Man has two aspects: the physical, which is subject to nature, and the merciful or divine, which is connected with God. If the physical or natural disposition in him should overcome the heavenly and merciful, he is, then, the most degraded of animal beings; and if the divine and spiritual should triumph over the human and natural, he is, verily, an angel. The Prophets come into the world to guide and educate humanity so that the animal nature of man may disappear and the divinity of his powers become awakened. The divine aspect or spiritual nature consists of the breaths of the Holy Spirit. The second birth of which Jesus has spoken refers to the appearance of this heavenly nature in man. It is expressed in the baptism of the Holy Spirit, and he who is baptized by the Holy Spirit is a veritable manifestation of divine mercy to mankind. Then he becomes just and kind to all humanity; he entertains prejudice and ill will toward none; he shuns no nation or people.

6   The foundations of the divine religions are one. If we investigate these foundations, we discover much ground for agreement, but if we consider the imitations of forms and ancestral beliefs, we find points of disagreement and division; for these imitations differ, while the sources and foundations are one and the same. That is to say, the fundamentals are conducive to unity, but imitations are the cause of disunion and dismemberment. Whosoever is lacking in love for humanity or manifests hatred and bigotry toward any part of it violates the foundation and source of his own belief and is holding to forms and imitations. Jesus Christ declares that the sun rises upon the evil and the good, and the rain descends upon the just and the unjust—upon all humanity alike. Christ was a divine mercy which shone upon all mankind, the medium for the descent of the bounty of God, and the bounty of God is transcendent, unrestricted, universal.

7   The revered minister read from the words of the Gospel, "I have yet many things to say unto you, but ye cannot bear them now. Howbeit when he, the Spirit of truth, is come, he will guide you into all truth." The century has dawned when the Spirit of Truth can reveal these verities to mankind, proclaim that very Word, establish the real foundations of Christianity and deliver the nations and peoples from the bondage of forms and imitations. The cause of discord, prejudice and animosity will be removed, the basis of love and amity be established. Therefore, all of you must strive with heart and soul in order that enmity may disappear entirely and that strife and hatred

pass away absolutely from the midst of the human world. You must listen to the admonition of this Spirit of Truth. You must follow the example and footprints of Jesus Christ. Read the Gospels. Jesus Christ was mercy itself, was love itself. He even prayed in behalf of His executioners—for those who crucified Him—saying, "Father, forgive them; for they know not what they do." If they knew what they were doing, they would not have done it. Consider how kind Jesus Christ was, that even upon the cross He prayed for His oppressors. We must follow His example. We must emulate the Prophets of God. We must follow Jesus Christ. We must free ourselves from all these imitations which are the source of darkness in the world.

I shall ask you a question: Did God create us for love or for enmity? Did He create us for peace or discord? Surely He has created us for love; therefore, we should live in accordance with His will. Do not listen to anything that is prejudiced, for self-interest prompts men to be prejudiced. They are thoughtful only of their own will and purposes. They live and move in darkness. Consider how many different nations and divergent religious beliefs existed when Christ appeared. Enmity and strife prevailed among them—Romans, Greeks, Assyrians, Egyptians—all warring and hostile toward each other. Christ, through the breaths of the Holy Spirit, united them, established fellowship among them so that no trace of strife remained. Under His standard they became united and lived in peace through His teachings. Which is preferable and more commendable? To follow the example of Jesus Christ or to manifest the satanic instinct? Let us strive with all our powers to unite the East and West so that the nations of the world may be advanced and that all may live according to the one foundation of the religions of God. The essentials of the divine religion are one reality, indivisible and not multiple. It is one. And when through investigation we find it to be single, we have a basis for the oneness of the world of

8

humanity. I will pray for you, asking confirmation and assistance in your behalf.

4

22 April 1912

*Talk at Home of Mr. and Mrs. Arthur J. Parsons
1700 Eighteenth Street, NW, Washington, D.C.*

Notes by Joseph H. Hannen

1   SEE how good Bahá'u'lláh is to us, how great the power of His Word! From what distant parts of the world He has brought us together in this house and caused us to meet at this heavenly table, for love has prepared a feast and bidden 'Abdu'l-Bahá to let this entertainment be in His name. What a union of hearts and what a confirmation of Bahá'u'lláh between East and West has been established! How His bounty has embraced all! How His favors have been perfected for all!

2   When the Muslims conquered Persia, the chief of the Zoroastrian high priests went to drink wine. According to Muslim law wine is forbidden, and he who drinks it must be punished by eighty-one strokes of the whip. Therefore, the Muslims arrested the high priest and whipped him. At that time the Arabs were considered very low and degraded by the Persians, scarcely to be accounted as human beings. As Muḥammad was an Arab, the Persians looked upon Him with disdain; but when the high priest saw the evidences of a power in Muḥammad which controlled these despised people, he cried out, "O thou Arabian Muḥammad, what hast thou done? What hast thou done which

58

has made thy people arrest the chief high priest of the Zoroastrians for committing something unlawful in thy religion?" By this circumstance the prejudice which caused the Zoroastrian to shun the Muslim had been overcome, for he recognized in what had happened to him the great influence Muḥammad exercised over these people.

Today in this meeting we have an evidence of how Bahá'u'lláh 3 through the power of the love of God has exercised a wonderful spiritual influence throughout the world. From the remotest parts of Persia and the Orient He has caused men to come to this table to meet with the people of the West in the utmost love and affection, union and harmony. Behold how the power of Bahá'u'lláh has brought the East and West together. And 'Abdu'l-Bahá is standing, serving you. There is neither rod nor blow, whip nor sword; but the power of the love of God has accomplished this.

In this world we judge a cause or movement by its progress 4 and development. Some movements appear, manifest a brief period of activity, then discontinue. Others show forth a greater measure of growth and strength, but before attaining mature development, weaken, disintegrate and are lost in oblivion. Neither of these mentioned are progressive and permanent.

There is still another kind of movement or cause which from a 5 very small, inconspicuous beginning goes forward with sure and steady progress, gradually broadening and widening until it has assumed universal dimensions. The Bahá'í Movement is of this nature. For instance, when Bahá'u'lláh was exiled from Persia with 'Abdu'l-Bahá and the rest of His family, they traveled the long road from Ṭihrán to Baghdád, passing through many towns and villages. During the whole of that journey and distance they did not meet a single believer in the Cause for which they had been banished. At that time very little was known about it in any part of the world. Even in Baghdád there was but one believer who had been taught by Bahá'u'lláh Himself in Persia. Later on, two or three others appeared. You will see, therefore, that at the beginning the Cause of Bahá'u'lláh was almost unknown, but on account of being a divine Movement it grew and developed with irresistible spiritual power until in this day, wherever you travel—East or West—and in whatever country you journey, you will meet Bahá'í assemblies and institutions. This is an evidence that the Bahá'ís are spreading the blessings of unity and progressive development throughout the world under the direction of divine guidance and purpose, while other movements which are only temporary in their activities and accomplishments have no real, universal significance.

5

23 April 1912

Talk at Howard University
Washington, D.C.

TRANSLATED BY AMIN BANANI

1 TODAY I am most happy, for I see here a gathering of the servants of God. I see white and black sitting together. There are no whites and blacks before God. All colors are one, and that is the color of servitude to God. Scent and color are not important. The heart is important. If the heart is pure, white or black or any color makes no difference. God does not look at colors; He looks at the hearts. He whose heart is pure is better. He whose character is better is more pleasing. He who turns more to the Abhá Kingdom is more advanced.

60

In the realm of existence colors are of no importance. Observe 2
in the mineral kingdom colors are not the cause of discord. In the
vegetable kingdom the colors of multicolored flowers are not the
cause of discord. Rather, colors are the cause of the adornment
of the garden because a single color has no appeal; but when you
observe many-colored flowers, there is charm and display.

The world of humanity, too, is like a garden, and humankind 3
are like the many-colored flowers. Therefore, different colors
constitute an adornment. In the same way, there are many colors
in the realm of animals. Doves are of many colors; nevertheless,
they live in utmost harmony. They never look at color; instead,
they look at the species. How often white doves fly with black
ones. In the same way, other birds and varicolored animals never
look at color; they look at the species.

Now ponder this: Animals, despite the fact that they lack 4
reason and understanding, do not make colors the cause of
conflict. Why should man, who has reason, create conflict? This
is wholly unworthy of him. Especially white and black are the
descendants of the same Adam; they belong to one household.
In origin they were one; they were the same color. Adam was of
one color. Eve had one color. All humanity is descended from
them. Therefore, in origin they are one. These colors developed
later due to climates and regions; they have no significance
whatsoever. Therefore, today I am very happy that white and
black have gathered together in this meeting. I hope this coming
together and harmony reaches such a degree that no distinctions
shall remain between them, and they shall be together in the
utmost harmony and love.

But I wish to say one thing in order that the blacks may 5
become grateful to the whites and the whites become loving toward the blacks. If you go to Africa and see the blacks of Africa,
you will realize how much progress you have made. Praise be
to God! You are like the whites; there are no great distinctions

left. But the blacks of Africa are treated as servants. The first proclamation of emancipation for the blacks was made by the whites of America. How they fought and sacrificed until they freed the blacks! Then it spread to other places. The blacks of Africa were in complete bondage, but your emancipation led to their freedom also—that is, the European states emulated the Americans, and the emancipation proclamation became universal. It was for your sake that the whites of America made such an effort. Were it not for this effort, universal emancipation would not have been proclaimed.

6 Therefore, you must be very grateful to the whites of America, and the whites must become very loving toward you so that you may progress in all human grades. Strive jointly to make extraordinary progress and mix together completely. In short, you must be very thankful to the whites who were the cause of your freedom in America. Had you not been freed, other blacks would not have been freed either. Now—praise be to God!—everyone is free and lives in tranquillity. I pray that you attain to such a degree of good character and behavior that the names of black and white shall vanish. All shall be called human, just as the name for a flight of doves is dove. They are not called black and white. Likewise with other birds.

7 I hope that you attain to such a high degree—and this is impossible except through love. You must try to create love between yourselves; and this love does not come about unless you are grateful to the whites, and the whites are loving toward you, and endeavor to promote your advancement and enhance your honor. This will be the cause of love. Differences between black and white will be completely obliterated; indeed, ethnic and national differences will all disappear.

8 I am very happy to see you and thank God that this meeting is composed of people of both races and that both are gathered in perfect love and harmony. I hope this becomes the example of

universal harmony and love until no title remains except that of humanity. Such a title demonstrates the perfection of the human world and is the cause of eternal glory and human happiness. I pray that you be with one another in utmost harmony and love and strive to enable each other to live in comfort.

6

23 April 1912

Talk at Home of Mr. and Mrs. Arthur J. Parsons
1700 Eighteenth Street, NW, Washington, D.C.

NOTES BY JOSEPH H. HANNEN

TODAY I have been speaking from dawn until now, yet because   1
of love, fellowship and desire to be with you, I have come here
to speak again briefly. Within the last few days a terrible event
has happened in the world, an event saddening to every heart
and grieving every spirit. I refer to the Titanic disaster, in which
many of our fellow human beings were drowned, a number of
beautiful souls passed beyond this earthly life. Although such
an event is indeed regrettable, we must realize that everything
which happens is due to some wisdom and that nothing happens without a reason. Therein is a mystery; but whatever the
reason and mystery, it was a very sad occurrence, one which
brought tears to many eyes and distress to many souls. I was
greatly affected by this disaster. Some of those who were lost
voyaged on the Cedric with us as far as Naples and afterward
sailed upon the other ship. When I think of them, I am very sad
indeed. But when I consider this calamity in another aspect, I am
consoled by the realization that the worlds of God are infinite;

that though they were deprived of this existence, they have other opportunities in the life beyond, even as Christ has said, "In my Father's house are many mansions." They were called away from the temporary and transferred to the eternal; they abandoned this material existence and entered the portals of the spiritual world. Foregoing the pleasures and comforts of the earthly, they now partake of a joy and happiness far more abiding and real, for they have hastened to the Kingdom of God. The mercy of God is infinite, and it is our duty to remember these departed souls in our prayers and supplications that they may draw nearer and nearer to the Source itself.

2   These human conditions may be likened to the matrix of the mother from which a child is to be born into the spacious outer world. At first the infant finds it very difficult to reconcile itself to its new existence. It cries as if not wishing to be separated from its narrow abode and imagining that life is restricted to that limited space. It is reluctant to leave its home, but nature forces it into this world. Having come into its new conditions, it finds that it has passed from darkness into a sphere of radiance; from gloomy and restricted surroundings it has been transferred to a spacious and delightful environment. Its nourishment was the blood of the mother; now it finds delicious food to enjoy. Its new life is filled with brightness and beauty; it looks with wonder and delight upon the mountains, meadows and fields of green, the rivers and fountains, the wonderful stars; it breathes the life-quickening atmosphere; and then it praises God for its release from the confinement of its former condition and attainment to the freedom of a new realm. This analogy expresses the relation of the temporal world to the life hereafter—the transition of the soul of man from darkness and uncertainty to the light and reality of the eternal Kingdom. At first it is very difficult to welcome death, but after attaining its new condition the soul is grateful, for it has been released from the bondage of

the limited to enjoy the liberties of the unlimited. It has been freed from a world of sorrow, grief and trials to live in a world of unending bliss and joy. The phenomenal and physical have been abandoned in order that it may attain the opportunities of the ideal and spiritual. Therefore, the souls of those who have passed away from earth and completed their span of mortal pilgrimage in the Titanic disaster have hastened to a world superior to this. They have soared away from these conditions of darkness and dim vision into the realm of light. These are the only considerations which can comfort and console those whom they have left behind.

Furthermore, these events have deeper reasons. Their object 3 and purpose is to teach man certain lessons. We are living in a day of reliance upon material conditions. Men imagine that the great size and strength of a ship, the perfection of machinery or the skill of a navigator will ensure safety, but these disasters sometimes take place that men may know that God is the real Protector. If it be the will of God to protect man, a little ship may escape destruction, whereas the greatest and most perfectly constructed vessel with the best and most skillful navigator may not survive a danger such as was present on the ocean. The purpose is that the people of the world may turn to God, the One Protector; that human souls may rely upon His preservation and know that He is the real safety. These events happen in order that man's faith may be increased and strengthened. Therefore, although we feel sad and disheartened, we must supplicate God to turn our hearts to the Kingdom and pray for these departed souls with faith in His infinite mercy so that, although they have been deprived of this earthly life, they may enjoy a new existence in the supreme mansions of the Heavenly Father.

Let no one imagine that these words imply that man should 4 not be thorough and careful in his undertakings. God has endowed man with intelligence so that he may safeguard and protect himself. Therefore, he must provide and surround himself with all that scientific skill can produce. He must be deliberate, thoughtful and thorough in his purposes, build the best ship and provide the most experienced captain; yet, withal, let him rely upon God and consider God as the one Keeper. If God protects, nothing can imperil man's safety; and if it be not His will to safeguard, no amount of preparation and precaution will avail.

7

23 April 1912

Talk to Bethel Literary Society
Metropolitan African Methodist Episcopal Church
M Street, NW, Washington, D.C.

NOTES BY JOSEPH H. HANNEN

1 As I stand here tonight and look upon this assembly, I am reminded curiously of a beautiful bouquet of violets gathered together in varying colors, dark and light. This is an evidence and indication that the United States of America is a just and free government, for I see black and white seated together in perfect harmony and agreement. Hearts are united. This just government makes such a meeting possible. You should thank God continually that you enjoy the security and protection of a government which furthers your development and rules with impartial equity and equality toward all, even as a father; for in the human world there is no greater blessing. This evening I will speak to you upon scientific subjects.

2 The virtues of humanity are many, but science is the most noble of them all. The distinction which man enjoys above and

beyond the station of the animal is due to this paramount virtue. It is a bestowal of God; it is not material; it is divine. Science is an effulgence of the Sun of Reality, the power of investigating and discovering the verities of the universe, the means by which man finds a pathway to God. All the powers and attributes of man are human and hereditary in origin—outcomes of nature's processes—except the intellect, which is supernatural. Through intellectual and intelligent inquiry science is the discoverer of all things. It unites present and past, reveals the history of bygone nations and events, and confers upon man today the essence of all human knowledge and attainment throughout the ages. By intellectual processes and logical deductions of reason this superpower in man can penetrate the mysteries of the future and anticipate its happenings.

Science is the first emanation from God toward man. All cre- 3 ated beings embody the potentiality of material perfection, but the power of intellectual investigation and scientific acquisition is a higher virtue specialized to man alone. Other beings and organisms are deprived of this potentiality and attainment. God has created or deposited this love of reality in man. The development and progress of a nation is according to the measure and degree of that nation's scientific attainments. Through this means its greatness is continually increased, and day by day the welfare and prosperity of its people are assured.

All blessings are divine in origin, but none can be compared 4 with this power of intellectual investigation and research, which is an eternal gift producing fruits of unending delight. Man is ever partaking of these fruits. All other blessings are temporary; this is an everlasting possession. Even sovereignty has its limitations and overthrow; this is a kingship and dominion which none may usurp or destroy. Briefly, it is an eternal blessing and divine bestowal, the supreme gift of God to man. Therefore, you should put forward your most earnest efforts toward the acquisition of science and arts. The greater your attainment, the higher your standard in the divine purpose. The man of science is perceiving and endowed with vision, whereas he who is ignorant and neglectful of this development is blind. The investigating mind is attentive, alive; the callous and indifferent mind is deaf and dead. A scientific man is a true index and representative of humanity, for through processes of inductive reasoning and research he is informed of all that appertains to humanity, its status, conditions and happenings. He studies the human body politic, understands social problems and weaves the web and texture of civilization. In fact, science may be likened to a mirror wherein the infinite forms and images of existing things are revealed and reflected. It is the very foundation of all individual and national development. Without this basis of investigation, development is impossible. Therefore, seek with diligent endeavor the knowledge and attainment of all that lies within the power of this wonderful bestowal.

5   We have already stated that science or the attribute of scientific penetration is supernatural and that all other blessings of God are within the boundary of nature. What is the proof of this? All created things except man are captives of nature. The stars and suns swinging through infinite space, all earthly forms of life and existence—whether mineral, vegetable or animal—come under the dominion and control of natural law. Man through scientific knowledge and power rules nature and utilizes her laws to do his bidding. According to natural limitations he is a creature of earth, restricted to life upon its surface, but through scientific utilization of material laws he soars in the sky, sails upon the ocean and dives beneath it. The products of his invention and discovery, so familiar to us in daily life, were once mysteries of nature. For instance, man has brought electricity out of the plane of the invisible into the plane of the visible,

harnessed and imprisoned that mysterious natural agent and made it the servant of his needs and wishes. Similar instances are many, but we will not prolong this. Man, as it were, takes the sword out of nature's hand and with it for his scepter of authority dominates nature itself. Nature is without the crown of human faculties and attributes. Man possesses conscious intelligence and reflection; nature does not. This is an established fundamental among philosophers. Man is endowed with volition and memory; nature has neither. Man can seek out the mysteries latent in nature, whereas nature is not conscious of her own hidden phenomena. Man is progressive; nature is stationary, without the power of progression or retrogression. Man is endowed with ideal virtues—for example, intellection, volition, faith, confession and acknowledgment of God—while nature is devoid of all these. The ideal faculties of man, including the capacity for scientific acquisition, are beyond nature's ken. These are powers whereby man is differentiated and distinguished from all other forms of life. This is the bestowal of divine idealism, the crown adorning human heads. Notwithstanding the gift of this supernatural power, it is most amazing that materialists still consider themselves within the bonds and captivity of nature. The truth is that God has endowed man with virtues, powers and ideal faculties of which nature is entirely bereft and by which man is elevated, distinguished and superior. We must thank God for these bestowals, for these powers He has given us, for this crown He has placed upon our heads.

How shall we utilize these gifts and expend these bounties? 6 By directing our efforts toward the unification of the human race. We must use these powers in establishing the oneness of the world of humanity, appreciate these virtues by accomplishing the unity of whites and blacks, devote this divine intelligence to the perfecting of amity and accord among all branches of the human family so that under the protection and providence of God the East and West may hold each other's hands and become as lovers. Then will mankind be as one nation, one race and kind—as waves of one ocean. Although these waves may differ in form and shape, they are waves of the same sea. Flowers may be variegated in colors, but they are all flowers of one garden. Trees differ though they grow in the same orchard. All are nourished and quickened into life by the bounty of the same rain, all grow and develop by the heat and light of the one sun, all are refreshed and exhilarated by the same breeze that they may bring forth varied fruits. This is according to the creative wisdom. If all trees bore the same kind of fruit, it would cease to be delicious. In their never-ending variety man finds enjoyment instead of monotony.

7   And now as I look into your faces, I am reminded of trees varying in color and form but all bearing luscious and delectable fruits, fragrant and delightful to the inner and outer senses. The radiance and spirituality of this meeting is through the favor of God. Our hearts are uplifted in thankfulness to Him. Praise be to God! You are living upon the great continent of the West, enjoying the perfect liberty, security and peace of this just government. There is no cause for sorrow or unhappiness anywhere; every means of happiness and enjoyment is about you, for in this human world there is no greater blessing than liberty. You do not know. I, who for forty years have been a prisoner, do know. I do know the value and blessing of liberty. For you have been and are now living in freedom, and you have no fear of anybody. Is there a greater blessing than this? Freedom! Liberty! Security! These are the great bestowals of God. Therefore, praise ye God! I will now pray in your behalf.

8

24 April 1912

Talk at Children's Reception
Studio Hall
1219 Connecticut Avenue, Washington, D.C.

NOTES BY JOSEPH H. HANNEN

WHAT a wonderful meeting this is! These are the children of the 1
Kingdom. The song we have just listened to was very beautiful
in melody and words. The art of music is divine and effective.
It is the food of the soul and spirit. Through the power and
charm of music the spirit of man is uplifted. It has wonderful
sway and effect in the hearts of children, for their hearts are
pure, and melodies have great influence in them. The latent
talents with which the hearts of these children are endowed will
find expression through the medium of music. Therefore, you
must exert yourselves to make them proficient; teach them to
sing with excellence and effect. It is incumbent upon each child
to know something of music, for without knowledge of this art
the melodies of instrument and voice cannot be rightly enjoyed.
Likewise, it is necessary that the schools teach it in order that the
souls and hearts of the pupils may become vivified and exhilarated
and their lives be brightened with enjoyment.

Today illumined and spiritual children are gathered in this 2
meeting. They are the children of the Kingdom. The Kingdom
of heaven is for such souls as these, for they are near to God. They
have pure hearts. They have spiritual faces. The effect of the divine
teachings is manifest in the perfect purity of their hearts. That is
why Christ has addressed the world, saying, "Except ye be con-

verted, and become as little children, ye shall not enter into the kingdom of heaven"—that is, men must become pure in heart to know God. The teachings have had great effect. Spiritual souls! Tender souls! The hearts of all children are of the utmost purity. They are mirrors upon which no dust has fallen. But this purity is on account of weakness and innocence, not on account of any strength and testing, for as this is the early period of their childhood, their hearts and minds are unsullied by the world. They cannot display any great intelligence. They have neither hypocrisy nor deceit. This is on account of the child's weakness, whereas the man becomes pure through his strength. Through the power of intelligence he becomes simple; through the great power of reason and understanding and not through the power of weakness he becomes sincere. When he attains to the state of perfection, he will receive these qualities; his heart becomes purified, his spirit enlightened, his soul is sensitized and tender—all through his great strength. This is the difference between the perfect man and the child. Both have the underlying qualities of simplicity and sincerity—the child through the power of weakness and the man through the power of strength.

3   I pray in behalf of these children and beg confirmation and assistance for them from the Kingdom of Abhá so that each one may be trained under the shadow of the protection of God, each may become like a lighted candle in the world of humanity, a tender and growing plant in the rose garden of Abhá; that these children may be so trained and educated that they shall give life to the world of humanity; that they may receive insight; that they may bestow hearing upon the people of the world; that they may sow the seeds of eternal life and be accepted in the threshold of God; that they may become characterized with such virtues, perfections and qualities that their mothers, fathers and relatives will be thankful to God, well pleased and hopeful. This is my wish and prayer.

I give you my advice, and it is this: Train these children with 4
divine exhortations. From their childhood instill in their hearts
the love of God so they may manifest in their lives the fear of
God and have confidence in the bestowals of God. Teach them
to free themselves from human imperfections and to acquire the
divine perfections latent in the heart of man. The life of man
is useful if he attains the perfections of man. If he becomes the
center of the imperfections of the world of humanity, death
is better than life, and nonexistence better than existence.
Therefore, make ye an effort in order that these children may
be rightly trained and educated and that each one of them may
attain perfection in the world of humanity. Know ye the value
of these children, for they are all my children.

9

24 April 1912

Talk at Home of Mr. and Mrs. Arthur J. Parsons
1700 Eighteenth Street, NW, Washington, D.C.

NOTES BY JOSEPH H. HANNEN

YOU are welcome this afternoon, most welcome. I am ever happy 1
to see you. I ask God that meeting me may be productive of
results; that it may not be like ordinary gatherings, for those
who hold meetings where groups of people assemble usually
have some interest to further. Praise be to God! I have no personal interests. I have an interest in the Kingdom, and this is a
sincere intention. I have perfect love for you; therefore, I have
traveled this long distance to meet and greet you. I hope that
these gatherings may be productive of great results, and there

is no greater result than the love of God. There is no greater result than bonds of service in the divine Kingdom and attainment to the good pleasure of the Lord. Therefore, I desire that your hearts may be directed to the Kingdom of God, that your intentions may be pure and sincere, your purposes turned toward altruistic accomplishment unmindful of your own welfare; nay, rather, may all your intentions center in the welfare of humanity, and may you seek to sacrifice yourselves in the pathway of devotion to mankind. Even as Jesus Christ forfeited His life, may you, likewise, offer yourselves in the threshold of sacrifice for the betterment of the world; and just as Bahá'u'lláh suffered severe ordeals and calamities nearly fifty years for you, may you be willing to undergo difficulties and withstand catastrophes for humanity in general. May you bear these trials and tests most willingly and joyously, for every night is followed by a day, and every day has a night. Every spring has an autumn, and every autumn has its spring. The coming of a Manifestation of God is the season of spiritual spring. For instance, the appearance of Christ was a divine springtime. Therefore, it caused a great commotion and vibrant movement in the world of humanity. The Sun of Reality dawned, the cloud of mercy poured down its rain, the breezes of providence moved, the world became a new world, mankind reflected an extraordinary radiance, souls were educated, minds were developed, intelligences became acute, and the human world attained a new freshness of life, like unto the advent of spring. Then gradually that spring was followed by the autumn of death and decay. The teachings of Christ were forgotten. The Christly bounties ceased. Divine moralities disappeared. Day ended in night. The people became negligent and oblivious. Minds weakened until conditions reached such a crisis that material science rose in the ascendant. Knowledge and sciences of the Kingdom became obsolete, the mysteries of God deepened, and the traces of the bounties of Christ were completely obliterated. The nations were enmeshed in superstition and blind imitation. Discord and disagreement arose, culminating in strife, war and bloodshed. Hearts were torn asunder in violence. Various denominations appeared, diverse sects and creeds arose, and the whole world was plunged into darkness.

At such a time as this Bahá'u'lláh dawned from the horizon of 2 Persia. He reformed and renewed the fundamentals and realities of Christ's teachings. He endured the greatest difficulties and underwent the severest ordeals.

Praise be to God that the teachings of God are revoiced, the 3 light of reality has dawned again, the effulgence is increasing daily, and the radiance is shining more gloriously in the zenith. From the cloud of mercy a deluge is descending; the Sun of Reality is brilliant in its eternal station. Again we are hopeful that the same springtime may pitch its tent and that these boundless bestowals may appear once more among us. Through your efforts and sincerity this is made possible. If you arise in the Cause of God with divine power, heavenly grace, the sincerity of the Kingdom, a merciful heart and decisive intention, it is certain that the world of humanity will be entirely illumined, the moralities of mankind will become merciful, the foundations of the Most Great Peace will be laid, and the oneness of the kingdom of man will become a reality. This is the great bounty I desire for you, and I pray and supplicate the divine threshold, imploring in your behalf.

O Thou merciful God! O Thou Who art mighty and power- 4 ful! O Thou most kind Father! These servants have gathered together, turning to Thee, supplicating Thy threshold, desiring Thine endless bounties from Thy great assurance. They have no purpose save Thy good pleasure. They have no intention save service to the world of humanity.

O God! Make this assemblage radiant. Make the hearts merci- 5 ful. Confer the bounties of the Holy Spirit. Endow them with a

75

power from heaven. Bless them with heavenly minds. Increase their sincerity, so that with all humility and contrition they may turn to Thy kingdom and be occupied with service to the world of humanity. May each one become a radiant candle. May each one become a brilliant star. May each one become beautiful in color and redolent of fragrance in the Kingdom of God.

6   O kind Father! Confer Thy blessings. Consider not our shortcomings. Shelter us under Thy protection. Remember not our sins. Heal us with Thy mercy. We are weak; Thou art mighty. We are poor; Thou art rich. We are sick; Thou art the Physician. We are needy; Thou art most generous.

7   O God! Endow us with Thy providence. Thou art the Powerful. Thou art the Giver. Thou art the Beneficent.

10

24 April 1912

Talk at Home of Mrs. Andrew J. Dyer
1937 Thirteenth Street, NW, Washington, D.C.

NOTES BY JOSEPH H. HANNEN

1   A MEETING such as this seems like a beautiful cluster of precious jewels—pearls, rubies, diamonds, sapphires. It is a source of joy and delight. Whatever is conducive to the unity of the world of mankind is most acceptable and praiseworthy; whatever is the cause of discord and disunion is saddening and deplorable. Consider the significance of unity and harmony.

2   This evening I will speak to you upon the subject of existence and nonexistence, life and death. Existence is the expression and outcome of composition and combination. Nonexistence is the

expression and outcome of division and disintegration. If we study the forms of existence in the material universe, we find that all created things are the result of composition. Material elements have grouped together in infinite variety and endless forms. Each organism is a compound; each object is an expression of elemental affinity. We find the complex human organism simply an aggregation of cellular structure; the tree is a composite of plant cells; the animal, a combination and grouping of cellular atoms or units, and so on. Existence or the expression of being is, therefore, composition; and nonexistence is decomposition, division, disintegration. When elements have been brought together in a certain plan of combination, the result is the human organism; when these elements separate and disperse, the outcome is death and nonexistence. Life is, therefore, the product of composition; and death signifies decomposition.

Likewise, in the world of minds and souls, fellowship, which 3 is an expression of composition, is conducive to life, whereas discord, which is an expression of decomposition, is the equivalent of death. Without cohesion among the individual elements which compose the body politic, disintegration and decay must inevitably follow and life be extinguished. Ferocious animals have no fellowship. The vultures and tigers are solitary, whereas domestic animals live together in complete harmony. The sheep, black and white, associate without discord. Birds of various species and colors wing their flight and feed together without a trace of enmity or disagreement. Therefore, in the world of humanity it is wise and seemly that all the individual members should manifest unity and affinity. In the clustered jewels of the races may the blacks be as sapphires and rubies and the whites as diamonds and pearls. The composite beauty of humanity will be witnessed in their unity and blending. How glorious the spectacle of real unity among mankind! How conducive to peace, confidence and happiness if races and nations were united in fellowship and accord! The Prophets of God were sent into the world upon this mission of unity and agreement: that these long-separated sheep might flock together. When the sheep separate, they are exposed to danger, but in a flock and under protection of the shepherd they are safe from the attack of all ferocious enemies.

4   When the racial elements of the American nation unite in actual fellowship and accord, the lights of the oneness of humanity will shine, the day of eternal glory and bliss will dawn, the spirit of God encompass, and the divine favors descend. Under the leadership and training of God, the real Shepherd, all will be protected and preserved. He will lead them in green pastures of happiness and sustenance, and they will attain to the real goal of existence. This is the blessing and benefit of unity; this is the outcome of love. This is the sign of the Most Great Peace; this is the star of the oneness of the human world. Consider how blessed this condition will be. I pray for you and ask the confirmation and assistance of God in your behalf.

11

25 April 1912

Talk to Theosophical Society
Home of Mr. and Mrs. Arthur J. Parsons
1700 Eighteenth Street, NW, Washington, D.C.

NOTES BY JOSEPH H. HANNEN

1   THE greatest power in the realm and range of human existence is spirit—the divine breath which animates and pervades all things. It is manifested throughout creation in different degrees

or kingdoms. In the vegetable kingdom it is the augmentative spirit or power of growth, the animus of life and development in plants, trees and organisms of the floral world. In this degree of its manifestation spirit is unconscious of the powers which qualify the kingdom of the animal. The distinctive virtue or plus of the animal is sense perception; it sees, hears, smells, tastes and feels but is incapable, in turn, of conscious ideation or reflection which characterizes and differentiates the human kingdom. The animal neither exercises nor apprehends this distinctive human power and gift. From the visible it cannot draw conclusions regarding the invisible, whereas the human mind from visible and known premises attains knowledge of the unknown and invisible. For instance, Christopher Columbus from information based upon known and provable facts drew conclusions which led him unerringly across the vast ocean to the unknown continent of America. Such power of accomplishment is beyond the range of animal intelligence. Therefore, this power is a distinctive attribute of the human spirit and kingdom. The animal spirit cannot penetrate and discover the mysteries of things. It is a captive of the senses. No amount of teaching, for instance, would enable it to grasp the fact that the sun is stationary, and the earth moves around it. Likewise, the human spirit has its limitations. It cannot comprehend the phenomena of the Kingdom transcending the human station, for it is a captive of powers and life forces which have their operation upon its own plane of existence, and it cannot go beyond that boundary.

There is, however, another Spirit, which may be termed the Divine, to which Jesus Christ refers when He declares that man must be born of its quickening and baptized with its living fire. Souls deprived of that Spirit are accounted as dead, though they are possessed of the human spirit. Jesus Christ has pronounced them dead inasmuch as they have no portion of the Divine Spirit. He says, "Let the dead bury their dead." In another instance He declares, "That which is born of the flesh is flesh; and that which is born of the Spirit is spirit." By this He means that souls, though alive in the human kingdom, are nevertheless dead if devoid of this particular spirit of divine quickening. They have not partaken of the divine life of the higher Kingdom, for the soul which partakes of the power of the Divine Spirit is, verily, living.

3   This quickening spirit emanates spontaneously from the Sun of Truth, from the reality of Divinity, and is not a revelation or a manifestation. It is like the rays of the sun. The rays are emanations from the sun. This does not mean that the sun has become divisible, that a part of the sun has come out into space. This plant beside me has risen from the seed; therefore, it is a manifestation and unfoldment of the seed. The seed, as you can see, has unfolded in manifestation, and the result is this plant. Every leaf of the plant is a part of the seed. But the reality of Divinity is indivisible, and each individual of humankind cannot be a part of it as is often claimed. Nay, rather, the individual realities of mankind, when spiritually born, are emanations from the reality of Divinity, just as the flame, heat and light of the sun are the effulgence of the sun and not a part of the sun itself. Therefore, a spirit has emanated from the reality of Divinity, and its effulgences have become visible in human entities or realities. This ray and this heat are permanent. There is no cessation in the effulgence. As long as the sun exists, the heat and light will exist, and inasmuch as eternality is a property of Divinity, this emanation is everlasting. There is no cessation in its outpouring. The more the world of humanity develops, the more the effulgences or emanations of Divinity will become revealed, just as the stone, when it becomes polished and pure as a mirror, will reflect in fuller degree the glory and splendor of the sun.

The mission of the Prophets, the revelation of the Holy   4
Books, the manifestation of the heavenly Teachers and the
purpose of divine philosophy all center in the training of the human realities so that they may become clear and pure as mirrors
and reflect the light and love of the Sun of Reality. Therefore, I
hope that—whether you be in the East or the West—you will
strive with heart and soul in order that day by day the world of
humanity may become glorified, more spiritual, more sanctified;
and that the splendor of the Sun of Reality may be revealed fully
in human hearts as in a mirror. This is worthy of the world of
mankind. This is the true evolution and progress of humanity.
This is the supreme bestowal. Otherwise, by simple development along material lines man is not perfected. At most, the
physical aspect of man, his natural or material conditions, may
become stabilized and improved, but he will remain deprived of
the spiritual or divine bestowal. He is then like a body without
a spirit, a lamp without the light, an eye without the power of
vision, an ear that hears no sound, a mind incapable of perceiving, an intellect minus the power of reason.

Man has two powers; and his development, two aspects.   5
One power is connected with the material world, and by it he
is capable of material advancement. The other power is spiritual, and through its development his inner, potential nature
is awakened. These powers are like two wings. Both must be
developed, for flight is impossible with one wing. Praise be to
God! Material advancement has been evident in the world, but
there is need of spiritual advancement in like proportion. We
must strive unceasingly and without rest to accomplish the
development of the spiritual nature in man, and endeavor with
tireless energy to advance humanity toward the nobility of its
true and intended station. For the body of man is accidental; it
is of no importance. The time of its disintegration will inevitably

come. But the spirit of man is essential and, therefore, eternal. It is a divine bounty. It is the effulgence of the Sun of Reality and, therefore, of greater importance than the physical body.

6   I pray for you. You have come to visit me, and I am most grateful. I shall ask confirmation and assistance for you from God, the Generous, the Bestower, that you may be aided in serving the world of humanity.

12

25 April 1912

Message to Esperantists
Home of Mr. and Mrs. Arthur J. Parsons
1700 Eighteenth Street, NW, Washington, D.C.

NOTES BY JOSEPH H. HANNEN

1   TODAY the greatest need of the world of humanity is discontinuance of the existing misunderstandings among nations. This can be accomplished through the unity of language. Unless the unity of languages is realized, the Most Great Peace and the oneness of the human world cannot be effectively organized and established because the function of language is to portray the mysteries and secrets of human hearts. The heart is like a box, and language is the key. Only by using the key can we open the box and observe the gems it contains. Therefore, the question of an auxiliary international tongue has the utmost importance. Through this means international education and training become possible; the evidence and history of the past can be acquired. The spread of the known facts of the human world depends upon language. The explanation of divine teach-

ings can only be through this medium. As long as diversity of tongues and lack of comprehension of other languages continue, these glorious aims cannot be realized. Therefore, the very first service to the world of man is to establish this auxiliary international means of communication. It will become the cause of the tranquillity of the human commonwealth. Through it sciences and arts will be spread among the nations, and it will prove to be the means of the progress and development of all races. We must endeavor with all our powers to establish this international auxiliary language throughout the world. It is my hope that it may be perfected through the bounties of God and that intelligent men may be selected from the various countries of the world to organize an international congress whose chief aim will be the promotion of this universal medium of speech.

13

25 April 1912

Talk at Home of Mr. and Mrs. Arthur J. Parsons
1700 Eighteenth Street, NW, Washington, D.C.

NOTES BY JOSEPH H. HANNEN

IN the world of existence the greatest bestowals of God are His 1 teachings. The other bounties of God are limited as regards their benefits and provision. Human existence itself is a divine bestowal, but it is circumscribed with limitations. Sight and hearing are bounties of God; both are limited. And so it is with all the other bestowals; the circle of their operation is confined, restricted, whereas the sphere of the divine teachings is boundless. Centuries and ages pass away, but their efficacy continues like the spirit of life which animates the world of existence. Without the teachings of God the world of humanity is like the animal kingdom. What difference is there between the animal and man? The difference is this: that the animal is not capable of apprehending the divine teachings, whereas man is worthy of them and possesses the capacity to understand. In the animal kingdom there is no such bestowal; therefore, there is limited progression. At most, evolution in that kingdom is a development of the organism. In the beginning it is small, undeveloped; it develops, becomes larger; but its sphere of intellectual growth is limited. Therefore, the teachings of God are the bestowals specialized for man.

2   Although the divine teachings are truth and reality, yet with the passage of time thick clouds envelop and obscure them. These clouds are imitations and superstitions; they are not the fundamentals. Then the Sun of Truth, the Word of God, arises again, shines forth once more in the glory of its power and disperses the enveloping darkness.

3   For a long time the divine precepts of the effulgent Word were obscured by clouds of superstition and error until Bahá'u'lláh appeared upon the horizon of humanity, rent the shadows, scattered the clouds and revealed anew the foundations of the teachings of God.

4   The first teaching of Bahá'u'lláh is the duty incumbent upon all to investigate reality. What does it mean to investigate reality? It means that man must forget all hearsay and examine truth himself, for he does not know whether statements he hears are in accordance with reality or not. Wherever he finds truth or reality, he must hold to it, forsaking, discarding all else; for outside of reality there is naught but superstition and imagination. For example, during the days of Jesus Christ the Jews were expecting the appearance of the Messiah, praying and beseeching God day and night that the Promised One might

appear. Why did they reject Him when He did appear? They denied Him absolutely, refused to believe in Him. There was no abuse and persecution which they did not heap upon Him. They reviled Him with curses, placed a crown of thorns upon His head, led Him through the streets in scorn and derision and finally crucified Him. Why did they do this? Because they did not investigate the truth or reality of Christ and were not able to recognize Him as the Messiah of God. Had they investigated sincerely for themselves, they would surely have believed in Him, respected Him and bowed before Him in reverence. They would have considered His manifestation the greatest bestowal upon mankind. They would have accepted Him as the very Savior of man; but, alas, they were veiled, they held to imitations of ancestral beliefs and hearsay and did not investigate the truth of Christ. They were submerged in the sea of superstitions and were, therefore, deprived of witnessing that glorious bounty; they were withheld from the fragrances or breaths of the Holy Spirit and suffered in themselves the greatest debasement and degradation.

Reality or truth is one, yet there are many religious beliefs,   5 denominations, creeds and differing opinions in the world today. Why should these differences exist? Because they do not investigate and examine the fundamental unity, which is one and unchangeable. If they seek reality itself, they will agree and be united; for reality is indivisible and not multiple. It is evident, therefore, that there is nothing of greater importance to mankind than the investigation of truth.

The second teaching of Bahá'u'lláh is the oneness of the world   6 of humanity. Every human creature is the servant of God. All have been created and reared by the power and favor of God; all have been blessed with the bounties of the same Sun of divine truth; all have quaffed from the fountain of the infinite mercy of God; and all in His estimation and love are equal as servants. He is beneficent and kind to all. Therefore, no one should glorify himself over another; no one should manifest pride or superiority toward another; no one should look upon another with scorn and contempt; and no one should deprive or oppress a fellow creature. All must be considered as submerged in the ocean of God's mercy. We must associate with all humanity in gentleness and kindliness. We must love all with love of the heart. Some are ignorant; they must be trained and educated. One is sick; he must be healed. Another is as a child; we must assist him to attain maturity. We must not detest him who is ailing, neither shun him, scorn nor curse him, but care for him with the utmost kindness and tenderness. An infant must not be treated with disdain simply because it is an infant. Our responsibility is to train, educate and develop it in order that it may advance toward maturity.

7   The third teaching or principle of Bahá'u'lláh is that religion and science are in complete agreement. Every religion which is not in accordance with established science is superstition. Religion must be reasonable. If it does not square with reason, it is superstition and without foundation. It is like a mirage, which deceives man by leading him to think it is a body of water. God has endowed man with reason that he may perceive what is true. If we insist that such and such a subject is not to be reasoned out and tested according to the established logical modes of the intellect, what is the use of the reason which God has given man? The eye is the organ of sense by which we view the world of outer phenomena; hearing is the faculty for distinguishing sounds; taste senses the properties of objects, such as bitter, sweet; smell detects and differentiates odors; touch reveals attributes of matter and perfects our communication with the outer world; yet after all, the circle and range of perception by the five senses is exceedingly limited. But the intellectual faculty of man is unlimited in its sphere of action. The eye views details

perhaps a mile, but the intellect can perceive the far East and West. The ear may hear tone modulations at one thousand feet, but the mind of man can detect the harmonies of the heavenly spheres as they swing in their courses. Mind makes geological discoveries in subterranean depths and determines the processes of creation in the earth's lowest strata. The sciences and arts, all inventions, crafts, trades and their products have come forth from the intellect of man. It is evident that within the human organism the intellect occupies the supreme station. Therefore, if religious belief, principle or creed is not in accordance with the intellect and the power of reason, it is surely superstition.

At another time I shall speak further of the principles revealed 8 in the teachings of Bahá'u'lláh.

Talks 'Abdu'l-Bahá Delivered in Chicago, Wilmette, and Evanston

30 April 1912

*Talk at Public Meeting Concluding Convention of
Bahá'í Temple Unity
Drill Hall, Masonic Temple, Chicago, Illinois*

NOTES BY JOSEPH H. HANNEN

AMONG the institutes of the Holy Books is that of the foundation   1
of places of worship. That is to say, an edifice or temple is to be
built in order that humanity might find a place of meeting, and
this is to be conducive to unity and fellowship among them.
The real temple is the very Word of God; for to it all humanity
must turn, and it is the center of unity for all mankind. It is
the collective center, the cause of accord and communion of
hearts, the sign of the solidarity of the human race, the source
of eternal life. Temples are the symbols of the divine uniting
force so that when the people gather there in the House of God
they may recall the fact that the law has been revealed for them
and that the law is to unite them. They will realize that just as
this temple was founded for the unification of mankind, the
law preceding and creating it came forth in the manifest Word.
Jesus Christ, addressing Peter, said, "Thou art Peter, and upon
this rock I will build my church." This utterance was indicative
of the faith of Peter, signifying: This faith of thine, O Peter, is
the very cause and message of unity to the nations; it shall be
the bond of union between the hearts of men and the foundation of the oneness of the world of humanity. In brief, the origi-

nal purpose of temples and houses of worship is simply that of unity—places of meeting where various peoples, different races and souls of every capacity may come together in order that love and agreement should be manifest between them. That is why Bahá'u'lláh has commanded that a place of worship be built for all the religionists of the world; that all religions, races and sects may come together within its universal shelter; that the proclamation of the oneness of mankind shall go forth from its open courts of holiness—the announcement that humanity is the servant of God and that all are submerged in the ocean of His mercy. It is the Mashriqu'l-Adhkár. The world of existence may be likened to this temple and place of worship. For just as the external world is a place where the people of all races and colors, varying faiths, denominations and conditions come together—just as they are submerged in the same sea of divine favors—so, likewise, all may meet under the dome of the Mashriqu'l-Adhkár and adore the one God in the same spirit of truth; for the ages of darkness have passed away, and the century of light has come. Ignorant prejudices are being dispelled, and the light of unity is shining. The differences existing between nations and peoples will soon be annulled, and the fundamentals of the divine religions, which are no other than the oneness and solidarity of the human race, are being established. For thousands of years the human race has been at war. It is enough. Now let mankind, for a time at least, consort in amity and peace. Enmity and hatred have ruled. Let the world, for a period, exercise love. For thousands of years the nations have denied each other, considering each other as infidel and inferior. It is sufficient. We must now realize that we are the servants of one God, that we turn to one beneficent Father, live under one divine law, seek one reality and have one desire. Thus may we live in the utmost friendship and love, and in return the favors and bounties of God shall surround us; the world of humanity will be reformed; mankind, enjoy a new life; eternal light will illumine, and heavenly moralities become manifest.

Then divine policy shall govern the world, for the divine 2 policy is the oneness of humanity. God is just and kind to all. He considers all as His servants. He excludes none, and His judgments are correct and true. No matter how complete human policy and foresight may appear, they are imperfect. If we do not seek the counsel of God or if we refuse to follow His dictates, it is presumptive evidence that we are knowing and wise, whereas God is ignorant; that we are sagacious and God is not. God forbid! We seek shelter in His mercy for this suggestion! No matter how far the human intelligence may advance, it is still but a drop, while divine omniscience is the ocean. Shall we say that a drop is imbued or endowed with qualities of which the ocean is devoid? Shall we believe that the policy and plan of this atom of a human soul are superior to the wisdom of the Omniscient? There is no greater ignorance than this. Briefly, some are mere children; with the utmost love we must educate them to make them wise. Others are sick and ailing; we must tenderly treat them until they recover. Some have unworthy morals; we must train them toward the standard of true morality. Other than this we are all the servants of one God and under the providence and protection of one Father.

These are the institutions of God and the foundations of His 3 temple, the Mashriqu'l-Adhkár. The outer edifice is a symbol of the inner. May the people be admonished thereby.

I pray in your behalf that your hearts may be enlightened 4 with the light of the love of God; that your minds may develop daily; that your spirits may become aglow with the fire and illumination of His glad tidings, until these divine foundations may become established throughout the human world. The first of these institutions and foundations is the oneness of humanity and love among mankind. The second is the Most Great Peace. Praise be to God! This American democracy manifests capacity, showing forth readiness to become the standard-bearer of the Most Great Peace. May its hosts be the hosts of the oneness of humanity. May they serve the threshold of God and spread the message of the good pleasure of God.

5   O Thou kind Lord! This gathering is turning to Thee. These hearts are radiant with Thy love. These minds and spirits are exhilarated by the message of Thy glad tidings. O God! Let this American democracy become glorious in spiritual degrees even as it has aspired to material degrees, and render this just government victorious. Confirm this revered nation to upraise the standard of the oneness of humanity, to promulgate the Most Great Peace, to become thereby most glorious and praiseworthy among all the nations of the world. O God! This American nation is worthy of Thy favors and is deserving of Thy mercy. Make it precious and near to Thee through Thy bounty and bestowal.

2

30 April 1912

Talk at Hull House
Chicago, Illinois

NOTES BY JOSEPH H. HANNEN

1   WHEN we view the world of creation, we find that all living things may be classified under two aspects of existence. First, they possess bodies composed of material substance common to all—whether vegetable, animal or human. This is their point of agreement or, as it is philosophically termed, their point of

contact. Second, they vary and differ from each other in degree and function—that is to say, in their respective kingdoms. This is their point of distinction and differentiation. For instance, the vegetable and animal are alike in the fact that their bodies are composed of the same material elements but widely different in their kingdoms and powers. Man is like the animal in physical structure but otherwise immeasurably separated and superior.

In the human kingdom itself there are points of contact, properties common to all mankind; likewise, there are points of distinction which separate race from race, individual from individual. If the points of contact, which are the common properties of humanity, overcome the peculiar points of distinction, unity is assured. On the other hand, if the points of differentiation overcome the points of agreement, disunion and weakness result. One of the important questions which affect the unity and the solidarity of mankind is the fellowship and equality of the white and colored races. Between these two races certain points of agreement and points of distinction exist which warrant just and mutual consideration. The points of contact are many; for in the material or physical plane of being, both are constituted alike and exist under the same law of growth and bodily development. Furthermore, both live and move in the plane of the senses and are endowed with human intelligence. There are many other mutual qualifications. In this country, the United States of America, patriotism is common to both races; all have equal rights to citizenship, speak one language, receive the blessings of the same civilization, and follow the precepts of the same religion. In fact numerous points of partnership and agreement exist between the two races; whereas the one point of distinction is that of color. Shall this, the least of all distinctions, be allowed to separate you as races and individuals? In physical bodies, in the law of growth, in sense endowment, intelligence, patriotism, language, citizenship, civilization and religion you are one and the same. A single point of distinction exists—that of racial color. God is not pleased with—neither should any reasonable or intelligent man be willing to recognize—inequality in the races because of this distinction.

3   But there is need of a superior power to overcome human prejudices, a power which nothing in the world of mankind can withstand and which will overshadow the effect of all other forces at work in human conditions. That irresistible power is the love of God. It is my hope and prayer that it may destroy the prejudice of this one point of distinction between you and unite you all permanently under its hallowed protection. Bahá'u'lláh has proclaimed the oneness of the world of humanity. He has caused various nations and divergent creeds to unite. He has declared that difference of race and color is like the variegated beauty of flowers in a garden. If you enter a garden, you will see yellow, white, blue, red flowers in profusion and beauty—each radiant within itself and although different from the others, lending its own charm to them. Racial difference in the human kingdom is similar. If all the flowers in a garden were of the same color, the effect would be monotonous and wearying to the eye.

4   Therefore, Bahá'u'lláh hath said that the various races of humankind lend a composite harmony and beauty of color to the whole. Let all associate, therefore, in this great human garden even as flowers grow and blend together side by side without discord or disagreement between them.

3

30 April 1912

Talk at Fourth Annual Conference of the National Association
for the Advancement of Colored People
Handel Hall, Chicago, Illinois

NOTES BY JOSEPH H. HANNEN

ACCORDING to the words of the Old Testament God has said,   1
"Let us make man in our image, after our likeness." This indicates that man is of the image and likeness of God—that is to
say, the perfections of God, the divine virtues, are reflected or
revealed in the human reality. Just as the light and effulgence
of the sun when cast upon a polished mirror are reflected fully,
gloriously, so, likewise, the qualities and attributes of Divinity
are radiated from the depths of a pure human heart. This is an
evidence that man is the most noble of God's creatures.

Each kingdom of creation is endowed with its necessary   2
complement of attributes and powers. The mineral possesses
inherent virtues of its own kingdom in the scale of existence.
The vegetable possesses the qualities of the mineral plus an augmentative virtue, or power of growth. The animal is endowed
with the virtues of both the mineral and vegetable plane plus
the power of intellect. The human kingdom is replete with the
perfections of all the kingdoms below it with the addition of
powers peculiar to man alone. Man is, therefore, superior to all
the creatures below him, the loftiest and most glorious being of
creation. Man is the microcosm; and the infinite universe, the
macrocosm. The mysteries of the greater world, or macrocosm,
are expressed or revealed in the lesser world, the microcosm. The

tree, so to speak, is the greater world, and the seed in its relation to the tree is the lesser world. But the whole of the great tree is potentially latent and hidden in the little seed. When this seed is planted and cultivated, the tree is revealed. Likewise, the greater world, the macrocosm, is latent and miniatured in the lesser world, or microcosm, of man. This constitutes the universality or perfection of virtues potential in mankind. Therefore, it is said that man has been created in the image and likeness of God.

3   Let us now discover more specifically how he is the image and likeness of God and what is the standard or criterion by which he can be measured and estimated. This standard can be no other than the divine virtues which are revealed in him. Therefore, every man imbued with divine qualities, who reflects heavenly moralities and perfections, who is the expression of ideal and praiseworthy attributes, is, verily, in the image and likeness of God. If a man possesses wealth, can we call him an image and likeness of God? Or is human honor and notoriety the criterion of divine nearness? Can we apply the test of racial color and say that man of a certain hue—white, black, brown, yellow, red—is the true image of his Creator? We must conclude that color is not the standard and estimate of judgment and that it is of no importance, for color is accidental in nature. The spirit and intelligence of man is essential, and that is the manifestation of divine virtues, the merciful bestowals of God, the eternal life and baptism through the Holy Spirit. Therefore, be it known that color or race is of no importance. He who is the image and likeness of God, who is the manifestation of the bestowals of God, is acceptable at the threshold of God—whether his color be white, black or brown; it matters not. Man is not man simply because of bodily attributes. The standard of divine measure and judgment is his intelligence and spirit.

4   Therefore, let this be the only criterion and estimate, for this is the image and likeness of God. A man's heart may be pure

and white though his outer skin be black; or his heart be dark
and sinful though his racial color is white. The character and
purity of the heart is of all importance. The heart illumined by
the light of God is nearest and dearest to God, and inasmuch
as God has endowed man with such favor that he is called the
image of God, this is truly a supreme perfection of attainment,
a divine station which is not to be sacrificed by the mere ac-
cident of color.

4

1 May 1912

Talk at Dedication of the Mashriqu'l-Adhkár Grounds
Wilmette, Illinois

NOTES BY JOSEPH H. HANNEN

THE power which has gathered you here today notwithstanding   1
the cold and windy weather is, indeed, mighty and wonderful.
It is the power of God, the divine favor of Bahá'u'lláh which has
drawn you together. We praise God that through His constraining love human souls are assembled and associated in this way.

Thousands of Mashriqu'l-Adhkárs, dawning points of praise   2
and mention of God for all religionists will be built in the East
and in the West, but this, being the first one erected in the
Occident, has great importance. In the future there will be
many here and elsewhere—in Asia, Europe, even in Africa,
New Zealand and Australia—but this edifice in Chicago is
of especial significance. It has the same importance as the
Mashriqu'l-Adhkár in 'Ishqábád, Caucasus, Russia, the first
one built there. In Persia there are many; some are houses which

have been utilized for the purpose, others are homes entirely devoted to the divine Cause, and in some places temporary structures have been erected. In all the cities of Persia there are Ma<u>sh</u>riqu'l-A<u>dh</u>kárs, but the great dawning point was founded in 'I<u>sh</u>qábád. It possesses superlative importance because it was the first Ma<u>sh</u>riqu'l-A<u>dh</u>kár built. All the Bahá'í friends agreed and contributed their utmost assistance and effort. The Afnán devoted his wealth, gave all he had to it. From such a mighty and combined effort a beautiful edifice arose. Notwithstanding their contributions to that building, they have assisted the fund here in Chicago as well. The Ma<u>sh</u>riqu'l-A<u>dh</u>kár in 'I<u>sh</u>qábád is almost completed. It is centrally located, nine avenues leading into it, nine gardens, nine fountains; all the arrangement and construction is according to the principle and proportion of the number nine. It is like a beautiful bouquet. Imagine a very lofty, imposing edifice surrounded completely by gardens of variegated flowers, with nine avenues leading through them, nine fountains and pools of water. Such is its matchless, beautiful design. Now they are building a hospital, a school for orphans, a home for cripples, a hospice and a large dispensary. God willing, when it is fully completed, it will be a paradise.

3   I hope the Ma<u>sh</u>riqu'l-A<u>dh</u>kár in Chicago will be like this. Endeavor to have the grounds circular in shape. If possible, adjust and exchange the plots in order to make the dimensions and boundaries circular. The Ma<u>sh</u>riqu'l-A<u>dh</u>kár cannot be triangular in shape. It must be in the form of a circle.

5

2 May 1912

Talk at Hotel Plaza
Chicago, Illinois

NOTES BY JOSEPH H. HANNEN

IN this Cause consultation is of vital importance, but spiritual conference and not the mere voicing of personal views is intended. In France I was present at a session of the senate, but the experience was not impressive. Parliamentary procedure should have for its object the attainment of the light of truth upon questions presented and not furnish a battleground for opposition and self-opinion. Antagonism and contradiction are unfortunate and always destructive to truth. In the parliamentary meeting mentioned, altercation and useless quibbling were frequent; the result, mostly confusion and turmoil; even in one instance a physical encounter took place between two members. It was not consultation but comedy.

The purpose is to emphasize the statement that consultation must have for its object the investigation of truth. He who expresses an opinion should not voice it as correct and right but set it forth as a contribution to the consensus of opinion, for the light of reality becomes apparent when two opinions coincide. A spark is produced when flint and steel come together. Man should weigh his opinions with the utmost serenity, calmness and composure. Before expressing his own views he should carefully consider the views already advanced by others. If he finds that a previously expressed opinion is more true and worthy, he should accept it immediately and not willfully hold to an opinion

1

2

99

of his own. By this excellent method he endeavors to arrive at unity and truth. Opposition and division are deplorable. It is better then to have the opinion of a wise, sagacious man; otherwise, contradiction and altercation, in which varied and divergent views are presented, will make it necessary for a judicial body to render decision upon the question. Even a majority opinion or consensus may be incorrect. A thousand people may hold to one view and be mistaken, whereas one sagacious person may be right. Therefore, true consultation is spiritual conference in the attitude and atmosphere of love. Members must love each other in the spirit of fellowship in order that good results may be forthcoming. Love and fellowship are the foundation.

3   The most memorable instance of spiritual consultation was the meeting of the disciples of Jesus Christ upon the mount after His ascension. They said, "Jesus Christ has been crucified, and we have no longer association and intercourse with Him in His physical body; therefore, we must be loyal and faithful to Him, we must be grateful and appreciate Him, for He has raised us from the dead, He made us wise, He has given us eternal life. What shall we do to be faithful to Him?" And so they held council. One of them said, "We must detach ourselves from the chains and fetters of the world; otherwise, we cannot be faithful." The others replied, "That is so." Another said, "Either we must be married and faithful to our wives and children or serve our Lord free from these ties. We cannot be occupied with the care and provision for families and at the same time herald the Kingdom in the wilderness. Therefore, let those who are unmarried remain so, and those who have married provide means of sustenance and comfort for their families and then go forth to spread the message of glad tidings." There were no dissenting voices; all agreed, saying, "That is right." A third disciple said, "To perform worthy deeds in the Kingdom we must be further

self-sacrificing. From now on we should forego ease and bodily comfort, accept every difficulty, forget self and teach the Cause of God." This found acceptance and approval by all the others. Finally a fourth disciple said, "There is still another aspect to our faith and unity. For Jesus' sake we shall be beaten, imprisoned and exiled. They may kill us. Let us receive this lesson now. Let us realize and resolve that though we are beaten, banished, cursed, spat upon and led forth to be killed, we shall accept all this joyfully, loving those who hate and wound us." All the disciples replied, "Surely we will—it is agreed; this is right." Then they descended from the summit of the mountain, and each went forth in a different direction upon his divine mission.

This was true consultation. This was spiritual consultation 4 and not the mere voicing of personal views in parliamentary opposition and debate.

6

2 May 1912

Talk to Federation of Women's Clubs
Hotel La Salle, Chicago, Illinois

NOTES BY JOSEPH H. HANNEN

ONE of the functions of the sun is to quicken and reveal the 1 hidden realities of the kingdoms of existence. Through the light and heat of the great central luminary, all that is potential in the earth is awakened and comes forth into the realm of the visible. The fruit hidden in the tree appears upon its branches in response to the power of the sun; man and all other organisms live, move and have their being under its developing rays; nature is resplendent with countless evolutionary forms through its pervading impulse—so that we can say a function of the sun is the revelation of the mysteries and creative purposes hidden within the phenomenal world.

2   The outer sun is a sign or symbol of the inner and ideal Sun of Truth, the Word of God. Inasmuch as this is the century of light, it is evident that the Sun of Reality, the Word, has revealed itself to all humankind. One of the potentialities hidden in the realm of humanity was the capability or capacity of womanhood. Through the effulgent rays of divine illumination the capacity of woman has become so awakened and manifest in this age that equality of man and woman is an established fact. In past ages woman was wronged and oppressed. This was especially the case in Asia and Africa. In certain parts of Asia women were not considered as members of humankind. They were looked upon as inferior, unworthy creatures, subordinate and subject to man. A certain people known as the Nusayris held to the belief for a long period that woman was the incarnation of the evil spirit, or Satan, and that man alone was the manifestation of God, the Merciful. At last this century of light dawned, the realities shone forth, and the mysteries long hidden from human vision were revealed. Among these revealed realities was the great principle of the equality of man and woman, which is now finding recognition throughout the whole world—America, Europe and the Orient.

3   History records the appearance in the world of women who have been signs of guidance, power and accomplishment. Some were notable poets, some philosophers and scientists, others courageous upon the field of battle. Qurratu'l-'Ayn, a Bahá'í, was a poetess. She discomfited the learned men of Persia by her brilliancy and fervor. When she entered a meeting, even

the learned were silent. She was so well versed in philosophy and science that those in her presence always considered and consulted her first. Her courage was unparalleled; she faced her enemies fearlessly until she was killed. She withstood a despotic king, the S͟háh of Persia, who had the power to decree the death of any of his subjects. There was not a day during which he did not command the execution of some. This woman singly and alone withstood such a despot until her last breath, then gave her life for her faith.

4

Consider the mysteries revealed during the last half century, all due to the effulgence of the Sun of Reality, which has been so gloriously manifested in this age and cycle. In this day man must investigate reality impartially and without prejudice in order to reach the true knowledge and conclusions. What, then, constitutes the inequality between man and woman? Both are human. In powers and function each is the complement of the other. At most it is this: that woman has been denied the opportunities which man has so long enjoyed, especially the privilege of education. But even this is not always a shortcoming. Shall we consider it an imperfection and weakness in her nature that she is not proficient in the school of military tactics, that she cannot go forth to the field of battle and kill, that she is not able to handle a deadly weapon? Nay, rather, is it not a compliment when we say that in hardness of heart and cruelty she is inferior to man? The woman who is asked to arm herself and kill her fellow creatures will say, "I cannot." Is this to be considered a fault and lack of qualification as man's equal? Yet be it known that if woman had been taught and trained in the military science of slaughter, she would have been the equivalent of man even in this accomplishment. But God forbid! May woman never attain this proficiency; may she never wield weapons of war, for the destruction of humanity is not a glorious achievement. The

103

upbuilding of a home, the bringing of joy and comfort into human hearts are truly glories of mankind. Let not a man glory in this, that he can kill his fellow creatures; nay, rather, let him glory in this, that he can love them.

5   When we consider the kingdoms of existence below man, we find no distinction or estimate of superiority and inferiority between male and female. Among the myriad organisms of the vegetable and animal kingdoms sex exists, but there is no differentiation whatever as to relative importance and value in the equation of life. If we investigate impartially, we may even find species in which the female is superior or preferable to the male. For instance, there are trees such as the fig, the male of which is fruitless while the female is fruitful. The male of the date palm is valueless while the female bears abundantly. Inasmuch as we find no ground for distinction or superiority according to the creative wisdom in the lower kingdoms, is it logical or becoming of man to make such distinction in regard to himself? The male of the animal kingdom does not glory in its being male and superior to the female. In fact, equality exists and is recognized. Why should man, a higher and more intelligent creature, deny and deprive himself of this equality the animals enjoy? His surest index and guide as to the creative intention concerning himself are the conditions and analogies of the kingdoms below him where equality of the sexes is fundamental.

6   The truth is that all mankind are the creatures and servants of one God, and in His estimate all are human. Man is a generic term applying to all humanity. The biblical statement "Let us make man in our image, after our likeness" does not mean that woman was not created. The image and likeness of God apply to her as well. In Persian and Arabic there are two distinct words translated into English as man: one meaning man and woman collectively, the other distinguishing man as male from woman the female.

The first word and its pronoun are generic, collective; the other is restricted to the male. This is the same in Hebrew.

To accept and observe a distinction which God has not in- 7 tended in creation is ignorance and superstition. The fact which is to be considered, however, is that woman, having formerly been deprived, must now be allowed equal opportunities with man for education and training. There must be no difference in their education. Until the reality of equality between man and woman is fully established and attained, the highest social development of mankind is not possible. Even granted that woman is inferior to man in some degree of capacity or accomplishment, this or any other distinction would continue to be productive of discord and trouble. The only remedy is education, opportunity; for equality means equal qualification. In brief, the assumption of superiority by man will continue to be depressing to the ambition of woman, as if her attainment to equality was creationally impossible; woman's aspiration toward advancement will be checked by it, and she will gradually become hopeless. On the contrary, we must declare that her capacity is equal, even greater than man's. This will inspire her with hope and ambition, and her susceptibilities for advancement will continually increase. She must not be told and taught that she is weaker and inferior in capacity and qualification. If a pupil is told that his intelligence is less than his fellow pupils, it is a very great drawback and handicap to his progress. He must be encouraged to advance by the statement, "You are most capable, and if you endeavor, you will attain the highest degree."

It is my hope that the banner of equality may be raised throughout the five continents where as yet it is not fully 8 recognized and established. In this enlightened world of the West woman has advanced an immeasurable degree beyond the women of the Orient. And let it be known once more that until woman and man recognize and realize equality, social and political progress here or anywhere will not be possible. For the world of humanity consists of two parts or members: one is woman; the other is man. Until these two members are equal in strength, the oneness of humanity cannot be established, and the happiness and felicity of mankind will not be a reality. God willing, this is to be so.

7

2 May 1912

Talk at Bahá'í Women's Reception
Hotel La Salle, Chicago, Illinois

NOTES BY JOSEPH H. HANNEN

1 WHEN we look upon the kingdoms of creation below man, we find three forms or planes of existence which await education and development. For instance, the function of a gardener is to till the soil of the mineral kingdom and plant a tree which under his training and cultivation will attain perfection of growth. If it be wild and fruitless, it may be made fruitful and prolific by grafting. If small and unsightly, it will become lofty, beautiful and verdant under the gardener's training, whereas a tree bereft of his cultivation retrogresses daily, its fruit grows acrid and bitter as the trees of the jungle, or it may become entirely barren and bereft of its fruitage. Likewise, we observe that animals which have undergone training in their sphere of limitation will progress and advance unmistakably, become more beautiful in appearance and increase in intelligence. For instance, how intelligent and knowing the Arabian horse has

become through training, even how polite this horse has become through education. As to the human world: It is more in need of guidance and education than the lower creatures. Reflect upon the vast difference between the inhabitants of Africa and those of America. Here the people have been civilized and uplifted; there they are in the utmost and abject state of savagery. What is the cause of their savagery and the reason of your civilization? It is evident that this difference is due to education and the lack of education. Consider, then, the effectiveness of education in the human kingdom. It makes the ignorant wise, the tyrant merciful, the blind seeing, the deaf attentive, even the imbecile intelligent. How vast this difference. How wide the chasm which separates the educated man from the man who lacks teaching and training. This is the effect when the teacher is merely an ordinary teacher.

But—praise be to God!—your Teacher and Instructor is   2
Bahá'u'lláh. He is the Educator of the Orient and Occident. He is the Teacher of the very world of divinity and spirituality, the Sun of Truth, the Word of God. The lights of His education are radiating even as the sun. See what it has accomplished, how it is developing all humanity so that I, a Persian, have come to this meeting of revered souls upon the American continent and am standing here expounding to you in the greatest love. This is through the training of Bahá'u'lláh, which can unite and has united these hearts. In this way it has enlightened the world. Even so it has breathed the spirit of God into men. Even so it has resuscitated the hearts of men.

Therefore, praise be to God that you have been brought under   3
the education of this One Who is the very Sun of Reality and Who is shining resplendently upon all humankind, endowing all with a life that is everlasting.

Praise be to God a thousand times!   4

8

2 May 1912

Talk at Hotel Plaza
Chicago, Illinois

NOTES BY MARZIEH MOSS

1   THIS morning the city is enveloped in fog and mist. How beautiful is a city brilliant with sunshine. Just as these mists and vapors conceal the phenomenal sun, so human imaginations obscure the Sun of Truth. Consider the radiant glory of the great solar center of our planetary system: how wonderful the sight, how its splendor illumines vision until clouds and mists veil it from the eye. In the same way, the Sun of Truth becomes veiled and hidden by the superstitions and imaginations of human minds. When the sun rises, no matter from what dawning point on the horizon it appears—northeast, east, southeast—the haze and mists disperse, and we have clear vision of its glory mounting to the zenith. Similarly, the nations have been directed to the dawning points of the Sun of Reality, each to a particular rising place from which the light of religion has become manifest; but after a time the dawning point has become the object of worship instead of the Sun itself, which is ever one Sun and stationary in the heavens of the divine Will. Differences have arisen because of this, causing clouds and darkness to overshadow again the glorious luminary of Reality. When the mists and darkness of superstition and prejudice are dispersed, all will see the Sun aright and alike. Then will all nations become as one in its radiance.

2   Inasmuch as these clouds and human vapors of superstition hide the light of the spiritual Sun, we must put forth our utmost endeavor to dispel them. May we unite in this and be enlight-

ened to accomplish it, for the Sun is one and its radiance and bounty universal. All the inhabitants of earth are recipients of the bounty of the one phenomenal sun, and none are preferred above others; so, likewise, all receive the heavenly bestowals of the Word of God; none are specialized as favorites; all are under its protection and universal effulgence. Human strife and religious disagreement complex and disfigure the simple purity and beauty of the divine Cause until clouds obscure the light of reality and disunion results. Therefore, make use of intelligence and reason so that you may dispel these dense clouds from the horizon of human hearts and all hold to the one reality of all the Prophets. It is most certain that if human souls exercise their respective reason and intelligence upon the divine questions, the power of God will dispel every difficulty, and the eternal realities will appear as one light, one truth, one love, one God and a peace that is universal.

9

2 May 1912

Talk at Hotel Plaza
Chicago, Illinois

Notes by Henrietta C. Wagner

WHEN we carefully investigate the kingdoms of existence and observe the phenomena of the universe about us, we discover the absolute order and perfection of creation. The dull minerals in their affinities, plants and vegetables with power of growth, animals in their instinct, man with conscious intellect and the heavenly orbs moving obediently through limitless space are all

1

found subject to universal law, most complete, most perfect. That is why a wise philosopher has said, "There is no greater or more perfect system of creation than that which already exists." The materialists and atheists declare that this order and symmetry is due to nature and its forces; that composition and decomposition which constitute life and existence are exigencies of nature; that man himself is an exigency of nature; that nature rules and governs creation; and that all existing things are captives of nature. Let us consider these statements. Inasmuch as we find all phenomena subject to an exact order and under control of universal law, the question is whether this is due to nature or to divine and omnipotent rule. The materialists believe that it is an exigency of nature for the rain to fall and that unless rain fell the earth would not become verdant. They reason that if clouds cause a downpour, if the sun sends forth heat and light and the earth is endowed with capacity, vegetation must inevitably follow; therefore, plant life is a property of these natural forces and is a sign of nature; just as combustion is the natural property of fire, therefore, fire burns, and we cannot conceive of fire without its burning.

2   In reply to these statements we say that from the premises advanced by materialists, the conclusions are drawn that nature is the ruler and governor of existence and that all virtues and perfections are natural exigencies and outcomes. Furthermore, it follows that man is but a part or member of that whereof nature is the whole.

3   Man possesses certain virtues of which nature is deprived. He exercises volition; nature is without will. For instance, an exigency of the sun is the giving of light. It is controlled—it cannot do otherwise than radiate light—but it is not volitional. An exigency of the phenomenon of electricity is that it is revealed in sparks and flashes under certain conditions, but it cannot voluntarily furnish

illumination. An exigency or property of water is humidity; it cannot separate itself from this property by its own will. Likewise, all the properties of nature are inherent and obedient, not volitional; therefore, it is philosophically predicated that nature is without volition and innate perception. In this statement and principle we agree with the materialists. But the question which presents food for reflection is this: How is it that man, who is a part of the universal plan, is possessed of certain qualities whereof nature is devoid? Is it conceivable that a drop should be imbued with qualities of which the ocean is completely deprived? The drop is a part; the ocean is the whole. Could there be a phenomenon of combustion or illumination which the great luminary the sun itself did not manifest? Is it possible for a stone to possess inherent properties of which the aggregate mineral kingdom is lacking? For example, could the fingernail which is a part of human anatomy be endowed with cellular properties of which the brain is deprived?

Man is intelligent, instinctively and consciously intelligent; 4 nature is not. Man is fortified with memory; nature does not possess it. Man is the discoverer of the mysteries of nature; nature is not conscious of those mysteries herself. It is evident, therefore, that man is dual in aspect: as an animal he is subject to nature, but in his spiritual or conscious being he transcends the world of material existence. His spiritual powers, being nobler and higher, possess virtues of which nature intrinsically has no evidence; therefore, they triumph over natural conditions. These ideal virtues or powers in man surpass or surround nature, comprehend natural laws and phenomena, penetrate the mysteries of the unknown and invisible and bring them forth into the realm of the known and visible. All the existing arts and sciences were once hidden secrets of nature. By his command and control of nature man took them out of the plane of the invisible and revealed them in the plane of visibility, whereas according to the exigencies of nature these secrets should have remained latent and concealed. According to the exigencies of nature electricity should be a hidden, mysterious power; but the penetrating intellect of man has discovered it, taken it out of the realm of mystery and made it an obedient human servant. In his physical body and its functions man is a captive of nature; for instance, he cannot continue his existence without sleep, an exigency of nature; he must partake of food and drink, which nature demands and requires. But in his spiritual being and intelligence man dominates and controls nature, the ruler of his physical being. Notwithstanding this, contrary opinions and materialistic views are set forth which would relegate man completely to physical subservience to nature's laws. This is equivalent to saying that the comparative degree exceeds the superlative, that the imperfect includes the perfect, that the pupil surpasses the teacher—all of which is illogical and impossible. When it is clearly manifest and evident that the intelligence of man, his constructive faculty, his power of penetration and discovery transcend nature, how can we say he is nature's thrall and captive? This would indicate that man is deprived of the bounties of God, that he is retrograding toward the station of the animal, that his keen superintelligence is without function and that he estimates himself as an animal, without distinction between his own and the animal's kingdom.

5   I was once conversing with a famous philosopher of the materialistic school in Alexandria. He was strongly opinioned upon the point that man and the other kingdoms of existence are under the control of nature and that, after all, man is only a social animal, often very much of an animal. When he was discomfited in argument, he said impetuously, "I see no difference between myself and the donkey, and I am not willing to admit distinctions which I cannot perceive." 'Abdu'l-Bahá

replied, "No, I consider you quite different and distinct; I call you a man and the donkey but an animal. I perceive that you are highly intelligent, whereas the donkey is not. I know that you are well versed in philosophy, and I also know that the donkey is entirely deficient in it; therefore, I am not willing to accept your statement."

Consider the lady beside me who is writing in this little book. 6 It seems a very trifling, ordinary matter; but upon intelligent reflection you will conclude that what has been written presupposes and proves the existence of a writer. These words have not written themselves, and these letters have not come together of their own volition. It is evident there must be a writer.

And now consider this infinite universe. Is it possible that it 7 could have been created without a Creator? Or that the Creator and cause of this infinite congeries of worlds should be without intelligence? Is the idea tenable that the Creator has no comprehension of what is manifested in creation? Man, the creature, has volition and certain virtues. Is it possible that his Creator is deprived of these? A child could not accept this belief and statement. It is perfectly evident that man did not create himself and that he cannot do so. How could man of his own weakness create such a mighty being? Therefore, the Creator of man must be more perfect and powerful than man. If the creative cause of man be simply on the same level with man, then man himself should be able to create, whereas we know very well that we cannot create even our own likeness. Therefore, the Creator of man must be endowed with superlative intelligence and power in all points that creation involves and implies. We are weak; He is mighty, because, were He not mighty, He could not have created us. We are ignorant; He is wise. We are poor; He is rich. Otherwise, He would have been incapable of our creation.

8   Among the proofs of the existence of a divine power is this: that things are often known by their opposites. Were it not for darkness, light could not be sensed. Were it not for death, life could not be known. If ignorance did not exist, knowledge would not be a reality. It is necessary that each should exist in order that the other should have reality. Night and day must be in order that each may be distinguished. Night itself is an indication and evidence of day which follows, and day itself indicates the coming night. Unless night were a reality, there could not be day. Were it not for death, there could be no life. Things are known by their opposites.

9   Therefore, our weakness is an evidence that there is might; our ignorance proves the reality of knowledge; our need is an indication of supply and wealth. Were it not for wealth, this need would not exist; were it not for knowledge, ignorance would be unknown; were it not for power, there would be no impotence. In other words, demand and supply is the law, and undoubtedly all virtues have a center and source. That source is God, from Whom all these bounties emanate.

10

3 May 1912

Talk at Hotel Plaza
Chicago, Illinois

Notes by Marzieh Moss

1   I was in the Orient, and from the Orient to this part of the world is a long distance. Travel is difficult, especially difficult for me on account of my infirmities of body, increased by forty

years in prison. My physical powers are weak; it is the power of will that sustains me. Realize from this how great has been my exertion and how strong my purpose in accomplishing this journey through the will of God. May it be the cause of great illumination in the Occident.

In this western world with its stimulating climate, its capacities for knowledge and lofty ideals, the message of peace should be easily spread. The people are not so influenced by imitations and prejudices, and through their comprehension of the real and unreal they should attain the truth. They should become leaders in the effort to establish the oneness of humankind. What is higher than this responsibility? In the Kingdom of God no service is greater, and in the estimation of the Prophets, including Jesus Christ, there is no deed so estimable.

Yet even now warfare prevails. Envy and hatred have arisen between nations. But because I find the American nation so capable of achievement and this government the fairest of western governments, its institutions superior to others, my wish and hope is that the banner of international reconciliation may first be raised on this continent and the standard of the Most Great Peace be unfurled here. May the American people and their government unite in their efforts in order that this light may dawn from this point and spread to all regions, for this is one of the greatest bestowals of God. In order that America may avail herself of this opportunity, I beg that you strive and pray with heart and soul, devoting all your energies to this end: that the banner of international peace may be upraised here and that this democracy may be the cause of the cessation of warfare in all other countries.

Observe what is taking place in Tripoli: men cutting each other into pieces, bombardment from the sea, attacks from the land and the hail of dynamite from the very heaven itself. The contending armies are thirsting for each other's blood. How

115

they can do this is inconceivable. They have fathers, mothers, children; they are human. What of their wives and families? Think of their anguish and suffering. How unjust, how terrible! Human beings should prevent and forbid this. These kings, rulers and chieftains should strive for the good of their subjects instead of their destruction. These shepherds should bring their sheep within the fold, comfort them and give them pasture instead of death and slaughter.

5   I supplicate the divine Kingdom and ask that you may be instrumental in establishing the great peace in this country and that this government and nation may spread it to all the world.

11

3 May 1912

Talk at Hotel Plaza
Chicago, Illinois

NOTES BY MARZIEH MOSS

1   ACCORDING to the statement of philosophers the difference in degree of humankind from lowest to highest is due to education. The proofs they advance are these. The civilization of Europe and America is an evidence and outcome of education, whereas the semicivilized and barbarous peoples of Africa bear witness in their condition that they have been deprived of its advantages. Education makes the ignorant wise, the tyrant just, promotes happiness, strengthens the mind, develops the will and makes fruitless trees of humanity fruitful. Therefore, in the human world some have attained lofty degrees, while others grope in

the abyss of despair. Nevertheless, the highest attainment is possible for every member of the human race even to the station of the Prophets. This is the statement and reasoning of the philosophers.

The Prophets of God are the first Educators. They bestow 2 universal education upon man and cause him to rise from the lowest levels of savagery to the highest pinnacles of spiritual development. The philosophers, too, are educators along lines of intellectual training. At most, they have only been able to educate themselves and a limited number about them, to improve their own morals and, so to speak, civilize themselves; but they have been incapable of universal education. They have failed to cause an advancement for any given nation from savagery to civilization.

It is evident that although education improves the morals 3 of mankind, confers the advantages of civilization and elevates man from lowest degrees to the station of sublimity, there is, nevertheless, a difference in the intrinsic or natal capacity of individuals. Ten children of the same age, with equal station of birth, taught in the same school, partaking of the same food, in all respects subject to the same environment, their interests equal and in common, will evidence separate and distinct degrees of capability and advancement; some will be exceedingly intelligent and progressive, some of mediocre ability, others limited and incapable. One may become a learned professor, while another under the same course of education proves dull and stupid. From all standpoints the opportunities have been equal, but the results and outcomes vary from the highest to lowest degree of advancement. It is evident, therefore, that mankind differs in natal capacity and intrinsic intellectual endowment. Nevertheless, although capacities are not the same, every member of the human race is capable of education.

4   Jesus Christ was an Educator of humanity. His teachings were altruistic; His bestowal, universal. He taught mankind by the power of the Holy Spirit and not through human agency, for the human power is limited, whereas the divine power is illimitable and infinite. The influence and accomplishment of Christ will attest this. Galen, the Greek physician and philosopher who lived in the second century A.D., wrote a treatise upon the civilization of nations. He was not a Christian, but he bore testimony that religious beliefs exercise an extraordinary effect upon the problems of civilization. In substance he said, "There are certain people among us, followers of Jesus, the Nazarene, who was killed in Jerusalem. These people are truly imbued with moral principles which are the envy of philosophers. They believe in God and fear Him. They have hopes in His favors; therefore, they shun all unworthy deeds and actions and incline to praiseworthy ethics and morals. Day and night they strive that their deeds may be commendable and that they may contribute to the welfare of humanity; therefore, each one of them is virtually a philosopher, for these people have attained unto that which is the essence and purport of philosophy. These people have praiseworthy morals, even though they may be illiterate."

5   The purpose of this is to show that the holy Manifestations of God, the divine Prophets, are the first Teachers of the human race. They are universal Educators, and the fundamental principles they have laid down are the causes and factors of the advancement of nations. Forms and imitations which creep in afterward are not conducive to that progress. On the contrary, these are destroyers of human foundations established by the heavenly Educators. These are clouds which obscure the Sun of Reality. If you reflect upon the essential teachings of Jesus, you will realize that they are the light of the world. Nobody can question their truth. They are the very source of life and the cause of happiness to the human race. The forms and supersti-

tions which appeared and obscured the light did not affect the reality of Christ. For example, Jesus Christ said, "Put up thy sword into the sheath." The meaning is that warfare is forbidden and abrogated; but consider the Christian wars which took place afterward. Christian hostility and inquisition spared not even the learned; he who proclaimed the revolution of the earth was imprisoned; he who announced the new astronomical system was persecuted as a heretic; scholars and scientists became objects of fanatical hatred, and many were killed and tortured. How do these actions conform with the teachings of Jesus Christ, and what relation do they bear to His own example? For Christ declared, "Love your enemies, . . . and pray for them which . . . persecute you; that you may be the children of your Father which is in heaven: for he maketh his sun to rise on the evil and on the good, and sendeth rain on the just and on the unjust." How can hatred, hostility and persecution be reconciled with Christ and His teachings?

Therefore, there is need of turning back to the original foundation. The fundamental principles of the Prophets are correct and true. The imitations and superstitions which have crept in are at wide variance with the original precepts and commands. Bahá'u'lláh has revoiced and reestablished the quintessence of the teachings of all the Prophets, setting aside the accessories and purifying religion from human interpretation. He has written a book entitled the Hidden Words. The preface announces that it contains the essences of the words of the Prophets of the past, clothed in the garment of brevity, for the teaching and spiritual guidance of the people of the world. Read it that you may understand the true foundations of religion and reflect upon the inspiration of the Messengers of God. It is light upon light. 6

We must not look for truth in the deeds and actions of nations; we must investigate truth at its divine source and summon all mankind to unity in reality itself. 7

12

4 May 1912

Talk to Theosophical Society
Northwestern University Hall, Evanston, Illinois

NOTES BY MARZIEH MOSS

1   I AM very happy in being present at this meeting. Praise be to God! I see before me the faces of those who are endowed with capacity to know and who desire to investigate truth. This is conducive to the greatest joy.

2   According to divine philosophy there are two important and universal conditions in the world of material phenomena: one which concerns life, the other concerning death; one relative to existence, the other nonexistence; one manifest in composition, the other in decomposition. Some define existence as the expression of reality or being and nonexistence as nonbeing, imagining that death is annihilation. This is a mistaken idea, for total annihilation is an impossibility. At most, composition is ever subject to decomposition or disintegration—that is to say, existence implies the grouping of material elements in a form or body, and nonexistence is simply the decomposing of these groupings. This is the law of creation in its endless forms and infinite variety of expression. Certain elements have formed the composite creature man. This composite association of the elements in the form of a human body is, therefore, subject to disintegration, which we call death, but after disintegration the elements themselves persist unchanged. Therefore, total annihilation is an impossibility, and existence can never become nonexistence. This would be equivalent to saying that light can

become darkness, which is manifestly untrue and impossible. As existence can never become nonexistence, there is no death for man; nay, rather, man is everlasting and ever-living. The rational proof of this is that the atoms of the material elements are transferable from one form of existence to another, from one degree and kingdom to another, lower or higher. For example, an atom of the soil or dust of earth may traverse the kingdoms from mineral to man by successive incorporations into the bodies of the organisms of those kingdoms. At one time it enters into the formation of the mineral or rock; it is then absorbed by the vegetable kingdom and becomes a constituent of the body and fibre of a tree; again it is appropriated by the animal, and at a still later period is found in the body of man. Throughout these degrees of its traversing the kingdoms from one form of phenomenal being to another, it retains its atomic existence and is never annihilated nor relegated to nonexistence.

Nonexistence, therefore, is an expression applied to change of form, but this transformation can never be rightly considered annihilation, for the elements of composition are ever present and existent as we have seen in the journey of the atom through successive kingdoms, unimpaired; hence, there is no death; life is everlasting. So to speak, when the atom entered into the composition of the tree, it died to the mineral kingdom, and when consumed by the animal, it died to the vegetable kingdom, and so on until its transference or transmutation into the kingdom of man; but throughout its traversing it was subject to transformation and not annihilation. Death, therefore, is applicable to a change or transference from one degree or condition to another. In the mineral realm there was a spirit of existence; in the world of plant life and organisms it reappeared as the vegetative spirit; thence it attained the animal spirit and finally aspired to the human spirit. These are degrees and changes but not obliteration, and this is a rational proof that man is everlasting, ever-living. Therefore, death is only a relative term implying change. For example, we will say that this light before me, having reappeared in another incandescent lamp, has died in the one and lives in the other. This is not death in reality. The perfections of the mineral are translated into the vegetable and from thence into the animal, the virtue always attaining a superlative degree in the upward change. In each kingdom we find the same virtues manifesting themselves more fully, proving that the reality has been transferred from a lower to a higher form and kingdom of being. Therefore, nonexistence is only relative and absolute nonexistence inconceivable. This rose in my hand will become disintegrated and its symmetry destroyed, but the elements of its composition remain changeless; nothing affects their elemental integrity. They cannot become nonexistent; they are simply transferred from one state to another.

4   Through his ignorance man fears death, but the death he shrinks from is imaginary and absolutely unreal; it is only human imagination.

5   The bestowal and grace of God have quickened the realm of existence with life and being. For existence there is neither change nor transformation; existence is ever existence; it can never be translated into nonexistence. It is gradation; a degree below a higher degree is considered as nonexistence. This dust beneath our feet, as compared with our being, is nonexistent. When the human body crumbles into dust, we can say it has become nonexistent; therefore, its dust in relation to living forms of human being is as nonexistent, but in its own sphere it is existent, it has its mineral being. Therefore, it is well proved that absolute nonexistence is impossible; it is only relative.

6   The purpose is this: that the everlasting bestowal of God vouchsafed to man is never subject to corruption. Inasmuch as

He has endowed the phenomenal world with being, it is impossible for that world to become nonbeing, for it is the very genesis of God; it is in the realm of origination; it is a creational and not a subjective world, and the bounty descending upon it is continuous and permanent. Therefore, man, the highest creature of the phenomenal world, is endowed with that continuous bounty bestowed by divine generosity without cessation. For instance, the rays of the sun are continuous, the heat of the sun emanates from it without cessation; no discontinuance of it is conceivable. Even so, the bestowal of God is descending upon the world of humanity, never ceasing, continuous, forever. If we say that the bestowal of existence ceases or falters, it is equivalent to saying that the sun can exist with cessation of its effulgence. Is this possible? Therefore, the effulgences of existence are ever present and continuous.

The conception of annihilation is a factor in human degradation, a cause of human debasement and lowliness, a source of human fear and abjection. It has been conducive to the dispersion and weakening of human thought, whereas the realization of existence and continuity has upraised man to sublimity of ideals, established the foundations of human progress and stimulated the development of heavenly virtues; therefore, it behooves man to abandon thoughts of nonexistence and death, which are absolutely imaginary, and see himself ever-living, everlasting in the divine purpose of his creation. He must turn away from ideas which degrade the human soul so that day by day and hour by hour he may advance upward and higher to spiritual perception of the continuity of the human reality. If he dwells upon the thought of nonexistence, he will become utterly incompetent; with weakened willpower his ambition for progress will be lessened and the acquisition of human virtues will cease.

8 Therefore, you must thank God that He has bestowed upon you the blessing of life and existence in the human kingdom. Strive diligently to acquire virtues befitting your degree and station. Be as lights of the world which cannot be hid and which have no setting in horizons of darkness. Ascend to the zenith of an existence which is never beclouded by the fears and forebodings of nonexistence. When man is not endowed with inner perception, he is not informed of these important mysteries. The retina of outer vision, though sensitive and delicate, may, nevertheless, be a hindrance to the inner eye which alone can perceive. The bestowals of God which are manifest in all phenomenal life are sometimes hidden by intervening veils of mental and mortal vision which render man spiritually blind and incapable, but when those scales are removed and the veils rent asunder, then the great signs of God will become visible, and he will witness the eternal light filling the world. The bestowals of God are all and always manifest. The promises of heaven are ever present. The favors of God are all-surrounding, but should the conscious eye of the soul of man remain veiled and darkened, he will be led to deny these universal signs and remain deprived of these manifestations of divine bounty. Therefore, we must endeavor with heart and soul in order that the veil covering the eye of inner vision may be removed, that we may behold the manifestations of the signs of God, discern His mysterious graces and realize that material blessings as compared with spiritual bounties are as nothing. The spiritual blessings of God are greatest. When we were in the mineral kingdom, although we were endowed with certain gifts and powers, they were not to be compared with the blessings of the human kingdom. In the matrix of the mother we were the recipients of endowments and blessings of God, yet these were as nothing compared to the powers and graces bestowed upon us after birth into this

human world. Likewise, if we are born from the matrix of this physical and phenomenal environment into the freedom and loftiness of the spiritual life and vision, we shall consider this mortal existence and its blessings as worthless by comparison.

In the spiritual world the divine bestowals are infinite, for in that realm there is neither separation nor disintegration, which characterize the world of material existence. Spiritual existence is absolute immortality, completeness and unchangeable being. Therefore, we must thank God that He has created for us both material blessings and spiritual bestowals. He has given us material gifts and spiritual graces, outer sight to view the lights of the sun and inner vision by which we may perceive the glory of God. He has designed the outer ear to enjoy the melodies of sound and the inner hearing wherewith we may hear the voice of our Creator. We must strive with energies of heart, soul and mind to develop and manifest the perfections and virtues latent within the realities of the phenomenal world, for the human reality may be compared to a seed. If we sow the seed, a mighty tree appears from it. The virtues of the seed are revealed in the tree; it puts forth branches, leaves, blossoms, and produces fruits. All these virtues were hidden and potential in the seed. Through the blessing and bounty of cultivation these virtues became apparent. Similarly, the merciful God, our Creator, has deposited within human realities certain latent and potential virtues. Through education and culture these virtues deposited by the loving God will become apparent in the human reality, even as the unfoldment of the tree from within the germinating seed. I will pray for you.

O Thou kind Lord! These are Thy servants who have gathered in this meeting, have turned unto Thy Kingdom and are in need of Thy bestowal and blessing. O thou God! Manifest and make evident the signs of Thy oneness which have been deposited in all the realities of life. Reveal and unfold the virtues which Thou hast made latent and concealed in these human realities.

11 O God! We are as plants, and Thy bounty is as the rain; refresh and cause these plants to grow through Thy bestowal. We are Thy servants; free us from the fetters of material existence. We are ignorant; make us wise. We are dead; make us alive. We are material; endow us with spirit. We are deprived; make us the intimates of Thy mysteries. We are needy; enrich and bless us from Thy boundless treasury. O God! Resuscitate us; give us sight; give us hearing; familiarize us with the mysteries of life, so that the secrets of Thy kingdom may become revealed to us in this world of existence and we may confess Thy oneness. Every bestowal emanates from Thee; every benediction is Thine.

12 Thou art mighty. Thou art powerful. Thou art the Giver, and Thou art the Ever-Bounteous.

13

5 May 1912

Talk at Children's Meeting
Hotel Plaza
Chicago, Illinois

NOTES BY MARZIEH MOSS

1 YOU are the children of whom Christ has said, "Of such is the kingdom of God"; and according to the words of Bahá'u'lláh you are the very lamps or candles of the world of humanity, for your hearts are exceedingly pure and your spirits most sensitive. You are near the source; you have not yet become contaminated.

You are the lambs of the heavenly Shepherd. You are as polished mirrors reflecting pure light. My hope is that your parents may educate you spiritually and give you thorough moral training. May you develop so that each one of you shall become imbued with all the virtues of the human world. May you advance in all material and spiritual degrees. May you become learned in sciences, acquire the arts and crafts, prove to be useful members of human society and assist the progress of human civilization. May you be a cause of the manifestation of divine bestowals— each one of you a shining star radiating the light of the oneness of humanity toward the horizons of the East and West. May you be devoted to the love and unity of mankind, and through your efforts may the reality deposited in the human heart find its divine expression. I pray for you, asking the assistance and confirmation of God in your behalf.

You are all my children, my spiritual children. Spiritual 2 children are dearer than physical children, for it is possible for physical children to turn away from the Spirit of God, but you are spiritual children and, therefore, you are most beloved. I wish for you progress in every degree of development. May God assist you. May you be surrounded by the beneficent light of His countenance, and may you attain maturity under His nurture and protection. You are all blessed.

(To the Friends)

I am going away, but you must arise to serve the Word of 3 God. Your hearts must be pure and your intentions sincere in order that you may become recipients of the divine bestowals. Consider that although the sun shines equally upon all things, yet in the clear mirror its reflection is most brilliant and not in the black stone. This great effulgence and heat have been produced by the crystal clearness of the glass. If there were no clearness and purity, these effects would not be witnessed. Should rain fall upon salty, stony earth, it will never have effect; but when it falls upon good pure soil, green and verdant growth follows, and fruits are produced.

4   This is the day when pure hearts have a portion of the everlasting bounties and sanctified souls are being illumined by the eternal manifestations. Praise be to God! You are believers in God, assured by the words of God and turning to the Kingdom of God. You have heard the divine call. Your hearts are moved by the breezes of the paradise of Abhá. You have good intentions; your purpose is the good pleasure of God; you desire to serve in the Kingdom of the Merciful One. Therefore, arise in the utmost power. Be in perfect unity. Never become angry with one another. Let your eyes be directed toward the kingdom of truth and not toward the world of creation. Love the creatures for the sake of God and not for themselves. You will never become angry or impatient if you love them for the sake of God. Humanity is not perfect. There are imperfections in every human being, and you will always become unhappy if you look toward the people themselves. But if you look toward God, you will love them and be kind to them, for the world of God is the world of perfection and complete mercy. Therefore, do not look at the shortcomings of anybody; see with the sight of forgiveness. The imperfect eye beholds imperfections. The eye that covers faults looks toward the Creator of souls. He created them, trains and provides for them, endows them with capacity and life, sight and hearing; therefore, they are the signs of His grandeur. You must love and be kind to everybody, care for the poor, protect the weak, heal the sick, teach and educate the ignorant.

5   It is my hope that the unity and harmony of the friends in Chicago may be the cause of the unity of the friends throughout America and that all people may become recipients of their love

and kindness. May they be an example for mankind. Then the confirmations of the Kingdom of Abhá and the bestowals of the Sun of Reality will be all-encircling.

14

5 May 1912

Talk at Plymouth Congregational Church
935 East Fiftieth Street
Chicago, Illinois

NOTES BY MARZIEH MOSS

I OFFER thanks to God for the privilege of being present in an   1
assemblage which is commemorating Him, whose members have no thought or intention save His good pleasure and the unbiased investigation of reality. I praise God for this meeting of human souls free from the bondage of imitations and prejudice, willing to examine reasonably and accept that which is found to be true.

In our solar system the center of illumination is the sun itself.   2
Through the will of God this central luminary is the one source of the existence and development of all phenomenal things. When we observe the organisms of the material kingdoms, we find that their growth and training are dependent upon the heat and light of the sun. Without this quickening impulse there would be no growth of tree or vegetation; neither would the existence of animal or human being be possible; in fact, no forms of created life would be manifest upon the earth. But if we reflect deeply, we will perceive that the great bestower and giver of life is God; the sun is the intermediary of His will and plan.

Without the bounty of the sun, therefore, the world would be in darkness. All illumination of our planetary system proceeds or emanates from the solar center.

3   Likewise, in the spiritual realm of intelligence and idealism there must be a center of illumination, and that center is the everlasting, ever-shining Sun, the Word of God. Its lights are the lights of reality which have shone upon humanity, illumining the realm of thought and morals, conferring the bounties of the divine world upon man. These lights are the cause of the education of souls and the source of the enlightenment of hearts, sending forth in effulgent radiance the message of the glad tidings of the kingdom of God. In brief, the moral and ethical world and the world of spiritual regeneration are dependent for their progressive being upon that heavenly Center of illumination. It gives forth the light of religion and bestows the life of the spirit, imbues humanity with archetypal virtues and confers eternal splendors. This Sun of Reality, this Center of effulgences, is the Prophet or Manifestation of God. Just as the phenomenal sun shines upon the material world producing life and growth, likewise, the spiritual or prophetic Sun confers illumination upon the human world of thought and intelligence, and unless it rose upon the horizon of human existence, the kingdom of man would become dark and extinguished.

4   The Sun of Reality is one Sun, but it has different dawning places, just as the phenomenal sun is one although it appears at various points of the horizon. During the time of summer the luminary of the physical world rises far to the north of the equinoctial, in spring and fall it dawns midway, and in winter it appears in the most southerly point of its zodiacal journey. These daysprings or dawning points differ widely, but the sun is ever the same sun—whether it be the phenomenal or spiritual luminary. Souls who focus their vision upon the Sun of Real-

ity will be the recipients of light no matter from what point it rises, but those who are fettered by adoration of the dawning point are deprived when it appears in a different station upon the spiritual horizon.

Furthermore, just as the solar cycle has its four seasons, the 5 cycle of the Sun of Reality has its distinct and successive periods. Each brings its vernal season or springtime. When the Sun of Reality returns to quicken the world of mankind, a divine bounty descends from the heaven of generosity. The realm of thoughts and ideals is set in motion and blessed with new life. Minds are developed, hopes brighten, aspirations become spiritual, the virtues of the human world appear with freshened power of growth, and the image and likeness of God become visible in man. It is the springtime of the inner world. After the spring, summer comes with its fullness and spiritual fruitage; autumn follows with its withering winds which chill the soul; the Sun seems to be going away, until at last the mantle of winter overspreads, and only faint traces of the effulgence of that divine Sun remain. Just as the surface of the material world becomes dark and dreary, the soil dormant, the trees naked and bare and no beauty or freshness remains to cheer the darkness and desolation, so the winter of the spiritual cycle witnesses the death and disappearance of divine growth and extinction of the light and love of God. But again the cycle begins and a new springtime appears. In it the former springtime has returned; the world is resuscitated, illumined and attains spirituality; religion is renewed and reorganized, hearts are turned to God, the summons of God is heard, and life is again bestowed upon man. For a long time the religious world had been weakened and materialism had advanced; the spiritual forces of life were waning, moralities were becoming degraded, composure and peace had vanished from souls, and satanic qualities were dominating hearts; strife and hatred overshadowed humanity, bloodshed and violence prevailed. God was neglected; the Sun of Reality seemed to have gone completely; deprivation of the bounties of heaven was a fact; and so the season of winter fell upon mankind. But in the generosity of God a new springtime dawned, the lights of God shone forth, the effulgent Sun of Reality returned and became manifest, the realm of thoughts and kingdom of hearts became exhilarated, a new spirit of life breathed into the body of the world, and continuous advancement became apparent.

6   I hope that the lights of the Sun of Reality will illumine the whole world so that no strife and warfare, no battles and bloodshed remain. May fanaticism and religious bigotry be unknown, all humanity enter the bond of brotherhood, souls consort in perfect agreement, the nations of earth at last hoist the banner of truth, and the religions of the world enter the divine temple of oneness, for the foundations of the heavenly religions are one reality. Reality is not divisible; it does not admit multiplicity. All the holy Manifestations of God have proclaimed and promulgated the same reality. They have summoned mankind to reality itself, and reality is one. The clouds and mists of imitations have obscured the Sun of Truth. We must forsake these imitations, dispel these clouds and mists and free the Sun from the darkness of superstition. Then will the Sun of Truth shine most gloriously; then all the inhabitants of the world will be united, the religions will be one, sects and denominations will reconcile, all nationalities will flow together in the recognition of one Fatherhood, and all degrees of humankind will gather in the shelter of the same tabernacle, under the same banner.

7   Until the heavenly civilization is founded, no result will be forthcoming from material civilization, even as you observe. See what catastrophes overwhelm mankind. Consider the wars which disturb the world. Consider the enmity and hatred. The

existence of these wars and conditions indicates and proves that the heavenly civilization has not yet been established. If the civilization of the Kingdom be spread to all the nations, this dust of disagreement will be dispelled, these clouds will pass away, and the Sun of Reality in its greatest effulgence and glory will shine upon mankind.

O God! O Thou Who givest! This congregation is turning to Thee, casting their glances toward Thy Kingdom and favor, longing to behold the lights of Thy face. O God! Bless this nation. Confirm this government. Reveal Thy glory unto this people and confer upon them life eternal. O God! Illumine the faces, render the hearts radiant, exhilarate the breasts, crown the heads with the diadem of Thy providence, cause them to soar in Thy pure atmosphere so they may reach the highest pinnacles of Thy splendor. Assist them in order that this world may ever find the light and effulgence of Thy presence. O God! Shelter this congregation and admonish this nation. Render them progressive in all degrees. May they become leaders in the world of humanity. May they be Thine examples among humankind. May they be manifestations of Thy grace. May they be filled with the inspiration of Thy Word. Thou art the Powerful. Thou art the Mighty. Thou art the Giver, and Thou art the Omniscient.

15

5 May 1912

Talk at All-Souls Church
Lincoln Center, Chicago, Illinois

Notes by Marzieh Moss

1 THE divine religions were founded for the purpose of unifying humanity and establishing universal peace. Any movement which brings about peace and agreement in human society is truly a divine movement; any reform which causes people to come together under the shelter of the same tabernacle is surely animated by heavenly motives. At all times and in all ages of the world, religion has been a factor in cementing together the hearts of men and in uniting various and divergent creeds. It is the peace element in religion that blends mankind and makes for unity. Warfare has ever been the cause of separation, disunion and discord.

2 Consider how Jesus Christ united the divergent peoples, sects and denominations of the early days. It is evident that the fundamentals of religion are intended to unify and bind together; their purpose is universal, everlasting peace. Prior to the time of Jesus Christ the Word of God had unified opposite types and conflicting elements of human society; and since His appearance the divine Teachers of the primal principles of the law of God have all intended this universal outcome. In Persia Bahá'u'lláh was able to unite people of varying thought, creed and denomination. The inhabitants of that country were Christians, Muslims, Jews, Zoroastrians and a great variety of subdivided forms and beliefs together with racial distinctions

such as Semitic, Arabic, Persian, Turk, etc.; but through the power and efficacy of religion Bahá'u'lláh united these differing peoples and caused them to consort together in perfect agreement. Such unity and accord became manifest among them that they were considered as one people and one kind.

The cause of this fellowship and unity lies in the fact that the 3 divine law has two distinct aspects or functions: one the essential or fundamental, the other the material or accidental. The first aspect of the revealed religion of God is that which concerns the ethical development and spiritual progress of mankind, the awakening of potential human susceptibilities and the descent of divine bestowals. These ordinances are changeless, essential, eternal. The second function of the divine religion deals with material conditions, the laws of human intercourse and social regulation. These are subject to change and transformation in accordance with the time, place and conditions. The essential ordinances of religion were the same during the time of Abraham, the day of Moses and the cycle of Jesus, but the accidental or material laws were abrogated and superseded according to the exigency and requirement of each succeeding age. For example, in the law of Moses there were ten distinct commandments in regard to murder, which were revealed according to the requirement and capacity of the people, but in the day of Jesus these were abrogated and superseded in conformity with the changed and advanced human conditions.

The central purpose of the divine religions is the establish- 4 ment of peace and unity among mankind. Their reality is one; therefore, their accomplishment is one and universal—whether it be through the essential or material ordinances of God. There is but one light of the material sun, one ocean, one rain, one atmosphere. Similarly, in the spiritual world there is one divine reality forming the center and altruistic basis for peace and reconciliation among various and conflicting nations and peoples. Consider how the Roman Empire and Greek nation were at war in enmity and hatred after the Messianic day, how the hostilities of Egypt and Assyria, though subdued in intensity, still flamed in the warring element of these ancient and declining nations. But the teachings of Jesus Christ proved to be the cement by which they were united; warfare ceased, strife and hatred passed away, and these belligerent peoples associated in love and friendship. For strife and warfare are the very destroyers of human foundations, whereas peace and amity are the builders and safeguards of human welfare. As an instance, two nations which have remained at peace for centuries declare war against each other. What destruction and loss befalls both in one year of strife and conflict—the undoing of centuries. How urgent their necessity and demand for peace, with its comfort and progress, instead of war, which blasts and destroys the foundation of all human attainment.

5   The body politic may be likened to the human organism. As long as the various members and parts of that organism are coordinated and cooperating in harmony, we have as a result the expression of life in its fullest degree. When these members lack coordination and harmony, we have the reverse, which in the human organism is disease, dissolution, death. Similarly, in the body politic of humanity dissension, discord and warfare are always destructive and inevitably fatal. All created beings are dependent upon peace and coordination, for every contingent and phenomenal being is a composition of distinct elements. As long as there is affinity and cohesion among these constituent elements, strength and life are manifest; but when dissension and repulsion arise among them, disintegration follows. This is proof that peace and amity, which God has willed for His children, are the saving factors of human society, whereas war and strife, which violate His ordinances, are the cause of death and

136

destruction. Therefore, God has sent His Prophets to announce the message of goodwill, peace and life to the world of mankind.

Inasmuch as the essential reality of the religions is one and their seeming variance and plurality is adherence to forms and imitations which have arisen, it is evident that these causes of difference and divergence must be abandoned in order that the underlying reality may unite mankind in its enlightenment and upbuilding. All who hold fast to the one reality will be in agreement and unity. Then shall the religions summon people to the oneness of the world of humanity and to universal justice; then will they proclaim equality of rights and exhort men to virtue and to faith in the loving mercy of God. The underlying foundation of the religions is one; there is no intrinsic difference between them. Therefore, if the essential and fundamental ordinances of the religions be observed, peace and unity will dawn, and all the differences of sects and denominations will disappear. 6

And now let us consider the various peoples of the world. All the nations—American, British, French, German, Turkish, Persian, Arab—are children of the same Adam, members of the same human household. Why should dissension exist among them? The surface of the earth is one native land, and that native land was provided for all. God has not set these boundaries and race limitations. Why should imaginary barriers which God has not originally destined be made a cause of contention? God has created and provided for all. He is the Preserver of all, and all are submerged in the ocean of His mercy. Not a single soul is deprived. Inasmuch as we have such a loving God and Creator, why should we be at war with each other? Now that His light is shining universally, why should we cast ourselves into darkness? As His table is spread for all His children, why should we deprive each other of its sustenance? As His effulgence is shining upon all, why should we seek to live among the shadows? There is no doubt that the only cause is ignorance and that the 7 result is perdition. Discord deprives humanity of the eternal favors of God; therefore, we must forget all imaginary causes of difference and seek the very fundamentals of the divine religions in order that we may associate in perfect love and accord and consider humankind as one family, the surface of the earth as one nationality and all races as one humanity. Let us live under the protection of God, attaining eternal happiness in this world and everlasting life in the world to come.

8 O Thou kind Lord! Thou hast created all humanity from the same stock. Thou hast decreed that all shall belong to the same household. In Thy Holy Presence they are all Thy servants, and all mankind are sheltered beneath Thy Tabernacle; all have gathered together at Thy Table of Bounty; all are illumined through the light of Thy Providence.

9 O God! Thou art kind to all, Thou hast provided for all, dost shelter all, conferrest life upon all. Thou hast endowed each and all with talents and faculties, and all are submerged in the Ocean of Thy Mercy.

10 O Thou kind Lord! Unite all. Let the religions agree and make the nations one, so that they may see each other as one family and the whole earth as one home. May they all live together in perfect harmony.

11 O God! Raise aloft the banner of the oneness of mankind.

12 O God! Establish the Most Great Peace.

13 Cement Thou, O God, the hearts together.

14 O Thou kind Father, God! Gladden our hearts through the fragrance of Thy love. Brighten our eyes through the Light of Thy Guidance. Delight our ears with the melody of Thy Word, and shelter us all in the Stronghold of Thy Providence.

15 Thou art the Mighty and Powerful, Thou art the Forgiving and Thou art the One Who overlooketh the shortcomings of all mankind.

Talks 'Abdu'l-Bahá Delivered in Cleveland

6 May 1912

Talk at Euclid Hall
Cleveland, Ohio

FROM STENOGRAPHIC NOTES

THIS is a very joyous evening, an evidence in itself of the possibil- 1
ity of uniting the East and the West—an eastern man appearing
before an assemblage of reverent western people. The East and
West, the Orient and Occident, shall be united. If we search
history, we shall not find the record of such an occasion where
one has traveled from the far East to the far West to address
a meeting of this universal character. This is a miracle of the
twentieth century which proves that the seemingly impossible
may become real and possible in the kingdom of man. Praise
be to God! The dark ages have disappeared, and the age of light
has at last arrived. The Sun of Reality has dawned with supreme
effulgence, the realities of things have become manifest and
renewed, the mysteries of the unknown have been revealed,
and great inventions and discoveries mark this period as a most
wonderful age.

Through the ingenuity and inventions of man it is possible 2
to cross the wide oceans, fly through the air and travel in submarine depths. At any moment the Orient and Occident can
communicate with each other. Trains speed across the continents.
The human voice has been arrested and reproduced, and now
man can speak at long distances from any point. These are
some of the signs of this glorious century. The great progress

mentioned has taken place in the material world. Remarkable signs and evidences have become manifest. Hidden realities and mysteries have been disclosed. This is the time for man to strive and put forth his greatest efforts in spiritual directions. Material civilization has reached an advanced plane, but now there is need of spiritual civilization. Material civilization alone will not satisfy; it cannot meet the conditions and requirements of the present age; its benefits are limited to the world of matter. There is no limitation to the spirit of man, for spirit in itself is progressive, and if the divine civilization be established, the spirit of man will advance. Every developed susceptibility will increase the effectiveness of man. Discoveries of the real will become more and more possible, and the influence of divine guidance will be increasingly recognized. All this is conducive to the divine form of civilization. This is what is meant in the Bible by the descent of the New Jerusalem. The heavenly Jerusalem is none other than divine civilization, and it is now ready. It is to be and shall be organized, and the oneness of humankind will be a visible fact. Humanity will then be brought together as one. The various religions will be united, and different races will be known as one kind. The Orient and Occident will be conjoined, and the banner of international peace will be unfurled. The world shall at last find peace, and the equalities and rights of men shall be established. The capacity of humankind will be tested, and a degree shall be attained where equality is a reality.

3   All the peoples of the world will enjoy like interests, and the poor shall possess a portion of the comforts of life. Just as the rich are surrounded by their luxuries in palaces, the poor will have at least their comfortable and pleasant places of abode; and just as the wealthy enjoy a variety of food, the needy shall have their necessities and no longer live in poverty. In short, a readjustment of the economic order will come about, the divine

Sonship will attract, the Sun of Reality will shine forth, and all phenomenal being will attain a portion.

Consider: What is this material civilization of the day giving forth? Has it not produced the instruments of warfare and destruction? In olden times the weapon of war was the sword; today it is the smokeless gun. Warships a century ago were sailing vessels; now we have dreadnoughts. Instruments and means of human destruction have enormously multiplied in this era of material civilization. But if material civilization shall become organized in conjunction with divine civilization, if the man of moral integrity and intellectual acumen shall unite for human betterment and uplift with the man of spiritual capacity, the happiness and progress of the human race will be assured. All the nations of the world will then be closely related and companionable, and the religions will merge into one, for the divine reality within them all is one reality. Abraham proclaimed this reality; Jesus promulgated it; all the Prophets who have appeared in the world have founded Their teachings upon it. Therefore, the people of the world have this one true, unchangeable basis for peace and agreement, and war, which has raged for thousands of years, will pass away.

For centuries and cycles humanity has been engaged in war and conflict. At one time the pretext for war has been religion, at another time patriotism, racial prejudice, national politics, territorial conquest or commercial expansion; in brief, humanity has never been at peace during the period of known history. What blood has been shed! How many fathers have mourned the loss of sons; how many sons have wept for fathers, and mothers for dear ones! Human beings have been the food and targets of the battlefield, and everywhere warfare and strife have been the theme and burden of history. Ferocity has characterized men even more than animals. The lion, tiger, bear and wolf are ferocious because of their needs. Unless they are fierce, cruel and unrelenting, they will die of starvation. The lion cannot graze; its teeth are fitted only for food of flesh. This is also true of other wild animals. Ferocity is natural to them as their means of subsistence; but human ferocity proceeds from selfishness, greed and oppression. It springs from no natural necessity. Man needlessly kills a thousand fellow creatures, becomes a hero and is glorified through centuries of posterity. A great city is destroyed in one day by a commanding general. How ignorant, how inconsistent is humankind! If a man slays another man, we brand him as a murderer and criminal and sentence him to capital punishment, but if he kills one hundred thousand men, he is a military genius, a great celebrity, a Napoleon idolized by his nation. If a man steals one dollar, he is called a thief and put into prison; if he rapes and pillages an innocent country by military invasion, he is crowned a hero. How ignorant is humankind! Ferocity does not belong to the kingdom of man. It is the province of man to confer life, not death. It behooves him to be the cause of human welfare, but inasmuch as he glories in the savagery of animalism, it is an evidence that divine civilization has not been established in human society. Material civilization has advanced unmistakably, but because it is not associated with divine civilization, evil and wickedness abound. In ancient times if two nations were at war twelve months, not over twenty thousand men would be killed; now the instruments of death have become so multiplied and perfected that one hundred thousand can be destroyed in a day. In three months during the Russo-Japanese War one million perished. This was undreamed of in former cycles. The cause is the absence of divine civilization.

6   This revered American nation presents evidences of greatness and worth. It is my hope that this just government will stand for peace so that warfare may be abolished throughout the world and the standards of national unity and reconciliation be upraised.

142

This is the greatest attainment of the world of humanity. This American nation is equipped and empowered to accomplish that which will adorn the pages of history, to become the envy of the world and be blest in the East and the West for the triumph of its democracy. I pray that this may come to pass, and I ask the blessing of God in behalf of you all.

2

6 May 1912

Talk at Sanatorium of Dr. C. M. Swingle
Cleveland, Ohio

NOTES BY SIGEL T. BROOKS

THIS is a beautiful city; the climate is pleasant; the views are 1 charming. All the cities of America seem to be large and beautiful, and the people appear prosperous. The American continent gives signs and evidences of very great advancement; its future is even more promising, for its influence and illumination are far-reaching, and it will lead all nations spiritually. The flag of freedom and banner of liberty have been unfurled here, but the prosperity and advancement of a city, the happiness and greatness of a country depend upon its hearing and obeying the call of God. The light of reality must shine therein and divine civilization be founded; then the radiance of the Kingdom will be diffused and heavenly influences surround. Material civilization is likened to the body, whereas divine civilization is the spirit in that body. A body not manifesting the spirit is dead; a fruitless tree is worthless. Jesus declares that there is spiritual capacity in some people, for all are not submerged in the sea of materialism. They seek the Divine Spirit; they turn to God; they long for the Kingdom. It is my hope that these revered people present may attain both material and spiritual progress. As they have advanced wonderfully in material degrees, so may they, likewise, advance in spiritual development until the body shall become refined and beautiful through the wealth of spiritual potentiality and efficiency.

2   Praise be to God! The Sun of Reality has dawned, and its effulgences are shining from all horizons. The signs of God are resplendent, and the teachings of the heavenly Messengers are being spread. May the hearts be directed to the Kingdom of God and become illuminated by witnessing the lights of God in order that all created beings may obtain a portion of the divine bestowals. May the spirit of life be restored through the divine graces of the Almighty, and may the East and West be bound together. May oneness and harmony become manifest in all regions. May the people of the world become as one family and obtain the everlasting bounty. May the doors of the Kingdom be opened from all directions and the praise of the name Abhá be heard throughout the earth.

Talk 'Abdu'l-Bahá Delivered in Pittsburgh

7 May 1912

Talk at Hotel Schenley
Pittsburgh, Pennsylvania

NOTES BY SUZANNE BEATTY

I HAVE come from the Orient to visit your country. Surely this 1
continent is praiseworthy from all points of view, and there are
signs of prosperity everywhere. The people show refinement,
and evidences of progressive civilization abound. I will give you
a brief exposition of the fundamental principles of Bahá'u'lláh's
teachings in order that you may be informed of the nature and
significance of the Bahá'í movement.

About sixty years ago the greatest enmity and strife existed 2
among the various peoples and religious denominations of
Persia. Throughout the world generally war and dissension
prevailed. At this time Bahá'u'lláh appeared in Persia and began
devoting Himself to the uplift and education of the people.
He united divergent sects and creeds, removed religious, racial,
patriotic and political prejudices and established a strong bond
of unity and reconciliation among varying degrees and classes
of mankind. The enmity then existing among the people was
so bitter and intense that even ordinary association was out
of the question. They would not meet and consult with each
other at all. Through the power of the teachings of Bahá'u'lláh
the most wonderful results were witnessed. He removed the
prejudices and hatred from human hearts and wrought such
transformation in their attitudes toward each other that today

in Persia there is perfect accord among hitherto bigoted religionists, varying sects and divergent classes. This was not an easy accomplishment, for Bahá'u'lláh underwent severe trials, great difficulties and violent persecution. He was imprisoned, tortures were inflicted upon Him, and finally He was banished from His native land. He bore every ordeal and infliction cheerfully. In His successive exiles from country to country up to the time of His ascension from this world, He was enabled to promulgate His teachings, even from prison. Wherever His oppressors sent Him, He hoisted the standard of the oneness of the world of humanity and promulgated the principles of the unity of mankind. Some of these principles are as follows. First, it is incumbent upon all mankind to investigate truth. If such investigation be made, all should agree and be united, for truth or reality is not multiple; it is not divisible. The different religions have one truth underlying them; therefore, their reality is one.

3   Each of the divine religions embodies two kinds of ordinances. The first is those which concern spiritual susceptibilities, the development of moral principles and the quickening of the conscience of man. These are essential or fundamental, one and the same in all religions, changeless and eternal—reality not subject to transformation. Abraham heralded this reality, Moses promulgated it, and Jesus Christ established it in the world of mankind. All the divine Prophets and Messengers were the instruments and channels of this same eternal, essential truth.

4   The second kind of ordinances in the divine religions is those which relate to the material affairs of humankind. These are the material or accidental laws which are subject to change in each day of manifestation, according to exigencies of the time, conditions and differing capacities of humanity. For instance, in the day of Moses ten commandments in regard to murder were revealed by Him. These commandments were in accordance with

146

the requirements of that day and time. Other laws embodying drastic punishments were enacted by Moses—an eye for an eye, a tooth for a tooth. The penalty for theft was amputation of the hand. These laws and penalties were applicable to the degree of the Israelitish people of that period, who dwelt in the wilderness and desert under conditions where severity was necessary and justifiable. But in the time of Jesus Christ this kind of law was not expedient; therefore, Christ abrogated and superseded the commands of Moses.

In brief, every one of the divine religions contains essential 5 ordinances, which are not subject to change, and material ordinances, which are abrogated according to the exigencies of time. But the people of the world have forsaken the divine teachings and followed forms and imitations of the truth. Inasmuch as these human interpretations and superstitions differ, dissensions and bigotry have arisen, and strife and warfare have prevailed. By investigating the truth or foundation of reality underlying their own and other beliefs, all would be united and agreed, for this reality is one; it is not multiple and not divisible.

The second principle or teaching of Bahá'u'lláh is the proc- 6 lamation of the oneness of the world of humanity—that all are servants of God and belong to one family; that God has created all and, therefore, His bestowals are universal; and that His providence, training, sustenance and loving-kindness surround all mankind.

This is the divine policy, and it is impossible for man to lay 7 the foundation of a better plan and policy than that which God has instituted. Therefore, we must recognize and assist the purpose of the glorious Lord. Inasmuch as God is kind and loving to all, why should we be unkind? As this human world is one household, why should its members be occupied with animosity and contention? Therefore, humanity must be looked upon with the eye of equal estimate and in the same attitude of love. The noblest of men is he who serves humankind, and he is nearest the threshold of God who is the least of His servants. The glory and majesty of man are dependent upon his servitude to his fellow creatures and not upon the exercise of hostility and hatred.

8   The third principle or teaching of Bahá'u'lláh is the oneness of religion and science. Any religious belief which is not conformable with scientific proof and investigation is superstition, for true science is reason and reality, and religion is essentially reality and pure reason; therefore, the two must correspond. Religious teaching which is at variance with science and reason is human invention and imagination unworthy of acceptance, for the antithesis and opposite of knowledge is superstition born of the ignorance of man. If we say religion is opposed to science, we lack knowledge of either true science or true religion, for both are founded upon the premises and conclusions of reason, and both must bear its test.

9   The fourth principle or teaching of Bahá'u'lláh is the readjustment and equalization of the economic standards of mankind. This deals with the question of human livelihood. It is evident that under present systems and conditions of government the poor are subject to the greatest need and distress while others more fortunate live in luxury and plenty far beyond their actual necessities. This inequality of portion and privilege is one of the deep and vital problems of human society. That there is need of an equalization and apportionment by which all may possess the comforts and privileges of life is evident. The remedy must be legislative readjustment of conditions. The rich too must be merciful to the poor, contributing from willing hearts to their needs without being forced or compelled to do so. The composure of the world will be assured by the establishment of this principle in the religious life of mankind.

The fifth principle or teaching of Bahá'u'lláh is the abandon- 10 ing of religious, racial, patriotic and political prejudices, which destroy the foundations of human society. All mankind are creatures and servants of the one God. The surface of the earth is one home; humanity is one family and household. Distinctions and boundaries are artificial, human. Why should there be discord and strife among men? All must become united and coordinated in service to the world of humanity.

The sixth principle or teaching of Bahá'u'lláh concerns the 11 equality of man and woman. He has declared that in the estimation of God there is no distinction of sex. The one whose heart is most pure, whose deeds and service in the Cause of God are greater and nobler, is most acceptable before the divine threshold—whether male or female. In the vegetable and animal kingdoms sex exists in perfect equality and without distinction or invidious estimate. The animal, although inferior to man in intelligence and reason, recognizes sex equality. Why should man, who is endowed with the sense of justice and sensibilities of conscience, be willing that one of the members of the human family should be rated and considered as subordinate? Such differentiation is neither intelligent nor conscientious; therefore, the principle of religion has been revealed by Bahá'u'lláh that woman must be given the privilege of equal education with man and full right to his prerogatives. That is to say, there must be no difference in the education of male and female in order that womankind may develop equal capacity and importance with man in the social and economic equation. Then the world will attain unity and harmony. In past ages humanity has been defective and inefficient because it has been incomplete. War and its ravages have blighted the world; the education of woman will be a mighty step toward its abolition and ending, for she will use her whole influence against war. Woman rears the child and educates the youth to maturity. She will refuse to give her sons for sacrifice upon the field of battle. In truth, she will be the greatest factor in establishing universal peace and international arbitration. Assuredly, woman will abolish warfare among mankind. Inasmuch as human society consists of two parts, the male and female, each the complement of the other, the happiness and stability of humanity cannot be assured unless both are perfected. Therefore, the standard and status of man and woman must become equalized.

12 Among other teachings and principles Bahá'u'lláh counsels the education of all members of society. No individual should be denied or deprived of intellectual training, although each should receive according to capacity. None must be left in the grades of ignorance, for ignorance is a defect in the human world. All mankind must be given a knowledge of science and philosophy—that is, as much as may be deemed necessary. All cannot be scientists and philosophers, but each should be educated according to his needs and deserts.

13 Bahá'u'lláh teaches that the world of humanity is in need of the breath of the Holy Spirit, for in spiritual quickening and enlightenment true oneness is attained with God and man. The Most Great Peace cannot be assured through racial force and effort; it cannot be established by patriotic devotion and sacrifice; for nations differ widely and local patriotism has limitations. Furthermore, it is evident that political power and diplomatic ability are not conducive to universal agreement, for the interests of governments are varied and selfish; nor will international harmony and reconciliation be an outcome of human opinions concentrated upon it, for opinions are faulty and intrinsically diverse. Universal peace is an impossibility through human and material agencies; it must be through spiritual power. There is need of a universal impelling force which will establish the oneness of humanity and destroy the foundations of war and

strife. None other than the divine power can do this; therefore, it will be accomplished through the breath of the Holy Spirit.

No matter how far the material world advances, it cannot 14 establish the happiness of mankind. Only when material and spiritual civilization are linked and coordinated will happiness be assured. Then material civilization will not contribute its energies to the forces of evil in destroying the oneness of humanity, for in material civilization good and evil advance together and maintain the same pace. For example, consider the material progress of man in the last decade. Schools and colleges, hospitals, philanthropic institutions, scientific academies and temples of philosophy have been founded, but hand in hand with these evidences of development, the invention and production of means and weapons for human destruction have correspondingly increased. In early days the weapon of war was the sword; now it is the magazine rifle. Among the ancients, men fought with javelins and daggers; now they employ shells and bombs. Dreadnoughts are built, torpedoes invented, and every few days new ammunition is forthcoming.

All this is the outcome of material civilization; therefore, 15 although material advancement furthers good purposes in life, at the same time it serves evil ends. The divine civilization is good because it cultivates morals. Consider what the Prophets of God have contributed to human morality. Jesus Christ summoned all to the Most Great Peace through the acquisition of pure morals. If the moral precepts and foundations of divine civilization become united with the material advancement of man, there is no doubt that the happiness of the human world will be attained and that from every direction the glad tidings of peace upon earth will be announced. Then humankind will achieve extraordinary progress, the sphere of human intelligence will be immeasurably enlarged, wonderful inventions will appear, and the spirit of God will reveal itself; all men will consort in joy and fragrance, and eternal life will be conferred upon the children of the Kingdom. Then will the power of the divine make itself effective and the breath of the Holy Spirit penetrate the essence of all things. Therefore, the material and the divine, or merciful, civilizations must progress together until the highest aspirations and desires of humanity shall become realized.

16   These are a few of the teachings and principles of Bahá'u'lláh, briefly presented so that you may be informed of their significance and purpose and find them a stimulus to your knowledge and actions. I ask God to assist this prosperous and progressive nation and to bestow His blessings upon this just government and wonderful continent of the West.

Talks 'Abdu'l-Bahá Delivered in New York, Montclair, and Jersey City

11 May 1912

Talk at 227 Riverside Drive, New York

NOTES BY JOHN G. GRUNDY

IT is only three weeks that we have been away from the New   1
York friends, yet so great has been the longing to see you that it
seems like three months. We have had no rest by day or night
since we left you—either traveling, moving about or speaking—yet it was all so pleasantly done, and we have been most
happy. Praise be to God! Everywhere and all the time it has been
harakat, harakat, harakat ("motion, motion, motion").

The friends in America are very good. All the people we have   2
met here are kind and pleasant. They are polite and not antagonistic, although somewhat inquisitive. A small minority of them seem
prejudiced, yet even these have their good points. The American
people have a real love for advancement. They are not content to
stand still. They are most energetic and progressive. When you
see a tree growing and developing, be hopeful of its outcome. It
will blossom and bear fruit eventually. If you see dry wood or old
trees, there is no hope whatever of fruitage.

The questions asked us have been opportune and to the point.   3
Our answers have not been utilized for controversy and argument. We met savants and learned men and satisfied them with
our explanations. Important people expressed their satisfaction
and pleasure at our replies to their inquiries. In brief, it would

be difficult to find in the aggregate of people we met anyone who was dissatisfied. Some scholastic minds aimed only at fruitless discussion. In Chicago we met two clergymen—delivering an address at the church of one and having dinner with the other. Both manifested great love. Likewise, among all the people we met, not a single soul arose in opposition or went away disappointed.

4   Yesterday in Washington we met a group of important people. One prominent in political circles came with a justice of the Supreme Court. There were many ladies of the diplomatic circle present. After we had spoken, the politician referred to raised the point that the foundation of all religions from time immemorial had been peace, love and accord—principles conducive to fellowship and unification—yet Jesus, he declared, had been "the cause of discord and strife and not a factor in the realization of unity." "Therefore," he said, "I cannot accept your statements and explanations that religion has been the source of human betterment." After we explained further he said, "What you have stated may cause me to change my views and agree with you." During this time the justice remained silent. Fearing he might have some feeling of dissatisfaction, we asked if anything presented had been objectionable to his opinion. He replied, "Not at all! Not at all! It's all right! It's all right!" This is the characteristic expression of the Occident—"All right! All right!"

5   There were also present at this meeting several cabinet officers, United States senators, many from the foreign diplomatic service, army and navy officials and other dignitaries. The servant of God, our hostess, experienced much trouble in preparation and entertainment but was always active and energetic in service, inviting important and influential people to the gatherings. We spoke to all from their own standpoints with most satisfactory results; we were working day and night so there was very little time for individual and private interviews.

In Washington, too, we called a meeting of the blacks and   6
whites. The attendance was very large, the blacks predominat-
ing. At our second gathering this was reversed, but at the third
meeting we were unable to say which color predominated. These
meetings were a great practical lesson upon the unity of colors
and races in the Bahá'í teaching.

We said in part: The black man must ever be grateful to the   7
white man, for he has manifested great courage and self-sacrifice
in behalf of the black race. Four years he fought their cause,
enduring severe hardships, sacrificing life, family, treasure, all for
his black brother until the great war ended in the proclamation
of freedom. By this effort and accomplishment the black race
throughout the world was influenced and benefited. Had this not
been accomplished, the black man in Africa would still be bound
by the chains of slavery. Therefore, his race should everywhere be
grateful, for no greater evidence of humanism and courageous
devotion could be shown than the white man has displayed. If
the blacks of the United States forget this sacrifice, zeal and manhood on the part of the whites, no ingratitude could be greater or
more censurable. If they could see the wretched conditions and
surroundings of the black people of Africa today, the contrast
would be apparent and the fact clearly evident that the black
race in America enjoys incomparable advantages. The comfort
and civilization under which they live here are due to the white
man's effort and sacrifice. Had this sacrifice not been made, they
would still be in the bonds and chains of slavery, scarcely lifted
out of an aboriginal condition. Therefore, always show forth
your gratitude to the white man. Eventually all differences will
disappear, and you will completely win his friendship.

God maketh no distinction between the white and the black.   8
If the hearts are pure both are acceptable unto Him. God is
no respecter of persons on account of either color or race. All

colors are acceptable to Him, be they white, black, or yellow. Inasmuch as all were created in the image of God, we must bring ourselves to realize that all embody divine possibilities. If you go into a garden and find all the flowers alike in form, species and color, the effect is wearisome to the eye. The garden is more beautiful when the flowers are many-colored and different; the variety lends charm and adornment. In a flock of doves some are white, some black, red, blue; yet they make no distinction among themselves. All are doves no matter what the color.

9   This variety in forms and colorings which is manifest in all the kingdoms is according to creative wisdom and has a divine purpose. Nevertheless, whether the creatures be all alike or all different should not be the cause of strife and quarreling among them. Especially why should man find cause for discord in the color or race of his fellow creature? No educated or illumined mind will allow that this differentiation and discord should exist or that there is any ground for it. Therefore, the whites should be just and kind to the blacks, who in turn should reflect an equal measure of appreciation and gratitude. Then will the world become as one great garden of flowering humanity, variegated and multicolored, rivaling each other only in the virtues and graces which are spiritual.

2

12 May 1912

*Talk at Unity Church
Montclair, New Jersey*

NOTES BY ESTHER FOSTER

I WISH to speak upon the subject of divine unity, the oneness   1
of God, before this revered assemblage.

It is a self-evident fact that phenomenal existence can never   2
grasp nor comprehend the ancient and essential Reality. Utter
weakness cannot understand absolute strength. When we view
the world of creation, we discover differences in degree which
make it impossible for the lower to comprehend the higher.
For example, the mineral kingdom, no matter how much it
may advance, can never comprehend the phenomena of the
vegetable kingdom. Whatever development the vegetable may
attain, it can have no message from nor come in touch with the
kingdom of the animal. However perfect may be the growth of
a tree, it cannot realize the sensation of sight, hearing, smell,
taste and touch; these are beyond its limitation. Although it
is the possessor of existence in the world of creation, a tree,
nevertheless, has no knowledge of the superior degree of the
animal kingdom. Likewise, no matter how great the advancement of the animal, it can have no idea of the human plane,
no knowledge of intellect and spirit. Difference in degree is
an obstacle to this comprehension. A lower degree cannot
comprehend a higher although all are in the same world of
creation—whether mineral, vegetable or animal. Degree is the
barrier and limitation. In the human plane of existence we can

157

say we have knowledge of a vegetable, its qualities and product; but the vegetable has no knowledge or comprehension whatever of us. No matter how near perfection this rose may advance in its own sphere, it can never possess hearing and sight. Inasmuch as in the creational world, which is phenomenal, difference of degree is an obstacle or hindrance to comprehension, how can the human being, which is a created exigency, comprehend the ancient divine Reality, which is essential? This is impossible because the reality of Divinity is sanctified beyond the comprehension of the created being, man.

3   Furthermore, that which man can grasp is finite to man, and man to it is as infinite. Is it possible then for the reality of Divinity to be finite and the human creature infinite? On the contrary, the reverse is true; the human is finite while the essence of Divinity is infinite. Whatever comes within the sphere of human comprehension must be limited and finite. As the essence of Divinity transcends the comprehension of man, therefore God brings forth certain Manifestations of the divine Reality upon Whom He bestows heavenly effulgences in order that They may be intermediaries between humanity and Himself. These holy Manifestations or Prophets of God are as mirrors which have acquired illumination from the Sun of Truth, but the Sun does not descend from its high zenith and does not effect entrance within the mirror. In truth, this mirror has attained complete polish and purity until the utmost capacity of reflection has been developed in it; therefore, the Sun of Reality with its fullest effulgence and splendor is revealed therein. These mirrors are earthly, whereas the reality of Divinity is in its highest apogee. Although its lights are shining and its heat is manifest in them, although these mirrors are telling their story of its effulgence, the Sun, nevertheless, remains in its own lofty station; it does not descend; it does not effect entrance, because it is holy and sanctified.

The Sun of Divinity and of Reality has revealed itself in vari-   4
ous mirrors. Though these mirrors are many, yet the Sun is one.
The bestowals of God are one; the reality of the divine religion
is one. Consider how one and the same light has reflected itself
in the different mirrors or manifestations of it. There are certain
souls who are lovers of the Sun; they perceive the effulgence of
the Sun from every mirror. They are not fettered or attached to
the mirrors; they are attached to the Sun itself and adore it, no
matter from what point it may shine. But those who adore the
mirror and are attached to it become deprived of witnessing
the light of the Sun when it shines forth from another mirror.
For instance, the Sun of Reality revealed itself from the Mosaic
mirror. The people who were sincere accepted and believed in it.
When the same Sun shone from the Messianic mirror, the Jews
who were not lovers of the Sun and who were fettered by their
adoration of the mirror of Moses did not perceive the lights and
effulgences of the Sun of Reality resplendent in Jesus; therefore,
they were deprived of its bestowals. Yet the Sun of Reality, the
Word of God, shone from the Messianic mirror through the
wonderful channel of Jesus Christ more fully and more wonderfully. Its effulgences were manifestly radiant, but even to this
day the Jews are holding to the Mosaic mirror. Therefore, they
are bereft of witnessing the lights of eternity in Jesus.

In brief, the sun is one sun, the light is one light which shines   5
upon all phenomenal beings. Every creature has a portion thereof,
but the pure mirror can reveal the story of its bounty more fully
and completely. Therefore, we must adore the light of the Sun,
no matter through what mirror it may be revealed. We must not
entertain prejudice, for prejudice is an obstacle to realization.
Inasmuch as the effulgence is one effulgence, the human realities
must all become recipients of the same light, recognizing in it the
compelling force that unites them in its illumination.

6   As this is the radiant century, it is my hope that the Sun of Truth may illumine all humanity. May the eyes be opened and the ears become attentive; may souls become resuscitated and consort together in the utmost harmony as recipients of the same light. Perchance, God will remove this strife and warfare of thousands of years. May this bloodshed pass away, this tyranny and oppression cease, this warfare be ended. May the light of love shine forth and illumine hearts, and may human lives be cemented and connected until all of us may find agreement and tranquillity beneath the same tabernacle and with the standard of the Most Great Peace above us move steadily onward.

7   O Thou kind Lord! O Thou Who art generous and merciful! We are the servants of Thy threshold and are gathered beneath the sheltering shadow of Thy divine unity. The sun of Thy mercy is shining upon all, and the clouds of Thy bounty shower upon all. Thy gifts encompass all, Thy loving providence sustains all, Thy protection overshadows all, and the glances of Thy favor are cast upon all. O Lord! Grant Thine infinite bestowals, and let the light of Thy guidance shine. Illumine the eyes, gladden the hearts with abiding joy. Confer a new spirit upon all people and bestow upon them eternal life. Unlock the gates of true understanding and let the light of faith shine resplendent. Gather all people beneath the shadow of Thy bounty and cause them to unite in harmony, so that they may become as the rays of one sun, as the waves of one ocean, and as the fruit of one tree. May they drink from the same fountain. May they be refreshed by the same breeze. May they receive illumination from the same source of light. Thou art the Giver, the Merciful, the Omnipotent.

3

12 May 1912

Talk at Meeting of International Peace Forum
Grace Methodist Episcopal Church
West 104th Street, New York

NOTES BY ESTHER FOSTER

WHEN we review history from the beginning down to the present 1
day, we find that strife and warfare have prevailed throughout
the human world. Wars—religious, racial or political—have
arisen from human ignorance, misunderstanding and lack of
education. We will first consider religious strife and conflict.

It is evident that the divine Prophets have appeared in the world 2
to establish love and agreement among mankind. They have been
the Shepherds and not the wolves. The Shepherd comes forth to
gather and lead his flock and not to disperse them by creating
strife. Every divine Shepherd has assembled a flock which had
formerly been scattered. Among the Shepherds was Moses. At
a time when the tribes of Israel were wandering and dispersed,
He assembled, united and educated them to higher degrees of
capacity and progress until they passed out of the wilderness of
discipline into the holy land of possession. He transformed their
degradation into glory, changed their poverty into wealth and
replaced their vices by virtues until they rose to such a zenith that
the splendor of the sovereignty of Solomon was made possible,
and the fame of their civilization extended to the East and the
West. It is evident, therefore, that Moses was a divine Shepherd,
for He gathered the tribes of Israel together and united them in
the power and strength of a great nationhood.

3   When the Messianic star of Jesus Christ dawned, He declared He had come to gather together the lost tribes or scattered sheep of Moses. He not only shepherded the flock of Israel but brought together people of Chaldea, Egypt, Syria, ancient Assyria and Phoenicia. These people were in a state of utmost hostility, thirsting for the blood of each other with the ferocity of animals; but Jesus Christ brought them together, cemented and united them in His Cause and established such a bond of love among them that enmity and warfare were abandoned. It is evident, therefore, that the divine teachings are intended to create a bond of unity in the human world and establish the foundations of love and fellowship among mankind. Divine religion is not a cause for discord and disagreement. If religion becomes the source of antagonism and strife, the absence of religion is to be preferred. Religion is meant to be the quickening life of the body politic; if it be the cause of death to humanity, its nonexistence would be a blessing and benefit to man. Therefore, in this day the divine teachings must be sought, for they are the remedies for the present conditions of the world of humanity. The purpose of a remedy is to heal and cure. If it be productive of worse symptoms, its absence or discontinuance is preferable.

4   At a time when the Arabian tribes and nomadic peoples were widely separated, living in the deserts under lawless conditions, strife and bloodshed continual among them, no tribe free from the menace of attack and destruction by another—at such a critical time Muḥammad appeared. He gathered these wild tribes of the desert together, reconciled, united and caused them to agree so that enmity and warfare ceased. The Arabian nation immediately advanced until its dominion extended westward to Spain and Andalusia.

5   From these facts and premises we may conclude that the establishing of the divine religions is for peace, not for war and

the shedding of blood. Inasmuch as all are founded upon one reality which is love and unity, the wars and dissensions which have characterized the history of religion have been due to imitations and superstitions which arise afterward. Religion is reality, and reality is one. The fundamentals of the religion of God are, therefore, one in reality. There is neither difference nor change in the fundamentals. Variance is caused by blind imitations, prejudices and adherence to forms which appear later; and inasmuch as these differ, discord and strife result. If the religions of the world would forsake these causes of difficulty and seek the fundamentals, all would agree, and strife and dissension would pass away; for religion and reality are one and not multiple.

Other wars are caused by purely imaginary racial differences; 6 for humanity is one kind, one race and progeny, inhabiting the same globe. In the creative plan there is no racial distinction and separation such as Frenchman, Englishman, American, German, Italian or Spaniard; all belong to one household. These boundaries and distinctions are human and artificial, not natural and original. All mankind are the fruits of one tree, flowers of the same garden, waves of one sea. In the animal kingdom no such distinction and separation are observed. The sheep of the East and the sheep of the West would associate peacefully. The Oriental flock would not look surprised as if saying, "These are sheep of the Occident; they do not belong to our country." All would gather in harmony and enjoy the same pasture without evidence of local or racial distinction. The birds of different countries mingle in friendliness. We find these virtues in the animal kingdom. Shall man deprive himself of these virtues? Man is endowed with superior reasoning power and the faculty of perception; he is the manifestation of divine bestowals. Shall racial ideas prevail and obscure the creative purpose of unity in his kingdom? Shall he say, "I am a German," "I am a Frenchman" or an "Englishman" and declare war because of this imaginary and human distinction? God forbid! This earth is one household and the native land of all humanity; therefore, the human race should ignore distinctions and boundaries which are artificial and conducive to disagreement and hostility. We have come from the East. Praise be to God! We find this continent prosperous, the climate salubrious and delightful, the inhabitants genial and courteous, the government equitable and just. Shall we entertain any other thought and feeling than that of love for you? Shall we say, "This is not our native land; therefore, everything is objectionable"? This would be gross ignorance to which man must not subject himself. Man is endowed with powers to investigate reality, and the reality is that humanity is one in kind and equal in the creative plan. Therefore, false distinctions of race and native land, which are factors and causes of warfare, must be abandoned.

7   Consider what is happening in Tripoli: how the poor are being killed and the blood of the helpless is being shed upon both sides; children, made fatherless; fathers, lamenting the death of their sons; mothers, bewailing the loss of dear ones. And what is the benefit after all? Nothing conceivable. Is it, therefore, justifiable? The domestic animals do not manifest hatred and cruelty toward each other; that is the attribute of the wild and ferocious beasts. In a flock of one thousand sheep you will witness no bloodshed. Numberless species of birds are peaceful in flocks. Wolves, lions, tigers are ferocious because it is their natural and necessary means for obtaining food. Man has no need of such ferocity; his food is provided in other ways. Therefore, it is evident that warfare, cruelty and bloodshed in the kingdom of man are caused by human greed, hatred and selfishness. The kings and rulers of nations enjoy luxury and ease in their palaces and send the common people to the

battlefield—offer them as the food and targets of cannon. Each day they invent new instruments for the more complete destruction of the foundations of the human race. They are callous and merciless toward their fellow creatures. What shall atone for the sufferings and grief of mothers who have so tenderly cared for their sons? What sleepless nights they have spent, and what days of devotion and love they have given to bring their children to maturity! Yet the savagery of these warring rulers causes great numbers of their victims to be torn and mutilated in a day. What ignorance and degradation, yea even greater than the ferocious beasts themselves! For a wolf will carry away and devour one sheep at a time, whereas an ambitious tyrant may cause the death of one hundred thousand men in a battle and glory in his military prowess, saying, "I am commander in chief; I have won this mighty victory." Consider the ignorance and inconsistency of the human race. If a man kills another, no matter what the cause may be, he is pronounced a murderer, imprisoned or executed; but the brutal oppressor who has slain one hundred thousand is idolized as a hero, conqueror or military genius. A man steals a small sum of money; he is called a thief and sent to the penitentiary; but the military leader who invades and pillages a whole kingdom is acclaimed heroic and a mighty man of valor. How base and ignorant is man!

In Persia previous to the middle of the nineteenth century 8 among the various tribes and peoples, sects and denominations there existed the greatest animosity, strife and hatred. At that time, too, all the other nations of the East were in the same condition. Religionists were hostile and bigoted, sects were at enmity, races hated each other, tribes were constantly at war; everywhere antagonism and conflict prevailed. Men shunned and were suspicious of each other. The man who could kill a number of his fellow creatures was glorified for his heroism and strength. Among religionists it was esteemed a praiseworthy deed to take the life of one who held an opposite belief. At this time Bahá'u'lláh arose and declared His mission. He founded the oneness of the world of humanity, proclaimed that all are servants of the loving and merciful God Who has created, nourished and provided for all; therefore, why should men be unjust and unkind to each other, showing forth that which is contrary to God? As He loves us, why should we entertain animosity and hate? If God did not love all, He would not have created, trained and provided for all. Loving-kindness is the divine policy. Shall we consider human policy and attitude superior to the wisdom and policy of God? This would be inconceivable, impossible. Therefore, we must emulate and follow the divine policy, dealing with each other in the utmost love and tenderness.

9   Bahá'u'lláh declared the Most Great Peace and international arbitration. He voiced these principles in numerous Epistles which were circulated broadcast throughout the East. He wrote to all the kings and rulers, encouraging, advising and admonishing them in regard to the establishment of peace, making it evident by conclusive proofs that the happiness and glory of humanity can only be assured through disarmament and arbitration. This was nearly fifty years ago. Because He promulgated the message of universal peace and international agreement, the kings of the Orient arose against Him, for they did not find their personal and national benefits advanced by His admonition and teaching. They persecuted Him bitterly, inflicted upon Him every torment, imprisoned, bastinadoed, banished Him and eventually confined Him in a fortress. Then they arose against His followers. For the establishment of international peace the blood of twenty thousand Bahá'ís was spilled. Their homes were destroyed, their children made captives and their possessions

pillaged, yet none of these people waxed cold or wavered in devotion. Even to this day the Bahá'ís are persecuted, and quite recently a number were killed, for wherever they are found they put forth the greatest efforts to establish the peace of the world. They not only promulgate principles; they are people of action.

In Persia today through the teachings of Bahá'u'lláh you will find people of various beliefs and denominations living together in the utmost peace and agreement. The former enmities and hatred have passed away, and they exercise the utmost love toward all mankind, for they realize and know that all are the creatures and servants of one God. This is directly due to the divine teachings. At most it is simply this: that the ignorant must be educated, the ailing must be healed, those who are as children in the scale of development must be helped to reach the age of maturity. We must not be unfriendly to anyone because of ignorance; neither must we reject the immature or turn away from the sick but administer the remedy for each human need until all are united in the providence of God. Therefore, it is evident that the essential foundations of the divine religions are unity and love. If religion be productive of discord among mankind, it is a destroyer and not divine, for religion implies unity and binding together and not separation. Mere knowledge of principles is not sufficient. We all know and admit that justice is good, but there is need of volition and action to carry out and manifest it. For example, we might think it good to build a church, but simply thinking of it as a good thing will not help its erection. The ways and means must be provided; we must will to build it and then proceed with the construction. All of us know that international peace is good, that it is conducive to human welfare and the glory of man, but volition and action are necessary before it can be established. Action is essential. Inasmuch as this century is a century of light, capacity for ac-

10

tion is assured to mankind. Necessarily the divine principles will be spread among men until the time of action arrives. Surely this has been so, and truly the time and conditions are ripe for action now. All men know that, verily, war is a destroyer of human foundations, and in every country of the world this is admitted and apparent. I find the United States of America an exceedingly progressive nation, the government just, the people in a state of readiness and the principle of equality established to an extraordinary degree. Therefore, it is my hope that, inasmuch as the standard of international peace must be upraised, it may be upraised upon this continent, for this nation is more deserving and has greater capacity for such an initial step than any other. If other nations should attempt to do this, the motive would be misunderstood. For instance, if Great Britain should declare for international peace, it would be said that it has been done to ensure the safety of her colonies. If France should hoist the standard, other nations would declare some hidden diplomatic policy underlies the action; Russia would be suspected of national designs if the first step were taken by that people, and so on with all the European and eastern governments. But the United States of America could not be accused of any such selfish interest. Your government has, strictly speaking, no colonies to protect. You are not endeavoring to extend your domain, nor have you need of territorial expansion. Therefore, if America takes the first step toward the establishing of world peace, it is certain to be ascribed to unselfishness and altruism. The world will say, "There is no other motive than altruism and service to humanity in this action by the United States." Therefore, it is my hope that you may stand forth as the first herald of peace and hoist this banner, for this banner will be hoisted. Raise it aloft, for you are the most qualified and deserving of nations. The other countries await this summons, expect this call to the standard of reconciliation, for the whole world is distressed because of the excessive burden and irreparable damage of war. Taxes are levied to meet its drain. Every year the burden increases, and the people have come to their end. Just now Europe is a battlefield of ammunition ready for a spark, and one spark will set aflame the whole world. Before these complications and cataclysmic events happen, take the step to prevent it.

The foundations of all the divine religions are peace and 11 agreement, but misunderstandings and ignorance have developed. If these are caused to disappear, you will see that all the religious agencies will work for peace and promulgate the oneness of humankind. For the foundation of all is reality, and reality is not multiple or divisible. Moses founded it, Jesus raised its tent, and its brilliant light has shone forth in all the religions. Bahá'u'lláh proclaimed this one reality and spread the message of the Most Great Peace. Even in prison He rested not until He lighted this lamp in the East. Praise be to God! All who have accepted His teachings are lovers of peace, peacemakers ready to sacrifice their lives and expend their possessions for it. Now let this standard be upraised in the West, and many will respond to the call. America has become renowned for her discoveries, inventions and artistic skill, famous for equity of government and stupendous undertakings; now may she also become noted and celebrated as the herald and messenger of universal peace. Let this be her mission and undertaking, and may its blessed impetus spread to all countries. I pray for all of you that you may render this service to the world of humanity.

4

13 May 1912

Talk at Reception by New York Peace Society
Hotel Astor, New York

NOTES BY ESTHER FOSTER

1   ALTHOUGH I felt indisposed this afternoon, yet because I attach great importance to this assembly and was longing to see your faces, I have come. The expression of kindly feelings and the spirit of hospitality manifested by the former speakers are most grateful. I am thankful for the susceptibilities of your hearts, for it is an evidence that your greatest desire is the establishment of international peace. You are lovers of the oneness of humanity, seekers after the good pleasure of the Lord, investigators of the foundations of the divine religions.

2   Today there is no greater glory for man than that of service in the cause of the Most Great Peace. Peace is light, whereas war is darkness. Peace is life; war is death. Peace is guidance; war is error. Peace is the foundation of God; war is a satanic institution. Peace is the illumination of the world of humanity; war is the destroyer of human foundations. When we consider outcomes in the world of existence, we find that peace and fellowship are factors of upbuilding and betterment, whereas war and strife are the causes of destruction and disintegration. All created things are expressions of the affinity and cohesion of elementary substances, and nonexistence is the absence of their attraction and agreement. Various elements unite harmoniously in composition, but when these elements become discordant, repelling each other, decomposition and nonexistence result. Everything partakes of this nature and is subject to this principle, for the

creative foundation in all its degrees and kingdoms is an expression or outcome of love. Consider the restlessness and agitation of the human world today because of war. Peace is health and construction; war is disease and dissolution. When the banner of truth is raised, peace becomes the cause of the welfare and advancement of the human world. In all cycles and ages war has been a factor of derangement and discomfort, whereas peace and brotherhood have brought security and consideration of human interests. This distinction is especially pronounced in the present world conditions, for warfare in former centuries had not attained the degree of savagery and destructiveness which now characterizes it. If two nations were at war in olden times, ten or twenty thousand would be sacrificed, but in this century the destruction of one hundred thousand lives in a day is quite possible. So perfected has the science of killing become and so efficient the means and instruments of its accomplishment that a whole nation can be obliterated in a short time. Therefore, comparison with the methods and results of ancient warfare is out of the question.

According to an intrinsic law all phenomena of being attain to a summit and degree of consummation, after which a new order and condition is established. As the instruments and science of war have reached the degree of thoroughness and proficiency, it is hoped that the transformation of the human world is at hand and that in the coming centuries all the energies and inventions of man will be utilized in promoting the interests of peace and brotherhood. Therefore, may this esteemed and worthy society for the establishment of international peace be confirmed in its sincere intentions and empowered by God. Then will it hasten the time when the banner of universal agreement will be raised and international welfare will be proclaimed and consummated so that the darkness which now encompasses the world shall pass away.

4   Sixty years ago Bahá'u'lláh was in Persia. Seventy years ago the Báb appeared there. These two Blessed Souls devoted Their lives to the foundation of international peace and love among mankind. They strove with heart and soul to establish the teachings by which divergent people might be brought together and no strife, rancor or hatred prevail. Bahá'u'lláh, addressing all humanity, said that Adam, the parent of mankind, may be likened to the tree of nativity upon which you are the leaves and blossoms. Inasmuch as your origin was one, you must now be united and agreed; you must consort with each other in joy and fragrance. He pronounced prejudice—whether religious, racial, patriotic, political—the destroyer of the body politic. He said that man must recognize the oneness of humanity, for all in origin belong to the same household, and all are servants of the same God. Therefore, mankind must continue in the state of fellowship and love, emulating the institutions of God and turning away from satanic promptings, for the divine bestowals bring forth unity and agreement, whereas satanic leadings induce hatred and war.

5   This remarkable Personage was able by these principles to establish a bond of unity among the differing sects and divergent people of Persia. Those who followed His teachings, no matter from what denomination or faction they came, were conjoined by the ties of love, until now they cooperate and live together in peace and agreement. They are real brothers and sisters. No distinctions of class are observed among them, and complete harmony prevails. Daily this bond of affinity is strengthening, and their spiritual fellowship continually develops. In order to ensure the progress of mankind and to establish these principles Bahá'u'lláh suffered every ordeal and difficulty. The Báb became a martyr, and over twenty thousand men and women sacrificed their lives for their faith. Bahá'u'lláh was imprisoned and sub-

jected to severe persecutions. Finally, He was exiled from Persia to Mesopotamia; from Baghdád He was sent to Constantinople and Adrianople and from thence to the prison of 'Akká in Syria. Through all these ordeals He strove day and night to proclaim the oneness of humanity and promulgate the message of universal peace. From the prison of 'Akká He addressed the kings and rulers of the earth in lengthy letters, summoning them to international agreement and explicitly stating that the standard of the Most Great Peace would surely be upraised in the world.

This has come to pass. The powers of earth cannot withstand 6 the privileges and bestowals which God has ordained for this great and glorious century. It is a need and exigency of the time. Man can withstand anything except that which is divinely intended and indicated for the age and its requirements. Now—praise be to God!—in all countries of the world, lovers of peace are to be found, and these principles are being spread among mankind, especially in this country. Praise be to God! This thought is prevailing, and souls are continually arising as defenders of the oneness of humanity, endeavoring to assist and establish international peace. There is no doubt that this wonderful democracy will be able to realize it, and the banner of international agreement will be unfurled here to spread onward and outward among all the nations of the world. I give thanks to God that I find you imbued with such susceptibilities and lofty aspirations, and I hope that you will be the means of spreading this light to all men. Thus may the Sun of Reality shine upon the East and West. The enveloping clouds shall pass away, and the heat of the divine rays will dispel the mist. The reality of man shall develop and come forth as the image of God, his Creator. The thoughts of man shall take such upward flight that former accomplishments shall appear as the play of children, for the ideas and beliefs of the past and the prejudices regarding race and religion have ever lowered and been destructive to human evolution. I am most hopeful that in this century these lofty thoughts shall be conducive to human welfare. Let this century be the sun of previous centuries, the effulgences of which shall last forever, so that in times to come they shall glorify the twentieth century, saying the twentieth century was the century of lights, the twentieth century was the century of life, the twentieth century was the century of international peace, the twentieth century was the century of divine bestowals, and the twentieth century has left traces which shall last forever.

5

19 May 1912

Talk at Church of the Divine Paternity
Central Park West, New York

NOTES BY ESTHER FOSTER

1 RELIGIONS are many, but the reality of religion is one. The days are many, but the sun is one. The fountains are many, but the fountainhead is one. The branches are many, but the tree is one.

2 The foundation of the divine religions is reality; were there no reality, there would be no religions. Abraham heralded reality. Moses promulgated reality. Christ established reality. Muḥammad was the Messenger of reality. The Báb was the door of reality. Bahá'u'lláh was the splendor of reality. Reality is one; it does not admit multiplicity or division. Reality is as the sun, which shines forth from different dawning points; it is as the light, which has illumined many lanterns.

Therefore, if the religions investigate reality and seek the   3
essential truth of their own foundations, they will agree and
no difference will be found. But inasmuch as religions are submerged in dogmatic imitations, forsaking the original foundations, and as imitations differ widely, therefore, the religions are
divergent and antagonistic. These imitations may be likened
to clouds which obscure the sunrise; but reality is the sun. If
the clouds disperse, the Sun of Reality shines upon all, and
no difference of vision will exist. The religions will then agree,
for fundamentally they are the same. The subject is one, but
predicates are many.

The divine religions are like the progression of the seasons   4
of the year. When the earth becomes dead and desolate and
because of frost and cold no trace of vanished spring remains,
the springtime dawns again and clothes everything with a new
garment of life. The meadows become fresh and green, the trees
are adorned with verdure and fruits appear upon them. Then
the winter comes again, and all the traces of spring disappear.
This is the continuous cycle of the seasons—spring, winter, then
the return of spring. But though the calendar changes and the
years move forward, each springtime that comes is the return
of the springtime that has gone; this spring is the renewal of
the former spring. Springtime is springtime, no matter when
or how often it comes. The divine Prophets are as the coming
of spring, each renewing and quickening the teachings of the
Prophet Who came before Him. Just as all seasons of spring are
essentially one as to newness of life, vernal showers and beauty,
so the essence of the mission and accomplishment of all the
Prophets is one and the same. Now the people of religion have
lost sight of the essential reality of the spiritual springtime. They
have held tenaciously to ancestral forms and imitations, and
because of this there is variance, strife and altercation among

them. Therefore, we must now abandon these imitations and seek the foundation of the divine teachings; and inasmuch as the foundation is one reality, the divergent religionists must agree in it so that love and unity will be established among all people and denominations.

5   At a time when the Orient was rent by religious dissension Bahá'u'lláh appeared. He founded teachings which became the means of uniting the various and divergent peoples. He promulgated principles which removed the cause of their dissension, until today in Persia those who had been constantly at war are united. Christians, Muslims, Zoroastrians, Jews—people of every belief and denomination who have followed the teachings of Bahá'u'lláh—have attained complete fellowship and spiritual agreement. Former differences and dissensions have passed away entirely. Some of the principles of Bahá'u'lláh's teaching are as follows:

6   First, that the oneness of humanity shall be recognized and established. All men are the servants of God. He has created all; He is the Provider and Preserver; He is loving to all. Inasmuch as He is just and kind, why should we be unjust toward each other? As God has quickened us with life, why should we be the cause of death? As He has comforted us, why should we be the cause of anxiety and suffering? Can humanity conceive a plan and policy better and superior to that of God? It is certain that no matter how capable man may be in origination of plan and organization of purpose, his efforts will be inadequate when compared with the divine plan and purpose; for the policy of God is perfect. Therefore, we must follow the will and plan of God. As He is kind to all, we must be likewise; and it is certain that this will be most acceptable to God.

7   Second, that truth or reality must be investigated; for reality is one, and by investigating it all will find love and unity.

Those who are ignorant must be educated, the ailing must be healed, the undeveloped must be brought to maturity. Shall we reject or oppose the ignorant, sick or immature because of their incapacity? Is it not better to be kind and gentle and to provide the means of remedy? Therefore, under no circumstances whatsoever should we assume any attitude except that of gentleness and humility.

Third, that religion is in harmony with science. The fundamental principles of the Prophets are scientific, but the forms and imitations which have appeared are opposed to science. If religion does not agree with science, it is superstition and ignorance; for God has endowed man with reason in order that he may perceive reality. The foundations of religion are reasonable. God has created us with intelligence to perceive them. If they are opposed to science and reason, how could they be believed and followed? 8

Fourth, that religion must be conducive to love and unity among mankind; for if it be the cause of enmity and strife, the absence of religion is preferable. When Moses appeared, the tribes of Israel were in a state of disunion as captives of the Pharaohs. Moses gathered them together, and the divine law established fellowship among them. They became as one people, united, consolidated, after which they were rescued from bondage. They passed into the promised land, advanced in all degrees, developed sciences and arts, progressed in material affairs, increased in divine or spiritual civilization until their nation rose to its zenith in the sovereignty of Solomon. It is evident, therefore, that religion is the cause of unity, fellowship and progress among mankind. The function of a shepherd is to gather the sheep together and not to scatter them. Then Christ appeared. He united varying and divergent creeds and warring people of His time. He brought together Greeks and Romans, 9 reconciled Egyptians and Assyrians, Chaldeans and Phoenicians. Christ established unity and agreement among people of these hostile and warring nations. Therefore, it is again evident that the purpose of religion is peace and concord. Likewise, Muḥammad appeared at a time when the peoples and tribes of Arabia were divergent and in a state of continual warfare. They killed each other, pillaged and took captive wives and children. Muḥammad united these fierce tribes, established a foundation of fellowship among them so that they gave up warring against each other absolutely and established communities. The result was that the Arabian tribes freed themselves from the Persian yoke and Roman control, established an independent sovereignty which rose to a high degree of civilization, advanced in sciences and arts, extended the Saracen dominion as far west as Spain and Andalusia and became famous throughout the world. Therefore, it is proved once more that the religion of God is intended to be the cause of advancement and solidarity and not of enmity and dissolution. If it becomes the cause of hatred and strife, its absence is preferable. Its purpose is unity, and its foundations are one.

10   When Bahá'u'lláh appeared in Persia, violent strife and hatred separated the peoples and tribes of that country. They would not come together for any purpose except war; they would not partake of the same food, or drink of the same water; association and intercourse were impossible. Bahá'u'lláh founded the oneness of humanity among these people and bound their hearts together with such ties of love that they were completely united. He reestablished the prophetic foundations, reformed and renewed the principles laid down by the Messengers of God who had preceded Him. And now it is hoped that through His life and teachings the East and West shall become so united that no trace of enmity, strife and discord shall remain.

6

19 May 1912

Talk at Brotherhood Church
Bergen and Fairview Avenues, Jersey City, New Jersey

NOTES BY ESTHER FOSTER

BECAUSE this is called the Church of Brotherhood, I wish to   1
speak upon the brotherhood of mankind. There is perfect
brotherhood underlying humanity, for all are servants of one
God and belong to one family under the protection of divine
providence. The bond of fraternity exists in humanity because
all are intelligent beings created in the realm of evolutionary
growth. There is brotherhood potential in humanity because
all inhabit this earthly globe under the one canopy of heaven.
There is brotherhood natal in mankind because all are elements
of one human society subject to the necessity of agreement and
cooperation. There is brotherhood intended in humanity because all are waves of one sea, leaves and fruit of one tree. This
is physical fellowship which ensures material happiness in the
human world. The stronger it becomes, the more will mankind
advance and the circle of materiality be enlarged.

The real brotherhood is spiritual, for physical brotherhood is   2
subject to separation. The wars of the outer world of existence
separate humankind, but in the eternal world of spiritual brotherhood separation is unknown. Material or physical association
is based upon earthly interests, but divine fellowship owes its
existence to the breaths of the Holy Spirit. Spiritual brotherhood may be likened to the light, while the souls of humankind
are as lanterns. The incandescent lamps here are many, yet the
light is one.

3   At a time in the Orient when even physical brotherhood was not in existence Bahá'u'lláh appeared. At first He set forth the principles of physical brotherhood and afterward founded the spiritual brotherhood. He breathed such a spirit into the countries of the Orient that various peoples and warring tribes were blended in unity. Their bestowals and susceptibilities became one, their purposes one purpose, their desires one desire to such a degree that they sacrificed themselves for each other, forfeiting name, possessions and comfort. Their fellowship became indissoluble. This is eternal, spiritual fellowship, heavenly and divine brotherhood, which defies dissolution. Material civilization advances through the physical association of mankind. The progress you observe in the outer world is founded mainly upon the fraternity of material interests. Were it not for this physical and mental association, civilization would not have progressed. Now—praise be to God!—the indissoluble spiritual association is evident; therefore, it is certain that divine civilization has been founded, and the world will progress and advance spiritually. In this radiant century divine knowledge, merciful attributes and spiritual virtues will attain the highest degree of advancement. The traces have become manifest in Persia. Souls have advanced to such a degree as to forfeit life and possessions for each other. Their spiritual perceptions have developed; their intelligence has quickened; their souls are awakened. The utmost love has been manifested. Therefore, it is my hope that spiritual fraternity shall unite the East and the West and bring about the complete abolition of warfare among mankind. May it bind together individuals and members of the human family and be the cause of advancing minds, illuminating hearts and allowing divine bestowals to encompass us from all directions. May spiritual susceptibilities set hearts aglow with the message of glad tidings. May spiritual brotherhood cause rebirth and regeneration, for its creative quickening emanates from the

breaths of the Holy Spirit and is founded by the power of God. Surely that which is founded through the divine power of the Holy Spirit is permanent in its potency and lasting in its effect.

Material brotherhood does not prevent nor remove warfare; 4 it does not dispel differences among mankind. But spiritual alliance destroys the very foundation of war, effaces differences entirely, promulgates the oneness of humanity, revivifies mankind, causes hearts to turn to the Kingdom of God and baptizes souls with the Holy Spirit. Through this divine brotherhood the material world will become resplendent with the lights of Divinity, the mirror of materiality will acquire its lights from heaven, and justice will be established in the world so that no trace of darkness, hatred and enmity shall be visible. Humanity shall come within the bounds of security, the Prophethood of all the Messengers of God shall be established, Zion shall leap and dance, Jerusalem shall rejoice, the Mosaic flame shall ignite, the Messianic light shall shine, the world will become another world, and humanity shall put on another power. This is the greatest divine bestowal; this is the effulgence of the Kingdom of God; this is the day of illumination; this is the merciful century. We must appreciate these things and strive in order that the utmost desire of the Prophets may now be realized and all the glad tidings be fulfilled. Trust in the favor of God. Look not at your own capacities, for the divine bestowal can transform a drop into an ocean; it can make a tiny seed a lofty tree. Verily, divine bestowals are like the sea, and we are the fishes of that sea. The fishes must not look at themselves; they must behold the ocean, which is vast and wonderful. Provision for the sustenance of all is in this ocean; therefore, the divine bounties encompass all, and love eternal shines upon all.

The question has been asked: Will the spiritual progress of 5 the world equal and keep pace with material progress in the future? In a living organism the full measure of its development is not known or realized at the time of its inception or birth. Development and progression imply gradual stages or degrees. For example, spiritual advancement may be likened to the light of the early dawn. Although this dawn light is dim and pale, a wise man who views the march of the sunrise at its very beginning can foretell the ascendancy of the sun in its full glory and effulgence. He knows for a certainty that it is the beginning of its manifestation and that later it will assume great power and potency. Again, for example, if he takes a seed and observes that it is sprouting, he will know assuredly that it will ultimately become a tree. Now is the beginning of the manifestation of the spiritual power, and inevitably the potency of its life forces will assume greater and greater proportions. Therefore, this twentieth century is the dawn, or beginning, of spiritual illumination, and it is evident that day by day it will advance. It will reach such a degree that spiritual effulgences will overcome the physical, so that divine susceptibilities will overpower material intelligence and the heavenly light dispel and banish earthly darkness. Divine healing shall purify all ills, and the cloud of mercy will pour down its rain. The Sun of Reality will shine, and all the earth shall put on its beautiful green carpet. Among the results of the manifestation of spiritual forces will be that the human world will adapt itself to a new social form, the justice of God will become manifest throughout human affairs, and human equality will be universally established. The poor will receive a great bestowal, and the rich attain eternal happiness. For although at the present time the rich enjoy the greatest luxury and comfort, they are nevertheless deprived of eternal happiness; for eternal happiness is contingent upon giving, and the poor are everywhere in the state of abject need. Through the manifestation of God's great equity the poor of the world will be rewarded and assisted fully, and there will be a readjustment in the economic conditions of mankind so that in the future there will not be the abnormally rich nor the abject poor. The rich will enjoy the privilege of this new economic condition as well as the poor, for owing to certain provisions and restrictions they will not be able to accumulate so much as to be burdened by its management, while the poor will be relieved from the stress of want and misery. The rich will enjoy his palace, and the poor will have his comfortable cottage.

The essence of the matter is that divine justice will become manifest in human conditions and affairs, and all mankind will find comfort and enjoyment in life. It is not meant that all will be equal, for inequality in degree and capacity is a property of nature. Necessarily there will be rich people and also those who will be in want of their livelihood, but in the aggregate community there will be equalization and readjustment of values and interests. In the future there will be no very rich nor extremely poor. There will be an equilibrium of interests, and a condition will be established which will make both rich and poor comfortable and content. This will be an eternal and blessed outcome of the glorious twentieth century which will be realized universally. The significance of it is that the glad tidings of great joy revealed in the promises of the Holy Books will be fulfilled. Await ye this consummation.

6

7

20 May 1912

Talk at Woman's Suffrage Meeting
Metropolitan Temple
Seventh Avenue and Fourteenth Street, New York

NOTES BY ESTHER FOSTER

1   TODAY questions of the utmost importance are facing humanity, questions peculiar to this radiant century. In former centuries there was not even mention of them. Inasmuch as this is the century of illumination, the century of humanity, the century of divine bestowals, these questions are being presented for the expression of public opinion, and in all the countries of the world, discussion is taking place looking to their solution.

2   One of these questions concerns the rights of woman and her equality with man. In past ages it was held that woman and man were not equal—that is to say, woman was considered inferior to man, even from the standpoint of her anatomy and creation. She was considered especially inferior in intelligence, and the idea prevailed universally that it was not allowable for her to step into the arena of important affairs. In some countries man went so far as to believe and teach that woman belonged to a sphere lower than human. But in this century, which is the century of light and the revelation of mysteries, God is proving to the satisfaction of humanity that all this is ignorance and error; nay, rather, it is well established that mankind and womankind as parts of composite humanity are coequal and that no difference in estimate is allowable, for all are human. The conditions in past centuries were due to woman's lack of opportunity. She was denied the right and privilege of educa-

tion and left in her undeveloped state. Naturally, she could not and did not advance. In reality, God has created all mankind, and in the estimation of God there is no distinction as to male and female. The one whose heart is pure is acceptable in His sight, be that one man or woman. God does not inquire, "Art thou woman or art thou man?" He judges human actions. If these are acceptable in the threshold of the Glorious One, man and woman will be equally recognized and rewarded.

Furthermore, the education of woman is more necessary 3 and important than that of man, for woman is the trainer of the child from its infancy. If she be defective and imperfect herself, the child will necessarily be deficient; therefore, imperfection of woman implies a condition of imperfection in all mankind, for it is the mother who rears, nurtures and guides the growth of the child. This is not the function of the father. If the educator be incompetent, the educated will be correspondingly lacking. This is evident and incontrovertible. Could the student be brilliant and accomplished if the teacher is illiterate and ignorant? The mothers are the first educators of mankind; if they be imperfect, alas for the condition and future of the race.

Again, it is well established in history that where woman 4 has not participated in human affairs the outcomes have never attained a state of completion and perfection. On the other hand, every influential undertaking of the human world wherein woman has been a participant has attained importance. This is historically true and beyond disproof even in religion. Jesus Christ had twelve disciples and among His followers a woman known as Mary Magdalene. Judas Iscariot had become a traitor and hypocrite, and after the crucifixion the remaining eleven disciples were wavering and undecided. It is certain from the evidence of the Gospels that the one who comforted them and reestablished their faith was Mary Magdalene.

5   The world of humanity consists of two parts: male and female. Each is the complement of the other. Therefore, if one is defective, the other will necessarily be incomplete, and perfection cannot be attained. There is a right hand and a left hand in the human body, functionally equal in service and administration. If either proves defective, the defect will naturally extend to the other by involving the completeness of the whole; for accomplishment is not normal unless both are perfect. If we say one hand is deficient, we prove the inability and incapacity of the other; for single-handed there is no full accomplishment. Just as physical accomplishment is complete with two hands, so man and woman, the two parts of the social body, must be perfect. It is not natural that either should remain undeveloped; and until both are perfected, the happiness of the human world will not be realized.

6   The most momentous question of this day is international peace and arbitration, and universal peace is impossible without universal suffrage. Children are educated by the women. The mother bears the troubles and anxieties of rearing the child, undergoes the ordeal of its birth and training. Therefore, it is most difficult for mothers to send to the battlefield those upon whom they have lavished such love and care. Consider a son reared and trained twenty years by a devoted mother. What sleepless nights and restless, anxious days she has spent! Having brought him through dangers and difficulties to the age of maturity, how agonizing then to sacrifice him upon the battlefield! Therefore, the mothers will not sanction war nor be satisfied with it. So it will come to pass that when women participate fully and equally in the affairs of the world, when they enter confidently and capably the great arena of laws and politics, war will cease; for woman will be the obstacle and hindrance to it. This is true and without doubt.

It has been objected by some that woman is not equally   7
capable with man and that she is deficient by creation. This is
pure imagination. The difference in capability between man and
woman is due entirely to opportunity and education. Heretofore woman has been denied the right and privilege of equal
development. If equal opportunity be granted her, there is no
doubt she would be the peer of man. History will evidence this.
In past ages noted women have arisen in the affairs of nations
and surpassed men in their accomplishments. Among them was
Zenobia, Queen of the East, whose capital was Palmyra. Even
today the site of that city bears witness to her greatness, ability
and sovereignty; for there the traveler will find ruins of palaces
and fortifications of the utmost strength and solidity built by
this remarkable woman in the third century after Christ. She was
the wife of the governor-general of Athens. After her husband's
death she assumed control of the government in his stead and
ruled her province most efficiently. Afterward she conquered
Syria, subdued Egypt and founded a most wonderful kingdom
with political sagacity and thoroughness. The Roman Empire
sent a great army against her. When this army replete with
martial splendor reached Syria, Zenobia herself appeared upon
the field leading her forces. On the day of battle she arrayed
herself in regal garments, placed a crown upon her head and
rode forth, sword in hand, to meet the invading legions. By her
courage and military strategy the Roman army was routed and
so completely dispersed that they were not able to reorganize
in retreat. The government of Rome held consultation, saying,
"No matter what commander we send, we cannot overcome
her; therefore, the Emperor Aurelian himself must go to lead
the legions of Rome against Zenobia." Aurelian marched into
Syria with two hundred thousand soldiers. The army of Zenobia
was greatly inferior in size. The Romans besieged her in Palmyra

two years without success. Finally, Aurelian was able to cut off the city's supply of provisions so that she and her people were compelled by starvation to surrender. She was not defeated in battle. Aurelian carried her captive to Rome. On the day of his entry into the city he arranged a triumphal procession—first elephants, then lions, tigers, birds, monkeys—and after the monkeys, Zenobia. A crown was upon her head, a chain of gold about her neck. With queenly dignity and unconscious of humiliation, looking to the right and left, she said, "Verily, I glory in being a woman and in having withstood the Roman Empire." (At that time the dominion of Rome covered half the known earth.) "And this chain about my neck is a sign not of humiliation but of glorification. This is a symbol of my power, not of my defeat."

8   Among other historical women was Catherine I, wife of Peter the Great. Russia and Turkey were at war. Muḥammad Páshá, commander of the Turkish forces, had defeated Peter and was about to take St. Petersburg. The Russians were in a most critical position. Catherine, the wife of Peter, said, "I will arrange this matter." She had an interview with Muḥammad Páshá, negotiated a treaty of peace and induced him to turn back. She saved her husband and her nation. This was a great accomplishment. Afterward she was crowned Empress of Russia and ruled with wisdom until her death.

9   The discovery of America by Columbus was during the reign of Isabella of Spain, to whose intelligence and assistance this wonderful accomplishment was largely due. In brief, many remarkable women have appeared in the history of the world, but further mention of them is not necessary.

10   Today among the Bahá'ís of Persia there are many women who are the very pride and envy of the men. They are imbued with all the virtues and excellences of humanity. They are eloquent; they

are poets and scholars and embody the quintessence of humility. In political ability and acumen they have been able to cope and compete with representative men. They have consecrated their lives and forfeited their possessions in martyrdom for the sake of humanity, and the traces of their glory will last forever. The pages of the history of Persia are illumined by the lives and records of these women.

The purpose, in brief, is this: that if woman be fully educated 11 and granted her rights, she will attain the capacity for wonderful accomplishments and prove herself the equal of man. She is the coadjutor of man, his complement and helpmeet. Both are human; both are endowed with potentialities of intelligence and embody the virtues of humanity. In all human powers and functions they are partners and coequals. At present in spheres of human activity woman does not manifest her natal prerogatives, owing to lack of education and opportunity. Without doubt education will establish her equality with men. Consider the animal kingdom, where no distinction is observed between male and female. They are equal in powers and privileges. Among birds of the air no distinction is evidenced. Their powers are equal; they dwell together in complete unity and mutual recognition of rights. Shall we not enjoy the same equality? Its absence is not befitting to mankind.

Talks 'Abdu'l-Bahá Delivered in Cambridge and Boston

22 May 1912

Talk at the Tremont Temple at the Unitarian Conference
Boston, Massachusetts

FROM STENOGRAPHIC NOTES

CREATION is the expression of motion. Motion is life. A moving 1
object is a living object, whereas that which is motionless and
inert is as dead. All created forms are progressive in their planes,
or kingdoms of existence, under the stimulus of the power
or spirit of life. The universal energy is dynamic. Nothing is
stationary in the material world of outer phenomena or in the
inner world of intellect and consciousness.

Religion is the outer expression of the divine reality. There- 2
fore, it must be living, vitalized, moving and progressive. If it
be without motion and nonprogressive, it is without the divine
life; it is dead. The divine institutes are continuously active
and evolutionary; therefore, the revelation of them must be
progressive and continuous. All things are subject to reformation. This is a century of life and renewal. Sciences and arts,
industry and invention have been reformed. Law and ethics have
been reconstituted, reorganized. The world of thought has been
regenerated. Sciences of former ages and philosophies of the
past are useless today. Present exigencies demand new methods
of solution; world problems are without precedent. Old ideas
and modes of thought are fast becoming obsolete. Ancient laws
and archaic ethical systems will not meet the requirements of

modern conditions, for this is clearly the century of a new life, the century of the revelation of reality and, therefore, the greatest of all centuries. Consider how the scientific developments of fifty years have surpassed and eclipsed the knowledge and achievements of all the former ages combined. Would the announcements and theories of ancient astronomers explain our present knowledge of the suns and planetary systems? Would the mask of obscurity which beclouded medieval centuries meet the demand for clear-eyed vision and understanding which characterizes the world today? Will the despotism of former governments answer the call for freedom which has risen from the heart of humanity in this cycle of illumination? It is evident that no vital results are now forthcoming from the customs, institutions and standpoints of the past. In view of this, shall blind imitations of ancestral forms and theological interpretations continue to guide and control the religious life and spiritual development of humanity today? Shall man, gifted with the power of reason, unthinkingly follow and adhere to dogma, creeds and hereditary beliefs which will not bear the analysis of reason in this century of effulgent reality? Unquestionably this will not satisfy men of science, for when they find premise or conclusion contrary to present standards of proof and without real foundation, they reject that which has been formerly accepted as standard and correct and move forward from new foundations.

3   The divine Prophets have revealed and founded religion. They have laid down certain laws and heavenly principles for the guidance of mankind. They have taught and promulgated the knowledge of God, established praiseworthy ethical ideals and inculcated the highest standards of virtues in the human world. Gradually these heavenly teachings and foundations of reality have been beclouded by human interpretations and dogmatic imitations of ancestral beliefs. The essential realities, which the Prophets labored so hard to establish in human hearts and minds

while undergoing ordeals and suffering tortures of persecution, have now well nigh vanished. Some of these heavenly Messengers have been killed, some imprisoned, all of Them despised and rejected while proclaiming the reality of Divinity. Soon after Their departure from this world, the essential truth of Their teachings was lost sight of and dogmatic imitations adhered to.

Inasmuch as human interpretations and blind imitations 4 differ widely, religious strife and disagreement have arisen among mankind, the light of true religion has been extinguished and the unity of the world of humanity destroyed. The Prophets of God voiced the spirit of unity and agreement. They have been the Founders of divine reality. Therefore, if the nations of the world forsake imitations and investigate the reality underlying the revealed Word of God, they will agree and become reconciled. For reality is one and not multiple.

The nations and religions are steeped in blind and bigoted 5 imitations. A man is a Jew because his father was a Jew. The Muslim follows implicitly the footsteps of his ancestors in belief and observance. The Buddhist is true to his heredity as a Buddhist. That is to say, they profess religious belief blindly and without investigation, making unity and agreement impossible. It is evident, therefore, that this condition will not be remedied without a reformation in the world of religion. In other words, the fundamental reality of the divine religions must be renewed, reformed, revoiced to mankind.

From the seed of reality religion has grown into a tree which 6 has put forth leaves and branches, blossoms and fruit. After a time this tree has fallen into a condition of decay. The leaves and blossoms have withered and perished; the tree has become stricken and fruitless. It is not reasonable that man should hold to the old tree, claiming that its life forces are undiminished, its fruit unequaled, its existence eternal. The seed of reality must be sown again in human hearts in order that a new tree may grow therefrom and new divine fruits refresh the world. By this means the nations and peoples now divergent in religion will be brought into unity, imitations will be forsaken, and a universal brotherhood in reality itself will be established. Warfare and strife will cease among mankind; all will be reconciled as servants of God. For all are sheltered beneath the tree of His providence and mercy. God is kind to all; He is the giver of bounty to all alike, even as Jesus Christ has declared that God "sendeth rain on the just and on the unjust"—that is to say, the mercy of God is universal. All humanity is under the protection of His love and favor, and unto all He has pointed the way of guidance and progress. Progress is of two kinds: material and spiritual. The former is attained through observation of the surrounding existence and constitutes the foundation of civilization. Spiritual progress is through the breaths of the Holy Spirit and is the awakening of the conscious soul of man to perceive the reality of Divinity. Material progress ensures the happiness of the human world. Spiritual progress ensures the happiness and eternal continuance of the soul. The Prophets of God have founded the laws of divine civilization. They have been the root and fundamental source of all knowledge. They have established the principles of human brotherhood, of fraternity, which is of various kinds—such as the fraternity of family, of race, of nation and of ethical motives. These forms of fraternity, these bonds of brotherhood, are merely temporal and transient in association. They do not ensure harmony and are usually productive of disagreement. They do not prevent warfare and strife; on the contrary, they are selfish, restricted and fruitful causes of enmity and hatred among mankind. The spiritual brotherhood which is enkindled and established through the breaths of the Holy Spirit unites nations and removes the cause of warfare and strife. It transforms mankind into one great family and establishes the foundations of the oneness of humanity. It promulgates the spirit of international agreement and ensures universal peace. Therefore, we must investigate the foundation of this heavenly fraternity. We must forsake all imitations and promote the reality of the divine teachings. In accordance with these principles and actions and by the assistance of the Holy Spirit, both material and spiritual happiness shall become realized. Until all nations and peoples become united by the bonds of the Holy Spirit in this real fraternity, until national and international prejudices are effaced in the reality of this spiritual brotherhood, true progress, prosperity and lasting happiness will not be attained by man. This is the century of new and universal nationhood. Sciences have advanced; industries have progressed; politics have been reformed; liberty has been proclaimed; justice is awakening. This is the century of motion, divine stimulus and accomplishment, the century of human solidarity and altruistic service, the century of universal peace and the reality of the divine Kingdom.

2

23 May 1912

Talk at Home of Mr. and Mrs. Francis W. Breed
367 Harvard Street, Cambridge, Massachusetts

FROM STENOGRAPHIC NOTES

SCIENTIFIC knowledge is the highest attainment upon the human 1
plane, for science is the discoverer of realities. It is of two kinds: material and spiritual. Material science is the investigation of natural phenomena; divine science is the discovery and realiza-

tion of spiritual verities. The world of humanity must acquire both. A bird has two wings; it cannot fly with one. Material and spiritual science are the two wings of human uplift and attainment. Both are necessary—one the natural, the other supernatural; one material, the other divine. By the divine we mean the discovery of the mysteries of God, the comprehension of spiritual realities, the wisdom of God, inner significances of the heavenly religions and foundation of the law.

2   This is 23 May, the anniversary of the message and Declaration of the Báb. It is a blessed day and the dawn of manifestation, for the appearance of the Báb was the early light of the true morn, whereas the manifestation of the Blessed Beauty, Bahá'u'lláh, was the shining forth of the sun. Therefore, it is a blessed day, the inception of the heavenly bounty, the beginning of the divine effulgence. On this day in 1844 the Báb was sent forth heralding and proclaiming the Kingdom of God, announcing the glad tidings of the coming of Bahá'u'lláh and withstanding the opposition of the whole Persian nation. Some of the Persians followed Him. For this they suffered the most grievous difficulties and severe ordeals. They withstood the tests with wonderful power and sublime heroism. Thousands were cast into prison, punished, persecuted and martyred. Their homes were pillaged and destroyed, their possessions confiscated. They sacrificed their lives most willingly and remained unshaken in their faith to the very end. Those wonderful souls are the lamps of God, the stars of sanctity shining gloriously from the eternal horizon of the will of God.

3   The Báb was subjected to bitter persecution in Shíráz, where He first proclaimed His mission and message. A period of famine afflicted that region, and the Báb journeyed to Iṣfahán. There the learned men rose against Him in great hostility. He was arrested and sent to Tabríz. From thence He was transferred to

Mákú and finally imprisoned in the strong castle of <u>Ch</u>ihríq. Afterward He was martyred in Tabríz.

This is merely an outline of the history of the Báb. He with-   4 stood all persecutions and bore every suffering and ordeal with unflinching strength. The more His enemies endeavored to extinguish that flame, the brighter it became. Day by day His Cause spread and strengthened. During the time when He was among the people He was constantly heralding the coming of Bahá'u'lláh. In all His Books and Tablets He mentioned Bahá'-u'lláh and announced the glad tidings of His manifestation, prophesying that He would reveal Himself in the ninth year. He said that in the ninth year "you will attain to all happiness"; in the ninth year "you will be blessed with the meeting of the Promised One of Whom I have spoken." He mentioned the Blessed Perfection, Bahá'u'lláh, by the title "Him Whom God shall make manifest." In brief, that blessed Soul offered His very life in the pathway of Bahá'u'lláh, even as it is recorded in historical writings and records. In His first Book, the Best of Stories, He says, "O Remnant of God! I am wholly sacrificed to Thee; I am content with curses in Thy path; I crave nought but to be slain in Thy love; and God, the Supreme, sufficeth as an eternal protection."

Consider how the Báb endured difficulties and tribulations;   5 how He gave His life in the Cause of God; how He was attracted to the love of the Blessed Beauty, Bahá'u'lláh; and how He announced the glad tidings of His manifestation. We must follow His heavenly example; we must be self-sacrificing and aglow with the fire of the love of God. We must partake of the bounty and grace of the Lord, for the Báb has admonished us to arise in service to the Cause of God, to be absolutely severed from all else save God during the day of the Blessed Perfection, Bahá'u'lláh, to be completely attracted by the love of Bahá'u'lláh, to love all humanity for His sake, to be lenient and merciful to all for Him and to upbuild the oneness of the world of humanity. Therefore, this day, 23 May, is the anniversary of a blessed event.

3

25 May 1912

Huntington Chambers
Boston, Massachusetts

From Stenographic Notes

1   I AM going away from your city, but I leave my heart with you. My spirit will be here; I will not forget you. I ask confirmation for you from the Kingdom of Bahá'u'lláh. I pray that you may advance continually in spiritual susceptibilities, that day by day you may grow more radiant and draw nearer to God until you become instrumental in illumining the world of humanity. May these confirmations of the Kingdom of God encompass you. This is my hope, my prayer.

2   In the estimation of historians this radiant century is equivalent to one hundred centuries of the past. If comparison be made with the sum total of all former human achievements, it will be found that the discoveries, scientific advancement and material civilization of this present century have equaled, yea far exceeded the progress and outcome of one hundred former centuries. The production of books and compilations of literature alone bears witness that the output of the human mind in this century has been greater and more enlightening than all the past centuries together. It is evident, therefore, that this century is of paramount importance. Reflect upon the miracles of accom-

plishment which have already characterized it: the discoveries in every realm of human research. Inventions, scientific knowledge, ethical reforms and regulations established for the welfare of humanity, mysteries of nature explored, invisible forces brought into visibility and subjection—a veritable wonder-world of new phenomena and conditions heretofore unknown to man now open to his uses and further investigation. The East and West can communicate instantly. A human being can soar in the skies or speed in submarine depths. The power of steam has linked the continents. Trains cross the deserts and pierce the barriers of mountains; ships find unerring pathways upon the trackless oceans. Day by day discoveries are increasing. What a wonderful century this is! It is an age of universal reformation. Laws and statutes of civil and federal governments are in process of change and transformation. Sciences and arts are being molded anew. Thoughts are metamorphosed. The foundations of human society are changing and strengthening. Today sciences of the past are useless. The Ptolemaic system of astronomy and numberless other systems and theories of scientific and philosophical explanation are discarded, known to be false and worthless. Ethical precedents and principles cannot be applied to the needs of the modern world. Thoughts and theories of past ages are fruitless now. Thrones and governments are crumbling and falling. All conditions and requisites of the past unfitted and inadequate for the present time are undergoing radical reform. It is evident, therefore, that counterfeit and spurious religious teaching, antiquated forms of belief and ancestral imitations which are at variance with the foundations of divine reality must also pass away and be reformed. They must be abandoned and new conditions be recognized. The morals of humanity must undergo change. New remedies and solutions for human problems must be adopted. Human intellects themselves must change and be subject to the universal reformation. Just as the thoughts and hypotheses of past ages are fruitless today, likewise dogmas and codes of human invention are obsolete and barren of product in religion. Nay, it is true that they are the cause of enmity and conducive to strife in the world of humanity; war and bloodshed proceed from them, and the oneness of mankind finds no recognition in their observance. Therefore, it is our duty in this radiant century to investigate the essentials of divine religion, seek the realities underlying the oneness of the world of humanity and discover the source of fellowship and agreement which will unite mankind in the heavenly bond of love. This unity is the radiance of eternity, the divine spirituality, the effulgence of God and the bounty of the Kingdom. We must investigate the divine source of these heavenly bestowals and adhere unto them steadfastly. For if we remain fettered and restricted by human inventions and dogmas, day by day the world of mankind will be degraded, day by day warfare and strife will increase and satanic forces converge toward the destruction of the human race.

3   If love and agreement are manifest in a single family, that family will advance, become illumined and spiritual; but if enmity and hatred exist within it, destruction and dispersion are inevitable. This is, likewise, true of a city. If those who dwell within it manifest a spirit of accord and fellowship, it will progress steadily and human conditions become brighter, whereas through enmity and strife it will be degraded and its inhabitants scattered. In the same way, the people of a nation develop and advance toward civilization and enlightenment through love and accord and are disintegrated by war and strife. Finally, this is true of humanity itself in the aggregate. When love is realized and the ideal spiritual bonds unite the hearts of men, the whole human race will be uplifted, the world will continually grow more spiritual and radiant and the happiness and tranquillity of mankind be immeasurably increased. Warfare and strife will be uprooted, disagreement

and dissension pass away and universal peace unite the nations and peoples of the world. All mankind will dwell together as one family, blend as the waves of one sea, shine as stars of one firmament and appear as fruits of the same tree. This is the happiness and felicity of humankind. This is the illumination of man, the eternal glory and everlasting life; this is the divine bestowal. I desire this station for you, and I pray God that the people of America may achieve this great end in order that the virtue of this democracy may be ensured and their names be glorified eternally. May the confirmations of God uphold them in all things and their memories become revered throughout the East and the West. May they become the servants of the Most High God, near and dear to Him in the oneness of the heavenly Kingdom.

Bahá'u'lláh endured ordeals and hardships sixty years. There 4 was no persecution, vicissitude or suffering He did not experience at the hand of His enemies and oppressors. All the days of His life were passed in difficulty and tribulation—at one time in prison, another in exile, sometimes in chains. He willingly endured these difficulties for the unity of mankind, praying that the world of humanity might realize the radiance of God, the oneness of humankind become a reality, strife and warfare cease and peace and tranquillity be realized by all. In prison He hoisted the banner of human solidarity, proclaiming universal peace, writing to the kings and rulers of nations, summoning them to international unity and counseling arbitration. His life was a vortex of persecution and difficulty; yet catastrophes, extreme ordeals and vicissitudes did not hinder the accomplishment of His work and mission. Nay, on the contrary, His power became greater and greater, His efficiency and influence spread and increased until His glorious light shone throughout the Orient, love and unity were established, and the differing religions found a center of contact and reconciliation.

5 Therefore, we also must strive in this pathway of love and service, sacrificing life and possessions, passing our days in devotion, consecrating our efforts wholly to the Cause of God so that, God willing, the ensign of universal religion may be uplifted in the world of mankind and the oneness of the world of humanity be established.

6 In your hearts I have beheld the reflection of a great and wonderful love. The Americans have shown me uniform kindness, and I entertain a deep spiritual love for them. I am pleased with the susceptibilities of your hearts. I will pray for you, asking divine assistance, and then say farewell.

7 O my God! O my God! Verily, these servants are turning to Thee, supplicating Thy kingdom of mercy. Verily, they are attracted by Thy holiness and set aglow with the fire of Thy love, seeking confirmation from Thy wondrous kingdom, and hoping for attainment in Thy heavenly realm. Verily, they long for the descent of Thy bestowal, desiring illumination from the Sun of Reality. O Lord! Make them radiant lamps, merciful signs, fruitful trees and shining stars. May they come forth in Thy service and be connected with Thee by the bonds and ties of Thy love, longing for the lights of Thy favor. O Lord! Make them signs of guidance, standards of Thine immortal kingdom, waves of the sea of Thy mercy, mirrors of the light of Thy majesty.

8 Verily, Thou art the Generous. Verily, Thou art the Merciful. Verily, Thou art the Precious, the Beloved.

Talks 'Abdu'l-Bahá Delivered in New York and Fanwood

26 May 1912

Talk at Mount Morris Baptist Church
Fifth Avenue and 126th Street, New York

NOTES BY ESTHER FOSTER

As I entered the church this evening, I heard the hymn "Nearer   1
my God, to Thee." The greatest attainment in the world of humanity is nearness to God. Every lasting glory, honor, grace and
beauty which comes to man comes through nearness to God. All
the Prophets and apostles longed and prayed for nearness to the
Creator. How many nights they passed in sleepless yearning for
this station; how many days they devoted to supplication for this
attainment, seeking ever to draw nigh unto Him! But nearness
to God is not an easy accomplishment. During the time Jesus
Christ was upon the earth mankind sought nearness to God,
but in that day no one attained it save a very few—His disciples.
Those blessed souls were confirmed with divine nearness through
the love of God. Divine nearness is dependent upon attainment
to the knowledge of God, upon severance from all else save God.
It is contingent upon self-sacrifice and to be found only through
forfeiting wealth and worldly possessions. It is made possible
through the baptism of water and fire revealed in the Gospels.
Water symbolizes the water of life, which is knowledge, and fire
is the fire of the love of God; therefore, man must be baptized
with the water of life, the Holy Spirit and the fire of the love
of the Kingdom. Until he attains these three degrees, nearness

to God is not possible. This is the process by which the Bahá'ís of Persia have attained it. They gave their lives for this station, sacrificed honor, comfort and possessions, hastened with the utmost joy to the place of martyrdom; their blood was spilled, their bodies were tortured and destroyed, their homes pillaged, their children carried into captivity. They endured all these conditions joyfully and willingly. Through such sacrifice nearness to God is made possible. And be it known that this nearness is not dependent upon time or place. Nearness to God is dependent upon purity of the heart and exhilaration of the spirit through the glad tidings of the Kingdom. Consider how a pure, well-polished mirror fully reflects the effulgence of the sun, no matter how distant the sun may be. As soon as the mirror is cleaned and purified, the sun will manifest itself. The more pure and sanctified the heart of man becomes, the nearer it draws to God, and the light of the Sun of Reality is revealed within it. This light sets hearts aglow with the fire of the love of God, opens in them the doors of knowledge and unseals the divine mysteries so that spiritual discoveries are made possible. All the Prophets have drawn near to God through severance. We must emulate those Holy Souls and renounce our own wishes and desires. We must purify ourselves from the mire and soil of earthly contact until our hearts become as mirrors in clearness and the light of the most great guidance reveals itself in them.

2   Bahá'u'lláh proclaims in the Hidden Words that God inspires His servants and is revealed through them. He says, "Thy heart is My home; sanctify it for My descent. Thy spirit is My place of revelation; cleanse it for My manifestation." Therefore, we learn that nearness to God is possible through devotion to Him, through entrance into the Kingdom and service to humanity; it is attained by unity with mankind and through loving-kindness to all; it is dependent upon investigation of truth, acquisition

of praiseworthy virtues, service in the cause of universal peace and personal sanctification. In a word, nearness to God necessitates sacrifice of self, severance and the giving up of all to Him. Nearness is likeness.

Behold how the sun shines upon all creation, but only surfaces 3 that are pure and polished can reflect its glory and light. The darkened soul has no portion of the revelation of the glorious effulgence of reality; and the soil of self, unable to take advantage of that light, does not produce growth. The eyes of the blind cannot behold the rays of the sun; only pure eyes with sound and perfect sight can receive them. Green and living trees can absorb the bounty of the sun; dead roots and withered branches are destroyed by it. Therefore, man must seek capacity and develop readiness. As long as he lacks susceptibility to divine influences, he is incapable of reflecting the light and assimilating its benefits. Sterile soil will produce nothing, even if the cloud of mercy pours rain upon it a thousand years. We must make the soil of our hearts receptive and fertile by tilling in order that the rain of divine mercy may refresh them and bring forth roses and hyacinths of heavenly planting. We must have perceiving eyes in order to see the light of the sun. We must cleanse the nostril in order to scent the fragrances of the divine rose garden. We must render the ears attentive in order to hear the summons of the supreme Kingdom. No matter how beautiful the melody, the ear that is deaf cannot hear it, cannot receive the call of the Supreme Concourse. The nostril that is clogged with dust cannot inhale the fragrant odors of the blossoms. Therefore, we must ever strive for capacity and seek readiness. As long as we lack susceptibility, the beauties and bounties of God cannot penetrate. Christ spoke a parable in which He said His words were like the seeds of the sower; some fall upon stony ground, some upon sterile soil, some are choked by thorns and thistles, but some fall upon the ready, receptive and fertile ground of human hearts. When seeds are cast upon sterile soil, no growth follows. Those cast upon stony ground will grow a short time, but lacking deep roots will wither away. Thorns and thistles destroy others completely, but the seed cast in good ground brings forth harvest and fruitage.

4   In the same way, the words I speak to you here tonight may produce no effect whatever. Some hearts may be affected, then soon forget; others owing to superstitious ideas and imaginations may even fail to hear and understand; but the blessed souls who are attentive to my exhortation and admonition, listening with the ear of acceptance, allowing my words to penetrate effectively, will advance day by day toward full fruition, yea even to the Supreme Concourse. Consider how the parable makes attainment dependent upon capacity. Unless capacity is developed, the summons of the Kingdom cannot reach the ear, the light of the Sun of Truth will not be observed, and the fragrances of the rose garden of inner significance will be lost. Let us endeavor to attain capacity, susceptibility and worthiness that we may hear the call of the glad tidings of the Kingdom, become revivified by the breaths of the Holy Spirit, hoist the standard of the oneness of humanity, establish human brotherhood, and under the protection of divine grace attain the everlasting and eternal life.

5   O Thou forgiving God! These servants are turning to Thy kingdom and seeking Thy grace and bounty. O God! Make their hearts good and pure in order that they may become worthy of Thy love. Purify and sanctify the spirits that the light of the Sun of Reality may shine upon them. Purify and sanctify the eyes that they may perceive Thy light. Purify and sanctify the ears in order that they may hear the call of Thy kingdom.

6   O Lord! Verily, we are weak, but Thou art mighty. Verily, we are poor, but Thou art rich. We are the seekers, and Thou art

the One sought. O Lord! Have compassion upon us and forgive us; bestow upon us such capacity and receptiveness that we may be worthy of Thy favors and become attracted to Thy kingdom, that we may drink deep of the water of life, may be enkindled by the fire of Thy love, and be resuscitated through the breaths of the Holy Spirit in this radiant century.

O God, my God! Cast upon this gathering the glances of 7 Thy loving-kindness. Keep safe each and all in Thy custody and under Thy protection. Send down upon these souls Thy heavenly blessings. Immerse them in the ocean of Thy mercy and quicken them through the breaths of the Holy Spirit.

O Lord! Bestow Thy gracious aid and confirmation upon 8 this just government. This country lieth beneath the sheltering shadow of Thy protection and this people is in Thy service. O Lord! Confer upon them Thy heavenly bounty and render the outpourings of Thy grace and favor copious and abundant. Suffer this esteemed nation to be held in honor and enable it to be admitted into Thy kingdom.

Thou art the Powerful, the Omnipotent, the Merciful, and 9 Thou art the Generous, the Beneficent, the Lord of grace abounding.

2

28 May 1912

Talk at Reception at Metropolitan Temple
Seventh Avenue and Fourteenth Street, New York

NOTES BY ESTHER FOSTER

1 THE Fatherhood of God, His loving-kindness and beneficence are apparent to all. In His mercy He provides fully and amply for His creatures, and if any soul sins, He does not suspend His bounty. All created things are visible manifestations of His Fatherhood, mercy and heavenly bestowals. Human brotherhood is, likewise, as clear and evident as the sun, for all are servants of one God, belong to one humankind, inhabit the same globe, are sheltered beneath the overshadowing dome of heaven and submerged in the sea of divine mercy. Human brotherhood and dependence exist because mutual helpfulness and cooperation are the two necessary principles underlying human welfare. This is the physical relationship of mankind. There is another brotherhood—the spiritual—which is higher, holier and superior to all others. It is heavenly; it emanates from the breaths of the Holy Spirit and the effulgence of merciful attributes; it is founded upon spiritual susceptibilities. This brotherhood is established by the Manifestations of the Holy One.

2 The divine Manifestations since the day of Adam have striven to unite humanity so that all may be accounted as one soul. The function and purpose of a shepherd is to gather and not disperse his flock. The Prophets of God have been divine Shepherds of humanity. They have established a bond of love and unity among mankind, made scattered peoples one nation and wandering

tribes a mighty kingdom. They have laid the foundation of the oneness of God and summoned all to universal peace. All these holy, divine Manifestations are one. They have served one God, promulgated the same truth, founded the same institutions and reflected the same light. Their appearances have been successive and correlated; each One has announced and extolled the One Who was to follow, and all laid the foundation of reality. They summoned and invited the people to love and made the human world a mirror of the Word of God. Therefore, the divine religions They established have one foundation; Their teachings, proofs and evidences are one; in name and form They differ, but in reality They agree and are the same. These holy Manifestations have been as the coming of springtime in the world. Although the spring-time of this year is designated by another name according to the changing calendar, yet as regards its life and quickening it is the same as the springtime of last year. For each spring is the time of a new creation, the effects, bestowals, perfections and life-giving forces of which are the same as those of the former vernal seasons, although the names are many and various. This is 1912, last year was 1911 and so on, but in fundamental reality no difference is apparent. The sun is one, but the dawning points of the sun are numerous and changing. The ocean is one body of water, but different parts of it have particular designations—Atlantic, Pacific, Mediterranean, Antarctic, etc. If we consider the names, there is differentiation; but the water, the ocean itself, is one reality.

Likewise, the divine religions of the holy Manifestations of God are in reality one, though in name and nomenclature they differ. Man must be a lover of the light, no matter from what dayspring it may appear. He must be a lover of the rose, no matter in what soil it may be growing. He must be a seeker of the truth, no matter from what source it come. Attachment to the lantern is not loving the light. Attachment to the earth is not befitting, but enjoyment of the rose which develops from the soil is worthy. Devotion to the tree is profitless, but partaking of the fruit is beneficial. Luscious fruits, no matter upon what tree they grow or where they may be found, must be enjoyed. The word of truth, no matter which tongue utters it, must be sanctioned. Absolute verities, no matter in what book they be recorded, must be accepted. If we harbor prejudice, it will be the cause of deprivation and ignorance. The strife between religions, nations and races arises from misunderstanding. If we investigate the religions to discover the principles underlying their foundations, we will find they agree; for the fundamental reality of them is one and not multiple. By this means the religionists of the world will reach their point of unity and reconciliation. They will ascertain the truth that the purpose of religion is the acquisition of praiseworthy virtues, the betterment of morals, the spiritual development of mankind, the real life and divine bestowals. All the Prophets have been the promoters of these principles; none of Them has been the promoter of corruption, vice or evil. They have summoned mankind to all good. They have united people in the love of God, invited them to the religions of the unity of mankind and exhorted them to amity and agreement. For example, we mention Abraham and Moses. By this mention we do not mean the limitation implied in the mere names but intend the virtues which these names embody. When we say Abraham, we mean thereby a manifestation of divine guidance, a center of human virtues, a source of heavenly bestowals to mankind, a dawning point of divine inspiration and perfections. These perfections and graces are not limited to names and boundaries. When we find these virtues, qualities and attributes in any personality, we recognize the same reality shining from within and bow in acknowledgment of the Abrahamic perfections. Similarly, we acknowledge and adore the beauty of Moses. Some souls were lovers of the name Abraham, loving the lantern instead of the light, and when they saw this same light shining from another lantern, they were so attached to the former lantern that they did not recognize its later appearance and illumination. Therefore, those who were attached and held tenaciously to the name Abraham were deprived when the Abrahamic virtues reappeared in Moses. Similarly, the Jews were believers in Moses, awaiting the coming of the Messiah. The virtues and perfections of Moses became apparent in Jesus Christ most effulgently, but the Jews held to the name Moses, not adoring the virtues and perfections manifest in Him. Had they been adoring these virtues and seeking these perfections, they would assuredly have believed in Jesus Christ when the same virtues and perfections shone in Him. If we are lovers of the light, we adore it in whatever lamp it may become manifest, but if we love the lamp itself and the light is transferred to another lamp, we will neither accept nor sanction it. Therefore, we must follow and adore the virtues revealed in the Messengers of God—whether in Abraham, Moses, Jesus or other Prophets—but we must not adhere to and adore the lamp. We must recognize the sun, no matter from what dawning point it may shine forth, be it Mosaic, Abrahamic or any personal point of orientation whatever, for we are lovers of sunlight and not of orientation. We are lovers of illumination and not of lamps and candles. We are seekers for water, no matter from what rock it may gush forth. We are in need of fruit in whatsoever orchard it may be ripened. We long for rain; it matters not which cloud pours it down. We must not be fettered. If we renounce these fetters, we shall agree, for all are seekers of reality. The counterfeit or imitation of true religion has adulterated human belief, and the foundations have been lost sight of. The variance of these imitations has produced enmity and strife, war and bloodshed. Now the glorious and brilliant twentieth century has dawned, and the divine bounty is radiating universally. The Sun of Truth is shining forth in intense enkindlement. This is, verily, the century when these imitations must be forsaken, superstitions abandoned and God alone worshiped. We must look at the reality of the Prophets and Their teachings in order that we may agree.

4   Praise be to God! The springtime of God is at hand. This century is, verily, the spring season. The world of mind and kingdom of soul have become fresh and verdant by its bestowals. It has resuscitated the whole realm of existence. On one hand, the lights of reality are shining; on the other, the clouds of divine mercy are pouring down the fullness of heavenly bounty. Wonderful material progress is evident, and great spiritual discoveries are being made. Truly, this can be called the miracle of centuries, for it is replete with manifestations of the miraculous. The time has come when all mankind shall be united, when all races shall be loyal to one fatherland, all religions become one religion, and racial and religious bias pass away. It is a day in which the oneness of humankind shall uplift its standard and international peace, like the true morning, flood the world with its light. Therefore, we offer supplications to God, asking Him to dispel these gloomy clouds and uproot these imitations in order that the East and West may become radiant with love and unity, that the nations of the world shall embrace each other and the ideal spiritual brotherhood illumine the world like the glorious sun of the high heavens. This is our hope, our wish and desire. We pray that through the bounty and grace of God we may attain thereto. I am very happy to be present at this meeting which has innate radiance, intelligence, perception and longing to investigate reality. Such meetings are the glory of the world of mankind. I ask the blessing of God in your behalf.

3

29 May 1912

Talk at Home of Mr. and Mrs. Edward B. Kinney
780 West End Avenue, New York

Notes by Howard MacNutt

THE divine Manifestations have been iconoclastic in Their 1
teachings, uprooting error, destroying false religious beliefs
and summoning mankind anew to the fundamental oneness
of God. All of Them have, likewise, proclaimed the oneness
of the world of humanity. The essential teaching of Moses was
the law of Sinai, the Ten Commandments. Christ renewed and
again revealed the commands of the one God and precepts of
human action. In Muḥammad, although the circle was wider,
the intention of His teaching was likewise to uplift and unify
humanity in the knowledge of the one God. In the Báb the
circle was again very much enlarged, but the essential teaching
was the same. The Books of Bahá'u'lláh number more than one
hundred. Each one is an evident proof sufficient for mankind;
each one from foundation to apex proclaims the essential unity
of God and humanity, the love of God, the abolition of war and
the divine standard of peace. Each one also inculcates divine
morality, the manifestation of lordly graces—in every word a
book of meanings. For the Word of God is collective wisdom,
absolute knowledge and eternal truth.

Consider the statement recorded in the first chapter of the 2
book of John: "In the beginning was the Word, and the Word was
with God, and the Word was God." This statement is brief but
replete with the greatest meanings. Its applications are illimitable
and beyond the power of books or words to contain and express.

Heretofore the doctors of theology have not expounded it but have restricted it to Jesus as "the Word made flesh," the separation of Jesus from God, the Father, and His descent upon the earth. In this way the individualized separation of the godhead came to be taught.

3   The essential oneness of Father, Son and Spirit has many meanings and constitutes the foundation of Christianity. Today we will merely give a synopsis of explanation. Why was Jesus the Word?

4   In the universe of creation all phenomenal beings are as letters. Letters in themselves are meaningless and express nothing of thought or ideal—as, for instance, a, b, etc. Likewise, all phenomenal beings are without independent meaning. But a word is composed of letters and has independent sense and meaning. Therefore, as Christ conveyed the perfect meaning of divine reality and embodied independent significance, He was the Word. He was as the station of reality compared to the station of metaphor. There is no intrinsic meaning in the leaves of a book, but the thought they convey leads you to reflect upon reality. The reality of Jesus was the perfect meaning, the Christhood in Him which in the Holy Books is symbolized as the Word.

5   "The Word was with God." The Christhood means not the body of Jesus but the perfection of divine virtues manifest in Him. Therefore, it is written, "He is God." This does not imply separation from God, even as it is not possible to separate the rays of the sun from the sun. The reality of Christ was the embodiment of divine virtues and attributes of God. For in Divinity there is no duality. All adjectives, nouns and pronouns in that court of sanctity are one; there is neither multiplicity nor division. The intention of this explanation is to show that the Words of God have innumerable significances and mysteries of meanings—each one a thousand and more.

The Tablets of Bahá'u'lláh are many. The precepts and teach- 6
ings they contain are universal, covering every subject. He has
revealed scientific explanations ranging throughout all the realms
of human inquiry and investigation—astronomy, biology,
medical science, etc. In the Kitáb-i-Íqán He has given expositions of the meanings of the Gospel and other heavenly Books.
He wrote lengthy Tablets upon civilization, sociology and government. Every subject is considered. His Tablets are matchless
in beauty and profundity. Even His enemies acknowledge the
greatness of Bahá'u'lláh, saying He was the miracle of humanity. This was their confession although they did not believe in
Him. He was eulogized by Christians, Jews, Zoroastrians and
Muslims who denied His claim. They frequently said, "He is
matchless, unique." A Christian poet in the Orient wrote, "Do
not believe him a manifestation of God, yet his miracles are as
great as the sun." Mírzá Abu'l-Faḍl has mentioned many poems
of this kind, and there are numerous others. The testimony of
His enemies witnessed that He was the "miracle of mankind,"
that He "walked in a special pathway of knowledge" and was
"peerless in personality." His teachings are universal and the
standard for human action. They are not merely theoretical and
intended to remain in books. They are the principles of action.
Results follow action. Mere theory is fruitless. Of what use is a
book upon medicine if it is never taken from the library shelf?
When practical activity has been manifested, the teachings of
God have borne fruit.

The great and fundamental teachings of Bahá'u'lláh are 7
the oneness of God and unity of mankind. This is the bond
of union among Bahá'ís all over the world. They become
united among themselves, then unite others. It is impossible to unite unless united. Christ said, "Ye are the salt of
the earth; but if the salt has lost his savor, wherewith shall
it be salted?" This proves there were dissensions and lack of

unity among His followers. Hence His admonition to unity of action.

8   Now must we, likewise, bind ourselves together in the utmost unity, be kind and loving to each other, sacrificing all our possessions, our honor, yea, even our lives for each other. Then will it be proved that we have acted according to the teachings of God, that we have been real believers in the oneness of God and unity of mankind.

4

30 May 1912

Talk at Theosophical Lodge
Broadway and Seventy-ninth Street, New York

Notes by Howard MacNutt

1   I AM greatly pleased with these expressions of kindly feeling and evidences of spiritual susceptibility. Tonight I am very happy in the realization that our aims and purposes are the same, our desires and longings are one. This is a reflection and evidence of the oneness of the world of humanity and the intention toward accomplishment of the Most Great Peace. Therefore, we are united in will and purpose. In the world of existence there are no greater questions than these. Oneness of the world of humanity ensures the glorification of man. International peace is the assurance of the welfare of all humankind. There are no greater motives and purposes in the human soul. As we are agreed upon them, the certainty of unity and concord between Bahá'ís and Theosophists is most hopeful. Their purposes are one,

their desires one, and spiritual susceptibilities are common to both. Their attention is devoted to the divine Kingdom; they partake alike of its bounty.

Today the human world is in need of a great power by which 2 these glorious principles and purposes may be executed. The cause of peace is a very great cause; it is the Cause of God, and all the forces of the world are opposed to it. Governments, for instance, consider militarism as the step to human progress, that division among men and nations is the cause of patriotism and honor, that if one nation attack and conquer another, gaining wealth, territory and glory thereby, this warfare and conquest, this bloodshed and cruelty are the cause of that victorious nation's advancement and prosperity. This is an utter mistake. Compare the nations of the world to the members of a family. A family is a nation in miniature. Simply enlarge the circle of the household, and you have the nation. Enlarge the circle of nations, and you have all humanity. The conditions surrounding the family surround the nation. The happenings in the family are the happenings in the life of the nation. Would it add to the progress and advancement of a family if dissensions should arise among its members, all fighting, pillaging each other, jealous and revengeful of injury, seeking selfish advantage? Nay, this would be the cause of the effacement of progress and advancement. So it is in the great family of nations, for nations are but an aggregate of families. Therefore, as strife and dissension destroy a family and prevent its progress, so nations are destroyed and advancement hindered.

All the heavenly Books, divine Prophets, sages and philosophers 3 agree that warfare is destructive to human development, and peace constructive. They agree that war and strife strike at the foundations of humanity. Therefore, a power is needed to prevent war and to proclaim and establish the oneness of humanity.

4   But knowledge of the need of this power is not sufficient. Realizing that wealth is desirable is not becoming wealthy. The admission that scientific attainment is praiseworthy does not confer scientific knowledge. Acknowledgment of the excellence of honor does not make a man honorable. Knowledge of human conditions and the needed remedy for them is not the cause of their betterment. To admit that health is good does not constitute health. A skilled physician is needed to remedy existing human conditions. As a physician is required to have complete knowledge of pathology, diagnosis, therapeutics and treatment, so this World Physician must be wise, skillful and capable before health will result. His mere knowledge is not health; it must be applied and the remedy carried out.

5   The attainment of any object is conditioned upon knowledge, volition and action. Unless these three conditions are forthcoming, there is no execution or accomplishment. In the erection of a house it is first necessary to know the ground, and design the house suitable for it; second, to obtain the means or funds necessary for the construction; third, actually to build it. Therefore, a power is needed to carry out and execute what is known and admitted to be the remedy for human conditions—namely, the unification of mankind. Furthermore, it is evident that this cannot be realized through material process and means. The accomplishment of this unification cannot be through racial power, for races are different and diverse in tendencies. It cannot be through patriotic power, for nationalities are unlike. Nor can it be effected through political power since the policies of governments and nations are various. That is to say, any effort toward unification through these material means would benefit one and injure another because of unequal and individual interests. Some may believe this great remedy can be found in dogmatic insistence upon imitations and interpretations. This

would likewise be without foundation and result. Therefore, it is evident that no means but an ideal means, a spiritual power, divine bestowals and the breaths of the Holy Spirit will heal this world sickness of war, dissension and discord. Nothing else is possible; nothing can be conceived of. But through spiritual means and the divine power it is possible and practicable.

Consider history. What has brought unity to nations, moral-   6
ity to peoples and benefits to mankind? If we reflect upon it, we will find that establishing the divine religions has been the greatest means toward accomplishing the oneness of humanity. The foundation of divine reality in religion has done this, not imitations of ancestral religious forms. Imitations are opposed to each other and have ever been the cause of strife, enmity, jealousy and war. The divine religions are collective centers in which diverse standpoints may meet, agree and unify. They accomplish oneness of native lands, races and policies. For instance, Christ united various nations, brought peace to warring peoples and established the oneness of humankind. The conquering Greeks and Romans, the prejudiced Egyptians and Assyrians were all in a condition of strife, enmity and war, but Christ gathered these varied peoples together and removed the foundations of discord—not through racial, patriotic or political power, but through divine power, the power of the Holy Spirit. This was not otherwise possible. All other efforts of men and nations remain as mere mention in history, without accomplishment.

As this great result is contingent upon divine power and   7
bestowals, where shall the world obtain that power? God is eternal and ancient—not a new God. His sovereignty is of old, not recent—not merely existent these five or six thousand years. This infinite universe is from everlasting. The sovereignty, power, names and attributes of God are eternal, ancient. His names presuppose creation and predicate His existence and

will. We say God is Creator. This name Creator appears when we connote creation. We say God is the Provider. This name presupposes and proves the existence of the provided. God is Love. This name proves the existence of the beloved. In the same way God is Mercy, God is Justice, God is Life, etc. Therefore, as God is Creator, eternal and ancient, there were always creatures and subjects existing and provided for. There is no doubt that divine sovereignty is eternal. Sovereignty necessitates subjects, ministers, trustees and others subordinate to sovereignty. Could there be a king without country, subjects and armies? If we conceive of a time when there were no creatures, no servants, no subjects of divine lordship, we dethrone God and predicate a time when God was not. It would be as if He had been recently appointed and man had given these names to Him. The divine sovereignty is ancient, eternal. God from everlasting was Love, Justice, Power, Creator, Provider, the Omniscient, the Bountiful.

8   As the divine entity is eternal, the divine attributes are coexistent, coeternal. The divine bestowals are, therefore, without beginning, without end. God is infinite; the works of God are infinite; the bestowals of God are infinite. As His divinity is eternal, His lordship and perfections are without end. As the bounty of the Holy Spirit is eternal, we can never say that His bestowals terminate, else He terminates. If we think of the sun and then try to conceive of the cessation of the solar flame and heat, we have predicated the nonexistence of the sun. For separation of the sun from its rays and heat is inconceivable. Therefore, if we limit the bestowals of God, we limit the attributes of God and limit God.

9   Let us then trust in the bounty and bestowal of God. Let us be exhilarated with the divine breath, illumined and exalted by the heavenly glad tidings. God has ever dealt with man in mercy and kindness. He Who conferred the divine spirit in former times is abundantly able and capable at all times and periods

to grant the same bestowals. Therefore, let us be hopeful. The God Who gave to the world formerly will do so now and in the future. God Who breathed the breath of the Holy Spirit upon His servants will breathe it upon them now and hereafter. There is no cessation to His bounty. The Divine Spirit is penetrating from eternity to eternity, for it is the bounty of God, and the bounty of God is eternal. Can you conceive of limitation of the divine power in atomic verities or cessation of the divine bounty in existing organisms? Could you conceive the power now manifest in this glass in cohesion of its atoms becoming nonexistent? The energy by which the water of the sea is constituted failing to exert itself and the sea disappearing? A shower of rain today and no more showers afterward? The effulgence of the sun terminated and no more light or heat?

When we observe that in the kingdom of minerals the divine 10 bounties are continuous, how much more shall we expect and realize in the divine spiritual Kingdom! How much greater the radiation of the lights of God and the bounty of everlasting life upon the soul of man! As the body of the universe is continuous, indestructible, the bounties and bestowals of the divine spirit are everlasting.

I praise God that I am privileged to be present in this revered 11 assembly which is quickened with spiritual susceptibilities and heavenly attraction—its members investigating reality, their utmost hope the establishment of international peace and their greatest purpose service to the world of humanity.

When we observe the world of created phenomena, we 12 discover that each atom of the atoms of substance is moving through the various degrees and kingdoms of organic life. For instance, consider the ethereal element which is penetrating and traveling through all the contingent realities. When there is vibration or movement in the ethereal element, the eye is affected by that vibration and beholds what is known as light.

13 In the same manner the bestowals of God are moving and circulating throughout all created things. This illimitable divine bounty has no beginning and will have no ending. It is moving, circulating and becomes effective wherever capacity is developed to receive it. In every station there is a specialized capacity. Therefore, we must be hopeful that through the bounty and favor of God this spirit of life infusing all created beings shall quicken humanity, and from its bestowals the human world shall become a divine world, this earthly kingdom become the mirror of the realm of Divinity, the virtues and perfections of the world of humanity become unveiled and the image and likeness of God be reflected from this temple.

14 I am most grateful to the president of this society and express my most respectful greetings to him. It is my hope that all of you may be assisted in attaining the good pleasure of God. The spiritual susceptibility of those present has made me very happy, and I beg of God assistance and confirmation for all.

5

31 May 1912

Talk at Town Hall
Fanwood, New Jersey

FROM PERSIAN NOTES

1 THE material world is subject to change and transformation. The Cause of the Kingdom is eternal; therefore, it is the most important. But, alas, day by day the power of the Kingdom in human hearts is weakened, and material forces gain the ascendancy. The divine signs are becoming less and less, and human

evidences grow stronger. They have reached such a degree that materialists are advancing and aggressive while divine forces are waning and vanishing. Irreligion has conquered religion. The cause of the chaotic condition lies in the differences among the religions and finds its origin in the animosity and hatred existing between sects and denominations. The materialists have availed themselves of this dissension amongst the religions and are constantly attacking them, intending to uproot the tree of divine planting. Owing to strife and contention among themselves, the religions are being weakened and vanquished. If a commander is at variance with his army in the execution of military tactics, there is no doubt he will be defeated by the enemy. Today the religions are at variance; enmity, strife and recrimination prevail among them; they refuse to associate; nay, rather, if necessary they shed each other's blood. Read history and record to see what dreadful events have happened in the name of religion. For instance, the Hebrew prophets were sent to announce Christ, but unfortunately the Talmud and its superstitions veiled Him so completely that they crucified their promised Messiah. Had they renounced the talmudic traditions and investigated the reality of the religion of Moses, they would have become believers in Christ. Blind adherence to forms and imitations of ancestral beliefs deprived them of their messianic bounty. They were not refreshed by the downpouring rain of mercy, nor were they illumined by the rays of the Sun of Truth.

Imitation destroys the foundation of religion, extinguishes the spirituality of the human world, transforms heavenly illumination into darkness and deprives man of the knowledge of God. It is the cause of the victory of materialism and infidelity over religion; it is the denial of Divinity and the law of revelation; it refuses Prophethood and rejects the Kingdom of God. When materialists subject imitations to the intellectual analysis of reason, they find them to be mere superstitions; therefore, they deny religion.

2

For instance, the Jews have ideas as to the purity and impurity of religion, but when you subject these ideas to scientific scrutiny, they are found to be without foundation.

3   Is it impossible for us to receive the infinite bounties of God? Is it impossible to attain the virtues of the spiritual world because we are not living in the time of Moses, the period of the prophets or the era of Christ? Those were spiritual cycles. Can we not develop spiritually because we are far from them and are living in a materialistic age? The God of Moses and Jesus is able to bestow the same favors, nay, greater favors upon His people in this day. For example, in past ages He bestowed reason, intelligence and understanding upon His servants. Can we say He is not able to confer His bounties in this century? Would it be just if He sent Moses for the guidance of past nations and entirely neglected those living now? Could it be possible that this present period has been deprived of divine bounties while past ages of tyranny and barbarism received an inexhaustible portion of them? The same merciful God Who bestowed His favors in the past has opened the doors of His Kingdom to us. The rays of His sun are shining; the breath of the Holy Spirit is quickening. That omniscient God still assists and confirms us, illumines our hearts, gladdens our souls and perfumes our nostrils with the fragrances of holiness. Divine wisdom and providence have encircled all and spread the heavenly table before us. We must take a bountiful share of this generous favor.

4   The work of the shepherd is to bring together the scattered sheep. If he disperses the united flock, he is not the shepherd. As the Prophets fulfilled Their mission in this respect, They are the true Shepherds. When Moses appeared, the Israelitish people were disorganized. Enmity and discord increased their disunion. With divine power He assembled and united this scattered flock, placed within their hearts the pearl of love, freed them from captivity and led them out of Egypt into the Holy Land. They

made wonderful progress in sciences and arts. Bonds of social and national strength cemented them. Their progress in human virtues was so rapid and wonderful that they rose to the zenith of the Solomonic sovereignty. Could it be said that Moses was not a real Shepherd and that He did not gather these scattered people together?

Christ was a real Shepherd. At the time of His manifestation, 5 the Greeks, Romans, Assyrians and Egyptians were like so many scattered flocks. Christ breathed upon them the spirit of unity and harmonized them.

Therefore, it is evident that the Prophets of God have come 6 to unite the children of men and not to disperse them, to establish the law of love and not enmity. Consequently, we must lay aside all prejudice—whether it be religious, racial, political or patriotic; we must become the cause of the unification of the human race. Strive for universal peace, seek the means of love, and destroy the basis of disagreement so that this material world may become divine, the world of matter become the realm of the Kingdom and humanity attain to the world of perfection.

6

2 June 1912

*Talk at Church of the Ascension
Fifth Avenue and Tenth Street, New York*

NOTES BY ESTHER FOSTER

IN the terminology of the Holy Books the church has been 1 called the house of the covenant for the reason that the church is a place where people of different thoughts and divergent tendencies—where all races and nations—may come together in a covenant of permanent fellowship. In the temple of the Lord, in the house of God, man must be submissive to God. He must enter into a covenant with his Lord in order that he shall obey the divine commands and become unified with his fellow-man. He must not consider divergence of races nor difference of nationalities; he must not view variation in denomination and creed, nor should he take into account the differing degrees of thoughts; nay, rather, he should look upon all as mankind and realize that all must become united and agreed. He must recognize all as one family, one race, one native land; he must see all as the servants of one God, dwelling beneath the shelter of His mercy. The purport of this is that the church is a collective center. Temples are symbols of the reality and divinity of God—the collective center of mankind. Consider how within a temple every race and people is seen and represented—all in the presence of the Lord, covenanting together in a covenant of love and fellowship, all offering the same melody, prayer and supplication to God. Therefore, it is evident that the church is a collective center for mankind. For this reason there have been churches and temples in all the divine religions; but the real Collective Centers are the Manifestations of God, of Whom the church or temple is a symbol and expression. That is to say, the Manifestation of God is the real divine temple and Collective Center of which the outer church is but a symbol.

2   Recall the statement of Jesus Christ in the Gospel. Addressing Peter, He said, "Thou art Peter, and upon this rock I will build my church." It is evident, therefore, that the church of God is the law of God and that the actual edifice is but one symbol thereof. For the law of God is a collective center which unites various peoples, native lands, tongues and opinions. All find shelter in its protection and become attracted by it. For example, Moses and the Mosaic law were the unifying center for the scat-

tered sheep of Israel. He united these wandering flocks, brought them under control of divine law, educated and unified them, caused them to agree and uplifted them to a superlative degree of development. At a time when they were debased, they became glorified; ignorant, they were made knowing; in the bonds of captivity, they were given freedom; in short, they were unified. Day by day they advanced until they attained the highest degree of progress witnessed in that age. We prove, therefore, that the Manifestation of God and the law of God accomplish unity.

It is self-evident that humanity is at variance. Human tastes differ; 3 thoughts, native lands, races and tongues are many. The need of a collective center by which these differences may be counterbalanced and the people of the world be unified is obvious. Consider how nothing but a spiritual power can bring about this unification, for material conditions and mental aspects are so widely different that agreement and unity are not possible through outer means. It is possible, however, for all to become unified through one spirit, just as all may receive light from one sun. Therefore, assisted by the collective and divine center which is the law of God and the reality of His Manifestation, we can overcome these conditions until they pass away entirely and the races advance.

Consider the time of Christ. Peoples, races and governments 4 were many; religions, sects and denominations were various; but when Christ appeared, the Messianic reality proved to be the collective center which unified them beneath the same tabernacle of agreement. Reflect upon this. Could Jesus Christ have united these divergent factors or brought about such results through political power? Was this unity and agreement possible through material forces? It is evident that it was not; nay, rather, these various peoples were brought together through a divine power, through the breaths of the Holy Spirit. They were blended and quickened by the infusion of a new life. The spirituality of Christ overcame their difficulties so that their disagreements passed away completely. In this way these divergent peoples were unified and became welded in a bond of love which alone can unite hearts. Therefore, it is shown that the divine Manifestations, the holy Mouthpieces of God, are the Collective Centers of God. These heavenly Messengers are the real Shepherds of humanity, for whenever They appear in the world They unite the scattered sheep. The Collective Center has always appeared in the Orient. Abraham, Moses, Jesus Christ, Muḥammad were Collective Centers of Their day and time, and all arose in the East. Today Bahá'u'lláh is the Collective Center of unity for all mankind, and the splendor of His light has likewise dawned from the East. He founded the oneness of humanity in Persia. He established harmony and agreement among the various peoples of religious beliefs, denominations, sects and cults by freeing them from the fetters of past imitations and superstitions, leading them to the very foundation of the divine religions. From this foundation shines forth the radiance of spirituality, which is unity, the love of God, the knowledge of God, praiseworthy morals and the virtues of the human world. Bahá'u'lláh renewed these principles, just as the coming of spring refreshes the earth and confers new life upon all phenomenal beings. For the freshness of the former springtimes had waned, the vivification had ceased, the life-giving breezes were no longer wafting their fragrances, winter and the season of darkness had come. Bahá'u'lláh came to renew the life of the world with this new and divine springtime, which has pitched its tent in the countries of the Orient in the utmost power and glory. It has refreshed the world of the Orient, and there is no doubt that if the world of the Occident should abandon dogmas of the past, turn away from empty imitations and superstitions, investigate the reality of the divine religions, holding fast to the example of Jesus Christ, acting in accordance with the teachings of God and becoming unified with the Orient, an eternal happiness and felicity would be attained.

In the western world material civilization has attained the 5
highest point of development, but divine civilization was
founded in the land of the East. The East must acquire material
civilization from the West, and the West must receive spiritual
civilization from the East. This will establish a mutual bond.
When these two come together, the world of humanity will present a glorious aspect, and extraordinary progress will be achieved.
This is clear and evident; no proof is needed. The degree of
material civilization in the Occident cannot be denied; nor can
anyone fail to confirm the spiritual civilization of the Orient,
for all the divine foundations of human uplift have appeared
in the East. This, likewise, is clear and evident. Therefore, you
must assist the East in order that it may attain material progress.
The East must, likewise, promulgate the principles of spiritual
civilization in the western world. By this commingling and union
the human race will attain the highest degree of prosperity and
development. Material civilization alone is not sufficient and
will not prove productive. The physical happiness of material
conditions was allotted to the animal. Consider how the animal
has attained the fullest degree of physical felicity. A bird perches
upon the loftiest branch and builds there its nest with consummate beauty and skill. All the grains and seeds of the meadows
are its wealth and food; all the fresh water of mountain springs
and rivers of the plain are for its enjoyment. Truly, this is the
acme of material happiness, to which even a human creature
cannot attain. This is the honor of the animal kingdom. But
the honor of the human kingdom is the attainment of spiritual
happiness in the human world, the acquisition of the knowledge
and love of God. The honor allotted to man is the acquisition of
the supreme virtues of the human world. This is his real happiness and felicity. But if material happiness and spiritual felicity
be conjoined, it will be "delight upon delight," as the Arabs say.
We pray that God will unite the East and the West in order that

these two civilizations may be exchanged and mutually enjoyed. I am sure it will come to pass, for this is the radiant century. This is an age for the outpouring of divine mercy upon the exigency of this new century—the unity of the East and the West. It will surely be accomplished.

6   *Question:* What is the status of woman in the Orient?

7   *Answer:* The status of woman in former times was exceedingly deplorable, for it was the belief of the Orient that it was best for woman to be ignorant. It was considered preferable that she should not know reading or writing in order that she might not be informed of events in the world. Woman was considered to be created for rearing children and attending to the duties of the household. If she pursued educational courses, it was deemed contrary to chastity; hence women were made prisoners of the household. The houses did not even have windows opening upon the outside world. Bahá'u'lláh destroyed these ideas and proclaimed the equality of man and woman. He made woman respected by commanding that all women be educated, that there be no difference in the education of the two sexes and that man and woman share the same rights. In the estimation of God there is no distinction of sex. One whose thought is pure, whose education is superior, whose scientific attainments are greater, whose deeds of philanthropy excel, be that one man or woman, white or colored, is entitled to full rights and recognition; there is no differentiation whatsoever. Therefore, the status of women in the East has undergone change. At present they attend schools and colleges, pursue the ordinary curriculum and day by day are becoming indispensable to men and equal to them. This is the present condition of womankind in Persia.

8   *Question:* What relation do you sustain to the founder of your belief? Are you his successor in the same manner as the Pope of Rome?

230

Answer: I am the servant of Bahá'u'lláh, the Founder; and in 9 this I glory. No honor do I consider greater than this, and it is my hope that I may be confirmed in servitude to Bahá'u'lláh. This is my station.

Question: Is it not a fact that universal peace cannot be ac- 10 complished until there is political democracy in all the countries of the world?

Answer: It is very evident that in the future there shall be no 11 centralization in the countries of the world, be they constitutional in government, republican or democratic in form. The United States may be held up as the example of future government—that is to say, each province will be independent in itself, but there will be federal union protecting the interests of the various independent states. It may not be a republican or a democratic form. To cast aside centralization which promotes despotism is the exigency of the time. This will be productive of international peace. Another fact of equal importance in bringing about international peace is woman's suffrage. That is to say, when perfect equality shall be established between men and women, peace may be realized for the simple reason that womankind in general will never favor warfare. Women will not be willing to allow those whom they have so tenderly cared for to go to the battlefield. When they shall have a vote, they will oppose any cause of warfare. Another factor which will bring about universal peace is the linking together of the Orient and the Occident.

Question: What is your belief about reincarnation? 12

Answer: The subject of reincarnation has two aspects. One 13 is that which the Hindustani people believe, and even that is subdivided into two: reincarnation and metempsychosis. According to one belief the soul goes and then returns in certain reincarnations; therefore, they say that a sick person is sick

231

because of actions in a previous incarnation and that this is retribution. The other school of Hinduism believes that man sometimes appears as an animal—a donkey, for instance—and that this is retribution for past acts. I am referring to the beliefs in that country, the beliefs of the schools. There is a reincarnation of the prophetic mission. Jesus Christ, speaking of John the Baptist, declared he was Elias. When John the Baptist was questioned, "Art thou Elias?" he said, "I am not." These two statements are apparently contradictory, but in reality they do not contradict. The light is one light. The light which illumined this lamp last night is illuminating it tonight. This does not mean that the identical rays of light have reappeared but the virtues of illumination. The light which revealed itself through the glass reveals itself again so that we can say the light of this evening is the light of last evening relighted. This is as regards its virtues and not as regards its former identity. This is our view of reincarnation. We believe in that which Jesus Christ and all the Prophets have believed. For example, the Báb states, "I am the return of all the Prophets." This is significant of the oneness of the prophetic virtues, the oneness of power, the oneness of bestowal, the oneness of radiation, the oneness of expression, the oneness of revelation.

14   *Question:* What is the attitude of your belief toward the family?

15   *Answer:* According to the teachings of Bahá'u'lláh the family, being a human unit, must be educated according to the rules of sanctity. All the virtues must be taught the family. The integrity of the family bond must be constantly considered, and the rights of the individual members must not be transgressed. The rights of the son, the father, the mother—none of them must be transgressed, none of them must be arbitrary. Just as the son has certain obligations to his father, the father, likewise, has certain obligations to his son. The mother, the sister and other

members of the household have their certain prerogatives. All these rights and prerogatives must be conserved, yet the unity of the family must be sustained. The injury of one shall be considered the injury of all; the comfort of each, the comfort of all; the honor of one, the honor of all.

Question: What is the relation of the Bahá'í teaching to the ancient Zoroastrian religion? 16

Answer: The religions of God have the same foundation, but 17 the dogmas appearing later have differed. Each of the divine religions has two aspects. The first is essential. It concerns morality and development of the virtues of the human world. This aspect is common to all. It is fundamental; it is one; there is no difference, no variation in it. As regards the inculcation of morality and the development of human virtues, there is no difference whatsoever between the teachings of Zoroaster, Jesus and Bahá'u'lláh. In this they agree; they are one. The second aspect of the divine religions is nonessential. It concerns human needs and undergoes change in every cycle according to the exigency of the time. For example, in the time of Moses divorce was conformable to the needs and conditions; Moses, therefore, established it. But in the time of Christ, divorces were numerous and the cause of corruption; as they were not suitable for the time, he made divorce unlawful and likewise changed other laws. These are needs and conditions which have to do with the conduct of society; therefore, they undergo change according to the exigency of the time. Moses dwelt in the desert. As there were no penitentiaries, no means of restitution in the desert and wilderness, the laws of God were an eye for an eye, a tooth for a tooth. Could this be carried out now? If a man destroys another man's eye, are you willing to destroy the eye of the offender? If a man's teeth are broken or his ear cut off, will you demand a corresponding mutilation of his assailant? This would not be conformable to conditions of humanity at the present time. If a man steals, shall his hand be cut off? This punishment was just and right in the law of Moses, but it was applicable to the desert, where there were no prisons and reformatory institutions of later and higher forms of government. Today you have government and organization, a police system, a judge and trial by jury. The punishment and penalty is now different. Therefore, the nonessentials which deal with details of community are changed according to the exigency of the time and conditions. But the essential foundation of the teachings of Moses, Zoroaster, Jesus and Bahá'u'lláh is identical, is one; there is no difference whatsoever.

18   *Question:* Is peace a greater word than love?

19   *Answer:* No! Love is greater than peace, for peace is founded upon love. Love is the objective point of peace, and peace is an outcome of love. Until love is attained, peace cannot be; but there is a so-called peace without love. The love which is from God is the fundamental. This love is the object of all human attainment, the radiance of heaven, the light of man.

20   *Question:* Will you state the tenets of your faith?

21   *Answer:* First, investigate reality. Man must leave imitation and seek reality. The contemporaneous religious beliefs differ because of their allegiance to dogma. It is necessary, therefore, to abandon imitations and seek their fundamental reality.

22   Second, the oneness of humanity. All human creatures are the servants of God. All are submerged in the sea of His mercy. The Creator of all is one God; the Provider, the Giver, the Protector of all is one God. He is kind to all; why should we be unkind? All live beneath the shadow of His love; why should we hate each other? There are certain people who are ignorant; they must be educated. Some are like children; they must be trained and educated until they reach maturity. Others are sickly,

intellectually ill, spiritually ill; they must be treated and healed. But all are the servants of God.

Third, religion must be conducive to love of all, the cause of fellowship, unity and light. If it be the cause of enmity, bloodshed and hatred, its nonbeing is better than its being, its nonexistence better than its existence. Religion and science conform and agree. If a question of religion violates reason and does not agree with science, it is imagination and not worthy of credence. 23

Fourth, equality between men and women. In all degrees they are equal. The readjustment of the economic laws for the livelihood of man must be effected in order that all humanity may live in the greatest happiness according to their respective degrees. 24

Fifth, spiritual brotherhood. All mankind must attain to spiritual fraternity—that is to say, fraternity in the Holy Spirit—for patriotic, racial and political fraternity are of no avail. Their results are meager; but divine fraternity, spiritual fraternity, is the cause of unity and amity among mankind. As heretofore material civilization has been extended, the divine civilization must now be promulgated. Until the two agree, real happiness among mankind will be unknown. By mere intellectual development and power of reason, man cannot attain to his fullest degree— that is to say, by means of intellect alone he cannot accomplish the progress effected by religion. For the philosophers of the past strove in vain to revivify the world of mankind through the intellectual faculty. The most of which they were capable was educating themselves and a limited number of disciples; they themselves have confessed failure. Therefore, the world of humanity must be confirmed by the breath of the Holy Spirit in order to receive universal education. Through the infusion of divine power all nations and peoples become quickened, and universal happiness is possible. 25

26   These are some of the principles of the Bahá'ís.

27   *Question:* Will women or men aid this new religion most? Which will be more capable?

28   *Answer:* In Persia the men have aided it more, but in the West perchance the women. In the West women evidently have precedence in religion, but in the East men surpass the women.

29   *Question:* What will be the food of the united people?

30   *Answer:* As humanity progresses, meat will be used less and less, for the teeth of man are not carnivorous. For example, the lion is endowed with carnivorous teeth, which are intended for meat, and if meat be not found, the lion starves. The lion cannot graze; its teeth are of different shape. The digestive system of the lion is such that it cannot receive nourishment save through meat. The eagle has a crooked beak, the lower part shorter than the upper. It cannot pick up grain; it cannot graze; therefore, it is compelled to partake of meat. The domestic animals have herbivorous teeth formed to cut grass, which is their fodder. The human teeth, the molars, are formed to grind grain. The front teeth, the incisors, are for fruits, etc. It is, therefore, quite apparent according to the implements for eating that man's food is intended to be grain and not meat. When mankind is more fully developed, the eating of meat will gradually cease.

7

8 June 1912

Talk at 309 West Seventy-eighth Street, New York

Notes by John G. Grundy

THE body politic today is greatly in need of a physician. It is   1
similar to a human body afflicted with severe ailments. A doctor diagnoses the case and prescribes treatment. He does not
prescribe, however, until he has made the diagnosis. The disease
which afflicts the body politic is lack of love and absence of altruism. In the hearts of men no real love is found, and the condition
is such that, unless their susceptibilities are quickened by some
power so that unity, love and accord may develop within them,
there can be no healing, no agreement among mankind. Love
and unity are the needs of the body politic today. Without these
there can be no progress or prosperity attained. Therefore, the
friends of God must adhere to the power which will create this
love and unity in the hearts of the sons of men. Science cannot
cure the illness of the body politic. Science cannot create amity
and fellowship in human hearts. Neither can patriotism nor
racial allegiance effect a remedy. It must be accomplished solely
through the divine bounties and spiritual bestowals which have
descended from God in this day for that purpose. This is an
exigency of the times, and the divine remedy has been provided.
The spiritual teachings of the religion of God can alone create
this love, unity and accord in human hearts.

Therefore, hold to these heavenly agencies which God has   2
provided so that through the love of God this soul-bond may be
established, this heart-attachment realized and the light of the

reality of unity be reflected from you throughout the universe. If we do not hold fast to these divine agencies and means, no result will be possible. Let us pray to God that He will exhilarate our spirits so we may behold the descent of His bounties, illumine our eyes to witness His great guidance and attune our ears to enjoy the celestial melodies of the heavenly Word. This is our greatest hope. This is our ultimate purpose.

Talks 'Abdu'l-Bahá Delivered in Philadelphia

9 June 1912

Talk at Unitarian Church
Fifteenth Street and Girard Avenue, Philadelphia, Pennsylvania

NOTES BY EDNA MCKINNEY

I HAVE come from distant countries of the Orient where the lights 1
of heaven have ever shone forth, from regions where the Manifestations of God have appeared and the radiance and power of
God have been revealed to mankind. The purpose and intention
of my visit is that, perchance, a bond of unity and agreement may
be established between the East and West, that divine love may
encompass all nations, divine radiance enlighten both continents
and the bounties of the Holy Spirit revivify the body of the world.
Therefore, I supplicate the threshold of God that the Orient
and Occident may become as one, that the various peoples and
religions be unified and souls be blended as the waves of one sea.
May they become as trees, flowers and roses which adorn and
beautify the same garden.

The realm of Divinity is an indivisible oneness, wholly sancti- 2
fied above human comprehension; for intellectual knowledge of
creation is finite, whereas comprehension of Divinity is infinite.
How can the finite comprehend the infinite? We are utter poverty, whereas the reality of Divinity is absolute wealth. How can
utter poverty understand absolute wealth? We are utter weakness,
whereas the reality of Divinity is absolute power. Utter weakness
can never attain nor apprehend absolute power. The phenomenal

beings, which are captives of limitations, are ever subject to transformation and change in condition. How can such phenomenal beings ever grasp the heavenly, eternal, unchanging reality? Assuredly this is an absolute impossibility, for when we study the creational world, we see that the difference of degree is a barrier to such knowing. An inferior degree can never comprehend a higher degree or kingdom. The mineral, no matter how far it may advance, can never attain knowledge of the vegetable. No matter how the plant or vegetable may progress, it cannot perceive the reality of the animal kingdom—in other words, it cannot grasp a world of life that is endowed with the power of the senses. The animal may develop a wonderful degree of intelligence, but it can never attain the powers of ideation and conscious reflection which belong to man. It is evident, therefore, that difference in degree is ever an obstacle to comprehension of the higher by the lower, the superior by the inferior. This flower, so beautiful, fresh, fragrant and delicately scented, although it may have attained perfection in its own kingdom, nevertheless cannot comprehend the human reality, cannot possess sight and hearing; therefore, it exists unaware of the world of man, although man and itself are both accidental or conditional beings. The difference is difference of degree. The limitation of an inferior degree is the barrier to comprehension.

3   This being so, how can the human reality, which is limited, comprehend the eternal, unmanifest Creator? How can man comprehend the omniscient, omnipresent Lord? Undoubtedly, he cannot, for whatever comes within the grasp of human mind is man's limited conception, whereas the divine Kingdom is unlimited, infinite. But although the reality of Divinity is sanctified beyond the comprehension of its creatures, it has bestowed its bounties upon all kingdoms of the phenomenal world, and evidences of spiritual manifestation are witnessed throughout the realms of contingent existence. The lights of

God illumine the world of man, even as the effulgences of the sun shine gloriously upon the material creation. The Sun of Reality is one; its bestowal is one; its heat is one; its rays are one; it shines upon all the phenomenal world, but the capacity for comprehending it differs according to the kingdoms, each kingdom receiving the light and bounty of the eternal Sun according to its capacity. The black stone receives the light of the material sun; the trees and animals likewise are recipients of it. All exist and are developed by that one bounty. The perfect soul of man—that is to say, the perfect individual—is like a mirror wherein the Sun of Reality is reflected. The perfections, the image and light of that Sun have been revealed in the mirror; its heat and illumination are manifest therein, for that pure soul is a perfect expression of the Sun.

These mirrors are the Messengers of God Who tell the story 4 of Divinity, just as the material mirror reflects the light and disc of the outer sun in the skies. In this way the image and effulgence of the Sun of Reality appear in the mirrors of the Manifestations of God. This is what Jesus Christ meant when He declared, "the father is in the son," the purpose being that the reality of that eternal Sun had become reflected in its glory in Christ Himself. It does not signify that the Sun of Reality had descended from its place in heaven or that its essential being had effected an entrance into the mirror, for there is neither entrance nor exit for the reality of Divinity; there is no ingress or egress; it is sanctified above all things and ever occupies its own holy station. Changes and transformations are not applicable to that eternal reality. Transformation from condition to condition is the attribute of contingent realities.

At a time when warfare and strife prevailed among nations, 5 when enmity and hatred separated sects and denominations and human differences were very great, Bahá'u'lláh appeared upon the horizon of the East, proclaiming the oneness of God and the unity of the world of humanity. He promulgated the teaching that all mankind are the servants of one God; that all have come into being through the bestowal of the one Creator; that God is kind to all, nurtures, rears and protects all, provides for all and extends His love and mercy to all races and people. Inasmuch as God is loving, why should we be unjust and unkind? As God manifests loyalty and mercy, why should we show forth enmity and hatred? Surely the divine policy is more perfect than human plan and theory; for no matter how wise and sagacious man may become, he can never attain a policy that is superior to the policy of God. Therefore, we must emulate the attitude of God, love all people, be just and kind to every human creature. We must consider all as the leaves, branches and fruit of one tree, children of one household; for all are the progeny of Adam. We are waves of one sea, grass of the same meadow, stars in the same heaven; and we find shelter in the universal divine Protector. If one be sick, he must be treated; the ignorant must be educated; the sleeping must be awakened; the dead must be quickened with life. These were principles of the teachings of Bahá'u'lláh.

6 In proclaiming the oneness of mankind He taught that men and women are equal in the sight of God and that there is no distinction to be made between them. The only difference between them now is due to lack of education and training. If woman is given equal opportunity of education, distinction and estimate of inferiority will disappear. The world of humanity has two wings, as it were: One is the female; the other is the male. If one wing be defective, the strong perfect wing will not be capable of flight. The world of humanity has two hands. If one be imperfect, the capable hand is restricted and unable to perform its duties. God is the Creator of mankind. He has endowed both sexes with perfections and intelligence, given them physical members and organs of sense, without differentiation or distinction as to superiority; therefore, why should woman be considered inferior?

This is not according to the plan and justice of God. He has created them equal; in His estimate there is no question of sex. The one whose heart is purest, whose deeds are most perfect, is acceptable to God, male or female. Often in history women have been the pride of humanity—for example, Mary, the mother of Jesus. She was the glory of mankind. Mary Magdalene, Ásíyih, daughter of Pharaoh, Sarah, wife of Abraham, and innumerable others have glorified the human race by their excellences. In this day there are women among the Bahá'ís who far outshine men. They are wise, talented, well-informed, progressive, most intelligent and the light of men. They surpass men in courage. When they speak in meetings, the men listen with great respect. Furthermore, the education of women is of greater importance than the education of men, for they are the mothers of the race, and mothers rear the children. The first teachers of children are the mothers. Therefore, they must be capably trained in order to educate both sons and daughters. There are many provisions in the words of Bahá'u'lláh in regard to this.

He promulgated the adoption of the same course of educa- 7
tion for man and woman. Daughters and sons must follow the same curriculum of study, thereby promoting unity of the sexes. When all mankind shall receive the same opportunity of education and the equality of men and women be realized, the foundations of war will be utterly destroyed. Without equality this will be impossible because all differences and distinction are conducive to discord and strife. Equality between men and women is conducive to the abolition of warfare for the reason that women will never be willing to sanction it. Mothers will not give their sons as sacrifices upon the battlefield after twenty years of anxiety and loving devotion in rearing them from infancy, no matter what cause they are called upon to defend. There is no doubt that when women obtain equality of rights, war will entirely cease among mankind.

8   Bahá'u'lláh promulgated the fundamental oneness of religion. He taught that reality is one and not multiple, that it underlies all divine precepts and that the foundations of the religions are, therefore, the same. Certain forms and imitations have gradually arisen. As these vary, they cause differences among religionists. If we set aside these imitations and seek the fundamental reality underlying our beliefs, we reach a basis of agreement because it is one and not multiple.

9   Among other principles of Bahá'u'lláh's teachings was the harmony of science and religion. Religion must stand the analysis of reason. It must agree with scientific fact and proof so that science will sanction religion and religion fortify science. Both are indissolubly welded and joined in reality. If statements and teachings of religion are found to be unreasonable and contrary to science, they are outcomes of superstition and imagination. Innumerable doctrines and beliefs of this character have arisen in the past ages. Consider the superstitions and mythology of the Romans, Greeks and Egyptians; all were contrary to religion and science. It is now evident that the beliefs of these nations were superstitions, but in those times they held to them most tenaciously. For example, one of the many Egyptian idols was to those people an authenticated miracle, whereas in reality it was a piece of stone. As science could not sanction the miraculous origin and nature of a piece of rock, the belief in it must have been superstition. It is now evident that it was superstition. Therefore, we must cast aside such beliefs and investigate reality. That which is found to be real and conformable to reason must be accepted, and whatever science and reason cannot support must be rejected as imitation and not reality. Then differences of belief will disappear. All will become as one family, one people, and the same susceptibility to the divine bounty and education will be witnessed among mankind.

O Thou forgiving Lord! Thou art the shelter of all these Thy 10 servants. Thou knowest the secrets and art aware of all things. We are all helpless, and Thou art the Mighty, the Omnipotent. We are all sinners, and Thou art the Forgiver of sins, the Merciful, the Compassionate. O Lord! Look not at our shortcomings. Deal with us according to Thy grace and bounty. Our shortcomings are many, but the ocean of Thy forgiveness is boundless. Our weakness is grievous, but the evidences of Thine aid and assistance are clear. Therefore, confirm and strengthen us. Enable us to do that which is worthy of Thy holy Threshold. Illumine our hearts, grant us discerning eyes and attentive ears. Resuscitate the dead and heal the sick. Bestow wealth upon the poor and give peace and security to the fearful. Accept us in Thy kingdom and illumine us with the light of guidance. Thou art the Powerful and the Omnipotent. Thou art the Generous. Thou art the Clement. Thou art the Kind.

2

9 June 1912

Talk at Baptist Temple
Broad and Berks Streets, Philadelphia, Pennsylvania

NOTES BY EDNA McKINNEY

I AM greatly pleased to be present this evening. Truly this is a 1 spiritual gathering. I perceive the fragrances of the heavenly Kingdom among you—devotion to God, sincere intention and spiritual love. Glad tidings!

2   From the time of the creation of Adam to this day there have been two pathways in the world of humanity: one the natural or materialistic, the other the religious or spiritual. The pathway of nature is the pathway of the animal realm. The animal acts in accordance with the requirements of nature, follows its own instincts and desires. Whatever its impulses and proclivities may be, it has the liberty to gratify them; yet it is a captive of nature. It cannot deviate in the least degree from the road nature has established. It is utterly lacking spiritual susceptibilities, ignorant of divine religion and without knowledge of the Kingdom of God. The animal possesses no power of ideation or conscious intelligence; it is a captive of the senses and deprived of that which lies beyond them. It is subject to what the eye sees, the ear hears, the nostrils sense, the taste detects and touch reveals. These sensations are acceptable and sufficient for the animal. But that which is beyond the range of the senses, that realm of phenomena through which the conscious pathway to the Kingdom of God leads, the world of spiritual susceptibilities and divine religion—of these the animal is completely unaware, for in its highest station it is a captive of nature.

3   One of the strangest things witnessed is that the materialists of today are proud of their natural instincts and bondage. They state that nothing is entitled to belief and acceptance except that which is sensible or tangible. By their own statements they are captives of nature, unconscious of the spiritual world, uninformed of the divine Kingdom and unaware of heavenly bestowals. If this be a virtue, the animal has attained it to a superlative degree, for the animal is absolutely ignorant of the realm of spirit and out of touch with the inner world of conscious realization. The animal would agree with the materialist in denying the existence of that which transcends the senses. If we admit that being limited to the plane of the senses is a virtue, the animal is indeed more virtuous than man, for it is

246

entirely bereft of that which lies beyond, absolutely oblivious of the Kingdom of God and its traces, whereas God has deposited within the human creature an illimitable power by which he can rule the world of nature.

Consider how all other phenomenal existence and beings are 4 captives of nature. The sun, that colossal center of our solar system, the giant stars and planets, the towering mountains, the earth itself and its kingdoms of life lower than the human—all are captives of nature except man. No other created thing can deviate in the slightest degree from obedience to natural law. The sun in its glory and greatness millions of miles away is held prisoner in its orbit of universal revolution, captive of universal natural control. Man is the ruler of nature. According to natural law and limitation he should remain upon the earth, but behold how he violates this command and soars above the mountains in airplanes. He sails in ships upon the surface of the ocean and dives into its depths in submarines. Man makes nature his servant; he harnesses the mighty energy of electricity, for instance, and imprisons it in a small lamp for his uses and convenience. He speaks from the East to the West through a wire. He is able to store and preserve his voice in a phonograph. Though he is a dweller upon earth, he penetrates the mysteries of starry worlds inconceivably distant. He discovers latent realities within the bosom of the earth, uncovers treasures, penetrates secrets and mysteries of the phenomenal world and brings to light that which according to nature's jealous laws should remain hidden, unknown and unfathomable. Through an ideal inner power man brings these realities forth from the invisible plane to the visible. This is contrary to nature's law.

It is evident, therefore, that man is ruler over nature's sphere 5 and province. Nature is inert; man is progressive. Nature has no consciousness; man is endowed with it. Nature is without volition and acts perforce, whereas man possesses a mighty will.

Nature is incapable of discovering mysteries or realities, whereas man is especially fitted to do so. Nature is not in touch with the realm of God; man is attuned to its evidences. Nature is uninformed of God; man is conscious of Him. Man acquires divine virtues; nature is denied them. Man can voluntarily discontinue vices; nature has no power to modify the influence of its instincts. Altogether it is evident that man is more noble and superior, that in him there is an ideal power surpassing nature. He has consciousness, volition, memory, intelligent power, divine attributes and virtues of which nature is completely deprived and bereft; therefore, man is higher and nobler by reason of the ideal and heavenly force latent and manifest in him.

6   How strange then it seems that man, notwithstanding his endowment with this ideal power, will descend to a level beneath him and declare himself no greater than that which is manifestly inferior to his real station. God has created such a conscious spirit within him that he is the most wonderful of all contingent beings. In ignoring these virtues he descends to the material plane, considers matter the ruler of existence and denies that which lies beyond. Is this virtue? In its fullest sense this is animalistic, for the animal realizes nothing more. In fact, from this standpoint the animal is the greater philosopher because it is completely ignorant of the Kingdom of God, possesses no spiritual susceptibilities and is uninformed of the heavenly world. In brief, this is a view of the pathway of nature.

7   The second pathway is that of religion, the road of the divine Kingdom. It involves the acquisition of praiseworthy attributes, heavenly illumination and righteous actions in the world of humanity. This pathway is conducive to the progress and uplift of the world. It is the source of human enlightenment, training and ethical improvement—the magnet which attracts the love of God because of the knowledge of God it bestows. This is

the road of the holy Manifestations of God; for They are, in reality, the foundation of the divine religion of oneness. There is no change or transformation in this pathway. It is the cause of human betterment, the acquisition of heavenly virtues and the illumination of mankind.

Alas that humanity is completely submerged in imitations and unrealities, notwithstanding that the truth of divine religion has ever remained the same. Superstitions have obscured the fundamental reality, the world is darkened, and the light of religion is not apparent. This darkness is conducive to differences and dissensions; rites and dogmas are many and various; therefore, discord has arisen among the religious systems, whereas religion is for the unification of mankind. True religion is the source of love and agreement amongst men, the cause of the development of praiseworthy qualities, but the people are holding to the counterfeit and imitation, negligent of the reality which unifies, so they are bereft and deprived of the radiance of religion. They follow superstitions inherited from their fathers and ancestors. To such an extent has this prevailed that they have taken away the heavenly light of divine truth and sit in the darkness of imitations and imaginations. That which was meant to be conducive to life has become the cause of death; that which should have been an evidence of knowledge is now a proof of ignorance; that which was a factor in the sublimity of human nature has proved to be its degradation. Therefore, the realm of the religionist has gradually narrowed and darkened, and the sphere of the materialist has widened and advanced; for the religionist has held to imitation and counterfeit, neglecting and discarding holiness and the sacred reality of religion. When the sun sets, it is the time for bats to fly. They come forth because they are creatures of the night. When the lights of religion become darkened, the materialists appear. They are the bats of night. The decline of

8

249

religion is their time of activity; they seek the shadows when the world is darkened and clouds have spread over it.

9   Bahá'u'lláh has risen from the eastern horizon. Like the glory of the sun He has come into the world. He has reflected the reality of divine religion, dispelled the darkness of imitations, laid the foundation of new teachings and resuscitated the world.

10   The first teaching of Bahá'u'lláh is the investigation of reality. Man must seek reality himself, forsaking imitations and adherence to mere hereditary forms. As the nations of the world are following imitations in lieu of truth and as imitations are many and various, differences of belief have been productive of strife and warfare. So long as these imitations remain, the oneness of the world of humanity is impossible. Therefore, we must investigate reality in order that by its light the clouds and darkness may be dispelled. Reality is one reality; it does not admit multiplicity or division. If the nations of the world investigate reality, they will agree and become united. Many people and sects in Persia have sought reality through the guidance and teaching of Bahá'u'lláh. They have become united and now live in a state of agreement and love; among them there is no longer the least trace of enmity and strife.

11   The Jews were expecting the appearance of the Messiah, looking forward to it with devotion of heart and soul, but because they were submerged in imitations, they did not believe in Jesus Christ when He appeared. Finally they rose against Him even to the extreme of persecution and shedding His blood. Had they investigated reality, they would have accepted their promised Messiah. These blind imitations and hereditary prejudices have invariably become the cause of bitterness and hatred and have filled the world with darkness and violence of war. Therefore, we must seek the fundamental truth in order to extricate ourselves from such conditions and then with illumined faces find the pathway to the Kingdom of God.

The second teaching of Bahá'u'lláh concerns the unity of 12
mankind. All are the servants of God and members of one human family. God has created all, and all are His children. He
rears, nourishes, provides for and is kind to all. Why should
we be unjust and unkind? This is the policy of God, the lights
of which have shone throughout the world. His sun bestows
its effulgence unsparingly upon all; His clouds send down rain
without distinction or favor; His breezes refresh the whole earth.
It is evident that humankind without exception is sheltered
beneath His mercy and protection. Some are imperfect; they
must be perfected. The ignorant must be taught, the sick healed,
the sleepers awakened. The child must not be oppressed or cen-
sured because it is undeveloped; it must be patiently trained.
The sick must not be neglected because they are ailing; nay,
rather, we must have compassion upon them and bring them
healing. Briefly, the old conditions of animosity, bigotry and
hatred between the religious systems must be dispelled and the
new conditions of love, agreement and spiritual brotherhood
be established among them.

The third teaching of Bahá'u'lláh is that religion must be the 13
source of fellowship, the cause of unity and the nearness of God
to man. If it rouses hatred and strife, it is evident that absence
of religion is preferable and an irreligious man better than one
who professes it. According to the divine Will and intention
religion should be the cause of love and agreement, a bond to
unify all mankind, for it is a message of peace and goodwill to
man from God.

The fourth teaching of Bahá'u'lláh is the agreement of religion 14
and science. God has endowed man with intelligence and reason
whereby he is required to determine the verity of questions and
propositions. If religious beliefs and opinions are found contrary
to the standards of science, they are mere superstitions and
imaginations; for the antithesis of knowledge is ignorance, and

251

the child of ignorance is superstition. Unquestionably there must be agreement between true religion and science. If a question be found contrary to reason, faith and belief in it are impossible, and there is no outcome but wavering and vacillation.

15   Bahá'u'lláh also taught that prejudices—whether religious, racial, patriotic or political—are destructive to the foundations of human development. Prejudices of any kind are the destroyers of human happiness and welfare. Until they are dispelled, the advancement of the world of humanity is not possible; yet racial, religious and national biases are observed everywhere. For thousands of years the world of humanity has been agitated and disturbed by prejudices. As long as it prevails, warfare, animosity and hatred will continue. Therefore, if we seek to establish peace, we must cast aside this obstacle; for otherwise, agreement and composure are not to be attained.

16   Sixth, Bahá'u'lláh set forth principles of guidance and teaching for economic readjustment. Regulations were revealed by Him which ensure the welfare of the commonwealth. As the rich man enjoys his life surrounded by ease and luxuries, so the poor man must, likewise, have a home and be provided with sustenance and comforts commensurate with his needs. This readjustment of the social economy is of the greatest importance inasmuch as it ensures the stability of the world of humanity; and until it is effected, happiness and prosperity are impossible.

17   Seventh, Bahá'u'lláh taught that an equal standard of human rights must be recognized and adopted. In the estimation of God all men are equal; there is no distinction or preferment for any soul in the dominion of His justice and equity.

18   Eighth, education is essential, and all standards of training and teaching throughout the world of mankind should be brought into conformity and agreement; a universal curriculum should be established, and the basis of ethics be the same.

Ninth, a universal language shall be adopted and be taught   19
by all the schools and institutions of the world. A committee
appointed by national bodies of learning shall select a suitable
language to be used as a medium of international communication. All must acquire it. This is one of the great factors in the
unification of man.

Tenth, Bahá'u'lláh emphasized and established the equality   20
of man and woman. Sex is not particularized to humanity; it
exists throughout the animate kingdoms but without distinction or preference. In the vegetable kingdom there is complete
equality between male and female of species. Likewise, in the
animal plane equality exists; all are under the protection of
God. Is it becoming to man that he, the noblest of creatures,
should observe and insist upon such distinction? Woman's lack
of progress and proficiency has been due to her need of equal
education and opportunity. Had she been allowed this equality,
there is no doubt she would be the counterpart of man in ability
and capacity. The happiness of mankind will be realized when
women and men coordinate and advance equally, for each is the
complement and helpmeet of the other.

The world of humanity cannot advance through mere physi-   21
cal powers and intellectual attainments; nay, rather, the Holy
Spirit is essential. The divine Father must assist the human world
to attain maturity. The body of man is in need of physical and
mental energy, but his spirit requires the life and fortification
of the Holy Spirit. Without its protection and quickening the
human world would be extinguished. Jesus Christ declared,
"Let the dead bury their dead." He also said, "That which is
born of the flesh is flesh; and that which is born of the Spirit
is spirit." It is evident, therefore, according to Christ that the
human spirit which is not fortified by the presence of the Holy
Spirit is dead and in need of resurrection by that divine power;

otherwise, though materially advanced to high degrees, man cannot attain full and complete progress.

Talks 'Abdu'l-Bahá Delivered in New York and Brooklyn

11 June 1912

Talk at Open Committee Meeting
Home of Mr. and Mrs. Edward B. Kinney
780 West End Avenue, New York

NOTES BY HOWARD MACNUTT

IT is my hope that the meetings of the Bahá'í Assembly in New York shall become like meetings of the Supreme Concourse. When you assemble, you must reflect the lights of the heavenly Kingdom. Let your hearts be as mirrors in which the radiance of the Sun of Reality is visible. Each bosom must be a telegraph station—one terminus of the wire attached to the soul, the other fixed in the Supreme Concourse—so that inspiration may descend from the Kingdom of Abhá and questions of reality be discussed. Then opinions will coincide with truth; day by day there will be progression, and the meetings will become more radiant and spiritual. This attainment is conditioned upon unity and agreement. The more perfect the love and agreement, the more the divine confirmations and assistance of the Blessed Perfection will descend. May this prove to be a divine meeting, and may boundless bestowals come down upon you. Strive with all your hearts and with the very power of life that unity and love may continually increase. In discussions look toward the reality without being self-opinionated. Let no one assert and insist upon his own mere opinion; nay, rather, let each investigate reality with the greatest love and fellowship. Consult upon every matter, and when one presents the point of view of reality itself, that shall be acceptable to all. Then will spiritual unity increase among you, individual illumination will be greater, happiness will be more abundant, and you will draw nearer and nearer to the Kingdom of God.

2

11 June 1912

Talk at 309 West Seventy-eighth Street, New York

NOTES BY HOWARD MACNUTT

1 WE have just returned from a visit to Philadelphia, spending two nights there and speaking in two large churches. The weather proved unpleasant and affected my health. The purpose in these movements here and there is a single purpose—it is to spread the light of truth in this dark world. On account of my age it is difficult to journey. Sometimes the difficulties are arduous, but out of love for the friends of God and with desire to sacrifice myself in the pathway of God, I bear them in gladness. The purpose is the result which is accomplished—love and unity among mankind. For the world is dark with discord and selfishness, hearts are negligent, souls are bereft of God and His heavenly bestowals. Man is submerged in the affairs of this world. His aims, objects and attainments are mortal, whereas God desires for him immortal accomplishments. In his heart there is no thought of God. He has sacrificed his portion and birthright of divine spirituality. Desire and passion, like two unmanageable horses, have wrested the reins of control from him and are galloping madly in the wilderness. This is the cause of the degradation of

the world of humanity. This is the cause of its retrogression into the appetites and passions of the animal kingdom. Instead of divine advancement we find sensual captivity and debasement of heavenly virtues of the soul. By devotion to the carnal, mortal world human susceptibilities sink to the level of animalism.

What are the animals' propensities? To eat, drink, wander about and sleep. The thoughts, the minds of the animals are confined to these. They are captives in the bonds of these desires. Man becomes a prisoner and slave to them when his ultimate desire is no higher than his welfare in this world of the senses. Consider how difficult for man is the attainment of pleasures and happiness in this mortal world. How easy it is for the animal. Look upon the fields and flowers, prairies, streams, forests and mountains. The grazing animals, the birds of the air, the fishes neither toil nor undergo hardships; they sow not, nor are they concerned about the reaping; they have no anxiety about business or politics—no trouble or worry whatsoever. All the fields and grasses, all the meadows of fruits and grains, all the mountain slopes and streams of salubrious water belong to them. They do not labor for their livelihood and happiness because everything is provided and made possible for them. If the life of man be confined to this physical, material outlook, the animal's life is a hundred times better, easier and more productive of comfort and contentment. The animal is nobler, more serene and confident because each hour is free from anxiety and worriment; but man, restless and dissatisfied, runs from morn till eve, sailing the seas, diving beneath them in submarines, flying aloft in airplanes, delving into the lowest strata of the earth to obtain his livelihood—all with the greatest difficulty, anxiety and unrest. Therefore, in this respect the animal is nobler, more serene, poised and confident. Consider the birds in the forest and jungle: how they build their nests high in the swaying treetops, build them with the utmost skill and beauty—swinging, rocking in the morning breezes, drinking the pure, sweet water, enjoying the most enchanting views as they fly here and there high overhead, singing joyously—all without labor, free from worry, care and forebodings. If man's life be confined to the elemental, physical world of enjoyment, one lark is nobler, more admirable than all humanity because its livelihood is prepared, its condition complete, its accomplishment perfect and natural.

3   But the life of man is not so restricted; it is divine, eternal, not mortal and sensual. For him a spiritual existence and livelihood is prepared and ordained in the divine creative plan. His life is intended to be a life of spiritual enjoyment to which the animal can never attain. This enjoyment depends upon the acquisition of heavenly virtues. The sublimity of man is his attainment of the knowledge of God. The bliss of man is the acquiring of heavenly bestowals, which descend upon him in the outflow of the bounty of God. The happiness of man is in the fragrance of the love of God. This is the highest pinnacle of attainment in the human world. How preferable to the animal and its hopeless kingdom!

4   Therefore, consider how base a nature it reveals in man that, notwithstanding the favors showered upon him by God, he should lower himself into the animal sphere, be wholly occupied with material needs, attached to this mortal realm, imagining that the greatest happiness is to attain wealth in this world. How purposeless! How debased is such a nature! God has created man in order that he may be a dove of the Kingdom, a heavenly candle, a recipient of eternal life. God has created man in order that he may be resuscitated through the breaths of the Holy Spirit and become the light of the world. How debased the soul which can find enjoyment in this darkness, occupied with itself, the captive of self and passion, wallowing in the mire of the material world!

How degraded is such a nature! What an ignorance this is! What a blindness! How glorious the station of man who has partaken of the heavenly food and built the temple of his everlasting residence in the world of heaven!

The Manifestations of God have come into the world to free 5 man from these bonds and chains of the world of nature. Although They walked upon the earth, They lived in heaven. They were not concerned about material sustenance and prosperity of this world. Their bodies were subjected to inconceivable distress, but Their spirits ever soared in the highest realms of ecstasy. The purpose of Their coming, Their teaching and suffering was the freedom of man from himself. Shall we, therefore, follow in Their footsteps, escape from this cage of the body or continue subject to its tyranny? Shall we pursue the phantom of a mortal happiness which does not exist or turn toward the tree of life and the joys of its eternal fruits?

I have come to this country in the advanced years of my life, 6 undergoing difficulties of health and climate because of excessive love for the friends of God. It is my wish that they may be assisted to become servants of the heavenly Kingdom, captives in the service of the will of God. This captivity is freedom; this sacrifice is glorification; this labor is reward; this need is bestowal. For service in love for mankind is unity with God. He who serves has already entered the Kingdom and is seated at the right hand of his Lord.

3

11 June 1912

Talk at 309 West Seventy-eighth Street, New York

NOTES BY EMMA C. MELICK

1   MAN must be lofty in endeavor. He must seek to become heavenly and spiritual, to find the pathway to the threshold of God and become acceptable in the sight of God. This is eternal glory—to be near to God. This is eternal sovereignty—to be imbued with the virtues of the human world. This is boundless blessing—to be entirely sanctified and holy above every stain and dross.

2   Consider the human world. See how nations have come and gone. They have been of all minds and purposes. Some were mere captives of self and desire, engulfed in the passions of the lower nature. They attained to wealth, to the comforts of life, to fame. And what was the final outcome? Utter evanescence and oblivion. Reflect upon this. Look upon it with the eye of admonition. No trace of them remains, no fruit, no result, no benefit; they have gone utterly—complete effacement.

3   Souls have appeared in the world who were pure and undefiled, who have directed their attention toward God, seeking the reward of God, attaining nearness to the threshold of God, acceptable in the good pleasure of God. They have been the lights of guidance and stars of the Supreme Concourse. Consider these souls, shining like stars in the horizon of sanctity forevermore.

4   It must not be implied that one should give up avocation and attainment to livelihood. On the contrary, in the Cause of

Bahá'u'lláh monasticism and asceticism are not sanctioned. In this great Cause the light of guidance is shining and radiant. Bahá'u'lláh has even said that occupation and labor are devotion. All humanity must obtain a livelihood by sweat of the brow and bodily exertion, at the same time seeking to lift the burden of others, striving to be the source of comfort to souls and facilitating the means of living. This in itself is devotion to God. Bahá'u'lláh has thereby encouraged action and stimulated service. But the energies of the heart must not be attached to these things; the soul must not be completely occupied with them. Though the mind is busy, the heart must be attracted toward the Kingdom of God in order that the virtues of humanity may be attained from every direction and source.

We have forsaken the path of God; we have given up attention to the divine Kingdom; we have not severed the heart from worldly attractions; we have become defiled with qualities which are not praiseworthy in the sight of God; we are so completely steeped in material issues and tendencies that we are not partakers of the virtues of humanity.

Little reflection, little admonition is necessary for us to realize the purpose of our creation. What a heavenly potentiality God has deposited within us! What a power God has given our spirits! He has endowed us with a power to penetrate the realities of things; but we must be self-abnegating, we must have pure spirits, pure intentions, and strive with heart and soul while in the human world to attain everlasting glory.

I have come for the purpose of admonition and voicing the teachings of Bahá'u'lláh. It is my hope that His will and guidance may influence your spirits, souls and hearts, causing them to become pure, holy, sanctified and illumined and making you lamps of heavenly illumination to the world. This is my desire; this is my hope through the assistance of God.

4

12 June 1912

Talk at 309 West Seventy-eighth Street, New York

NOTES BY MARY J. MACNUTT

1 YOU are all exceedingly welcome. Do you realize how much you should thank God for His blessings? If you should thank Him a thousand times with each breath, it would not be sufficient because God has created and trained you. He has protected you from every affliction and prepared every gift and bestowal. Consider what a kind Father He is. He bestows His gift before you ask. We were not in the world of existence, but as soon as we were born, we found everything prepared for our needs and comfort without question on our part. He has given us a kind father and compassionate mother, provided for us two springs of salubrious milk, pure atmosphere, refreshing water, gentle breezes and the sun shining above our heads. In brief, He has supplied all the necessities of life although we did not ask for any of these great gifts. With pure mercy and bounty He has prepared this great table. It is a mercy which precedes asking. There is another kind of mercy, which is realized after questioning and supplication. He has bestowed both upon us—without asking and with supplication. He has created us in this radiant century, a century longed for and expected by all the sanctified souls in past periods. It is a blessed century; it is a blessed day. The philosophers of history have agreed that this century is equal to one hundred past centuries. This is true from every standpoint. This is the century of science, inventions, discoveries and universal laws. This is the century of the revelation

of the mysteries of God. This is the century of the effulgence of the rays of the Sun of Truth. Therefore, you must render thanks and glorification to God that you were born in this age. Furthermore, you have listened to the call of Bahá'u'lláh. Your nostrils are perfumed with the breezes of the paradise of Abhá. You have caught glimpses of the light from the horizon of the Orient. You were asleep; you are awakened. Your ears are attentive; your hearts are informed. You have acquired the love of God. You have attained to the knowledge of God. This is the most great bestowal of God. This is the breath of the Holy Spirit, and this consists of faith and assurance. This eternal life is the second birth; this is the baptism of the Holy Spirit. God has destined this station for you all. He has prepared this for you. You must appreciate the value of this bounty and engage your time in mentioning and thanking the True One. You must live in the utmost happiness. If any trouble or vicissitude comes into your lives, if your heart is depressed on account of health, livelihood or vocation, let not these things affect you. They should not cause unhappiness, for Bahá'u'lláh has brought you divine happiness. He has prepared heavenly food for you; He has destined eternal bounty for you; He has bestowed everlasting glory upon you. Therefore, these glad tidings should cause you to soar in the atmosphere of joy forever and ever. Render continual thanks unto God so that the confirmations of God may encircle you all.

5

15 June 1912

Talk at 309 West Seventy-eighth Street, New York

NOTES BY HOWARD MACNUTT

1 I HAVE made you wait awhile, but as I was tired, I slept. While I was sleeping, I was conversing with you as though speaking at the top of my voice. Then through the effect of my own voice I awoke. As I awoke, one word was upon my lips—the word *imtíyáz* ("distinction"). So I will speak to you upon that subject this morning.

2 When we look upon the world of existence, we realize that all material things have a common bond; and yet, on the other hand, there are certain points of distinction between them. For instance, all earthly objects have common bodily ties. The minerals, vegetables and animals have elemental bodies in common with each other. Likewise, they have place in the order of creation. This is the common tie or point of contact between them. All of them pass through the process of composition and decomposition; this is a natural law to which all are subject. This law is ruling throughout creation and constitutes a bond of connection among created things. But at the same time there are certain distinguishing features between these objects. For instance, between the mineral and vegetable, the vegetable and animal, the animal and human, points of distinction exist which are unmistakable and significant. Likewise, there are distinctions between kinds and species of each kingdom. When we consider the mineral kingdom in detail, we observe not only points of similarity between objects but points of distinction as

well. Some are immovable bodies, some hard and solid; some have the power of expansion and contraction; some are liquid, some gaseous; some have weight; others, like fire and electricity, have not. So there are many points of distinction among these kinds of elements.

In the vegetable kingdom also we observe distinction between 3 the various sorts and species of organisms. Each has its own form, color and fragrance. In the animal kingdom the same law rules as many distinctions in form, color and function are noticeable. It is the same in the human kingdom. From the standpoint of color there are white, black, yellow and red people. From the standpoint of physiognomy there is a wide difference and distinction among races. The Asian, African and American have different physiognomies; the men of the North and men of the South are very different in type and features. From an economic standpoint in the law of living there is a great deal of difference. Some are poor, others wealthy; some are wise, others ignorant; some are patient and serene, some impatient and excitable; some are prone to justice, others practice injustice and oppression; some are meek, others arrogant. In brief, there are many points of distinction among humankind.

I desire distinction for you. The Bahá'ís must be distin- 4 guished from others of humanity. But this distinction must not depend upon wealth—that they should become more affluent than other people. I do not desire for you financial distinction. It is not an ordinary distinction I desire; not scientific, commercial, industrial distinction. For you I desire spiritual distinction—that is, you must become eminent and distinguished in morals. In the love of God you must become distinguished from all else. You must become distinguished for loving humanity, for unity and accord, for love and justice. In brief, you must become distinguished in all the virtues of the human world—for faithfulness and sincerity, for justice and fidelity, for firmness and steadfastness, for philanthropic deeds and service to the human world, for love toward every human being, for unity and accord with all people, for removing prejudices and promoting international peace. Finally, you must become distinguished for heavenly illumination and for acquiring the bestowals of God. I desire this distinction for you. This must be the point of distinction among you.

6

16 June 1912

Talk at Fourth Unitarian Church
Beverly Road, Flatbush, Brooklyn, New York

NOTES BY ESTHER FOSTER

1 THIS is a Unitarian church, and in the Arabic tongue this day may well be called *Yawm-al' Ittiḥád* ("the Unitarian Day"). Therefore, I consider it appropriate to speak to you upon the subject of unity.

2 What is real unity? When we observe the human world, we find various collective expressions of unity therein. For instance, man is distinguished from the animal by his degree, or kingdom. This comprehensive distinction includes all the posterity of Adam and constitutes one great household or human family, which may be considered the fundamental or physical unity of mankind. Furthermore, a distinction exists between various groups of humankind according to lineage, each group forming a racial unity separate from the others. There is also the unity of

tongue among those who use the same language as a means of communication; national unity where various peoples live under one form of government such as French, German, British, etc.; and political unity, which conserves the civil rights of parties or factions of the same government. All these unities are imaginary and without real foundation, for no real result proceeds from them. The purpose of true unity is real and divine outcomes. From these limited unities mentioned only limited outcomes proceed, whereas unlimited unity produces unlimited result. For instance, from the limited unity of race or nationality the results at most are limited. It is like a family living alone and solitary; there are no unlimited or universal outcomes from it.

The unity which is productive of unlimited results is first a 3 unity of mankind which recognizes that all are sheltered beneath the overshadowing glory of the All-Glorious, that all are servants of one God; for all breathe the same atmosphere, live upon the same earth, move beneath the same heavens, receive effulgence from the same sun and are under the protection of one God. This is the most great unity, and its results are lasting if humanity adheres to it; but mankind has hitherto violated it, adhering to sectarian or other limited unities such as racial, patriotic or unity of self-interests; therefore, no great results have been forthcoming. Nevertheless, it is certain that the radiance and favors of God are encompassing, minds have developed, perceptions have become acute, sciences and arts are widespread, and capacity exists for the proclamation and promulgation of the real and ultimate unity of mankind, which will bring forth marvelous results. It will reconcile all religions, make warring nations loving, cause hostile kings to become friendly and bring peace and happiness to the human world. It will cement together the Orient and Occident, remove forever the foundations of war and upraise the ensign of the Most Great Peace. These limited unities are, therefore, signs of that great unity which will make all the human family one by being productive of the attractions of conscience in mankind.

4   Another unity is the spiritual unity which emanates from the breaths of the Holy Spirit. This is greater than the unity of mankind. Human unity or solidarity may be likened to the body, whereas unity from the breaths of the Holy Spirit is the spirit animating the body. This is a perfect unity. It creates such a condition in mankind that each one will make sacrifices for the other, and the utmost desire will be to forfeit life and all that pertains to it in behalf of another's good. This is the unity which existed among the disciples of Jesus Christ and bound together the Prophets and holy Souls of the past. It is the unity which through the influence of the divine spirit is permeating the Bahá'ís so that each offers his life for the other and strives with all sincerity to attain his good pleasure. This is the unity which caused twenty thousand people in Persia to give their lives in love and devotion to it. It made the Báb the target of a thousand arrows and caused Bahá'u'lláh to suffer exile and imprisonment forty years. This unity is the very spirit of the body of the world. It is impossible for the body of the world to become quickened with life without its vivification. Jesus Christ—may my life be a sacrifice to Him!—promulgated this unity among mankind. Every soul who believed in Jesus Christ became revivified and resuscitated through this spirit, attained to the zenith of eternal glory, realized the everlasting life, experienced the second birth and rose to the acme of good fortune.

5   In the Word of God there is still another unity—the oneness of the Manifestations of God, Abraham, Moses, Jesus Christ, Muḥammad, the Báb and Bahá'u'lláh. This is a unity divine, heavenly, radiant, merciful—the one reality appearing in its successive Manifestations. For instance, the sun is one and the same, but its points of dawning are various. During the sum-

mer season it rises from the northern point of the ecliptic; in winter it appears from the southern point of rising. Each month between, it appears from a certain zodiacal position. Although these dawning points are different, the sun is the same sun which has appeared from them all. The significance is the reality of Prophethood which is symbolized by the sun, and the holy Manifestations are the dawning places or zodiacal points.

There is also the divine unity or entity, which is sanctified above all concept of humanity. It cannot be comprehended nor conceived because it is infinite reality and cannot become finite. Human minds are incapable of surrounding that reality because all thoughts and conceptions of it are finite, intellectual creations and not the reality of Divine Being which alone knows itself. For example, if we form a conception of Divinity as a living, almighty, self-subsisting, eternal Being, this is only a concept apprehended by a human intellectual reality. It would not be the outward, visible reality, which is beyond the power of human mind to conceive or encompass. We ourselves have an external, visible entity; but even our concept of it is the product of our own brain and limited comprehension. The reality of Divinity is sanctified above this degree of knowing and realization. It has ever been hidden and secluded in its own holiness and sanctity above our comprehending. Although it transcends our realization, its lights, bestowals, traces and virtues have become manifest in the realities of the Prophets, even as the sun becomes resplendent in various mirrors. These holy realities are as reflectors, and the reality of Divinity is as the sun, which, although it is reflected from the mirrors, and its virtues and perfections become resplendent therein, does not stoop from its own station of majesty and glory and seek abode in the mirrors; it remains in its heaven of sanctity. At most it is this: that its lights become manifest and evident in its mirrors or manifestations. Therefore, its bounty proceeding from them is one bounty, but the recipients of that bounty are many. This is the unity of God; this is oneness—unity of Divinity, holy above ascent or descent, embodiment, comprehension or idealization—divine unity. The Prophets are its mirrors; its lights are revealed through Them; its virtues become resplendent in Them, but the Sun of Reality never descends from its own highest point and station. This is unity, oneness, sanctity; this is glorification whereby we praise and adore God.

7   O my God! O my God! Verily, these are servants at the threshold of Thy mercy, and maidservants at the door of Thy oneness. Verily, they have gathered in this temple to turn to Thy face of glory, holding to the hem of Thy garment and to Thy singleness, seeking Thy good pleasure and ascent into Thy Kingdom. They receive effulgence from the Sun of Reality in this glorious century, and they long for Thy goodwill in all great affairs. O Lord! Illumine their sight with a vision of Thy signs and riches, and quicken their ears with hearkening to Thy Word. Render their hearts replete with Thy love, and gladden their spirits with Thy meeting. Deign to bestow upon them spiritual good in Thine earth and heaven, and make them signs of unity among Thy servants in order that the real unity may appear and all may become one in Thy Cause and Kingdom. Verily, Thou art the Generous. Verily, Thou art the Mighty, the Spiritual. Thou art the Merciful, the Clement.

(To the children in the Sunday School)

8   I am glad to see these bright, radiant children. God willing, all of them may realize the hopes and aspirations of their parents.

9   Praise be to God! I see before me these beautiful children of the Kingdom. Their hearts are pure, their faces are shining. They shall soon become the sons and daughters of the Kingdom. Thanks be to God! They are seeking to acquire virtues and will

be the cause of the attainment of the excellences of humanity. This is the cause of oneness in the Kingdom of God. Praise be to God! They have kind and revered teachers who train and educate them well and who long for confirmation in order that, God willing, like tender plants in the garden of God they may be refreshed by the downpour of the clouds of mercy, grow and become verdant. In the utmost perfection and delicacy may they at last bring forth fruit.

I supplicate God that these children may be reared under His 10 protection and that they may be nourished by His favor and grace until all, like beautiful flowers in the garden of human hopes and aspirations, shall blossom and become redolent of fragrance.

O God! Educate these children. These children are the plants 11 of Thine orchard, the flowers of Thy meadow, the roses of Thy garden. Let Thy rain fall upon them; let the Sun of Reality shine upon them with Thy love. Let Thy breeze refresh them in order that they may be trained, grow and develop, and appear in the utmost beauty. Thou art the Giver. Thou art the Compassionate.

7

16 June 1912

Talk at Home of Mr. and Mrs. Howard MacNutt
935 Eastern Parkway, Brooklyn, New York

NOTES BY ESTHER FOSTER

THIS is a splendid gathering, a meeting of the maidservants of 1 the Merciful and the beloved of God. Whenever such gatherings have taken place in this world, the results have been very great.

They have exerted an influence upon the world of hearts and minds. Wherever a lamp is lighted in the night, naturally people are attracted and gather around it. When you see such an assemblage as this, you may know that a light is illumining the darkness. There are lamps the light of which is limited. There are lamps the light of which is unlimited. There are lamps which illumine small places and lamps which illumine the horizons. The lamp of the guidance of God, wherever lighted, has shed its radiance throughout the East and the West. Praise be to God! It has been lighted in this country; day by day its radiance is becoming more resplendent and its effulgence more widespread. This is not known now, but later on its traces will become evident. Consider the days of Christ: how the light of guidance brightened twelve hearts. How limited it seemed, but how expansive it became afterward and illumined the world! You are not a large body of people, but because the lamp of guidance has been lighted in your hearts, the effects will be wonderful in the years to come. It is evident and manifest that the world will be illumined by this light; therefore, you must thank God that—praise be to God!—through His grace and favor the lamp of the most great guidance has been ignited in your hearts, and He has summoned you to His Kingdom. He has caused the call of the Supreme Concourse to reach your ears. The doors of heaven have been opened unto you. The Sun of Reality is shining upon you, the cloud of mercy is pouring down, and the breezes of providence are wafting through your souls. Although the bestowal is great and the grace is glorious, yet capacity and readiness are requisite. Without capacity and readiness the divine bounty will not become manifest and evident. No matter how much the cloud may rain, the sun may shine and the breezes blow, the soil that is sterile will give no growth. The ground that is pure and free from thorns and thistles receives and produces through the rain of the cloud of mercy. No matter how much the sun shines, it will have no effect upon the black rock, but in a pure and polished mirror its lights become resplendent. Therefore, we must develop capacity in order that the signs of the mercy of the Lord may be revealed in us. We must endeavor to free the soil of the hearts from useless weeds and sanctify it from the thorns of worthless thoughts in order that the cloud of mercy may bestow its power upon us. The doors of God are open, but we must be ready and fitted to enter. The ocean of divine providence is surging, but we must be able to swim. The bestowals of the Almighty are descending from the heaven of grace, but capacity to receive them is essential. The fountain of divine generosity is gushing forth, but we must have thirst for the living waters. Unless there be thirst, the salutary water will not assuage. Unless the soul hungers, the delicious foods of the heavenly table will not give sustenance. Unless the eyes of perception be opened, the lights of the sun will not be witnessed. Until the nostrils are purified, the fragrance of the divine rose garden will not be inhaled. Unless the heart be filled with longing, the favors of the Lord will not be evident. Unless a perfect melody be sung, the ears of the hearers will not be attracted. Therefore, we must endeavor night and day to purify the hearts from every dross, sanctify the souls from every restriction and become free from the discords of the human world. Then the divine bestowals will become evident in their fullness and glory. If we do not strive and sanctify ourselves from the defects and evil qualities of human nature, we will not partake of the bestowals of God. It is as if the sun is shining in its full glory, but no reflection is forthcoming from hearts that are black as stone. If an ocean of salubrious water is surging and we be not thirsty, what benefit do we receive? If the candle be lighted and we have no eyes, what enjoyment do we obtain from it? If melodious anthems should rise to the heavens and we are bereft of hearing, what enjoyment can we find?

2   Therefore, we must endeavor always, cry, supplicate and invoke the Kingdom of God to grant us full capacity in order that the bestowals of God may become revealed and manifest in us. And as we attain to these heavenly bounties, we shall offer thanks unto the threshold of oneness. Then shall we rejoice in the Lord that in this wonderful century and glorious age, under the shelter of the Kingdom of God we have enjoyed these bestowals and will arise in praise and thanksgiving. Therefore, I first exhort myself and then I entreat you to appreciate this great bestowal, recognize this most great guidance, accept these bounties of the Lord. You must endeavor day and night to become worthy of a generous portion of these gifts and realize full capacity of attainment. Praise be to God! Your hearts are illumined, your faces are turned toward the Kingdom of God. It is my hope that all of these degrees may be reached and these friends attain a station which shall be an example and stimulus for all friends in the world. May the love of God spread from here onward and outward; may the knowledge of God be sent broadcast from this place; may spiritual forces become effective here; may the lights of the Kingdom shine; may intelligent souls be found here so that with all power they may be occupied in the service of God, furthering the oneness of the human world and the cause of the Most Great Peace. May these souls be lighted candles and fruitful trees; may they be pearls of the shells of providence; may they be stars of heaven. This is my supplication to God. This is my request from the Beauty of Abhá: that He may submerge all of you in the ocean of His grace.

(Afterward, speaking of numbers)

3   Such suppositions regarding lucky or unlucky numbers are purely imaginary. The superstition concerning thirteen had its

origin in the fact that Jesus Christ was surrounded by twelve disciples and that Judas Iscariot was the thirteenth member of their gathering. This is the source of the superstition, but it is purely imaginary. Although Judas was outwardly a disciple, in reality he was not. Twelve is the original number of significance and completion. Jacob had twelve sons from whom descended twelve tribes. The disciples of Jesus were twelve; the Imáms of Muḥammad were twelve. The zodiacal signs are twelve; the months of the year are twelve, etc.

The mysteries of the Holy Books have become explained 4 in the manifestation of Bahá'u'lláh. Before He appeared, these mysteries were not understood. Bahá'u'lláh opened and unsealed these mysteries. It was my wish to come here today to have this meeting.

8

16 June 1912

Talk at Central Congregational Church
Hancock Street, Brooklyn, New York

NOTES BY ESTHER FOSTER

THIS is a goodly temple and congregation, for—praise be to 1 God!—this is a house of worship wherein conscientious opinion has free sway. Every religion and every religious aspiration may be freely voiced and expressed here. Just as in the world of politics there is need for free thought, likewise in the world of religion there should be the right of unrestricted individual belief. Consider what a vast difference exists between modern democracy and the old forms of despotism. Under an autocratic government the opinions of men are not free, and development is stifled, whereas in democracy, because thought and speech are not restricted, the greatest progress is witnessed. It is likewise true in the world of religion. When freedom of conscience, liberty of thought and right of speech prevail—that is to say, when every man according to his own idealization may give expression to his beliefs—development and growth are inevitable. Therefore, this is a blessed church because its pulpit is open to every religion, the ideals of which may be set forth with openness and freedom. For this reason I am most grateful to the reverend doctor; I find him indeed a servant of the oneness of humanity.

2   The holy Manifestations Who have been the Sources or Founders of the various religious systems were united and agreed in purpose and teaching. Abraham, Moses, Zoroaster, Buddha, Jesus, Muḥammad, the Báb and Bahá'u'lláh are one in spirit and reality. Moreover, each Prophet fulfilled the promise of the One Who came before Him and, likewise, Each announced the One Who would follow. Consider how Abraham foretold the coming of Moses, and Moses embodied the Abrahamic statement. Moses prophesied the Messianic cycle, and Christ fulfilled the law of Moses. It is evident, therefore, that the Holy Manifestations Who founded the religious systems are united and agreed; there is no differentiation possible in Their mission and teachings; all are reflectors of reality, and all are promulgators of the religion of God. The divine religion is reality, and reality is not multiple; it is one. Therefore, the foundations of the religious systems are one because all proceed from the indivisible reality; but the followers of these systems have disagreed; discord, strife and warfare have arisen among them, for they have forsaken the foundation and held to that which is but imitation and semblance. Inasmuch as imitations differ, enmity and dissension

have resulted. For example, Jesus Christ—may my spirit be a sacrifice unto Him!—laid the foundation of eternal reality, but after His departure many sects and divisions appeared in Christianity. What was the cause of this? There is no doubt that they originated in dogmatic imitations, for the foundations of Christ were reality itself, in which no divergence exists. When imitations appeared, sects and denominations were formed.

If Christians of all denominations and divisions should in- 3 vestigate reality, the foundations of Christ will unite them. No enmity or hatred will remain, for they will all be under the one guidance of reality itself. Likewise, in the wider field if all the existing religious systems will turn away from ancestral imitations and investigate reality, seeking the real meanings of the Holy Books, they will unite and agree upon the same foundation, reality itself. As long as they follow counterfeit doctrines or imitations instead of reality, animosity and discord will exist and increase. Let me illustrate this. Moses and the prophets of Israel announced the advent of the Messiah but expressed it in the language of symbols. When Christ appeared, the Jews rejected Him, although they were expecting His manifestation and in their temples and synagogues were crying and lamenting, saying, "O God, hasten the coming of the Messiah!" Why did they deny Him when He announced Himself? Because they had followed ancestral forms and interpretations and were blind to the reality of Christ. They had not perceived the inner significances of the Holy Bible. They voiced their objections, saying, "We are expecting Christ, but His coming is conditioned upon certain fulfillments and prophetic announcements. Among the signs of His appearance is one that He shall come from an unknown place, whereas now this claimant of Messiahship has come from Nazareth. We know his home, and we are acquainted with his mother.

4   "Second, one of the signs or Messianic conditions is that His scepter would be an iron rod, and this Christ has not even a wooden staff.

5   "Third, He was to be seated upon the throne of David, whereas this Messianic king is in the utmost state of poverty and has not even a mat.

6   "Fourth, He was to conquer the East and the West. This person has not even conquered a village. How can he be the Messiah?

7   "Fifth, He was to promulgate the laws of the Bible. This one has not only failed to promulgate the laws of the Bible, but he has broken the law of the sabbath.

8   "Sixth, the Messiah was to gather together all the Jews who were scattered in Palestine and restore them to honor and prestige, but this one has degraded the Jews instead of uplifting them.

9   "Seventh, during His sovereignty even the animals were to enjoy blessings and comfort, for according to the prophetic texts, He should establish peace to such a universal extent that the eagle and quail would live together, the lion and deer would feed in the same meadow, the wolf and lamb would lie down in the same pasture. In the human kingdom warfare was to cease entirely; spears would be turned into pruning hooks and swords into plowshares. Now we see in the day of this would-be Messiah such injustice prevails that even he himself is sacrificed. How could he be the promised Christ?"

10   And so they spoke infamous words regarding Him.

11   Now inasmuch as the Jews were submerged in the sea of ancestral imitations, they could not comprehend the meaning of these prophecies. All the words of the prophets were fulfilled, but because the Jews held tenaciously to hereditary interpretations, they did not understand the inner meanings of the Holy Bible;

therefore, they denied Jesus Christ, the Messiah. The purpose of the prophetic words was not the outward or literal meaning, but the inner symbolical significance. For example, it was announced that the Messiah was to come from an unknown place. This did not refer to the birthplace of the physical body of Jesus. It has reference to the reality of the Christ—that is to say, the Christ reality was to appear from the invisible realm—for the divine reality of Christ is holy and sanctified above place.

His sword was to be a sword of iron. This signified His tongue 12 which should separate the true from the false and by which great sword of attack He would conquer the kingdoms of hearts. He did not conquer by the physical power of an iron rod; He conquered the East and the West by the sword of His utterance.

He was seated upon the throne of David, but His sovereignty 13 was neither a Napoleonic sovereignty nor the vanishing dominion of a Pharaoh. The Christ Kingdom was everlasting, eternal in the heaven of the divine Will.

By His promulgating the laws of the Bible the reality of the 14 law of Moses was meant. The Sinaitic law is the foundation of the reality of Christianity. Christ promulgated it and gave it higher, spiritual expression.

He conquered and subdued the East and West. His conquest 15 was effected through the breaths of the Holy Spirit, which eliminated all boundaries and shone from all horizons.

In His day, according to prophecy, the wolf and the lamb 16 were to drink from the same fountain. This was realized in Christ. The fountain referred to was the Gospel, from which the water of life gushes forth. The wolf and lamb are opposed and divergent races symbolized by these animals. Their meeting and association were impossible, but having become believers in Jesus Christ those who were formerly as wolves and lambs became united through the words of the Gospel.

17   The purport is that all the meanings of the prophecies were fulfilled, but because the Jews were captives of ancestral imitations and did not perceive the reality of the meanings of these words, they denied Christ; nay, they even went so far as to crucify Him. Consider how harmful is imitation. These were interpretations handed down from fathers and ancestors, and because the Jews held fast to them, they were deprived.

18   It is evident, then, that we must forsake all such imitations and beliefs so that we may not commit this error. We must investigate reality, lay aside selfish notions and banish hearsay from our minds. The Jews consider Christ the enemy of Moses, whereas, on the contrary, Christ promoted the Word of Moses. He spread the name of Moses throughout the Orient and Occident. He promulgated the teachings of Moses. Had it not been for Christ, you would not have heard the name of Moses; and unless the manifestation of Messiah-ship had appeared in Christ, we would not have received the Old Testament.

19   The truth is that Christ fulfilled the Mosaic law and in every way upheld Moses; but the Jews, blinded by imitations and prejudices, considered Him the enemy of Moses.

20   Among the great religious systems of the world is Islám. About three hundred million people acknowledge it. For more than a thousand years there has been enmity and strife between Muslims and Christians, owing to misunderstanding and spiritual blindness. If prejudices and imitations were abandoned, there would be no enmity whatever between them, and these hundreds of millions of antagonistic religionists would adorn the world of humanity by their unity.

21   I wish now to call your attention to a most important point. All Islám considers the Qur'án the Word of God. In this sacred Book there are explicit texts which are not traditional, stating

that Christ was the Word of God, that He was the Spirit of God, that Jesus Christ came into this world through the quickening breaths of the Holy Spirit and that Mary, His mother, was holy and sanctified. In the Qur'án a whole chapter is devoted to the story of Jesus. It records that in the time of His youth He worshiped God in the temple at Jerusalem, that manna descended from heaven for His sustenance and that He uttered words immediately after His birth. In brief, in the Qur'án there is eulogy and commendation of Christ such as you do not find in the Gospel. The Gospel does not record that the child Jesus spoke at birth or that God caused sustenance to descend from heaven for Him, but in the Qur'án it is repeatedly stated that God sent down manna day by day as food for Him. Furthermore, it is significant and convincing that when Muḥammad proclaimed His work and mission, His first objection to His own followers was, "Why have you not believed on Jesus Christ? Why have you not accepted the Gospel? Why have you not believed in Moses? Why have you not followed the precepts of the Old Testament? Why have you not understood the prophets of Israel? Why have you not believed in the disciples of Christ? The first duty incumbent upon ye, O Arabians, is to accept and believe in these. You must consider Moses as a Prophet. You must accept Jesus Christ as the Word of God. You must know the Old and the New Testaments as the Word of God. You must believe in Jesus Christ as the product of the Holy Spirit." His people answered, "O Muḥammad! We will become believers although our fathers and ancestors were not believers, and we are proud of them. Tell us what is going to become of them?" Muḥammad replied, "I declare unto you that they occupy the lowest stratum of hell because they did not believe in Moses and Christ and because they did not accept the Bible; and although they are my own ancestors, yet they are in despair in hell." This is an explicit text of the Qur'án; it is not a story or tradition but from the Qur'án itself, which is in the hands of the people. Therefore, it is evident that ignorance and misunderstanding have caused so much warfare and strife between Christians and Muslims. If both should investigate the underlying truth of their religious beliefs, the outcome would be unity and agreement; strife and bitterness would pass away forever and the world of humanity find peace and composure. Consider that there are two hundred and fifty million Christians and three hundred million Muslims. How much blood has flowed in their wars; how many nations have been destroyed; how many children have been made fatherless; how many fathers and mothers have mourned the loss of children and dear ones! All this has been due to prejudice, misunderstanding and imitations of ancestral beliefs without investigation of reality. If the Holy Books were rightly understood, none of this discord and distress would have existed, but love and fellowship would have prevailed instead. This is true with all the other religions as well. The conditions I have named will apply equally to all. The essential purpose of the religion of God is to establish unity among mankind. The divine Manifestations were Founders of the means of fellowship and love. They did not come to create discord, strife and hatred in the world. The religion of God is the cause of love, but if it is made to be the source of enmity and bloodshed, surely its absence is preferable to its existence; for then it becomes satanic, detrimental and an obstacle to the human world.

22   In the Orient the various peoples and nations were in a state of antagonism and strife, manifesting the utmost enmity and hatred toward each other. Darkness encompassed the world of mankind. At such a time as this Bahá'u'lláh appeared. He removed all the imitations and prejudices which had caused separation and misunderstanding and laid the foundation of the

one religion of God. When this was accomplished, Muslims, Christians, Jews, Zoroastrians, Buddhists all were united in actual fellowship and love. The souls who followed Bahá'u'lláh from every nation have become as one family living in agreement and accord, willing to sacrifice life for each other. The Muslim will give his life for the Christian, the Christian for the Jew and all of them for the Zoroastrian. They live together in love, fellowship and unity. They have attained to the condition of rebirth in the Spirit of God. They have become revivified and regenerated through the breaths of the Holy Spirit. Praise be to God! This light has come forth from the East, and eventually there shall be no discord or enmity in the Orient. Through the power of Bahá'u'lláh all will be united. He upraised this standard of the oneness of humanity in prison. When subjected to banishment by two kings, while a refugee from enemies of all nations and during the days of His long imprisonment He wrote to the kings and rulers of the world in words of wonderful eloquence, arraigning them severely and summoning them to the divine standard of unity and justice. He exhorted them to peace and international agreement, making it incumbent upon them to establish a board of international arbitration—that from all nations and governments of the world there should be delegates selected for a congress of nations which should constitute a universal arbitral court of justice to settle international disputes. He wrote to Victoria, Queen of Great Britain, the Czar of Russia, the Emperor of Germany, Napoleon III of France and others, inviting them to world unity and peace. Through a heavenly power He was enabled to promulgate these ideals in the Orient. Kings could not withstand Him. They endeavored to extinguish His light but served only to increase its intensity and illumination. While in prison He stood against the S͟háh of Persia and Sulṭán of Turkey and promulgated His teachings until He firmly established the banner of truth and the oneness of humankind. I was a prisoner with Him for forty years until the Young Turks of the Committee of Union and Progress overthrew the despotism of 'Abdu'l-Ḥamíd, dethroned him and proclaimed liberty. This committee set me free from tyranny and oppression; otherwise, I should have been in prison until the days of my life were ended. The purport is this: that Bahá'u'lláh in prison was able to proclaim and establish the foundations of peace although two despotic kings were His enemies and oppressors. The King of Persia, Náṣiri'd-Dín Sháh, had killed twenty thousand Bahá'ís, martyrs who in absolute severance and complete willingness offered their lives joyfully for their faith. These two powerful and tyrannical kings could not withstand a prisoner; this Prisoner upheld the standard of humanity and brought the people of the Orient into agreement and unity. Today in the East, only those who have not followed Bahá'u'lláh are in opposition and enmity. The people of the nations who have accepted Him as the standard of divine guidance enjoy a condition of actual fellowship and love. If you should attend a meeting in the East, you could not distinguish between Christian and Muslim; you would not know which was Jew, Zoroastrian or Buddhist, so completely have they become fraternized and their religious differences been leveled. They associate in the utmost love and spiritual fragrance as if they belonged to one family, as if they were one people.

9

17 June 1912

Talk at 309 West Seventy-eighth Street, New York

NOTES BY EMMA C. MELICK

WE should all visit the sick. When they are in sorrow and   1
suffering, it is a real help and benefit to have a friend come.
Happiness is a great healer to those who are ill. In the East it is
the custom to call upon the patient often and meet him individually. The people in the East show the utmost kindness and
compassion to the sick and suffering. This has greater effect than
the remedy itself. You must always have this thought of love and
affection when you visit the ailing and afflicted.

The world of humanity may be likened to the individual   2
man himself; it has its illness and ailments. A patient must be
diagnosed by a skillful physician. The Prophets of God are the
real Physicians. In whatever age or time They appear They prescribe for human conditions. They know the sicknesses; They
discover the hidden sources of disease and indicate the necessary remedy. Whosoever is healed by that remedy finds eternal
health. For instance, in the day of Jesus Christ the world of
humanity was afflicted with various ailments. Jesus Christ was
the real Physician. He appeared, recognized the symptoms and
prescribed the real remedy. What was that remedy? It was His
revealed teaching especially applicable to that age. Later on many
new ailments and disorders appeared in the body politic. The
world became sick; other severe maladies appeared, especially
in the peninsula of Arabia. God manifested Muḥammad there.
He came and prescribed for the conditions so that the Arabs
became healthy, strong and virile in that time.

3   In this present age the world of humanity is afflicted with severe sicknesses and grave disorders which threaten death. Therefore, Bahá'u'lláh has appeared. He is the real Physician, bringing divine remedy and healing to the world of man. He has brought teachings for all ailments—the Hidden Words, Ishráqát, Ṭarázát, Tajallíyát, Words of Paradise, Glad Tidings, etc. These Holy Words and teachings are the remedy for the body politic, the divine prescription and real cure for the disorders which afflict the world. Therefore, we must accept and partake of this healing remedy in order that complete recovery may be assured. Every soul who lives according to the teachings of Bahá'u'lláh is free from the ailments and indispositions which prevail throughout the world of humanity; otherwise, selfish disorders, intellectual maladies, spiritual sicknesses, imperfections and vices will surround him, and he will not receive the life-giving bounties of God.

4   Bahá'u'lláh is the real Physician. He has diagnosed human conditions and indicated the necessary treatment. The essential principles of His healing remedies are the knowledge and love of God, severance from all else save God, turning our faces in sincerity toward the Kingdom of God, implicit faith, firmness and fidelity, loving-kindness toward all creatures and the acquisition of the divine virtues indicated for the human world. These are the fundamental principles of progress, civilization, international peace and the unity of mankind. These are the essentials of Bahá'u'lláh's teachings, the secret of everlasting health, the remedy and healing for man.

5   It is my hope that you may assist in healing the sick body of the world through these teachings so that eternal radiance may illumine all the nations of mankind.

10

18 June 1912

Talk at 309 West Seventy-eighth Street, New York

NOTES BY EMMA C. MELICK

No matter how much the world of humanity advances in mate- 1
rial civilization, it is nevertheless in need of the spiritual development mentioned in the Gospel. The virtues of the material world
are limited, whereas divine virtues are unlimited. Inasmuch as
material virtues are limited, man's need of the perfections of
the divine world is unlimited.

Throughout human history we find that although the very 2
apex of human virtues has been reached at various times, yet
they were limited, whereas divine attainments have ever been
unbounded and infinite. The limited is ever in need of the unlimited. The material must be correlated with the spiritual. The
material may be likened to the body, but divine virtues are the
breathings of the Holy Spirit itself. The body without spirit is
not capable of real accomplishment. Although it may be in the
utmost condition of beauty and excellence, it is, nevertheless,
in need of the spirit. The chimney of the lamp, no matter how
polished and perfect it be, is in need of the light. Without the
light, the lamp or candle is not illuminating. Without the spirit,
the body is not productive. The teacher of material principles
is limited. The philosophers who claimed to be the educators
of mankind were at most only able to train themselves. If they
educated others, it was within a restricted circle; they failed
to bestow general education and development. This has been
conferred upon humanity by the power of the Holy Spirit.

3   For example, Christ educated and developed mankind universally. He rescued nations and peoples from the bondage of superstition and idolatry. He summoned them all to the knowledge of the oneness of God. They were dark, they became illumined; they were material, they became spiritual; earthly they were, they became heavenly. He enlightened the world of morality. This general, universal development is not possible through the power of philosophy. It is only attainable through the pervading influence of the Holy Spirit. Therefore, no matter how far the world of humanity advances, it fails to attain the highest degree unless quickened by the education and divine bestowals of the Holy Spirit. This ensures human progress and prosperity.

4   Therefore, I exhort you to be devoted to your spiritual development. Just as you have striven along material lines and have attained to high degrees of worldly advancement, may you likewise become strengthened and proficient in the knowledge of God. May divine susceptibilities be increased and awakened; may your devotion to the heavenly Kingdom become intense. May you be the recipients of the impulses of the Holy Spirit, be assisted in the world of morality and attain ideal power so that the sublimity of the world of mankind may become apparent in you. Thus may you attain the highest happiness, the eternal life, the everlasting glory, the second birth, and become manifestations of the bestowals of God.

11

20 June 1912

Talk at 309 West Seventy-eighth Street, New York

NOTES BY HOWARD MACNUTT

I AM about to leave the city for a few days rest at Montclair. When 1
I return, it is my wish to give a large feast of unity. A place for it
has not yet been found. It must be outdoors under the trees, in
some location away from city noise—like a Persian garden. The
food will be Persian food. When the place is arranged, all will
be informed, and we will have a general meeting in which hearts
will be bound together, spirits blended and a new foundation
for unity established. All the friends will come. They will be my
guests. They will be as the parts and members of one body. The
spirit of life manifest in that body will be one spirit. The foundation of that temple of unity will be one foundation. Each will
be a stone in that foundation, solid and interdependent. Each
will be as a leaf, blossom or fruit upon one tree. For the sake of
fellowship and unity I desire this feast and spiritual gathering.

Whatsoever is conducive to unity is merciful and from the 2
divine bounty itself. Every universal affair is divine. Everything
which conduces to separation and estrangement is satanic
because it emanates from the purposes of self. Consider how
clearly it is shown in creation that the cause of existence is unity
and cohesion and the cause of nonexistence is separation and
dissension. By a divine power of creation the elements assemble
together in affinity, and the result is a composite being. Certain
of these elements have united, and man has come into existence. Certain other combinations produce plants and animals.

289

Therefore, this affinity of the inanimate elements is the cause of life and being. Through their commingling, therefore, human affinity, love and fellowship are made possible. If the elements were not assembled together in affinity to produce the body of man, the higher intelligent forces could not be manifest in the body. But when these elements separate, when their affinity and cohesion are overcome, death and dissolution of the body they have built inevitably follow. Therefore, affinity and unity among even these material elements mean life in the body of man, and their discord and disagreement mean death. Throughout all creation, in all the kingdoms, this law is written: that love and affinity are the cause of life, and discord and separation are the cause of death.

3   Consider the bodies of all the natural organisms. Certain elements have gathered and combine in chemical affinity. The tree, the man, the fish are due to this attraction and cohesion which have brought the elements together. A composition or composite being has resulted. The outcome of certain atomic grouping, for instance, is a mirror, table or clock because a cohesive power has magnetized and bound these atoms together. When that attracting power is withdrawn, dissolution and disintegration follow; no mirror, table or clock remain—no trace, no existence. Therefore, commingling of the atoms brings forth a reality, while dispersion or dissemination of them is equivalent to nonexistence.

4   Study the law of affinity among the domestic animals. They manifest fellowship, they live in flocks and herds; the love of association is evident among them. Among birds we see evidences of instinctive fellowship and love. But the ferocious animals and birds of prey are just the reverse of the domestic. Sheep, cows and horses graze together in concord and agreement, but ferocious animals are never seen associating in love and fellow-

ship. Each lives solitary and alone or with a single mate. When they see each other, they manifest the utmost ferocity. Dogs pounce upon dogs; wolves, tigers, lions rage, snarl and fight to the death. Their ferocity is instinctive. There is a creative reason for it. Birds of prey, like eagles and hawks, live solitary and build their nests apart, but doves fly in flocks and nest in the same branches. When an eagle meets another eagle, there is a furious battle. The meeting of two doves is a peace meeting. Therefore, it is evident that these blessed characteristics as well as the reverse are found among the creatures of a lower kingdom.

The great mass of humanity does not exercise real love and 5 fellowship. The elect of humanity are those who live together in love and unity. They are preferable before God because the divine attributes are already manifest in them. The supreme love and unity is witnessed in the divine Manifestations. Among Them unity is indissoluble, changeless, eternal and everlasting. Each One is expressive and representative of all. If we deny One of the Manifestations of God, we deny all. To inflict persecution upon One is to persecute the Others. In all degrees of existence each One praises and sanctifies the Others. Each of Them holds to the solidarity of mankind and promotes the unity of human hearts. Next to the divine Manifestations come the believers whose characteristics are agreement, fellowship and love. The Bahá'í friends in Persia attained such a brotherhood and love that it really became a hindrance in the conduct of material affairs. Each one into whatever house of the friends he went considered himself the owner of the house, so to speak. There was no duality but complete mutuality of interests and love. The visiting friend would have no hesitation in opening the provision box and taking out enough food for his needs. They wore each other's clothes as their own when necessary. If in need of a hat or cloak, they would take and use it. The owner of the clothing would be thankful and grateful that the garment had gone. When he returned home, he would perhaps be told, "So and so was here and took away your coat." He would reply, "Praise be to God! I am so grateful to him. Praise be to God! I am so thankful I have been given this opportunity of showing my love for him." To such an extreme degree this love and fellowship expressed itself that Bahá'u'lláh commanded that no one should take possession of another's belongings unless presented with them. The intention is to show to what an extent unity and love prevailed among the Bahá'í friends in the East.

6   I hope that this same degree and intensity of love may become manifest and apparent here; that the spirit of God shall so penetrate your hearts that each one of the beloved of God shall be considered as all; that each one may become a cause of unity and center of accord and all mankind be bound together in real fellowship and love.

Talks 'Abdu'l-Bahá Delivered in Montclair and West Englewood, New Jersey

23 June 1912

Talk at Montclair, New Jersey

NOTES BY FRANK E. OSBORNE

'Abdu'l-Bahá: You are always smiling. 1

Mr. Osborne: Surely our faces should reflect happiness in this 2
presence.

'Abdu'l-Bahá: Yes! This is the day of Bahá'u'lláh, the age of 3
the Blessed Perfection, the cycle of the Greatest Name. If you
do not smile now, for what time will you await and what greater
happiness could you expect? This is the springtime of manifestation. The vernal shower has descended from the cloud of divine
mercy; the life-giving breeze of the Holy Spirit is wafting the
perfume of blossoms. From field and meadow rises a fragrant
breath of thanksgiving like pure incense ascending to the throne
of God. The world has become a new world; souls are quickened,
spirits renewed, refreshed. Truly it is a time for happiness.

(To people coming in)

Welcome! Welcome! You are very welcome! 4

(The church bells begin to ring)

I was not feeling very well this morning, or I would have gone 5
to church. Everywhere we hear the call of the spiritual world; in

everything we behold the works of God. The church bells are pealing in memory of Jesus Christ although more than nineteen hundred years have passed since He lived upon the earth. This is through the power of the spirit. No material power could do this. Yet people in their blindness deny Christ, seeking to perpetuate their names in worldly deeds. Everyone wishes to be remembered. Through earthly and material accomplishments one will hardly be remembered nine years, while the memory and glory of Christ continue after nineteen hundred have passed. For His name is eternal and His glory everlasting. Therefore, man should hear with attentive ear the call of the spiritual world, seeking first the Kingdom of God and its perfections. This is eternal life; this is everlasting remembrance.

6   How great the difference between the glory of Christ and the glory of an earthly conqueror! It is related by historians that Napoleon Bonaparte I embarked secretly by night from Egypt. His destination was France. During his campaign in Palestine revolution had broken out and grave difficulties had arisen in the home government. Christian worship had been forbidden by the revolutionists. The priests of Christianity had fled in terror. France had become atheistic; anarchy prevailed. The ship sailed out into a night brilliant with the light of the moon. Napoleon was pacing up and down the deck. His officers were sitting together, talking. One of them spoke of the similarity between Bonaparte and Christ. Napoleon stopped and said grimly, "Do you think I am going back to France to establish religion?"

7   Jesus Christ established the religion of God through love. His sovereignty is everlasting. Napoleon overthrew governments in war and bloodshed. His dominion passed away; he himself was dethroned. Bonaparte destroyed human life; Christ was a Savior. Bonaparte controlled the physical bodies of men; Christ was a conqueror of human hearts. None of the Prophets of God were

famous men, but They were unique in spiritual power. Love is the eternal sovereignty. Love is the divine power. By it all the kings of earth are overthrown and conquered. What evidence of this could be greater than the accomplishment of Bahá'u'lláh? He appeared in the East and was exiled. He was sent to the prison of 'Akká in Palestine. Two powerful despotic kings arose against Him. During His exile and imprisonment He wrote Tablets of authority to the kings and rulers of the world, announcing His spiritual sovereignty, establishing the religion of God, upraising the heavenly banners of the Cause of God. One of these Tablets was sent to Napoleon III, Emperor of France. He received it with contempt and cast it behind his back. Bahá'u'lláh addressed a second Tablet to him, containing these words, "Hadst thou been sincere in thy words, thou wouldst have not cast behind thy back the Book of God, when it was sent unto thee. . . . We have proved thee through it, and found thee other than that which thou didst profess. Arise, and make amends for that which escaped thee. Erelong the world and all that thou possessest will perish, and the kingdom will remain unto God. . . . For what thou hast done, thy kingdom shall be thrown into confusion, and thine empire shall pass from thine hands, as a punishment for that which thou hast wrought. Then wilt thou know how thou hast plainly erred. . . . Thy pomp . . . shall soon pass away, unless thou holdest fast by this firm Cord. We see abasement hastening after thee. . . ." All this happened just as announced by Bahá'u'lláh. Napoleon III was dethroned and exiled. His empire passed away and became nonexistent while the dominion and sovereignty of Bahá'u'lláh, the Prisoner, has become eternal through the confirmation of God. This is as evident as the light of the sun at midday except to those who are spiritually blind. If we are afflicted with a cold, we cannot inhale the delicate fragrances emanating from the rose garden of the divine Kingdom.

8   In brief, the nations of the world are becoming united under the sovereignty of the divine Kingdom. The East and the West are embracing here in love and affection today. This is not a commercial or political unity, but unity through the love of God. We have crossed the sea to spread that love in America, to announce the call of the Kingdom, to establish the spiritual foundations of international peace. Although men may arise against the Kingdom, the dominion and sovereignty of God will be set up. It is an eternal Kingdom, a divine sovereignty. In His day Christ was called Satan, Beelzebub, but hear the bells now ringing for Him! He was the Word of God and not Satan. They mocked Him, led Him through the city upon a donkey, crowned Him with thorns, spat upon His blessed face and crucified Him, but He is now with God and in God because He was the Word and not Satan. Fifty years ago no one would touch the Christian Bible in Persia. Bahá'u'lláh came and asked, "Why?" They said, "It is not the Word of God." He said, "You must read it with understanding of its meanings, not as those who merely recite its words." Now Bahá'ís all over the East read the Bible and understand its spiritual teaching. Bahá'u'lláh spread the Cause of Christ and opened the book of the Christians and Jews. He removed the barriers of names. He proved that all the divine Prophets taught the same reality and that to deny One is to deny the Others, for all are in perfect oneness with God.

9   In London some of the Christians said we were deniers of Christ. We say Christ is the Word of God. We are gathered here this morning for His mention. The bells have called us together in love and unity. This house is the temple of God. All are welcome! Very welcome!

10   *Question:* How shall we determine the truth or error of certain biblical interpretation, as, for instance, the higher criticism and other present-day Christian teachings?

'Abdu'l-Bahá: Your question is an abstruse and important one. Complete answer to it would require a long time. I will reply to it briefly. The only true Explainer of the Book of God is the Holy Spirit, for no two minds are alike, no two can comprehend alike, no two can speak alike. That is to say, from the mere human standpoint of interpretation there could be neither truth nor agreement. 11

Question: Do you approve of the new thought in which the control of mind over matter is the central principle? 12

'Abdu'l-Bahá: Philosophy develops the mind. Christ and the Word of God are revealed through the Spirit. Plato says, "The mental conclusions are so and so." Christ says, "Be led of the Spirit." 13

Question: Should children be allowed to read the higher criticism? 14

'Abdu'l-Bahá: They should first be taught the reality of religion as a foundation. For instance, in the Catholic Church the child is taught that through some act of the priest the bread and wine of the sacrament become the flesh and blood of Jesus Christ. The mind cannot accept this. The child must be taught that this transformation is symbolical of the truth that Christ is the food from heaven, the eating of which produces eternal life. The Jews had memorized the Bible but failed to grasp its meanings. If they had understood the spiritual significances of the scriptures, they would have been the first believers in Christ. You are among the first believers in this country. You are the children of the Kingdom. Bahá'u'lláh has taught you the reality of religion. There are many of the Bahá'í friends in Persia whom we do not know, but we know you here in America. Turn your faces to the Sun of Reality. That Sun has always risen in the East. Find the answer to your questions in your heart. Be as little children. Until the soil is prepared, it cannot receive the benefit of planting. 15

2

29 June 1912

Talk at Unity Feast, Outdoors
West Englewood, New Jersey

NOTES BY ESTHER FOSTER

1   THIS is a delightful gathering; you have come here with sincere intentions, and the purpose of all present is the attainment of the virtues of God. The motive is attraction to the divine Kingdom. Since the desire of all is unity and agreement, it is certain that this meeting will be productive of great results. It will be the cause of attracting a new bounty, for we are turning to the Kingdom of Abhá, seeking the infinite bestowals of the Lord. This is a new Day, and this hour is a new Hour in which we have come together. Surely the Sun of Reality with its full effulgence will illumine us, and the darkness of disagreements will disappear. The utmost love and unity will result; the favors of God will encompass us; the pathway of the Kingdom will be made easy. Like candles these souls will become ignited and made radiant through the lights of supreme guidance. Such gatherings as this have no equal or likeness in the world of mankind, where people are drawn together by physical motives or in furtherance of material interests, for this meeting is a prototype of that inner and complete spiritual association in the eternal world of being.

2   True Bahá'í meetings are the mirrors of the Kingdom wherein images of the Supreme Concourse are reflected. In them the lights of the most great guidance are visible. They voice the summons of the heavenly Kingdom and echo the call of the

298

angelic hosts to every listening ear. The efficacy of such meetings as these is permanent throughout the ages. This assembly
has a name and significance which will last forever. Hundreds of
thousands of meetings shall be held to commemorate this occasion, and the very words I speak to you today shall be repeated
in them for ages to come. Therefore, be ye rejoiced, for ye are
sheltered beneath the providence of God. Be happy and joyous
because the bestowals of God are intended for you and the life
of the Holy Spirit is breathing upon you.

Rejoice, for the heavenly table is prepared for you. 3

Rejoice, for the angels of heaven are your assistants and helpers. 4

Rejoice, for the glance of the Blessed Beauty, Bahá'u'lláh, is 5
directed upon you.

Rejoice, for Bahá'u'lláh is your Protector. 6

Rejoice, for the everlasting glory is destined for you. 7

Rejoice, for the eternal life is awaiting you. 8

How many blessed souls have longed for this radiant century, 9
their utmost hopes and desires centered upon the happiness and
joy of one such day as this. Many the nights they passed sleepless and lamenting until the very morn in longing anticipation
of this age, yearning to realize even an hour of this time. God
has favored you in this century and has specialized you for the
realization of its blessings. Therefore, you must praise and thank
God with heart and soul in appreciation of this great opportunity
and the attainment of this infinite bestowal—that such doors
have been opened before your faces, that such abundance is
pouring down from the cloud of mercy and that these refreshing breezes from the paradise of Abhá are resuscitating you. You
must become of one heart, one spirit and one susceptibility. May
you become as the waves of one sea, stars of the same heaven,
fruits adorning the same tree, roses of one garden in order that
through you the oneness of humanity may establish its temple

in the world of mankind, for you are the ones who are called to uplift the cause of unity among the nations of the earth.

10   First, you must become united and agreed among yourselves. You must be exceedingly kind and loving toward each other, willing to forfeit life in the pathway of another's happiness. You must be ready to sacrifice your possessions in another's behalf. The rich among you must show compassion toward the poor, and the well-to-do must look after those in distress. In Persia the friends offer their lives for each other, striving to assist and advance the interests and welfare of all the rest. They live in a perfect state of unity and agreement. Like the Persian friends you must be perfectly agreed and united to the extent and limit of sacrificing life. Your utmost desire must be to confer happiness upon each other. Each one must be the servant of the others, thoughtful of their comfort and welfare. In the path of God one must forget himself entirely. He must not consider his own pleasure but seek the pleasure of others. He must not desire glory nor gifts of bounty for himself but seek these gifts and blessings for his brothers and sisters. It is my hope that you may become like this, that you may attain to the supreme bestowal and be imbued with such spiritual qualities as to forget yourselves entirely and with heart and soul offer yourselves as sacrifices for the Blessed Perfection. You should have neither will nor desire of your own but seek everything for the beloved of God and live together in complete love and fellowship. May the favors of Bahá'u'lláh surround you from all directions. This is the greatest bestowal and supreme bounty. These are the infinite favors of God.

Talks 'Abdu'l-Bahá Delivered in New York

1 July 1912

Talk at 309 West Seventy-eighth Street, New York

NOTES BY HOWARD MACNUTT

WHAT could be better before God than thinking of the poor?   1
For the poor are beloved by our heavenly Father. When Christ
came upon the earth, those who believed in Him and followed
Him were the poor and lowly, showing that the poor were near
to God. When a rich man believes and follows the Manifestation of God, it is a proof that his wealth is not an obstacle and
does not prevent him from attaining the pathway of salvation.
After he has been tested and tried, it will be seen whether his
possessions are a hindrance in his religious life. But the poor
are especially beloved of God. Their lives are full of difficulties,
their trials continual, their hopes are in God alone. Therefore,
you must assist the poor as much as possible, even by sacrifice
of yourself. No deed of man is greater before God than helping the poor. Spiritual conditions are not dependent upon the
possession of worldly treasures or the absence of them. When
one is physically destitute, spiritual thoughts are more likely.
Poverty is a stimulus toward God. Each one of you must have
great consideration for the poor and render them assistance.
Organize in an effort to help them and prevent increase of
poverty. The greatest means for prevention is that whereby the
laws of the community will be so framed and enacted that it will
not be possible for a few to be millionaires and many destitute.
One of Bahá'u'lláh's teachings is the adjustment of means of

livelihood in human society. Under this adjustment there can be no extremes in human conditions as regards wealth and sustenance. For the community needs financier, farmer, merchant and laborer just as an army must be composed of commander, officers and privates. All cannot be commanders; all cannot be officers or privates. Each in his station in the social fabric must be competent—each in his function according to ability but with justness of opportunity for all.

2 Lycurgus, King of Sparta, who lived long before the day of Christ, conceived the idea of absolute equality in government. He proclaimed laws by which all the people of Sparta were classified into certain divisions. Each division had its separate rights and function. First, farmers and tillers of the soil. Second, artisans and merchants. Third, leaders or grandees. Under the laws of Lycurgus, the latter were not required to engage in any labor or vocation, but it was incumbent upon them to defend the country in case of war and invasion. Then he divided Sparta into nine thousand equal parts or provinces, appointing nine thousand leaders or grandees to protect them. In this way the farmers of each province were assured of protection, but each farmer was compelled to pay a tax to support the grandee of that province. The farmers and merchants were not obliged to defend the country. In lieu of labor the grandees received the taxes. Lycurgus, in order to establish this forever as a law, brought nine thousand grandees together, told them he was going upon a long journey and wished this form of government to remain effective until his return. They swore an oath to protect and preserve his law. He then left his kingdom, went into voluntary exile and never came back. No man ever made such a sacrifice to ensure equality among his fellowmen. A few years passed, and the whole system of government he had founded collapsed, although established upon such a just and wise basis.

Difference of capacity in human individuals is fundamental. It is impossible for all to be alike, all to be equal, all to be wise. Bahá'u'lláh has revealed principles and laws which will accomplish the adjustment of varying human capacities. He has said that whatsoever is possible of accomplishment in human government will be effected through these principles. When the laws He has instituted are carried out, there will be no millionaires possible in the community and likewise no extremely poor. This will be effected and regulated by adjusting the different degrees of human capacity. The fundamental basis of the community is agriculture, tillage of the soil. All must be producers. Each person in the community whose need is equal to his individual producing capacity shall be exempt from taxation. But if his income is greater than his needs, he must pay a tax until an adjustment is effected. That is to say, a man's capacity for production and his needs will be equalized and reconciled through taxation. If his production exceeds, he will pay a tax; if his necessities exceed his production, he shall receive an amount sufficient to equalize or adjust. Therefore, taxation will be proportionate to capacity and production, and there will be no poor in the community. 3

Bahá'u'lláh, likewise, commanded the rich to give freely to the poor. In the Kitáb-i-Aqdas it is further written by Him that those who have a certain amount of income must give one-fifth of it to God, the Creator of heaven and earth. 4

2

1 July 1912

Talk at 309 West Seventy-eighth Street, New York

FROM STENOGRAPHIC NOTES

1   I DESIRE to make manifest among the friends in America a new light that they may become a new people, that a new foundation may be established and complete harmony be realized; for the foundation of Bahá'u'lláh is love. When you go to Green Acre, you must have infinite love for each other, each preferring the other before himself. The people must be so attracted to you that they will exclaim, "What happiness exists among you!" and will see in your faces the lights of the Kingdom; then in wonderment they will turn to you and seek the cause of your happiness. You must give the message through action and deed, not alone by word. Word must be conjoined with deed. You must love your friend better than yourself; yes, be willing to sacrifice yourself. The Cause of Bahá'u'lláh has not yet appeared in this country. I desire that you be ready to sacrifice everything for each other, even life itself; then I will know that the Cause of Bahá'u'lláh has been established. I will pray for you that you may become the cause of upraising the lights of God. May everyone point to you and ask, "Why are these people so happy?" I want you to be happy in Green Acre, to laugh, smile and rejoice in order that others may be made happy by you. I will pray for you.

3

5 July 1912

Talk at 309 West Seventy-eighth Street, New York

NOTES BY HOWARD MACNUTT

Question: You have stated that we are living in a universal cycle, 1
the first Manifestation of which was Adam and the universal
Manifestation of which is Bahá'u'lláh. Does this imply that
other universal cycles preceded this one and that all traces of
them have been effaced—cycles in which the ultimate purpose
was the divine spiritualization of man just as it is the creative
intention in this one?

THE divine sovereignty is an ancient sovereignty, not an ac- 2
cidental sovereignty.

If we imagine this world of existence has a beginning, we can 3
say the divine sovereignty is accidental—that is, there was a time
when it did not exist. A king without a kingdom is impossible.
He cannot be without a country, without subjects, without an
army, without dominion, or he would be without kingship. All
these exigencies or requirements of sovereignty must exist for a
king. When they do exist, we can apply the word sovereignty
to him. Otherwise, his sovereignty is imperfect, incomplete.
If none of these conditions exists, sovereignty does not exist.

If we acknowledge that there is a beginning for this world 4
of creation, we acknowledge that the sovereignty of God
is accidental—that is, we admit a time when the reality of
Divinity has been without dominion (lit. "defeated"). The
names and attributes of Divinity are requirements of this

world. The names the Powerful, the Living, the Provider, the Creator require and necessitate the existence of creatures. If there were no creatures, Creator would be meaningless. If there were none to provide for, we could not think of the Provider. If there were no life, the Living would be beyond the power of conception. Therefore, all the names and attributes of God require the existence of objects or creatures upon which they have been bestowed and in which they have become manifest. If there was a time when no creation existed, when there was none to provide for, it would imply a time when there was no existent One, no Trainer, and the attributes and qualities of God would have been meaningless and without significance. Therefore, the requirements of the attributes of God do not admit of cessation or interruption, for the names of God are actually and forever existing and not potential. Because they convey life, they are called Life-giving; because they provide, they are called Bountiful, the Provider; because they create, they are called Creator; because they educate and govern, the name Lord God is applied. That is to say, the divine names emanate from the eternal attributes of Divinity. Therefore, it is proved that the divine names presuppose the existence of objects or beings.

5 How then is a time conceivable when this sovereignty has not been existent? This divine sovereignty is not to be measured by six thousand years. This interminable, illimitable universe is not the result of that measured period. This stupendous laboratory and workshop has not been limited in its production to six thousand revolutions of the earth about the sun. With the slightest reflection man can be assured that this calculation and announcement is childish, especially in view of the fact that it is scientifically proved the terrestrial globe has been the habitation of man long prior to such a limited estimate.

As to the record in the Bible concerning Adam's entering 6
paradise, His eating from the tree and His expulsion through
the temptation of Satan: These are all symbols beneath which
there are wonderful and divine meanings not to be calculated
in years, dates and measurement of time. Likewise, the statement that God created the heaven and the earth in six days
is symbolic. We will not explain this further today. The texts
of the Holy Books are all symbolical, needing authoritative
interpretation.

When man casts even a cursory glance of reflection upon 7
the question of the universe, he discovers it is very ancient. A
Persian philosopher was looking up into the heavens, lost in
wonder. He said, "I have written a book containing seventy
proofs of the accidental appearance of the universe, but I still
find it very ancient."

Bahá'u'lláh says, "The universe hath neither beginning nor 8
ending." He has set aside the elaborate theories and exhaustive
opinions of scientists and material philosophers by the simple
statement, "There is no beginning, no ending." The theologians
and religionists advance plausible proofs that the creation of
the universe dates back six thousand years; the scientists bring
forth indisputable facts and say, "No! These evidences indicate
ten, twenty, fifty thousand years ago," etc. There are endless
discussions pro and con. Bahá'u'lláh sets aside these discussions
by one word and statement. He says, "The divine sovereignty
hath no beginning and no ending." By this announcement and
its demonstration He has established a standard of agreement
among those who reflect upon this question of divine sovereignty; He has brought reconciliation and peace in this war of
opinion and discussion.

Briefly, there were many universal cycles preceding this one 9
in which we are living. They were consummated, completed

and their traces obliterated. The divine and creative purpose in them was the evolution of spiritual man, just as it is in this cycle. The circle of existence is the same circle; it returns. The tree of life has ever borne the same heavenly fruit.

4

5 July 1912

Talk at 309 West Seventy-eighth Street, New York

NOTES BY EMMA C. MELICK AND HOWARD MACNUTT

1 YOU are very welcome, very welcome, all of you! In the divine Holy Books there are unmistakable prophecies giving the glad tidings of a certain Day in which the Promised One of all the Books would appear, a radiant dispensation be established, the banner of the Most Great Peace and conciliation be hoisted and the oneness of the world of humanity proclaimed. Among the various nations and peoples of the world no enmity or hatred should remain. All hearts were to be connected one with another. These things are recorded in the Torah, or Old Testament, in the Gospel, the Qur'án, the Zend-Avesta, and the books of Buddha. In brief, all the Holy Books contain these glad tidings. They announce that after the world is surrounded by darkness, radiance shall appear. For just as the night, when it becomes excessively dark, precedes the dawn of a new day, so likewise when the darkness of religious apathy and heedlessness overtakes the world, when human souls become negligent of God, when materialistic ideas overshadow spirituality, when nations become submerged in the world of matter and forget

God—at such a time as this shall the divine Sun shine forth and the radiant morn appear.

Consider to what a remarkable extent the spirituality of people has been overcome by materialism so that spiritual susceptibility seems to have vanished, divine civilization become decadent, and guidance and knowledge of God no longer remain. All are submerged in the sea of materialism. Although some attend churches and temples of worship and devotion, it is in accordance with the traditions and imitations of their fathers and not for the investigation of reality. For it is evident they have not found reality and are not engaged in its adoration. They are holding to certain imitations which have descended to them from their fathers and ancestors. They have become accustomed to passing a certain length of time in temple worship and conforming to imitations and ceremonies. The proof of this is that the son of every Jewish father becomes a Jew and not a Christian; the son of every Muslim becomes a follower of Islám; the son of every Christian proves to be a Christian; the son of every Zoroastrian is a Zoroastrian, etc. Therefore, religious faith and belief is merely a remnant of blind imitations which have descended through fathers and ancestors. Because this man's father was a Jew, he considers himself a Jew. Not that he has investigated reality and proved satisfactorily to himself that Judaism is right—nay, rather, he is aware that his forefathers have followed this course; therefore, he has held to it himself.

The purpose of this is to explain that the darkness of imitations encompasses the world. Every nation is holding to its traditional religious forms. The light of reality is obscured. Were these various nations to investigate reality, there is no doubt they would attain to it. As reality is one, all nations would then become as one nation. So long as they adhere to various imitations and are deprived of reality, strife and warfare will continue and rancor and sedition prevail. If they investigate reality, neither enmity nor rancor will remain, and they will attain to the utmost concord among themselves.

4   During the years when the darkness of heedlessness was most intense in the Orient and the people were so submerged in imitations that nations were thirsting for the blood of each other, considering each other as contaminated and refusing to associate—at such a time as this Bahá'u'lláh appeared. He arose in the Orient, uprooting the very foundations of imitations, and brought the dawn of the light of reality. Through Him various nations became united because all desired reality. Inasmuch as they investigated reality in religion, they found that all men are the servants of God, the posterity of Adam, children of one household and that the foundations of all the Prophets are one. For inasmuch as the teachings of the Prophets are reality, Their foundations are one. The enmity and strife of nations, therefore, are due to religious imitations and not to the reality which underlies the teachings of the Prophets. Through Bahá'u'lláh the nations and peoples grew to understand and comprehend this. Therefore, hearts became united, and lives were cemented together. After centuries of hatred and bitterness the Christian, Jew, Zoroastrian, Muslim and Buddhist met in fellowship, all of them in the utmost love and unity. They became welded and cemented because they had perceived reality.

5   The divine Prophets are conjoined in the perfect state of love. Each One has given the glad tidings of His successor's coming and each successor has sanctioned the One Who preceded Him. They were in the utmost unity, but Their followers are in strife. For instance, Moses gave the message of the glad tidings of Christ, and Christ confirmed the Prophethood of Moses. Therefore, between Moses and Jesus there is no variation or conflict. They are in perfect unity, but between the Jew and the

Christian there is conflict. Now, therefore, if the Christian and Jewish peoples investigate the reality underlying their Prophets' teachings, they will become kind in their attitude toward each other and associate in the utmost love, for reality is one and not dual or multiple. If this investigation of reality becomes universal, the divergent nations will ratify all the divine Prophets and confirm all the Holy Books. No strife or rancor will then remain, and the world will become united. Then will we associate in the reality of love. We will become as fathers and sons, as brothers and sisters living together in complete unity, love and happiness; for this century is the century of light. It is not like former centuries. Former centuries were epochs of oppression. Now human intellects have developed, and human intelligence has increased. Each soul is investigating reality. This is not a time when we shall wage war and be hostile toward each other. We are living at a time when we should enjoy real friendship.

Fifty years ago Bahá'u'lláh sent Epistles to all the kings and nations of the world, at a time when there was no mention of international peace. One of these Epistles was sent by Him to the president of the American democracy. In these communications He summoned all to international peace and the oneness of the human world. He summoned mankind to the fundamentals of the teachings of all the Prophets. Some of the European kings were arrogant. Among them was Napoleon III. Bahá'u'lláh wrote a second Epistle to him, which was published thirty years ago. The context is this: "O Napoleon! Thou hast become haughty indeed. Thou hast become proud. Thou hast forgotten God. Thou dost imagine that this majesty is permanent for thee, that this dominion is abiding for thee. A letter have we sent unto thee for acceptance with thy greatest love; but, instead, thou hast shown arrogance. Therefore, God shall uproot the edifice of thy sovereignty; thy country shall flee away from thee. Thou

6

shalt find humiliation hastening after thee because thou didst not arise for that which was enjoined upon thee, whereas that which was a duty incumbent upon thee was the cause of life to the world. The punishment of God shall soon be dealt out to thee."

7   This Epistle was revealed in the year 1869, and after one year the foundations of the Napoleonic sovereignty were completely uprooted.

8   Among these Epistles was a very lengthy one to the Sháh of Persia. It was printed and spread broadcast throughout all the countries. This Epistle was revealed in the year 1870. In it Bahá'u'lláh admonished the Sháh of Persia to be kind to all his subjects, summoning him to dispense justice, counseling him to make no distinction between the religions, charging him to deal equally with Jew, Christian, Muslim and Zoroastrian and to remove the oppression prevailing in his country.

9   At that time the Jews were greatly oppressed in Persia. Bahá'u'lláh especially recommended justice for them, saying that all people are the servants of God, and in the eye of the government they should be equally estimated. "If justice is not dealt out, if these oppressions are not removed and if thou dost not obey God, the foundations of thy government will be razed, and thou shalt become evanescent, become as nothing. Thou shouldst gather all the learned men, and then summon Me. There I shall be present. I will then advance proofs and evidences as to My validity. I will manifest My proof and anything that you may ask. I am ready. But if no attention is paid to this book, thou, like unto the kings who became nonexistent, shalt likewise become nonexistent." The Sháh did not answer this Epistle of the Blessed Perfection. Then God destroyed the foundations of his sovereignty.

10   Among those to whom Bahá'u'lláh wrote was the Sultán of Turkey. In it He arraigned him, saying, "Verily, thou didst incarcerate and make Me a prisoner. Dost thou imagine that imprisonment

is a loss to Me, that imprisonment is a humiliation for Me? This imprisonment is a glory for Me because it is in the pathway of God. I have not committed a crime. It is for the sake of God that I have received this ordeal. Therefore, I am very happy; I am exceedingly joyous. But thou must wait; God will send thee a punishment; thou shalt receive retribution. Erelong thou shalt observe how ordeals shall descend upon thee like rain, and thou shalt become nonexistent." And even so it was.

Likewise, He sent messages to the other kings and crowned 11 heads of the earth, summoning all of them to love, equity, international peace and the oneness of humanity in order that mankind might become unified and agreed; that strife, warfare and sedition should pass away; that bitterness and enmity might cease and all arise to serve the one God.

In brief, two kings arose against Bahá'u'lláh: the Sháh of Persia 12 and the Sulṭán of Turkey. They imprisoned Him in the fortress of 'Akká in order to extinguish His light and exterminate His Cause. But Bahá'u'lláh while in prison wrote severe letters of arraignment to them. He declared that imprisonment was no obstacle to Him. He said, "This imprisonment will prove to be the means of the promotion of My Cause. This imprisonment shall be the incentive for the spreading of My teachings. No harm shall come to Me because I have sacrificed My life, I have sacrificed My blood, I have sacrificed My possessions, I have sacrificed all and for Me this imprisonment is no loss." And just as He declared, so it came to pass. In prison He hoisted His banner, and His Cause spread throughout the world. It has reached America. Now the Cause of Bahá'u'lláh is extending to all nations of the earth. You go to Asia, and wherever you travel you will find Bahá'ís. You go to Africa, Europe; there you will find the Cause of Bahá'u'lláh. In America it is just beginning to grow and spread.

These two kings could not do anything to withstand Bahá'- 13 u'lláh, but God through Him was capable of destroying both of them. I, too, was in prison. God removed the chains from my neck and placed them around the neck of 'Abdu'l-Ḥamíd. It was done suddenly—not a long time, in a moment as it were. The same hour that the Young Turks declared liberty, the Committee of Union and Progress set me free. They lifted the chains from my neck and threw them around the neck of 'Abdu'l-Ḥamíd. That which he did to me was inflicted upon him. Now the position is precisely reversed. His days are spent in prison just as I passed the days in prison at 'Akká, with this difference: that I was happy in imprisonment. I was in the utmost elation because I was not a criminal. They had imprisoned me in the path of God. Every time I thought of this, that I was a prisoner in the pathway of God, the utmost elation overcame me. 'Abdu'l-Ḥamíd is now suffering punishment for his deeds. Because of the sins he committed, he is now in prison. This is retribution for his acts. Every hour he is mortified anew and his ignominy revived. He is in the utmost sorrow and disappointment while I am in perfect happiness. I was happy that—praise be to God!—I was a prisoner in the Cause of God, that my life was not wasted, that it was spent in the divine service. Nobody who saw me imagined that I was in prison. They beheld me in the utmost joy, complete thankfulness and health, paying no attention to the prison.

5

6 July 1912

Talk at 309 West Seventy-eighth Street, New York

NOTES BY EMMA C. MELICK

IN the world of existence man has traversed successive degrees   1
until he has attained the human kingdom. In each degree of
his progression he has developed capacity for advancement to
the next station and condition. While in the kingdom of the
mineral he was attaining the capacity for promotion into the
degree of the vegetable. In the kingdom of the vegetable he
underwent preparation for the world of the animal, and from
thence he has come onward to the human degree, or kingdom.
Throughout this journey of progression he has ever and always
been potentially man.

In the beginning of his human life man was embryonic in   2
the world of the matrix. There he received capacity and endowment for the reality of human existence. The forces and powers
necessary for this world were bestowed upon him in that limited
condition. In this world he needed eyes; he received them potentially in the other. He needed ears; he obtained them there
in readiness and preparation for his new existence. The powers
requisite in this world were conferred upon him in the world of
the matrix so that when he entered this realm of real existence
he not only possessed all necessary functions and powers but
found provision for his material sustenance awaiting him.

Therefore, in this world he must prepare himself for the life   3
beyond. That which he needs in the world of the Kingdom must
be obtained here. Just as he prepared himself in the world of the

matrix by acquiring forces necessary in this sphere of existence, so, likewise, the indispensable forces of the divine existence must be potentially attained in this world.

4   What is he in need of in the Kingdom which transcends the life and limitation of this mortal sphere? That world beyond is a world of sanctity and radiance; therefore, it is necessary that in this world he should acquire these divine attributes. In that world there is need of spirituality, faith, assurance, the knowledge and love of God. These he must attain in this world so that after his ascension from the earthly to the heavenly Kingdom he shall find all that is needful in that eternal life ready for him.

5   That divine world is manifestly a world of lights; therefore, man has need of illumination here. That is a world of love; the love of God is essential. It is a world of perfections; virtues, or perfections, must be acquired. That world is vivified by the breaths of the Holy Spirit; in this world we must seek them. That is the Kingdom of everlasting life; it must be attained during this vanishing existence.

6   By what means can man acquire these things? How shall he obtain these merciful gifts and powers? First, through the knowledge of God. Second, through the love of God. Third, through faith. Fourth, through philanthropic deeds. Fifth, through self-sacrifice. Sixth, through severance from this world. Seventh, through sanctity and holiness. Unless he acquires these forces and attains to these requirements, he will surely be deprived of the life that is eternal. But if he possesses the knowledge of God, becomes ignited through the fire of the love of God, witnesses the great and mighty signs of the Kingdom, becomes the cause of love among mankind and lives in the utmost state of sanctity and holiness, he shall surely attain to second birth, be baptized by the Holy Spirit and enjoy everlasting existence.

7   Is it not astonishing that although man has been created for the knowledge and love of God, for the virtues of the human

world, for spirituality, heavenly illumination and eternal life, nevertheless, he continues ignorant and negligent of all this? Consider how he seeks knowledge of everything except knowledge of God. For instance, his utmost desire is to penetrate the mysteries of the lowest strata of the earth. Day by day he strives to know what can be found ten meters below the surface, what he can discover within the stone, what he can learn by archaeological research in the dust. He puts forth arduous labors to fathom terrestrial mysteries but is not at all concerned about knowing the mysteries of the Kingdom, traversing the illimitable fields of the eternal world, becoming informed of the divine realities, discovering the secrets of God, attaining the knowledge of God, witnessing the splendors of the Sun of Truth and realizing the glories of everlasting life. He is unmindful and thoughtless of these. How much he is attracted to the mysteries of matter, and how completely unaware he is of the mysteries of Divinity! Nay, he is utterly negligent and oblivious of the secrets of Divinity. How great his ignorance! How conducive to his degradation! It is as if a kind and loving father had provided a library of wonderful books for his son in order that he might be informed of the mysteries of creation, at the same time surrounding him with every means of comfort and enjoyment, but the son amuses himself with pebbles and playthings, neglectful of all his father's gifts and provision. How ignorant and heedless is man! The Father has willed for him eternal glory, and he is content with blindness and deprivation. The Father has built for him a royal palace, but he is playing with the dust; prepared for him garments of silk, but he prefers to remain unclothed; provided for him delicious foods and fruits, while he seeks sustenance in the grasses of the field.

Praise be to God! You have heard the call of the Kingdom. 8 Your eyes are opened; you have turned to God. Your purpose is the good pleasure of God, the understanding of the mysteries of the heart and investigation of the realities. Day and night you must strive that you may attain to the significances of the heavenly Kingdom, perceive the signs of Divinity, acquire certainty of knowledge and realize that this world has a Creator, a Vivifier, a Provider, an Architect—knowing this through proofs and evidences and not through susceptibilities, nay, rather, through decisive arguments and real vision—that is to say, visualizing it as clearly as the outer eye beholds the sun. In this way may you behold the presence of God and attain to the knowledge of the holy, divine Manifestations.

9   You must come into the knowledge of the divine Manifestations and Their teachings through proofs and evidences. You must unseal the mysteries of the supreme Kingdom and become capable of discovering the inner realities of things. Then shall you be the manifestations of the mercy of God and true believers, firm and steadfast in the Cause of God.

10   Praise be to God! The door of divine knowledge has been opened by Bahá'u'lláh, for He has laid the foundation whereby man may become acquainted with the verities of heaven and earth and has bestowed the utmost confirmation in this day. He is our Teacher and Adviser; He is our Seer and the One clement toward us. He has prepared His gifts and vouchsafed His bounties, revealed every admonition and behest, prepared for us the means of eternal glory, breathed upon us the life-quickening breaths of the Holy Spirit, opened before our faces the doors of the paradise of Abhá and caused the lights of the Sun of Truth to shine upon us. The clouds of mercy have poured down their precious rain. The sea of favor is swelling and surging toward us.

11   The spiritual springtime has come. Infinite bounties and graces have appeared. What bestowal is greater than this? We must appreciate the divine generosity and act in accordance with

the teachings of Bahá'u'lláh so that all good may be stored up for us and in both worlds we shall become precious and acceptable to God, attain to everlasting blessings, taste the delicacy of the love of God, find the sweetness of the knowledge of God, perceive the heavenly bestowal and witness the power of the Holy Spirit. This is my advice, and this is my admonition. 12

6

14 July 1912

Talk at All Souls Unitarian Church
Fourth Avenue and Twentieth Street, New York

NOTES BY JOHN G. GRUNDY AND HOWARD MACNUTT

TODAY I wish to speak to you upon the subject of the oneness 1 of humanity, for in this great century the most important accomplishment is the unity of mankind. Although in former centuries and times this subject received some measure of mention and consideration, it has now become the paramount issue and question in the religious and political conditions of the world. History shows that throughout the past there has been continual warfare and strife among the various nations, peoples and sects; but now—praise be to God!—in this century of illumination, hearts are inclined toward agreement and fellowship, and minds are thoughtful upon the question of the unification of mankind. There is an emanation of the universal consciousness today which clearly indicates the dawn of a great unity.

In the investigation of a subject the right method of approach 2 is to carefully examine its premises. Therefore, we must go back to the foundation upon which human solidarity rests—namely, that all are the progeny of Adam, the creatures and servants of one God; that God is the Protector and Provider; that all are submerged in the sea of divine mercy and grace and God is loving toward all.

3   Humanity shares in common the intellectual and spiritual faculties of a created endowment. All are equally subject to the various exigencies of human life and are similarly occupied in acquiring the means of earthly subsistence. From the viewpoint of creation human beings stand upon the same footing in every respect, subject to the same requirements and seeking the enjoyment and comfort of earthly conditions. Therefore, the things humanity shares in common are numerous and manifest. This equal participation in the physical, intellectual and spiritual problems of human existence is a valid basis for the unification of mankind.

4   Consider how discord and dissension have prevailed in this great human family for thousands of years. Its members have ever been engaged in war and bloodshed. Up to the present time in history the world of humanity has neither attained nor enjoyed any measure of peace, owing to incessant conditions of hostility and strife. History is a continuous and consecutive record of warfare brought about by religious, sectarian, racial, patriotic and political causes. The world of humanity has found no rest. Mankind has always been in conflict, engaged in destroying the foundations, pillaging the properties and possessing the lands and territory of each other, especially in the earlier periods of savagery and barbarism where whole races and peoples were carried away captive by their conquerors. Who shall measure or estimate the tremendous destruction of human life resulting from this hostility and strife? What human powers and forces have been employed in the prosecution of war and applied to inhuman purposes of

battle and bloodshed? In this most radiant century it has become necessary to divert these energies and utilize them in other directions, to seek the new path of fellowship and unity, to unlearn the science of war and devote supreme human forces to the blessed arts of peace. After long trial and experience we are convinced of the harmful and satanic outcomes of dissension; now we must seek after means by which the benefits of agreement and concord may be enjoyed. When such means are found, we must give them a trial.

Consider the harmful effect of discord and dissension in a 5 family; then reflect upon the favors and blessings which descend upon that family when unity exists among its various members. What incalculable benefits and blessings would descend upon the great human family if unity and brotherhood were established! In this century when the beneficent results of unity and the ill effects of discord are so clearly apparent, the means for the attainment and accomplishment of human fellowship have appeared in the world. Bahá'u'lláh has proclaimed and provided the way by which hostility and dissension may be removed from the human world. He has left no ground or possibility for strife and disagreement.

First, He has proclaimed the oneness of mankind and spe- 6 cialized religious teachings for existing human conditions. The first form of dissension arises from religious differences. Bahá'-u'lláh has given full teachings to the world which are conducive to fellowship and unity in religion. Throughout past centuries each system of religious belief has boasted of its own superiority and excellence, abasing and scorning the validity of all others. Each has proclaimed its own belief as the light and all others as darkness. Religionists have considered the world of humanity as two trees: one divine and merciful, the other satanic; they themselves the branches, leaves and fruit of the divine tree and all others who differ from them in belief the product of the tree which is satanic. Therefore, sedition and warfare, bloodshed and strife have been continuous among them. The greatest cause of human alienation has been religion because each party has considered the belief of the other as anathema and deprived of the mercy of God.

7   The teachings specialized in Bahá'u'lláh are addressed to humanity. He says, "Ye are all the leaves of one tree." He does not say, "Ye are the leaves of two trees: one divine, the other satanic." He has declared that each individual member of the human family is a leaf or branch upon the Adamic tree; that all are sheltered beneath the protecting mercy and providence of God; that all are the children of God, fruit upon the one tree of His love. God is equally compassionate and kind to all the leaves, branches and fruit of this tree. Therefore, there is no satanic tree whatever—Satan being a product of human minds and of instinctive human tendencies toward error. God alone is Creator, and all are creatures of His might. Therefore, we must love mankind as His creatures, realizing that all are growing upon the tree of His mercy, servants of His omnipotent will and manifestations of His good pleasure.

8   Even though we find a defective branch or leaf upon this tree of humanity or an imperfect blossom, it, nevertheless, belongs to this tree and not to another. Therefore, it is our duty to protect and cultivate this tree until it reaches perfection. If we examine its fruit and find it imperfect, we must strive to make it perfect. There are souls in the human world who are ignorant; we must make them knowing. Some growing upon the tree are weak and ailing; we must assist them toward health and recovery. If they are as infants in development, we must minister to them until they attain maturity. We should never detest and shun them as objectionable and unworthy. We must treat them with honor,

respect and kindness; for God has created them and not Satan. They are not manifestations of the wrath of God but evidences of His divine favor. God, the Creator, has endowed them with physical, mental and spiritual qualities that they may seek to know and do His will; therefore, they are not objects of His wrath and condemnation. In brief, all humanity must be looked upon with love, kindness and respect; for what we behold in them are none other than the signs and traces of God Himself. All are evidences of God; therefore, how shall we be justified in debasing and belittling them, uttering anathema and preventing them from drawing near unto His mercy? This is ignorance and injustice, displeasing to God; for in His sight all are His servants.

Another cause of dissension and disagreement is the fact that 9 religion has been pronounced at variance with science. Between scientists and the followers of religion there has always been controversy and strife for the reason that the latter have proclaimed religion superior in authority to science and considered scientific announcement opposed to the teachings of religion. Bahá'u'lláh declared that religion is in complete harmony with science and reason. If religious belief and doctrine is at variance with reason, it proceeds from the limited mind of man and not from God; therefore, it is unworthy of belief and not deserving of attention; the heart finds no rest in it, and real faith is impossible. How can man believe that which he knows to be opposed to reason? Is this possible? Can the heart accept that which reason denies? Reason is the first faculty of man, and the religion of God is in harmony with it. Bahá'u'lláh has removed this form of dissension and discord from among mankind and reconciled science with religion by revealing the pure teachings of the divine reality. This accomplishment is specialized to Him in this Day.

Still another cause of disagreement and dissension has been 10 the formation of religious sects and denominations. Bahá'u'lláh

323

said that God has sent religion for the purpose of establishing fellowship among humankind and not to create strife and discord, for all religion is founded upon the love of humanity. Abraham promulgated this principle, Moses summoned all to its recognition, Christ established it, and Muḥammad directed mankind to its standard. This is the reality of religion. If we abandon hearsay and investigate the reality and inner significance of the heavenly teachings, we will find the same divine foundation of love for humanity. The purport is that religion is intended to be the cause of unity, love and fellowship and not discord, enmity and estrangement. Man has forsaken the foundation of divine religion and adhered to blind imitations. Each nation has clung to its own imitations, and because these are at variance, warfare, bloodshed and destruction of the foundation of humanity have resulted. True religion is based upon love and agreement. Bahá'u'lláh has said, "If religion and faith are the causes of enmity and sedition, it is far better to be nonreligious, and the absence of religion would be preferable; for we desire religion to be the cause of amity and fellowship. If enmity and hatred exist, irreligion is preferable." Therefore, the removal of this dissension has been specialized in Bahá'u'lláh, for religion is the divine remedy for human antagonism and discord. But when we make the remedy the cause of the disease, it would be better to do without the remedy.

11   Other sources of human dissension are political, racial and patriotic prejudices. These have been removed by Bahá'u'lláh. He has said, and has guarded His statement by rational proofs from the Holy Books, that the world of humanity is one race, the surface of the earth one place of residence and that these imaginary racial barriers and political boundaries are without right or foundation. Man is degraded in becoming the captive of his own illusions and suppositions. The earth is one earth, and

the same atmosphere surrounds it. No difference or preference has been made by God for its human inhabitants; but man has laid the foundation of prejudice, hatred and discord with his fellowman by considering nationalities separate in importance and races different in rights and privileges.

Diversity of languages has been a fruitful cause of discord. 12 The function of language is to convey the thought and purpose of one to another. Therefore, it matters not what language man speaks or employs. Sixty years ago Bahá'u'lláh advocated one language as the greatest means of unity and the basis of international conference. He wrote to the kings and rulers of the various nations, recommending that one language should be sanctioned and adopted by all governments. According to this each nation should acquire the universal language in addition to its native tongue. The world would then be in close communication, consultation would become general, and dissensions due to diversity of speech would be removed.

Another teaching of Bahá'u'lláh is in relation to universal peace: 13 that all mankind must be awakened to and become conscious of the harm of war, that they should be brought to realize the benefits of peace and know that peace is from God while warfare is satanic. Man must emulate the merciful God and turn away from satanic promptings in order that universal inclination shall be toward peace, love and unity and the discord of war vanish.

Lack of equality between man and woman is, likewise, a 14 cause of human dissension. Bahá'u'lláh has named this as an important factor of discord and separation, for so long as humankind remains unequally divided in right and importance between male and female, no unity can be established. In a perfect human body it is not possible for one organ to be complete and another defective. In the great body of human society it is impossible to establish unity and coordination if one part is considered perfect and the other imperfect. When the perfect functions of both parts are in operation, harmony will prevail. God has created man and woman equal as to faculties. He has made no distinction between them. Woman has not reached the level of man in human accomplishment because of the lack of opportunity and education. If educational opportunities were made equal and similar, the two parts, man and woman, would equalize in attainment. God has intended no difference between them that should be productive of discord. He has endowed all with human faculties, and all are manifestations of His mercy. If we say man and woman differ in creational endowment, it is contrary to divine justice and intention. Both are human. If God has created one perfect and the other defective, He is unjust. But God is just; all are perfect in His intention and creative endowment. To assume imperfection in the creature is to presuppose imperfection in the almighty Creator. The soul that excels in attainment of His attributes and graces is most acceptable before God.

15   We are considering the divine plan for the reconciliation of the religious systems of the world. Bahá'u'lláh has said that if one intelligent member be selected from each of the varying religious systems, and these representatives come together seeking to investigate the reality of religion, they would establish an interreligious body before which all disputes and differences of belief could be presented for consideration and settlement. Such questions could then be weighed and viewed from the standpoint of reality and all imitations be discarded. By this method and procedure all sects, denominations and systems would become one.

16   Do not question the practicability of this, and be not astonished. It has been accomplished and effected in Persia. In that country the various religionists have conjoined in investigating reality and have united in complete fellowship and love. No traces

of discord or differences remain among them; now affection and unity are manifest instead. They live together in harmony and accord like a single family. Antagonism and strife have passed away; love and agreement have taken the place of hatred and animosity. Furthermore, those souls who have followed Bahá'u'lláh and attained this condition of fellowship and affiliation are Muslims, Jews, Christians, Zoroastrians, Buddhists, Nestorians, Sunnites, Shiites and others. No discord exists among them. This is a proof of the possibility of unification among the religionists of the world through practical means. Imitations and prejudices which have held men apart have been discarded, and the reality of religion envelops them in a perfect unity. When reality envelops the soul of man, love is possible. The divine purpose in religion is pure love and agreement. The Prophets of God manifested complete love for all. Each One announced the glad tidings of His successor, and each subsequent One confirmed the teachings and prophecies of the Prophet Who preceded Him. There was no disagreement or variance in the reality of Their teaching and mission. Discord has arisen among Their followers, who have lost sight of reality and hold fast to imitations. If imitations be done away with and the radiant shining reality dawn in the souls of men, love and unity must prevail. In this way humanity will be rescued from the strife and wars which have prevailed for thousands of years; dissensions will pass away and the illumination of unity dawn. Consider how all the Prophets of God were persecuted and what hardships They experienced. Jesus Christ endured affliction and accepted martyrdom upon the cross in order to summon mankind to unity and love. What sacrifice could be greater? He brought the religion of love and fellowship into the world. Shall we make use of it to create discord, violence and hatred among mankind?

Moses was persecuted and driven out into the desert, Abraham was banished, Muḥammad took refuge in caves, the Báb 17

327

was killed and Bahá'u'lláh was exiled and imprisoned forty years. Yet all of Them desired fellowship and love among men. They endured hardships, suffered persecution and death for our sakes that we might be taught to love one another and be united and affiliated instead of discordant and at variance. Enough of these long centuries which have brought such vicissitudes and hardships into the world through strife and hatred. Now in this radiant century let us try to do the will of God that we may be rescued from these things of darkness and come forth into the boundless illumination of heaven, shunning division and welcoming the divine oneness of humanity. Perchance, God willing, this terrestrial world may become as a celestial mirror upon which we may behold the imprint of the traces of Divinity, and the fundamental qualities of a new creation may be reflected from the reality of love shining in human hearts. From the light and semblance of God in us may it be, indeed, proved and witnessed that God has created man after His own image and likeness.

18   O my God! O my God! Verily, I invoke Thee and supplicate before Thy threshold, asking Thee that all Thy mercies may descend upon these souls. Specialize them for Thy favor and Thy truth.

19   O Lord! Unite and bind together the hearts, join in accord all the souls, and exhilarate the spirits through the signs of Thy sanctity and oneness. O Lord! Make these faces radiant through the light of Thy oneness. Strengthen the loins of Thy servants in the service of Thy kingdom.

20   O Lord, Thou possessor of infinite mercy! O Lord of forgiveness and pardon! Forgive our sins, pardon our shortcomings, and cause us to turn to the kingdom of Thy clemency, invoking the kingdom of might and power, humble at Thy shrine and submissive before the glory of Thine evidences.

21   O Lord God! Make us as waves of the sea, as flowers of the garden, united, agreed through the bounties of Thy love. O

Lord! Dilate the breasts through the signs of Thy oneness, and make all mankind as stars shining from the same height of glory, as perfect fruits growing upon Thy tree of life.

Verily, Thou art the Almighty, the Self-Subsistent, the 22 Giver, the Forgiving, the Pardoner, the Omniscient, the One Creator.

7

15 July 1912

Talk at Home of Dr. and Mrs. Florian Krug
830 Park Avenue, New York

NOTES BY HOWARD MACNUTT

I AM greatly pleased to see you. Your hearts are illumined by 1 the lights of Bahá. This meeting is in reality a divine, celestial assembly under the favor of God, for we have no other purpose than praising and meeting God. The prayer you have just offered is a prayer of thankfulness.

Thankfulness is of various kinds. There is a verbal thanksgiv- 2 ing which is confined to a mere utterance of gratitude. This is of no importance because perchance the tongue may give thanks while the heart is unaware of it. Many who offer thanks to God are of this type, their spirits and hearts unconscious of thanksgiving. This is mere usage, just as when we meet, receive a gift and say thank you, speaking the words without significance. One may say thank you a thousand times while the heart remains thankless, ungrateful. Therefore, mere verbal thanksgiving is without effect. But real thankfulness is a cordial giving of thanks from the heart. When man in response to the favors of God manifests susceptibilities of conscience, the heart is happy, the spirit is exhilarated. These spiritual susceptibilities are ideal thanksgiving.

3   There is a cordial thanksgiving, too, which expresses itself in the deeds and actions of man when his heart is filled with gratitude. For example, God has conferred upon man the gift of guidance, and in thankfulness for this great gift certain deeds must emanate from him. To express his gratitude for the favors of God man must show forth praiseworthy actions. In response to these bestowals he must render good deeds, be self-sacrificing, loving the servants of God, forfeiting even life for them, showing kindness to all the creatures. He must be severed from the world, attracted to the Kingdom of Abhá, the face radiant, the tongue eloquent, the ear attentive, striving day and night to attain the good pleasure of God. Whatsoever he wishes to do must be in harmony with the good pleasure of God. He must observe and see what is the will of God and act accordingly. There can be no doubt that such commendable deeds are thankfulness for the favors of God.

4   Consider how grateful anyone becomes when healed from sickness, when treated kindly by another or when a service is rendered by another, even though it may be of the least consequence. If we forget such favors, it is an evidence of ingratitude. Then it will be said a loving-kindness has been done, but we are thankless, not appreciating this love and favor. Physically and spiritually we are submerged in the sea of God's favor. He has provided our foods, drink and other requirements; His favors encompass us from all directions. The sustenances provided for man are blessings. Sight, hearing and all his faculties are wonderful gifts. These blessings are innumerable; no matter how many are mentioned, they are still endless. Spiritual blessings are likewise endless—spirit, consciousness, thought, memory, perception, ideation and other endowments. By these He has

guided us, and we enter His Kingdom. He has opened the doors of all good before our faces. He has vouchsafed eternal glory. He has summoned us to the Kingdom of heaven. He has enriched us by the bestowals of God. Every day he has proclaimed new glad tidings. Every hour fresh bounties descend.

Consider how all the people are asleep, and ye are awake. They are dead, and ye are alive through the breaths of the Holy Spirit. They are blind while ye are endowed with perceptive sight. They are deprived of the love of God, but in your hearts it exists and is glowing. Consider these bestowals and favors. 5

Therefore, in thanksgiving for them ye must act in accordance with the teachings of Bahá'u'lláh. Ye must read the Tablets—the Hidden Words, Ishráqát, Glad Tidings—all the holy utterances, and act according to them. This is real thanksgiving, to live in accord with these utterances. This is true thankfulness and the divine bestowal. This is thanksgiving and glorification of God. 6

I hope you all may attain thereto, be mindful of these favors of God and be attentive. It is my hope that I may go away from New York with a happy heart, and my heart is happy when the friends of God love each other, when they manifest the mercy of God to all people. If I see this, I shall go away happy. 7

Salutations! 8

331

Talks 'Abdu'l-Bahá Delivered in Boston

23 July 1912

Talk at Hotel Victoria
Boston, Massachusetts

NOTES BY EDNA MCKINNEY

THE Bahá'ís must not engage in political movements which 1
lead to sedition. They must interest themselves in movements
which conduce to law and order. In Persia at the present time
the Bahá'ís have no part in the revolutionary upheavals which
have terminated in lawlessness and rebellion. Nevertheless, a
Bahá'í may hold a political office and be interested in politics
of the right type. Ministers, state officials and governor-generals
in Persia are Bahá'ís, and there are many other Bahá'ís holding
governmental positions; but nowhere throughout the world
should the followers of Bahá'u'lláh be engaged in seditious
movements. For example, if there should be an uprising here in
America having for its purpose the establishment of a despotic
government, the Bahá'ís should not be connected with it.

The Bahá'í Cause covers all economic and social questions 2
under the heading and ruling of its laws. The essence of the
Bahá'í spirit is that, in order to establish a better social order and
economic condition, there must be allegiance to the laws and
principles of government. Under the laws which are to govern
the world, the socialists may justly demand human rights but
without resort to force and violence. The governments will
enact these laws, establishing just legislation and economics in

order that all humanity may enjoy a full measure of welfare and privilege; but this will always be according to legal protection and procedure. Without legislative administration, rights and demands fail, and the welfare of the commonwealth cannot be realized. Today the method of demand is the strike and resort to force, which is manifestly wrong and destructive of human foundations. Rightful privilege and demand must be set forth in laws and regulations.

3   While thousands are considering these questions, we have more essential purposes. The fundamentals of the whole economic condition are divine in nature and are associated with the world of the heart and spirit. This is fully explained in the Bahá'í teaching, and without knowledge of its principles no improvement in the economic state can be realized. The Bahá'ís will bring about this improvement and betterment but not through sedition and appeal to physical force—not through warfare, but welfare. Hearts must be so cemented together, love must become so dominant that the rich shall most willingly extend assistance to the poor and take steps to establish these economic adjustments permanently. If it is accomplished in this way, it will be most praiseworthy because then it will be for the sake of God and in the pathway of His service. For example, it will be as if the rich inhabitants of a city should say, "It is neither just nor lawful that we should possess great wealth while there is abject poverty in this community," and then willingly give their wealth to the poor, retaining only as much as will enable them to live comfortably.

4   Strive, therefore, to create love in the hearts in order that they may become glowing and radiant. When that love is shining, it will permeate other hearts even as this electric light illumines its surroundings. When the love of God is established, everything else will be realized. This is the true foundation of all economics.

Reflect upon it. Endeavor to become the cause of the attraction of souls rather than to enforce minds. Manifest true economics to the people. Show what love is, what kindness is, what true severance is and generosity. This is the important thing for you to do. Act in accordance with the teachings of Bahá'u'lláh. All His Books will be translated. Now is the time for you to live in accordance with His words. Let your deeds be the real translation of their meaning. Economic questions will not attract hearts. The love of God alone will attract them. Economic questions are most interesting; but the power which moves, controls and attracts the hearts of men is the love of God.

2

24 July 1912

Talk to Theosophical Society
The Kensington
Exeter and Boylston Streets, Boston, Massachusetts

NOTES BY EDNA McKINNEY

IN the world of existence there is nothing so important as spirit, 1 nothing so essential as the spirit of man. The spirit of man is the most noble of phenomena. The spirit of man is the meeting between man and God. The spirit of man is the animus of human life and the collective center of all human virtues. The spirit of man is the cause of the illumination of this world. The world may be likened to the body; man is the spirit of the body, because the light of the world is the human spirit. Man is the life of the world, and the life of man is the spirit. The happiness of the world depends upon man, and the happiness of man is dependent upon the spirit. The world may be likened to the lamp chimney, whereas man is the light. Man himself may be likened to the lamp; his spirit is the light within the lamp. Therefore, we will speak of this spirit.

2 The philosophers of the world are divided into two classes: materialists, who deny the spirit and its immortality, and the divine philosophers, the wise men of God, the true illuminati who believe in the spirit and its continuance hereafter. The ancient philosophers taught that man consists simply of the material elements which compose his cellular structure and that when this composition is disintegrated the life of man becomes extinct. They reasoned that man is body only, and from this elemental composition the organs and their functions, the senses, powers and attributes which characterize man have proceeded, and that these disappear completely with the physical body. This is practically the statement of all the materialists.

3 The divine philosophers proclaim that the spirit of man is ever-living and eternal, and because of the objections of the materialists, these wise men of God have advanced rational proofs to support the validity of their statement. Inasmuch as the materialistic philosophers deny the Books of God, scriptural demonstration is not evidence to them, and materialistic proofs are necessary. Answering them, the men of divine knowledge have said that all existing phenomena may be resolved into grades or kingdoms, classified progressively as mineral, vegetable, animal and human, each of which possesses its degree of function and intelligence. When we consider the mineral, we find that it exists and is possessed of the power of affinity or combination. The vegetable possesses the qualities of the mineral plus the augmentative virtue or power of growth. It is, therefore, evident that the vegetable kingdom is superior to the mineral.

The animal kingdom in turn possesses the qualities of the mineral and vegetable plus the five senses of perception whereof the kingdoms below it are lacking. Likewise, the power of memory inherent in the animal does not exist in the lower kingdoms.

Just as the animal is more noble than the vegetable and mineral, so man is superior to the animal. The animal is bereft of ideality—that is to say, it is a captive of the world of nature and not in touch with that which lies within and beyond nature; it is without spiritual susceptibilities, deprived of the attractions of consciousness, unconscious of the world of God and incapable of deviating from the law of nature. It is different with man. Man is possessed of the emanations of consciousness; he has perception, ideality and is capable of discovering the mysteries of the universe. All the industries, inventions and facilities surrounding our daily life were at one time hidden secrets of nature, but the reality of man penetrated them and made them subject to his purposes. According to nature's laws they should have remained latent and hidden; but man, having transcended those laws, discovered these mysteries and brought them out of the plane of the invisible into the realm of the known and visible. How wonderful is the spirit of man! One of the mysteries of natural phenomena is electricity. Man has discovered this illimitable power and made it captive to his uses. How many of nature's secrets have been penetrated and revealed! Columbus, while in Spain, discovered America. Man has accurately determined that the sun is stationary while the earth revolves about it. The animal cannot do this. Man perceives the mirage to be an illusion. This is beyond the power of the animal. The animal can only know through sense impressions and cannot grasp intellectual realities. The animal cannot conceive of the power of thought. This is an abstract intellectual matter and not limited to the senses. The animal is incapable of knowing

4

that the earth is round. In brief, abstract intellectual phenomena are human powers. All creation below the kingdom of man is the captive of nature; it cannot deviate in the slightest degree from nature's laws. But man wrests the sword of dominion from nature's hand and uses it upon nature's head. For example, it is a natural exigency that man should be a dweller upon the earth, but the power of the human spirit transcends this limitation, and he soars aloft in airplanes. This is contrary to the law and requirement of nature. He sails at high speed upon the ocean and dives beneath its surface in submarines. He imprisons the human voice in a phonograph and communicates in the twinkling of an eye from East to West. These are things we know to be contrary to the limitations of natural law. Man transcends nature, while the mineral, vegetable and animal are helplessly subject to it. This can be done only through the power of the spirit, because the spirit is the reality.

5   In the physical powers and senses, however, man and the animal are partners. In fact, the animal is often superior to man in sense perception. For instance, the vision of some animals is exceedingly keen and the hearing of others most acute. Consider the instinct of a dog: how much greater than that of man. But, although the animal shares with man all the physical virtues and senses, a spiritual power has been bestowed upon man of which the animal is devoid. This is a proof that there is something in man above and beyond the endowment of the animal—a faculty and virtue peculiar to the human kingdom which is lacking in the lower kingdoms of existence. This is the spirit of man. All these wonderful human accomplishments are due to the efficacy and penetrating power of the spirit of man. If man were bereft of this spirit, none of these accomplishments would have been possible. This is as evident as the sun at midday.

6   All the organisms of material creation are limited to an image or form. That is to say, each created material being is possessed

of a form; it cannot possess two forms at the same time. For example, a body may be spherical, triangular or square; but it is impossible for it to be two of these shapes simultaneously. It may be triangular, but if it is to become square, it must first rid itself of the triangular shape. It is absolutely impossible for it to be both at the same time. Therefore, it is evident in the reality of material organisms that different forms cannot be simultaneously possessed. In the spiritual reality of man, however, all geometrical figures can be simultaneously conceived, while in physical realities one image must be forsaken in order that another may be possible. This is the law of change and transformation, and change and transformation are precursors of mortality. Were it not for this change in form, phenomena would be immortal; but because the phenomenal existence is subject to transformation, it is mortal. The reality of man, however, is possessed of all virtues; it is not necessary for him to give up one image for another as mere physical bodies do. Therefore, in that reality there is no change or transformation; it is immortal and everlasting. The body of man may be in America while his spirit is laboring and working in the Far East, discovering, organizing and planning. While occupied in governing, making laws and erecting a building in Russia, his body is still here in America. What is this power which, notwithstanding that it is embodied in America, is operating at the same time in the Orient, organizing, destroying, upbuilding? It is the spirit of man. This is irrefutable.

When you wish to reflect upon or consider a matter, you consult something within you. You say, shall I do it, or shall I not do it? Is it better to make this journey or abandon it? Whom do you consult? Who is within you deciding this question? Surely there is a distinct power, an intelligent ego. Were it not distinct from your ego, you would not be consulting it. It is greater than the faculty of thought. It is your spirit which teaches you, which advises and decides upon matters. Who is it that interrogates? Who is it that answers? There is no doubt that it is the spirit and that there is no change or transformation in it, for it is not a composition of elements, and anything that is not composed of elements is eternal. Change and transformation are peculiarities of composition. There is no change and transformation in the spirit. In proof of this, the body may become weakened in its members. It may be dismembered, or one of its members may be incapacitated. The whole body may be paralyzed; and yet the mind, the spirit, remains ever the same. The mind decides; the thought is perfect; and yet the hand is withered, the feet have become useless, the spinal column is paralyzed, and there is no muscular movement at all, but the spirit is in the same status. Dismember a healthy man; the spirit is not dismembered. Amputate his feet; his spirit is there. He may become lame; the spirit is not affected. The spirit is ever the same; no change or transformation can you perceive, and because there is no change or transformation, it is everlasting and permanent.

8   Consider man while in the state of sleep; it is evident that all his parts and members are at a standstill, are functionless. His eye does not see, his ear does not hear, his feet and hands are motionless; but, nevertheless, he does see in the world of dreams, he does hear, he speaks, he walks, he may even fly in an airplane. Therefore, it becomes evident that though the body be dead, yet the spirit is alive and permanent. Nay, the perceptions may be keener when man's body is asleep, the flight may be higher, the hearing may be more acute; all the functions are there, and yet the body is at a standstill. Hence it is proof that there is a spirit in the man, and in this spirit there is no distinction as to whether the body be asleep or absolutely dead and dependent. The spirit is not incapacitated by these conditions; it is not bereft of its existence; it is not bereft of its perfections. The proofs are many, innumerable.

340

These are all rational proofs. Nobody can refute them. As we   9
have shown that there is a spirit and that this spirit is permanent
and everlasting, we must strive to learn of it. May you become
informed of its power, hasten to render it divine, to have it
become sanctified and holy and make it the very light of the
world illumining the East and the West.

3

25 July 1912

Talk at Hotel Victoria
Boston, Massachusetts

Notes by Edna McKinney

I AM very happy to greet you here today. This is the second time   1
the breeze of God has wafted over Boston. I am expecting results
from this visit and hope that my coming may not be fruitless.
The results I expect are these: that the individual soul shall be
released from self and desire and freed from the bondage of
satanic suggestions. May the mirrors of hearts be cleansed from
dust in order that the Sun of Truth may be reflected therein.

Man possesses two kinds of susceptibilities: the natural   2
emotions, which are like dust upon the mirror, and spiritual
susceptibilities, which are merciful and heavenly characteristics.

There is a power which purifies the mirror from dust and   3
transforms its reflection into intense brilliancy and radiance so
that spiritual susceptibilities may chasten the hearts and heavenly bestowals sanctify them. What is the dust which obscures
the mirror? It is attachment to the world, avarice, envy, love of
luxury and comfort, haughtiness and self-desire; this is the dust

which prevents reflection of the rays of the Sun of Reality in the mirror. The natural emotions are blameworthy and are like rust which deprives the heart of the bounties of God. But sincerity, justice, humility, severance, and love for the believers of God will purify the mirror and make it radiant with reflected rays from the Sun of Truth.

4   It is my hope that you may consider this matter, that you may search out your own imperfections and not think of the imperfections of anybody else. Strive with all your power to be free from imperfections. Heedless souls are always seeking faults in others. What can the hypocrite know of others' faults when he is blind to his own? This is the meaning of the words in the Seven Valleys. It is a guide for human conduct. As long as a man does not find his own faults, he can never become perfect. Nothing is more fruitful for man than the knowledge of his own shortcomings. The Blessed Perfection says, "I wonder at the man who does not find his own imperfections."

Talks 'Abdu'l-Bahá Delivered in Dublin

5 August 1912

Talk at Dublin Inn
Dublin, New Hampshire

NOTES BY HOWARD MACNUTT

THE people of Christianity have clung to literal interpretation of the statement in the Gospel that Christ came from heaven. The Jews, likewise, at the time of His manifestation held to outward and visible expectation of the fulfillment of the prophecies. They said, "The Messiah shall appear from heaven. This man came from Nazareth; we know his house; we know his parents and people. It is only hearsay that he descended from heaven; this cannot be proved." 1

The text of the Gospel states that He came from heaven although physically born of the mother. The meaning is that the divine reality of Christ was from heaven, but the body was born of Mary. Therefore, He came according to the prophecies of the Holy Book and, likewise, according to natural law—His reality from heaven, His body earthly. As He came before, so must He come this time in the same way. But some arise with objections, saying, "We must have literal proof of this through the senses." 2

The reality of Christ was always in heaven and will always be. This is the intention of the text of the Gospel. For while Jesus Christ walked upon the earth, He said, "The Son of Man is in heaven." Therefore, holding to literal interpretation and visible fulfillment of the text of the Holy Books is simply imitation of 3

343

ancestral forms and beliefs; for when we perceive the reality of Christ, these texts and statements become clear and perfectly reconcilable with each other. Unless we perceive reality, we cannot understand the meanings of the Holy Books, for these meanings are symbolical and spiritual—such as, for instance, the raising of Lazarus, which has spiritual interpretation. We must first establish the fact that the power of God is infinite, unlimited, and that it is within that power to accomplish anything.

4   Second, we must understand the interpretation of Christ's words concerning the dead. A certain disciple came to Christ and asked permission to go and bury his father. He answered, "Let the dead bury their dead." Therefore, Christ designated as dead some who were still living—that is, let the living dead, the spiritually dead, bury your father. They were dead because they were not believers in Christ. Although physically alive, they were dead spiritually. This is the meaning of Christ's words, "That which is born of flesh is flesh; and that which is born of Spirit is spirit." He meant that those who were simply born of the human body were dead spiritually, while those quickened by the breaths of the Holy Spirit were living and eternally alive. These are the interpretations of Christ Himself. Reflect upon them, and the meanings of the Holy Books will become clear as the sun at midday.

5   The Holy Books have their special terminologies which must be known and understood. Physicians have their own peculiar terms; architects, philosophers have their characteristic expressions; poets have their phrases; and scientists, their nomenclature. In the scripture we read that Zion is dancing. It is evident that this has other than literal interpretation. The meaning is that the people of Zion shall rejoice. The Jews said Christ was not the Messiah but Antichrist, because one of the signs of the Messiah's coming was the dancing of Mount Zion, which had not yet come to pass. In reality, when Christ appeared, not only Mount Zion but all Palestine danced and rejoiced. Again

in scriptures it is said, "The trees of the field shall clap their hands." This is symbolical. There are terms and expressions of usage in every language which cannot be taken literally. For instance, in oriental countries it is customary to say, "When my friend entered the house, the doors and walls began to sing and dance." In Persia they say, "Get at the head," meaning engage in the matter according to its own terms and usages. All these have other and inner meanings.

You have asked concerning approval of Christian Science treatment and healing. Spirit has influence; prayer has spiritual effect. Therefore, we pray, "O God! Heal this sick one!" Perchance God will answer. Does it matter who prays? God will answer the prayer of every servant if that prayer is urgent. His mercy is vast, illimitable. He answers the prayers of all His servants. He answers the prayer of this plant. The plant prays potentially, "O God! Send me rain!" God answers the prayer, and the plant grows. God will answer anyone. He answers prayers potentially. Before we were born into this world did we not pray, "O God! Give me a mother; give me two fountains of bright milk; purify the air for my breathing; grant me rest and comfort; prepare food for my sustenance and living"? Did we not pray potentially for these needed blessings before we were created? When we came into this world, did we not find our prayers answered? Did we not find mother, father, food, light, home and every other necessity and blessing, although we did not actually ask for them? Therefore, it is natural that God will give to us when we ask Him. His mercy is all-encircling. 6

But we ask for things which the divine wisdom does not desire for us, and there is no answer to our prayer. His wisdom does not sanction what we wish. We pray, "O God! Make me wealthy!" If this prayer were universally answered, human affairs would be at a standstill. There would be none left to work in the streets, none to till the soil, none to build, none to run the 7 trains. Therefore, it is evident that it would not be well for us if all prayers were answered. The affairs of the world would be interfered with, energies crippled and progress hindered. But whatever we ask for which is in accord with divine wisdom, God will answer. Assuredly!

8   For instance, a very feeble patient may ask the doctor to give him food which would be positively dangerous to his life and condition. He may beg for roast meat. The doctor is kind and wise. He knows it would be dangerous to his patient so he refuses to allow it. The doctor is merciful; the patient, ignorant. Through the doctor's kindness the patient recovers; his life is saved. Yet the patient may cry out that the doctor is unkind, not good, because he refuses to answer his pleading.

9   God is merciful. In His mercy He answers the prayers of all His servants when according to His supreme wisdom it is necessary.

2

6 August 1912

Talk at Home of Mr. and Mrs. Arthur J. Parsons
Dublin, New Hampshire

NOTES BY HOWARD MACNUTT

1   TODAY we are enjoying temperate weather. As there are many strangers present, we will answer questions.

2   *Question:* Are not all Christians Bahá'ís? Is there any difference?

3   *Answer:* When Christians act according to the teachings of Christ, they are called Bahá'ís. For the foundations of Christian-

346

ity and the religion of Bahá'u'lláh are one. The foundations of all
the divine Prophets and Holy Books are one. The difference among
them is one of terminology only. Each springtime is identical with
the former springtime. The distinction between them is only one
of the calendar—1911, 1912 and so on. The difference between
a Christian and a Bahá'í, therefore, is this: There was a former
springtime, and there is a springtime now. No other difference exists
because the foundations are the same. Whoever acts completely in
accordance with the teachings of Christ is a Bahá'í. The purpose is
the essential meaning of Christian, not the mere word. The purpose
is the sun itself and not the dawning points. For though the sun
is one sun, its dawning points are many. We must not adore the
dawning points but worship the sun. We must adore the reality of
religion and not blindly cling to the appellation Christianity. The
Sun of Reality must be worshiped and followed. We must seek the
fragrance of the rose from whatever bush it is blooming—whether
oriental or western. Be seekers of light, no matter from which lantern
it shines forth. Be not lovers of the lantern. At one time the light has
shone from a lantern in the East, now in the West. If it comes from
North, South, from whatever direction it proceeds, follow the light.
Let me illustrate further. A certain person bestowed a coin upon
five beggars. They resolved to spend it for food. The Englishman
said, "Buy grapes." The Turk wanted *uzum*, the Arab *'anab*, the
Greek *stafi' li*, the Persian *angúr*. Not understanding each other's
language, they quarreled and fought. A stranger came along. He
was familiar with all five languages. He said, "Give me the coin;
I will buy what you wish." When he brought them grapes, they
were all satisfied. They wanted the same thing but differed in the
term only. Briefly, when reality dawns in the midst of the religions,
all will be unified and reconciled.

    Question: Does 'Abdu'l-Bahá find Christianity is not lived up   4
to and carried out in America?

5   *Answer:* My meaning is that it should be completely carried out and lived up to. Man needs eyes, ears, arms, a head, feet and various other members. When he possesses all and all work together, there is symmetry and perfection in him. So Christ said, "Be ye therefore perfect, even as your Father which is in heaven is perfect," meaning that perfection is the requirement of Christianity. Be the image and likeness of God. This is not easy. It necessitates the focalization of all heavenly virtues. It requires that we become recipients of all the perfections of God. Then we become His image and likeness. For in the Bible it is stated, "Let us make man in our image, after our likeness." The attainment of this is most difficult.

6   When Christ appeared with those marvelous breaths of the Holy Spirit, the children of Israel said, "We are quite independent of him; we can do without him and follow Moses; we have a book and in it are found the teachings of God; what need, therefore, have we of this man?" Christ said to them, "The book sufficeth you not." It is possible for a man to hold to a book of medicine and say, "I have no need of a doctor; I will act according to the book; in it every disease is named, all symptoms are explained, the diagnosis of each ailment is completely written out, and a prescription for each malady is furnished; therefore, why do I need a doctor?" This is sheer ignorance. A physician is needed to prescribe. Through his skill the principles of the book are correctly and effectively applied until the patient is restored to health. Christ was a heavenly Physician. He brought spiritual health and healing into the world. Bahá'u'lláh is, likewise, a divine Physician. He has revealed prescriptions for removing disease from the body politic and has remedied human conditions by spiritual power.

7   Therefore, mere knowledge is not sufficient for complete human attainment. The teachings of the Holy Books need a

heavenly power and divine potency to carry them out. A house is not built by mere acquaintance with the plans. Money must be forthcoming; volition is necessary to construct it; a carpenter must be employed in its erection. It is not enough to say, "The plan and purpose of this house are very good; I will live in it." There are no walls of protection, there is no roof of shelter in this mere statement; the house must be actually built before we can live in it.

Briefly, the teachings of the Holy Books need a divine potency to complete their accomplishment in human hearts. In Persia Bahá'u'lláh reared and taught souls, established a bond of affiliation among various peoples and united divergent religious beliefs to such an extent that twenty thousand devoted ones sacrificed themselves for the Cause of God in the glorious unity of martyrdom. No differences whatever remained among these blessed souls—Christians, Jews, Muslims, Zoroastrians, all blended, unified and agreed through the potency of His heavenly power, not by mere words, not by merely saying, "Unity is good, and love is praiseworthy." 8

Bahá'u'lláh not only proclaimed this unity and love; He established it. As a heavenly Physician He not only gave prescriptions for these ailments of discord and hatred but accomplished the actual healing. We may read in a medical book that a certain form of illness requires such and such a remedy. While this may be absolutely true, the remedy is useless unless there be volition and executive force to apply it. Every man in the king's army can give a command; but when the king speaks, it is carried out. This one, that one, may say, "Go conquer a country"; but when the king says, "Go!", the army advances. Therefore, it is evident that the confirmation of the Holy Spirit and impelling influence of a heavenly power are needed to accomplish the divine purpose in human hearts and conditions. Jesus Christ, single, solitary and 9 alone, accomplished what all the kings of the earth could not have carried out. If all the kingdoms and nations of the world had combined to effect it, they would have failed.

10 It is, therefore, evident and proved that an effort must be put forward to complete the purpose and plan of the teachings of God in order that in this great Day of days the world may be reformed, souls resuscitated, a new spirit of life found, hearts become illumined, mankind rescued from the bondage of nature, saved from the baseness of materialism and attain spirituality and radiance in attraction toward the divine Kingdom. This is necessary; this is needful. Mere reading of the Holy Books and texts will not suffice.

11 Many years ago in Baghdád I saw a certain officer sitting upon the ground. Before him a large paper was placed into which he was sticking needles tipped with small red and white flags. First he would stick them into the paper, then thoughtfully pull them out and change their position. I watched him with curious interest for a long time, then asked, "What are you doing?" He replied, "I have in mind something which is historically related of Napoleon I during his war against Austria. One day, it is said, his secretary found him sitting upon the ground as I am now doing, sticking needles into a paper before him. His secretary inquired what it meant. Napoleon answered, 'I am on the battlefield figuring out my next victory. You see, Italy and Austria are defeated, and France is triumphant.' In the great campaign which followed, everything came out just as he said. His army carried his plans to a complete success. Now, I am doing the same as Napoleon, figuring out a great campaign of military conquest." I said, "Where is your army? Napoleon had an army already equipped when he figured out his victory. You have no army. Your forces exist only on paper. You have no power to conquer countries. First get ready your army, then sit

upon the ground with your needles." We need an army to attain victory in the spiritual world; mere plans are not sufficient; ideas and principles are helpless without a divine power to put them into effect.

Aside from all this, there is need of the stimulus of the joy 12 of glad tidings in human hearts. Certain spiritual attraction is requisite in order that hearts may willingly take the step forward in the divine Cause. We must become attracted to God. The breaths of the Holy Spirit must take effect. Unless this is so, it is impossible for the teachings of God to accomplish in us. An ideal power is necessary. The people of America have remarkably quick perception, intelligence and understanding. Their thoughts are free and not fettered by the yoke of governmental tyranny. They should investigate reality and not be occupied with ancestral forms and imitations. Consider what Christ accomplished. He caused souls to attain a station where with complete willingness and joy they laid down their lives. What a power! Thousands of human souls, in the utmost joy because of their spiritual susceptibilities, were so attracted to God that they were dispossessed of volition, deprived of will in His path. If they had been told simply that sacrifice in the path of God was good and praiseworthy, this would never have happened. They would not have acted. Christ attracted them, wrested the reins of control from them, and they went forth in ecstasy to sacrifice themselves.

Qurratu'l-'Ayn was a Persian woman without fame and im- 13 portance—unknown, like all other Persian women. When she saw Bahá'u'lláh, she changed completely, visibly, and looked within another world. The reins of volition were taken out of her hands by heavenly attraction. She was so overcome that physical susceptibilities ceased. Her husband, her sons and her family arose in the greatest hostility against Bahá'u'lláh. She became so attracted to the divine threshold that she forsook everything and went forth to the plain of Bada_sh_t, no fear in her heart, dauntless, intrepid, openly proclaiming the message of light which had come to her. The Persian government stood against her. They made every effort to quiet her, they imprisoned her in the governor's house, but she continued to speak. Then she was taken and killed. To her very last breath she spoke with fervid eloquence and so became famous for her complete attraction in the path of God. If she had not seen Bahá'u'lláh, no such effect would have been produced. She had read and heard the teachings of scriptures all her life, but the action and enkindlement were missing. All women in Persia are enveloped in veils in public. So completely covered are they that even the hand is not visible. This rigid veiling is unspeakable. Qurratu'l-'Ayn tore off her veils and went forth fearlessly. She was like a lioness. Her action caused a great turmoil throughout the land of Persia. So excessive and compulsory is the requirement for veiling in the East that the people in the West have no idea of the excitement and indignation produced by the appearance of an unveiled woman. Qurratu'l-'Ayn lost all thought of herself and was unconscious of fear in her attraction to God.

14   *Question:* Do the Bahá'í women go without veils in the East?

15   *Answer:* It is not possible for them to do so universally yet, but the conditions are not nearly so restrictive as they were. The Bahá'í men and women meet together. This is the beginning of woman's emancipation from the thralldom of centuries. Qurratu'l-'Ayn was really the liberator of all Persian women.

Talks 'Abdu'l-Bahá Delivered at Green Acre

16 August 1912

Talk at Green Acre
Eliot, Maine

NOTES BY EDNA MCKINNEY

EVERY subject presented to a thoughtful audience must be sup-   1
ported by rational proofs and logical arguments. Proofs are of
four kinds: first, through sense perception; second, through the
reasoning faculty; third, from traditional or scriptural authority;
fourth, through the medium of inspiration. That is to say, there
are four criteria or standards of judgment by which the human
mind reaches its conclusions. We will first consider the criterion
of the senses. This is a standard still held to by the materialistic
philosophers of the world. They believe that whatever is perceptible to the senses is a verity, a certainty and without doubt
existent. For example, they say, "Here is a lamp which you see,
and because it is perceptible to the sense of sight, you cannot
doubt its existence. There is a tree; your sense of vision assures
you of its reality, which is beyond question. This is a man; you
see that he is a man; therefore, he exists." In a word, everything
confirmed by the senses is assumed to be as undoubted and
unquestioned as the product of five multiplied by five; it cannot be twenty-six nor less than twenty-five. Consequently, the
materialistic philosophers consider the criterion of the senses
to be first and foremost.

But in the estimation of the divine philosophers this proof and   2
assurance is not reliable; nay, rather, they deem the standard of

the senses to be false because it is imperfect. Sight, for instance, is one of the most important of the senses, yet it is subject to many aberrations and inaccuracies. The eye sees the mirage as a body of water; it regards images in the mirror as realities when they are but reflections. A man sailing upon the river imagines that objects upon the shore are moving, whereas he is in motion, and they are stationary. To the eye the earth appears fixed, while the sun and stars revolve about it. As a matter of fact, the heavenly orbs are stationary, and the earth is turning upon its axis. The colossal suns, planets and constellations which shine in the heavens appear small, nay, infinitesimal to human vision, whereas in reality they are vastly greater than the earth in dimension and volume. A whirling spark appears to the sight as a circle of fire. There are numberless instances of this kind which show the error and inaccuracy of the senses. Therefore, the divine philosophers have considered this standard of judgment to be defective and unreliable.

3   The second criterion is that of the intellect. The ancient philosophers in particular considered the intellect to be the most important agency of judgment. Among the wise men of Greece, Rome, Persia and Egypt the criterion of true proof was reason. They held that every matter submitted to the reasoning faculty could be proved true or false and must be accepted or rejected accordingly. But in the estimation of the people of insight this criterion is likewise defective and unreliable, for these same philosophers who held to reason or intellect as the standard of human judgment have differed widely among themselves upon every subject of investigation. The statements of the Greek philosophers are contradictory to the conclusions of the Persian sages. Even among the Greek philosophers themselves there is continual variance and lack of agreement upon any given subject. Great difference of thought also prevailed between the

wise men of Greece and Rome. Therefore, if the criterion of reason or intellect constituted a correct and infallible standard of judgment, those who tested and applied it should have arrived at the same conclusions. As they differ and are contradictory in conclusions, it is an evidence that the method and standard of test must have been faulty and insufficient.

The third criterion or standard of proof is traditional or 4 scriptural—namely, that every statement or conclusion should be supported by traditions recorded in certain religious books. When we come to consider even the Holy Books—the Books of God—we are led to ask, "Who understands these books? By what authority of explanation may these Books be understood?" It must be the authority of human reason, and if reason or intellect finds itself incapable of explaining certain questions, or if the possessors of intellect contradict each other in the interpretation of traditions, how can such a criterion be relied upon for accurate conclusions?

The fourth standard is that of inspiration. In past centuries 5 many philosophers have claimed illumination or revelation, prefacing their statements by the announcement that "this subject has been revealed through me" or "thus do I speak by inspiration." Of this class were the philosophers of the Illuminati. Inspirations are the promptings or susceptibilities of the human heart. The promptings of the heart are sometimes satanic. How are we to differentiate them? How are we to tell whether a given statement is an inspiration and prompting of the heart through the merciful assistance or through the satanic agency?

Consequently, it has become evident that the four criteria or 6 standards of judgment by which the human mind reaches its conclusions are faulty and inaccurate. All of them are liable to mistake and error in conclusions. But a statement presented to the mind accompanied by proofs which the senses can perceive to be correct, which the faculty of reason can accept, which is in accord with traditional authority and sanctioned by the promptings of the heart, can be adjudged and relied upon as perfectly correct, for it has been proved and tested by all the standards of judgment and found to be complete. When we apply but one test, there are possibilities of mistake. This is self-evident and manifest.

7   We will now consider the subject of love which has been suggested, submitting it to the four standards of judgment and thereby reaching our conclusions.

8   We declare that love is the cause of the existence of all phenomena and that the absence of love is the cause of disintegration or nonexistence. Love is the conscious bestowal of God, the bond of affiliation in all phenomena. We will first consider the proof of this through sense perception. As we look upon the universe, we observe that all composite beings or existing phenomena are made up primarily of single elements bound together by a power of attraction. Through this power of attraction cohesion has become manifest between atoms of these composing elements. The resultant being is a phenomenon of the lower contingent type. The power of cohesion expressed in the mineral kingdom is in reality love or affinity manifested in a low degree according to the exigencies of the mineral world. We take a step higher into the vegetable kingdom where we find an increased power of attraction has become manifest among the composing elements which form phenomena. Through this degree of attraction a cellular admixture is produced among these elements which make up the body of a plant. Therefore, in the degree of the vegetable kingdom there is love. We enter the animal kingdom and find the attractive power binding together single elements as in the mineral, plus the cellular admixture as in the vegetable, plus the phenomena of feelings or

susceptibilities. We observe that the animals are susceptible to certain affiliation and fellowship and that they exercise natural selection. This elemental attraction, this admixture and selective affinity is love manifest in the degree of the animal kingdom.

Finally, we come to the kingdom of man. As this is the superior kingdom, the light of love is more resplendent. In man we find the power of attraction among the elements which compose his material body, plus the attraction which produces cellular admixture or augmentative power, plus the attraction which characterizes the sensibilities of the animal kingdom, but still beyond and above all these lower powers we discover in the being of man the attraction of heart, the susceptibilities and affinities which bind men together, enabling them to live and associate in friendship and solidarity. It is, therefore, evident that in the world of humanity the greatest king and sovereign is love. If love were extinguished, the power of attraction dispelled, the affinity of human hearts destroyed, the phenomena of human life would disappear. 9

This is a proof perceptible to the senses, acceptable to reason, in accord with traditions and teachings of the Holy Books and verified by the promptings of human hearts themselves. It is a proof upon which we can absolutely rely and declare to be complete. But these are only degrees of love which exist in the natural or physical world. Their manifestation is ever according to the requirement of natural conditions and standards. 10

Real love is the love which exists between God and His servants, the love which binds together holy souls. This is the love of the spiritual world, not the love of physical bodies and organisms. For example, consider and observe how the bestowals of God successively descend upon mankind, how the divine effulgences ever shine upon the human world. There can be no doubt that these bestowals, these bounties, these effulgences 11 emanate from love. Unless love be the divine motive, it would be impossible for the heart of man to attain or receive them. Unless love exists, the divine blessing could not descend upon any object or thing. Unless there be love, the recipient of divine effulgence could not radiate and reflect that effulgence upon other objects. If we are of those who perceive, we realize that the bounties of God manifest themselves continuously, even as the rays of the sun unceasingly emanate from the solar center. The phenomenal world through the resplendent effulgence of the sun is radiant and bright. In the same way the realm of hearts and spirits is illumined and resuscitated through the shining rays of the Sun of Reality and the bounties of the love of God. Thereby the world of existence, the kingdom of hearts and spirits, is ever quickened into life. Were it not for the love of God, hearts would be inanimate, spirits would wither, and the reality of man would be bereft of the everlasting bestowals.

12   Consider to what extent the love of God makes itself manifest. Among the signs of His love which appear in the world are the dawning points of His Manifestations. What an infinite degree of love is reflected by the divine Manifestations toward mankind! For the sake of guiding the people They have willingly forfeited Their lives to resuscitate human hearts. They have accepted the cross. To enable human souls to attain the supreme degree of advancement, They have suffered during Their limited years extreme ordeals and difficulties. If Jesus Christ had not possessed love for the world of humanity, surely He would not have welcomed the cross. He was crucified for the love of mankind. Consider the infinite degree of that love. Without love for humanity John the Baptist would not have offered his life. It has been likewise with all the Prophets and Holy Souls. If the Báb had not manifested love for mankind, surely He would not have offered His breast for a thousand bullets. If Bahá'u'lláh

had not been aflame with love for humanity, He would not have willingly accepted forty years' imprisonment.

Observe how rarely human souls sacrifice their pleasure or comfort for others, how improbable that a man would offer his eye or suffer himself to be dismembered for the benefit of another. Yet all the divine Manifestations suffered, offered Their lives and blood, sacrificed Their existence, comfort and all They possessed for the sake of mankind. Therefore, consider how much They love. Were it not for Their love for humanity, spiritual love would be mere nomenclature. Were it not for Their illumination, human souls would not be radiant. How effective is Their love! This is a sign of the love of God, a ray of the Sun of Reality.

Therefore, we must give praise unto God, for it is the light of His bounty which has shone upon us through His love which is everlasting. His divine Manifestations have offered Their lives through love for us. Consider, then, what the love of God means. Were it not for the love of God, all the spirits would be inanimate. The meaning of this is not physical death; nay, rather, it is that condition concerning which Christ declared, "Let the dead bury their dead," for "That which is born of the flesh is flesh; and that which is born of the Spirit is spirit." Were it not for the love of God, the hearts would not be illumined. Were it not for the love of God, the pathway of the Kingdom would not be opened. Were it not for the love of God, the Holy Books would not have been revealed. Were it not for the love of God, the divine Prophets would not have been sent to the world. The foundation of all these bestowals is the love of God. Therefore, in the human world there is no greater power than the love of God. It is the love of God which has brought us together here tonight. It is the love of God which is affiliating the East and the West. It is the love of God which has resuscitated the world.

Now we must offer thanks to God that such a great bestowal and effulgence has been revealed to us.

15   We come to another aspect of our subject: Are the workings and effects of love confined to this world, or do they extend on and on to another existence? Will its influence affect our existence here only, or will it extend to the everlasting life? When we look upon the human kingdom, we readily observe that it is superior to all others. In the differentiation of life in the world of existence, there are four degrees or kingdoms: the mineral, vegetable, animal and human. The mineral kingdom is possessed of a certain virtue which we term cohesion. The vegetable kingdom possesses cohesive properties plus the power of growth, or augmentative power. The animal kingdom is possessed of the virtues of the mineral and vegetable plus the powers of the senses. But the animal, although gifted with sensibilities, is utterly bereft of consciousness, absolutely out of touch with the world of consciousness and spirit. The animal possesses no powers by which it can make discoveries which lie beyond the realm of the senses. It has no power of intellectual origination. For example, an animal located in Europe is not capable of discovering the continent of America. It understands only phenomena which come within the range of its senses and instinct. It cannot abstractly reason out anything. The animal cannot conceive of the earth being spherical or revolving upon its axis. It cannot apprehend that the little stars in the heavens are tremendous worlds vastly greater than the earth. The animal cannot abstractly conceive of intellect. Of these powers it is bereft. Therefore, these powers are peculiar to man, and it is made evident that in the human kingdom there is a reality of which the animal is lacking. What is that reality? It is the spirit of man. By it man is distinguished above all the other phenomenal kingdoms. Although he possesses all the virtues of the lower

kingdoms, he is further endowed with the spiritual faculty, the heavenly gift of consciousness.

All material phenomena are subject to nature. All material 16 organisms are captives of nature. None of them can deviate in the slightest from the laws of nature. This earth, these great mountains, the animals with their wonderful powers and instincts cannot go beyond natural limitations. All things are captives of nature except man. Man is the sovereign of nature; he breaks nature's laws. Though an animal fitted by nature to live upon the surface of the earth, he flies in the air like a bird, sails upon the ocean and dives deep beneath its waves in submarines. Man is gifted with a power whereby he penetrates and discovers the laws of nature, brings them forth from the world of invisibility into the plane of visibility. Electricity was once a latent force of nature. According to nature's laws it should remain a hidden secret, but the spirit of man discovered it, brought it forth from its secret depository and made its phenomena visible. It is evident and manifest that man is capable of breaking nature's laws. How does he accomplish it? Through a spirit with which God has endowed him at creation. This is a proof that the spirit of man differentiates and distinguishes him above all the lower kingdoms. It is this spirit to which the verse in the Old Testament refers when it states, "And God said, Let us make man in our image, after our likeness." The spirit of man alone penetrates the realities of God and partakes of the divine bounties.

This great power must evidently be differentiated from the 17 physical body or temple in which it is manifested. Observe and understand how this human body changes; nevertheless, the spirit of man remains ever in the same condition. For instance, the body sometimes grows weak, it becomes strong or stout, sometimes it grows smaller or may be dismembered, but there is no effect upon the spirit. The eye may become blind, the foot may be amputated, but no imperfection afflicts the spirit. This is proof that the spirit of man is distinct from his body. Defects in the body or its members do not imply defects in the spirit. This leads to the accurate conclusion that if the whole body should be subjected to a radical change, the spirit will survive that change; that even if the body of man is destroyed and becomes nonexistent, the spirit of man remains unaffected. For the spirit of man is everlasting. Sometimes the body sleeps, the eyes do not see, the ears do not hear, the members cease to act, every function is as inactive as death; nevertheless, the spirit sees, hears and soars on high. For it is possessed of these faculties which operate without the instrumentality of the body. In the world of thought it sees without eyes, hears without ears and travels without the motion of foot. Without physical force it exercises every function. This makes it evident that during sleep the spirit is alive though the body is as dead. In the world of dreams the body becomes absolutely passive, but the spirit still functions actively, possessed of all susceptibilities. This leads to the conclusion that the life of the spirit is neither conditional nor dependent upon the life of the body. At most it can be said that the body is a mere garment utilized by the spirit. If that garment be destroyed, the wearer is not affected but is, in fact, protected.

18   Furthermore, all phenomena are subject to changes from one condition to another, and the revolution caused by this trans-formation produces a form of nonexistence. For instance, when a man is transformed from the human kingdom to the mineral, we say that he is dead, for he has relinquished the physical form of man and assumed the condition of the mineral substances. This transformation or transmutation is called death. Therefore, it follows that no phenomenal organism can be possessed of two forms at the same time. If an object or phenomenon presents a

triangular shape, it cannot simultaneously possess the shape of a square. If it is spherical, it cannot at the same time be pentagonal or hexagonal. In order to assume any given figure or form it must relinquish its previous shape or dimension. Thus the triangular must be abandoned to assume the square; the square must change to become a pentagon. These transformations or changes from one condition to another are equivalent to death. But the reality of man, the human spirit, is simultaneously possessed of all forms and figures without being bereft of any of them. It does not require transformation from one concept to another. Were it to be bereft of one or all figures, we would then say it has been transferred to another, and this would be equivalent to death. But as the human spirit possesses all the figures simultaneously, it has no transformation or death.

Again, according to natural philosophy it is an assured fact 19 that single or simple elements are indestructible. As nature is indestructible, every simple element of nature is lasting and permanent. Death and annihilation affect only compounds and compositions. That is to say, compositions are destructible. When decomposition takes place, death occurs. For example, certain single elements have combined to make this flower. When this combination is disintegrated, this composition decomposed, the flower dies as an organism of the vegetable kingdom. But the single elements of which this flower is composed do not suffer death, for all single elements are permanent, everlasting and not subject to destruction. They are indestructible because they are single and not compound. Thus they cannot disintegrate nor become separated in their component atoms but are single, simple and, therefore, everlasting.

If an elementary substance is possessed of immortality, how 20 can the human spirit or reality, which is wholly above combination and composition, be destroyed? Nay, rather, that spirit, which is all in all, is a unit and not a compound. Its destruction, therefore, is not possible. The spirit of man transcends the qualities and attributes of any natural element. It is greater in attributes than gold, silver or iron, which are single elements and indestructible. As they are free from destruction and qualified with permanence, how much more so is the human spirit free and immortal. How will that ever be destroyed? This is a subject of great importance. There are innumerable proofs in support of it. I hope we may continue it at another time.

21   Before we leave, I desire to offer a prayer in behalf of Miss Farmer; for, verily, she has been the founder of this organization, the source of this loving fellowship and assemblage.

22   O Thou kind God! Encircle these servants with the glances of Thy providence. Set aglow the hearts of this assemblage with the fire of Thy love. Illumine these faces with the light of heaven. Enlighten these hearts with the light of the most great guidance.

23   O God! The clouds of superstitions have covered the horizons of the hearts. O Lord! Dispel these clouds so that the lights of the Sun of Reality may shine. O Lord! Illumine our eyes so that we may behold Thy light. O Lord! Attune our ears so that we may hear the call of the Supreme Concourse. O Lord! Render our tongues eloquent so that we may become engaged in Thy commemoration. O Lord! Sanctify and purify the hearts so that the effulgence of Thy love may shine therein.

24   O Thou kind Lord! Bestow quick recovery through Thy power and bounty upon the founder of this Association. O Lord! This woman has served Thee, has turned her face toward Thy Kingdom and has established these conferences in order that reality might be investigated and the light of reality shine.

25   O Lord! Be Thou ever her support. O Lord! Be Thou ever her comforter. O Lord! Bestow upon her quick healing. Verily, Thou art the Clement. Verily, Thou art the Merciful. Verily, Thou art the Generous.

2

17 August 1912

Talk at Green Acre
Eliot, Maine

NOTES BY EDNA MCKINNEY

THE physical beauty of this place is very wonderful. We hope 1
that a spiritual charm may surround and halo it; then its beauty
will be perfect. There is a spiritual atmosphere manifest here
particularly at sunset.

In cities like New York the people are submerged in the sea of 2
materialism. Their sensibilities are attuned to material forces, their
perceptions purely physical. The animal energies predominate in
their activities; all their thoughts are directed to material things; day
and night they are devoted to the attractions of this world, without
aspiration beyond the life that is vanishing and mortal. In schools
and temples of learning knowledge of the sciences acquired is based
upon material observations only; there is no realization of Divinity
in their methods and conclusions—all have reference to the world
of matter. They are not interested in attaining knowledge of the
mysteries of God or understanding the secrets of the heavenly Kingdom; what they acquire is based altogether upon visible and tangible
evidences. Beyond these evidences they are without susceptibilities;
they have no idea of the world of inner significances and are
utterly out of touch with God, considering this an indication
of reasonable attitude and philosophical judgement whereof
they are self-sufficient and proud.

As a matter of fact, this supposed excellence is possessed in 3
its superlative degree by the animals. The animals are without
knowledge of God; so to speak, they are deniers of Divinity and

understand nothing of the Kingdom and its heavenly mysteries. As deniers of the Kingdom, they are utterly ignorant of spiritual things and uninformed of the supernatural world. Therefore, if it be a perfection and virtue to be without knowledge of God and His Kingdom, the animals have attained the highest degree of excellence and proficiency. Then the donkey is the greatest scientist and the cow an accomplished naturalist, for they have obtained what they know without schooling and years of laborious study in colleges, trusting implicitly to the evidence of the senses and relying solely upon intuitive virtues. The cow, for instance, is a lover of the visible and a believer in the tangible, contented and happy when pasture is plenty, perfectly serene, a blissful exponent of the transcendental school of philosophy. Such is the status of the material philosophers, who glory in sharing the condition of the cow, imagining themselves in a lofty station. Reflect upon their ignorance and blindness.

4   Nay, rather, the virtue of man is this: that he can investigate the ideals of the Kingdom and attain knowledge which is denied the animal in its limitation. The station of man is this: that he has the power to attain those ideals and thereby differentiate and consciously distinguish himself an infinite degree above the kingdoms of existence below him.

5   The station of man is great, very great. God has created man after His own image and likeness. He has endowed him with a mighty power which is capable of discovering the mysteries of phenomena. Through its use man is able to arrive at ideal conclusions instead of being restricted to the mere plane of sense impressions. As he possesses sense endowment in common with the animals, it is evident that he is distinguished above them by his conscious power of penetrating abstract realities. He acquires divine wisdom; he searches out the mysteries of creation; he witnesses the radiance of omnipotence; he attains the second

birth—that is to say, he is born out of the material world just as he is born of the mother; he attains to everlasting life; he draws nearer to God; his heart is replete with the love of God. This is the foundation of the world of humanity; this is the image and likeness of God; this is the reality of man; otherwise, he is an animal. Verily, God has created the animal in the image and likeness of man, for though man outwardly is human, yet in nature he possesses animal tendencies.

You must endeavor to understand the mysteries of God, attain   6
the ideal knowledge and arrive at the station of vision, acquiring directly from the Sun of Reality and receiving a destined portion from the ancient bestowal of God.

3

17 August 1912

Talk at Green Acre
Eliot, Maine

NOTES BY EDNA MCKINNEY

ALTHOUGH the body was weak and not fitted to undergo the vicis-   1
situdes of crossing the Atlantic, yet love assisted us, and we came here. At certain times the spirit must assist the body. We cannot accomplish really great things through physical force alone; the spirit must fortify our bodily strength. For example, the body of man may be able to withstand the ordeal of imprisonment for ten or fifteen years under temperate conditions of climate and restful physical routine. During our imprisonment in 'Akká means of comfort were lacking, troubles and persecutions of

all kinds surrounded us, yet notwithstanding such distressful conditions, we were able to endure these trials for forty years. The climate was very bad, necessities and conveniences of life were denied us, yet we endured this narrow prison forty years. What was the reason? The spirit was strengthening and resuscitating the body constantly. We lived through this long, difficult period in the utmost love and heavenly servitude. The spirit must assist the body under certain conditions which surround us, because the body of itself cannot endure the extreme strain of such hardships.

2   The human body is in reality very weak; there is no physical body more delicately constituted. One mosquito will distress it; the smallest quantity of poison will destroy it; if respiration ceases for a moment, it will die. What instrument could be weaker and more delicate? A blade of grass severed from the root may live an hour, whereas a human body deprived of its forces may die in one minute. But in the proportion that the human body is weak, the spirit of man is strong. It can control natural phenomena; it is a supernatural power which transcends all contingent beings. It has immortal life, which nothing can destroy or pervert. If all the kingdoms of life arise against the immortal spirit of man and seek its destruction, this immortal spirit, singly and alone, can withstand their attacks in fearless firmness and resolution because it is indestructible and empowered with supreme natural virtues. For this reason we say that the spirit of man can penetrate and discover the realities of all things, can solve the secrets and mysteries of all created objects. While living upon the earth, it discovers the stars and their satellites; it travels underground, finds the metals in their hidden depths and unlocks the secrets of geological ages. It can cross the abysses of interstellar space and discover the motion of inconceivably distant suns. How wonderful it is! It can attain to the Kingdom of God. It can penetrate the mysteries of the divine

Kingdom and attain to everlasting life. It receives illumination from the light of God and reflects it to the whole universe. How wonderful it is! How powerful the spirit of man, while his body is so weak! If the susceptibilities of the spirit control him, there is no created being more heroic, more undaunted than man; but if physical forces dominate, you cannot find a more cowardly or fearful object because the body is so weak and incapable. Therefore, it is divinely intended that the spiritual susceptibilities of man should gain precedence and overrule his physical forces. In this way he becomes fitted to dominate the human world by his nobility and stand forth fearless and free, endowed with the attributes of eternal life.

4

17 August 1912

Talk at Green Acre
Eliot, Maine

Notes by Edna McKinney

ARE you all well and happy? This is a delightful spot; the scenery 1 is beautiful, and an atmosphere of spirituality haloes everything. In the future, God willing, Green Acre shall become a great center, the cause of the unity of the world of humanity, the cause of uniting hearts and binding together the East and the West. This is my hope.

Tonight I wish to speak upon the oneness of the world of 2 humanity. This is one of the important subjects of the present period. If the oneness of the human world were established, all the differences which separate mankind would be eradicated.

Strife and warfare would cease, and the world of humanity would find repose. Universal peace would be promoted, and the East and West would be conjoined in a strong bond. All men would be sheltered beneath one tabernacle. Native lands would become one; races and religions would be unified. The people of the world would live together in harmony, and their well-being would be assured.

3   From the beginning of human history down to the present time the various religions of the world have anathematized and accused each other of falsity. Each religion has considered the others bereft of the face of God, deprived of His mercy and in the direct line of divine wrath. Therefore, they have shunned each other most rigidly, exercising mutual animosity and rancor. Consider the record of religious warfare, the battles between nations, the bloodshed and destruction in the name of religion. One of the greatest religious wars, the Crusades, extended over a period of two hundred years. In this succession of great campaigns the western crusaders were constantly invading the Orient, bent upon recovering the Holy City from the hands of the Islamic people. Army after army raised in Europe poured its fanatical legions into the East. The kings of European nations personally led these Crusades, killing and shedding the blood of the Orientals. During this period of two hundred years the East and West were in a state of violence and commotion. Sometimes the crusaders were successful, killing, pillaging and taking captive the Muslim people; sometimes the Muslims were victorious, inflicting bloodshed, death and ruin in turn upon the invaders. So they continued for two centuries, alternately fighting with fury and relaxing from weakness, until the European religionists withdrew from the East, leaving ashes of desolation behind them and finding their own nations in a condition of turbulence and upheaval. Hundreds of thousands of human beings were killed

and untold wealth wasted in this fruitless religious warfare. How many fathers mourned the loss of their sons! How many mothers and wives lamented the absence of their dear ones! Yet this was only one of the "holy" wars. Consider and reflect.

Religious wars have been many. Nine hundred thousand 4 martyrs to the Protestant cause was the record of conflict and difference between that sect of Christians and the Catholics. Consult history and confirm this. How many languished in prisons! How merciless the treatment of captives! All in the name of religion! Consider and estimate the outcome of other wars between the people and sects of religious belief.

From the beginning of human history down to this time the 5 world of humanity has not enjoyed a day of absolute rest and relaxation from conflict and strife. Most of the wars have been caused by religious prejudice, fanaticism and sectarian hatred. Religionists have anathematized religionists, each considering the other as deprived of the mercy of God, abiding in gross darkness and the children of Satan. For example, the Christians and Muslims considered the Jews satanic and the enemies of God. Therefore, they cursed and persecuted them. Great numbers of Jews were killed, their houses burned and pillaged, their children carried into captivity. The Jews in turn regarded the Christians as infidels and the Muslims as enemies and destroyers of the law of Moses. Therefore, they call down vengeance upon them and curse them even to this day.

Consider what injuries, ordeals and calamities have been 6 inflicted upon mankind since the beginning of history. Every city, country, nation and people has been subjected to the destruction and havoc of war. Each one of the divine religions considers itself as belonging to a goodly and blessed tree, the tree of the Merciful, and all other religious systems as belonging to a tree of evil, the tree of Satan. For this reason they heap execration and abuse upon each other. This is clearly apparent in books of historical record and prevailed until the time of the appearance of Bahá'u'lláh.

7   When the light of Bahá'u'lláh dawned from the East, He proclaimed the promise of the oneness of humanity. He addressed all mankind, saying, "Ye are all the fruits of one tree. There are not two trees: one a tree of divine mercy, the other the tree of Satan." Again He said, "Ye are all the fruits of one tree, the leaves of one branch." This was His announcement; this was His promise of the oneness of the world of humanity. Anathema and execration were utterly abrogated. He said, "It is not becoming in man to curse another; it is not befitting that man should attribute darkness to another; it is not meet that one human being should consider another human being as bad; nay, rather, all mankind are the servants of one God; God is the Father of all; there is not a single exception to that law. There are no people of Satan; all belong to the Merciful. There is no darkness; all is light. All are the servants of God, and man must love humanity from his heart. He must, verily, behold humanity as submerged in the divine mercy."

8   Bahá'u'lláh has made no exception to this rule. He said that among mankind there may be those who are ignorant; they must be trained. Some are sick; they must be treated. Some are immature; they must be helped to attain maturity. In other respects humanity is submerged in the ocean of divine mercy. God is the Father of all. He educates, provides for and loves all; for they are His servants and His creation. Surely the Creator loves His creatures. It would be impossible to find an artist who does not love his own production. Have you ever seen a man who did not love his own actions? Even though they be bad actions, he loves them. How ignorant, therefore, the thought that God, Who created man, educated and nurtured him, surrounded him

with all blessings, made the sun and all phenomenal existence for his benefit, bestowed upon him tenderness and kindness and then did not love him. This is palpable ignorance, for no matter to what religion a man belongs, even though he be an atheist or materialist, nevertheless, God nurtures him, bestows His kindness and sheds upon him His light. How then can we believe God is wrathful and unloving? How can we even imagine this, when as a matter of fact we are witnesses of the tenderness and mercy of God upon every hand? All about us we behold manifestations of the love of God. If, therefore, God be loving, what should we do? We have nothing else to do but to emulate Him. Just as God loves all and is kind to all, so must we really love and be kind to everybody. We must consider none bad, none worthy of detestation, no one as an enemy. We must love all; nay, we must consider everyone as related to us, for all are the servants of one God. All are under the instructions of one Educator. We must strive day and night that love and amity may increase, that this bond of unity may be strengthened, that joy and happiness may more and more prevail, that in unity and solidarity all mankind may gather beneath the shadow of God, that people may turn to God for their sustenance, finding in Him the life that is everlasting. Thus may they be confirmed in the Kingdom of God and live forever through His grace and bounty.

Bahá'u'lláh has clearly said in His Tablets that if you have an enemy, consider him not as an enemy. Do not simply be long-suffering; nay, rather, love him. Your treatment of him should be that which is becoming to lovers. Do not even say that he is your enemy. Do not see any enemies. Though he be your murderer, see no enemy. Look upon him with the eye of friendship. Be mindful that you do not consider him as an enemy and simply tolerate him, for that is but stratagem and hypocrisy. To consider a man your enemy and love him is hypocrisy. This is not becoming of any soul. You must behold him as a friend. You must treat him well. This is right.

10   We return to the subject. When we observe the phenomena of the universe, we realize that the axis around which life revolves is love, while the axis around which death and destruction revolve is animosity and hatred. Let us view the mineral kingdom. Here we see that if attraction did not exist between the atoms, the composite substance of matter would not be possible. Every existent phenomenon is composed of elements and cellular particles. This is scientifically true and correct. If attraction did not exist between the elements and among the cellular particles, the composition of that phenomenon would never have been possible. For instance, the stone is an existent phenomenon, a composition of elements. A bond of attraction has brought them together, and through this cohesion of ingredients this petrous object has been formed. This stone is the lowest degree of phenomena, but nevertheless within it a power of attraction is manifest without which the stone could not exist. This power of attraction in the mineral world is love, the only expression of love the stone can manifest.

11   Look now upon the next highest stage of life, the vegetable kingdom. Here we see that the plant is the result of cohesion among various elements, just as the mineral is in its kingdom; but, furthermore, the plant has the power of absorption from the earth. This is a higher degree of attraction which differentiates the plant from the mineral. In the kingdom of the vegetable this is an expression of love, the highest capacity of expression the vegetable possesses. By this power of attraction, or augmentation, the plant grows day by day. Therefore, in this kingdom, also, love is the cause of life. If repulsion existed among the elements instead of attraction, the result would be disintegration, destruction and nonexistence. Because cohesion exists

among the elements and cellular attraction is manifest, the plant appears. When this attraction is dispelled and the ingredients separate, the plant ceases to exist.

Then we come to the animal world, which is still higher in 12 degree than the vegetable kingdom. In it the power of love makes itself still more manifest. The light of love is more resplendent in the animal kingdom because the power of attraction whereby elements cohere and cellular atoms commingle now reveals itself in certain emotions and sensibilities which produce instinctive fellowship and association. The animals are imbued with kindness and affinity which manifests itself among those of the same species.

Finally, we reach the kingdom of man. Here we find that all 13 the degrees of the mineral, vegetable and animal expressions of love are present plus unmistakable attractions of consciousness. That is to say, man is the possessor of a degree of attraction which is conscious and spiritual. Here is an immeasurable advance. In the human kingdom spiritual susceptibilities come into view, love exercises its superlative degree, and this is the cause of human life.

The proof is clear that in all degrees and kingdoms unity and 14 agreement, love and fellowship are the cause of life, whereas dissension, animosity and separation are ever conducive to death. Therefore, we must strive with life and soul in order that day by day unity and agreement may be increased among mankind and that love and affinity may become more resplendently glorious and manifest. In the animal kingdom you will observe that domestic species live together in the utmost fellowship. See how sociable and friendly sheep gather together in a flock. Look at the doves and other domestic birds. There is no partisanship among them, no separation due to notions of patriotism. They live together in the utmost love and unity, flying, feeding, associating.

Ferocious animals—beasts of prey such as the wolf, bear, tiger and hyena—are never amicable and do not associate together. They attack one another. Whenever they meet, they fight. Three wolves are never seen associating happily. If you see them together, it is with some ferocious intent. They are like selfish, brutal men who are inimical, cursing and killing each other. Better that man should resemble the domestic animals than the ferocious beasts of prey, for in the estimation of God love is acceptable, whereas hatred and animosity are rejected. Why should we act contrary to the good pleasure of God? Why should we be as ferocious animals, constantly shedding blood, pillaging and destroying? Because we belong to one race or family of humankind, why should we consider all others bad and inferior, deserving of death, pillage and invasion—people of darkness, worthy of hatred and detestation by God? Why does man show forth such attitude and actions toward his fellowman? We see that God is kind to all. Just as He loves us, He loves all others; just as He provides for us, He provides for the rest. He nurtures and trains all with equal solicitude.

15   God is great! God is kind! He does not behold human short-comings; He does not regard human weaknesses. Man is a creature of His mercy, and to His mercy He summons all. Why then should we despise or detest His creatures because this one is a Jew, another a Buddhist or Zoroastrian and so on? This is ignorance, for the oneness of humanity as servants of God is an assured and certain fact.

16   Bahá'u'lláh has proclaimed the promise of the oneness of humanity. Therefore, we must exercise the utmost love toward each other. We must be loving to all the people of the world. We must not consider any people the people of Satan, but know and recognize all as the servants of the one God. At most it is this: Some do not know; they must be guided and trained. They must be taught to love their fellow creatures and be en-

couraged in the acquisition of virtues. Some are ignorant; they must be informed. Some are as children, undeveloped; they must be helped to reach maturity. Some are ailing, their moral condition is unhealthy; they must be treated until their morals are purified. But the sick man is not to be hated because he is sick, the child must not be shunned because he is a child, the ignorant one is not to be despised because he lacks knowledge. They must all be treated, educated, trained and assisted in love. Everything must be done in order that humanity may live under the shadow of God in the utmost security, enjoying happiness in its highest degree.

5

17 August 1912

Talk at Green Acre
Eliot, Maine

NOTES BY EDNA MCKINNEY

THE worlds of God are in perfect harmony and correspondence 1
one with another. Each world in this limitless universe is, as it were, a mirror reflecting the history and nature of all the rest. The physical universe is, likewise, in perfect correspondence with the spiritual or divine realm. The world of matter is an outer expression or facsimile of the inner kingdom of spirit. The world of minds corresponds with the world of hearts.

If we look reflectively upon the material world, we realize that 2
all outer phenomena are dependent upon the sun. Without the sun the phenomenal world would be in a state of utter darkness and devoid of life. All earthly creation—whether mineral,

vegetable, animal or human—is dependent upon the heat, light and splendor of the great central solar body for training and development. Were it not for the solar heat and sunlight, no minerals would have been formed, no vegetable, animal and human organisms would or could have become existent. It is clearly evident, therefore, that the sun is the source of life to all earthly and outer phenomena.

3   In the inner world, the world of the Kingdom, the Sun of Reality is the Trainer and Educator of minds, souls and spirits. Were it not for the effulgent rays of the Sun of Reality, they would be deprived of growth and development; nay, rather, they would be nonexistent. For just as the physical sun is the trainer of all outer and phenomenal forms of being through the radiation of its light and heat, so the radiation of the light and heat of the Sun of Reality gives growth, education and evolution to minds, souls and spirits toward the station of perfection.

4   Christ was the Sun of Reality which shone from the heavenly horizon of Christianity, training, protecting, confirming minds, souls and spirits until they came into harmony with the divine Kingdom and attained capacity for descent of the infinite bounties of God. Were it not for the appearance of His splendor, they would have remained in the darkness of imperfection and remoteness from God. But because that Sun of Reality shone forth and flooded its light into the world of minds, souls and spirits, they became radiant. He conferred a new and eternal life upon them.

5   When the phenomenal sun appears from the vernal point of dawning in the zodiac, a wondrous and vibrant commotion is set up in the body of the earthly world. The withered trees are quickened with animation, the black soil becomes verdant with new growth, fresh and fragrant flowers bloom, the world of dust is refreshed, renewed life forces surge through the veins of every animate being, and a new springtime carpets the mead-

ows, plains, mountains and valleys with wondrous forms of life. That which was dead and desolate is revived and resuscitated; that which was withered, faded and stricken is transformed by the spirit of a new creation. In the same way the Sun of Reality, when it illumines the horizon of the inner world, animates, vivifies and quickens with a divine and wonderful power. The trees of human minds clothe themselves in new and verdant robes, putting on leaves and blossoms and bearing spiritual fruits of the heavenly glad tidings. Then fragrant flowers of inner significances appear from the soil of human souls, and the whole being of man awakens to a new and divine activity. This is the growth and development of the inner world through the effulgent light of divine guidance and the heat of the fire of the love of God.

The physical sun has its rising and its setting. The earthly   6 world has its day and its night. After each sunset there is a sunrise and the coming of a new dawn. The Sun of Reality, likewise, has its rising and setting. There is a day and a night in the world of spirituality. After each departure there is a return and the dawning light of a new day.

Furthermore, the reality of Divinity is characterized by   7 certain names and attributes. Among these names are Creator, Resuscitator, Provider, the All-Present, Almighty, Omniscient and Giver. These names and attributes of Divinity are eternal and not accidental. This is a very subtle point which demands close attention. Their existence is proved and necessitated by the appearance of phenomena. For example, Creator presupposes creation, Resuscitator implies resuscitation, Provider necessitates provision; otherwise, these would be empty and impossible names. Merciful evidences an object upon which mercy is bestowed. If mercy were not manifest, this attribute of God would not be realized. The name Lord proves the existence of subjects over whom sovereignty is exercised. The name

Omniscient demands the objects of all-knowing. Unless these objects existed, omniscience would be meaningless and without function. The name the Wise necessitates objects for the exercise of wisdom; and unless wisdom comprehended them, this name would be inconceivable. Therefore, the divine names and attributes presuppose the existence of phenomena implied by those names and attributes. And vice versa—the sovereignty of God is proved and established through their verity and being.

8   Reflect then carefully that the sovereignty of God is not accidental but everlasting and eternal, and that it necessitates the existence of phenomenal being. Kingship necessitates a kingdom, an army, a treasury, subjects, a court and ministers. How could there be a king without subjects, dominion and wealth? Otherwise, anybody could claim to be a king. "Where is your army?" "I do not need one." "Where is your country?" "It is unnecessary. I am a king without a kingdom, without army, subjects or sovereignty." Is this possible?

9   Therefore, divine sovereignty necessitates a creation over which its dominion is exercised. There must be evidences of sovereignty. If we try to conceive of a time when creation was nonexistent, when there were no subjects or creatures under divine dominion and control, Divinity itself would disappear; there would be a cessation of the bounty of God, just as the kingship and favor of an earthly monarch would disappear if his kingdom did not exist. The sovereignty of God is eternal. There has been no beginning; there will be no end. This is as evident as the sun at midday, even to one endowed with limited reason.

10   When we consider the phenomenal sun, we see that its heat and light are continuous. There is no cessation to the solar bounty. If the sun at any time were without light or heat, it would not be the sun. How do we recognize the sun? Through its heat and effulgence. If it be deprived of its rays and heat, it is no longer a sun; it is merely a dark globe or sphere in the

380

heavens. The bounties of the sun must be perpetual in order that it may be qualified as a solar center of energy, illumination and attraction.

Likewise, the divine bounties of the Sun of Reality are perpetual. Its light is forever shining. Its love is forever radiating. Its bounty never ceases. It could not be said that the power and effulgence of God was ever subject to cessation. It could not be claimed that the divinity of the Almighty One had come to an end. For the divinity of God is eternal. Therefore, the divine bounties—whether phenomenal and accidental or spiritual and ideal—are perpetual. But the people of religion are of two kinds: Some worship the sun, and some adore the dawning points from which the sun rises. For instance, the Jews adore the Mosaic point of dawning, the Zoroastrians that of Zoroaster. The people of Abraham turned to the point of rising in Abraham. When the Sun of Reality transferred its illumination from the Abrahamic to the Mosaic point of dawning, the people of Abraham denied its appearance because they were turning toward the point and not to the Sun of Reality itself. When that Sun of Reality with its divine bestowal, its heavenly glow and effulgence transferred to the Messianic point of rising, the Jews denied its appearance in Jesus, for they were not worshipers of the Sun itself but adored its rising in Moses. Had they been worshipers of the Sun of Reality, they would have turned to Christ instead of denying Him as the Messiah.

What was the reason of this deprivation? It was simply because they were imitating fathers and ancestors in forms of belief instead of turning toward the Sun of Divinity. For this reason they were deprived of the bounty which dawned in the Messianic dayspring. Holding tenaciously to the former dawning point, they still remain in this position of deprivation. Consider the people and nations of the earth today and observe this same tenacious allegiance to ancestral belief. He whose father was a

Zoroastrian is a Zoroastrian. He whose father was a Buddhist remains a Buddhist. The son of a Muslim continues a Muslim, and so on throughout. Why is this? Because they are slaves and captives of mere imitation. They have not investigated the reality of religion and arrived at its fundamentals and conclusions. The Jew, for instance, has not proved the validity of Moses by investigating reality. He is a Jew because his father was a Jew. He imitates the forms and belief of his fathers and ancestors. There is no thought or mention of reality. And so it is with the other peoples of religion. This is the purpose of our statement that they worship the dawning point rather than the Sun of Reality itself.

13   If in the day of Jesus Christ the Jews had forsaken imitation and investigated reality, they would assuredly have believed in and accepted Him, for the Messianic effulgence was far greater than the Mosaic. The Sun of Reality, when it appeared from the dawning point of Christ, was as the midsummer sun in brilliancy and beauty.

14   Now, therefore, we must be admonished and realize that mere imitation of fathers and ancestors is fruitless. Nay, rather, we must exert ourselves to the utmost in investigating and turning toward the Sun of Reality, no matter from what dayspring or dawning point it may appear. The phenomenal sun is one sun. If tomorrow it should rise in the West, it is the same sun. We cannot say, "This is not the sun because it has appeared in the West." For East and West are but earthly and imaginary directions. In the station of the sun there is neither East nor West. It is ever shining from its place in the heavens. In the focal point of the solar circle there is no rising, no setting. Therefore, sunrise and sunset have relation to earthly observation and not to the luminary itself. Nay, rather, night in the solar orb is inconceivable. In that center of effulgence, constant light and illumination prevail. Its risings and settings are, therefore, only apparent and not actual. They have relation to our earthly point of view.

We could not consider it the sun if there were a cessation of its light, heat and splendor. To do so would be equivalent to calling a black stone a diamond. This would be meaningless. If a man is a miser and you call him generous, it will produce no change in him.

The purport of this is that God is almighty, but His greatness 15 cannot be brought within the grasp of human limitation. We cannot limit God to a boundary. Man is limited, but the world of Divinity is unlimited. Prescribing limitation to God is human ignorance. God is the Ancient, the Almighty; His attributes are infinite. He is God because His light, His sovereignty, is infinite. If He can be limited to human ideas, He is not God. Strange it is that, notwithstanding these are self-evident truths, man continues to build walls and fences of limitation about God, about Divinity so glorious, illimitable, boundless. Consider the endless phenomena of His creation. They are infinite; the universe is infinite. Who shall declare its height, its depth and length? It is absolutely infinite. How could an almighty sovereignty, a Divinity so wondrous, be brought within the limitations of faulty human minds even as to terms and definition? Shall we then say that God has performed a certain thing and He will never be able to perform it again? That the Sun of His effulgence once shone upon the world but now has set forever? That His mercy, His grace, His bounty once descended but now have ceased? Is this possible? No! We can never say nor believe with truth that His Manifestation, the adored verity, the Sun of Reality, shall cease to shine upon the world.

O God! Thou Who art kind. Verily, certain souls have gath- 16 ered in this meeting turning to Thee with their hearts and spirits. They are seeking the everlasting bounty. They are in need of Thine infinite mercy.

O Lord! Remove the veils from their eyes, and dispel the dark- 17 ness of ignorance. Confer upon them the light of knowledge

383

and wisdom. Illumine these contrite hearts with the radiance of the Sun of Reality. Make these eyes perceptive through witnessing the lights of Thy sovereignty. Suffer these spirits to rejoice through the great glad tidings, and receive these souls into Thy supreme Kingdom.

18   O Lord! Verily, we are weak; make us mighty. We are poor; assist us from the treasury of Thy munificence. We are dead; resuscitate us through the breath of the Holy Spirit. We lack patience in tests and in long-suffering; permit us to attain the lights of oneness.

19   O Lord! Make this assemblage the cause of upraising the standard of the oneness of the world of humanity, and confirm these souls so that they may become the promoters of international peace.

20   O Lord! Verily, the people are veiled and in a state of contention with each other, shedding the blood and destroying the possessions of each other. Throughout the world there is war and conflict. In every direction there is strife, bloodshed and ferocity.

21   O Lord! Guide human souls in order that they may turn away from warfare and battle, that they may become loving and kind to each other, that they may enter into affiliation and serve the oneness and solidarity of humanity.

22   O Lord! The horizons of the world are darkened by this dissension. O God! Illumine them, and through the lights of Thy love let the hearts become radiant. Through the blessing of Thy bestowal resuscitate the spirits until every soul shall perceive and act in accordance with Thy teachings. Thou art the Almighty. Thou art the Omniscient. Thou art the Seer. O Lord, be compassionate to all.

Talks 'Abdu'l-Bahá Delivered in Boston and Malden

25 August 1912

Talk at the New Thought Forum
Metaphysical Club
Boston, Massachusetts

NOTES BY EDNA MCKINNEY

O THOU kind God! In the utmost state of humility and sub- 1
mission do we entreat and supplicate at Thy threshold, seeking
Thine endless confirmations and illimitable assistance. O Thou
Lord! Regenerate these souls, and confer upon them a new life.
Animate the spirits, inform the hearts, open the eyes, and make
the ears attentive. From Thine ancient treasury confer a new
being and animus, and from Thy preexistent abode assist them
to attain to new confirmations.

O God! Verily, the world is in need of reformation. Bestow 2
upon it a new existence. Give it newness of thoughts, and reveal
unto it heavenly sciences. Breathe into it a fresh spirit, and grant
unto it a holier and higher purpose.

O God! Verily, Thou hast made this century radiant, and in it 3
Thou hast manifested Thy merciful effulgence. Thou hast effaced
the darkness of superstitions and permitted the light of assurance
to shine. O God! Grant that these servants may be acceptable at
Thy threshold. Reveal a new heaven, and spread out a new earth
for habitation. Let a new Jerusalem descend from on high. Bestow
new thoughts, new life upon mankind. Endow souls with new
perceptions, and confer upon them new virtues. Verily, Thou art
the Almighty, the Powerful. Thou art the Giver, the Generous.

4   It is easy to bring human bodies under control. A king can bring under his rule and authority the bodies of his subjects throughout a whole country. In former centuries kings and rulers have absolutely dominated millions of men and have been thereby enabled to carry out whatsoever they desire. If they willed to bestow happiness and peace, they could do so; and if they determined to inflict suffering and discomfort, they were equally capable. If they desired to send men to the field of battle, none could oppose their authority; and if they decreed their kingdoms should enjoy the bliss and serenity of immunity from war, this condition prevailed. In a word, kings and rulers have been able to control millions of human beings and have exercised that dominion with the utmost despotism and tyranny.

5   The point is this: that to gain control over physical bodies is an extremely easy matter, but to bring spirits within the bonds of serenity is a most arduous undertaking. This is not the work of everybody. It necessitates a divine and holy potency, the potency of inspiration, the power of the Holy Spirit. For example, Christ was capable of leading spirits into that abode of serenity. He was capable of guiding hearts into that haven of rest. From the day of His manifestation to the present time He has been resuscitating hearts and quickening spirits. He has exercised that vivifying influence in the realm of hearts and spirits; therefore, His resuscitating is everlasting.

6   In this century of the latter times Bahá'u'lláh has appeared and so resuscitated spirits that they have manifested powers more than human. Thousands of His followers have given their lives; and while under the sword, shedding their blood, they have proclaimed, "Yá Bahá'u'l-Abhá!" Such resuscitation is impossible except through a heavenly potency, a supernatural power, the divine power of the Holy Spirit. Through a natural and mere human power this is impossible. Therefore, the question arises: How is this resuscitation to be accomplished?

There are certain means for its accomplishment by which   7
mankind is regenerated and quickened with a new birth. This
is the second birth mentioned in the heavenly Books. Its accomplishment is through the baptism of the Holy Spirit. The
resuscitation or rebirth of the spirit of man is through the science
of the love of God. It is through the efficacy of the water of life.
This life and quickening is the regeneration of the phenomenal
world. After the coming of the spiritual springtime, the falling
of the vernal showers, the shining of the Sun of Reality, the
blowing of the breezes of perfection, all phenomena become
imbued with the life of a new creation and are reformed in the
process of a new genesis. Reflect upon the material springtime.
When winter comes, the trees are leafless, the fields and meadows
withered, the flowers die away into dustheaps; in prairie, mountain
and garden no freshness lingers, no beauty is visible, no verdure
can be seen. Everything is clad in the robe of death. Wherever
you look around, you will find the expression of death and decay.
But when the spring comes, the showers descend, the sun floods
the meadows and plains with light; you will observe creation
clad in a new robe of expression. The showers have made the
meadows green and verdant. The warm breezes have caused the
trees to put on their garments of leaves. They have blossomed
and soon will produce new, fresh and delightful fruits. Everything appears endowed with a newness of life; a new animus
and spirit is everywhere visible. The spring has resuscitated all
phenomena and has adorned the earth with beauty as it willeth.

Even so is the spiritual springtime when it comes. When the   8
holy, divine Manifestations or Prophets appear in the world, a
cycle of radiance, an age of mercy dawns. Everything is renewed.
Minds, hearts and all human forces are reformed, perfections are
quickened, sciences, discoveries and investigations are stimulated
afresh, and everything appertaining to the virtues of the human
world is revitalized. Consider this present century of radiance,

and compare it with the past centuries. What a vast difference exists between them! How minds have developed! How perceptions have deepened! How discoveries have increased! What great projects have been accomplished! How many realities have become manifest! How many mysteries of creation have been probed and penetrated! What is the cause of this? It is through the efficacy of the spiritual springtime in which we are living. Day by day the world attains a new bounty. In this radiant century neither the old customs nor the old sciences, crafts, laws and regulations have remained. The old political principles are undergoing change, and a new body politic is in process of formation. Nevertheless, some whose thoughts are congealed and whose souls are bereft of the light of the Sun of Reality seek to arrest this development in the world of the minds of men. Is this possible?

9   In the unmistakable and universal reformation we are witnessing, when outer conditions of humanity are receiving such impetus, when human life is assuming a new aspect, when sciences are stimulated afresh, inventions and discoveries increasing, civic laws undergoing change and moralities evidencing uplift and betterment, is it possible that spiritual impulses and influences should not be renewed and reformed? Naturally, new spiritual thoughts and inclinations must also become manifest. If spirituality be not renewed, what fruits come from mere physical reformation? For instance, the body of man may improve, the quality of bone and sinew may advance, the hand may develop, other limbs and members may increase in excellence, but if the mind fails to develop, of what use is the rest? The important factor in human improvement is the mind. In the world of the mind there must needs be development and improvement. There must be reformation in the kingdom of the human spirit; otherwise, no result will be attained from betterment of the mere physical structure.

In this new year new fruits must be forthcoming, for that is the   10
provision and intention of spiritual reformation. The renewal of
the leaf is fruitless. From the reformation of bark or branch no
fruit will come forth. The renewal of verdure produces nothing.
If there be no renewal of fruit from the tree, of what avail is the
reformation of bark, blossom, branch and trunk? For a fruitless
tree is of no special value. Similarly, of what avail is the reformation of physical conditions unless they are concomitant with
spiritual reformations? For the essential reality is the spirit, the
foundation is the spirit, the life of man is due to the spirit; the
happiness, the animus, the radiance, the glory of man—all are
due to the spirit; and if in the spirit no reformation takes place,
there will be no result to human existence.

Therefore, we must strive with life and heart that the material   11
and physical world may be reformed, human perception become
keener, the merciful effulgence manifest and the radiance of
reality shine. Then the star of love shall appear and the world
of humanity become illumined. The purpose is that the world
of existence is dependent for its progress upon reformation;
otherwise, it will be as dead. Consider: If a new springtime
failed to appear, what would be the effect upon this globe, the
earth? Undoubtedly it would become desolate and life extinct.
The earth has need of an annual coming of spring. It is necessary that a new bounty should be forthcoming. If it comes
not, life would be effaced. In the same way the world of spirit
needs new life, the world of mind necessitates new animus and
development, the world of souls a new bounty, the world of
morality a reformation, the world of divine effulgence ever new
bestowals. Were it not for this replenishment, the life of the
world would become effaced and extinguished. If this room is
not ventilated and the air freshened, respiration will cease after
a length of time. If no rain falls, all life organisms will perish.

If new light does not come, the darkness of death will envelop the earth. If a new springtime does not arrive, life upon this globe will be obliterated.

12   Therefore, thoughts must be lofty and ideals uplifted in order that the world of humanity may become assisted in new conditions of reform. When this reformation affects every degree, then will come the very Day of the Lord of which all the prophets have spoken. That is the Day wherein the whole world will be regenerated. Consider: Are the laws of past ages applicable to present human conditions? Evidently they are not. For example, the laws of former centuries sanctioned despotic forms of government. Are the laws of despotic control fitted for present-day conditions? How could they be applied to solve the questions surrounding modern nations? Similarly, we ask: Would the status of ancient thought, the crudeness of arts and crafts, the insufficiency of scientific attainment serve us today? Would the agricultural methods of the ancients suffice in the twentieth century? Transportation in the former ages was restricted to conveyance by animals. How would it provide for human needs today? If modes of transportation had not been reformed, the teeming millions now upon the earth would die of starvation. Without the railway and the fast-going steamship, the world of the present day would be as dead. How could great cities such as New York and London subsist if dependent upon ancient means of conveyance? It is also true of other things which have been reformed in proportion to the needs of the present time. Had they not been reformed, man could not find subsistence.

13   If these material tendencies are in such need of reformation, how much greater the need in the world of the human spirit, the world of human thought, perception, virtues and bounties! Is it possible that that need has remained stationary while the world has been advancing in every other condition and direction? It is impossible.

Therefore, we must invoke and supplicate God and strive with   14
the utmost effort in order that the world of human existence in all
its degrees may receive a mighty impulse, complete human happiness be attained and the resuscitation of all spirits and emanations
be realized through the boundless favor of the mercy of God.

2

26 August 1912

Talk at Franklin Square House
Boston, Massachusetts

NOTES BY EDNA MCKINNEY

AMONG the teachings of Bahá'u'lláh is the principle of equality of   1
man and woman. Bahá'u'lláh has said that both belong to humankind and that in the estimation of God they are equal, for each is
the complement of the other in the divine creative plan. The only
distinction between them in the sight of God is the purity and
righteousness of their deeds and actions, for that one is preferred
by God who is most nearly in the spiritual image and likeness of
the Creator. Throughout the kingdoms of living organisms there
is sex differentiation in function, but no preference or distinction
is made in favor of either male or female. In the animal kingdom
individual sex exists, but rights are equal and without distinction.
Likewise, in the plane or kingdom of the vegetable sex appears,
but equality of function and right is evident. Inasmuch as sex
distinction and preference are not observed in these kingdoms of
inferior intelligence, is it befitting the superior station of man that
he should make such differentiation and estimate, when as a matter of fact there is no difference indicated in the law of creation?

391

2   In ancient times and medieval ages woman was completely subordinated to man. The cause of this estimate of her inferiority was her lack of education. A woman's life and intellect were limited to the household. Glimpses of this may be found even in the Epistles of Saint Paul. In later centuries the scope and opportunities of a woman's life broadened and increased. Her mind unfolded and developed; her perceptions awakened and deepened. The question concerning her was: Why should a woman be left mentally undeveloped? Science is praiseworthy—whether investigated by the intellect of man or woman. So, little by little, woman advanced, giving increasing evidence of equal capabilities with man—whether in scientific research, political ability or any other sphere of human activity. The conclusion is evident that woman has been outdistanced through lack of education and intellectual facilities. If given the same educational opportunities or course of study, she would develop the same capacity and abilities.

3   There are some who declare that woman is not naturally endowed or imbued with the same capabilities as man; that she is intellectually inferior to man, weaker in willpower and lacking his courage. This theory is completely contradicted by history and facts of record. Certain women of superlative capacity and determination have appeared in the world, peers of man in intellect and equally courageous. Zenobia was the wife of the governor-general of Athens. Her husband died, and like the Russian Queen, Catherine, she manifested the highest degree of capability in the administration of public affairs. The Roman government appointed her to succeed her husband. Afterward she conquered Syria, conducted a successful campaign in Egypt and established a memorable sovereignty. Rome sent an army against her under direction of distinguished commanders. When the two forces met in battle, Zenobia arrayed herself in gorgeous apparel, placed the crown of her kingdom upon her head

and rode forth at the head of her army, defeating the Roman legions so completely that they were not able to reorganize. The Emperor of Rome himself took command of the next army of one hundred thousand soldiers and marched into Syria. At that time Rome was at the zenith of greatness and was the strongest military power in the world. Zenobia withdrew with her forces to Palmyra and fortified it to withstand a siege. After two years the Roman Emperor cut off her supplies, and she was forced to surrender.

The Romans returned in triumphal procession and pageant to their own country. They entered Rome in great pomp and splendor, led by African elephants. After the elephants there were lions, then tigers, bears and monkeys, and after the monkeys, Zenobia—barefooted, walking, a chain of gold about her neck and a crown in her hand, dignified, majestic, queenly and courageous notwithstanding her downfall and defeat. 4

Among other noted women of history was Cleopatra, Queen of Egypt, who held her kingdom against the armies of Rome for a long time. Catherine, wife of Peter the Great, displayed courage and military strategy of the very highest order during the war between Russia and Muḥammad Páshá. When the cause of Russia seemed hopeless, she took her jewels and went before the Turkish victor, presented them to him and pled the justice of her country's cause with such convincing skill and diplomacy that peace was declared. 5

Victoria, Queen of England, was really superior to all the kings of Europe in ability, justness and equitable administration. During her long and brilliant reign the British Empire was immensely extended and enriched, due to her political sagacity, skill and foresight. 6

The history of religion, likewise, furnishes eloquent examples of woman's capability under conditions of great difficulty and necessity. The conquest of the Holy Land by the Israelites after 7 forty years' wandering in the desert and wilderness of Judea was accomplished through the strategy and cunning of a woman.

8   After the martyrdom of Christ, to Whom be glory, the disciples were greatly disturbed and disheartened. Even Peter had denied Christ and tried to shun Him. It was a woman, Mary Magdalene, who confirmed the wavering disciples in their faith, saying, "Was it the body of Christ or the reality of Christ that ye have seen crucified? Surely it was His body. His reality is everlasting and eternal; it hath neither beginning nor ending. Therefore, why are ye perplexed and discouraged? Christ always spoke of His being crucified." Mary Magdalene was a mere villager, a peasant woman; yet she became the means of consolation and confirmation to the disciples of Christ.

9   In the Cause of Bahá'u'lláh there have been women who were superior to men in illumination, intellect, divine virtues and devotion to God. Among them was Qurratu'l-'Ayn. When she spoke, she was listened to reverently by the most learned men. They were most respectful in her presence, and none dared to contradict her. Among the Bahá'í women in Persia today there are Rúḥu'lláh and others who are gifted with knowledge, invincible steadfastness, courage, virtue and power of will. They are superior to men and well-known throughout Persia.

10   Briefly, history furnishes evidence that during the past centuries there have been great women as well as great men; but in general, owing to lack of educational advantages, women have been restricted and deprived of opportunity to become fully qualified and representative of humankind. When given the opportunity for acquiring education, they have shown equal capacity with men. Some philosophers and writers have considered woman naturally and by creation inferior to man, claiming as a proof that the brain of man is larger and heavier than that of woman. This is frail and faulty evidence, inasmuch

as small brains are often found coupled with superior intellect and large brains possessed by those who are ignorant, even imbecilic. The truth is that God has endowed all humankind with intelligence and perception and has confirmed all as His servants and children; therefore, in the plan and estimate of God there is no distinction between male or female. The soul that manifests pure deeds and spiritual graces is most precious in His sight and nearer to Him in its attainments.

The realities of things have been revealed in this radiant century, 11 and that which is true must come to the surface. Among these realities is the principle of the equality of man and woman— equal rights and prerogatives in all things appertaining to humanity. Bahá'u'lláh declared this reality over fifty years ago. But while this principle of equality is true, it is likewise true that woman must prove her capacity and aptitude, must show forth the evidences of equality. She must become proficient in the arts and sciences and prove by her accomplishments that her abilities and powers have merely been latent. Demonstrations of force, such as are now taking place in England, are neither becoming nor effective in the cause of womanhood and equality. Woman must especially devote her energies and abilities toward the industrial and agricultural sciences, seeking to assist mankind in that which is most needful. By this means she will demonstrate capability and ensure recognition of equality in the social and economic equation. Undoubtedly God will confirm her in her efforts and endeavors, for in this century of radiance Bahá'u'lláh has proclaimed the reality of the oneness of the world of humanity and announced that all nations, peoples and races are one. He has shown that although individuals may differ in development and capacity, they are essentially and intrinsically equal as human beings, just as the waves of the sea are innumerable and different, but the reality of the sea is one.

The plurality of humanity may be likened to the waves, but the reality of humankind is like the sea itself. All the waves are of the same water; all are waves of one ocean.

12 Therefore, strive to show in the human world that women are most capable and efficient, that their hearts are more tender and susceptible than the hearts of men, that they are more philanthropic and responsive toward the needy and suffering, that they are inflexibly opposed to war and are lovers of peace. Strive that the ideal of international peace may become realized through the efforts of womankind, for man is more inclined to war than woman, and a real evidence of woman's superiority will be her service and efficiency in the establishment of universal peace.

3

27 August 1912

Talk at Metaphysical Club
Boston, Massachusetts

NOTES BY EDNA MCKINNEY

1 UPON the faces of those present I behold the expression of thoughtfulness and wisdom; therefore, I shall discourse upon a subject involving one of the divine questions, a question of religious and metaphysical importance—namely, the progressive and perpetual motion of elemental atoms throughout the various degrees of phenomena and the kingdoms of existence. It will be demonstrated and become evident that the origin and outcome of phenomena are identical and that there is an essential oneness in all existing things. This is a subtle principle appertaining to divine philosophy and requiring close analysis and attention.

The elemental atoms which constitute all phenomenal existence 2
and being in this illimitable universe are in perpetual motion,
undergoing continuous degrees of progression. For instance, let us
conceive of an atom in the mineral kingdom progressing upward
to the kingdom of the vegetable by entering into the composition and fibre of a tree or plant. From thence it is assimilated
and transferred into the kingdom of the animal and finally,
by the law and process of composition, becomes a part of the
body of man. That is to say, it has traversed the intermediate
degrees and stations of phenomenal existence, entering into the
composition of various organisms in its journey. This motion
or transference is progressive and perpetual, for after disintegration of the human body into which it has entered, it returns
to the mineral kingdom whence it came and will continue to
traverse the kingdoms of phenomena as before. This is an illus-
tration designed to show that the constituent elemental atoms
of phenomena undergo progressive transference and motion
throughout the material kingdoms.

In its ceaseless progression and journeyings the atom becomes 3
imbued with the virtues and powers of each degree or kingdom
it traverses. In the degree of the mineral it possessed mineral
affinities; in the kingdom of the vegetable it manifested the
augmentative virtue or power of growth; in the animal organism
it reflected the intelligence of that degree; and in the kingdom
of man it was qualified with human attributes or virtues.

Furthermore, the forms and organisms of phenomenal being 4
and existence in each of the kingdoms of the universe are myriad
and numberless. The vegetable plane or kingdom, for instance,
has its infinite variety of types and material structures of plant
life—each distinct and different within itself, no two exactly
alike in composition and detail—for there are no repetitions in
nature, and the augmentative virtue cannot be confined to any
given image or shape. Each leaf has its own particular identity—

so to speak, its own individuality as a leaf. Therefore, each atom of the innumerable elemental atoms, during its ceaseless motion through the kingdoms of existence as a constituent of organic composition, not only becomes imbued with the powers and virtues of the kingdoms it traverses but also reflects the attributes and qualities of the forms and organisms of those kingdoms. As each of these forms has its individual and particular virtue, therefore, each elemental atom of the universe has the opportunity of expressing an infinite variety of those individual virtues. No atom is bereft or deprived of this opportunity or right of expression. Nor can it be said of any given atom that it is denied equal opportunities with other atoms; nay, all are privileged to possess the virtues existent in these kingdoms and to reflect the attributes of their organisms. In the various transformations or passages from kingdom to kingdom the virtues expressed by the atoms in each degree are peculiar to that degree. For example, in the world of the mineral the atom does not express the vegetable form and organism, and when through the process of transmutation it assumes the virtues of the vegetable degree, it does not reflect the attributes of animal organisms, and so on.

5   It is evident, then, that each elemental atom of the universe is possessed of a capacity to express all the virtues of the universe. This is a subtle and abstract realization. Meditate upon it, for within it lies the true explanation of pantheism. From this point of view and perception pantheism is a truth, for every atom in the universe possesses or reflects all the virtues of life, the manifestation of which is effected through change and transformation. Therefore, the origin and outcome of phenomena is, verily, the omnipresent God; for the reality of all phenomenal existence is through Him. There is neither reality nor the manifestation of reality without the instrumentality of God. Existence is realized and possible through the bounty of God, just as the ray or flame emanating from this lamp is realized

through the bounty of the lamp, from which it originates. Even so, all phenomena are realized through the divine bounty, and the explanation of true pantheistic statement and principle is that the phenomena of the universe find realization through the one power animating and dominating all things, and all things are but manifestations of its energy and bounty. The virtue of being and existence is through no other agency. Therefore, in the words of Bahá'u'lláh, the first teaching is the oneness of the world of humanity.

When the man who is spiritually sagacious and possessed of insight views the world of humanity, he will observe that the lights of the divine bounty are flooding all mankind, just as the lights of the sun shed their splendor upon all existing things. All phenomena of material existence are revealed through the ray emanating from the sun. Without light nothing would be visible. Similarly, all phenomena in the inner world of reality receive the bounties of God from the source of divine bestowal. This human plane, or kingdom, is one creation, and all souls are the signs and traces of the divine bounty. In this plane there are no exceptions; all have been recipients of their bestowals through the heavenly bounty. Can you find a soul bereft of the nearness of God? Can you find one whom God has deprived of its daily sustenance? This is impossible. God is kind and loving to all, and all are manifestations of the divine bounty. This is the oneness of the world of humanity. 6

But some souls are weak; we must endeavor to strengthen them. Some are ignorant, uninformed of the bounties of God; we must strive to make them knowing. Some are ailing; we must seek to restore them to health. Some are immature as children; they must be trained and assisted to attain maturity. We nurse the sick in tenderness and the kindly spirit of love; we do not despise them because they are ill. Therefore, we must exercise extreme patience, sympathy and love toward all mankind, considering 7 no soul as rejected. If we look upon a soul as rejected, we have disobeyed the teachings of God. God is loving to all. Shall we be unjust or unkind to anyone? Is this allowable in the sight of God? God provides for all. Is it befitting for us to prevent the flow of His merciful provisions for mankind? God has created all in His image and likeness. Shall we manifest hatred for His creatures and servants? This would be contrary to the will of God and according to the will of Satan, by which we mean the natural inclinations of the lower nature. This lower nature in man is symbolized as Satan—the evil ego within us, not an evil personality outside.

8 Bahá'u'lláh teaches that the foundations of the divine religion are one reality which does not admit of multiplicity or division. Therefore, the commandments and teachings of God are one. The religious differences and divisions which exist in the world are due to blind imitations of forms without knowledge or investigation of the fundamental divine reality which underlies all the religions. Inasmuch as these imitations of ancestral forms are various, dissensions have arisen among the people of religion. Therefore, it is necessary to free mankind from this subjection to blind belief by pointing the way of guidance to reality itself, which is the only basis of unity.

9 Bahá'u'lláh says that religion must be conducive to love and unity. If it proves to be the source of hatred and enmity, its absence is preferable; for the will and law of God is love, and love is the bond between human hearts. Religion is the light of the world. If it is made the cause of darkness through human misunderstanding and ignorance, it would be better to do without it.

10 Religion must conform to science and reason; otherwise, it is superstition. God has created man in order that he may perceive the verity of existence and endowed him with mind or reason to discover truth. Therefore, scientific knowledge and religious

belief must be conformable to the analysis of this divine faculty in man.

Prejudices of all kinds—whether religious, racial, patriotic or 11 political—are destructive of divine foundations in man. All the warfare and bloodshed in human history have been the outcome of prejudice. This earth is one home and native land. God has created mankind with equal endowment and right to live upon the earth. As a city is the home of all its inhabitants although each may have his individual place of residence therein, so the earth's surface is one wide native land or home for all races of humankind. Racial prejudice or separation into nations such as French, German, American and so on is unnatural and proceeds from human motive and ignorance. All are the children and servants of God. Why should we be separated by artificial and imaginary boundaries? In the animal kingdom the doves flock together in harmony and agreement. They have no prejudices. We are human and superior in intelligence. Is it befitting that lower creatures should manifest virtues which lack expression in man?

Bahá'u'lláh has proclaimed and promulgated the foundation 12 of international peace. For thousands of years men and nations have gone forth to the battlefield to settle their differences. The cause of this has been ignorance and degeneracy. Praise be to God! In this radiant century minds have developed, perceptions have become keener, eyes are illumined and ears attentive. Therefore, it will be impossible for war to continue. Consider human ignorance and inconsistency. A man who kills another man is punished by execution, but a military genius who kills one hundred thousand of his fellow creatures is immortalized as a hero. One man steals a small sum of money and is imprisoned as a thief. Another pillages a whole country and is honored as a patriot and conqueror. A single falsehood brings reproach and censure, but the wiles of politicians and diplomats excite the admiration and praise of a nation. Consider the ignorance and inconsistency of mankind. How darkened and savage are the instincts of humanity!

13   Bahá'u'lláh has announced that no matter how far the world of humanity may advance in material civilization, it is nevertheless in need of spiritual virtues and the bounties of God. The spirit of man is not illumined and quickened through material sources. It is not resuscitated by investigating phenomena of the world of matter. The spirit of man is in need of the protection of the Holy Spirit. Just as he advances by progressive stages from the mere physical world of being into the intellectual realm, so must he develop upward in moral attributes and spiritual graces. In the process of this attainment he is ever in need of the bestowals of the Holy Spirit. Material development may be likened to the glass of a lamp, whereas divine virtues and spiritual susceptibilities are the light within the glass. The lamp chimney is worthless without the light; likewise, man in his material condition requires the radiance and vivification of the divine graces and merciful attributes. Without the presence of the Holy Spirit he is lifeless. Although physically and mentally alive, he is spiritually dead. Christ announced, "That which is born of the flesh is flesh; and that which is born of the Spirit is spirit," meaning that man must be born again. As the babe is born into the light of this physical world, so must the physical and intellectual man be born into the light of the world of Divinity. In the matrix of the mother the unborn child was deprived and unconscious of the world of material existence, but after its birth it beheld the wonders and beauties of a new realm of life and being. In the world of the matrix it was utterly ignorant and unable to conceive of these new conditions, but after its transformation it discovers the radiant sun, trees, flowers and an infinite range

of blessings and bounties awaiting it. In the human plane and kingdom man is a captive of nature and ignorant of the divine world until born of the breaths of the Holy Spirit out of physical conditions of limitation and deprivation. Then he beholds the reality of the spiritual realm and Kingdom, realizes the narrow restrictions of the mere human world of existence and becomes conscious of the unlimited and infinite glories of the world of God. Therefore, no matter how man may advance upon the physical and intellectual plane, he is ever in need of the boundless virtues of Divinity, the protection of the Holy Spirit and the face of God.

4

29 August 1912

Talk at Home of Madame Morey
34 Hillside Avenue, Malden, Massachusetts

NOTES BY EDNA MCKINNEY

IN the Books of the Prophets certain glad tidings are recorded   1
which are absolutely true and free from doubt. The East has ever been the dawning point of the Sun of Reality. All the Prophets of God have appeared there. The religions of God have been promulgated, the teachings of God have been spread and the law of God founded in the East. The Orient has always been the center of lights. The West has acquired illumination from the East, but in some respects the reflection of the light has been greater in the Occident. This is especially true of Christianity. Christ appeared in Palestine, and His teachings were founded

there. Although the doors of the Kingdom were opened in that country and the bestowals of Divinity were spread broadcast from its center, the people of the West have embraced and promulgated Christianity more fully than those in the East. The Sun of Reality shone forth from the horizon of the East, but its heat and ray are most resplendent in the West, where the radiant standard of Christ has been upraised. I have great hopes that the lights of Bahá'u'lláh's appearance may also find the fullest manifestation and reflection in these western regions, for the teachings of Bahá'u'lláh are especially applicable to the conditions of the people here. The western nations are endowed with the capability of understanding the rational and peerless words of Bahá'u'lláh and realizing that the essence of the teachings of all the former Prophets can be found in His utterance.

2 The teachings of Christ have been promulgated by Bahá'u'lláh, Who has also revealed new teachings applicable to present conditions in the world of humanity. He has trained the people of the East through the power and protection of the Holy Spirit, cemented the souls of humanity together and established the foundations of international unity.

3 Through the power of His words the hearts of the people of all religions have been attuned in harmony. For instance, among the Bahá'ís in Persia there are Christians, Muslims, Zoroastrians, Jews and many others of varying denominations and beliefs who have been brought together in unity and love in the Cause of Bahá'u'lláh. Although these people were formerly hostile and antagonistic, filled with hatred and bitterness toward each other, bloodthirsty and pillaging, considering that animosity and attack were the means of attaining the good pleasure of God, they have now become loving and filled with the radiant zeal of fellowship and brotherhood, the purpose of them all being service to the world of humanity, promotion of international

peace, the unification of the divine religions and deeds of universal philanthropy. By their words and actions they are proving the verity of Bahá'u'lláh.

Consider the animosity and hatred existing today between the 4 various nations of the world. What disagreements and hostilities arise, what warfare and contention, how much bloodshed, what injustice and tyranny! Just now there is war in eastern Turkey, also war between Turkey and Italy. Nations are devoted to conquest and bloodshed, filled with the animus of religious hatred, seeking the good pleasure of God by killing and destroying those whom in their blindness they consider enemies. How ignorant they are! That which is forbidden by God they consider acceptable to Him. God is love; God seeketh fellowship, purity, sanctity and long-suffering; these are the attributes of Divinity. Therefore, these warring, raging nations have arisen against Divinity, imagining they are serving God. What gross ignorance this is! What injustice, blindness and lack of realization! Briefly, we must strive with heart and soul in order that this darkness of the contingent world may be dispelled, that the lights of the Kingdom shall shine upon all the horizons, the world of humanity become illumined, the image of God become apparent in human mirrors, the law of God be well established and that all regions of the world shall enjoy peace, comfort and composure beneath the equitable protection of God. My admonition and exhortation to you is this: Be kind to all people, love humanity, consider all mankind as your relations and servants of the most high God. Strive day and night that animosity and contention may pass away from the hearts of men, that all religions shall become reconciled and the nations love each other so that no racial, religious or political prejudice may remain and the world of humanity behold God as the beginning and end of all existence. God has created all, and all return to God. Therefore, love humanity with all your heart and soul. If you meet a poor man, assist him; if you see the sick, heal him; reassure the affrighted one, render the cowardly noble and courageous, educate the ignorant, associate with the stranger. Emulate God. Consider how kindly, how lovingly He deals with all, and follow His example. You must treat people in accordance with the divine precepts—in other words, treat them as kindly as God treats them, for this is the greatest attainment possible for the world of humanity.

5   Furthermore, know ye that God has created in man the power of reason, whereby man is enabled to investigate reality. God has not intended man to imitate blindly his fathers and ancestors. He has endowed him with mind, or the faculty of reasoning, by the exercise of which he is to investigate and discover the truth, and that which he finds real and true he must accept. He must not be an imitator or blind follower of any soul. He must not rely implicitly upon the opinion of any man without investigation; nay, each soul must seek intelligently and independently, arriving at a real conclusion and bound only by that reality. The greatest cause of bereavement and disheartening in the world of humanity is ignorance based upon blind imitation. It is due to this that wars and battles prevail; from this cause hatred and animosity arise continually among mankind. Through failure to investigate reality the Jews rejected Jesus Christ. They were expecting His coming; by day and night they mourned and lamented, saying, "O God! Hasten Thou the day of the advent of Christ," expressing most intense longing for the Messiah; but when Christ appeared, they denied and rejected Him, treated Him with arrogant contempt, sentenced Him to death and finally crucified Him. Why did this happen? Because they were blindly following imitations, believing that which had descended to them as a heritage from their fathers and ancestors, tenaciously

holding to it and refusing to investigate the reality of Christ. Therefore, they were deprived of the bounties of Christ, whereas if they had forsaken imitations and investigated the reality of the Messiah, they would have surely been guided to believing in Him. Instead of this they said, "We have heard from our fathers and have read in the Old Testament that Christ must come from an unknown place; now we find that this one has come from Nazareth." Steeped in the literal interpretation and imitating the beliefs of fathers and ancestors, they failed to understand the fact that although the body of Jesus came from Nazareth, the reality of the Christ came from the unknown place of the divine Kingdom. They also said that the scepter of Christ would be of iron—that is to say, He should wield a sword. When Christ appeared, He did possess a sword; but it was the sword of His tongue with which He separated the false from the true. But the Jews were blind to the spiritual significance and symbolism of the prophetic words. They also expected that the Messiah would sit upon the throne of David, whereas Christ had neither throne nor semblance of sovereignty; nay, rather, He was a poor man, apparently abject and vanquished; therefore, how could He be the veritable Christ? This was one of their most insistent objections based upon ancestral interpretation and teaching. In reality, Christ was glorified with an eternal sovereignty and everlasting dominion—spiritual and not temporal. His throne and Kingdom were established in human hearts, where He reigns with power and authority without end. Notwithstanding the fulfillment of all the prophetic signs in Christ, the Jews denied Him and entered the period of their deprivation because of their allegiance to imitations and ancestral forms.

Among other objections they said, "We are promised through 6 the tongue of the prophets that Christ at the time of His coming would proclaim the law of the Torah, whereas now we see this person abrogating the commands of the Pentateuch, disturbing our blessed Sabbath and abolishing the law of divorce. He has left nothing of the ancient law of Moses; therefore, he is the enemy of Moses." In reality, Christ proclaimed and completed the law of Moses. He was the very helper and assister of Moses. He spread the Book of Moses throughout the world and established anew the fundamentals of the law revealed by Him. He abolished certain unimportant laws and forms which were no longer compatible with the exigencies of the time, such as divorce and plurality of wives. The Jews did not comprehend this, and the cause of their ignorance was blind and tenacious adherence to imitations of ancient forms and teachings; therefore, they finally sentenced Christ to death.

7   They, likewise, said, "Through the tongues of the prophets it was announced that during the time of Christ's appearance the justice of God would prevail throughout the world, tyranny and oppression would be unknown, justice would even extend to the animal kingdom, ferocious beasts would associate in gentleness and peace, the wolf and the lamb would drink from the same spring, the lion and the deer meet in the same meadow, the eagle and quail dwell together in the same nest; but instead of this, we see that during the time of this supposed Christ the Romans have conquered Palestine and are ruling it with extreme tyranny, justice is nowhere apparent, and signs of peace in the animal kingdom are conspicuously absent." These statements and attitudes of the Jews were inherited from their fathers—blind allegiance to literal expectations which did not come to pass during the time of Jesus Christ. The real purport of these prophetic statements was that various peoples, symbolized by the wolf and lamb, between whom love and fellowship were impossible would come together during the Messiah's reign, drink from the same fountain of life in His teachings and

become His devoted followers. This was realized when peoples of all religions, nationalities and dispositions became united in their beliefs and followed Christ in humility, associating in love and brotherhood under the shadow of His divine protection. The Jews, being blind to this and holding to their bigoted imitations, were insolent and arrogant toward Christ and crucified Him. Had they investigated the reality of Christ, they would have beheld His beauty and truth.

God has given man the eye of investigation by which he may see and recognize truth. He has endowed man with ears that he may hear the message of reality and conferred upon him the gift of reason by which he may discover things for himself. This is his endowment and equipment for the investigation of reality. Man is not intended to see through the eyes of another, hear through another's ears nor comprehend with another's brain. Each human creature has individual endowment, power and responsibility in the creative plan of God. Therefore, depend upon your own reason and judgment and adhere to the outcome of your own investigation; otherwise, you will be utterly submerged in the sea of ignorance and deprived of all the bounties of God. Turn to God, supplicate humbly at His threshold, seeking assistance and confirmation, that God may rend asunder the veils that obscure your vision. Then will your eyes be filled with illumination, face to face you will behold the reality of God and your heart become completely purified from the dross of ignorance, reflecting the glories and bounties of the Kingdom.

Holy souls are like soil which has been plowed and tilled with much earnest labor, the thorns and thistles cast aside and all weeds uprooted. Such soil is most fruitful, and the harvest from it will prove full and plenteous. In this same way man must free himself from the weeds of ignorance, thorns of superstitions and thistles of imitations that he may discover reality in the harvests of true knowledge. Otherwise, the discovery of reality is impossible, contention and divergence of religious belief will always remain, and mankind, like ferocious wolves, will rage and attack each other in hatred and antagonism. We supplicate God that He may destroy the veils which limit our vision and that these becloudings, which darken the way of the manifestation of the shining lights, may be dispelled in order that the effulgent Sun of Reality may shine forth. We implore and invoke God, seeking His assistance and confirmation. Man is a child of God, most noble, lofty and beloved by God, his Creator. Therefore, he must ever strive that the divine bounties and virtues bestowed upon him may prevail and control him. Just now the soil of human hearts seems like black earth, but in the innermost substance of this dark soil there are thousands of fragrant flowers latent. We must endeavor to cultivate and awaken these potentialities, discover the secret treasure in this very mine and depository of God, bring forth these resplendent powers long hidden in human hearts. Then will the glories of both worlds be blended and increased and the quintessence of human existence be made manifest.

10   We must not be content with simply following a certain course because we find our fathers pursued that course. It is the duty of everyone to investigate reality, and investigation of reality by another will not do for us. If all in the world were rich and one man poor, of what use are these riches to that man? If all the world be virtuous and a man steeped in vice, what good results are forthcoming from him? If all the world be resplendent and a man blind, where are his benefits? If all the world be in plenty and a man hungry, what sustenance does he derive? Therefore, every man must be an investigator for himself. Ideas and beliefs left by his fathers and ancestors as a heritage will not suffice, for adherence to these are but imitations, and imitations have ever

been a cause of disappointment and misguidance. Be investigators of reality that you may attain the verity of truth and life.

You have asked why it was necessary for the soul that was 11 from God to make this journey back to God? Would you like to understand the reality of this question just as I teach it, or do you wish to hear it as the world teaches it? For if I should answer you according to the latter way, this would be but imitation and would not make the subject clear.

The reality underlying this question is that the evil spirit, 12 Satan or whatever is interpreted as evil, refers to the lower nature in man. This baser nature is symbolized in various ways. In man there are two expressions: One is the expression of nature; the other, the expression of the spiritual realm. The world of nature is defective. Look at it clearly, casting aside all superstition and imagination. If you should leave a man uneducated and barbarous in the wilds of Africa, would there be any doubt about his remaining ignorant? God has never created an evil spirit; all such ideas and nomenclature are symbols expressing the mere human or earthly nature of man. It is an essential condition of the soil of earth that thorns, weeds and fruitless trees may grow from it. Relatively speaking, this is evil; it is simply the lower state and baser product of nature.

It is evident, therefore, that man is in need of divine education 13 and inspiration, that the spirit and bounties of God are essential to his development. That is to say, the teachings of Christ and the Prophets are necessary for his education and guidance. Why? Because They are the divine Gardeners Who till the earth of human hearts and minds. They educate man, uproot the weeds, burn the thorns and remodel the waste places into gardens and orchards where fruitful trees grow. The wisdom and purpose of Their training is that man must pass from degree to degree of progressive unfoldment until perfection is attained. For instance, if a man should live his entire life in one city, he cannot gain a knowledge of the whole world. To become perfectly informed he must visit other cities, see the mountains and valleys, cross the rivers and traverse the plains. In other words, without progressive and universal education perfection will not be attained.

14   Man must walk in many paths and be subjected to various processes in his evolution upward. Physically he is not born in full stature but passes through consecutive stages of fetus, infant, childhood, youth, maturity and old age. Suppose he had the power to remain young throughout his life. He then would not understand the meaning of old age and could not believe it existed. If he could not realize the condition of old age, he would not know that he was young. He would not know the difference between young and old without experiencing the old. Unless you have passed through the state of infancy, how would you know this was an infant beside you? If there were no wrong, how would you recognize the right? If it were not for sin, how would you appreciate virtue? If evil deeds were unknown, how could you commend good actions? If sickness did not exist, how would you understand health? Evil is nonexistent; it is the absence of good. Sickness is the loss of health; poverty, the lack of riches. When wealth disappears, you are poor; you look within the treasure box but find nothing there. Without knowledge there is ignorance; therefore, ignorance is simply the lack of knowledge. Death is the absence of life. Therefore, on the one hand, we have existence; on the other, nonexistence, negation or absence of existence.

15   Briefly, the journey of the soul is necessary. The pathway of life is the road which leads to divine knowledge and attainment. Without training and guidance the soul could never progress beyond the conditions of its lower nature, which is ignorant and defective.

Talks 'Abdu'l-Bahá Delivered in Montreal

1 September 1912

Talk at Church of the Messiah
Montreal, Canada

FROM STENOGRAPHIC NOTES

GOD, the Almighty, has created all mankind from the dust   1
of earth. He has fashioned them all from the same elements;
they are descended from the same race and live upon the same
globe. He has created them to dwell beneath the one heaven.
As members of the human family and His children He has endowed them with equal susceptibilities. He maintains, protects
and is kind to all. He has made no distinction in mercies and
graces among His children. With impartial love and wisdom
He has sent forth His Prophets and divine teachings. His teachings are the means of establishing union and fellowship among
mankind and awakening love and kindness in human hearts. He
proclaims the oneness of the kingdom of humanity. He rebukes
those things which create differences and destroy harmony; He
commends and praises every means that will conduce to the
solidarity of the human race. He encourages man in every step
of advancement which leads to ultimate union. The Prophets
of God have been inspired with the message of love and unity.
The Books of God have been revealed for the upbuilding of fellowship and union. The Prophets of God have been the servants
of reality; Their teachings constitute the science of reality. Reality is one; it does not admit plurality. We conclude, therefore,
that the foundation of the religions of God is one foundation.
Notwithstanding this, certain forms and imitations have been

413

persistently adhered to which have nothing to do with the foundation of the teachings of the Prophets of God. As these imitations are various and different, contention and strife prevail among the people of religious beliefs, and the foundation of the religion of God has become obscured. Like beasts of prey, men are warring and killing each other, destroying cities and homes, devastating countries and kingdoms.

2   God has created His servants in order that they may love and associate with each other. He has revealed the glorious splendor of His sun of love in the world of humanity. The cause of the creation of the phenomenal world is love. All the Prophets have promulgated the law of love. Man has opposed the will of God and acted in opposition to the plan of God. Therefore, from the beginning of history to the present time the world of humanity has had no lasting rest; warfare and strife have continuously prevailed, and hearts have manifested hatred toward each other. The cause of bloodshed and battle, strife and hatred throughout the past has been either religious, racial, patriotic or political prejudice. Therefore, the world of humanity has ever been in torment. These prejudices are more pronounced in the Orient, where freedom is restricted. In the nineteenth century the nations of the East were restless and in a state of inner commotion. The darkness of imitations and forms had enveloped religious belief. The people of religions were in constant warfare, filled with enmity, hatred and bitterness. In the midst of these conditions Bahá'u'lláh appeared. He proclaimed the oneness of the world of humanity and announced that all are the servants of God. He taught that all the religions are beneath the shadow and pro-tection of the Almighty, that God is compassionate and loving to all, that the revelations of all the Prophets of the past have been in perfect unity and agreement, that the heavenly Books have confirmed each other; therefore, why should contention and strife exist among the people?

As all mankind have been created by the one God, we are 3
sheep under the care and protection of one Shepherd. Therefore, as His sheep we must associate in accord and agreement.
If one single lamb becomes separated from the flock, the
thoughts and efforts of all the others must be to bring it back
again. Consequently, Bahá'u'lláh proclaimed that, inasmuch
as God is the one heavenly Shepherd and all mankind are the
sheep of His fold, the religion or guidance of God must be the
means of love and fellowship in the world. If religion proves to
be the source of hatred, enmity and contention, if it becomes
the cause of warfare and strife and influences men to kill each
other, its absence is preferable. For that which is productive of
hatred amongst the people is rejected by God, and that which
establishes fellowship is beloved and sanctioned by Him. Religion and divine teachings are like unto a remedy. A remedy
must produce the condition of health. If it occasions sickness,
it is wiser and better to have no remedy whatever. This is the
significance of the statement that if religion becomes the cause
of warfare and bloodshed, irreligion and the absence of religion
are preferable among mankind.

Bahá'u'lláh has declared that religion must be in accord with 4
science and reason. If it does not correspond with scientific
principles and the processes of reason, it is superstition. For God
has endowed us with faculties by which we may comprehend
the realities of things, contemplate reality itself. If religion is
opposed to reason and science, faith is impossible; and when
faith and confidence in the divine religion are not manifest in
the heart, there can be no spiritual attainment.

According to the teachings of Bahá'u'lláh all religious, racial, 5
patriotic and political prejudice must be abandoned, for these
are the destroyers of the real foundation of humanity. He has
announced that the religion of God is one, for all revelations of
it are based upon reality. Abraham summoned the people to real-

ity; Moses proclaimed reality; Christ founded reality. Likewise, all the Prophets were the servants and promulgators of reality. Reality is one and indivisible. Therefore, the prejudices and bigotries which exist today among the religions are not justifiable, inasmuch as they are opposed to reality. All prejudices are against the will and plan of God. Consider, for instance, racial distinction and enmity. All humanity are the children of God; they belong to the same family, to the same original race. There can be no multiplicity of races, since all are the descendants of Adam. This signifies that racial assumption and distinction are nothing but superstition. In the estimate of God there are no English, French, Germans, Turkish or Persians. All these in the presence of God are equal; they are of one race and creation; God did not make these divisions. These distinctions have had their origin in man himself. Therefore, as they are against the plan and purpose of reality, they are false and imaginary. We are of one physical race, even as we are of one physical plan of material body—each endowed with two eyes, two ears, one head, two feet. Among the animals racial prejudice does not exist. Consider the doves; there is no distinction as to whether it is an oriental or an occidental dove. The sheep are all of one race; there is no assumption of distinction between an eastern and a western sheep. When they meet, they associate with perfect fellowship. If a dove from the West should go to the Orient, it will associate with the eastern doves unhesitatingly. There will be no attitude of unwillingness as if saying, "You belong to the East; I am from the West." Is it reasonable or allowable that a racial prejudice which is not observed by the animal kingdom should be entertained by man?

6   Consider the prejudice of patriotism. This is one globe, one land, one country. God did not divide it into national boundaries. He created all the continents without national divisions.

Why should we make such division ourselves? These are but imaginary lines and boundaries. Europe is a continent; it is not naturally divided; man has drawn the lines and established the limits of kingdoms and empires. Man declares a river to be a boundary line between two countries, calling this side French and the other side German, whereas the river was created for both and is a natural artery for all. Is it not imagination and ignorance which impels man to violate the divine intention and make the very bounties of God the cause of war, bloodshed and destruction? Therefore, all prejudices between man and man are falsehoods and violations of the will of God. God desires unity and love; He commands harmony and fellowship. Enmity is human disobedience; God Himself is love.

Bahá'u'lláh has announced that inasmuch as ignorance and 7 lack of education are barriers of separation among mankind, all must receive training and instruction. Through this provision the lack of mutual understanding will be remedied and the unity of mankind furthered and advanced. Universal education is a universal law. It is, therefore, incumbent upon every father to teach and instruct his children according to his possibilities. If he is unable to educate them, the body politic, the representative of the people, must provide the means for their education.

In the Orient women were degraded and considered subordi- 8 nate to man. Bahá'u'lláh proclaimed equality of the sexes—that both man and woman are servants of God before Whom there is no distinction. Whosoever has a pure heart and renders good deeds is nearer to God and the object of His favor—whether man or woman. The sex distinction which exists in the human world is due to the lack of education for woman, who has been denied equal opportunity for development and advancement. Equality of the sexes will be established in proportion to the increased opportunities afforded woman in this age, for man

417

and woman are equally the recipients of powers and endowments from God, the Creator. God has not ordained distinction between them in His consummate purpose.

9   Bahá'u'lláh has proclaimed the adoption of a universal language. A language shall be agreed upon by which unity will be established in the world. Each person will require training in two languages: his native tongue and the universal auxiliary form of speech. This will facilitate intercommunication and dispel the misunderstandings which the barriers of language have occasioned in the world. All people worship the same God and are alike His servants. When they are able to communicate freely, they will associate in friendship and concord, entertain the greatest love and fellowship for each other, and in reality the Orient and Occident will embrace in unity and agreement.

10   The world is in greatest need of international peace. Until it is established, mankind will not attain composure and tranquillity. It is necessary that the nations and governments organize an international tribunal to which all their disputes and differences shall be referred. The decision of that tribunal shall be final. Individual controversy will be adjudged by a local tribunal. International questions will come before the universal tribunal, and so the cause of warfare will be taken away.

11   Fifty years ago Bahá'u'lláh wrote Epistles to the kings and rulers of the world in which the teachings and principles revealed by Him were embodied and set forth. These Epistles were printed in India forty years ago and spread broadcast.

12   Briefly, by the promulgation of these principles Bahá'u'lláh has caused the prejudices which afflicted the people of the Orient to disappear. The communities which have accepted His teachings are now living together in the greatest love and harmony. When you enter a meeting of these people, you will find Christians, Jews, Muslims, Zoroastrians, Buddhists gathered

together in perfect fellowship and agreement. In their discussions the greatest spirit of tolerance and friendship has supplanted the former hostility and hatred witnessed among them.

I have visited America and find everywhere the evidences of 13 just and equitable government. Therefore, I pray God that these western peoples may become the means of establishing international peace and spreading the oneness of the world of humanity. May you become the cause of unity and agreement among the nations. May a lamp be lighted here which will illumine the whole universe with the oneness of the world of humanity, with love between the hearts of the children of men, and the unity of all mankind. I hope that you may become assisted in this supreme accomplishment, that you may raise the flag of international peace and reconciliation upon this continent, that this government and people may be the means of spreading these lofty ideals in order that the world of man may find rest, in order that the good pleasure of the Most High God shall be attained and His favors encircle the Orient and Occident.

O Thou compassionate, almighty One! This assemblage of 14 souls have turned their faces unto Thee in supplication. With the utmost humility and submission they look toward Thy Kingdom and beg Thee for pardon and forgiveness. O God! Endear this assembly to Thyself. Sanctify these souls, and cast upon them the rays of Thy guidance. Illumine their hearts, and gladden their spirits with Thy glad tidings. Receive all of them in Thy holy Kingdom; confer upon them Thine inexhaustible bounty; make them happy in this world and in the world to come. O God! We are weak; give us strength. We are poor; bestow upon us Thine illimitable treasures. We are sick; grant unto us Thy divine healing. We are impotent; give us Thy heavenly power. O Lord! Make us useful in this world; free us from the condition of self and desire. O Lord! Make us brethren in Thy love, and cause us to be loving toward all Thy children. Confirm us in service to the world of humanity so that we may become the servants of Thy servants, that we may love all Thy creatures and become compassionate to all Thy people. O Lord, Thou art the Almighty. Thou art the Merciful. Thou art the Forgiver. Thou art the Omnipotent.

2

1 September 1912

Talk at Home of Mr. and Mrs. William Sutherland Maxwell
716 Pine Avenue West, Montreal, Canada

FROM STENOGRAPHIC NOTES

1   I AM exceedingly happy to meet you. Praise be to God! I see before me souls who have unusual capability and the power of spiritual advancement. In reality, the people of this continent possess great capacity; they are the cause of my happiness, and I ever pray that God may confirm and assist them to progress in all the degrees of existence. As they have advanced along material lines, may they develop in idealistic degrees, for material advancement is fruitless without spiritual progress and not productive of everlasting results. For example, no matter how much the physical body of man is trained and developed, there will be no real progression in the human station unless the mind correspondingly advances. No matter how much man may acquire material virtues, he will not be able to realize and express the highest possibilities of life without spiritual graces. God has created all earthly things under a law of progression

in material degrees, but He has created man and endowed him with powers of advancement toward spiritual and transcendental kingdoms. He has not created material phenomena after His own image and likeness, but He has created man after that image and with potential power to attain that likeness. He has distinguished man above all other created things. All created things except man are captives of nature and the sense world, but in man there has been created an ideal power by which he may perceive intellectual or spiritual realities. He has brought forth everything necessary for the life of this world, but man is a creation intended for the reflection of divine virtues. Consider that the highest type of creation below man is the animal, which is superior to all degrees of life except man. Manifestly, the animal has been created for the life of this world. Its highest virtue is to express excellence in the material plane of existence. The animal is perfect when its body is healthy and its physical senses are whole. When it is characterized by the attributes of physical health, when its physical forces are in working order, when food and surrounding conditions minister to its needs, it has attained the ultimate perfection of its kingdom. But man does not depend upon these things for his virtues. No matter how perfect his health and physical powers, if that is all, he has not yet risen above the degree of a perfect animal. Beyond and above this, God has opened the doors of ideal virtues and attainments before the face of man. He has created in his being the mysteries of the divine Kingdom. He has bestowed upon him the power of intellect so that through the attribute of reason, when fortified by the Holy Spirit, he may penetrate and discover ideal realities and become informed of the mysteries of the world of significances. As this power to penetrate the ideal knowledges is superhuman, supernatural, man becomes the collective center of spiritual as well as material forces so that the divine spirit may manifest itself in his being, the effulgences of the Kingdom shine within the sanctuary of his heart, the signs of the attributes and perfections of God reveal themselves in a newness of life, the everlasting glory and eternal existence be attained, the knowledge of God illumine, and the mysteries of the realm of might be unsealed.

2   Man is like unto this lamp, but the effulgences of the Kingdom are like the rays of the lamp. Man is like unto the glass, but spiritual splendors are like unto the light within the glass. No matter how translucent the glass may be, as long as there is no light within, it remains dark. Likewise, man, no matter how much he advances in material accomplishments, will remain like the glass without light if he is deprived of the spiritual virtues. Material virtues are like unto a perfect body, but this body is in need of the spirit. No matter how handsome and perfect the body may be, if it is deprived of the spirit and its animus, it is dead. But when that same body is affiliated with the spirit and expressing life, perfection and virtue become realized in it. Deprived of the Holy Spirit and its bounties, man is spiritually dead.

3   Children, for instance, no matter how good and pure, no matter how healthy their bodies, are, nevertheless, considered imperfect because the power of intellect is not fully manifest in them. When the intellectual power fully displays its influences and they attain to the age of maturity, they are considered as perfect. Likewise, man, no matter how much he may advance in worldly affairs and make progress in material civilization, is imperfect unless he is quickened by the bounties of the Holy Spirit; for it is evident that until he receives that divine impetus he is ignorant and deprived. For this reason Jesus Christ said, "Except a man be born of water and of the Spirit, he cannot enter into the kingdom of God." By this Christ meant that unless man is released from the material world, freed from the captivity of materialism and receiving a portion of the bounties

of the spiritual world, he shall be deprived of the bestowals and favors of the Kingdom of God, and the utmost we can say of him is that he is a perfect animal. No one can rightly call him a man. In another place He said, "That which is born of the flesh is flesh; and that which is born of the Spirit is spirit." The meaning of this is that if man is a captive of nature, he is like unto an animal because he is only a body physically born—that is, he belongs to the world of matter and remains subject to the law and control of nature. But if he is baptized with the Holy Spirit, if he is freed from the bondage of nature, released from animalistic tendencies and advanced in the human realm, he is fitted to enter into the divine Kingdom. The world of the Kingdom is the realm of divine bestowals and the bounties of God. It is attainment of the highest virtues of humanity; it is nearness to God; it is capacity to receive the bounties of the ancient Lord. When man advances to this station, he attains the second birth. Before his first or physical birth man was in the world of the matrix. He had no knowledge of this world; his eyes could not see; his ears could not hear. When he was born from the world of the matrix, he beheld another world. The sun was shining with its splendors, the moon radiant in the heavens, the stars twinkling in the expansive firmament, the seas surging, trees verdant and green, all kinds of creatures enjoying life here, infinite bounties prepared for him. In the world of the matrix none of these things existed. In that world he had no knowledge of this vast range of existence; nay, rather, he would have denied the reality of this world. But after his birth he began to open his eyes and behold the wonders of this illimitable universe. Similarly, as long as man is in the matrix of the human world, as long as he is the captive of nature, he is out of touch and without knowledge of the universe of the Kingdom. If he attains rebirth while in the world of nature, he will become informed of the divine world. He will observe that another and a higher world exists. Wonderful bounties descend; eternal life awaits; everlasting glory surrounds him. All the signs of reality and greatness are there. He will see the lights of God. All these experiences will be his when he is born out of the world of nature into the divine world. Therefore, for the perfect man there are two kinds of birth: the first, physical birth, is from the matrix of the mother; the second, or spiritual birth, is from the world of nature. In both he is without knowledge of the new world of existence he is entering. Therefore, rebirth means his release from the captivity of nature, freedom from attachment to this mortal and material life. This is the second, or spiritual, birth of which Jesus Christ spoke in the Gospels.

4   The majority of people are captives in the matrix of nature, submerged in the sea of materiality. We must pray that they may be reborn, that they may attain insight and spiritual hearing, that they may receive the gift of another heart, a new transcendent power, and in the eternal world the unending bestowal of divine bounties.

5   Today the world of humanity is walking in darkness because it is out of touch with the world of God. That is why we do not see the signs of God in the hearts of men. The power of the Holy Spirit has no influence. When a divine spiritual illumination becomes manifest in the world of humanity, when divine instruction and guidance appear, then enlightenment follows, a new spirit is realized within, a new power descends, and a new life is given. It is like the birth from the animal kingdom into the kingdom of man. When man acquires these virtues, the oneness of the world of humanity will be revealed, the banner of international peace will be upraised, equality between all mankind will be realized, and the Orient and Occident will become one. Then will the justice of God become manifest, all humanity will appear as the members of one family, and every member of that family will be consecrated to cooperation and

mutual assistance. The lights of the love of God will shine; eternal happiness will be unveiled; everlasting joy and spiritual delight will be attained.

I will pray, and you must pray, likewise, that such heavenly 6 bounty may be realized; that strife and enmity may be banished, warfare and bloodshed taken away; that hearts may attain ideal communication and that all people may drink from the same fountain. May they receive their knowledge from the same divine source. May all hearts become illumined with the rays of the Sun of Reality; may all of them enter the university of God, acquire spiritual virtues and seek for themselves heavenly bounties. Then this material, phenomenal world will become the mirror of the world of God, and within this pure mirror the divine virtues of the realm of might will be reflected.

3

1 September 1912

Talk at Home of Mr. and Mrs. William Sutherland Maxwell
716 Pine Avenue West, Montreal, Canada

FROM STENOGRAPHIC NOTES

THE subject of immortality has been suggested. 1

Life is the expression of composition; and death, the expres- 2 sion of decomposition. In the world or kingdom of the minerals certain materials or elemental substances exist. When through the law of creation they enter into composition, a being or organism comes into existence. For example, certain material atoms are brought together, and man is the result. When this composition is destroyed and disintegrated, decomposition takes place; this is mortality, or death. When certain elements are composed, an animal comes into being. When these elements are scattered or decomposed, this is called the death of the animal. Again, certain atoms are bound together by chemical affinity; a composition called a flower appears. When these atoms are dispersed and the composition they have formed is disintegrated, the flower has come to its end; it is dead. Therefore, it is evident that life is the expression of composition, and mortality, or death, is equivalent to decomposition. As the spirit of man is not composed of material elements, it is not subject to decomposition and, therefore, has no death. It is self-evident that the human spirit is simple, single and not composed in order that it may come to immortality, and it is a philosophical axiom that the individual or indivisible atom is indestructible. At most, it passes through a process of construction and reconstruction. For example, these individual atoms are brought together in a composition, and through this composition a given organism—such as a man, an animal or a plant—is created. When this composition is decomposed, that created organism is brought to an end, but the component atoms are not annihilated; they continue to exist because they are single, individual and not composed. Therefore, it may be said that these individual atoms are eternal. Likewise, the human spirit, inasmuch as it is not composed of individual elements or atoms—as it is sanctified above these elements—is eternal. This is a self-evident proof of its immortality.

3   Second, consider the world of dreams, wherein the body of man is immovable, seemingly dead, not subject to sensation; the eyes do not see, the ears do not hear nor the tongue speak. But the spirit of man is not asleep; it sees, hears, moves, perceives and discovers realities. Therefore, it is evident that the spirit of man is not affected by the change or condition of the body.

Even though the material body should die, the spirit continues eternally alive, just as it exists and functions in the inert body in the realm of dreams. That is to say, the spirit is immortal and will continue its existence after the destruction of the body.

Third, the human body has one form. In its composition it 4 has been transferred from one form to another but never possesses two forms at the same time. For example, it has existed in the elemental substances of the mineral kingdom. From the mineral kingdom it has traversed the vegetable kingdom and its constituent substances; from the vegetable kingdom it has risen by evolution into the kingdom of the animal and from thence attained the kingdom of man. After its disintegration and decomposition it will return again to the mineral kingdom, leaving its human form and taking a new form unto itself. During these progressions one form succeeds another, but at no time does the body possess more than one.

The spirit of man, however, can manifest itself in all forms 5 at the same time. For example, we say that a material body is either square or spherical, triangular or hexagonal. While it is triangular, it cannot be square; and while it is square, it is not triangular. Similarly, it cannot be spherical and hexagonal at the same time. These various forms or shapes cannot be manifest at the same instant in one material object. Therefore, the form of the physical body of man must be destroyed and abandoned before it can assume or take unto itself another. Mortality, therefore, means transference from one form to another—that is, transference from the human kingdom to the kingdom of the mineral. When the physical man is dead, he will return to dust; and this transference is equivalent to nonexistence. But the human spirit in itself contains all these forms, shapes and figures. It is not possible to break or destroy one form so that it may transfer itself into another. As an evidence of this, at the present moment in the human spirit you have the shape of a square and the figure of a triangle. Simultaneously also you can conceive a hexagonal form. All these can be conceived at the same moment in the human spirit, and not one of them needs to be destroyed or broken in order that the spirit of man may be transferred to another. There is no annihilation, no destruction; therefore, the human spirit is immortal because it is not transferred from one body into another body.

6   Consider another proof: Every cause is followed by an effect and vice versa; there could be no effect without a cause preceding it. Sight is an effect; there is no doubt that behind that effect there is a cause. When we hear a discourse, there is a speaker. We could not hear words unless they proceeded from the tongue of a speaker. Motion without a mover or cause of motion is inconceivable. Jesus Christ lived two thousand years ago. Today we behold His manifest signs; His light is shining; His sovereignty is established; His traces are apparent; His bounties are effulgent. Can we say that Christ did not exist? We can absolutely conclude that Christ existed and that from Him these traces proceeded.

7   Still another proof: The body of man becomes lean or fat; it is afflicted with disease, suffers mutilation; perhaps the eyes become blind, the ears deaf; but none of these imperfections and failings afflict or affect the spirit. The spirit of man remains in the same condition, unchanged. A man is blinded, but his spirit continues the same. He loses his hearing, his hand is cut off, his foot amputated; but his spirit remains the same. He becomes lethargic, he is afflicted with apoplexy; but there is no difference, change or alteration in his spirit. This is proof that death is only destruction of the body, while the spirit remains immortal, eternal.

8   Again, all phenomena of the material world are subject to mortality and death, but the immortal spirit does not belong

to the phenomenal world; it is holy and sanctified above material existence. If the spirit of man belonged to the elemental existence, the eye could see it, the ear hear it, the hand touch. As long as these five senses cannot perceive it, the proof is unquestioned that it does not belong to the elemental world and, therefore, is beyond death or mortality, which are inseparable from that material realm of existence. If being is not subject to the limitation of material life, it is not subject to mortality.

There are many other proofs of the immortality of the spirit 9 of man. These are but a few of them. Salutations!

4

2 September 1912

*Talk at Home of Mr. and Mrs. William Sutherland Maxwell
716 Pine Avenue West, Montreal, Canada*

FROM STENOGRAPHIC NOTES

NATURE is the material world. When we look upon it, we see 1 that it is dark and imperfect. For instance, if we allow a piece of land to remain in its natural condition, we will find it covered with thorns and thistles; useless weeds and wild vegetation will flourish upon it, and it will become like a jungle. The trees will be fruitless, lacking beauty and symmetry; wild animals, noxious insects and reptiles will abound in its dark recesses. This is the incompleteness and imperfection of the world of nature. To change these conditions, we must clear the ground and cultivate it so that flowers may grow instead of thorns and weeds—that is to say, we must illumine the dark world of nature. In their primal natural state, the forests are dim, gloomy, impenetrable. Man opens them to the light, clears away the tangled underbrush and plants fruitful trees. Soon the wild woodlands and jungle are changed into productive orchards and beautiful gardens; order has replaced chaos; the dark realm of nature has become illumined and brightened by cultivation.

2   If man himself is left in his natural state, he will become lower than the animal and continue to grow more ignorant and imperfect. The savage tribes of central Africa are evidences of this. Left in their natural condition, they have sunk to the lowest depths and degrees of barbarism, dimly groping in a world of mental and moral obscurity. If we wish to illumine this dark plane of human existence, we must bring man forth from the hopeless captivity of nature, educate him and show him the pathway of light and knowledge, until, uplifted from his condition of ignorance, he becomes wise and knowing; no longer savage and revengeful, he becomes civilized and kind; once evil and sinister, he is endowed with the attributes of heaven. But left in his natural condition without education and training, it is certain that he will become more depraved and vicious than the animal, even to the extreme degree witnessed among African tribes who practice cannibalism. It is evident, therefore, that the world of nature is incomplete, imperfect until awakened and illumined by the light and stimulus of education.

3   In these days there are new schools of philosophy blindly claiming that the world of nature is perfect. If this is true, why are children trained and educated in schools, and what is the need of extended courses in sciences, arts and letters in colleges and universities? What would be the result if humanity were left in its natural condition without education or training? All scientific discoveries and attainments are the outcomes of knowledge and education. The telegraph, phonograph, telephone were

latent and potential in the world of nature but would never have come forth into the realm of visibility unless man through education had penetrated and discovered the laws which control them. All the marvelous developments and miracles of what we call civilization would have remained hidden, unknown and, so to speak, nonexistent, if man had remained in his natural condition, deprived of the bounties, blessings and benefits of education and mental culture. The intrinsic difference between the ignorant man and the astute philosopher is that the former has not been lifted out of his natural condition, while the latter has undergone systematic training and education in schools and colleges until his mind has awakened and unfolded to higher realms of thought and perception; otherwise, both are human and natural.

God has sent forth the Prophets for the purpose of quicken- 4
ing the soul of man into higher and divine recognitions. He has revealed the heavenly Books for this great purpose. For this the breaths of the Holy Spirit have been wafted through the gardens of human hearts, the doors of the divine Kingdom opened to mankind and the invisible inspirations sent forth from on high. This divine and ideal power has been bestowed upon man in order that he may purify himself from the imperfections of nature and uplift his soul to the realm of might and power. God has purposed that the darkness of the world of nature shall be dispelled and the imperfect attributes of the natal self be effaced in the effulgent reflection of the Sun of Truth. The mission of the Prophets of God has been to train the souls of humanity and free them from the thralldom of natural instincts and physical tendencies. They are like unto Gardeners, and the world of humanity is the field of Their cultivation, the wilderness and untrained jungle growth wherein They proceed to labor. They cause the crooked branches to become straightened, the fruitless

trees to become fruitful, and gradually transform this great wild, uncultivated field into a beautiful orchard producing wonderful abundance and outcome.

5   If the world of nature were perfect and complete in itself, there would be no need of such training and cultivation in the human world—no need of teachers, schools and universities, arts and crafts. The revelations of the Prophets of God would not have been necessary, and the heavenly Books would have been superfluous. If the world of nature were perfect and sufficient for mankind, we would have no need of God and our belief in Him. Therefore, the bestowal of all these great helps and accessories to the attainment of divine life is because the world of nature is incomplete and imperfect. Consider this Canadian country during the early history of Montreal when the land was in its wild, uncultivated and natural condition. The soil was unproductive, rocky and almost uninhabitable—vast forests stretching in every direction. What invisible power caused this great metropolis to spring up amid such savage and forbidding conditions? It was the human mind. Therefore, nature and the effect of nature's laws were imperfect. The mind of man remedied and removed this imperfect condition, until now we behold a great city instead of a savage unbroken wilderness. Before the coming of Columbus America itself was a wild, uncultivated expanse of primeval forest, mountains and rivers—a very world of nature. Now it has become the world of man. It was dark, forbidding and savage; now it has become illumined with a great civilization and prosperity. Instead of forests, we behold productive farms, beautiful gardens and prolific orchards. Instead of thorns and useless vegetation, we find flowers, domestic animals and fields awaiting harvest. If the world of nature were perfect, the condition of this great country would have been left unchanged.

6   If a child is left in its natural state and deprived of education, there is no doubt that it will grow up in ignorance and

illiteracy, its mental faculties dulled and dimmed; in fact, it will become like an animal. This is evident among the savages of central Africa, who are scarcely higher than the beast in mental development.

The conclusion is irresistible that the splendors of the Sun 7 of Truth, the Word of God, have been the source and cause of human upbuilding and civilization. The world of nature is the kingdom of the animal. In its natural condition and plane of limitation the animal is perfect. The ferocious beasts of prey have been completely subject to the laws of nature in their development. They are without education or training; they have no power of abstract reasoning and intellectual ideals; they have no touch with the spiritual world and are without conception of God or the Holy Spirit. The animal can neither recognize nor apprehend the spiritual power of man and makes no distinction between man and itself, for the reason that its susceptibilities are limited to the plane of the senses. It lives under the bondage of nature and nature's laws. All the animals are materialists. They are deniers of God and without realization of a transcendent power in the universe. They have no knowledge of the divine Prophets and Holy Books—mere captives of nature and the sense world. In reality they are like the great philosophers of this day who are not in touch with God and the Holy Spirit—deniers of the Prophets, ignorant of spiritual susceptibilities, deprived of the heavenly bounties and without belief in the supernatural power. The animal lives this kind of life blissfully and untroubled, whereas the material philosophers labor and study for ten or twenty years in schools and colleges, denying God, the Holy Spirit and divine inspirations. The animal is even a greater philosopher, for it attains the ability to do this without labor and study. For instance, the cow denies God and the Holy Spirit, knows nothing of divine inspirations, heavenly bounties or spiritual emotions and is a stranger to the world of hearts. Like the philosophers, the cow is a captive of nature and knows nothing beyond the range of the senses. The philosophers, however, glory in this, saying, "We are not captives of superstitions; we have implicit faith in the impressions of the senses and know nothing beyond the realm of nature, which contains and covers everything." But the cow, without study or proficiency in the sciences, modestly and quietly views life from the same standpoint, living in harmony with nature's laws in the utmost dignity and nobility.

8   This is not the glory of man. The glory of man is in the knowledge of God, spiritual susceptibilities, attainment to transcendent powers and the bounties of the Holy Spirit. The glory of man is in being informed of the teachings of God. This is the glory of humanity. Ignorance is not glory but darkness. Can these souls who are steeped in the lower strata of ignorance become informed of the mysteries of God and the realities of existence while Jesus Christ was without knowledge of them? Is the intellect of these people greater than the intellect of Christ? Christ was heavenly, divine and belonged to the world of the Kingdom. He was the embodiment of spiritual knowledge. His intellect was superior to these philosophers, His comprehension deeper, His perception keener, His knowledge more perfect. How is it that He overlooked and denied Himself everything in this world? He attached little importance to this material life, denying Himself rest and composure, accepting trials and voluntarily suffering vicissitudes because He was endowed with spiritual susceptibilities and the power of the Holy Spirit. He beheld the splendors of the divine Kingdom, embodied the bounties of God and possessed ideal powers. He was illumined with love and mercy, and so, likewise, were all the Prophets of God.

5

3 September 1912

'Abdu'l-Bahá's address to Socialists and Labor leaders
in Coronation Hall
Montreal, Canada

It seems as though all creatures can exist singly and alone. For   1
example, a tree can exist solitary and alone on a given prairie or
in a valley or on the mountainside. An animal upon a mountain
or a bird soaring in the air might live a solitary life. They are
not in need of cooperation or solidarity. Such animated beings
enjoy the greatest comfort and happiness in their respective
solitary lives.

On the contrary, man cannot live singly and alone. He is in   2
need of continuous cooperation and mutual help. For example,
a man living alone in the wilderness will eventually starve. He
can never, singly and alone, provide himself with all the necessities of existence. Therefore, he is in need of cooperation and
reciprocity. The mystery of this phenomenon, the cause thereof
is this: that mankind has been created from one single origin,
has branched off from one family. Thus, in reality, all mankind
represents one family. God has not created any difference. He
has created all as one that thus this family might live in perfect
happiness and well-being.

Regarding reciprocity and cooperation, each member of   3
the body politic should live in the utmost comfort and welfare
because each individual member of humanity is a member of
the body politic, and if one member is in distress or is afflicted
with some disease, all the other members must necessarily suffer.
For example, a member of the human organism is the eye. If

435

the eye should be affected, that affliction would affect the whole nervous system. Hence, if a member of the body politic becomes afflicted, in reality, from the standpoint of sympathetic connection, all will share that affliction since this [one afflicted] is a member of the group of members, a part of the whole. Is it possible for one member or part to be in distress and the other members to be at ease? It is impossible! Hence, God has desired that in the body politic of humanity each one shall enjoy perfect welfare and comfort.

4   Although the body politic is one family, yet, because of lack of harmonious relations some members are comfortable and some in direst misery; some members are satisfied and some are hungry; some members are clothed in most costly garments and some families are in need of food and shelter. Why? Because this family lacks the necessary reciprocity and symmetry. This household is not well arranged. This household is not living under a perfect law. All the laws which are legislated do not ensure happiness. They do not provide comfort. Therefore, a law must be given to this family by means of which all the members of this family will enjoy equal well-being and happiness.

5   Is it possible for one member of a family to be subjected to the utmost misery and to abject poverty and for the rest of the family to be comfortable? It is impossible unless those members of the family be senseless, atrophied, inhospitable, unkind. Then they would say, "Though these members do belong to our family, let them alone. Let us look after ourselves. Let them die. So long as I am comfortable, I am honored, I am happy—this, my brother—let him die. If he be in misery, let him remain in misery, so long as I am comfortable. If he is hungry, let him remain so; I am satisfied. If he is without clothes, so long as I am clothed, let him remain as he is. If he is shelterless, homeless, so long as I have a home, let him remain in the wilderness."

Such utter indifference in the human family is due to lack   6
of control, to lack of a working law, to lack of kindness in its
midst. If kindness had been shown to the members of this family, surely all the members thereof would have enjoyed comfort
and happiness.

Bahá'u'lláh has given instructions regarding every one of the   7
questions confronting humanity. He has given teachings and
instructions with regard to every one of the problems with which
man struggles. Among them are [the teachings] concerning the
question of economics, that all the members of the body politic
may enjoy through the working out of this solution the greatest happiness, welfare and comfort without any harm or injury
attacking the general order of things. Thereby no difference or
dissension will occur. No sedition or contention will take place.
This solution is this:

First and foremost is the principle that to all the members of   8
the body politic shall be given the greatest achievements of the
world of humanity. Each one shall have the utmost welfare and
well-being. To solve this problem we must begin with the farmer;
there will we lay a foundation for system and order because the
peasant class and the agricultural class exceed other classes in the
importance of their service. In every village there must be established a general storehouse which will have a number of revenues.

The first revenue will be that of the tenth or tithes.   9

The second revenue [will be derived] from the animals.   10

The third revenue, from the minerals; that is to say, every   11
mine prospected or discovered, a third thereof will go to this
vast storehouse.

The fourth is this: whosoever dies without leaving any heirs,   12
all his heritage will go to the general storehouse.

Fifth, if any treasures shall be found on the land, they should   13
be devoted to this storehouse.

14   All these revenues will be assembled in this storehouse.

15   As to the first, the tenths or tithes: We will consider a farmer, one of the peasants. We will look into his income. We will find out for instance, what is his annual revenue and also what are his expenditures. Now, if his income be equal to his expenditures, from such a farmer nothing whatever will be taken. That is, he will not be subjected to taxation of any sort, needing as he does all his income. Another farmer may have expenses running up to one thousand dollars, we will say, and his income is two thousand dollars. From such an one a tenth will be required, because he has a surplus. But if his income be ten thousand dollars and his expenses one thousand dollars or his income twenty thousand dollars, he will have to pay as taxes, one fourth. If his income be one hundred thousand dollars, and his expenses five thousand, one third will he have to pay because he has still a surplus since his expenses are five thousand and his income one hundred thousand. If he pays, say, thirty-five thousand dollars, in addition to the expenditure of five thousand he still has sixty thousand left. But if his expenses be ten thousand and his income two hundred thousand, then he must give an even half because ninety thousand will be in that case the sum remaining. Such a scale as this will determine allotment of taxes. All the income from such revenues will go to this general storehouse.

16   Then there must be considered such emergencies as follows: A certain farmer whose expenses run up to ten thousand dollars and whose income is only five thousand will receive necessary expenses from the storehouse. Five thousand dollars will be allotted to him so he will not be in need.

17   Then the orphans will be looked after, all of whose expenses will be taken care of. The cripples in the village—all their expenses will be looked after. The poor in the village—their necessary expenses will be defrayed. And other members who

for valid reasons are incapacitated—the blind, the old, the deaf—their comfort must be looked after. In the village no one will remain in need or in want. All will live in the utmost comfort and welfare. Yet no schism will assail the general order of the body politic.

Hence, the expenses or expenditures of the general storehouse 18 are now made clear and its activities made manifest. The income of this general storehouse has been shown. Certain trustees will be elected by the people in a given village to look after these transactions. The farmers will be taken care of, and, if after all these expenses are defrayed, any surplus is found in the storehouse, it must be transferred to the national treasury.

This system is all thus ordered so that in the village the very 19 poor will be comfortable, the orphans will live happily and well; in a word, no one will be left destitute. All the individual members of the body politic will thus live comfortably and well.

For larger cities, naturally, there will be a system on a larger 20 scale. Were I to go into that solution the details thereof would be very lengthy.

The result of this [system] will be that each individual 21 member of the body politic will live most comfortably and happily under obligation to no one. Nevertheless, there will be preservation of degree because in the world of humanity there must needs be degrees. The body politic may well be likened to an army. In this army there must be a general, there must be a sergeant, there must be a marshal, there must be the infantry; but all must enjoy the greatest comfort and welfare.

God is not partial and is no respecter of persons. He has made 22 provision for all. The harvest comes forth for everyone. The rain showers upon everybody and the heat of the sun is destined to warm everyone. The verdure of the earth is for everyone. Therefore, there should be for all humanity the utmost happiness, the utmost comfort, the utmost well-being.

23   But if conditions are such that some are happy and comfortable and some in misery, some are accumulating exorbitant wealth and others are in dire want—under such a system it is impossible for man to be happy and impossible for him to win the good pleasure of God. God is kind to all. The good pleasure of God consists in the welfare of all the individual members of mankind.

24   A Persian king was one night in his palace, living in the greatest luxury and comfort. Through excessive joy and gladness he addressed a certain man, saying, "Of all my life this is the happiest moment. Praise be to God, from every point prosperity appears and fortune smiles! My treasury is full and the army is well taken care of. My palaces are many; my land unlimited; my family is well off; my honor and sovereignty are great. What more could I want?"

25   The poor man at the gate of his palace spoke out, saying: "O kind king! Assuming that you are from every point of view so happy, free from every worry and sadness, do you not worry for us? You say that on your own account you have no worries, but do you never worry about the poor in your land? Is it becoming or meet that you should be so well off and we in such dire want and need? In view of our needs and troubles, how can you rest in your palace, how can you even say that you are free from worries and sorrows? As a ruler you must not be so egoistic as to think of yourself alone, but you must think of those who are your subjects. When we are comfortable, then you will be comfortable; when we are in misery, how can you, as a king, be in happiness?"

26   The purport is this, that we are all inhabiting one globe of earth. In reality we are one family, and each one of us is a member of this family. We must all be in the greatest happiness and comfort, under a just rule and regulation which is according to the good pleasure of God, thus causing us to be happy, for this life is fleeting.

If man were to care for himself only he would be nothing but 27
an animal, for only the animals are thus egoistic. If you bring a
thousand sheep to a well to kill nine hundred and ninety-nine,
the one remaining sheep would go on grazing, not thinking of
the others and worrying not at all about the lost, never bothering
that its own kind had passed away, or had perished or been killed.
To look after one's self only is, therefore, an animal propensity.
It is the animal propensity to live solitary and alone. It is the
animal proclivity to look after one's own comfort. But man was
created to be a man—to be fair, to be just, to be merciful, to be
kind to all his species, never to be willing that he himself be well
off while others are in misery and distress. This is an attribute of
the animal and not of man. Nay, rather, man should be willing
to accept hardships for himself in order that others may enjoy
wealth; he should enjoy trouble for himself that others may
enjoy happiness and well-being. This is the attribute of man.
This is becoming of man. Otherwise man is not man—he is
less than the animal.

The man who thinks only of himself and is thoughtless of 28
others is undoubtedly inferior to the animal because the animal
is not possessed of the reasoning faculty. The animal is excused;
but in man there is reason, the faculty of justice, the faculty of
mercifulness. Possessing all these faculties, he must not leave
them unused. He who is so hard-hearted as to think only of his
own comfort, such an one will not be called man.

Man is he who forgets his own interests for the sake of oth- 29
ers. His own comfort he forfeits for the well-being of all. Nay,
rather, his own life must he be willing to forfeit for the life of
mankind. Such a man is the honor of the world of humanity. Such a man is the glory of the world of mankind. Such a
man is the one who wins eternal bliss. Such a man is near to
the threshold of God. Such a man is the very manifestation of
eternal happiness. Otherwise, men are like animals, exhibiting

the same proclivities and propensities as the world of animals. What distinction is there? What prerogatives, what perfection? None whatever! Animals are better even—thinking only of themselves and negligent of the needs of others.

30　　Consider how the greatest men in the world—whether among prophets or philosophers—all have forfeited their own comfort, have sacrificed their own pleasure for the well-being of humanity. They have sacrificed their own lives for the body politic. They have sacrificed their own wealth for that of the general welfare. They have forfeited their own honor for the honor of mankind. Therefore, it becomes evident that this is the highest attainment for the world of humanity.

31　　We ask God to endow human souls with justice so that they may be fair, and may strive to provide for the comfort of all, that each member of humanity may pass his life in the utmost comfort and welfare. Then this material world will become the very paradise of the Kingdom, this elemental earth will be in a heavenly state and all the servants of God will live in the utmost joy, happiness and gladness. We must all strive and concentrate all our thoughts in order that such happiness may accrue to the world of humanity.

32　　The question of socialization is very important. It will not be solved by strikes for wages. All the governments of the world must be united and organize an assembly the members of which should be elected from the parliaments and the nobles of the nations. These must plan with utmost wisdom and power so that neither the capitalist suffer from enormous losses nor the laborers become needy. In the utmost moderation they should make the law; then announce to the public that the rights of the working people are to be strongly preserved. Also the rights of the capitalists are to be protected. When such a general plan is adopted by the will of both sides, should a strike occur, all the governments of the world collectively should resist it. Otherwise, the labor problem will lead to much destruction, especially in Europe. Terrible things will take place.

For instance, the owners of properties, mines and factories 33 should share their incomes with their employees and give a fairly certain percentage of their products to their workingmen in order that the employees may receive, beside their wages, some of the general income of the factory so that the employee may strive with his soul in the work.

No more trusts will remain in the future. The question 34 of the trusts will be wiped away entirely. Also, every factory that has ten thousand shares will give two thousand shares of these ten thousand to its employees and will write the shares in their names, so that they may have them, and the rest will belong to the capitalists. Then at the end of the month or year whatever they may earn after the expenses and wages are paid, according to the number of shares, should be divided among both. In reality, so far great injustice has befallen the common people. Laws must be made because it is impossible for the laborers to be satisfied with the present system. They will strike every month and every year. Finally, the capitalists will lose. In ancient times a strike occurred among the Turkish soldiers. They said to the government: "Our wages are very small and they should be increased." The government was forced to give them their demands. Shortly afterwards they struck again. Finally all the incomes went to the pockets of the soldiers to the extent that they killed the king, saying: "Why didst thou not increase the income so that we might have received more?"

It is impossible for a country to live properly without laws. 35 To solve this problem rigorous laws must be made, so that all the governments of the world will be the protectors thereof.

36   In the Bolshevistic principles equality is effected through force. The masses who are opposed to the people of rank and to the wealthy class desire to partake of their advantages.

37   But in the divine teachings equality is brought about through a ready willingness to share. It is commanded as regards wealth that the rich among the people, and the aristocrats should, by their own free will and for the sake of their own happiness, concern themselves with and care for the poor. This equality is the result of the lofty characteristics and noble attributes of mankind.

6

5 September 1912

Talk at St. James Methodist Church
Montreal, Canada

FROM STENOGRAPHIC NOTES

1   PRAISE be to God! It is with a deep realization of happiness that I am present here this evening, for I am looking upon the faces of those who are earnest in their search for reality and who sincerely long to attain knowledge of truth. God has created man and endowed him with the power of reason whereby he may arrive at valid conclusions. Therefore, man must endeavor in all things to investigate the fundamental reality. If he does not independently investigate, he has failed to utilize the talent God has bestowed upon him. I am pleased with the American people because, as a rule, they are independent seekers of the truth; their minds are actively employed instead of remaining idle and unproductive. This is most praiseworthy.

Some souls imagine that there is a cessation to the bounties 2
of God, as if at one time the divine bestowals are poured out,
at another time withheld from mankind and ceasing. If we
carefully reflect upon this matter, we find that such a statement
is in fact a denial of Divinity, for the reality of Divinity is evidenced by virtue of its outpourings or bestowals. The cessation
of the bestowals of God at any time would be equivalent to the
cessation of the sovereignty of God. The sun is the sun because
of its ray and heat; it is the sun because of its bestowal; but if
at any time its effulgence, splendor and radiance should cease
to emanate, it would no longer be the sun. Consequently, it
is inconceivable that the bounties of Divinity should cease,
for the attributes of Divinity are everexistent. God has ever
been divine; He hath ever exercised His sovereignty and still
possesses everlasting divinity and sovereignty. He is like the
sun, which has ever had its splendor, heat and radiance and
will continue to possess these bounties and attributes. If at any
time its splendor and heat should cease, it would no longer
be pronounced the sun. Therefore, the sound reasoning mind
concludes that the bounties of the Holy Spirit are continuous and that holy souls are ever the recipients of these divine
emanations. The potency of the Holy Spirit is everlasting, not
temporary; for the sanctity of the Holy Spirit is its power and
efficacy manifest in the spirits it quickens. We pray that all
of us may become recipients of its bestowals, that we may be
illumined by the lights of heaven, edified through the teachings of God and imbued with the virtues of divine character, as
mirrors reflecting the light of the sun. Unless the mirror reflects
the sunlight, it is only dark, inanimate matter. Likewise, the
hearts and spirits of mankind, when deprived and without their
portion of the bounties of the Holy Spirit, linger in the abyss
of darkness and ignorance.

3   From time immemorial the divine teachings have been successively revealed, and the bounties of the Holy Spirit have ever been emanating. All the teachings are one reality, for reality is single and does not admit multiplicity. Therefore, the divine Prophets are one, inasmuch as They reveal the one reality, the Word of God. Abraham announced teachings founded upon reality, Moses proclaimed reality, Christ established reality and Bahá'u'lláh was the Messenger and Herald of reality. But humanity, having forsaken the one essential and fundamental reality which underlies the religion of God, and holding blindly to imitations of ancestral forms and interpretations of belief, is separated and divided in the strife, contention and bigotry of various sects and religious factions. If all should be true to the original reality of the Prophet and His teaching, the peoples and nations of the world would become unified, and these differences which cause separation would be lost sight of. To accomplish this great and needful unity in reality, Bahá'u'lláh appeared in the Orient and renewed the foundations of the divine teachings. His revelation of the Word embodies completely the teachings of all the Prophets, expressed in principles and precepts applicable to the needs and conditions of the modern world, amplified and adapted to present-day questions and critical human problems. That is to say, the words of Bahá'u'lláh are the essences of the words of the Prophets of the past. They are the very spirit of the age and the cause of the unity and illumination of the East and the West. The followers of His teachings are in conformity with the precepts and commands of all the former heavenly Messengers. Differences and dissensions, which destroy the foundations of the world of humanity and are contrary to the will and good pleasure of God, disappear completely in the light of the revelation of Bahá'u'lláh; difficult problems are solved, unity and love are established. For the good pleasure of God is the effulgence of love and the establishment of unity and fellow-

ship in the human world, whereas discord, contention, warfare and strife are satanic outcomes and contrary to the will of the Merciful. In order that human souls, minds and spirits may attain advancement, tranquillity and vision in broader horizons of unity and knowledge, Bahá'u'lláh proclaimed certain principles or teachings, some of which I will mention.

First, man must independently investigate reality, for the disagreements and dissensions which afflict and affect humanity primarily proceed from imitations of ancestral beliefs and adherences to hereditary forms of worship. These imitations are accidental and without sanction in the Holy Books. They are the outcomes of human interpretations and teachings which have arisen, gradually obscuring the real light of divine meaning and causing men to differ and dissent. The reality proclaimed in the heavenly Books and divine teachings is ever conducive to love, unity and fellowship.

Second, the oneness of the world of humanity shall be realized, accepted and established. When we reflect upon this blessed principle, it will become evident and manifest that it is the healing remedy for all human conditions. All mankind are the servants of the glorious God, our Creator. He has created all. Assuredly He must have loved them equally; otherwise, He would not have created them. He protects all. Assuredly He loves His creatures; otherwise, He would not protect them. He provides for all, proving His love for all without distinction or preference. He manifests His perfect goodness and loving-kindness toward all. He does not punish us for our sins and shortcomings, and we are all immersed in the ocean of His infinite mercy. Inasmuch as God is clement and loving to His children, lenient and merciful toward our shortcomings, why should we be unkind and unforgiving toward each other? As He loves humanity without distinction or preference, why should we not love all? Can we conceive of a plan and policy superior

4

5

447

to the divine purpose? Manifestly, we cannot. Therefore, we must strive to do the will of the glorious Lord and emulate His policy of loving all mankind. The wisdom and policy of God are reality and truth, whereas human policy is accidental and limited to our finite understanding. The policy of God is infinite. We must emulate His example. If a soul be ailing and infirm, we must produce remedies; if ignorant, we must provide education; if defective, we must train and perfect that which is lacking; if immature and undeveloped, we must supply the means of attainment to maturity. No soul should be hated, none neglected; nay, rather, their very imperfections should demand greater kindness and tender compassion. Therefore, if we follow the example of the Lord of divinity, we will love all mankind from our hearts, and the means of the unity of the world of humanity will become as evident and manifest to us as the light of the sun. And from our example the light of the love of God will be enkindled among men. For God is love, and all phenomena find source and emanation in that divine current of creation. The love of God haloes all created things. Were it not for the love of God, no animate being would exist. This is clear, manifest vision and truth unless a man is veiled by superstitions and a captive to imaginations, differentiating mankind according to his own estimate, loving some and hating others. Such an attitude is most unworthy and ignoble.

6   Third, religion must be the mainspring and source of love in the world, for religion is the revelation of the will of God, the divine fundamental of which is love. Therefore, if religion should prove to be the cause of enmity and hatred instead of love, its absence is preferable to its existence.

7   Fourth, religion must reconcile and be in harmony with science and reason. If the religious beliefs of mankind are contrary to science and opposed to reason, they are none other than superstitions and without divine authority, for the Lord God has

endowed man with the faculty of reason in order that through its exercise he may arrive at the verities of existence. Reason is the discoverer of the realities of things, and that which conflicts with its conclusions is the product of human fancy and imagination.

Fifth, prejudice—whether it be religious, racial, patriotic or political in its origin and aspect—is the destroyer of human foundations and opposed to the commands of God. God has sent forth His Prophets for the sole purpose of creating love and unity in the world of human hearts. All the heavenly Books are the written word of love. If they prove to be the cause of prejudice and human estrangement, they have become fruitless. Therefore, religious prejudice is especially opposed to the will and command of God. Racial and national prejudices which separate mankind into groups and branches, likewise, have a false and unjustifiable foundation, for all men are the children of Adam and essentially of one family. There should be no racial alienation or national division among humankind. Such distinctions as French, German, Persian, Anglo-Saxon are human and artificial; they have neither significance nor recognition in the estimation of God. In His estimate all are one, the children of one family; and God is equally kind to them. The earth has one surface. God has not divided this surface by boundaries and barriers to separate races and peoples. Man has set up and established these imaginary lines, giving to each restricted area a name and the limitation of a native land or nationhood. By this division and separation into groups and branches of mankind, prejudice is engendered which becomes a fruitful source of war and strife. Impelled by this prejudice, races and nations declare war against each other; the blood of the innocent is poured out, and the earth torn by violence. Therefore, it has been decreed by God in this day that these prejudices and differences shall be laid aside. All are commanded to seek the good pleasure of the Lord of unity, to follow His command and obey His will;

in this way the world of humanity shall become illumined with the reality of love and reconciliation.

9   Sixth, the world of humanity is in need of the confirmations of the Holy Spirit. True distinction among mankind is through divine bestowals and receiving the intuitions of the Holy Spirit. If man does not become the recipient of the heavenly bestowals and spiritual bounties, he remains in the plane and kingdom of the animal. For the distinction between the animal and man is that man is endowed with the potentiality of divinity in his nature, whereas the animal is entirely bereft of that gift and attainment. Therefore, if a man is bereft of the intuitive breathings of the Holy Spirit, deprived of divine bestowals, out of touch with the heavenly world and negligent of the eternal truths, though in image and likeness he is human, in reality he is an animal; even as Christ declared, "That which is born of the flesh is flesh; and that which is born of the Spirit is spirit." This means that if man be a captive of physical susceptibilities and be lacking the quickening of spiritual emotions, he is merely an animal. But every soul who possesses spiritual susceptibilities and has attained a goodly portion of the bestowals of the Holy Spirit is alive with the divine life of the higher Kingdom. The soul that is portionless and bereft is as dead. Therefore, He said, "Let the dead bury their dead." Just as the physical body of man is in need of its force of life, even so the human soul is in need of the divine animus and vivification emanating from the Holy Spirit. Without this vivification and sustenance, man would be an animal, nay, rather, dead.

10   Seventh, the necessity of education for all mankind is evident. Children especially must be trained and taught. If the parent cannot afford to do this owing to lack of means, the body politic must make necessary provision for its accomplishment. Through the broadening spirit of education illiteracy will disappear, and misunderstandings due to ignorance will pass away.

Eighth, universal peace will be established among the na- 11
tions of the world by international agreement. The greatest
catastrophe in the world of humanity today is war. Europe is a
storehouse of explosives awaiting a spark. All the European nations are on edge, and a single flame will set on fire the whole of
that continent. Implements of war and death are multiplied and
increased to an inconceivable degree, and the burden of military
maintenance is taxing the various countries beyond the point of
endurance. Armies and navies devour the substance and possessions of the people; the toiling poor, the innocent and helpless
are forced by taxation to provide munitions and armament for
governments bent upon conquest of territory and defense against
powerful rival nations. There is no greater or more woeful ordeal
in the world of humanity today than impending war. Therefore,
international peace is a crucial necessity. An arbitral court of
justice shall be established by which international disputes are
to be settled. Through this means all possibility of discord and
war between the nations will be obviated.

Ninth, there must be an equality of rights between men and 12
women. Women shall receive an equal privilege of education.
This will enable them to qualify and progress in all degrees of
occupation and accomplishment. For the world of humanity
possesses two wings: man and woman. If one wing remains
incapable and defective, it will restrict the power of the other,
and full flight will be impossible. Therefore, the completeness
and perfection of the human world are dependent upon the
equal development of these two wings.

Tenth, there shall be an equality of rights and prerogatives 13
for all mankind.

Eleventh, one language must be selected as an international 14
medium of speech and communication. Through this means
misunderstandings will be lessened, fellowship established and
unity assured.

15   These are a few of the principles proclaimed by Bahá'u'lláh. He has provided the remedy for the ailments which now afflict the human world, solved the difficult problems of individual, social, national and universal welfare and laid the foundation of divine reality upon which material and spiritual civilization are to be founded throughout the centuries before us.

16   Praise be to God! I find these two great American nations highly capable and advanced in all that appertains to progress and civilization. These governments are fair and equitable. The motives and purposes of these people are lofty and inspiring. Therefore, it is my hope that these revered nations may become prominent factors in the establishment of international peace and the oneness of the world of humanity; that they may lay the foundations of equality and spiritual brotherhood among mankind; that they may manifest the highest virtues of the human world, revere the divine lights of the Prophets of God and establish the reality of unity so necessary today in the affairs of nations. I pray that the nations of the East and West shall become one flock under the care and guidance of the divine Shepherd. Verily, this is the bestowal of God and the greatest honor of man. This is the glory of humanity. This is the good pleasure of God. I ask God for this with a contrite heart.

17   O my Lord! Thou Who art ever-forgiving! Verily, this assembly hath turned its face toward Thy Kingdom. Verily, they are all of Thy flock, and Thou art the one Shepherd of all. O Thou real Shepherd! Educate and train Thy sheep in Thy green and verdant pastures. Suffer these birds of Thine to build their nests in Thy rose garden. Adorn Thine orchard with these fresh plants and flowers. Refresh these human trees by Thy shower of beneficence and favor. O God! Verily, we are all Thy servants—all Thine—and Thou art the One Lord. We all adore Thee, and Thou art the beneficent Master. O Lord! Render the eyes perceptive that they may witness the lights of Thy King-

dom. Render the ears attentive that they may hear the heavenly summons. Resuscitate the spirits that they may be exhilarated through the breath of the Holy Spirit. O Lord! Verily, we are weak, but Thou art almighty. We are poor, but Thou art rich. Have mercy upon us. Apportion unto us a goodly share of Thy realities, and lead us into the arena of Thine attainments. Thou art the Powerful. Thou art the Able. Thou art the kind Lord.

Talk 'Abdu'l-Bahá Delivered in Chicago

16 September 1912

Talk at Home of Mrs. Corinne True
5338 Kenmore Avenue, Chicago, Illinois

NOTES BY GERTRUDE BUIKEMA

ALLÁH-U-ABHÁ! Praise be to God! I have spent a number of   1
days among you, associating with you in love and fragrance.
Praise be to God! Your hearts are pure, your faces radiant, your
spirits exhilarated through the glad tidings of God. I pray in
your behalf, seeking heavenly confirmations for you that each
one may become a radiant candle, shedding light in the world
of humanity. May you become the quintessence of love. May
you prove to be the effulgence of God, replete with the efficacy
of the Holy Spirit and the cause of unity and fellowship in the
world of humanity, for today mankind has the greatest need of
love and agreement. If the world should remain as it is today,
great danger will face it. But if reconciliation and unity are witnessed, if security and confidence be established, if with heart
and soul we strive in order that the teachings of Bahá'u'lláh
may find effective penetration in the realities of humankind,
inducing fellowship and accord, binding together the hearts of
the various religions and uniting divergent peoples, the world of
mankind shall attain peace and composure, the will of God will
become the will of man and the earth a veritable habitation of
angels. Souls shall be educated, vice be dispelled, the virtues of
the world of humanity prevail, materialism pass away, religion

be strengthened and prove to be the bond which shall cement together the hearts of men.

2   In the world of existence there are various bonds which unite human hearts, but not one of these bonds is completely effective. The first and foremost is the bond of family relationship, which is not an efficient unity, for how often it happens that disagreement and divergence rend asunder this close tie of association. The bond of patriotism may be a means of fellowship and agreement, but oneness of native land will not completely cement human hearts; for if we review history, we shall find that people of the same race and native land have frequently waged war against each other. Often in civil strife they have shed the same racial blood and destroyed the possessions of their own native kind. Therefore, this bond is not sufficient. Another means of seeming unity is the bond of political association, where governments and rulers have been allied for reasons of intercourse and mutual protection, but which agreement and union afterward became subject to change and violent hatred even to the extreme of war and bloodshed. It is evident that political oneness is not permanently effective.

3   The source of perfect unity and love in the world of existence is the bond and oneness of reality. When the divine and fundamental reality enters human hearts and lives, it conserves and protects all states and conditions of mankind, establishing that intrinsic oneness of the world of humanity which can only come into being through the efficacy of the Holy Spirit. For the Holy Spirit is like unto the life in the human body, which blends all differences of parts and members in unity and agreement. Consider how numerous are these parts and members, but the oneness of the animating spirit of life unites them all in perfect combination. It establishes such a unity in the bodily organism that if any part is subjected to injury or becomes diseased, all the

other parts and functions sympathetically respond and suffer, owing to the perfect oneness existing. Just as the human spirit of life is the cause of coordination among the various parts of the human organism, the Holy Spirit is the controlling cause of the unity and coordination of mankind. That is to say, the bond or oneness of humanity cannot be effectively established save through the power of the Holy Spirit, for the world of humanity is a composite body, and the Holy Spirit is the animating principle of its life.

Therefore, we must strive in order that the power of the Holy 4 Spirit may become effective throughout the world of mankind, that it may confer a new quickening life upon the body politic of the nations and peoples and that all may be guided to the protection and shelter of the Word of God. Then this human world will become angelic, earthly darkness pass away and celestial illumination flood the horizons, human defects be effaced and divine virtues become resplendent. This is possible and real, but only through the power of the Holy Spirit. Today the greatest need of the world is the animating, unifying presence of the Holy Spirit. Until it becomes effective, penetrating and interpenetrating hearts and spirits, and until perfect, reasoning faith shall be implanted in the minds of men, it will be impossible for the social body to be inspired with security and confidence. Nay, on the contrary, enmity and strife will increase day by day, and the differences and divergences of nations will be woefully augmented. Continual additions to the armies and navies of the world will be made, and the fear and certainty of the great pandemic war—the war unparalleled in history—will be intensified; for armament, heretofore limited, is now being increased upon a colossal scale. Conditions are becoming acute, drawing nigh unto the degree of men warring upon the seas, warring upon the plains, warring in the very atmosphere with a violence unknown in former centuries. With the growth of armament and preparation the dangers are increasingly great.

5   We must use our utmost endeavors in order that the Holy Spirit may influence minds and hearts toward peace, the bounties of God surround, the divine effulgences become successive, human souls advance, minds expand in wider vision, souls become more holy and the world of humanity be rid of its great menace. For the betterment of the world Bahá'u'lláh endured all the hardships, ordeals and vicissitudes of life, sacrificing His very being and comfort, forfeiting His estates, possessions and honor—all that pertains to human existence—not for one year, nay, rather, for nearly fifty years. During this long period He was subjected to persecution and abuse, was cast into prison, was banished from His native land, underwent severities and humiliation and was exiled four times. He was first exiled from Persia to Baghdád, thence to Constantinople, thence to Rumelia and finally to the great prison-fortress of 'Akká in Syria, where He passed the remainder of His life. Every day a new oppression and abuse was heaped upon Him until He winged His flight from the dungeon to the supreme world and returned to His Lord. He endured these ordeals and difficulties in order that this earthly human world might become heavenly, that the illumination of the divine Kingdom should become a reality in human hearts, that the individual members of mankind might progress, the power of the Holy Spirit increase its efficacy and penetration and the happiness of the world of humanity be assured. He desired for all tranquillity and composure and exercised loving-kindness toward the nations regardless of conditions and differences. He addressed humanity, saying, "O humankind! Verily, ye are all the leaves and fruits of one tree; ye are all one. Therefore, associate in friendship; love one another; abandon prejudices of race; dispel forever this gloomy darkness of human ignorance,

458

for the century of light, the Sun of Reality hath appeared. Now is the time for affiliation, and now is the period of unity and concord. For thousands of years ye have been contending in warfare and strife. It is enough. Now is the time for unity. Lay aside all self-purposes, and know for a certainty that all men are the servants of one God Who will bind them together in love and agreement."

Inasmuch as great differences and divergences of denomina- 6 tional belief had arisen throughout the past, every man with a new idea attributing it to God, Bahá'u'lláh desired that there should not be any ground or reason for disagreement among the Bahá'ís. Therefore, with His own pen He wrote the Book of His Covenant, addressing His relations and all people of the world, saying, "Verily, I have appointed One Who is the Center of My Covenant. All must obey Him; all must turn to Him; He is the Expounder of My Book, and He is informed of My purpose. All must turn to Him. Whatsoever He says is correct, for, verily, He knoweth the texts of My Book. Other than He, no one doth know My Book." The purpose of this statement is that there should never be discord and divergence among the Bahá'ís but that they should always be unified and agreed. In His prayers Bahá'u'lláh also said, "O God! Whosoever violates My Covenant, O God, humiliate him. Verily, whosoever violates My Covenant, O God, erase and efface him." In all His Tablets, among which is the Tablet of the Branch, He has mentioned and explained the attributes and qualities of the Personage to Whom He referred in the Book of His Covenant. He has fully expounded the function and potency of that Personage, so that no one shall say, "I understand this from the writings of Bahá'u'lláh," for He has appointed the Center, or Expounder, of the Book. He said, "Verily, He is the appointed one; other than He, there is none," intending that no sects or prejudices should be formed, and preventing every man here and there with a new thought from creating dissension and variance. It is as though a king should appoint a governor-general. Whosoever obeys him, obeys the king. Whosoever violates and disobeys him, violates the king. Therefore, whosoever obeys the Center of the Covenant appointed by Bahá'u'lláh has obeyed Bahá'u'lláh, and whosoever disobeys Him has disobeyed Bahá'u'lláh. It has nothing to do with Him ('Abdu'l-Bahá) at all—precisely as the governor-general appointed by the king—whosoever obeys the governor-general obeys the king; whosoever disobeys the governor-general disobeys the king.

7   Therefore, you must read the Tablets of Bahá'u'lláh. You must read the Tablet of the Branch and regard that which He has so clearly stated. Beware! Beware! lest anyone should speak from the authority of his own thoughts or create a new thing out of himself. Beware! Beware! According to the explicit Covenant of Bahá'u'lláh you should care nothing at all for such a person. Bahá'u'lláh shuns such souls. I have expounded these things for you, for the conservation and protection of the teachings of Bahá'u'lláh, in order that you may be informed, lest any souls shall deceive you and lest any souls shall cause suspicion among you. You must love all people, and yet if any souls put you in doubt, you must know that Bahá'u'lláh is severed from them. Whosoever works for unity and fellowship is a servant of Bahá'u'lláh, and Bahá'u'lláh is his assistant and helper. I ask God that He may cause you to be the very means of agreement and unity, that He may make you radiant, merciful, heavenly children of the divine Kingdom; that you may advance day by day; that you may become as bright as these lamps, bestowing light upon all humanity. Salutations and farewell!

Talk 'Abdu'l-Bahá Delivered in Minneapolis

20 September 1912

Talk at Home of Mr. Albert L. Hall
2030 Queen Avenue South, Minneapolis, Minnesota

NOTES BY ELLEN T. PURSELL

PRAISE be to God! This is a beautiful and radiant assemblage. It 1
is a merciful gathering, for you have met here in the utmost love
and spirituality. There are many meetings in the world, thousands of them perhaps being held at this very moment, mostly
for social, political, scientific or commercial purposes; but our
gathering here tonight is for God, for heavenly purposes. We
are neither attached to commerce nor is our interest scientific;
our spirit and motive are solely for the manifestation of divine
bestowals.

Man possesses two types of virtues: One is material, and the 2
other ideal in character. For example, the body of man expresses
certain material virtues, but the spirit of man manifests virtues
that are ideal. The sense of sight in man is a physical virtue; but
insight, the power of inner perception, is ideal in its nature. The
sense of hearing is a physical endowment, whereas memory in
man is ideal. Among other human forces the power of ideation,
or faculty of intellection, is material, but the power of love is
spiritual. The acquisition of the realities of phenomena is an
ideal virtue; likewise, the emotions of man and his ability to
prove the existence of God. Realization of moral standards and
the world of discovery involve virtues essentially ideal.

461

3   If we review history, we will observe that human advancement has been greatest in the development of material virtues. Civilization is the sign and evidence of this progression. Throughout the world, material civilization has attained truly wonderful heights and degrees of efficiency—that is to say, the outward powers and virtues of man have greatly developed, but the inner and ideal virtues have been correspondingly delayed and neglected. It is now the time in the history of the world for us to strive and give an impetus to the advancement and development of inner forces—that is to say, we must arise to service in the world of morality, for human morals are in need of readjustment. We must also render service to the world of intellectuality in order that the minds of men may increase in power and become keener in perception, assisting the intellect of man to attain its supremacy so that the ideal virtues may appear. Before a step is taken in this direction we must be able to prove Divinity from the standpoint of reason so that no doubt or objection may remain for the rationalist. Afterward, we must be able to prove the existence of the bounty of God—that the divine bounty encompasses humanity and that it is transcendental. Furthermore, we must demonstrate that the spirit of man is immortal, that it is not subject to disintegration and that it comprises the virtues of humanity.

4   Material virtues have attained great development, but ideal virtues have been left far behind. If you should ask a thousand persons, "What are the proofs of the reality of Divinity?" perhaps not one would be able to answer. If you should ask further, "What proofs have you regarding the essence of God?" "How do you explain inspiration and revelation?" "What are the evidences of conscious intelligence beyond the material universe?" "Can you suggest a plan and method for the betterment of human moralities?" "Can you clearly define and differentiate

the world of nature and the world of Divinity?"—you would
receive very little real knowledge and enlightenment upon
these questions. This is due to the fact that development of
the ideal virtues has been neglected. People speak of Divinity,
but the ideas and beliefs they have of Divinity are, in reality,
superstition. Divinity is the effulgence of the Sun of Reality,
the manifestation of spiritual virtues and ideal powers. The
intellectual proofs of Divinity are based upon observation and
evidence which constitute decisive argument, logically proving
the reality of Divinity, the effulgence of mercy, the certainty of
inspiration and immortality of the spirit. This is, in reality, the
science of Divinity. Divinity is not what is set forth in dogmas
and sermons of the church. Ordinarily when the word Divinity
is mentioned, it is associated in the minds of the hearers with
certain formulas and doctrines, whereas it essentially means the
wisdom and knowledge of God, the effulgence of the Sun of
Truth, the revelation of reality and divine philosophy.

Philosophy is of two kinds: natural and divine. Natural 5
philosophy seeks knowledge of physical verities and explains
material phenomena, whereas divine philosophy deals with
ideal verities and phenomena of the spirit. The field and scope
of natural philosophy have been greatly enlarged, and its accomplishments are most praiseworthy, for it has served humanity. But according to the evidence of present world conditions
divine philosophy—which has for its object the sublimation
of human nature, spiritual advancement, heavenly guidance
for the development of the human race, attainment to the
breaths of the Holy Spirit and knowledge of the verities of
God—has been outdistanced and neglected. Now is the time
for us to make an effort and enable it to advance apace with the
philosophy of material investigation so that awakening of the
ideal virtues may progress equally with the unfoldment of the

natural powers. In the same proportion that the body of man is developing, the spirit of man must be strengthened; and just as his outer perceptions have been quickened, his inner intellectual powers must be sensitized so that he need not rely wholly upon tradition and human precedent. In divine questions we must not depend entirely upon the heritage of tradition and former human experience; nay, rather, we must exercise reason, analyze and logically examine the facts presented so that confidence will be inspired and faith attained. Then and then only the reality of things will be revealed to us. The philosophers of Greece—such as Aristotle, Socrates, Plato and others—were devoted to the investigation of both natural and spiritual phenomena. In their schools of teaching they discoursed upon the world of nature as well as the supernatural world. Today the philosophy and logic of Aristotle are known throughout the world. Because they were interested in both natural and divine philosophy, furthering the development of the physical world of mankind as well as the intellectual, they rendered praiseworthy service to humanity. This was the reason of the triumph and survival of their teachings and principles. Man should continue both these lines of research and investigation so that all the human virtues, outer and inner, may become possible. The attainment of these virtues, both material and ideal, is conditioned upon intelligent investigation of reality, by which investigation the sublimity of man and his intellectual progress is accomplished. Forms must be set aside and renounced; reality must be sought. We must discover for ourselves where and what reality is. In religious beliefs nations and peoples today are imitators of ancestors and forefathers. If a man's father was a Christian, he himself is a Christian; a Buddhist is the son of a Buddhist, a Zoroastrian of a Zoroastrian. A gentile or an idolator follows the religious footsteps of his father and ancestry. This is absolute imitation.

The requirement in this day is that man must independently and impartially investigate every form of reality.

The great question appertaining to humanity is religion. 6 The first condition is that man must intelligently investigate its foundations. The second condition is that he must admit and acknowledge the oneness of the world of humanity. By this means the attainment of true fellowship among mankind is assured, and the alienation of races and individuals is prevented. All must be considered the servants of God; all must recognize God as the one kind Protector and Creator. In proportion to the acknowledgment of the oneness and solidarity of mankind, fellowship is possible, misunderstandings will be removed and reality become apparent. Then will the light of reality shine forth, and when reality illumines the world, the happiness of humankind will become a verity. Man must spiritually perceive that religion has been intended by God to be the means of grace, the source of life and cause of agreement. If it becomes the cause of discord, enmity and hatred, it is better that man should be without it. For in its teachings we seek the spirit of charity and love to bind the hearts of men together. If, on the contrary, we find it alienates and embitters human hearts, we are justified in casting it aside. Therefore, when man through sincere investigation discovers the fundamental reality of religion, his former prejudices disappear, and his new condition of enlightenment is conducive to the development of the world of humanity.

The purport of our subject is that, just as man is in need of 7 outward education, he is likewise in need of ideal refinement; just as the outer sense of sight is necessary to him, he should also possess insight and conscious perception; as he needs hearing, at the same time memory is essential; as a body is indispensable to him, likewise a mind is requisite; one is a material virtue, the other is ideal. As human creatures fitted and qualified with this dual endowment, we must endeavor through the assistance and grace of God and by the exercise of our ideal power of intellect to attain all lofty virtues, that we may witness the effulgence of the Sun of Reality, reflect the spirit of the Kingdom, behold the manifest evidences of the reality of Divinity, comprehend irrefutable proofs of the immortality of the soul, live in conscious at-one-ment with the eternal world and become quickened and awake with the life and love of God.

Talk 'Abdu'l-Bahá Delivered in St. Paul

20 September 1912

Talk at Home of Dr. and Mrs. Clement Woolson
870 Laurel Avenue, St. Paul, Minnesota

FROM STENOGRAPHIC NOTES

THE materialists hold to the opinion that the world of nature   1
is complete. The divine philosophers declare that the world of
nature is incomplete. There is a wide difference between the two.
The materialists call attention to the perfection of nature, the
sun, moon and stars, the trees in their adornment, the whole
earth and the sea—even unimportant phenomena revealing
the most perfect symmetry. The divine philosophers deny this
seeming perfection and completeness in nature's kingdom,
even though admitting the beauty of its scenes and aspects and
acknowledging the irresistible cosmic forces which control the
colossal suns and planets. They hold that while nature seems
perfect, it is, nevertheless, imperfect because it has need of
intelligence and education. In proof of this they say that man,
though he be a very god in the realm of material creation, is
himself in need of an educator. Man undeveloped by education
is savage, animalistic, brutal. Laws and regulations, schools, colleges and universities have for their purpose the training of man
and his uplift from the dark borderland of the animal kingdom.
What is the difference between the people of America and the
inhabitants of central Africa?

All are human beings. Why have the people of America   2
advanced to a high degree of civilization while the tribes of
central Africa remain in extreme ignorance and barbarism? The

difference and distinction between them is the degree of education. This is unquestioned. The people of Europe and America have been uplifted by education and training from the world of defects and have ascended toward the realm of perfection, whereas the people of Africa, denied educational development, remain in a natural condition of illiteracy and deprivation, for nature is incomplete and defective. Education is a necessity. If a piece of ground be left in its natural and original state, it will either become a thorny waste or be covered by worthless weeds. When cleared and cultivated, this same unproductive field will yield plentiful harvests of food for human sustenance.

3   This same difference is noticeable among animals; some have been domesticated, educated, others left wild. The proof is clear that the world of nature is imperfect, the world of education perfect. That is to say, man is rescued from the exigencies of nature by training and culture; consequently, education is necessary, obligatory. But education is of various kinds. There is a training and development of the physical body which ensures strength and growth. There is intellectual education or mental training for which schools and colleges are founded. The third kind of education is that of the spirit. Through the breaths of the Holy Spirit man is uplifted into the world of moralities and illumined by the lights of divine bestowals. The moral world is only attained through the effulgence of the Sun of Reality and the quickening life of the divine spirit. For this reason the holy Manifestations of God appear in the human world. They come to educate and illuminate mankind, to bestow spiritual susceptibilities, to quicken inner perceptions and thereby adorn the reality of man—the human temple—with divine graces. Through Them man may become the point of the emanations of God and the recipient of heavenly bounties. Under the influence of Their teachings he may become the manifestation of the

effulgences of God and a magnet attracting the lights of the supreme world. For this reason the holy, divine Manifestations are the first Teachers and Educators of humanity; Their traces are the highest evidences, and Their spiritual tuition is universal in its application to the world of mankind. Their influence and power are immeasurable and unlimited. One heavenly Personage has developed many nations. For example, Jesus Christ, single and unassisted, educated the Roman, Greek and Assyrian nations and all of Europe. It is evident, therefore, that the greatest education is that of the Spirit.

The spirit of man must acquire its bounties from the   4 Kingdom of God in order that it may become the mirror and manifestation of lights and the dawning point of divine traces, because the human reality is like the soil. If no bounty of rain descends from heaven upon the soil, if no heat of the sun penetrates, it will remain black, forbidding, unproductive; but when the moistening shower and the effulgent glow of the sun's rays fall upon it, beautiful and redolent flowers grow from its bosom. Similarly, the human spirit or reality of man, unless it becomes the recipient of the lights of the Kingdom, develops divine susceptibilities and consciously reflects the effulgence of God, will not be the manifestation of ideal bounties, for only the reality of man can become the mirror wherein the lights of God are revealed. The reality of man will then be as the spirit of this world, for just as the animus of life quickens the physical human body, so the body of the world will receive its vivification through the animating virtue of the sanctified spirit of man.

It is evident that the holy Manifestations and divine dawning   5 points are necessary, for these blessed and glorious Souls are the foremost Teachers and Educators of mankind, and all human souls are developed through Them by the bounty of the Holy Spirit of God.

6   During the ministry of Jesus Christ in Palestine He was surrounded by people of various nations, including the Jews, all of them living in the condition of extreme ignorance, bereft of the Word of God and darkened in consciousness. Christ educated these people and quickened them with the life of the Word so that they in turn became the instruments of educating the world, illumining the East and the West.

7   Consider the wonderful effect of spiritual education and training. By it the fisherman Peter was transformed into the greatest of teachers. Spiritual education made the disciples radiant lamps in the darkness of the world and caused the Christians of the first and second centuries to become renowned everywhere for their virtues. Even philosophers bore testimony to this. Among them was Galen, the physician, who wrote a book upon the subject of the progress of the nations. He was a celebrated philosopher of the Greeks, although not a Christian. In his book he stated that religious beliefs exercise a tremendous influence upon civilization and that the world is in need of such belief. In proof of this, he said, in substance, "In our time there is a certain people called Christians, who, though neither philosophers nor scholastically trained, are superior to all others as regards their morality. They are perfect in morals. Each one of them is like a great philosopher in morals, ethics and turning toward the Kingdom of God." This is evidence from the testimony of an intelligent outside observer that spiritual education is the light of the world of humanity and that its absence in the world is darkness itself.

8   Bahá'u'lláh appeared in Persia at a time when the darkness of ignorance enveloped the East, and there was no trace of human love and fellowship. Through divine education and the power of the breaths of the Holy Spirit He so refined the souls of the Persians who followed Him that they attained a station of high-

est intelligence and reflected the attributes of perfection to the world. Whereas formerly they were ignorant, they became knowing; they were weak, they became mighty; they were without integrity, they became conscientious; they were hostile toward all men, they developed love for humanity; they were spiritually negligent, they became mindful and attentive; they were sleeping, they became awakened; they disagreed among themselves, they united in love and are now striving to render service to the world of humankind. Service to God and mankind is their sole intention; they have neither wish nor desire save that which is in accordance with the good pleasure of God. The good pleasure of God is love for His creatures. The will and plan of God is that each individual member of humankind shall become illumined like unto a lamp, radiant with all the destined virtues of humanity, leading his fellow creatures out of natural darkness into the heavenly light. Therein rests the virtue and glory of the world of humanity. This is the perfection, honor and glory of man; otherwise, man is an animal and without differentiation from the creatures of that lower kingdom.

It is clearly evident that while man possesses powers in common with the animal, he is distinguished from the animal by intellectual attainment, spiritual perception, the acquisition of virtues, capacity to receive the bestowals of Divinity, lordly bounty and emanations of heavenly mercy. This is the adornment of man, his honor and sublimity. Humanity must strive toward this supreme station. Christ has interpreted this station as the second birth. Man is first born from a world of darkness, the matrix of the mother, into this physical world of light. In the dark world from whence he came he had no knowledge of the virtues of this existence. He has been liberated from a condition of darkness and brought into a new and spacious realm where there is sunlight, the stars are shining, the moon sheds its

9

radiance, there are beautiful views, gardens of roses, fruits and all the blessings of the present world. How did he attain these blessings? Through the agency of birth from the mother. Just as man has been physically born into this world, he may be reborn from the realm and matrix of nature, for the realm of nature is a condition of animalism, darkness and defect. In this second birth he attains the world of the Kingdom. There he witnesses and realizes that the world of nature is a world of gloom, whereas the Kingdom is a world of radiance; the world of nature is a world of defects, the Kingdom is a realm of perfection; the world of nature is a world without enlightenment, the Kingdom of spiritual humanity is a heaven of illumination. Great discoveries and revelations are now possible for him; he has attained the reality of perception; his circle of understanding is illimitably widened; he views the realities of creation, comprehends the divine bounties and unseals the mystery of phenomena. This is the station which Christ has interpreted as the second birth. He says that just as ye were physically born from the mother into this world, ye must be born again from the mother world of nature into the life of the divine Kingdom. May you all attain this second, spiritual birth. "That which is born of the flesh is flesh; and that which is born of the Spirit is spirit."

10   I pray that the confirmation of God may descend upon you. May you all be born again from this mortal world into the realm of the Kingdom. May you clearly witness the signs of God, sense the virtues of the divine, attain the eternal bounties and perceive the reality of everlasting life.

Talks 'Abdu'l-Bahá Delivered in Denver

24 September 1912

Talk at Home of Mrs. Sidney E. Roberts
Denver, Colorado

FROM STENOGRAPHIC NOTES

I HAVE come from distant lands of the East to visit you, crossing 1
the great ocean and traveling a long distance upon this continent. Consider how I have longed to meet you, for my body
is frail and weak, incapable of long endurance, yet—praise be
to God!—we have at last reached Denver. Such a gathering as
this is worthy of thanksgiving; it is peerless and unique among
meetings. Other meetings are held from motives of material
interests—such as social, political, commercial, educational—
but this assemblage has no other purpose than attainment to the
divine Kingdom; therefore, it is unique, unequaled. The hearts
have turned to God; spirits are exalted through the glad tidings
of God; the intentions of all are directed to God. What better
meeting could be imagined than this?

Such a gathering is fundamentally spiritual, sincere and 2
most important. But we must arise in the accomplishment of
its purposes, for our attention is directed toward the heavenly
Kingdom unto which we must render faithful service. Therefore,
all individuals present here must be in the attitude of perfect
love and fellowship, manifesting the utmost humility and self-
sacrifice, turning our thoughts toward the Kingdom of God so
that our meeting may be an expression of the glorified hosts of
the Supreme Concourse.

3   Praise be to God! We are living in a century of light. Praise be to God! We are upon earth in the day of divine effulgence. Praise be to God! We are alive in this time of the manifestation of divine love. Praise be to God that we live in the day of the outpouring of heavenly bounty. Praise be to God! This is a day wherein the lights and splendors have awakened progress throughout the East and the West. Many holy souls in former times longed to witness this century, lamenting night and day, yearning to be upon the earth in this cycle; but our presence and privilege is the beneficent gift of the Lord. In His divine mercy and absolute virtue He has bestowed this upon us, even as Christ declared, "Many are called but few are chosen." Verily, God has chosen you for His love and knowledge; God has chosen you for the worthy service of unifying mankind; God has chosen you for the purpose of investigating reality and promulgating international peace; God has chosen you for the progress and development of humanity, for spreading and proclaiming true education, for the expression of love toward your fellow creatures and the removal of prejudice; God has chosen you to blend together human hearts and give light to the human world. The doors of His generosity are wide, wide open to us; but we must be attentive, alert and mindful, occupied with service to all mankind, appreciating the bestowals of God and ever conforming to His will.

4   Observe how darkness has overspread the world. In every corner of the earth there is strife, discord and warfare of some kind. Mankind is submerged in the sea of materialism and occupied with the affairs of this world. They have no thought beyond earthly possessions and manifest no desire save the passions of this fleeting, mortal existence. Their utmost purpose is the attainment of material livelihood, physical comforts and worldly enjoyments such as constitute the happiness of the animal world rather than the world of man.

The honor of man is through the attainment of the knowl-　5
edge of God; his happiness is from the love of God; his joy is
in the glad tidings of God; his greatness is dependent upon
his servitude to God. The highest development of man is his
entrance into the divine Kingdom, and the outcome of this human existence is the nucleus and essence of eternal life. If man
is bereft of the divine bestowals and if his enjoyment and happiness are restricted to his material inclinations, what distinction
or difference is there between the animal and himself? In fact,
the animal's happiness is greater, for its wants are fewer and its
means of livelihood easier to acquire. Although it is necessary
for man to strive for material needs and comforts, his real need
is the acquisition of the bounties of God. If he is bereft of divine
bounties, spiritual susceptibilities and heavenly glad tidings, the
life of man in this world has not yielded any worthy fruit. While
possessing physical life, he should lay hold of the life spiritual,
and together with bodily comforts and happiness, he should
enjoy divine pleasures and content. Then is man worthy of the
title man; then will he be after the image and likeness of God,
for the image of the Merciful consists of the attributes of the
heavenly Kingdom. If no fruits of the Kingdom appear in the
garden of his soul, man is not in the image and likeness of God,
but if those fruits are forthcoming, he becomes the recipient
of ideal bestowals and is enkindled with the fire of the love of
God. If his morals become spiritual in character, his aspirations
heavenly and his actions conformable to the will of God, man
has attained the image and likeness of his Creator; otherwise,
he is the image and likeness of Satan. Therefore, Christ hath
said, "Ye shall know them by their fruits."

What are the fruits of the human world? They are the spiri-　6
tual attributes which appear in man. If man is bereft of those
attributes, he is like a fruitless tree. One whose aspiration is lofty

and who has developed self-reliance will not be content with a mere animal existence. He will seek the divine Kingdom; he will long to be in heaven although he still walks the earth in his material body, and though his outer visage be physical, his face of inner reflection will become spiritual and heavenly. Until this station is attained by man, his life will be utterly devoid of real outcomes. The span of his existence will pass away in eating, drinking and sleeping, without eternal fruits, heavenly traces or illumination—without spiritual potency, everlasting life or the lofty attainments intended for him during his pilgrimage through the human world. You must thank God that your efforts are high and noble, that your endeavors are worthy, that your intentions are centered upon the Kingdom of God and that your supreme desire is the acquisition of eternal virtues. You must act in accordance with these requirements. A man may be a Bahá'í in name only. If he is a Bahá'í in reality, his deeds and actions will be decisive proofs of it. What are the requirements? Love for mankind, sincerity toward all, reflecting the oneness of the world of humanity, philanthropy, becoming enkindled with the fire of the love of God, attainment to the knowledge of God and that which is conducive to human welfare.

7   This evening we were speaking of the fellowship and unity of the Persian Bahá'ís. They can truly be called lovers. For example, if one of the friends of God arrived in their city, all the friends would rejoice and assemble together in a meeting with him. If he were ill, they would care for him; if sad, they would comfort him. They would care for him in every way and give unmistakable evidence that there is a spiritual relationship amongst them.

8   Strangers and outsiders are astonished at this love and radiant affection existing among the Bahá'ís. They inquire about it. They observe the unity and agreement manifest among them. They say, "What a beautiful spirit shines in their faces!" All envy it and

wish that such a bond of love might be witnessed everywhere. Therefore, to you my first admonition is this: Associate most kindly with all; be as one family; pursue this same pathway. Let your intentions be one that your love may permeate and affect the hearts of others so that they may grow to love each other and all attain to this condition of oneness.

The world of humanity is filled with darkness; you are its 9 radiant candles. It is very poor; you must be the treasury of the Kingdom. It is exceedingly debased; you must be the cause of its exaltation. It is bereft of divine graces; you must give it impetus and spiritual quickening. According to the teachings of Bahá'u'lláh you must love and cherish each individual member of humanity.

The first sign of faith is love. The message of the holy, divine 10 Manifestations is love; the phenomena of creation are based upon love; the radiance of the world is due to love; the well-being and happiness of the world depend upon it. Therefore, I admonish you that you must strive throughout the human world to diffuse the light of love. The people of this world are thinking of warfare; you must be peacemakers. The nations are self-centered; you must be thoughtful of others rather than yourselves. They are neglectful; you must be mindful. They are asleep; you should be awake and alert. May each one of you be as a shining star in the horizon of eternal glory. This is my wish for you and my highest hope. I have come long distances that you may attain these attributes and divine favors. Praise be to God! I have attended this meeting which has for its purpose the commemoration of God.

2

25 September 1912

Talk at Second Divine Science Church
3929 West Thirty-eighth Avenue, Denver, Colorado

FROM STENOGRAPHIC NOTES

1 IN the Orient I was informed of the lofty purposes and wonderful attainments of the American people. When I arrived in this country, I realized that American ideals are indeed most praiseworthy and that the people here are lovers of truth. They investigate reality, and there is no trace of fanaticism among them. Today the nations of the world are on the verge of war, influenced and impelled by prejudices of ignorance and racial fanaticism. Praise be to God! You are free from such prejudice, for you believe in the oneness and solidarity of the world of humanity. There is no doubt that the divine confirmations will uphold you.

2 One of the forms of prejudice which afflict the world of mankind is religious bigotry and fanaticism. When this hatred burns in human hearts, it becomes the cause of revolution, destruction, abasement of humankind and deprivation of the mercy of God. For the holy Manifestations and divine Founders of religion Themselves were completely unified in love and agreement, whereas Their followers are characterized by bitter antagonism and attitudes of hostility toward each other. God has desired for mankind the effulgence of love, but through blindness and misapprehension man has enveloped himself in veils of discord, strife and hatred. The supreme need of humanity is cooperation and reciprocity. The stronger the ties of fellowship and solidarity

amongst men, the greater will be the power of constructiveness and accomplishment in all the planes of human activity. Without cooperation and reciprocal attitude the individual member of human society remains self-centered, uninspired by altruistic purposes, limited and solitary in development like the animal and plant organisms of the lower kingdoms. The lower creatures are not in need of cooperation and reciprocity. A tree can live solitary and alone, but this is impossible for man without retrogression. Therefore, every cooperative attitude and activity of human life is praiseworthy and foreintended by the will of God. The first expression of cooperation is family relationship, which is unreliable and uncertain in its potency, for it is subject to separation and does not permanently cement together the individual members of humanity. There is also a cooperation and oneness in nativity or race which is likewise not efficient, for although its members may agree in general, they differ radically in personal and particular points of view. Racial association, therefore, will not ensure the requirements of divine relationship. There are other means in the human world by which physical association is established, but these fail to weld together the hearts and spirits of men and are correspondingly inefficient. Therefore, it is evident that God has destined and intended religion to be the cause and means of cooperative effort and accomplishment among mankind. To this end He has sent the Prophets of God, the holy Manifestations of the Word, in order that the fundamental reality and religion of God may prove to be the bond of human unity, for the divine religions revealed by these holy Messengers have one and the same foundation. All will admit, therefore, that the divine religions are intended to be the means of true human cooperation, that they are united in the purpose of making humanity one family, for they rest upon the universal foundation of love, and love is the first effulgence of Divinity.

3   Each one of the divine religions has established two kinds of ordinances: the essential and the accidental. The essential ordinances rest upon the firm, unchanging, eternal foundations of the Word itself. They concern spiritualities, seek to stabilize morals, awaken intuitive susceptibilities, reveal the knowledge of God and inculcate the love of all mankind. The accidental laws concern the administration of outer human actions and relations, establishing rules and regulations requisite for the world of bodies and their control. These are ever subject to change and supersedure according to exigencies of time, place and condition. For example, during the time of Moses, ten commandments concerning the punishment of murder were revealed in His Book. Divorce was sanctioned and polygamy allowable to a certain extent. If a man committed theft, his hand was cut off. This was drastic law and severe punishment applicable to the time of Moses. But when the time of Christ came, minds had developed, realizations were keener and spiritual perceptions had advanced so that certain laws concerning murder, plurality of wives and divorce were abrogated. But the essential ordinances of the Mosaic dispensation remained unchanged. These were the fundamental realities of the knowledge of God and the holy Manifestations, the purification of morals, the awakening of spiritual susceptibilities—eternal principles in which there is no change or transformation. Briefly, the foundation of the divine religions is one eternal foundation, but the laws for temporary conditions and exigencies are subject to change. Therefore, by adherence to these temporary laws, blindly following and imitating ancestral forms, difference and divergence have arisen among followers of the various religions, resulting in disunion, strife and hatred. Blind imitations and dogmatic observances are conducive to alienation and disagreement; they lead to bloodshed and destruction of the foundations of human-

ity. Therefore, the religionists of the world must lay aside these imitations and investigate the essential foundation or reality itself, which is not subject to change or transformation. This is the divine means of agreement and unification.

The purpose of all the divine religions is the establishment of 4 the bonds of love and fellowship among men, and the heavenly phenomena of the revealed Word of God are intended to be a source of knowledge and illumination to humanity. So long as man persists in his adherence to ancestral forms and imitation of obsolete ceremonials, denying higher revelations of the divine light in the world, strife and contention will destroy the purpose of religion and make love and fellowship impossible. Each of the holy Manifestations announced the glad tidings of His successor, and each One confirmed the message of His predecessor. Therefore, inasmuch as They were agreed and united in purpose and teaching, it is incumbent upon Their followers to be likewise unified in love and spiritual fellowship. In no other way will discord and alienation disappear and the oneness of the world of humanity be established.

After we have proved the validity of the Manifestations of 5 the Word of God by investigating the divine teachings, we must discover for a certainty whether They have been real Educators of mankind. Among the revelators of the law of God was Moses. When He appeared, all the contemporaneous nations rejected Him. Notwithstanding this, single and alone He promulgated the divine teachings and liberated a nation from the lowest condition of degradation and bondage. The people of Israel were ignorant, lowly, debased in morals—a race of slaves under burdensome oppression. Moses led them out of captivity and brought them to the Holy Land. He educated and disciplined them, established among them the foundations of material and divine civilization. Through the education of Moses these

ignorant people attained an advanced degree of power and prestige, culminating in the glory of the reign of Solomon. From
the abyss of bereavement and slavery they were uplifted to the
highest plane of progress and civilized nationhood. It is evident,
therefore, that Moses was an Educator and Teacher. The purpose
and mission of the holy, divine Messengers is the training and
advancement of humanity, the cultivation of divine fruits in the
gardens of human hearts, the reflection of heavenly effulgence in
the mirrors of human souls, the quickening of mental capacity
and the increase of spiritual susceptibilities. When these results
and outcomes are witnessed in mankind, the function and mission
of the Manifestations are unmistakable. Christ, single and alone,
without schooling or outward education and trained to labor in the
shop of a carpenter, appeared in the world at the time when the
Jewish nation was in the greatest abasement. This radiant Youth,
without wealth, power of armies or prestige, rescued the Jews who
believed on Him from tyranny and degradation and lifted them
to the highest plane of development and glory. Peter, His disciple,
was a fisherman. Through the power of Christ he shed light upon
all the horizons of the world. Furthermore, various people of the
Greek, Roman, Egyptian and Assyrian nations were brought together in unity and agreement; where warfare and bloodshed had
existed, humility and love were manifest, and the foundations of
divine religion were established, never to be destroyed. This proves
that Christ was a heavenly Teacher and Educator of the world of
humanity, for such evidences are historical and irrefutable, not
based upon tradition and circumstantial report. The power of His
Word in cementing these nations together is as clear and evident
as the sun at midday. There is no need of further demonstration.

6   The proof of the validity of a Manifestation of God is the
penetration and potency of His Word, the cultivation of heavenly attributes in the hearts and lives of His followers and the

bestowal of divine education upon the world of humanity. This is absolute proof. The world is a school in which there must be Teachers of the Word of God. The evidence of the ability of these Teachers is efficient education of the graduating classes.

In the early part of the nineteenth century the horizon of 7 Persia was shrouded in great darkness and ignorance. The people of that country were in a condition of barbarism. Hatred and bigotry prevailed among the various religions; bloodshed and hostility were frequent among sects and denominations of belief. There were no evidences of affiliation and unity; violent prejudice and antagonism ruled the hearts of men. At such a time as this Bahá'u'lláh proclaimed the first principle of His mission and teaching—the oneness of the world of humanity. His second announcement was the investigation of reality; the third was the oneness of the foundations of the divine religions. Through spiritual education He led the people out of darkness and ignorance into the clear light of truth, illuminated their hearts with the splendor of knowledge, laid a true and universal basis for religious teachings, cultivated the virtues of humanity, conferred spiritual susceptibilities, awakened inner perceptions and changed the dishonor of prejudiced souls to the highest degree of honor and capacity. Today in Persia and the Orient you will find the followers of Bahá'u'lláh united in the closest ties of fellowship and love. They have abandoned religious prejudices and have become as one family. When you enter their meetings, you will find Christians, Muslims, Buddhists, Zoroastrians, Jews and representatives of other beliefs present, all conjoined in a wonderful unity without a trace of bigotry or fanaticism, and the light of the oneness of the world of humanity reflected in their faces. Day by day they are advancing, manifesting greater and still greater love for each other. Their faith is fixed upon the unification of mankind, and their highest purpose is the oneness of religious belief. They proclaim to all humanity the sheltering mercy and infinite grace of God. They teach the reconciliation of religion with science and reason. They show forth in words and deeds the reality of love for all mankind as the servants of one God and the recipients of His universal bounty. These are their thoughts, their beliefs, their guiding principles, their religion. No trace of religious, racial, patriotic or political prejudice can be found among them, for they are real servants of God and obedient to His will and command.

8   My highest hope and desire is that the strongest and most indissoluble bond shall be established between the American nation and the people of the Orient. This is my prayer to God. May the day come when through divine and spiritual activity in the human world the religions shall be reconciled and all races of mankind come together in unity and love. Fifty years ago Bahá'u'lláh proclaimed the peace of the nations and oneness of the divine religions, addressing His words to all the kings and rulers of the world in specific Tablets. Therefore, my supreme desire is the unity of the East and West, universal peace and the oneness of the world of humanity.

Talks 'Abdu'l-Bahá Delivered in Oakland, Palo Alto, San Francisco, and Sacramento

7 October 1912

Talk to Japanese Young Men's Christian Association
Japanese Independent Church, Oakland, California

NOTES BY BIJOU STRAUN

IT is a great happiness to be here this evening, especially for the   1
reason that the members of this Association have come from
the region of the Orient. For a long time I have entertained a
desire to meet some of the Japanese friends. That nation has
achieved extraordinary progress in a short space of time—a
progress and development which have astonished the world.
Inasmuch as they have advanced in material civilization, they
must assuredly possess the capacity for spiritual development.
For this reason, I have an excessive longing to meet them. Praise
be to God! This pleasure is now afforded me, for here in this
city I am face to face with a revered group of the Japanese.
According to report the people of the Japanese nation are not
prejudiced. They investigate reality. Wherever they find truth,
they prove to be its lovers. They are not attached tenaciously to
blind imitations of ancient beliefs and dogmas. Therefore, it is
my great desire to discourse with them upon a subject in order
that the unity and blending together of the nations of the East
and the nations of the West may be furthered and accomplished.
In this way religious, racial and political prejudice, partisan bias
and sectarianism will be dispelled amongst men. Any kind of
prejudice is destructive to the body politic.

485

2   When we review history from the beginning of human existence to the present age in which we live, it is evident all war and conflict, bloodshed and battle, every form of sedition has been due to some form of prejudice—whether religious, racial or national—to partisan bias and selfish prejudice of some sort. Even today we witness an upheaval in the Balkans, a war of religious prejudice. Some years ago when I was living in Rumelia, war broke out among the religious peoples. There was no attitude of justice or equity whatever amongst them. They pillaged the properties of each other, burning each others' homes and houses, slaughtering men, women and children, imagining that such warfare and bloodshed was the means of drawing near to God. This clearly proved that prejudice is a destroyer of the foundations of the world of humanity, whereas religion was meant to be the cause of fellowship and agreement.

3   Religion must be the cause of love. Religion must be the cause of justice, for the wisdom of the Manifestations of God is directed toward the establishing of the bond of a love which is indissoluble. The bonds which hold together the body politic are not sufficient. These bonds may be mentioned—for instance, the bond of patriotism. This is evidently not a sufficient bond, for how often it happens that people of the same nation wage civil war amongst themselves. The bond of fellowship may be racial, but history proves this is not sufficiently strong, for tremendous wars have broken out between peoples of the same racial lineage. Again, the bond holding men together may be political. How often it happens that the diplomacy of nations makes a treaty of peace one day and on the morrow a declaration of war! It is historically evident and manifest that these bonds are not self-sufficient.

4   The real bond of integrity is religious in character, for religion indicates the oneness of the world of humanity. Religion serves the world of morality. Religion purifies the hearts. Religion

impels men to achieve praiseworthy deeds. Religion becomes the cause of love in human hearts, for religion is a divine foundation, the foundation ever conducive to life. The teachings of God are the source of illumination to the people of the world. Religion is ever constructive, not destructive.

The foundation of all the divine religions is one. All are based upon reality. Reality does not admit plurality, yet amongst mankind there have arisen differences concerning the Manifestations of God. Some have been Zoroastrians, some are Buddhists, some Jews, Christians, Muslims and so on. This has become a source of divergence, whereas the teachings of the holy Souls Who founded the divine religions are one in essence and reality. All these have served the world of humanity. All have summoned souls to peace and accord. All have proclaimed the virtues of humanity. All have guided souls to the attainment of perfections, but among the nations certain imitations of ancestral forms of worship have arisen. These imitations are not the foundation and essence of the divine religions. Inasmuch as they differ from the reality and the essential teachings of the Manifestations of God, dissensions have arisen, and prejudice has developed. Religious prejudice thus becomes the cause of warfare and battle.

If we abandon these timeworn blind imitations and investigate reality, all of us will be unified. No discord will remain; antagonism will disappear. All will associate in fellowship. All will enjoy the cordial bonds of friendship. The world of creation will then attain composure. The dark and gloomy clouds of blind imitations and dogmatic variances will be scattered and dispelled; the Sun of Reality will shine most gloriously.

Verily, we should consider the divine Prophets as the intermediaries, but mankind has made use of Them as causes of dissension and pretexts for warfare and strife. In reality, They were the intermediaries of love and reconciliation. If They were not sources of love and fellowship amongst men, then undoubtedly They were not true, for the divine wisdom and purpose in sending the Prophets was the manifestation of love in human hearts. Therefore, we must investigate reality. First of all, let us determine whether these Prophets were valid or not by using rational proofs and shining arguments, not simply by quoting traditionary evidences, because traditions are divergent and the source of dissension.

8   Among the holy, divine Manifestations of God were Moses, Buddha, etc. The sending of Prophets has ever been for the training of humanity. They are the first Educators and Trainers. If Moses has developed the body politic, there is no doubt that He was a true Teacher and Educator. This will be proof and evidence that He was a Prophet. We shall consider how He was sent to the children of Israel when they were in the abyss of despair, in the lowest degree of ignorance and heedlessness, degraded and under conditions of bondage. Moses rescued these degraded people of Israel from that state of bondage. He raised them from that condition of ignorance, saved them from barbarism and led them into the Holy Land. He educated them, endowed them with sagacious instincts, made them worthy and honorable. He civilized them, raised them to a higher plane of existence until they were enabled to establish a national sovereignty, the great kingdom of Solomon. This proves that Moses was a Teacher and an Educator. He had neither army nor dominion; neither did He possess wealth. It was only through an idealistic power that He cemented them together, proving that He was a Prophet of God, an Educator and Trainer.

9   Likewise, must we set aside prejudice in considering other divine Educators by investigating reality. For instance, let us take Christ. He achieved results greater than Moses. He educated the body politic, trained mighty nations. There is no doubt whatever that such Souls were Prophets, for the mission of

Prophethood is education, and these wondrous Souls trained and educated mankind.

Christ was a unique Personage, without helper or assistant. 10 Single and solitary He arose to train great and mighty nations; the Romans, Greeks, Egyptians, Syrians, Chaldeans and Assyrians came under His influence. He was able to bind together many nations, melting them together, as it were, and pouring them into one mold, changing their enmity into love, war into peace. Under His influence satanic souls became veritable angels, tyrannical rulers became just, the human moral standard was raised. This proves that Christ was an Educator, a Teacher and Trainer of nations. If we deny this, it is nought but injustice.

Blessed souls—whether Moses, Jesus, Zoroaster, Krishna, 11 Buddha, Confucius or Muḥammad—were the cause of the illumination of the world of humanity. How can we deny such irrefutable proof? How can we be blind to such light? How can we dispute the validity of Christ? This is injustice. This is a denial of reality. Man must be just. We must set aside bias and prejudice. We must abandon the imitations of ancestors and forefathers. We ourselves must investigate reality and be fair in judgment.

The old nation of Persia denied all these facts, harboring the 12 utmost hatred and enmity toward other religious beliefs besides their own. We have investigated reality and found that these holy souls were all sent of God. All of them have sacrificed life, endured ordeals and tribulations in order that They might educate us. How can such love be forgotten? The light of Christ is evident. The candle of Buddha is shining. The star of Moses is sparkling. The flame ignited by Zoroaster is still burning. How can we deny Them? It is injustice. It is a denial of complete evidence. If we forsake imitations, all will become united, and no differences will remain to separate us.

We entertain no prejudice against Muḥammad. Outwardly 13 the Arabian nation was instrumental in overthrowing the Pársí dominion, the sovereignty of Persia. Therefore, the old Pársí nation manifested the utmost contempt toward the Arabs. But we deal justly and will never abandon the standard of fairness. The Arabians were in the utmost state of degradation. They were bloodthirsty and barbarous, so savage and degraded that the Arabian father often buried his own daughter alive. Consider: Could any barbarism be lower than this? The nation consisted of warring, hostile tribal peoples inhabiting the vast Arabian peninsula, and their business consisted in fighting and pillaging each other, making captive women and children, killing each other. Muḥammad appeared among such a people. He educated and unified these barbarous tribes, put an end to their shedding of blood. Through His education they reached such a degree of civilization that they subdued and governed continents and nations. What a great civilization was established in Spain by the Muslims! What a marvelous civilization was founded in Morocco by the Moors! What a powerful caliphate or successorship was set up in Baghdád! How much Islám served and furthered the cause of science! Why then should we deny Muḥammad? If we deny Him, we awaken enmity and hatred. By our prejudice we become the cause of war and bloodshed, for prejudice was the cause of the tremendous storm which swept through human history for thirteen hundred years and still continues. Even now in the Balkans a commotion is apparent, reflecting it.

14   The Christian people number nearly three hundred millions and the Muslims about the same. It is no small task to do away with such numbers. And furthermore, why should they be obliterated? For these are all servants of the one God. Let us strive to establish peace between Christians and Muslims. Is it not better? What is the benefit of war? What is its fruitage? For thirteen hundred years there has been warfare and hostility. What good result has been forthcoming? Is it not folly? Is God

pleased with it? Is Christ pleased? Is Muḥammad? It is evident that They are not. The Prophets have extolled each other to the utmost. Muḥammad declared Christ to be the Spirit of God. This is an explicit text of the Qur'án. He declared Christ to be the Word of God. He eulogized the disciples of Christ to the utmost. He bestowed upon Mary, the mother of Christ, the highest praise. Likewise, Christ extolled Moses. He spread broadcast the Old Testament, the Torah, and caused the name of Moses to reach unto the East and the West. The purpose is this: that the Prophets Themselves have manifested the utmost love toward each other, but the nations who believe and follow Them are hostile and antagonistic among themselves.

The world was in this condition of darkness when Baháʼuʼlláh 15 appeared upon the Persian horizon. He hoisted the banner of the oneness of the world of humanity. He proclaimed international peace. He admonished the Persian nation to investigate reality, announced that religion must be the cause of unity and love, that it must be the means of binding hearts together, the cause of life and illumination. If religion becomes the cause of enmity and bloodshed, then irreligion is to be preferred, for religion is the remedy for every ailment, and if a remedy should become the cause of ailment and difficulty, it is better to abandon it. Today in Persia you will see the Muslims, Christians, Zoroastrians, Buddhists assembled together in the same meeting, living in accordance with the teachings of Baháʼuʼlláh, manifesting utmost love and accord. Rancor, hatred, antagonism and violence have disappeared; they live together as one family.

And ye who are the people of the Orient—the Orient which 16 has ever been the dawning point of lights from whence the Sun of Reality has ever shone forth, casting its effulgence upon the West—ye, therefore, must become the manifestations of lights. Ye must become brilliant lamps. Ye must shine as stars radiating the light of love toward all mankind. May you be the cause of love amongst the nations. Thus may the world become witness that the Orient has ever been the dawning point of illumination, the source of love and reconciliation. Make peace with all the world. Love everybody; serve everybody. All are the servants of God. God has created all. He provideth for all. He is kind to all. Therefore, must we be kind to all.

17   I am greatly pleased with this meeting. I am joyous and happy, for here in these western regions I find Orientals seeking education and who are free from prejudice. May God assist you!

2

8 October 1912

Talk at Leland Stanford Junior University
Palo Alto, California

NOTES BY BIJOU STRAUN

1   THE greatest attainment in the world of humanity has ever been scientific in nature. It is the discovery of the realities of things. Inasmuch as I find myself in the home of science—for this is one of the great universities of the country and well known abroad—I feel a keen sense of joy.

2   The highest praise is due to men who devote their energies to science, and the noblest center is a center wherein the sciences and arts are taught and studied. Science ever tends to the illumination of the world of humanity. It is the cause of eternal honor to man, and its sovereignty is far greater than the sovereignty of kings. The dominion of kings has an ending; the king himself

may be dethroned; but the sovereignty of science is everlasting and without end. Consider the philosophers of former times. Their rule and dominion is still manifest in the world. The Greek and Roman kingdoms with all their grandeur passed away; the ancient sovereignties of the Orient are but memories, whereas the power and influence of Plato and Aristotle still continue. Even now in schools and universities of the world their names are revered and commemorated, but where do we hear the names of bygone kings extolled? They are forgotten and rest in the valley of oblivion. It is evident that the sovereignty of science is greater than the dominion of rulers. Kings have invaded countries and achieved conquest through the shedding of blood, but the scientist through his beneficent achievements invades the regions of ignorance, conquering the realm of minds and hearts. Therefore, his conquests are everlasting. May you attain extraordinary progress in this center of education. May you become radiant lights flooding the dark regions and recesses of ignorance with illumination.

Inasmuch as the fundamental principle of the teaching of Bahá'u'lláh is the oneness of the world of humanity, I will speak to you upon the intrinsic oneness of all phenomena. This is one of the abstruse subjects of divine philosophy. 3

Fundamentally all existing things pass through the same degrees and phases of development, and any given phenomenon embodies all others. An ancient statement of the Arabian philosophers declares that all things are involved in all things. It is evident that each material organism is an aggregate expression of single and simple elements, and a given cellular element or atom has its coursings or journeyings through various and myriad stages of life. For example, we will say the cellular elements which have entered into the composition of a human organism were at one time a component part of the animal kingdom; at another 4 time they entered into the composition of the vegetable, and prior to that they existed in the kingdom of the mineral. They have been subject to transference from one condition of life to another, passing through various forms and phases, exercising in each existence special functions. Their journeyings through material phenomena are continuous. Therefore, each phenomenon is the expression in degree of all other phenomena. The difference is one of successive transferences and the period of time involved in evolutionary process.

5   For example, it has taken a certain length of time for this cellular element in my hand to pass through the various periods of metabolism. At one period it was in the mineral kingdom subject to changes and transferences in the mineral state. Then it was transferred to the vegetable kingdom where it entered into different grades and stations. Afterward it reached the animal plane, appearing in forms of animal organisms until finally in its transferences and coursings it attained to the kingdom of man. Later on it will revert to its primordial elemental state in the mineral kingdom, being subject, as it were, to infinite journeyings from one degree of existence to another, passing through every stage of being and life. Whenever it appears in any distinct form or image, it has its opportunities, virtues and functions. As each component atom or element in the physical organisms of existence is subject to transference through endless forms and stages, possessing virtues peculiar to those forms and stations, it is evident that all phenomena of material being are fundamentally one. In the mineral kingdom this component atom or element possesses certain virtues of the mineral; in the kingdom of the vegetable it is imbued with vegetable qualities or virtues; in the plane of animal existence it is empowered with animal virtues—the senses; and in the kingdom of man it manifests qualities peculiar to the human station.

494

As this is true of material phenomena, how much more 6
evident and essential it is that oneness should characterize man
in the realm of idealism, which finds its expression only in the
human kingdom. Verily, the origin of all material life is one
and its termination likewise one. In view of this fundamental
unity and agreement of all phenomenal life, why should man
in his kingdom of existence wage war or indulge in hostility and
destructive strife against his fellowman? Man is the noblest of
the creatures. In his physical organism he possesses the virtues of
the mineral kingdom. Likewise, he embodies the augmentative
virtue, or power of growth, which characterizes the kingdom of
the vegetable. Furthermore, in his degree of physical existence
he is qualified with functions and powers peculiar to the animal,
beyond which lies the range of his distinctive human mental
and spiritual endowment. Considering this wonderful unity of
the kingdoms of existence and their embodiment in the highest and noblest creature, why should man be at variance and
in conflict with man? Is it fitting and justifiable that he should
be at war, when harmony and interdependence characterize
the kingdoms of phenomenal life below him? The elements
and lower organisms are synchronized in the great plan of life.
Shall man, infinitely above them in degree, be antagonistic and
a destroyer of that perfection? God forbid such a condition!

From the fellowship and commingling of the elemental atoms 7
life results. In their harmony and blending there is ever newness
of existence. It is radiance, completeness; it is consummation;
it is life itself. Just now the physical energies and natural forces
which come under our immediate observation are all at peace.
The sun is at peace with the earth upon which it shines. The soft
breathing winds are at peace with the trees. All the elements are
in harmony and equilibrium. A slight disturbance and discord
among them might bring another San Francisco earthquake and

fire. A physical clash, a little quarreling among the elements as it were, and a violent cataclysm of nature results. This happens in the mineral kingdom. Consider, then, the effect of discord and conflict in the kingdom of man, so superior to the realm of inanimate existence. How great the attendant catastrophe, especially when we realize that man is endowed by God with mind and intellect. Verily, mind is the supreme gift of God. Verily, intellect is the effulgence of God. This is manifest and self-evident.

8   For all created things except man are subjects or captives of nature; they cannot deviate in the slightest degree from nature's law and control. The colossal sun, center of our planetary system, is nature's captive, incapable of the least variation from the law of command. All the orbs and luminaries in this illimitable universe are, likewise, obedient to nature's regulation. Our planet, the earth, acknowledges nature's omnipresent sovereignty. The kingdoms of the mineral, vegetable and animal respond to nature's will and fiat of control. The great bulky elephant with its massive strength has no power to disobey the restrictions nature has laid upon him; but man, weak and diminutive in comparison, empowered by mind which is an effulgence of Divinity itself, can resist nature's control and apply natural laws to his own uses.

9   According to the limitations of his physical powers man was intended by creation to live upon the earth, but through the exercise of his mental faculties, he removes the restriction of this law and soars in the air like a bird. He penetrates the secrets of the sea in submarines and builds fleets to sail at will over the ocean's surface, commanding the laws of nature to do his will. All the sciences and arts we now enjoy and utilize were once mysteries, and according to the mandates of nature should have remained hidden and latent, but the human intellect has broken through the laws surrounding them and discovered the

underlying realities. The mind of man has taken these mysteries out of the plane of invisibility and brought them into the plane of the known and visible.

It has classified and adapted these laws to human needs and uses, this being contrary to the postulates of nature. For example, electricity was once a hidden, or latent, natural force. It would have remained hidden if the human intellect had not discovered it. Man has broken the law of its concealment, taken this energy out of the invisible treasury of the universe and brought it into visibility. Is it not an extraordinary accomplishment that this little creature, man, has imprisoned an irresistible cosmic force in an incandescent lamp? It is beyond the vision and power of nature itself to do this. The East can communicate with the West in a few minutes. This is a miracle transcending nature's control. Man takes the human voice and stores it in a phonograph. The voice naturally should be free and transient according to the law and phenomenon of sound, but man arrests its vibrations and puts it in a box in defiance of nature's laws. All human discoveries were once secrets and mysteries sealed and stored up in the bosom of the material universe until the mind of man, which is the greatest of divine effulgences, penetrated them and made them subservient to his will and purpose. In this sense man has broken the laws of nature and is constantly taking out of nature's laboratory new and wonderful things. Notwithstanding this supreme bestowal of God, which is the greatest power in the world of creation, man continues to war and fight, killing his fellowman with the ferocity of a wild animal. Is this in keeping with his exalted station? Nay, rather, this is contrary to the divine purpose manifest in his creation and endowment.

If the animals are savage and ferocious, it is simply a means for their subsistence and preservation. They are deprived of that

10

11

degree of intellect which can reason and discriminate between right and wrong, justice and injustice; they are justified in their actions and not responsible. When man is ferocious and cruel toward his fellowman, it is not for subsistence or safety. His motive is selfish advantage and willful wrong. It is neither seemly nor befitting that such a noble creature, endowed with intellect and lofty thoughts, capable of wonderful achievements and discoveries in sciences and arts, with potential for ever higher perceptions and the accomplishment of divine purposes in life, should seek the blood of his fellowmen upon the field of battle. Man is the temple of God. He is not a human temple. If you destroy a house, the owner of that house will be grieved and wrathful. How much greater is the wrong when man destroys a building planned and erected by God! Undoubtedly, he deserves the judgment and wrath of God.

12   God has created man lofty and noble, made him a dominant factor in creation. He has specialized man with supreme bestowals, conferred upon him mind, perception, memory, abstraction and the powers of the senses. These gifts of God to man were intended to make him the manifestation of divine virtues, a radiant light in the world of creation, a source of life and the agency of constructiveness in the infinite fields of existence. Shall we now destroy this great edifice and its very foundation, overthrow this temple of God, the body social or politic? When we are not captives of nature, when we possess the power to control ourselves, shall we become captives of nature and act according to its exigencies?

13   In nature there is the law of the survival of the fittest. Even if man be not educated, then according to the natural institutes this natural law will demand of man supremacy. The purpose and object of schools, colleges and universities is to educate man and thereby rescue and redeem him from the exigencies and defects of nature and to awaken within him the capabil-

ity of controlling and appropriating nature's bounties. If we should relegate this plot of ground to its natural state, allow it to return to its original condition, it would become a field of thorns and useless weeds, but by cultivation it will become fertile soil, yielding a harvest. Deprived of cultivation, the mountain slopes would be jungles and forests without fruitful trees. The gardens bring forth fruits and flowers in proportion to the care and tillage bestowed upon them by the gardener. Therefore, it is not intended that the world of humanity should be left to its natural state. It is in need of the education divinely provided for it. The holy, heavenly Manifestations of God have been the Teachers. They are the divine Gardeners Who transform the jungles of human nature into fruitful orchards and make the thorny places blossom as the rose. It is evident, then, that the intended and especial function of man is to rescue and redeem himself from the inherent defects of nature and become qualified with the ideal virtues of Divinity. Shall he sacrifice these ideal virtues and destroy these possibilities of advancement? God has endowed him with a power whereby he can even overcome the laws and phenomena of nature, wrest the sword from nature's hand and use it against nature itself. Shall he, then, remain its captive, even failing to qualify under the natural law which commands the survival of the fittest? That is to say, shall he continue to live upon the level of the animal kingdom without distinction between them and himself in natural impulses and ferocious instincts? There is no lower degree nor greater debasement for man than this natural condition of animalism. The battlefield is the acme of human degradation, the cause of the wrath of God, the destruction of the divine foundation of man.

Praise be to God! I find myself in an assemblage, the members 14 of which are peace loving and advocates of international unity. The thoughts of all present are centered upon the oneness of the world of mankind, and every ambition is to render service in the cause of human uplift and betterment. I supplicate God that He may confirm and assist you, that each one of you may become a professor emeritus in the world of scientific knowledge, a faithful standard-bearer of peace and bonds of agreement between the hearts of men.

15   Fifty years ago Bahá'u'lláh declared the necessity of peace among the nations and the reality of reconciliation between the religions of the world. He announced that the fundamental basis of all religion is one, that the essence of religion is human fellowship and that the differences in belief which exist are due to dogmatic interpretation and blind imitations which are at variance with the foundations established by the Prophets of God. He proclaimed that if the reality underlying religious teaching be investigated all religions would be unified, and the purpose of God, which is love and the blending of human hearts, would be accomplished. According to His teachings if religious belief proves to be the cause of discord and dissension, its absence would be preferable; for religion was intended to be the divine remedy and panacea for the ailments of humanity, the healing balm for the wounds of mankind. If its misapprehension and defilement have brought about warfare and bloodshed instead of remedy and cure, the world would be better under irreligious conditions.

16   Bahá'u'lláh especially emphasized international peace. He declared that all mankind is the one progeny of Adam and members of one great universal family. If the various races and distinct types of mankind had each proceeded from a different original paternity—in other words, if we had two or more Adams for our human fathers—there might be reasonable ground for difference and divergence in humanity today; but inasmuch as we belong to one progeny and one family, all names which seek

to differentiate and distinguish mankind as Italian, German, French, Russian and so on are without significance and sanction. We are all human, all servants of God and all come from Mr. Adam's family. Why, then, all these fallacious national and racial distinctions? These boundary lines and artificial barriers have been created by despots and conquerors who sought to attain dominion over mankind, thereby engendering patriotic feeling and rousing selfish devotion to merely local standards of government. As a rule they themselves enjoyed luxuries in palaces, surrounded by conditions of ease and affluence, while armies of soldiers, civilians and tillers of the soil fought and died at their command upon the field of battle, shedding their innocent blood for a delusion such as "we are Germans," "our enemies are French," etc., when, in reality, all are humankind, all belong to the one family and posterity of Adam, the original father. This prejudice or limited patriotism is prevalent throughout the world, while man is blind to patriotism in the larger sense which includes all races and native lands. From every real standpoint there must and should be peace among all nations.

God created one earth and one mankind to people it. Man 17 has no other habitation, but man himself has come forth and proclaimed imaginary boundary lines and territorial restrictions, naming them Germany, France, Russia, etc. And torrents of precious blood are spilled in defense of these imaginary divisions of our one human habitation, under the delusion of a fancied and limited patriotism.

After all, a claim and title to territory or native land is but a 18 claim and attachment to the dust of earth. We live upon this earth for a few days and then rest beneath it forever. So it is our graveyard eternally. Shall man fight for the tomb which devours him, for his eternal sepulcher? What ignorance could be greater than this? To fight over his grave, to kill another for his grave! What heedlessness! What a delusion!

19   It is my hope that you who are students in this university may never be called upon to fight for the dust of earth which is the tomb and sepulcher of all mankind, but that during the days of your life you may enjoy the most perfect companionship one with another, even as one family—as brothers, sisters, fathers, mothers—associating together in peace and true fellowship.

3

10 October 1912

Talk at Open Forum
San Francisco, California

NOTES BY BIJOU STRAUN

1   ALTHOUGH I was feeling indisposed this evening, yet owing to the love I entertain for you I have attended this meeting. For I have heard that this is an open forum, investigating reality; that you are free from blind imitations, desiring to arrive at the truth of things, and that your endeavors are lofty. Therefore, I have thought it expedient to discourse upon the subject of philosophy, which is alike interesting to the East and the West, enabling us to consider the analogies and differences between the philosophical teachings of the Orient and Occident.

2   The criterion of judgment in the estimation of western philosophers is sense perception. They consider that which is tangible or perceptible to the senses to be a reality—that there is

no doubt of its existence. For example, we prove the existence of this light through the sense of sight; we visualize this room; we see the sun, the green fields; we use our sense of sight to observe them. The opinion of these philosophers is that such perception is reality, that the senses are the highest standard of perception and judgment, in which there can neither be doubt nor uncertainty. In the estimation of the philosophers of the Orient, especially those of Greece and Persia, the standard of judgment is the intellect. They are of the opinion that the criterion of the senses is defective, and their proof is that the senses are often deceived and mistaken. That which is liable to mistake cannot be infallible, cannot be a true standard of judgment.

Among the senses the most powerful and reliable is that of 3 sight. This sense views a mirage as a body of water and is positive as to its character, whereas a mirage is nonexistent. The sense of vision, or sight, sees reflected images in a mirror as verities, when reason declares them to be nonexistent. The eye sees the sun and planets revolving around the earth, whereas in reality the sun is stationary, central, and the earth revolves upon its own axis. The sense of sight sees the earth as a plane, whereas the faculty of reason discovers it to be spherical. The eye views the heavenly bodies in boundless space as small and insignificant, whereas reason declares them to be colossal suns. The sense of sight beholds a whirling spark of fire as a circle of light and is without doubt as to it, whereas such a circle is nonexistent. A man sailing in a ship sees the banks on either side as if they were moving, whereas the ship is moving. Briefly, there are many instances and evidences which disprove the assertion that tangibilities and sense impressions are certainties, for the senses are misleading and often mistaken. How, then, can we rightly declare that they prove reality when the standard or criterion itself is defective?

4   The philosophers of the East consider the perfect criterion to be reason or intellect, and according to that standard the realities of all objects can be proved; for, they say, the standard of reason and intellect is perfect, and everything provable through reason is veritable. Therefore, those philosophers consider all philosophical deductions to be correct when weighed according to the standard of reason, and they state that the senses are the assistants and instruments of reason, and that although the investigation of realities may be conducted through the senses, the standard of knowing and judgment is reason itself. In this way the philosophers of the East and West differ and disagree. The materialistic philosophers of the West declare that man belongs to the animal kingdom, whereas the philosophers of the East—such as Plato, Aristotle and the Persians—divide the world of existence or phenomena of life into two general categories or kingdoms: one the animal kingdom, or world of nature, the other the human kingdom, or world of reason.

5   Man is distinguished above the animals through his reason. The perceptions of man are of two kinds: tangible, or sensible, and reasonable, whereas the animal perceptions are limited to the senses, the tangible only. The tangible perceptions may be likened to this candle, the reasonable perceptions to the light. Calculations of mathematical problems and determining the spherical form of the earth are through the reasonable perceptions. The center of gravity is a hypothesis of reason. Reason itself is not tangible, perceptible to the senses. Reason is an intellectual verity or reality. All qualities are ideal realities, not tangible realities. For instance, we say this man is a scholarly man. Knowledge is an ideal attainment not perceptible to the senses. When you see this scholarly man, your eye does not see his knowledge, your ear cannot hear his science, nor can you sense it by taste. It is not a tangible verity. Science itself is an

ideal verity. It is evident, therefore, that the perceptions of man are twofold: the reasonable and the tangible, or sensible.

As to the animal: It is endowed only with sense perception. It 6 is lacking the reasonable perception. It cannot apprehend ideal realities. The animal cannot conceive of the earth as a sphere. The intelligence of an animal located in Europe could never have planned the discovery of the continent of America. The animal kingdom is incapable of discovering the latent mysteries of nature—such as electricity—and bringing them forth from the invisible to the plane of visibility. It is evident that the discoveries and inventions transcend the animal intelligence. The animal cannot penetrate the secrets of genesis and creation. Its mind is incapable of conceiving the verity of ether. It cannot know the mysteries of magnetism because the bestowals of abstract reason and intellect are absent in its endowment. That is to say, the animal in its creation is a captive of the senses. Beyond the tangibilities and impressions of the senses it cannot accept anything. It denies everything. It is incapable of ideal perception and, therefore, a captive of the senses.

Virtue, or perfection, belongs to man, who possesses both 7 the capacity of the senses and ideal perception. For instance, astronomical discoveries are man's accomplishments. He has not gained this knowledge through his senses. The greater part of it has been attained through intellect, through the ideal senses. Man's inventions have appeared through the avenue of his reasonable faculties. All his scientific attainments have come through the faculty of reason. Briefly, the evidences of intellect or reason are manifest in man. By them he is differentiated from the animal. Therefore, the animal kingdom is distinct and inferior to the human kingdom. Notwithstanding this, the philosophers of the West have certain syllogisms, or demonstrations, whereby they endeavor to prove that man had his origin in the animal kingdom; that although he is now a vertebrate, he originally lived in the sea; from thence he was transferred to the land and became vertebrate; that gradually his feet and hands appeared in his anatomical development; then he began to walk upon all fours, after which he attained to human stature, walking erect. They find that his anatomy has undergone successive changes, finally assuming human form, and that these intermediate forms or changes are like links connected. Between man and the ape, however, there is one link missing, and to the present time scientists have not been able to discover it. Therefore, the greatest proof of this western theory of human evolution is anatomical, reasoning that there are certain vestiges of organs found in man which are peculiar to the ape and lower animals, and setting forth the conclusion that man at some time in his upward progression has possessed these organs which are no longer functioning but appear now as mere rudiments and vestiges.

8   For example, a serpent has a certain appendage which indicates that at one time it was possessed of long limbs, but as this creature began to find its habitation in the holes of the earth, these limbs, no longer needed, became atrophied and shrunk, leaving but a vestige, or appendage, as an evidence of the time when they were lengthy and serviceable. Likewise, it is claimed man had a certain appendage which shows that there was a time when his anatomical structure was different from his present organism and that there has been a corresponding transformation or change in that structure. The coccyx, or extremity of the human spinal column, is declared to be the vestige of a tail which man formerly possessed but which gradually disappeared when he walked erect and its utility ceased. These statements and demonstrations express the substance of western philosophy upon the question of human evolution.

9   The philosophers of the Orient in reply to those of the western world say: Let us suppose that the human anatomy was pri-

mordially different from its present form, that it was gradually transformed from one stage to another until it attained its present likeness, that at one time it was similar to a fish, later an invertebrate and finally human. This anatomical evolution or progression does not alter or affect the statement that the development of man was always human in type and biological in progression. For the human embryo when examined microscopically is at first a mere germ or worm. Gradually as it develops it shows certain divisions; rudiments of hands and feet appear—that is to say, an upper and a lower part are distinguishable. Afterward it undergoes certain distinct changes until it reaches its actual human form and is born into this world. But at all times, even when the embryo resembled a worm, it was human in potentiality and character, not animal. The forms assumed by the human embryo in its successive changes do not prove that it is animal in its essential character. Throughout this progression there has been a transference of type, a conservation of species or kind. Realizing this we may acknowledge the fact that at one time man was an inmate of the sea, at another period an invertebrate, then a vertebrate and finally a human being standing erect. Though we admit these changes, we cannot say man is an animal. In each one of these stages are signs and evidences of his human existence and destination. Proof of this lies in the fact that in the embryo man still resembles a worm. This embryo still progresses from one state to another, assuming different forms until that which was potential in it—namely, the human image—appears. Therefore, in the protoplasm, man is man. Conservation of species demands it.

The lost link of Darwinian theory is itself a proof that man 10 is not an animal. How is it possible to have all the links present and that important link absent? Its absence is an indication that man has never been an animal. It will never be found.

The significance is this: that the world of humanity is distinct 11 from the animal kingdom. This is the teaching of the philosophers of the Orient. They have a proof for it. The proof is that the animals are captives of nature. All existence and phenomena of the lower kingdoms are captives of nature; the mighty sun, the numberless stars, the kingdoms of the vegetable and mineral, none of these can deviate one hair's breadth from the limitation of nature's laws. They are, as it were, arrested by nature's hands. But man breaks the laws of nature and makes them subservient to his uses. For instance, man is an animate earthly being in common with the animals. The exigency of nature demands that he should be restricted to the earth; but he, by breaking the laws of nature, soars in the atmosphere high above it. By the application of his intellect he overcomes natural law and dives beneath the seas in submarines or sails across them in ships. He arrests a mighty force of nature such as electricity and imprisons it in an incandescent lamp. According to the law of nature he should be able to communicate at a distance of, say, one thousand feet; but through his inventions and discoveries he communicates with the East and with the West in a few moments. This is breaking the laws of nature. Man arrests the human voice and reproduces it in a phonograph. At most his voice should be heard only a few hundred feet away, but he invents an instrument which transmits it one thousand miles. In brief, all the present arts and sciences, inventions and discoveries man has brought forth were once mysteries which nature had decreed should remain hidden and latent, but man has taken them out of the plane of the invisible and brought them into the plane of the visible. This is contrary to nature's laws. Electricity should be a latent mystery, but man discovers it and makes it his servant. He wrests the sword from nature's hand and uses it against nature, proving that there is a power in him which is beyond nature, for it is capable of breaking and subduing the laws of nature. If this power were not supernatural and extraordinary, man's accomplishments would not have been possible.

Furthermore, it is evident that in the world of nature con-   12
scious knowledge is absent. Nature is without knowing, whereas man is conscious. Nature is devoid of memory; man possesses memory. Nature is without perception and volition; man possesses both. It is evident that virtues are inherent in man which are not present in the world of nature. This is provable from every standpoint.

If it be claimed that the intellectual reality of man belongs to   13
the world of nature—that it is a part of the whole—we ask is it possible for the part to contain virtues which the whole does not possess? For instance, is it possible for the drop to contain virtues of which the aggregate body of the sea is deprived? Is it possible for a leaf to be imbued with virtues which are lacking in the whole tree? Is it possible that the extraordinary faculty of reason in man is animal in character and quality? On the other hand, it is evident and true, though most astounding, that in man there is present this supernatural force or faculty which discovers the realities of things and which possesses the power of idealization or intellection. It is capable of discovering scientific laws, and science we know is not a tangible reality. Science exists in the mind of man as an ideal reality. The mind itself, reason itself, is an ideal reality and not tangible.

Notwithstanding this, some of the sagacious men declare: We   14
have attained to the superlative degree of knowledge; we have penetrated the laboratory of nature, studying sciences and arts; we have attained the highest station of knowledge in the human world; we have investigated the facts as they are and have arrived at the conclusion that nothing is rightly acceptable except the tangible, which alone is a reality worthy of credence; all that is not tangible is imagination and nonsense.

15   Strange indeed that after twenty years training in colleges and universities man should reach such a station wherein he will deny the existence of the ideal or that which is not perceptible to the senses. Have you ever stopped to think that the animal already has graduated from such a university? Have you ever realized that the cow is already a professor emeritus of that university? For the cow without hard labor and study is already a philosopher of the superlative degree in the school of nature. The cow denies everything that is not tangible, saying, "I can see! I can eat! Therefore, I believe only in that which is tangible!"

16   Then why should we go to the colleges? Let us go to the cow.

4

12 October 1912

Talk at Temple Emmanu-El
450 Sutter Street, San Francisco, California

NOTES BY BIJOU STRAUN

1   THE greatest bestowal of God in the world of humanity is religion, for assuredly the divine teachings of religion are above all other sources of instruction and development to man. Religion confers upon man eternal life and guides his footsteps in the world of morality. It opens the doors of unending happiness and bestows everlasting honor upon the human kingdom. It has been the basis of all civilization and progress in the history of mankind.

2   We will, therefore, investigate religion, seeking from an unprejudiced standpoint to discover whether it is the source

of illumination, the cause of development and the animating impulse of all human advancement. We will investigate independently, free from the restrictions of dogmatic beliefs, blind imitations of ancestral forms and the influence of mere human opinion; for as we enter this question, we will find some who declare that religion is a cause of uplift and betterment in the world, while others assert just as positively that it is a detriment and a source of degradation to mankind. We must give these questions thorough and impartial consideration so that no doubt or uncertainty may linger in our minds regarding them.

How shall we determine whether religion has been the cause 3 of human advancement or retrogression?

We will first consider the Founders of the religions—the 4 Prophets—review the story of Their lives, compare the conditions preceding Their appearance with those subsequent to Their departure, following historical records and irrefutable facts instead of relying upon traditionary statements which are open to both acceptance and denial.

Among the great Prophets was Abraham, Who, being an 5 iconoclast and a Herald of the oneness of God, was banished from His native land. He founded a family upon which the blessing of God descended, and it was owing to this religious basis and ordination that the Abrahamic house progressed and advanced. Through the divine benediction noteworthy and luminous prophets issued from His lineage. There appeared Isaac, Ishmael, Jacob, Joseph, Moses, Aaron, David and Solomon. The Holy Land was conquered by the power of the Covenant of God with Abraham, and the glory of the Solomonic wisdom and sovereignty dawned. All this was due to the religion of God which this blessed lineage established and upheld. It is evident that throughout the history of Abraham and His posterity this was the source of their honor, advancement and civilization.

Even today the descendants of His household and lineage are found throughout the world.

6   There is another and more significant aspect to this religious impulse and impetus. The children of Israel were in bondage and captivity in the land of Egypt four hundred years. They were in an extreme state of degradation and slavery under the tyranny and oppression of the Egyptians. While they were in the condition of abject poverty, in the lowest degree of abasement, ignorance and servility, Moses suddenly appeared among them. Although He was but a shepherd, such majesty, grandeur and efficiency became manifest in Him through the power of religion that His influence continues to this day. His Prophethood was established throughout the land, and the law of His Word became the foundation of the laws of the nations. This unique Personage, single and alone, rescued the children of Israel from bondage through the power of religious training and discipline. He led them to the Holy Land and founded there a great civilization which has become permanent and renowned and under which these people attained the highest degree of honor and glory. He freed them from bondage and captivity. He imbued them with qualities of progressiveness and capability. They proved to be a civilizing people with instincts toward education and scholastic attainment. Their philosophy became renowned; their industries were celebrated throughout the nations. In all lines of advancement which characterize a progressive people they achieved distinction. In the splendor of the reign of Solomon their sciences and arts advanced to such a degree that even the Greek philosophers journeyed to Jerusalem to sit at the feet of the Hebrew sages and acquire the basis of Israelitish law. According to eastern history this is an established fact. Even Socrates visited the Jewish doctors in the Holy Land, consorting with them and discussing the principles and basis of their

religious belief. After his return to Greece he formulated his philosophical teaching of divine unity and advanced his belief in the immortality of the spirit beyond the dissolution of the body. Without doubt, Socrates absorbed these verities from the wise men of the Jews with whom he came in contact. Hippocrates and other philosophers of the Greeks likewise visited Palestine and acquired wisdom from the Jewish prophets, studying the basis of ethics and morality, returning to their country with contributions which have made Greece famous.

When a movement fundamentally religious makes a weak nation strong, changes a nondescript tribal people into a mighty and powerful civilization, rescues them from captivity and elevates them to sovereignty, transforms their ignorance into knowledge and endows them with an impetus of advancement in all degrees of development (this is not theory, but historical fact), it becomes evident that religion is the cause of man's attainment to honor and sublimity. 7

But when we speak of religion, we mean the essential foundation or reality of religion, not the dogmas and blind imitations which have gradually encrusted it and which are the cause of the decline and effacement of a nation. These are inevitably destructive and a menace and hindrance to a nation's life—even as it is recorded in the Torah and confirmed in history that when the Jews became fettered by empty forms and imitations, the wrath of God became manifest. When they forsook the foundations of the law of God, Nebuchadnezzar came and conquered the Holy Land. He killed and made captive the people of Israel, laid waste the country and populous cities and burned the villages. Seventy thousand Jews were carried away captive to Babylon. He destroyed Jerusalem, despoiled the great Temple, desecrated the Holy of Holies and burned the Torah, the heavenly book of Scriptures. Therefore, we learn that allegiance to the essential 8 foundation of the divine religions is ever the cause of development and progress, whereas the abandonment and beclouding of that essential reality through blind imitations and adherence to dogmatic beliefs are the causes of a nation's debasement and degradation. After their conquest by the Babylonians the Jews were successively subjugated by the Greeks and Romans. Under the Roman general Titus in A.D. 70 the Holy Land was stripped and pillaged, Jerusalem razed to its foundations and the Israelites scattered broadcast throughout the world. So complete was their dispersion that they have continued without a country and government of their own to the present day.

9   From this review of the history of the Jewish people we learn that the foundation of the religion of God laid by Moses was the cause of their eternal honor and national prestige, the animating impulse of their advancement and racial supremacy and the source of that excellence which will always command the respect and reverence of those who understand their peculiar destiny and outcome. The dogmas and blind imitations which gradually obscured the reality of the religion of God proved to be Israel's destructive influences, causing the expulsion of these chosen people from the Holy Land of their Covenant and promise.

10   What, then, is the mission of the divine Prophets? Their mission is the education and advancement of the world of humanity. They are the real Teachers and Educators, the universal Instructors of mankind. If we wish to discover whether any one of these great Souls or Messengers was in reality a Prophet of God, we must investigate the facts surrounding His life and history, and the first point of our investigation will be the education He bestowed upon mankind. If He has been an Educator, if He has really trained a nation or people, causing it to rise from the lowest depths of ignorance to the highest station of knowledge, then we are sure that He was a Prophet. This is a

plain and clear method of procedure, proof that is irrefutable. We do not need to seek after other proofs. We do not need to mention miracles, saying that out of rock water gushed forth, for such miracles and statements may be denied and refused by those who hear them. The deeds of Moses are conclusive evidences of His Prophethood. If a man be fair, unbiased and willing to investigate reality, he will undoubtedly testify to the fact that Moses was, verily, a man of God and a great Personage.

In further consideration of this subject, I wish you to be 11 fair and reasonable in your judgment, setting aside all religious prejudices. We should earnestly seek and thoroughly investigate realities, recognizing that the purpose of the religion of God is the education of humanity and the unity and fellowship of mankind. Furthermore, we will establish the point that the foundations of the religions of God are one foundation. This foundation is not multiple, for it is reality itself. Reality does not admit of multiplicity, although each of the divine religions is separable into two divisions. One concerns the world of morality and the ethical training of human nature. It is directed to the advancement of the world of humanity in general; it reveals and inculcates the knowledge of God and makes possible the discovery of the verities of life. This is ideal and spiritual teaching, the essential quality of divine religion, and not subject to change or transformation. It is the one foundation of all the religions of God. Therefore, the religions are essentially one and the same.

The second classification or division comprises social laws 12 and regulations applicable to human conduct. This is not the essential spiritual quality of religion. It is subject to change and transformation according to the exigencies and requirements of time and place. For instance, in the time of Noah certain requirements made it necessary that all seafood be allowable or lawful. During the time of the Abrahamic Prophethood it was considered allowable, because of a certain exigency, that a man should marry his aunt, even as Sarah was the sister of Abraham's mother. During the cycle of Adam it was lawful and expedient for a man to marry his own sister, even as Abel, Cain and Seth, the sons of Adam, married their sisters. But in the law of the Pentateuch revealed by Moses these marriages were forbidden and their custom and sanction abrogated. Other laws formerly valid were annulled during the time of Moses. For example, it was lawful in Abraham's cycle to eat the flesh of the camel, but during the time of Jacob this was prohibited. Such changes and transformations in the teaching of religion are applicable to the ordinary conditions of life, but they are not important or essential. Moses lived in the wilderness of Sinai where crime necessitated direct punishment. There were no penitentiaries or penalties of imprisonment. Therefore, according to the exigency of the time and place it was a law of God that an eye should be given for an eye and a tooth for a tooth. It would not be prac-ticable to enforce this law at the present time—for instance, to blind a man who accidentally blinded you. In the Torah there are many commands concerning the punishment of a murderer. It would not be allowable or possible to carry out these ordinances today. Human conditions and exigencies are such that even the question of capital punishment—the one penalty which most nations have continued to enforce for murder—is now under discussion by wise men who are debating its advisability. In fact, laws for the ordinary conditions of life are only valid temporarily. The exigencies of the time of Moses justified cutting off a man's hand for theft, but such a penalty is not allowable now. Time changes conditions, and laws change to suit conditions. We must remember that these changing laws are not the essentials; they are the accidentals of religion. The essential ordinances established by a Manifestation of God are spiritual; they concern moralities, the ethical development of man and faith in God. They are ideal and necessarily permanent—expressions of the one foundation and not amenable to change or transformation. Therefore, the fundamental basis of the revealed religion of God is immutable, unchanging throughout the centuries, not subject to the varying conditions of the human world.

Christ ratified and proclaimed the foundation of the law of 13 Moses. Muḥammad and all the Prophets have revoiced that same foundation of reality. Therefore, the purposes and accomplishments of the divine Messengers have been one and the same. They were the source of advancement to the body politic and the cause of the honor and divine civilization of humanity, the foundation of which is one and the same in every dispensation. It is evident, then, that the proofs of the validity and inspiration of a Prophet of God are the deeds of beneficent accomplishment and greatness emanating from Him. If He proves to be instrumental in the elevation and betterment of mankind, He is undoubtedly a valid and heavenly Messenger.

I wish you to be reasonable and just in your consideration of 14 the following statements:

At the time when the Israelites had been dispersed by the 15 power of the Roman Empire and the national life of the Hebrew people had been effaced by their conquerors—when the law of God had seemingly passed from them and the foundation of the religion of God was apparently destroyed—Jesus Christ appeared. When He arose among the Jews, the first thing He did was to proclaim the validity of the Manifestation of Moses. He declared that the Torah, the Old Testament, was the Book of God and that all the prophets of Israel were valid and true. He extolled the mission of Moses, and through His proclamation the name of Moses was spread throughout the world. Through Christianity the greatness of Moses became known among all

517

nations. It is a fact that before the appearance of Christ, the name of Moses had not been heard in Persia. In India they had no knowledge of Judaism, and it was only through the Christianizing of Europe that the teachings of the Old Testament became spread in that region. Throughout Europe there was not a copy of the Old Testament. But consider this carefully and judge it aright: Through the instrumentality of Christ, through the translation of the New Testament, the little volume of the Gospel, the Old Testament, the Torah, has been translated into six hundred languages and spread everywhere in the world. The names of the Hebrew prophets became household words among the nations, who believed that the children of Israel were, verily, the chosen people of God, a holy nation under the especial blessing and protection of God, and that, therefore, the prophets who had arisen in Israel were the daysprings of revelation and brilliant stars in the heaven of the will of God.

16   Therefore, Christ really promulgated Judaism; for he was a Jew and not opposed to the Jews. He did not deny the Prophethood of Moses; on the contrary, He proclaimed and ratified it. He did not invalidate the Torah; He spread its teachings. That portion of the ordinances of Moses which concerned transactions and unimportant conditions underwent transformation, but the essential teachings of Moses were revoiced and confirmed by Christ without change. He left nothing unfinished or incomplete. Likewise, through the supreme efficacy and power of the Word of God He united most of the nations of the East and the West. This was accomplished at a time when these nations were opposed to each other in hostility and strife. He led them beneath the overshadowing tent of the oneness of humanity. He educated them until they became united and agreed, and through His spirit of conciliation the Roman, Greek, Chaldean and Egyptian were blended in a composite civilization. This

wonderful power and extraordinary efficacy of the Word prove conclusively the validity of Christ. Consider how His heavenly sovereignty is still permanent and lasting. Verily, this is conclusive proof and manifest evidence.

From another horizon we see Muḥammad, the Prophet of 17 Arabia, appearing. You may not know that the first address of Muḥammad to His tribe was the statement, "Verily, Moses was a Prophet of God, and the Torah is a Book of God. Verily, O ye people, ye must believe in the Torah, in Moses and the prophets. Ye must accept all the prophets of Israel as valid." In the Qur'án, the Muslim Bible, there are seven statements or repetitions of the Mosaic narrative, and in all the historic accounts Moses is praised. Muḥammad announces that Moses was the greatest Prophet of God, that God guided Him in the wilderness of Sinai, that through the light of guidance Moses hearkened to the summons of God, that He was the Interlocutor of God and the bearer of the tablet of the Ten Commandments, that all the contemporary nations of the world arose against Him and that eventually Moses conquered them, for falsehood and error are ever overcome by truth. There are many other instances of Muḥammad's confirmation of Moses. I am mentioning but a few. Consider that Muḥammad was born among the savage and barbarous tribes of Arabia, lived among them and was outwardly illiterate and uninformed of the Holy Books of God. The Arabian people were in the utmost ignorance and barbarism. They buried their infant daughters alive, considering this to be an evidence of a valorous and lofty nature. They lived in bondage and serfdom under the Persian and Roman governments and were scattered throughout the desert, engaged in continual strife and bloodshed. When the light of Muḥammad dawned, the darkness of ignorance was dispelled from the deserts of Arabia. In a short period of time those barbarous peoples attained a superlative degree of civilization which, with Baghdád as its center, extended as far westward as Spain and afterward influenced the greater part of Europe. What proof of Prophethood could be greater than this, unless we close our eyes to justice and remain obstinately opposed to reason?

18 Today the Christians are believers in Moses, accept Him as a Prophet of God and praise Him most highly. The Muslims are, likewise, believers in Moses, accept the validity of His Prophethood, at the same time believing in Christ. Could it be said that the acceptance of Moses by the Christians and Muslims has been harmful and detrimental to those people? On the contrary, it has been beneficial to them, proving that they have been fair-minded and just. What harm could result to the Jewish people, then, if they in return should accept Christ and acknowledge the validity of the Prophethood of Muḥammad? By this acceptance and praiseworthy attitude the enmity and hatred which have afflicted mankind so many centuries would be dispelled, fanaticism and bloodshed pass away and the world be blessed by unity and agreement. Christians and Muslims believe and admit that Moses was the Interlocutor of God. Why do you not say that Christ was the Word of God? Why do you not speak these few words that will do away with all this difficulty? Then there will be no more hatred and fanaticism, no more warfare and bloodshed in the Land of Promise. Then there will be peace among you forever.

19 Verily, I now declare to you that Moses was the Interlocutor of God and a most noteworthy Prophet, that Moses revealed the fundamental law of God and founded the real ethical basis of the civilization and progress of humanity. What harm is there in this? Have I lost anything by saying this to you and believing it as a Bahá'í? On the contrary, it benefits me; and Bahá'u'lláh, the Founder of the Bahá'í Movement, confirms me, saying, "You have been fair and just in your judgment; you have impartially

investigated the truth and arrived at a true conclusion; you have announced your belief in Moses, a Prophet of God, and accepted the Torah, the Book of God." Inasmuch as it is possible for me to sweep away all evidences of prejudice by such a liberal and universal statement of belief, why is it not possible for you to do likewise? Why not put an end to this religious strife and establish a bond of connection between the hearts of men? Why should not the followers of one religion praise the Founder or Teacher of another? The other religionists extol the greatness of Moses and admit that He was the Founder of Judaism. Why do the Hebrews refuse to praise and accept the other great Messengers Who have appeared in the world? What harm could there be in this? What rightful objection? None whatever. You would lose nothing by such action and statement. On the contrary, you would contribute to the welfare of mankind. You would be instrumental in establishing the happiness of the world of humanity. The eternal honor of man depends upon the liberalism of this modern age. Inasmuch as our God is one God and the Creator of all mankind, He provides for and protects all. We acknowledge Him as a God of kindness, justice and mercy. Why then should we, His children and followers, war and fight, bringing sorrow and grief into the hearts of each other? God is loving and merciful. His intention in religion has ever been the bond of unity and affinity between humankind.

Praise be to God! The medieval ages of darkness have passed 20 away and this century of radiance has dawned, this century wherein the reality of things is becoming evident, wherein science is penetrating the mysteries of the universe, the oneness of the world of humanity is being established, and service to mankind is the paramount motive of all existence. Shall we remain steeped in our fanaticisms and cling to our prejudices? Is it fitting that we should still be bound and restricted by ancient fables and superstitions of the past, be handicapped by superannuated beliefs and the ignorances of dark ages, waging religious wars, fighting and shedding blood, shunning and anathematizing each other? Is this becoming? Is it not better for us to be loving and considerate toward each other? Is it not preferable to enjoy fellowship and unity, join in anthems of praise to the most high God and extol all His Prophets in the spirit of acceptance and true vision? Then, indeed, this world will become a paradise, and the promised Day of God will dawn. Then, according to the prophecy of Isaiah, the wolf and the lamb will drink from the same stream, the owl and the vulture will nest together in the same branches, and the lion and the calf pasture in the same meadow. What does this mean? It means that fierce and contending religions, hostile creeds and divergent beliefs will reconcile and associate, notwithstanding their former hatreds and antagonism. Through the liberalism of human attitude demanded in this radiant century they will blend together in perfect fellowship and love. This is the spirit and meaning of Isaiah's words. There will never be a day when this prophecy will come to pass literally, for these animals by their natures cannot mingle and associate in kindness and love. Therefore, this prophecy symbolizes the unity and agreement of races, nations and peoples who will come together in attitudes of intelligence, illumination and spirituality.

21   The age has dawned when human fellowship will become a reality.

22   The century has come when all religions shall be unified.

23   The dispensation is at hand when all nations shall enjoy the blessings of international peace.

24   The cycle has arrived when racial prejudice will be abandoned by tribes and peoples of the world.

25   The epoch has begun wherein all native lands will be conjoined in one great human family.

For all mankind shall dwell in peace and security beneath the   26
shelter of the great tabernacle of the one living God.

5

25 October 1912

Talk at Hotel Sacramento
Sacramento, California

NOTES BY BIJOU STRAUN

WHEN Christ appeared, certain blessed souls followed His ex-   1
ample. They were with their Master, ever watching and observ-
ing His conduct, movements and thoughts. They witnessed the
persecutions which were heaped upon Him and were informed
of all the events appertaining to that marvelous life—recipients
of His kindness and favors. After the ascension of Christ they
hastened to various regions of the world, scattering broadcast the
teachings and instructions which He had given them. Through
their devotion and efforts other places and remote nations became
informed of the principles revealed by Him.

    Through their instrumentality the East was illumined, and   2
the light which flooded the East flooded the West. This light
was the cause of guiding great hosts of people. It proved to be
a preventive of warfare in many instances. This is evidenced in
the unification and conjoining of various nations which had formerly been hostile to each other—such as the Greeks, Romans,
Egyptians, Syrians, Chaldeans and Assyrians. Through Christ
the oneness of the world of humanity received its expression and
proved to be the cause of spiritual illumination for mankind.

The breaths of the Holy Spirit became effective in the hearts of people.

3   Now we have, likewise, come from the Orient, announcing the appearance of Bahá'u'lláh, Who shone from the horizon of the East. We have observed His life and beheld His deeds. We have been witnesses of His ordeals and sufferings, observers of His imprisonment and exile. We are fully acquainted with the persecutions heaped upon His blessed Personality. Therefore, we who are His disciples have been scattered throughout the world in order that His teachings may be widespread and be heard by every ear. Thus may the people receive the glad tidings of the dawn of His great dispensation, become aware of the divine evidences manifest in Him, be informed of the wonderful episodes of His marvelous life, the greatness of His power in withstanding the kings of the Orient, the might of His spirit in upholding under all circumstances the standard of the oneness of the world of mankind. Perchance you have heard or read of Him. I will give you a brief epitome of His life in order that you may be informed of the history of His great movement and know His teachings.

4   Bahá'u'lláh was a Persian personage descended from prominent lineage. During His early years a Youth Whose name was 'Alí-Muḥammad appeared in Persia. He was entitled the Báb, which means *door* or *gate*. The bearer of this title was a great Soul from Whom spiritual signs and evidences became manifest. He withstood the tests of time and lived contrary to the custom and usages of Persia. He revealed a new system of faith opposed to the beliefs in His country and promulgated certain principles contrary to the thoughts of the people. For this, that remarkable Personality was imprisoned by the Persian government. Eventually, by order of the government He was martyred. The account of this martyrdom, briefly stated, is as follows: He was suspended in a square as a target and shot to death. This

revered Personage foreshadowed the advent of another Soul of Whom He said, "When He cometh He shall reveal greater things unto you."

Thus, after the martyrdom of the Báb, Bahá'u'lláh appeared. 5 The government arose against Him. The priesthood in Persia opposed Him, subjecting Him to severe persecution. His possessions were confiscated, His relatives and friends were killed, and He was placed in a dungeon. For a long period He was imprisoned, chained and subjected to severest suffering. Afterward, He was exiled to 'Iráq, or Mesopotamia, from thence to Constantinople, then transferred to Adrianople and finally to 'Akká in Syria. He spent twenty-four years in the prison of 'Akká, where He underwent the severest ordeals and privations without a day or night of relaxation and repose. Notwithstanding this imprisonment and suffering, He manifested utmost spiritual power and majesty. Although imprisoned, He withstood two tyrant kings and eventually overcame both.

Shortly after His imprisonment He addressed Epistles, or Tab- 6 lets, to all the kings and rulers of the world, summoning them to universal peace, to unity and international brotherhood. Among these sovereigns was the Sháh of Persia, through whose instrumentality chiefly He had been imprisoned. In His letter to that ruler He arraigned him severely and prophesied his downfall, saying, "Thou art a tyrant; thy country will be laid waste; and thy family, humiliated and debased." He wrote to the Sultán of Turkey in similar terms, saying, "Thy dominion will pass away from thee." The Epistles to the kings and rulers summoning them to international peace were written by Bahá'u'lláh fifty years ago. Everything He wrote has come to pass. These letters were published in Bombay thirty years ago and are now spread broadcast throughout the world. Briefly, Bahá'u'lláh endured forty years of vicissitudes, ordeals and hardships for the purpose of spreading His teachings, which may be mentioned as follows:

7   The first teaching is that man should investigate reality, for reality is contrary to dogmatic interpretations and imitations of ancestral forms of belief to which all nations and peoples adhere so tenaciously. These blind imitations are contrary to the fundamental basis of the divine religions, for the divine religions in their central and essential teaching are based upon unity, love and peace, whereas these variations and imitations have ever been productive of warfare, sedition and strife. Therefore, all souls should consider it incumbent upon them to investigate reality. Reality is one; and when found, it will unify all mankind. Reality is the love of God. Reality is the knowledge of God. Reality is justice. Reality is the oneness or solidarity of mankind. Reality is international peace. Reality is the knowledge of verities. Reality unifies humanity.

8   In brief, His theme was that reality underlies all the great religious systems of the world. He summoned the nations and peoples of the world to it. Hostile nations because of their acceptance of the reality of His words became unified. Strife, discord and contention among them passed away; they attained a station of utmost love. At present in Asia those who have accepted His teachings and followed His example, although formerly most hostile and bitter toward each other, now associate in brotherhood and fellowship. The strife and warfare of past times have ceased among them. Jews, Zoroastrians, Christians, Muslims and others have attained to a superlative state of love and agreement through Bahá'u'lláh. They now consort together as one family. They have investigated reality. Reality does not accept multiplicity, nor is it subject to divisibility. These irreconcilable peoples have become unified and agreed.

9   The second teaching of Bahá'u'lláh is the principle of the oneness of the world of humanity. God is one; His servants are, likewise, one. God has created all; He is kind to all. Inasmuch as He is such a tender Father to all, why should His children

disagree? Why should they war and fight? Like the Heavenly Father we must live in love and unity. Man is the temple of God, the image and likeness of the Lord. Surely if one should destroy the temple of God, he will incur the displeasure of the Creator. For this reason, we must live together in amity and love. Bahá'u'lláh has addressed the world of humanity, saying, "Verily, ye are the fruits of one tree and the leaves of one branch." This signifies that the entire world of humanity is one tree. The various nations and peoples are the branches of that tree. Individual members of mankind are represented by the twigs and blossoms. Why should these parts of the same tree manifest strife and discord toward each other?

The third teaching of Bahá'u'lláh concerns universal peace 10 among the nations, among the religions, among the races and native lands. He has declared that so long as prejudice—whether religious, racial, patriotic, political or sectarian—continues to exist among mankind, universal peace cannot become a reality in the world. From the earliest history of man down to the present time all the wars and bloodshed which have taken place were caused either by religious, racial, political or sectarian bias. Therefore, it is evident that so long as these prejudices continue, the world of humanity cannot attain peace and composure.

Among the teachings of Bahá'u'lláh is His declaration that 11 religion must be the cause of love and fellowship, must be the source of unity in the hearts of men. If religion becomes a cause of enmity and hatred, it is evident that the abolition of religion is preferable to its promulgation; for religion is a remedy for human ills. If a remedy should be productive of disease, it is certainly advisable to abandon it.

Furthermore, the teachings of Bahá'u'lláh announce that reli- 12 gion must be in conformity with science and reason; otherwise, it is superstition; for science and reason are realities, and religion itself is the Divine Reality unto which true science and reason

527

must conform. God has bestowed the gift of mind upon man in order that he may weigh every fact or truth presented to him and adjudge whether it be reasonable. That which conforms to his reason he may accept as true, while that which reason and science cannot sanction may be discarded as imagination and superstition, as a phantom and not reality. Inasmuch as the blind imitations or dogmatic interpretations current among men do not coincide with the postulates of reason, and the mind and scientific investigation cannot acquiesce thereto, many souls in the human world today shun and deny religion. That is to say, imitations, when weighed in the scales of reason, will not conform to its standard and requirement. Therefore, these souls deny religion and become irreligious, whereas if the reality of the divine religions becomes manifest to them and the foundation of the heavenly teachings is revealed coinciding with facts and evident truths, reconciling with scientific knowledge and reasonable proof, all may acknowledge them, and irreligion will cease to exist. In this way all mankind may be brought to the foundation of religion, for reality is true reason and science, while all that is not conformable thereto is mere superstition.

13   The teachings of Bahá'u'lláh also proclaim equality between man and woman, for He has declared that all are the servants of God and endowed with capacity for the attainment of virtues and bestowals. All are the manifestations of the mercy of the Lord. In the creation of God no distinction obtains. All are His servants. In the estimation of God there is no gender. The one whose deeds are more worthy, whose sayings are better, whose accomplishments are more useful is nearest and dearest in the estimation of God, be that one male or female. When we look upon creation, we find the male and female principle apparent in all phenomena of existence. In the vegetable kingdom we find the male and female fig tree, the male and female palm, the mulberry tree and so on. All plant life is characterized by

this difference in gender, but no distinction or preference is evidenced. Nay, rather, there is perfect equality. Likewise, in the animal kingdom gender obtains; we have male and female, but no distinction or preference. Perfect equality is manifest. The animal, bereft of the degree of human reason and comprehension, is unable to appreciate the questions of suffrage, nor does it assert its prerogative. Man, endowed with his higher reason, accomplished in attainments and comprehending the realities of things, will surely not be willing to allow a great part of humanity to remain defective or deprived. This would be the utmost injustice. The world of humanity is possessed of two wings: the male and the female. So long as these two wings are not equivalent in strength, the bird will not fly. Until womankind reaches the same degree as man, until she enjoys the same arena of activity, extraordinary attainment for humanity will not be realized; humanity cannot wing its way to heights of real attainment. When the two wings or parts become equivalent in strength, enjoying the same prerogatives, the flight of man will be exceedingly lofty and extraordinary. Therefore, woman must receive the same education as man and all inequality be adjusted. Thus, imbued with the same virtues as man, rising through all the degrees of human attainment, women will become the peers of men, and until this equality is established, true progress and attainment for the human race will not be facilitated.

The evident reasons underlying this are as follows: Woman 14 by nature is opposed to war; she is an advocate of peace. Children are reared and brought up by the mothers who give them the first principles of education and labor assiduously in their behalf. Consider, for instance, a mother who has tenderly reared a son for twenty years to the age of maturity. Surely she will not consent to having that son torn asunder and killed in the field of battle. Therefore, as woman advances toward the degree of man in power and privilege, with the right of vote and control in human government, most assuredly war will cease; for woman is naturally the most devoted and staunch advocate of international peace.

15 Bahá'u'lláh teaches that material civilization is incomplete, insufficient and that divine civilization must be established. Material civilization concerns the world of matter or bodies, but divine civilization is the realm of ethics and moralities. Until the moral degree of the nations is advanced and human virtues attain a lofty level, happiness for mankind is impossible. The philosophers have founded material civilization. The Prophets have founded divine civilization. Christ was the Founder of heavenly civilization. Mankind receives the bounties of material civilization as well as divine civilization from the heavenly Prophets. The capacity for achieving extraordinary and praiseworthy progress is bestowed by Them through the breaths of the Holy Spirit, and heavenly civilization is not possible of attainment or accomplishment otherwise. This evidences the need of humanity for heavenly bestowals, and until these heavenly bestowals are received, eternal happiness cannot be realized.

16 In brief, the purport is this: The teachings of Bahá'u'lláh are boundless, innumerable; time will not allow us to mention them in detail. The foundation of progress and real prosperity in the human world is reality, for reality is the divine standard and the bestowal of God. Reality is reasonableness, and reasonableness is ever conducive to the honorable station of man. Reality is the guidance of God. Reality is the cause of illumination of mankind. Reality is love, ever working for the welfare of humanity. Reality is the bond which conjoins hearts. This ever uplifts man toward higher stages of progress and attainment. Reality is the unity of mankind, conferring everlasting life. Reality is perfect equality, the foundation of agreement between the nations, the first step toward international peace.

6

26 October 1912

Talk at Assembly Hall, Hotel Sacramento
Sacramento, California

NOTES BY BIJOU STRAUN

I HAVE visited your Capitol and its gardens. No other Capitol   1
has such beautiful surroundings. Just as it is imposing and
distinguished above all others, so may the people of California
become the most exalted and perfect altruists of the world.
California is, indeed, a blessed country. The climate is temperate, the sun ever shining, the fruits abundant and delicious. All
outer blessings are evident here. The Californians are a noble
people; therefore, I hope they may make extraordinary progress
and become renowned for their virtues.

The issue of paramount importance in the world today is   2
international peace. The European continent is like an arsenal,
a storehouse of explosives ready for ignition, and one spark will
set the whole of Europe aflame, particularly at this time when
the Balkan question is before the world. Even now war is raging furiously in some places, the blood of innocent people is
being shed, children are made captive, women are left without
support, and homes are being destroyed. Therefore, the greatest
need in the world today is international peace. The time is ripe.
It is time for the abolition of warfare, the unification of nations
and governments. It is the time for love. It is time for cementing
together the East and the West.

Inasmuch as the Californians seem peace loving and possessed   3
of great worthiness and capacity, I hope that advocates of peace

may daily increase among them until the whole population shall stand for that beneficent outcome. May the men of affairs in this democracy uphold the standard of international concilia- tion. Then may altruistic aims and thoughts radiate from this center toward all other regions of the earth, and may the glory of this accomplishment forever halo the history of this country. May the first flag of international peace be upraised in this state. May the first illumination of reality shine gloriously upon this soil. May this center and capital become distinguished in all degrees of accomplishment, for the virtues of humanity and the possibilities of human advancement are boundless. There is no end to them, and whatever be the degree to which humanity may attain, there are always degrees beyond. There is no attain- ment in the contingent realm of which it may be said, "Beyond this state of being and perfection there is no other," or "This has achieved the superlative degree." No matter how perfect it may appear, there is always a greater degree of attainment to be reached. Therefore, no matter how much humanity may advance, there are ever higher stations to be attained because virtues are unlimited. There is a consummation for everything except virtues, and although this country has achieved extraordinary progress, I hope that its attainment may be immeasurably greater, for the divine bounties are infinite and unlimited.

4   There are some who believe that the divine bounties are subject to cessation. For example, they think that the revela- tion of God, the effulgence of God and the bounties of God have ended. This is self-evidently a mistaken idea, for none of these is subject to termination. The reality of Divinity is like unto the sun, and revelation is like unto the rays thereof. If we should assert that the bounties of God are not everlasting, we are forced to believe that Divinity can come to an end, whereas the reality of Divinity enfolds all virtues and by reason of these bounties is perfect. Were it not possessed of all these perfections

or virtues, it could not be Divinity. The sun is the sun because of its rays, light and heat. If it could be dispossessed of them, it would not be the sun. Therefore, if we say that the divinity or sovereignty of God is accidental and subject to termination, we must perforce think that Divinity itself is accidental, without foundation and not essential.

God is the Creator. The word *creator* presupposes or con- 5 notes creation. God is the Provider. The word *provider* implies recipients of provision. Another name for the Creator is the Resuscitator, which demands the existence of creatures to be resuscitated. If He be not the Provider, how could we conceive of creatures to receive His bounty? If He be not the Lord, how could we conceive of subjects? If He be not the Knower, how could we conceive of those known? If we should say that there was a time in past ages when God was not possessed of His creation or that there was a beginning for the world, it would be a denial of creation and the Creator. Or if we should declare that a time may come when there will be a cessation of divine bounties, we should virtually deny the existence of Divinity. It is as though man should conceive of a king without country, army, treasury and all that constitutes sovereignty or kingdom. Is it possible to conceive of such a sovereign? A king must be possessed of a dominion, an army and all that appertains to sovereignty in order that his sovereignty may be a reality. It is even so with the reality of Divinity which enfolds all virtues. The sovereignty thereof is everlasting, and the creation thereof is without beginning and without end.

Among the bounties of God is revelation. Hence revelation 6 is progressive and continuous. It never ceases. It is necessary that the reality of Divinity with all its perfections and attributes should become resplendent in the human world. The reality of Divinity is like an endless ocean. Revelation may be likened to the rain. Can you imagine the cessation of rain? Ever on the face of the earth somewhere rain is pouring down. Briefly, the world of existence is progressive. It is subject to development and growth. Consider how great has been the progress in this radiant century. Civilization has unfolded. Nations have developed. Industrialism and jurisprudence have expanded. Sciences, inventions and discoveries have increased. All of these show that the world of existence is continuously progressing and developing; and therefore, assuredly, the virtues characterizing the maturity of man must, likewise, expand and grow.

7   The greatest bestowal of God to man is the capacity to attain human virtues. Therefore, the teachings of religion must be reformed and renewed because past teachings are not suitable for the present time. For example, the sciences of bygone centuries are not adequate for the present because sciences have undergone reform. The industrialism of the past will not ensure present efficiency because industrialism has advanced. The laws of the past are being superseded because they are not applicable to this time. All material conditions pertaining to the world of humanity have undergone reform, have achieved development, and the institutes of the past are not to be compared with those of this age. The laws and institutes of former governments cannot be current today, for legislation must be in conformity with the needs and requirements of the body politic at this time.

8   This has been the case also with the religious teachings so long set forth in the temples and churches, because they were not based upon the fundamental principles of the religions of God. In other words, the foundation of the divine religions had become obscured and nonessentials of form and ceremony were adhered to—that is, the kernel of religion had apparently disappeared, and only the shell remained. Consequently, it was necessary that the fundamental basis of all religious teaching should be restored, that the Sun of Reality which had set should rise again, that the springtime which had refreshed the arena

of life in ages gone by should appear anew, that the rain which had ceased should descend, that the breezes which had become stilled should blow once more.

Therefore, Bahá'u'lláh appeared from the horizon of the Orient and reestablished the essential foundation of the religious teachings of the world. The worn-out traditional beliefs current among men were removed. He caused fellowship and agreement to exist between the representatives of varying denominations so that love became manifest among the contending religions. He created a condition of harmony among hostile sects and upheld the banner of the oneness of the world of humanity. He established the foundation for international peace, caused the hearts of nations to be cemented together and conferred new life upon the various peoples of the East. Among those who have followed the teachings of Bahá'u'lláh no one says, "I am a Persian," "I am a Turk," "I am a Frenchman," or "I am an Englishman." No one says, "I am a Muslim, upholding the only true religion," "I am a Christian, loyal to my traditional and inherited beliefs," "I am a Jew, following talmudic interpretations," or "I am a Zoroastrian and opposed to all other religions." On the contrary, all have been rescued from religious, racial, political and patriotic prejudices and are now associating in fellowship and love to the extent that if you should attend one of their meetings you would be unable to observe any distinction between Christian and Muslim, Jew and Zoroastrian, Persian and Turk, Arab and European; for their meetings are based upon the essential foundations of religion, and real unity has been established among them. Former antagonisms have passed away; the centuries of sectarian hatred are ended; the period of aversion has gone by; the medieval conditions of ignorance have ceased to exist.

Verily, the century of radiance has dawned, minds are advanc- 10 ing, perceptions are broadening, realizations of human possibilities are becoming universal, susceptibilities are developing, the discovery of realities is progressing. Therefore, it is necessary that we should cast aside all the prejudices of ignorance, discard superannuated beliefs in traditions of past ages and raise aloft the banner of international agreement. Let us cooperate in love and through spiritual reciprocity enjoy eternal happiness and peace.

Talks 'Abdu'l-Bahá Delivered in Chicago

31 October 1912

Talk at Hotel Plaza
Chicago, Illinois

NOTES BY GERTRUDE BUIKEMA

IN Los Angeles and San Francisco great interest was manifested 1 in the teachings of Bahá'u'lláh by the newspapers, universities and churches. Our addresses were lengthy, the message of the Cause was proclaimed and arguments and evidences advanced. There was no dissent. All heard the glad tidings with complete acquiescence, and praise was unanimous, even including the ministers.

The friends in Los Angeles and San Francisco are very firm 2 in the Covenant. If they sense the least violation on the part of anyone, they shun him entirely; for they know that such a person is engaged in extinguishing the lamps of faith ignited by the light of the Covenant, thereby producing weakness and indifference in the divine Cause. For instance, the firm ones teach a person. Then the violators go to him and instill suspicion until he becomes lukewarm. There have been violators here in Chicago for twenty years. What have they done? Nothing. Have they been able to teach anybody? Have they been able to speak in churches or address audiences elsewhere? Have they been able to make anybody firm in the Cause? They are doing nothing except extinguishing the lamps we ignite. The friends in San Francisco are exceedingly firm. They do not receive violators in their homes. Recently a violator went to that city. The

Bahá'í friends turned him away, saying, "You are not with us; why do you try to come among us?" Today the most important principle of faith is firmness in the Covenant, because firmness in the Covenant wards off differences. Therefore, you must be firm as mountains.

3   After the departure of Christ many appeared who were instrumental in creating factions, schisms and discussions. It became difficult to know which one was following the right path. One of these disturbers was Nestorius, a Syrian, who proclaimed that Christ was not a Prophet of God. This created a division and sect called the Nestorians. The Catholics declared Jesus Christ to be the Son of God, even pronouncing Him to be Deity itself. The Protestants announced the doctrine that Christ embodied two elements: the human and the divine. In brief, divisions were created in the religion of God, and it was not known which was pursuing the right pathway because there was no appointed center to whom Christ referred everyone, no successor whose word was a gateway to the truth. If Christ had revealed a Covenant with some soul, commanding all to cling to his word and interpretation as correct, it would have been evident which belief and statement was valid and true.

4   Inasmuch as there was no appointed explainer of the Book of Christ, everyone made the claim to authority, saying, "This is the true pathway and others are not." To ward off such dissensions as these and prevent any person from creating a division or sect the Blessed Perfection, Bahá'u'lláh, appointed a central authoritative Personage, declaring Him to be the expounder of the Book. This implies that the people in general do not understand the meanings of the Book, but this appointed One does understand. Therefore, Bahá'u'lláh said, "He is the explainer of My Book and the Center of My Testament." In the last verses of the Book instructions are revealed, declaring that, "After Me,"

you must turn toward a special Personage and "whatsoever He says is correct." In the Book of the Covenant Bahá'u'lláh declares that by these two verses this Personage is meant. In all His Books and Tablets He has praised those who are firm in the Covenant and rebuked those who are not. He said, "Verily, shun those who are shaken in the Covenant. Verily, God is the Confirmer of the firm ones." In His prayers He has said, "O God! Render those who are firm in the Covenant blessed, and degrade those who are not. O God! Be the Protector of him who protecteth Him, and confirm him who confirms the Center of the Covenant." Many utterances are directed against the violators of the Covenant, the purpose being that no dissension should arise in the blessed Cause; that no one should say, "My opinion is this"; and that all may know Who is the authoritative expounder and whatsoever He says is correct. Bahá'u'lláh has not left any possible room for dissension. Naturally, there are some who are antagonistic, some who are followers of self-desire, others who hold to their own ideas and still others who wish to create dissension in the Cause. For example, Judas Iscariot was one of the disciples, yet he betrayed Christ. Such a thing has happened in the past, but in this day the Blessed Perfection has declared, "This person is the expounder of My Book and all must turn to Him." The purpose is to ward off dissension and differences among His followers. Notwithstanding this safeguard and provision against disagreement, there are certain souls here in America and a few in 'Akká who have violated this explicit command. For twenty years these violators have accomplished nothing. Have they accomplished anything in Chicago? The friends here must be like the friends in San Francisco. Whenever they sense the least violation from anyone, they should say, "Begone! You shall not associate with us."

2

1 November 1912

Talk at Home of Mrs. Corinne True
5338 Kenmore Avenue, Chicago, Illinois

NOTES BY GERTRUDE BUIKEMA

1   I AM well pleased with every person here this evening and most happy in meeting the friends of God and maidservants of the Merciful. Praise be to God! The faces are radiant, and the hearts are attracted to the Kingdom of Abhá. Faith is evident in the countenances of all, and this is a source of joy. The Blessed Perfection, Bahá'u'lláh, endured hardships and vicissitudes nearly fifty years. There was no ordeal or difficulty He did not experience, yet He endured all in perfect joy and happiness.

2   Those who beheld Him were assured of His great happiness, for no trace of sadness or sorrow was ever visible upon His face. Even in prison He was like a king enthroned in majesty and greatness, and He ever bore Himself with supreme confidence and dignity. When the officers and grandees of the government were presented to Him, they became respectful at once. His majesty and dignity were awe-inspiring. Remember: He was a prisoner—He was in prison. He endured ordeals and calamities for the sole purpose of illuminating us and in order that our hearts might be attracted to the Kingdom of God, our faces become radiant with the glad tidings of God; in order that we might be submerged in the ocean of lights and be as brilliant and shining candles, illuminating the dark recesses and flooding the regions with brightness. Now, as I look around, I observe that your faces—praise be to God!—are shining, your hearts

are filled with the love of God, and you are thinking of service in the Cause of God. Therefore, I am very happy to be here, and I hope that this happiness will be with you always—an eternal condition.

We visited San Francisco and from there went to Los Angeles. 3 In these places we found most devoted friends. Truly zealous and aglow with the fire of the love of God, their sole purpose is ever to serve the Kingdom of Abhá. I hope that you may serve even more faithfully and take precedence over all the other friends. May the fire of the love of God be so enkindled in Chicago that all the cities in America shall be ignited. This is my hope.

My third visit here expresses the degree of my longing to see 4 you and the extent of my love. It was thought that I should go direct from San Francisco to New York and thence to the Orient; but impelled by excessive love, I have visited Chicago again to associate with you in fellowship and fragrance. I hope that these three visits may be most productive of future results. May you all become signs of unity; may each one be a standard of Bahá'u'lláh, each one shine as a star, each one become precious and worthy in the Kingdom of God. May you attain such a condition of spirituality that the people will be astounded, saying, "Verily, these souls are proofs in themselves of the validity of Bahá'u'lláh, for through His training they have been completely regenerated. These souls are peerless; they are truly the people of the Kingdom; they are distinguished above the people about them. This is in reality a proof of Bahá'u'lláh. Behold how educated and illumined they have become."

When this Cause appeared in the Orient, the friends and fol- 5 lowers were self-sacrificing to the utmost, forfeiting everything. It is a significant and wonderful fact that, although the most precious thing on earth is life, yet twenty thousand people offered themselves willingly in the pathway of martyrdom. Recently, in Yazd two hundred of the Bahá'í friends were cruelly slain. They went to the place of martyrdom in the utmost ecstasy of attraction, smiling with joy and gratitude upon their persecutors. Some of them offered sweetmeats to their executioners, saying, "Taste of this in order that with sweetness and enjoyment you may bestow upon us the blessed cup of martyrdom." Among these beloved and glorified ones were a number of women who were subjected to the most cruel manner of execution. Some were cut to pieces; and their executioners, not content with such butchery, set others on fire, and their bodies were consumed. Throughout these terrible ordeals not a single soul among the Bahá'í friends objected or recanted. They offered no resistance, although the Bahá'ís in that city were most courageous and strong. In physical strength and fortitude one of these Bahá'ís could have withstood many of their enemies, but they accepted martyrdom in the spirit of complete resignation and nonresistance. Many of them died, crying out, "O Lord! Forgive them; they know not what they do. If they knew, they would not commit this wrong." In the throes of martyrdom they willingly offered all they possessed in this life.

6   It is stated in certain prophecies that when the standard of God appears in the East, its signs will become evident in the West. This is truly good news and glad tidings for you. I hope that this promise may be fulfilled in you and that all may be able to testify to the spirit and truth of the prophetic announcement, saying, "Verily, the standard of God did appear in the East, and its tokens have become resplendent in the West." This realization will be a source of great joy to all the friends in the Orient who anticipate the good news and await the glad tidings from the land of the Occident. They look forward to hearing that the friends in the West have become firm and steadfast, that they have distinguished themselves by establishing the oneness of the

world of humanity, that they are even offering their lives for the foundations of international peace, that they have become the lights of the Kingdom and have proved to be the manifestations of divine mercy, that the friends in the West are the expression of the favors of the Blessed Perfection, the very stars of the bestowal of God, blessed trees and flowers in the garden of His purity and sanctity. Any good news from here is the cause of rejoicing in the East and a source of deep gratitude to them. They hold a feast and praise God for the blessed tidings. If the occasion demanded, they would give their lives for you without the least hesitation. The friends in the East are all united and agreed.

There are none who waver in the East, none who oppose 7 the Covenant of God. There is not a single soul among the Bahá'ís in Persia who is opposed to the Covenant. They are all steadfast. If any soul wishes to speak in this Cause, they will ask, "Is this a word of your own, or is it by the authority of the Center of the Covenant? If you have the authority of the Center of the Covenant, produce it. Where is the letter from Him? Where is His signature?" If he produces the letter, they will accept it. If he fails to do so, they say, "We cannot accept your words because they emanate from you only and return to you. We have no command from the Blessed Perfection, Bahá'u'lláh, to obey you. He has revealed a Book in which He has covenanted with us to obey an appointed Center of the Covenant. He has not covenanted with us to obey you. Therefore, the statement you make is rejected. You must furnish proof of your authority and sanction. We are commanded to turn to one Center. We do not obey various centers. The Blessed Perfection has made a Covenant with us, and we are holding to this Covenant and Testament. We do not listen to anything else, for people may arise who speak words of their own, and we are commanded not to pay attention to them."

8   It was not so in former dispensations. Christ, for instance, did not appoint a center of authority and explanation. He did not say to His followers, "Obey the one whom I have chosen." Upon one occasion He asked His disciples, "Whom say ye that I am?" Simon Peter answered and said, "Thou art the Christ, the Son of the living God." Christ, wishing to make firm the faith of Peter, said, "Thou art Peter, and upon this rock I will build my church," meaning that the faith of Peter was the true faith. It was a sanction of Peter's faith. He did not say that all should turn to Peter. He did not say, "He is the branch extended from my ancient root." He did not say, "O God! Bless all who serve Peter. O God! Degrade those who are not obedient to him. Shun him who is a violator of the Covenant. O God! Thou knowest that I love all who are steadfast in the Covenant." This has been revealed, however, in all the Books, Writings and Epistles of Bahá'u'lláh regarding the appointed Center of the Covenant in this dispensation. Therefore, the Bahá'í dispensation is distinguished from all others in this fact, the purpose of Bahá'u'lláh being that no one could arise to cause differences and disunion. After the departure of Christ various sects and denominations arose, each one claiming to be the true channel of Christianity, but none of them possessed a written authority from Christ; none could produce proof from Him; yet all claimed His sanction and approval. Bahá'u'lláh has written a Covenant and Testament with His own pen, declaring that the One Whom He has appointed the Center of the Covenant shall be turned to and obeyed by all. Therefore, thank God that Bahá'u'lláh has made the pathway straight. He has clearly explained all things and opened every door for advancing souls. There is no reason for hesitation by anyone. The purpose of the Covenant was simply to ward off disunion and differences so that no one might say, "My opinion is the true and valid one."

9   Any opinion expressed by the Center of the Covenant is correct, and there is no reason for disobedience by anyone. Be

watchful, for perchance there may be violators (*náqidín*) of the Covenant among you. Do not listen to them. Read the Book of the Covenant. All have been commanded to obey the Covenant, and the first admonition is addressed to the sons of Bahá'u'lláh, the Branches: "You must turn to the appointed Center; He is the expounder of the Book."

Should any soul so clearly violate and disobey this command, 10 can he even say he is a Bahá'í? If anyone disobeys the explicit command of Christ, can he truthfully say he is a Christian?

In conclusion, I would say that I am greatly pleased with 11 this meeting. I shall pray for you, seeking confirmation from the Blessed Perfection. Praise be to God! You must be grateful that He has chosen you from among the people of the world, that such glorious bestowal and such endless graces and favors have been specialized for you. You must not look at present accomplishments, for this is but the beginning as it was at the time of Christ. Before long you will see that you will be distinguished among all people. In every way the divine confirmation will uphold you, and the radiance of the Kingdom of Bahá'u'lláh will illumine your countenances. Be truly grateful for all these blessings. I hope I may always hear good news of you, showing that the friends in Chicago are occupied with service in the divine Cause, filled with the joy of promoting the Word of God, engaged in spreading the teachings of Bahá'u'lláh and manifesting love and kindness to all humanity. This is my hope and anticipation. I am sure that you will endeavor to accomplish this so that the friends in Persia and I may experience the happiness of the good tidings. May you be a source of joy and happiness to us, a source of tranquillity and composure.

Talk 'Abdu'l-Bahá Delivered in Cincinnati

5 November 1912

Talk at Grand Hotel
Cincinnati, Ohio

FROM STENOGRAPHIC NOTES

As we are in Cincinnati, the home of President Taft, who has   1
rendered such noble service in the cause of peace, I will dictate a
statement for the people of Cincinnati and America generally. In
the Orient I was informed that there are many lovers of peace in
America. Therefore, I left my native land to associate here with
those who are the standard-bearers of international conciliation
and agreement. Having traveled from coast to coast, I find the
United States of America vast and progressive, the government
just and equitable, the nation noble and independent. I attended
many meetings where international peace was discussed and am
always extremely happy to witness the results of such meetings,
for one of the great principles of Bahá'u'lláh's teachings is the
establishment of agreement among the peoples of the world.
He founded and taught this principle in the Orient fifty years
ago. He proclaimed international unity, summoned the religions
of the world to harmony and reconciliation and established
fellowship among many races, sects and communities. At that
time He wrote Epistles to the kings and rulers of the world,
calling upon them to arise and cooperate with Him in spreading these principles, saying that the stability and advancement
of humanity could only be realized through the unity of the
nations. Through His efforts this principle of universal harmony
and agreement was practically demonstrated in Persia and other

countries. Today in Persia, for instance, there are many people of various races and religions who have followed the exhortations of Bahá'u'lláh and are living together in love and fellowship without religious, patriotic or racial prejudices—Muslims, Jews, Christians, Buddhists, Zoroastrians and many others.

2   America has arisen to spread the teachings of peace, to increase the illumination of humankind and bestow happiness and prosperity upon the children of men. These are the principles and evidences of divine civilization. America is a noble nation, the standard-bearer of peace throughout the world, shedding light to all regions. Foreign nations are not untrammeled and free from intrigues and complications like the United States; therefore, they are not able to bring about universal harmony. But America—praise be to God!—is at peace with all the world and is worthy of raising the flag of brotherhood and international agreement. When this is done, the rest of the world will accept. All nations will join in adopting the teachings of Bahá'u'lláh revealed more than fifty years ago. In His Epistles He asked the parliaments of the world to send their wisest and best men to an international world conference which should decide all questions between the peoples and establish universal peace. This would be the highest court of appeal, and the parliament of man so long dreamed of by poets and idealists would be realized. Its accomplishment would be more far-reaching than the Hague tribunal.

3   I am most grateful to President Taft for having extended his influence toward the establishment of universal peace. What he has accomplished in making treaties with various nations is very good, but when we have the interparliamentary body composed of delegates from all the nations of the world and devoted to the maintenance of agreement and goodwill, the utopian dream of sages and poets, the parliament of man, will be realized.

Talks 'Abdu'l-Bahá Delivered in Washington, D.C.

6 November 1912

Talk at Universalist Church
Thirteenth and L Streets, NW, Washington, D.C.

NOTES BY JOSEPH H. HANNEN

PRAISE be to God! The standard of liberty is held aloft in this land. You enjoy political liberty; you enjoy liberty of thought and speech, religious liberty, racial and personal liberty. Surely this is worthy of appreciation and thanksgiving. In this connection let me mention the freedom, hospitality and universal welcome extended to me during my recent travels throughout America. I wish also to reciprocate fully and completely the warm greeting and friendly attitude of the reverend doctor, pastor of this church, whose loving and quickened susceptibilities especially command acknowledgment. Surely men who are leaders of thought must conform to the example of his kindliness and goodwill. Liberalism is essential in this day—justness and equity toward all nations and people. Human attitudes must not be limited; for God is unlimited, and whosoever is the servant of the threshold of God must, likewise, be free from limitations. The world of existence is an emanation of the merciful attribute of God. God has shone forth upon the phenomena of being through His effulgence of mercy, and He is clement and kind to all His creation. Therefore, the world of humanity must ever be the recipient of bounties from His majesty, the eternal Lord, even as Christ has declared, "Be ye therefore perfect, even as your

1

549

Father which is in heaven is perfect." For His bounties, like the
light and heat of the sun in the material heavens, descend alike
upon all mankind. Consequently, man must learn the lesson of
kindness and beneficence from God Himself. Just as God is kind
to all humanity, man also must be kind to his fellow creatures.
If his attitude is just and loving toward his fellowmen, toward
all creation, then indeed is he worthy of being pronounced the
image and likeness of God.

2   Brotherhood, or fraternity, is of different kinds. It may be
family association, the intimate relationship of the household.
This is limited and subject to change and disruption. How often
it happens that in a family love and agreement are changed into
enmity and antagonism. Another form of fraternity is manifest
in patriotism. Man loves his fellowmen because they belong to
the same native land. This is also limited and subject to change
and disintegration as, for instance, when sons of the same fatherland are opposed to each other in war, bloodshed and battle.
Still another brotherhood, or fraternity, is that which arises from
racial unity, the oneness of racial origin, producing ties of affinity
and association. This, likewise, has its limitation and liability
to change, for often war and deadly strife have been witnessed
between people and nations of the same racial lineage. There is
a fourth kind of brotherhood, the attitude of man toward humanity itself, the altruistic love of humankind and recognition
of the fundamental human bond. Although this is unlimited,
it is, nevertheless, susceptible to change and destruction. Even
from this universal fraternal bond the looked-for result does not
appear. What is the looked-for result? Loving-kindness among
all human creatures and a firm, indestructible brotherhood
which includes all the divine possibilities and significances
in humanity. Therefore, it is evident that fraternity, love and
kindness based upon family, native land, race or an attitude of

altruism are neither sufficient nor permanent since all of them are limited, restricted and liable to change and disruption. For in the family there is discord and alienation; among sons of the same fatherland, strife and internecine warfare are witnessed; between those of a given race, hostility and hatred are frequent; and even among the altruists, varying aspects of opinion and lack of unselfish devotion give little promise of permanent and indestructible unity among mankind.

Therefore, the Lord of mankind has caused His holy, divine 3 Manifestations to come into the world. He has revealed His heavenly Books in order to establish spiritual brotherhood and through the power of the Holy Spirit has made it practicable for perfect fraternity to be realized among mankind. And when through the breaths of the Holy Spirit this perfect fraternity and agreement are established amongst men—this brotherhood and love being spiritual in character, this loving-kindness being heavenly, these constraining bonds being divine—a unity appears which is indissoluble, unchanging and never subject to transformation. It is ever the same and will forever remain the same. For example, consider the foundation of the brotherhood laid by Christ. Observe how that fraternity was conducive to unity and accord and how it brought various souls to a plane of uniform attainment where they were willing to sacrifice their lives for each other. They were content to renounce possessions and ready to forfeit joyously life itself. They lived together in such love and fellowship that even Galen, the famous Greek philosopher who was not a Christian, in his work entitled "The Progress of the Nations" said that religious beliefs are greatly conducive to the foundation of real civilization. As a proof thereof he said, "A certain number of people contemporaneous with us are known as Christians. These enjoy the superlative degree of moral civilization. Each one of them is as a great philosopher because they live together in the utmost love and good fellowship. They sacrifice life for each other. They offer worldly possessions for each other. You can say of the Christian people that they are as one person. There is a bond amongst them that is indissoluble in character."

4   It is evident, therefore, that the foundation of real brotherhood, the cause of loving cooperation and reciprocity and the source of real kindness and unselfish devotion is none other than the breaths of the Holy Spirit. Without this influence and animus it is impossible. We may be able to realize some degrees of fraternity through other motives, but these are limited associations and subject to change. When human brotherhood is founded upon the Holy Spirit, it is eternal, changeless, unlimited.

5   In various parts of the Orient there was a time when brotherhood, loving-kindness and all the praiseworthy qualities of mankind seemed to have disappeared. There was no evidence of patriotic, religious or racial fraternity; but conditions of bigotry, hatred and prejudice prevailed instead. The adherents of each religion were violent enemies of the others, filled with the spirit of hostility and eager for shedding of blood. The present war in the Balkans furnishes a parallel of these conditions. Consider the bloodshed, ferocity and oppression manifested there even in this enlightened century—all of it based fundamentally upon religious prejudice and disagreement. For the nations involved belong to the same races and native lands; nevertheless, they are savage and merciless toward each other. Similar deplorable conditions prevailed in Persia in the nineteenth century. Darkness and ignorant fanaticism were widespread; no trace of fellowship or brotherhood existed amongst the races. On the contrary, human hearts were filled with rage and hatred; darkness and gloom were manifest in human lives and conditions everywhere. At such a time as this Bahá'u'lláh appeared upon the divine horizon, even as the glory of the sun, and in that gross darkness

and hopelessness of the human world there shone a great light. He founded the oneness of the world of humanity, declaring that all mankind are as sheep and that God is the real and true Shepherd. The Shepherd is one, and all people are of His flock.

The world of humanity is one, and God is equally kind to 6 all. What, then, is the source of unkindness and hatred in the human world? This real Shepherd loves all His sheep. He leads them in green pastures. He rears and protects them. What, then, is the source of enmity and alienation among humankind? Whence this conflict and strife? The real underlying cause is lack of religious unity and association, for in each of the great religions we find superstition, blind imitation of creeds, and theological formulas adhered to instead of the divine fundamentals, causing difference and divergence among mankind instead of agreement and fellowship. Consequently, strife, hatred and warfare have arisen, based upon this divergence and separation. If we investigate the foundations of the divine religions, we find them to be one, absolutely changeless and never subject to transformation. For example, each of the divine religions contains two kinds of laws or ordinances. One division concerns the world of morality and ethical institutions. These are the essential ordinances. They instill and awaken the knowledge and love of God, love for humanity, the virtues of the world of mankind, the attributes of the divine Kingdom, rebirth and resurrection from the kingdom of nature. These constitute one kind of divine law which is common to all and never subject to change. From the dawn of the Adamic cycle to the present day this fundamental law of God has continued changeless. This is the foundation of divine religion.

The second division comprises laws and institutions which 7 provide for human needs and conditions according to exigencies of time and place. These are accidental, of no essential importance and should never have been made the cause and

553

source of human contention. For example, during the time of Moses—upon Him be peace!—according to the exigencies of that period, divorce was permissible. During the cycle of Christ, inasmuch as divorce was not in conformity with the time and conditions, Jesus Christ abrogated it. In the cycle of Moses plurality of wives was permissible. But during the time of Christ the exigency which had sanctioned it did not exist; therefore, it was forbidden. Moses lived in the wilderness and desert of Sinai; therefore, His ordinances and commandments were in conformity with those conditions. The penalty for theft was to cut off a man's hand. An ordinance of this kind was in keeping with desert life but is not compatible with conditions of the present day. Such ordinances, therefore, constitute the second or nonessential division of the divine religions and are not of importance, for they deal with human transactions which are ever changing according to the requirements of time and place. Therefore, the intrinsic foundations of the divine religions are one. As this is true, why should hostility and strife exist among them? Why should this hatred and warfare, ferocity and bloodshed continue? Is this allowable and justified? God forbid!

8   An essential principle of Bahá'u'lláh's teaching is that religion must be the cause of unity and love amongst men; that it is the supreme effulgence of Divinity, the stimulus of life, the source of honor and productive of eternal existence. Religion is not intended to arouse enmity and hatred nor to become the source of tyranny and injustice. Should it prove to be the cause of hostility, discord and the alienation of mankind, assuredly the absence of religion would be preferable. Religious teachings are like a course of treatment having for its purpose the cure and healing of mankind. If the only outcome of a course of treatment should be mere diagnosis and fruitless discussion of symptoms, it would be better to abandon and abolish it. In this

sense the absence of religion would be at least some progress toward unity.

Furthermore, religion must conform to reason and be in accord with the conclusions of science. For religion, reason and science are realities; therefore, these three, being realities, must conform and be reconciled. A question or principle which is religious in its nature must be sanctioned by science. Science must declare it to be valid, and reason must confirm it in order that it may inspire confidence. If religious teaching, however, be at variance with science and reason, it is unquestionably superstition. The Lord of mankind has bestowed upon us the faculty of reason whereby we may discern the realities of things. How then can man rightfully accept any proposition which is not in conformity with the processes of reason and the principles of science? Assuredly such a course cannot inspire man with confidence and real belief.

The teachings of Bahá'u'lláh embody many principles; I am giving you only a synopsis. One of these principles concerns equality between men and women. He declared that as all are created in the image and likeness of the one God, there is no distinction as to sex in the estimation of God. He who is purest in heart, whose knowledge exceeds and who excels in kindness to the servants of God, is nearest and dearest to the Lord, our Creator, irrespective of sex. In the lower kingdoms, the animal and vegetable, we find sex differentiation in function and organism. All plants, trees and animals are subject to that differentiation by creation, but among themselves there is absolute equality without further distinction as to sex. Why, then, should mankind make a distinction which the lower creatures do not regard? Especially so when we realize that all are of the same kingdom and kindred; that all are the leaves of one tree, the waves of one sea? The only reasonable explanation is that woman has not been afforded the same educational facilities as man. For if she had received the same opportunities for training and development as man has enjoyed, undoubtedly she would have attained the same station and level. In the estimate of God no distinction exists; both are as one and possess equal degrees of capacity. Therefore, through opportunity and development woman will merit and attain the same prerogatives. When Jesus Christ died upon the cross, the disciples who witnessed His crucifixion were disturbed and shaken. Even Peter, one of the greatest of His followers, denied Him thrice. Mary Magdalene brought them together and confirmed their faith, saying, "Why are ye doubting? Why have ye feared? O thou Peter! Why didst thou deny Him? For Christ was not crucified. The reality of Christ is ever-living, everlasting, eternal. For that divine reality there is no beginning, no ending, and, therefore, there can be no death. At most, only the body of Jesus has suffered death." In brief, this woman, singly and alone, was instrumental in transforming the disciples and making them steadfast. This is an evidence of extraordinary power and supreme attributes, a proof that woman is the equivalent and complement of man. The one who is better trained and educated, whose aptitude is greater and whose ideals are higher is most distinguished and worthy—whether man or woman.

11   Through the teachings of Bahá'u'lláh the horizon of the East was made radiant and glorious. Souls who have hearkened to His words and accepted His message live together today in complete fellowship and love. They even offer their lives for each other. They forego and renounce worldly possessions for one another, each preferring the other to himself. This has been due to the declaration and foundation of the oneness of the world of humanity. Today in Persia there are meetings and assemblages wherein souls who have become illumined by the teachings of Bahá'u'lláh—representative Muslims, Christians,

Jews, Zoroastrians, Buddhists and of the various denominations of each—mingle and conjoin in perfect fellowship and absolute agreement. A wonderful brotherhood and love is established among them, and all are united in spirit and service for international peace. More than twenty thousand Bahá'ís have given their lives in martyrdom for the Cause of God. The governments of the East arose against them, bent upon their extermination. They were killed relentlessly, but day by day their numbers have increased, day by day they have multiplied in strength and become more eloquent. They have been strengthened through the efficacy of a wonderful spiritual power. How savage and fearful the ferocity of man against his fellowman! Consider what is taking place now in the Balkans, what blood is being shed. Even the wild beasts and ferocious animals do not commit such acts. The most ferocious wolf kills but one sheep a day, and even that for his food. But now in the Balkans one man destroys ten fellow beings. The commanders of armies glory in having killed ten thousand men, not for food, nay, rather, for military control, territorial greed, fame and possession of the dust of the earth. They kill for national aggrandizement, notwithstanding this terrestrial globe is but a dark world of grossest matter. It is a world of sorrow and grief, a world of disappointment and unhappiness, a world of death. For after all, the earth is but the everlasting graveyard, the vast, universal cemetery of all mankind. Yet men fight to possess this graveyard, waging war and battle, killing each other. What ignorance! How spacious the earth is with room in plenty for all! How thoughtful the providence which has so allotted that every man may derive his sustenance from it! The Lord, our Creator, does not ordain that anyone should starve or live in want. All are intended to participate in the blessed and abundant bestowals of our God. Fundamentally, all warfare and bloodshed in the human world are due to the lack of unity between the religions, which through superstitions and adherence to theological dogmas have obscured the one reality which is the source and basis of them all.

12   As to the American people: This noble nation, intelligent, thoughtful, reflective, is not impelled by motives of territorial aggrandizement and lust for dominion. Its boundaries are insular and geographically separated from the other nations. Here we find a oneness of interest and unity of national policy. These are, indeed, United States. Therefore, this nation possesses the capacity and capability for holding aloft the banner of international peace. May this noble people be the cause of unifying humanity. May they spread broadcast the heavenly civilization and illumination, become the cause of the diffusion of the love of God, proclaim the solidarity of mankind and be the cause of the guidance of the human race. Therefore, I ask that you will give this all-important question your most serious consideration and efforts. May the world of humanity find peace and composure and this dark earth be transformed into a realm of radiance. May the East and West clasp hands together. May the oneness of God become reflected and fully revealed in the hearts of humanity and all mankind prove to be the manifestations of the favors of God.

13   Necessarily there will be some who are defective amongst men, but it is our duty to enable them by kind methods of guidance and teaching to become perfected. Some will be found who are morally sick; they should be treated in order that they may be healed. Others are immature and like children; they must be trained and educated so that they may become wise and mature. Those who are asleep must be awakened; the indifferent must become mindful and attentive. But all this must be accomplished in the spirit of kindness and love and not by strife, antagonism nor in a spirit of hostility and hatred, for this is contrary to the good pleasure of God. That which is acceptable in the sight of

God is love. Love is, in reality, the first effulgence of Divinity and the greatest splendor of God.

O Thou compassionate Lord, Thou Who art generous and able! We are servants of Thine sheltered beneath Thy providence. Cast Thy glance of favor upon us. Give light to our eyes, hearing to our ears, and understanding and love to our hearts. Render our souls joyous and happy through Thy glad tidings. O Lord! Point out to us the pathway of Thy kingdom and resuscitate all of us through the breaths of the Holy Spirit. Bestow upon us life everlasting and confer upon us never-ending honor. Unify mankind and illumine the world of humanity. May we all follow Thy pathway, long for Thy good pleasure and seek the mysteries of Thy kingdom. O God! Unite us and connect our hearts with Thine indissoluble bond. Verily, Thou art the Giver, Thou art the Kind One and Thou art the Almighty.

2

7 November 1912

*Talk at Home of Mr. and Mrs. Arthur J. Parsons
1700 Eighteenth Street, NW, Washington, D. C.*

NOTES BY JOSEPH H. HANNEN

CONSIDER events in the Balkans today where a great conflagration of war is furiously raging and so much blood is being shed. Virtually the whole world of humanity is mourning and lamenting because of the revival of these calamitous conditions. Governments are in the process of change and transformation. The sovereignty of oriental nations is tottering; outcomes are wrapped in the greatest uncertainty. I desire, therefore, to speak to you upon this subject.

2 I will call your attention more especially to the aspects of this war which Bahá'u'lláh prophesied forty years ago fully and completely. During His exile and while under surveillance in the prison of 'Akká He addressed a letter to the Sulṭán of Turkey. He, likewise, sent Epistles to Napoleon III and to the S͟háh of Persia. All His letters to the kings and rulers of the earth were compiled in a book published thirty-five years ago in Bombay, India. There were several editions of this book.

3 I have with me a copy of an edition published twenty-two years ago. In 1891 Professor E. G. Browne of Cambridge University, England, wrote a book detailing his visit to 'Akká. This was followed by a second volume in which he quoted extracts from Bahá'u'lláh's Epistles to the kings and rulers. There are also translations of some of these Epistles in your libraries. When you get them, you will read the remarkable statements made by Bahá'u'lláh.

4 I will read to you from the Arabic text the very words written by Bahá'u'lláh in His Epistle to the Sulṭán of Turkey. They will be translated to you as I read. "O King! Thou hast committed that by reason of which Muḥammad, the Prophet of God, lamenteth in the highest heaven. Verily, the world hath made thee proud so that thou hast turned away from the face of Him by Whose light the people of the supreme assembly are illuminated, and erelong thou shalt find thyself in manifest loss. Thou hast united with the Persian chief in opposition to Me after I came unto you from the rising place of greatness and might with a matter which has consoled the eyes of those near unto God. Verily, this is a day wherein the Fire speaketh through all things, declaring that the Beloved of the two worlds hath come, and on the part of everything an Interlocutor of the matter hath sprung up to

listen unto the Word of thy Lord, the Precious, the Knowing. Dost thou imagine that thou canst quench the fire which God hath kindled in the horizons? No! By Himself, the True One, wert thou of those who know. Rather, by that which thou hast done its burning is increased and its blaze augmented; and it shall encompass the earth and whosoever is thereupon. Thus the matter hath been decreed, and whosoever is in the heavens and upon the earth could not withstand His command.

"The day is approaching when the Land of Mystery [Adrianople], and what is beside it shall be changed, and shall pass out of the hands of the king, and commotions shall appear, and the voice of lamentation shall be raised, and the evidences of mischief shall be revealed on all sides, and confusion shall spread by reason of that which hath befallen these captives at the hands of the hosts of oppression. The course of things shall be altered, and conditions shall wax so grievous, that the very sands on the desolate hills will moan, and the trees on the mountain will weep, and blood will flow out of all things. Then wilt thou behold the people in sore distress. Was Pharaoh able to hinder God by exercising his dominion when he rebelled upon the earth and was of the disobedient? We have indeed manifested the Interlocutor [Moses] from his house in spite of his will; verily, we were able to do this. And remember when Nimrod kindled the fire of polytheism whereby he would burn the Friend of God [Abraham]. Verily, we extinguished the fire by the truth and brought upon Nimrod manifest grief. Verily, the oppressor [King of Persia] slew the Beloved of the Worlds [the Báb] that he might thereby extinguish the light of God among His creatures and deprive mankind of the pure water of life in the days of his Lord, the Mighty, the Kind. We have made the matter manifest in the country and elevated His mention among the unitarians. Verily, the Servant hath assuredly come to vivify the world and bring to union whosoever is upon the surface of the whole earth. That which God willeth shall overcome, and thou shalt see the earth as the garden of Abhá. Thus hath it been written by the pen of command in an irrevocable Tablet."

6 There are many other prophecies in this book, especially in the Epistle to the <u>Sh</u>áh of Persia, all of which prophecies have come to pass. As they are lengthy, we will not have time to quote them.

7 The purpose of these quotations is to show that Bahá'u'lláh's great endeavor in the East was to unify mankind, to cause them to agree and become reconciled, thereby manifesting the oneness of the world of humanity, preparing the way for international peace and establishing the foundations of happiness and welfare. But the nations have not hearkened to His summons and message. The Persian and Turkish governments arose against His Cause, and the result is that both these governments have been disintegrated and broken. Had they been attentive to His commands and received His admonitions, they would have been protected. They would have enjoyed happiness and prosperity. They would have been bound together in ties of fellowship and brotherhood, availing themselves of the wonderful bounties of love and unity and dwelling in the delectable paradise of the divine Kingdom. But, alas, the commands and guidance of the Blessed One have been neglected and ignored. Day by day they have followed their own devices and imaginations, until now this fire of war is raging most furiously.

3

7 November 1912

Talk at Home of Mr. and Mrs. Arthur J. Parsons
1700 Eighteenth Street, NW, Washington, D. C.

NOTES BY JOSEPH H. HANNEN

IN the world of nature we behold the living organisms in a ceaseless struggle for existence. Everywhere we are confronted by evidences of the physical survival of the fittest. This is the very source of error and misapprehension in the opinions and theories of men who fail to realize that the world of nature is inherently defective in cause and outcome and that the defects therein must be removed by education. For example, consider man himself. If we study human beings such as the aboriginal tribes of central Africa, who have been reared in complete subjection to nature's rule, we will find them deficient indeed. They are without religious education; neither do they give evidences of any advance whatever toward civilization. They have simply grown and developed in the natural plane of barbarism. We find them bloodthirsty, immoral and animalistic in type to such an extent that they even kill and devour each other. It is evident, therefore, that the world of nature unassisted is imperfect because it is a plane upon which the struggle for physical existence expresses itself.

If a piece of ground is left in its natural state, wild weeds, thorns and trees of the jungle will grow upon it. But if we cultivate that same piece of ground, the result will be that it will rid itself of natural imperfections and become transformed into a beautiful rose garden or an orchard of fruitful trees. This is proof that the world of nature is defective. The founding of schools and establishing of educational systems in the world are intended to replace the defects of nature with virtues and perfections. If there were no defects, there would be no need of training, culture and education, but inasmuch as we find that children need training and schooling, it is a conclusive proof that the world of nature must be developed. Many things show this clearly. One of the basic evidences is the survival of the fittest in the animal kingdom, their ignorance, sensuality and unbridled instincts and passions. Therefore, in the natural world there is need of an Educator and Teacher for mankind. He must be universal in his powers and accomplishments. Teachers are of two kinds: universal and special. The universal Instructors are the Prophets of God, and the special teachers are the philosophers. The philosophers are capable of educating and training a limited circle of human souls, whereas the holy, divine Manifestations of God confer general education upon humanity. They arise to bestow universal moral training. For example, Moses was a universal Teacher. He trained and disciplined the people of Israel, enabled them to rescue themselves from the lowest abyss of despair and ignorance and caused them to attain an advanced degree of knowledge and development. They were captives and in the bondage of slavery; through Him they became free. He led them out of Egypt into the Holy Land and opened the doors of their advancement into higher civilization. Through His training this oppressed and downtrodden people, slaves and captives of the Pharaohs, established the splendor of the Solomonic sovereignty. This is an example of a universal Teacher, a universal Educator. Again, consider Christ: how that marvelous expression of unity bestowed education and ethical training upon the Roman, Greek, Egyptian, Syrian and Assyrian nations and welded together a people from them in a permanent and indissoluble bond. These nations were formerly at enmity and in a state of continual hostility and strife. He cemented them together, caused them to agree, conferred tranquillity upon humanity and established the foundations of human welfare throughout the world. Therefore, He was a real Educator, the Instructor of reality.

When we review the conditions existing in the East prior to the rise of the Prophet of Arabia, we find that throughout the Arabian peninsula intense mental darkness and the utmost ignorance prevailed among its inhabitants. Those tribal peoples were constantly engaged in war, killing and shedding blood, burning and pillaging the homes of each other and living in conditions of the utmost debasement and immorality. They were lower and more brutal than the animals. Muḥammad appeared as a Prophet among such a people. He educated these barbarous tribes, lifted them out of their ignorance and savagery and put an end to the continuous strife and hatred which had existed among them. He established agreement and reconciliation among them, unified them and taught them to look upon each other as brothers. Through His training they advanced rapidly in prestige and civilization. They were formerly ignorant; they became wise. They were barbarous; they attained refinement and culture. They were debased and brutal; He uplifted and elevated them. They were humiliated and despised; their civilization and renown spread throughout the world. This is perfect proof that Muḥammad was an Educator and Teacher.

In the nineteenth century strife and hostility prevailed among the people of the Orient. Apathy and ignorance characterized the nations. They were indeed gloomy and dark, negligent of God and under the subjection of the baser instincts and passions of mankind. The struggle for existence was intense and universal. At such a time as this Bahá'u'lláh appeared among them like a luminary in the heavens. He flooded the East with light. He proclaimed new principles and teachings. He laid a basis for new institutions which are the very spirit of modernism, the light of the world, the development of the body politic and eternal honor. The souls who hearkened to these teachings among the various oriental nations immediately renounced the spirit of strife and hostility and began to associate in goodwill and fellowship. From extremes of animosity they attained the acme of love and brotherhood. They had been warring and quarreling; now they became loving and lived together in complete unity and agreement. Among them today you will find no religious, political or patriotic prejudice; they are friendly, loving and associate in the greatest happiness. They have no part in the war and strife which take place in the East; their attitude toward all men is that of goodwill and loving-kindness. A standard of universal peace has been unfurled among them. The light of guidance has flooded their souls. It is light upon light, love upon love. This is the education and training of Bahá'u'lláh. He has led these souls to this standard and given them teachings which ensure eternal illumination. Anyone who becomes well versed in His teachings will say, "Verily, I declare that these words constitute the illumination of humanity, that this is the everlasting honor, that these are heavenly precepts and the cause of never-ending life among men."

4

8 November 1912

Talk at Eighth Street Temple, Synagogue
Washington, D. C.

NOTES BY JOSEPH H. HANNEN

GOD is one, the effulgence of God is one, and humanity consti- 1
tutes the servants of that one God. God is kind to all. He creates
and provides for all, and all are under His care and protection.
The Sun of Truth, the Word of God, shines upon all mankind;
the divine cloud pours down its precious rain; the gentle zephyrs
of His mercy blow, and all humanity is submerged in the ocean
of His eternal justice and loving-kindness. God has created
mankind from the same progeny in order that they may associate in good fellowship, exercise love toward each other and live
together in unity and brotherhood.

But we have acted contrary to the will and good pleasure 2
of God. We have been the cause of enmity and disunion. We
have separated from each other and risen against each other in
opposition and strife. How many have been the wars between
peoples and nations! What bloodshed! Numberless are the cities and homes which have been laid waste. All of this has been
contrary to the good pleasure of God, for He hath willed love
for humanity. He is clement and merciful to all His creatures.
He hath ordained amity and fellowship amongst men.

Most regrettable of all is the state of difference and divergence 3
we have created between each other in the name of religion,
imagining that a paramount duty in our religious belief is that
of alienation and estrangement, that we should shun each other

and consider each other contaminated with error and infidelity. In reality, the foundations of the divine religions are one and the same. The differences which have arisen between us are due to blind imitations of dogmatic beliefs and adherence to ancestral forms of worship. Abraham was the founder of reality. Moses, Christ, Muḥammad were the manifestations of reality. Bahá'u'lláh was the glory of reality. This is not simply an assertion; it will be proved.

4   Let me ask your closest attention in considering this subject. The divine religions embody two kinds of ordinances. First, there are those which constitute essential, or spiritual, teachings of the Word of God. These are faith in God, the acquirement of the virtues which characterize perfect manhood, praiseworthy moralities, the acquisition of the bestowals and bounties emanating from the divine effulgences—in brief, the ordinances which concern the realm of morals and ethics. This is the fundamental aspect of the religion of God, and this is of the highest importance because knowledge of God is the fundamental requirement of man. Man must comprehend the oneness of Divinity. He must come to know and acknowledge the precepts of God and realize for a certainty that the ethical development of humanity is dependent upon religion. He must get rid of all defects and seek the attainment of heavenly virtues in order that he may prove to be the image and likeness of God. It is recorded in the Holy Bible that God said, "Let us make man in our image, after our likeness." It is self-evident that the image and likeness mentioned do not apply to the form and semblance of a human being because the reality of Divinity is not limited to any form or figure. Nay, rather, the attributes and characteristics of God are intended. Even as God is pronounced to be just, man must likewise be just. As God is loving and kind to all men, man must likewise manifest loving-kindness to all humanity.

As God is loyal and truthful, man must show forth the same attributes in the human world. Even as God exercises mercy toward all, man must prove himself to be the manifestation of mercy. In a word, the image and likeness of God constitute the virtues of God, and man is intended to become the recipient of the effulgences of divine attributes. This is the essential foundation of all the divine religions, the reality itself, common to all. Abraham promulgated this; Moses proclaimed it. Christ and all the Prophets upheld this standard and aspect of divine religion.

Second, there are laws and ordinances which are temporary and nonessential. These concern human transactions and relations. They are accidental and subject to change according to the exigencies of time and place. These ordinances are neither permanent nor fundamental. For instance, during the time of Noah it was expedient that seafood be considered as lawful; therefore, God commanded Noah to partake of all marine animal life. During the time of Moses this was not in accordance with the exigencies of Israel's existence; therefore, a second command was revealed partly abrogating the law concerning marine foods. During the time of Abraham—upon Him be peace!—camel's milk was considered a lawful and acceptable food; likewise, the flesh of the camel; but during Jacob's time, because of a certain vow He made, this became unlawful. These are nonessential, temporary laws. In the Holy Bible there are certain commandments which according to those bygone times constituted the very spirit of the age, the very light of that period. For example, according to the law of the Torah if a man committed theft of a certain amount, they cut off his hand. Is it practicable and reasonable in this present day to cut off a man's hand for the theft of a dollar? In the Torah there are ten ordinances concerning murder. Could these be made effective today? Unquestionably no; times have changed. According to the explicit text of the

Bible if a man should change or break the law of the Sabbath or if he should touch fire on the Sabbath, he must be killed. Today such a law is abrogated. The Torah declares that if a man should speak a disrespectful word to his father, he should suffer the penalty of death. Is this possible of enforcement now? No; human conditions have undergone changes. Likewise, during the time of Christ certain minor ordinances conformable to that period were enforced.

6   It has been shown conclusively, therefore, that the foundation of the religion of God remains permanent and unchanging. It is that fixed foundation which ensures the progress and stability of the body politic and the illumination of humanity. It has ever been the cause of love and justice amongst men. It works for the true fellowship and unification of all mankind, for it never changes and is not subject to supersedure. The accidental, or nonessential, laws which regulate the transactions of the social body and everyday affairs of life are changeable and subject to abrogation.

7   Let me ask: What is the purpose of Prophethood? Why has God sent the Prophets? It is self-evident that the Prophets are the Educators of men and the Teachers of the human race. They come to bestow universal education upon humanity, to give humanity training, to uplift the human race from the abyss of despair and desolation and to enable man to attain the apogee of advancement and glory. The people are in darkness; the Prophets bring them into the realm of light. They are in a state of utter imperfection; the Prophets imbue them with perfections. The purpose of the prophetic mission is none other than the education and guidance of the people. Therefore, we must regard and be on the lookout for the man who is thus qualified—that is to say, any soul who proves to be the Educator of mankind and the Teacher of the human race is undoubtedly the Prophet of His age.

For example, let us review the events connected with the history of Moses—upon Him be peace! He dwelt in Midian at a time when the children of Israel were in captivity and bondage in the land of Egypt, subjected to every tyranny and severe oppression. They were illiterate and ignorant, undergoing cruel ordeals and experiences. They were in such a state of helplessness and impotence that it was proverbial to state that one Egyptian could overcome ten Israelites. At such a time as this and under such forbidding conditions Moses appeared and shone forth with a heavenly radiance. He saved Israel from the bondage of Pharaoh and released them from captivity. He led them out of the land of Egypt and into the Holy Land. They had been scattered and broken; He unified and disciplined them, conferred upon them the blessing of wisdom and knowledge. They had been slaves; He made them princes. They were ignorant; He made them learned. They were imperfect; He enabled them to attain perfection. In a word, He led them out of their condition of hopelessness and brought them to efficiency in the plane of confidence and valor. They became renowned throughout the ancient world until finally in the zenith and splendor of their new civilization the glory of the sovereignty of Solomon was attained. Through the guidance and training of Moses these slaves and captives became the dominating people amongst the nations. Not only in physical and military superiority were they renowned, but in all the degrees of arts, letters and refinement their fame was widespread. Even the celebrated philosophers of Greece journeyed to Jerusalem in order to study with the Israelitish sages, and many were the lessons of philosophy and wisdom they received. Among these philosophers was the famous Socrates. He visited the Holy Land and studied with the prophets of Israel, acquiring principles of their philosophical teaching and a knowledge of their advanced arts and sciences. After his return to Greece he founded the system known as the unity of God. The Greek people rose against him, and at last he was poisoned in the presence of the king. Hippocrates and many other Greek philosophers sat at the feet of the learned Israelitish doctors and absorbed their expositions of wisdom and inner truth.

9   Inasmuch as Moses through the influence of His great mission was instrumental in releasing the Israelites from a low state of debasement and humiliation, establishing them in a station of prestige and glorification, disciplining and educating them, it is necessary for us to reach a fair and just judgment in regard to such a marvelous Teacher. For in this great accomplishment He stood single and alone. Could He have made such a change and brought about such a condition among these people without the sanction and assistance of a heavenly power? Could He have transformed a people from humiliation to glory without a holy and divine support?

10   None other than a divine power could have done this. Therein lies the proof of Prophethood because the mission of a Prophet is education of the human race such as this Personage accomplished, proving Him to be a mighty Prophet among the Prophets and His Book the very Book of God. This is a rational, direct and perfect proof.

11   In brief, Moses—upon Whom be peace!—founded the law of God, purified the morals of the people of Israel and gave them an impetus toward nobler and higher attainments. But after the departure of Moses, following the decline of the glory of Solomon's era and during the reign of Jeroboam there came a great change in this nation. The high ethical standards and spiritual perfections ceased to exist. Conditions and morals became corrupt, religion was debased, and the perfect principles of the Mosaic law were obscured in superstition and polytheism. War and strife arose among the tribes, and their unity

was destroyed. The followers of Jeroboam declared themselves rightful and valid in kingly succession, and the supporters of Rehoboam made the same claim. Finally, the tribes were torn asunder by hostility and hatred, the glory of Israel was eclipsed, and so complete was the degradation that a golden calf was set up as an object of worship in the city of Tyre. Thereupon God sent Elijah, the prophet, who redeemed the people, renewed the law of God and established an era of new life for Israel. History shows a still later change and transformation when this oneness and solidarity were followed by another dispersion of the tribes. Nebuchadnezzar, King of Babylon, invaded the Holy Land and carried away captive seventy thousand Israelites to Chaldea, where the greatest reverses, trials and suffering afflicted these unfortunate people. Then the prophets of God again reformed and reestablished the law of God, and the people in their humiliation again followed it. This resulted in their liberation, and under the edict of Cyrus, King of Persia, there was a return to the Holy City. Jerusalem and the Temple of Solomon were rebuilt, and the glory of Israel was restored. This lasted but a short time; the morality of the people declined, and conditions reached an extreme degree until the Roman general Titus took Jerusalem and razed it to its foundations. Pillage and conquest completed the desolation; Palestine became a waste and wilderness, and the Jews fled from the Holy Land of their ancestors. The cause of this disintegration and dispersion was the departure of Israel from the foundation of the law of God revealed by Moses—namely, the acquisition of divine virtues, morality, love, the development of arts and sciences and the spirit of the oneness of humanity.

I now wish you to examine certain facts and statements 12 which are worthy of consideration. My purpose and intention is to remove from the hearts of men the religious enmity and hatred which have fettered them and to bring all religions into agreement and unity. Inasmuch as this hatred and enmity, this bigotry and intolerance are outcomes of misunderstandings, the reality of religious unity will appear when these misunderstandings are dispelled. For the foundation of the divine religions is one foundation. This is the oneness of revelation or teaching. But, alas, we have turned away from that foundation, holding tenaciously to various dogmatic forms and blind imitation of ancestral beliefs. This is the real cause of enmity, hatred and bloodshed in the world—the reason of alienation and estrangement among mankind. Therefore, I wish you to be very just and fair in your judgment of the following statements.

13   During the time that the people of Israel were being tossed and afflicted by the conditions I have named, Jesus Christ appeared among them. Jesus of Nazareth was a Jew. He was single and unaided, alone and unique. He had no assistant. The Jews at once pronounced Him to be an enemy of Moses. They declared that He was the destroyer of the Mosaic laws and ordinances. Let us examine the facts as they are, investigate the truth and reality in order to arrive at a true opinion and conclusion. For a completely fair opinion upon this question we must lay aside all we have and investigate independently. This Personage, Jesus Christ, declared Moses to have been the Prophet of God and pronounced all the prophets of Israel as sent from God. He proclaimed the Torah the very Book of God, summoned all to conform to its precepts and follow its teachings. It is an historical fact that during a period of fifteen hundred years the kings of Israel were unable to promulgate broadcast the religion of Judaism. In fact, during that period the name and history of Moses were confined to the boundaries of Palestine and the Torah was a book well known only in that country. But through Christ, through the blessing of the New Testament of Jesus Christ, the Old Testament, the Torah, was translated

into six hundred different tongues and spread throughout the world. It was through Christianity that the Torah reached Persia. Before that time there was no knowledge in that country of such a book, but Christ caused its spread and acceptance. Through Him the name of Moses was elevated and revered. He was instrumental in publishing the name and greatness of the Israelitish prophets, and He proved to the world that the Israelites constituted the people of God. Which of the kings of Israel could have accomplished this? Were it not for Jesus Christ, would the Bible, the Torah have reached this land of America? Would the name of Moses be spread throughout the world? Refer to history. Everyone knows that when Christianity was spread, there was a simultaneous spread of the knowledge of Judaism and the Torah. Throughout the length and breadth of Persia there was not a single volume of the Old Testament until the religion of Jesus Christ caused it to appear everywhere so that today the Holy Bible is a household book in that country. It is evident, then, that Christ was a friend of Moses, that He loved and believed in Moses; otherwise, He would not have commemorated His name and Prophethood. This is self-evident. Therefore, Christians and Jews should have the greatest love for each other because the Founders of these two great religions have been in perfect agreement in Book and teaching. Their followers should be likewise.

We have already stated the valid proofs of Prophethood. We 14 find the very evidences of the validity of Moses were witnessed and duplicated in Christ. Christ was also a unique and single Personage born of the lineage of Israel. By the power of His Word He was able to unite people of the Roman, Greek, Chaldean, Egyptian and Assyrian nations. Whereas they had been cruel, bloodthirsty and hostile, killing, pillaging and taking each other captive, He cemented them together in a perfect bond of unity and love. He caused them to agree and become reconciled.

Such mighty effects were the results of the manifestation of one single Soul. This proves conclusively that Christ was assisted by God. Today all Christians admit and believe that Moses was a Prophet of God. They declare that His Book was the Book of God, that the prophets of Israel were true and valid and that the people of Israel constituted the people of God. What harm has come from this? What harm could come from a statement by the Jews that Jesus was also a Manifestation of the Word of God? Have the Christians suffered for their belief in Moses? Have they experienced any loss of religious enthusiasm or witnessed any defeat in their religious belief by declaring that Moses was a Prophet of God, that the Torah was a Book of God and that all the prophets of Israel were prophets of God? It is evident that no loss comes from this. And now it is time for the Jews to declare that Christ was the Word of God, and then this enmity between two great religions will pass away. For two thousand years this enmity and religious prejudice have continued. Blood has been shed, ordeals have been suffered. These few words will remedy the difficulty and unite two great religions. What harm could follow this: that just as the Christians glorify and praise the name of Moses, likewise the Jews should commemorate the name of Christ, declare Him to be the Word of God and consider Him as one of the chosen Messengers of God?

15   A few words concerning the Qur'án and the Muslims: When Muḥammad appeared, He spoke of Moses as the great Man of God. In the Qur'án He refers to the sayings of Moses in seven different places, proclaims Him a Prophet and the possessor of a Book, the Founder of the law and the Spirit of God. He said, "Whosoever believes in Him is acceptable in the estimation of God, and whosoever shuns Him or any of the prophets is rejected of God." Even in conclusion He calls upon His own relatives, saying, "Why have ye shunned and not believed in Moses? Why have ye not acknowledged the Torah? Why have

576

ye not believed in the Jewish prophets?" In a certain súrih of the Qur'án He mentions the names of twenty-eight of the prophets of Israel, praising each and all of them. To this great extent He has ratified and commended the prophets and religion of Israel. The purport is this: that Muḥammad praised and glorified Moses and confirmed Judaism. He declared that whosoever denies Moses is contaminated and even if he repents, his repentance will not be accepted. He pronounced His own relatives infidels and impure because they had denied the prophets. He said, "Because you have not believed in Christ, because you have not believed in Moses, because you have not believed in the Gospels, you are infidels and contaminated." In this way Muḥammad has praised the Torah, Moses, Christ and the prophets of the past. He appeared amongst the Arabs, who were a people nomadic and illiterate, barbarous in nature and bloodthirsty. He guided and trained them until they attained a high degree of development. Through His education and discipline they rose from the lowest levels of ignorance to the heights of knowledge, becoming masters of erudition and philosophy. We see, therefore that the proofs applicable to one Prophet are equally applicable to another.

In conclusion, since the Prophets themselves, the Founders, have loved, praised and testified of each other, why should we disagree and be alienated? God is one. He is the Shepherd of all. We are His sheep and, therefore, should live together in love and unity. We should manifest the spirit of justness and goodwill toward each other. Shall we do this, or shall we censure and pronounce anathema, praising ourselves and condemning all others? What possible good can come from such attitude and action? On the contrary, nothing but enmity and hatred, injustice and inhumanity can possibly result. Has not this been the greatest cause of bloodshed, woe and tribulation in the past?

16

577

17   Praise be to God! You are living in a land of freedom. You are blessed with men of learning, men who are well versed in the comparative study of religions. You realize the need of unity and know the great harm which comes from prejudice and superstition. I ask you, is not fellowship and brotherhood preferable to enmity and hatred in society and community? The answer is self-evident. Love and fellowship are absolutely needful to win the good pleasure of God, which is the goal of all human attainment. We must be united. We must love each other. We must ever praise each other. We must bestow commendation upon all people, thus removing the discord and hatred which have caused alienation amongst men. Otherwise, the conditions of the past will continue, praising ourselves and condemning others; religious wars will have no end, and religious prejudice, the prime cause of this havoc and tribulation, will increase. This must be abandoned, and the way to do it is to investigate the reality which underlies all the religions. This underlying reality is the love of humanity. For God is one and humanity is one, and the only creed of the Prophets is love and unity.

5

9 November 1912

Talk at Home of Mr. and Mrs. Arthur J. Parsons
1700 Eighteenth Street, NW, Washington, D. C.

NOTES BY JOSEPH H. HANNEN

THE address delivered last evening in the Jewish synagogue   1
evidently disturbed some of the people, including the revered
rabbi who called upon me this afternoon. Together we went
over the ground again, which I shall now review for your benefit.

It was not possible to make the subject completely plain to   2
the rabbi last night, as he was very much pressed for time, but
today the opportunity was sufficient for a reconsideration of the
statements in detail. I wish you to understand them thoroughly
and memorize them in order that you may discourse with the
Jews and thus, perchance, become instrumental in leading them
aright.

The quintessence of our subject was this: What is the mission   3
of the Prophet, and what is the object of a divine law? In answer
we stated: There is no doubt that the purpose of a divine law is
the education of the human race, the training of humanity. All
mankind may be considered as pupils or children who are in need
of a divine Educator, a real Teacher. The essential requirement
and qualification of Prophethood is the training and guidance
of the people. Therefore, we shall first consider the efficacy of
the teachings of those who have been followed and accepted as
the Prophets of God. The question that must be answered is:
Have They taught mankind? Have They proved Themselves
efficient Educators?

4   Among Them was Moses. We find that He appeared as the leader of the children of Israel during a period of their captivity. They were in a state of extreme humiliation, ignorance and heedlessness, living in a very lowly manner in Egypt under conditions of life worse than death. Imagine an ignorant people, downtrodden and oppressed, thoughtless, negligent and mentally darkened, held in subjection as slaves. Moses was appointed for their deliverance and training. He guided them, led them out of bondage into the Holy Land, uplifted them from ignorance and despair, trained them so that they rose from a condition of lowliness and subjection into one of honor and importance, and enabled them to reach a high degree of perfection. They became proficient in sciences and arts, attained a lofty plane of civilization, honorable and esteemed among nations, whereas formerly they had been lowly and despised. They were ignorant; they became intelligent, finally reaching that period of supremacy and power witnessed in the Solomonic sovereignty. Their name became widespread throughout the world, and they were esteemed for distinct virtues. Even the philosophers of Greece went to Palestine to drink from the fountains of their wisdom and sit at the feet of their sages. All these facts prove that Moses was a Prophet and a Teacher.

5   As to Christ: He was a single, unique and lowly individual Who appeared at a time when the Israelitish nation had fallen from the heights of its glory to the lowest condition of bondage and contempt, subject to the tyranny of the Roman Empire, living under a yoke of humiliation, ignorant and negligent of God. The historical records of the Holy Books confirm these statements. Christ—this single and unique Personage—appeared amongst these despised and degraded people, reflecting a divine power and the potency of the Holy Spirit. He unified the various peoples and nations of the world, brought them

together in fellowship and agreement and gathered them beneath the overshadowing protection of one Word. His prestige and mention were not confined to the children of Israel alone, who were at that time a limited race and people, but His spiritual power had also permeated and united great influential nations who had been warlike and hostile, such as the Romans, Greeks, Egyptians, Chaldeans, Syrians and Assyrians. He dispelled their hostility, healed their hatred, made them a united people, and by His Word created the utmost love amongst them so that they advanced immeasurably in the degrees of education and human perfection, thereby attaining a never-ending glory.

The Jews had become dispersed and widely scattered. This 6 single and unique Personage overcame all the then known world, founding an everlasting sovereignty, a mighty nation indeed. Such a result proved Him to be a great man, the first Educator of His time, the first Teacher of His period. What proofs could be greater than these? What would be more convincing than this evidence that a single individual resuscitated so many nations and peoples, unified so many tribes and sects, removed so much warfare and hatred? Undoubtedly, such accomplishment could be wrought only through the power of God and not by mere human effort, which is altogether incapable of producing these mighty results.

When Christ appeared, the Jews pronounced Him an enemy 7 of Moses. Pharisaical rabbis of that age declared Him to be the destroyer of the Mosaic law and the institutes of the Torah. They proclaimed that He would bring great misfortune to the people of Israel, considering Him the violator of the holy Sabbath and destroyer of the Temple of Solomon. Therefore, they turned away from Him. Let us investigate this and discover whether such accusations were true or false. We will find that in reality Christ caused the name and prestige of Moses to become widespread. Through His efforts and teaching the Book of Moses, the Bible, became known everywhere. In fifteen hundred years there had been but one translation of the Old Testament, the Torah, which translation was made from Hebrew into Greek. But through the instrumentality of Christ's message and teachings it was translated into six hundred tongues and spread to every part of the world. All the kings and prophets of Israel were unable to promulgate the teachings of Judaism and the name of Moses beyond the borders of Palestine, whereas through Christ Judaism became an established religion in Asia, Africa, Europe and the world generally. Through the message of Christ, Moses was everywhere proclaimed a Prophet of God and His Book the Book of God. Shall we consider this Personage an enemy or a friend of Moses?

8   Justice is needed; we must render fair judgment upon this question. Had He been an enemy, He would not have allowed the name and teachings of Moses to become widespread in the world. He would not have promulgated the law and principles of the Torah. Would there have been any mention of Moses in America? Could even the name of Judaism have reached this part of the world through any other instrumentality? Undoubtedly, it was owing to the blessed agency and influence of Christianity that Judaism became established in this western world. Moses had no better friend and sympathizer than Christ. Consider how the illiterate among the Israelites conceal the reality of these facts and continue the delusion that Christ was an enemy of Moses. All Christians believe in Moses. They declare that He was a Man of God, the Interlocutor and Prophet of God, that His Book was the Book of God, that the people of Israel were the people of God and that all the prophets of Israel were valid and true. They offer unlimited praise, sincere eulogy, and manifest unlimited love for the religion of Moses. What harm comes from

this? And if the Jews should say that Christ was also the Word of God, the Spirit of God, what harm could follow this statement? Just these few words would be the cause of reconciling the Christians and Jews. The Christians accept Moses and His Book. What harm have they suffered on account of this belief? Have they lost anything because of it?

In answer to all these questions the rabbi answered, "No." 9

We continued: What harm could result if the Jews were in a 10 similar attitude toward Christianity, declaring that Christ was the Word of God, that the Gospel is the Book of God? Such an attitude as this would cause the enmity of many centuries to pass away. If we declare that Moses was the Prophet of God and that His Book was the law of God, does it harm our religious standpoint? Not at all. Furthermore, every nation is proud of its great men and heroes even though those great ones may have been atheists or agnostics. Today France glorifies Napoleon Bonaparte, saying, "He was a French military genius," whereas, in reality, he was a tyrant. They say, "Voltaire was ours," although Voltaire was an atheist. "Rousseau was a great man of this nation," and yet Rousseau was irreligious. France is proud of these great men. Feasts are held commemorating them, their names are perpetuated in special days, their memories treasured in prominent places, and there is music and celebration in their honor. The nation is proud of them. And now, do you consider these great men of France greater than Jesus of Nazareth? It is evident that in comparison with Jesus Christ they are as nothing. Consider the grandeur and majesty of Jesus in contrast with such men as we have mentioned. Consider Him from the standpoint of fame and renown. Where is the station of Christ, and where is their station? What comparison is there? In reality, Christ is incomparable. What harm, then, could come from your declaration that Jesus of Nazareth was a great man of Israelitish

583

birth and, therefore, we love Him? That we have given to the world a great man indeed? That this mighty Personage, Whose Word has spread throughout the world, Who has conquered the East and the West, was an Israelite? Should you not be proud of Him? When you glorify and honor the memory of Christ, rest assured that the Christians will take your hands in real fellowship. All difficulty, hesitancy and restraint will vanish. Consider the troubles and persecutions heaped upon you in Russia for your fanaticism of unbelief. And you must not think that this is ended.

11   This humiliation will continue forever. The time may come when in Europe itself they will arise against the Jews. But your declaration that Christ was the Word of God will end all such trouble. My advice is that in order to become honorable, protected and secure among the nations of the world, in order that the Christians may love and safeguard the Israelitish people, you should be willing to announce your belief in Christ, the Word of God. This is a complete statement; there is nothing more. Is it not thoughtless, ignorant prejudice which restrains you from doing so? Declare that, verily, the Word of God was realized in Him, and all will be right.

12   The rabbi thoughtfully said, "I believe that what you have said is perfectly true, but I must ask one thing of you. Will you not tell the Christians to love us a little more?"

13   We replied, "We have advised them and will continue to do so."

6

9 November 1912

Talk at Home of Mr. and Mrs. Arthur J. Parsons
1700 Eighteenth Street, NW, Washington, D. C.

Notes by Joseph H. Hannen

Every composition is necessarily subject to destruction or disin-   1
tegration. For instance, this flower is a composition of various
elements; its decomposition is inevitable. When this composed
form undergoes decomposition—in other words, when these
elements separate and disintegrate—that is what we call the
death of the flower. For inasmuch as it is composed of single
elements, the grouping of multitudinous cellular atoms, it is
subject to disintegration. This is the mortality of the flower.
Similarly, the body of man is composed of various elements.
This composition of the elements has been given life. When
these elements disintegrate, life disappears, and that is death.
Existence in the various planes, or kingdoms, implies composition; and nonexistence, or death, is decomposition.

But the inner and essential reality of man is not composed   2
of elements and, therefore, cannot be decomposed. It is not an
elemental composition subject to disintegration or death. A true
and fundamental scientific principle is that an element itself never
dies and cannot be destroyed for the reason that it is single and
not composed. Therefore, it is not subject to decomposition.

Another evidence or proof of the indestructibility of the real-   3
ity of man is that it is not affected by the changes of the physical
body. These changing conditions of the bodily composition
are definite and continual. At one time it is normal, at another

time abnormal. Now it is weak, now strong. It suffers injury, a hand may be amputated, a limb broken, an eye destroyed, an ear deafened or some defect appear in a certain organ, but these changes do not affect the human spirit, the soul of man. If the body becomes stout or thin, decrepit or strong, the spirit or soul is unaffected thereby. If a part of the bodily organism be destroyed, even if it be dismembered completely, the soul continues to function, showing that no changes of the body affect its operation. We have seen that death and mortality are synonymous with change and disintegration. As we find the soul unaffected by this change and disintegration of the body, we, therefore, prove it to be immortal; for that which is changeable is accidental, evanescent.

4   Furthermore, this immortal human soul is endowed with two means of perception: One is effected through instrumentality; the other, independently. For instance, the soul sees through the instrumentality of the eye, hears with the ear, smells through the nostrils and grasps objects with the hands. These are the actions or operations of the soul through instruments. But in the world of dreams the soul sees when the eyes are closed. The man is seemingly dead, lies there as dead; the ears do not hear, yet he hears. The body lies there, but he—that is, the soul—travels, sees, observes. All the instruments of the body are inactive, all the functions seemingly useless. Notwithstanding this, there is an immediate and vivid perception by the soul. Exhilaration is experienced. The soul journeys, perceives, senses. It often happens that a man in a state of wakefulness has not been able to accomplish the solution of a problem, and when he goes to sleep, he will reach that solution in a dream. How often it has happened that he has dreamed, even as the prophets have dreamed, of the future; and events which have thus been foreshadowed have come to pass literally.

Therefore, we learn that the immortality of the soul, or spirit, 5
is not contingent or dependent upon the so-called immortality
of the body, because the body in the quiescent state, in the time
of sleep, may be as dead, unconscious, senseless; but the soul,
or spirit, is possessed of perceptions, sensations, motion and
discovery. Even inspiration and revelation are obtained by it.
How many were the prophets who have had marvelous visions
of the future while in that state! The spirit, or human soul, is
the rider; and the body is only the steed. If anything affects the
steed, the rider is not affected by it. The spirit may be likened
to the light within the lantern. The body is simply the outer
lantern. If the lantern should break, the light is ever the same
because the light could shine even without the lantern. The
spirit can conduct its affairs without the body. In the world of
dreams it is precisely as this light without the chimney glass. It
can shine without the glass. The human soul by means of this
body can perform its operations, and without the body it can,
likewise, have its control. Therefore, if the body be subject to
disintegration, the spirit is not affected by these changes or
transformations.

It is an evident fact that the body does not conduct the process 6
of intellection or thought radiation. It is only the medium of the
grossest sensations. This human body is purely animal in type
and, like the animal, it is subject only to the grosser sensibilities.
It is utterly bereft of ideation or intellection, utterly incapable
of the processes of reason. The animal perceives what its eye
sees and judges what the ear hears. It perceives according to its
animal senses, the scent of the nostril, the taste of the tongue.
It comprehends not beyond its sense perceptions. The animal
is confined to its feelings and sensibilities, a prisoner of the
senses. Beyond these, in the finer higher processes of reasoning,
the animal cannot go. For instance, the animal cannot conceive

of the earth whereon it stands as a spherical object because the spherical shape of the earth is a matter of conscious reasoning. It is not a matter of sense perception. An animal in Europe could not foresee and plan the discovery of America as Columbus did. It could not take the globe map of the earth and scan the various continents, saying, "This is the eastern hemisphere; there must be another, the western hemisphere." No animal could know these things for the reason that they are referable to intellection. The animal cannot become aware of the fact that the earth is revolving and the sun stationary. Only processes of reasoning can come to this conclusion. The outward eye sees the sun as revolving. It mistakes the stars and the planets as moving about the earth. But reason decides their orbit, knows that the earth is moving and the other worlds fixed, knows that the sun is the solar center and ever occupies the same place, proves that it is the earth which revolves around it. Such conclusions are entirely intellectual, not according to the senses.

7   Hence, we know that in the human organism there is a center of intellection, a power of intellectual operation which is the discoverer of the realities of things. This power can unravel the mysteries of phenomena. It can comprehend that which is knowable, not alone the sensible. All the inventions are its products. For all of these have been the mysteries of nature. There was a time when the energy of electricity was a mystery of nature, but that collective reality which is manifest in man discovered this mystery of nature, this latent force. Having discovered it, man brought it into the plane of visibility. All the sciences which we now utilize are the products of that wondrous reality. But the animal is deprived of its operations. The arts we now enjoy are the expressions of that marvelous reality. The animal is bereft of them because these conscious realities are peculiar to the human spirit. All the traces are the outcoming of the perfections which comprehend realities. The animal is bereft of these.

Such evidences prove conclusively that man is possessed of 8 two realities, as it were: a reality connected with the senses which is shared in common with the animal, and another reality which is conscious and ideal in character. This latter is the collective reality and the discoverer of mysteries. That which discovers the realities of things undoubtedly is not of the elemental substances. It is distinct from them. For mortality and disintegration are the properties inherent in compositions and are referable to things which are subject to sense perceptions, but the collective reality in man, not being so subject, is the discoverer of things. Therefore, it is real, eternal and does not have to undergo changes and transformations.

There are many other proofs concerning this vital subject, but 9 I shall conclude with the words of Jesus Christ: "That which is born of the Spirit is spirit" and is acceptable in the Kingdom of God. This means that just as in the first birth the fetus comes forth from the matrix of the mother into the conditions of the human kingdom, even so the spirit of man must be born out of the matrix of naturalism, out of the baser nature, in order that he may comprehend the great things of the Kingdom of God. He must be born out of mother earth to find the everlasting life. And this collective reality, or spirit, of man, being born out of the world of nature, possessing the attributes of God, will continue to live forever in the eternal realm.

7

9 November 1912

Talk at Bahá'í Banquet
Rauscher's Hall, Washington, D. C.

NOTES BY JOSEPH H. HANNEN

1 I FEEL a keen sense of joy in being present at this banquet this evening, for—praise be to God!—before me are radiant faces, ears attuned to the melodies of the Supreme Concourse, hearts aglow with the fire of the love of God, spirits exhilarated through the glad tidings of God, souls sheltered beneath the overshadowing power of the Kingdom of Abhá. I see before me an assemblage of souls who are of the chosen and not of the many called. And it is my hope that through the favors of Bahá'u'lláh He may continue to attract you to His Kingdom and render you victorious and triumphant in your service to the oneness and solidarity of mankind. May He assist all who are firm in establishing the unity of the inhabitants of this earth. May all of you thereby become my partners and coadjutors in servitude.

2 O Lord! Confirm and aid this assemblage. Confirm these souls through the breaths of Thy Holy Spirit. Enlighten the eyes by the vision of these radiant lights, and make the ears joyful through the anthems of Thy call to service. O God! Verily, we have gathered here in the fragrance of Thy love. We have turned to Thy Kingdom. We seek naught save Thee and desire nothing save Thy good pleasure. O God! Let this food be Thy manna from heaven, and grant that this assemblage may be a concourse of Thy supreme ones. May they be the quickening cause of love to humanity and the source of illumination to

the human race. May they be the instruments of Thy guidance upon earth. Verily, Thou art powerful. Thou art the Bestower. Thou art the Forgiver, and Thou art the Almighty.

In the world many banquets, assemblages and meetings have 3 been organized, but those gatherings have been commercial, political, educational or social in their purpose and motive. Meetings are held for the promotion of financial plans or promulgation of the arts and sciences. Others have sought to establish agricultural industries or consummate territorial agreements. Innumerable assemblages have been held for consultation upon subjects of learning and education. All such meetings have for their object the advancement of civilization. But—praise be to God!—this banquet and this assemblage are for none other purpose than love, for the purpose of announcing the divine Kingdom, for the manifestation of the ineffable traces of God, for reflecting the effulgences of the Kingdom of God, for binding hearts together, for service to the world of humanity, for the promulgation of humanitarian and altruistic realities, for the advancement and advocating of international peace, for the illumination of the whole world. Therefore, such an assemblage is matchless and peerless because other assemblages are held for a limited object and personal motive, whereas this meeting is for God and God only, for His love and purpose. It is for love of the hearts of men and the oneness of the world of humanity. Therefore, we should offer thanks to God, for He has confirmed us in attaining to the happiness of this occasion. He has appointed us servants of the human world, advocates of peace and unity among the religions, heralds of universal agreement among the races and nations, founders of divine reconciliation among all peoples.

It is my fond and fervent hope through the favor of God that 4 this present meeting may be instrumental in ushering in the day when the standard of the oneness of the world of humanity shall be held aloft in America. May it be the first real foundation of international peace, having for its object universal service to man. May it be divine philanthropy without distinctions or differentiations in humankind. May you consider all religions the instruments of God and regard all races as channels of divine manifestation. May you view mankind as the sheep of God and know for a certainty that He is the real Shepherd. Consider how this kind and tender Shepherd cares for all His flock; how He leads them in green pastures and beside the still waters. How well He protects them! Verily, this Shepherd makes no distinctions whatsoever; to all the sheep He is equally kind. Therefore, we must follow the example of God and strive in pathways of goodwill toward all humanity. May we endeavor with heart and soul to reconcile the religions of the earth, unify the peoples and races and blend the nations in a perfect solidarity. May we uphold the flag of international agreement and enkindle a light which shall illumine all regions with the radiance of oneness. May our purposes centralize in the earnest desire of attaining the good pleasure of God, and may our supreme energies be directed to welding together the human household. Let us not regard our own respective capacities; nay, rather, let us regard forever the favors and bounties of God. The drop must not estimate its own limited capacity; it must realize the volume and sufficiency of the ocean, which ever glorifieth the drop. The tender and simple seed, solitary though it may be, must not look upon its own lack of power. Nay, rather, its attention must ever be directed to the sun, in the rays of which it finds life and quickening; and it must ever consider the downpour of the cloud of mercy. For the bounty of the cloud, the effulgence and heat of the sun and the breath of the vernal zephyrs can transform the tiny seed and develop it into a mighty tree. And may you remember that a single infinitesimal atom in the ray of the sun through a shining beam of the solar energy becomes glorified and radiant.

Therefore, let us ever trust in God and seek confirmation and   5
assistance from Him. Let us have perfect and absolute confidence in the bounty of the Kingdom. Review the events surrounding souls of bygone times in the beginning of their day; and again consider them when, through the aid and assistance of God, they proved to be the mighty ones of God. Remember that Peter was a fisherman, but through the bounty of the Kingdom he became the great apostle. Mary Magdalene was a villager of lowly type, yet that selfsame Mary was transformed and became the means through which the confirmation of God descended upon the disciples. Verily, she served the Kingdom of God with such efficiency that she became well-known and oft mentioned by the tongues of men. Even today she is shining from the horizon of eternal majesty. Consider how infinite is the bounty of God that a woman such as Mary Magdalene should be selected by God to become the channel of confirmation to the disciples and a light of nearness in His Kingdom. Consequently, trust ye in the bounty and grace of God, and rest assured in the bestowals of His eternal outpouring. I hope that each one of you may become a shining light even as these electric lights are now brilliant in their intensity. Nay, may each one of you be a luminary like unto a sparkling star in the heaven of the divine Will. This is my supplication at the throne of God. This is my hope through the favors of Bahá'u'lláh. I offer this prayer in behalf of all of you and beg with a contrite heart that you may be assisted and glorified with an eternal bestowal.

8

10 November 1912

Talk at Home of Mr. and Mrs. Arthur J. Parsons
1700 Eighteenth Street, NW, Washington, D. C.

NOTES BY JOSEPH H. HANNEN

1 WHAT is the reality of Divinity, or what do we understand by God?

2 When we consider the world of existence, we find that the essential reality underlying any given phenomenon is unknown. Phenomenal, or created, things are known to us only by their attributes. Man discerns only manifestations, or attributes, of objects, while the identity, or reality, of them remains hidden. For example, we call this object a flower. What do we understand by this name and title? We understand that the qualities appertaining to this organism are perceptible to us, but the intrinsic elemental reality, or identity, of it remains unknown. Its external appearance and manifest attributes are knowable; but the inner being, the underlying reality or intrinsic identity, is still beyond the ken and perception of our human powers. Inasmuch as the realities of material phenomena are impenetrable and unknowable and are only apprehended through their properties or qualities, how much more this is true concerning the reality of Divinity, that holy essential reality which transcends the plane and grasp of mind and man? That which comes within human grasp is finite, and in relation to it we are infinite because we can grasp it. Assuredly, the finite is lesser than the infinite; the infinite is ever greater. If the reality of Divinity could be contained within the grasp of human mind, it would after all be possessed

594

of an intellectual existence only—a mere intellectual concept without extraneous existence, an image or likeness which had come within the comprehension of finite intellect. The mind of man would be transcendental thereto. How could it be possible that an image which has only intellectual existence is the reality of Divinity, which is infinite? Therefore, the reality of Divinity in its identity is beyond the range of human intellection because the human mind, the human intellect, the human thought are limited, whereas the reality of Divinity is unlimited. How can the limited grasp the unlimited and transcend it? Impossible. The unlimited always comprehends the limited. The limited can never comprehend, surround nor take in the unlimited. Therefore, every concept of Divinity which has come within the intellection of a human being is finite, or limited, and is a pure product of imagination, whereas the reality of Divinity is holy and sacred above and beyond all such concepts.

But the question may be asked: How shall we know God? [3] We know Him by His attributes. We know Him by His signs. We know Him by His names. We know not what the reality of the sun is, but we know the sun by the ray, by the heat, by its efficacy and penetration. We recognize the sun by its bounty and effulgence, but as to what constitutes the reality of the solar energy, that is unknowable to us. The attributes characterizing the sun, however, are knowable. If we wish to come in touch with the reality of Divinity, we do so by recognizing its phenomena, its attributes and traces, which are widespread in the universe. All things in the world of phenomena are expressive of that one reality. Its lights are shining, its heat is manifest, its power is expressive, and its education, or training, resplendent everywhere. What proof could there be greater than that of its functioning or its attributes which are manifest? This plant or this flower—we ask: Does it exist or not? Can this plant—this

595

flower—comprehend the reality of man? Can it put itself in touch with the human existence or reality? Evidently not. It is entirely out of tune with the human kingdom; it is not possessed of the capacity, although both man and the flower have been created. But the difference in the degrees between the vegetable and the human is ever a hindrance, an obstacle. Inasmuch as the degree of capacity appertaining to this plant is inferior to our human kingdom, it is entirely impossible for the plant, which is inferior, to comprehend man, who is superior, although both are accidental, or created. We are created; likewise, this plant is existent, this mineral exists, this wood exists. But can this flooring here comprehend those who are standing upon it? It cannot, because sight and hearing are properties or faculties belonging to a higher kingdom than the mineral. The difference between these two kingdoms, the vast difference between the mineral kingdom and the human kingdom, is a hindrance to comprehension.

4   How, then, can the reality of man, which is accidental, ever comprehend the Reality of God, which is eternal? It is self-evidently an impossibility. Hence we can observe the traces and attributes of God, which are resplendent in all phenomena and shining as the sun at midday, and know surely that these emanate from an infinite source. We know that they come from a source which is infinite indeed.

5   Furthermore, it is a philosophical principle that the existence of phenomena implies composition and that mortality, or nonexistence, is equivalent to decomposition. For example, certain elements have come together, and as a result of that composition man is here. Certain elements have entered into the structure of this flower. Certain organic or cellular elements have been utilized in the composition of every animal organism. Therefore, we can state that existence necessitates

composition, and death is another expression for decomposition. When there is disintegration amongst these composing elements, that is death; that is mortality. The elements which have gone into the body of this flower and which have given existence to this form and shape will finally disintegrate; this beautiful organism will decompose; and this we call mortality, death. Consequently, the conclusion is that life means composition, and death is equivalent to decomposition. On this account the materialists are of the opinion that life is the mere conjoining of elemental substances into myriad forms and shapes. The materialist comes to the conclusion that life, in other words, means composition; that wherever we find single elements combined in aggregate form, there we behold the phenomena of organic life; that every organic composition is organic life. Now if life means composition of elements, then the materialist may come to the conclusion of the nonnecessity of a composer, the nonnecessity of a creator; for composition is all there is to it, and that is accomplished by adhesion or cohesion. In response to this we say that composition must needs be of three kinds: One form of composition is termed philosophically the accidental, another the involuntary, and a third the voluntary. As to the first, or accidental, composition: This would signify that certain elements through inherent qualities and powers of attraction or affinity have been gathered together, have blended, and so composed a certain form, being or organism. This can be proven to be false; for composition is an effect, and philosophically no effect is conceivable without causation. No effect can be conceived of without some primal cause. For example, this heat is an effect; but that energy which gives forth this phenomenon of heat is the cause. This light is an effect, but back of it is the energy which is the cause. Is it possible for this light to be separated from the energy whereof it is a property? That is impossible and inconceivable. It is self-evidently false. Accidental composition is, therefore, a false theory and may be excluded.

6   As to the second form of composition—involuntary: This means that each element has within itself as an inherent property the power of composition. For example, the inherent quality of fire is burning, or heat; heat is a property of fire. Humidity is the inherent nature or property of water. You cannot conceive H_2O, which is the chemical form of water, without having humidity associated; for that is an inherent quality of water. The power of attraction has as its function attractive, or magnetic, qualities. We cannot separate attraction from that power. The power of repulsion has as its function repelling—sending off. You cannot separate the effect from the cause. If these premises be true—and they are self-evident—then it would be impossible for a composite being, for the elements which have gone into the makeup of a composite organism, ever to be decomposed because the inherent nature of each element would be to hold fast together. As fire cannot be separated from heat, likewise the elemental being could not be subjected to decomposition, and this does not hold true because we see decomposition everywhere. Hence this theory is untrue, inasmuch as we observe that after each composition there is a process of decomposition which forever ends it. By this we learn that composition as regards phenomena is neither accidental nor involuntary.

7   Then what have we left as a form of composition? It is the voluntary form of composition, which means that composition is effected through a superior will, that there is will expressed in this motive or action. It is thus proved that the existence of phenomena is effected through the eternal Will, the Will of the Living, Eternal and Self-subsistent, and this is a rational proof concerning composition whereof there is no doubt or uncertainty. Furthermore, it is quite evident that our kind of

life, our form of existence, is limited and that the reality of all accidental phenomena is, likewise, limited. The very fact that the reality of phenomena is limited well indicates that there must needs be an unlimited reality, for were there no unlimited, or infinite, reality in life, the finite being of objects would be inconceivable. To make it plainer for you, if there were no wealth in the world, you would not have poverty. If there were no light in the world, you could not conceive of darkness, for we know things philosophically by their antitheses. We know, for example, that poverty is the lack of wealth. Where there is no knowledge, there is no ignorance. What is ignorance? It is the absence of knowledge. Therefore, our limited existence is a conclusive proof that there is an unlimited reality, and this is a shining proof and evident argument. Many are the proofs concerning this matter, but there is not time to go into the subject further.

This is our last evening, and I ask God that His confirmations 8 may encompass you, that your hearts may become radiant, that your eyes become illumined through witnessing the signs of God, that your ears hearken to the anthems of heaven, that your faces be set aglow with the radiant light of the Word of God. May you all be united, may you be agreed, may you serve the solidarity of mankind. May you be well-wishers of all humanity. May you be assistants of every poor one. May you be nurses for the sick. May you be sources of comfort to the broken in heart. May you be a refuge for the wanderer. May you be a source of courage to the affrighted one. Thus, through the favor and assistance of God may the standard of the happiness of humanity be held aloft in the center of the world and the ensign of universal agreement be unfurled.

9

10 November 1912

Talk at Home of Mr. and Mrs. Joseph H. Hannen
1252 Eighth Street, NW, Washington, D. C.

NOTES BY JOSEPH H. HANNEN

1 THIS is a beautiful assembly. I am very happy that white and black are together. This is the cause of my happiness, for you all are the servants of one God and, therefore, brothers, sisters, mothers and fathers. In the sight of God there is no distinction between whites and blacks; all are as one. Anyone whose heart is pure is dear to God—whether white or black, red or yellow. Among the animals colors exist. The doves are white, black, red, blue; but notwithstanding this diversity of color they flock together in unity, happiness and fellowship, making no distinction among themselves, for they are all doves. Man is intelligent and thoughtful, endowed with powers of mind. Why, then, should he be influenced by distinction of color or race, since all belong to one human family? There is no sheep which shuns another as if saying, "I am white, and you are black." They graze together in complete unity, live together in fellowship and happiness. How then can man be limited and influenced by racial colors? The important thing is to realize that all are human, all are one progeny of Adam. Inasmuch as they are all one family, why should they be separated?

2 I had a servant who was black; his name was Isfandíyár. If a perfect man could be found in the world, that man was Isfandíyár. He was the essence of love, radiant with sanctity and perfection, luminous with light. Whenever I think of Isfandíyár, I am moved to tears, although he passed away fifty years ago.

He was the faithful servant of Bahá'u'lláh and was entrusted with His secrets. For this reason the Sháh of Persia wanted him and inquired continually as to his whereabouts. Bahá'u'lláh was in prison, but the Sháh had commanded many persons to find Isfandíyár. Perhaps more than one hundred officers were appointed to search for him. If they had succeeded in catching him, they would not have killed him at once. They would have cut his flesh into pieces to force him to tell them the secrets of Bahá'u'lláh. But Isfandíyár with the utmost dignity used to walk in the streets and bazaars. One day he came to us. My mother, my sister and myself lived in a house near a corner. Because our enemies frequently injured us, we were intending to go to a place where they did not know us. I was a child at that time. At midnight Isfandíyár came in. My mother said, "O Isfandíyár, there are a hundred policemen seeking for you. If they catch you, they will not kill you at once but will torture you with fire. They will cut off your fingers. They will cut off your ears. They will put out your eyes to force you to tell them the secrets of Bahá'u'lláh. Go away! Do not stay here." He said, "I cannot go because I owe money in the street and in the stores. How can I go? They will say that the servant of Bahá'u'lláh has bought and consumed the goods and supplies of the storekeepers without paying for them. Unless I pay all these obligations, I cannot go. But if they take me, never mind. If they punish me, there is no harm in that. If they kill me, do not be grieved. But to go away is impossible. I must remain until I pay all I owe. Then I will go." For one month Isfandíyár went about in the streets and bazaars. He had things to sell, and from his earnings he gradually paid his creditors. In fact, they were not his debts but the debts of the court, for all our properties had been confiscated. Everything we had was taken away from us. The only things that remained were our debts. Isfandíyár paid them in full; not a single penny remained unpaid. Then he came to us, said good-bye and went away. Afterward Bahá'u'lláh was released from prison. We went to Baghdád, and Isfandíyár came there. He wanted to stay in the same home. Bahá'u'lláh, the Blessed Perfection, said to him, "When you fled away, there was a Persian minister who gave you shelter at a time when no one else could give you protection. Because he gave you shelter and protected you, you must be faithful to him. If he is satisfied to have you go, then come to us; but if he does not want you to go, do not leave him." His master said, "I do not want to be separated from Isfandíyár. Where can I find another like him, with such sincerity, such faithfulness, such character, such power? Where can I find one? O Isfandíyár! I am not willing that you should go, yet if you wish to go, let it be according to your own will." But because the Blessed Perfection had said, "You must be faithful," Isfandíyár stayed with his master until he died. He was a point of light. Although his color was black, yet his character was luminous; his mind was luminous; his face was luminous. Truly, he was a point of light.

3   Then it is evident that excellence does not depend upon color. Character is the true criterion of humanity. Anyone who possesses a good character, who has faith in God and is firm, whose actions are good, whose speech is good—that one is accepted at the threshold of God no matter what color he may be. In short—praise be to God!—you are the servants of God. The love of Bahá'u'lláh is in your hearts. Your souls are rejoicing in the glad tidings of Bahá'u'lláh. My hope is that the white and the black will be united in perfect love and fellowship, with complete unity and brotherhood. Associate with each other, think of each other, and be like a rose garden. Anyone who goes into a rose garden will see various roses, white, pink, yellow, red, all growing together and replete with adornment. Each one accentuates the beauty of the other. Were all of one color, the

garden would be monotonous to the eye. If they were all white or yellow or red, the garden would lack variety and attractiveness; but when the colors are varied, white, pink, yellow, red, there will be the greatest beauty. Therefore, I hope that you will be like a rose garden. Although different in colors, yet—praise be to God!—you receive rays from the same sun. From one cloud the rain is poured upon you. You are under the training of one Gardener, and this Gardener is kind to all. Therefore, you must manifest the utmost kindness towards each other, and you may rest assured that whenever you are united, the confirmations of the Kingdom of Abhá will reach you, the heavenly favors will descend, the bounties of God will be bestowed, the Sun of Reality will shine, the cloud of mercy will pour its showers, and the breeze of divine generosity will waft its fragrances upon you.

I hope you will continue in unity and fellowship. How beauti- 4 ful to see blacks and whites together! I hope, God willing, the day may come when I shall see the red men, the Indians, with you, also Japanese and others. Then there will be white roses, yellow roses, red roses, and a very wonderful rose garden will appear in the world.

10

10 November 1912

Talk at 1901 Eighteenth Street, NW, Washington, D. C.

Notes by Joseph H. Hannen

1 I AM greatly pleased with the friends in Washington and experience real happiness in meeting them. Likewise, I am pleased
with the friends from Baltimore, for I have observed that their
hearts are attracted to the love of Bahá'u'lláh. Their vision is
extended toward the Kingdom of Bahá. Their spirits are rejoicing in the glad tidings of Abhá. Verily, they are servants of the
Cause of God. All are engaged in service, and the perfection of
their desire is to enter into the Kingdom of Abhá and draw near
unto God. For that reason I am very happy and well pleased with
them. I pray for you all. May the favors of the Blessed Beauty,
Bahá'u'lláh, encompass you, and may the lights of the Sun of
Reality be your illumination. May you all become united and
assured. May you serve the Cause of God as one single, united
force. I give you the glad tidings that the confirmations of God
will descend upon you. Be ye assured of this. Ye will become
illumined. Ye will become conquerors.

2 But after I leave, some people may arise in opposition,
heaping persecutions upon you in their bitterness, and in the
newspapers there may be articles published against the Cause.
Rest ye in the assurance of firmness. Be well poised and serene,
remembering that this is only as the harmless twittering of
sparrows and that it will soon pass away. If such things do not
happen, the fame of the Cause will not become widespread, and
the summons of God will not be heard. Consider the history of

604

the past. Recall, for instance, the days of Christ and the events subsequent thereto. How many were the books written against Him! What calumnies were attributed to Him! How violent were the utterances in the temples against Him! How many the accusations! What hatred and persecution! How they scoffed at Him in derision and contempt! Consider the titles and epithets they bestowed upon His majesty! They even designated Him Beelzebub—Satan. They said Beelzebub had been captured and crucified. They placed a crown of thorns upon Beelzebub's head and paraded Him through the streets. This was the name the Jews bestowed upon Christ; it is written in the Gospel. There were many other forms of reviling and persecution, spitting in His beautiful face, cursing and anathematizing, bowing backward toward Him, saying, "Peace be on thee, thou king of the Jews!" "Peace be on thee, thou destroyer of the temple!" "Peace be on thee, thou king and pretender who would restore the temple in three days!" The philosophers of the times, Romans and Greeks, wrote against Christ. Even the kings wrote books of abuse, calumny and contempt. One of these kings was a Caesar. He was also a philosopher. In his book he says, concerning the people of Christ, "The most degraded of people are the Christians. The most immoral of the people of this time are the Christians. Jesus of Nazareth has led them astray. O people! If you wish to know who Jesus is and what Christian means, go and ask his relatives. Go and ask the Jews who know him. See what a bad person he is, how degraded he is." There were many similar accounts. But remember that these statements did not affect the cause of Christianity. On the contrary, Christianity advanced daily in power and potency.

Day by day the majesty of Christ grew in splendor and effulgence. Therefore, my purpose is to warn and strengthen you against accusations, criticisms, revilings and derision in 3 newspaper articles or other publications. Be not disturbed by them. They are the very confirmation of the Cause, the very source of upbuilding to the Movement. May God confirm the day when a score of ministers of the churches may arise and with bared heads cry at the top of their voices that the Bahá'ís are misguided. I would like to see that day, for that is the time when the Cause of God will spread. Bahá'u'lláh has pronounced such as these the couriers of the Cause. They will proclaim from pulpits that the Bahá'ís are fools, that they are a wicked and unrighteous people, but be ye steadfast and unwavering in the Cause of God. They will spread the message of Bahá'u'lláh.

4   His Honor Mírzá Abu'l-Faḍl has written a treatise answering the criticisms of a London preacher. Each one of you should have a copy.* Read, memorize and reflect upon it. Then, when accusations and criticisms are advanced by those unfavorable to the Cause, you will be well armed.

---

* Mirza Abul Fazl Gulpaygan, *The Brilliant Proof* (Chicago: Press of Bahai News Service, 1912). The booklet was published under the direction of 'Abdu'l-Bahá while He was in America.

Talks 'Abdu'l-Bahá Delivered in New York

15 November 1912

Talk at Home of Miss Juliet Thompson
48 West Tenth Street, New York

NOTES BY HOOPER HARRIS

I HAVE spoken in the various Christian churches and in the   1
synagogues, and in no assemblage has there been a dissenting
voice. All have listened, and all have conceded that the teachings
of Bahá'u'lláh are superlative in character, acknowledging that
they constitute the very essence or spirit of this new age and
that there is no better pathway to the attainment of its ideals.
Not a single voice has been raised in objection. At most there
have been some who have refused to acknowledge the mission
of Bahá'u'lláh, although even these have admitted that He was
a great teacher, a most powerful soul, a very great man. Some
who could find no other pretext have said, "These teachings are
not new; they are old and familiar; we have heard them before."
Therefore, I will speak to you upon the distinctive characteristics of the manifestation of Bahá'u'lláh and prove that from
every standpoint His Cause is distinguished from all others. It
is distinguished by its didactic character and method of exposition, by its practical effects and application to present world
conditions, but especially distinguished from the standpoint
of its spread and progress.

When Bahá'u'lláh appeared in Persia, all the contemporane-   2
ous religious sects and systems rose against Him. His enemies
were kings. The enemies of Christ were the Jews, the Pharisees;

but the enemies of Bahá'u'lláh were rulers who could command armies and bring hundreds of thousands of soldiers into the arena of operation. These kings represented some fifty million people, all of whom under their influence and domination were opposed to Bahá'u'lláh. Therefore, in effect Bahá'u'lláh, singly and alone, virtually withstood fifty million enemies. Yet these great numbers, instead of being able to dominate Him, could not withstand His wonderful personality and the power and influence of His heavenly Cause. Although they were determined upon extinguishing the light in that most brilliant lantern, they were ultimately defeated and overthrown, and day by day His splendor became more radiant. They made every effort to lessen His greatness, but His prestige and renown grew in proportion to their endeavors to diminish it. Surrounded by enemies who were seeking His life, He never sought to conceal Himself, did nothing to protect Himself; on the contrary, in His spiritual might and power He was at all times visible before the faces of men, easy of access, serenely withstanding the multitudes who were opposing Him. At last His banner was upraised.

3 If we study historical record and review the pages of Holy Writ, we will find that none of the Prophets of the past ever spread His teachings or promulgated His Cause from a prison. But Bahá'u'lláh upheld the banner of the Cause of God while He was in a dungeon, addressing the kings of the earth from His prison cell, severely arraigning them for their oppression of their subjects and their misuse of power. The letter He sent to the Sháh of Persia under such conditions may now be read by anyone. His Epistles to the Sulṭán of Turkey, Napoleon III, Emperor of France, and to the other rulers of the world including the President of the United States are, likewise, current and available. The book containing these Epistles to the kings was published in India about thirty years ago and is known as

the Súratu'l-Haykal ("Discourse of the Temple"). Whatever is recorded in these Epistles has happened. Some of the prophecies contained in them came to pass after two years; others were fulfilled after five, ten and twenty years. The most important prophecies relative to events transpiring in the Balkans are being fulfilled at the present time though written long ago. For instance, in the Epistle which Bahá'u'lláh addressed to the Sultán of Turkey, the war and the occurrences of the present day were foretold by Him. These events were also prophesied in the Tablet He addressed to the city of Constantinople, even to the details of happenings now being witnessed in that city.

While addressing these powerful kings and rulers He was a   4
prisoner in a Turkish dungeon. Consider how marvelous it was for a prisoner under the eye and control of the Turks to arraign so boldly and severely the very king who was responsible for His imprisonment. What power this is! What greatness! Nowhere in history can the record of such a happening be found. In spite of the iron rule and absolute dominion of these kings, His function was to withstand them; and so constant and firm was He that He caused their banners to come down and His own standard to be upraised. For today the flags of both the Persian and the Ottoman Empires are trailing in the dust, whereas the ensign of Bahá'u'lláh is being held aloft in the world both in the East and in the West. Consider what a mighty power this is! What a decisive argument! Although a prisoner in a fortress, He paid no heed to these kings, regarded not their power of life and death, but, on the contrary, addressed them in plain and fearless language, announcing explicitly that the time would come when their sovereignty would be brought low and His own dominion be established.

He said in substance, "Erelong you will find yourselves in   5
manifest loss. Your sovereignties will be laid waste; your em-

pires will become a wilderness and a heap of ruins; hosts from without will invade and subdue your lands; lamentation and mourning will rise from your homes. There will be no throne; there will be no crown; there will be no palace; there will be no armies. Nay, rather, all these will be brought low; but the standard of the Cause of God will be held aloft. Then will you see that hosts and hosts will enter the Cause of God and that this mighty revelation will be spread throughout the world." Read the prophecies contained in the Súratu'l-Haykal and ponder carefully over them.

6   This is one of the characteristics of Bahá'u'lláh's message and teachings. Can you find events and happenings of this kind in any other prophetic dispensation? If so, in what cycle have similar things taken place? Do you find such specific prophecies and explicit statements concerning the future in the Holy Books of the past? We will now compare the teachings of Bahá'u'lláh with the Holy Words which have descended in the former cycles.

7   First among the great principles revealed by Him is that of the investigation of reality. The meaning is that every individual member of humankind is exhorted and commanded to set aside superstitious beliefs, traditions and blind imitation of ancestral forms in religion and investigate reality for himself. Inasmuch as the fundamental reality is one, all religions and nations of the world will become one through investigation of reality. The announcement of this principle is not found in any of the sacred Books of the past.

8   A second characteristic principle of the teachings of Bahá'u'lláh is that which commands recognition of the oneness of the world of humanity. Addressing all mankind, He says, "Ye are all the leaves of one tree." There are no differences or distinctions of race among you in the sight of God. Nay, rather, all are the servants of God, and all are submerged in the ocean of His oneness. Not a single soul is bereft. On the contrary, all are the

recipients of the bounties of God. Every human creature has a portion of His bestowals and a share of the effulgence of His reality. God is kind to all. Mankind are His sheep, and He is their real Shepherd. No other scriptures contain such breadth and universality of statement; no other teachings proclaim this unequivocal principle of the solidarity of humanity. As regards any possible distinctions, the utmost that Bahá'u'lláh says is that conditions among men vary, that some, for instance, are defective. Therefore, such souls must be educated in order that they may be brought to the degree of perfection. Some are sick and ailing; they must be treated and cared for until they are healed. Some are asleep; they need to be awakened. Some are immature as children; they should be helped to attain maturity. But all must be loved and cherished. The child must not be disliked simply because it is a child. Nay, rather, it should be patiently educated. The sick one must not be avoided nor slighted merely because he is ailing. Nay, rather, he must be regarded with sympathy and affection and treated until he is healed. The soul that is asleep must not be looked upon with contempt but awakened and led into the light.

Bahá'u'lláh teaches that religion must be in conformity with 9 science and reason. If belief and teaching are opposed to the analysis of reason and principles of science, they are not worthy of acceptance. This principle has not been revealed in any of the former Books of divine teaching.

Another fundamental announcement made by Bahá'u'lláh 10 is that religion must be the source of unity and fellowship in the world. If it is productive of enmity, hatred and bigotry, the absence of religion would be preferable. This is a new principle of revelation found only in the utterances of Bahá'u'lláh.

Again, Bahá'u'lláh declares that all forms of prejudice among 11 mankind must be abandoned and that until existing prejudices are entirely removed, the world of humanity will not and cannot attain peace, prosperity and composure. This principle cannot be found in any other sacred volume than the teachings of Bahá'u'lláh.

12   Another teaching is that there shall be perfect equality between men and women. Why should man create a distinction which God does not recognize? In the kingdoms below man sex exists, but the distinction between male and female is neither repressive nor restrictive. The mare, for instance, is as strong and often more speedy than the horse. Throughout the animal and vegetable kingdoms there is perfect equality between the sexes. In the kingdom of mankind this equality must likewise exist, and the one whose heart is purest, whose life and character are highest and nearest to the divine standard is most worthy and excellent in the sight of God. This is the only true and real distinction, be that one man or woman.

13   Bahá'u'lláh has announced the necessity for a universal language which shall serve as a means of international communication and thus remove misunderstandings and difficulties. This teaching is set forth in the Kitáb-i-Aqdas ("Most Holy Book") published fifty years ago.

14   He has also proclaimed the principle that all mankind shall be educated and that no illiteracy be allowed to remain. This practical remedy for the need of the world cannot be found in the text of any other sacred Books.

15   He teaches that it is incumbent upon all mankind to become fitted for some useful trade, craft or profession by which subsistence may be assured, and this efficiency is to be considered as an act of worship.

16   The teachings of Bahá'u'lláh are boundless and without end in their far-reaching benefit to mankind. The point and purpose of our statement today is that they are new and that they are not found in any of the religious Books of the past. This is in

answer to the question, "What has Bahá'u'lláh brought that we have not heard before?" Therefore, it is conclusive and evident that the Manifestation of God in this day is distinguished from all former appearances and revelations by His majesty, His power and the efficacy and application of His Word.

All the Prophets of God were scorned and persecuted. Consider 17 Moses. The people called Him a murderer. They said, "You killed a man and fled from punishment and retribution. Is it possible after your former deeds that you could become a Prophet?"

Many similar experiences are recorded concerning the holy, 18 divine Messengers. How bitter and severe was the persecution to which They were subjected! Consider how they endeavored to efface and belittle Christ. They placed upon His head a crown of thorns and paraded Him through the streets and bazaars in mockery crying, "Peace be upon thee, thou king of the Jews!" Some would bow to Him backward, saying in scornful tones, "Thou king of the Jews!" or "Lord of lords, peace be upon thee!" Still others would spit upon His blessed countenance. In brief, the persecutions which Christ suffered during the time of His manifestation are mentioned in the books of the old cycle, Jewish, Roman or Greek. No praises were bestowed upon Him. The only recognition and acceptance offered Him was from His believers and followers. Peter, for instance, was one who praised Him; and the other disciples spoke in His behalf. Numerous books were written against Him. In the history of the Church you will find record of the hatred and antagonism manifested by the Roman, Greek and Egyptian philosophers, attributing calumnies and ascribing imperfection to Him.

But during the manifestation of Bahá'u'lláh, from the day of 19 His appearance to the time of His departure, the people of all nations acknowledged His greatness, and even those who were His most bitter enemies have said of Him, "This man was truly great; his influence was mighty and wonderful. This personage was glorious; his power was tremendous, his speech most eloquent; but, alas, he was a misleader of the people." This was the essence of their praise, eulogy and denial. It is evident that the authors of such statements, although His enemies, were profoundly impressed by His greatness and majesty. Some of His enemies have even written poems about Him, which though intended for satire and sarcastic allusion, have in reality been praise. For instance, a certain poet opposed to His Cause has said, "Beware! Beware! lest ye approach this person, for he is possessed of such power and of such an eloquent tongue that he is a sorcerer. He charms men, he drugs them; he is a hypnotizer. Beware! Beware! lest you read his book follow his example and associate with his companions because they are the possessors of tremendous power and they are misleaders." That is to say, this poet used such characterizations, believing them to be terms of belittlement and disparagement, unaware that they were in reality praises, because a wise man, after reading such a warning, would say, "The power of this man must unquestionably be very great if even his enemies acknowledge it. Undoubtedly, such a power is heavenly in its nature." This was one of the reasons why so many were moved to investigate. The more His enemies wrote against Him, the more the people were attracted and the greater the number who came to inquire about the truth. They would say, "This is remarkable. This is a great man, and we must investigate. We must look into this cause to find out what it all means, to discover its purpose, examine its proofs and learn for ourselves what it signifies." In this way the malign and sinister statements of His enemies caused the people to become friendly and approach the Cause. In Persia the mullás went so far as to proclaim from the pulpits against the Cause of Bahá'u'lláh casting their turbans upon the ground—a sign of great agitation—and crying out, "O people! This Bahá'u'lláh is a sorcerer who is seeking to mesmerize you; he is alienating you from your own religion and making you his own followers. Beware! lest you read his book. Beware! lest you associate with his friends."

Bahá'u'lláh, speaking of these very ones who were attack- 20 ing and decrying Him, said, "They are My heralds; they are the ones who are proclaiming My message and spreading My Word. Pray that they may be multiplied, pray that their number may increase and that they may cry out more loudly. The more they abuse Me by their words and the greater their agitation, the more potent and mighty will be the efficacy of the Cause of God, the more luminous the light of the Word and the greater the radiance of the divine Sun. And eventually the gloomy darkness of the outer world will disappear, and the light of reality will shine until the whole earth will be effulgent with its glory."

2

16 November 1912

Talk at 309 West Seventy-eighth Street, New York

Notes by Edna McKinney

WHEREVER the mention of Bahá'u'lláh rises up, that is the 1 paradise of Abhá. Wherever purified, severed and illumined souls are found, that is the paradise of Bahá. Ṭihrán is the paradise of Bahá'u'lláh, for souls are found there you cannot call human; they are angels. In reality, the Bahá'í friends in that city are of the heavenly host. Whenever I think of them, I become happy.

2   The Blessed Perfection suffered innumerable ordeals and calamities, but during His lifetime He trained in all regions many souls who were peerless. The purpose of the appearance of the Manifestations of God is the training of the people. That is the only result of Their mission, the real outcome. The outcome of the whole life of Jesus was the training of eleven disciples and two women. Why did He suffer troubles, ordeals and calamities? For the training of these few followers. That was the result of His life. The product of the life of Christ was not the churches but the illumined souls of those who believed in Him. Afterward, they spread His teachings.

3   It is my hope that you all may become the product of the life of Bahá'u'lláh and the outcomes of His heavenly training. When the people ask you, "What has Bahá'u'lláh accomplished?" say to them, "He has created these; He has trained us."

3

17 November 1912

Talk at Genealogical Hall
252 West Fifty-eighth Street, New York

NOTES BY EDNA MCKINNEY

1   THIS is a blessed meeting, for these revered souls have come together in complete unity and with an intelligent purpose. It is an occasion of great joy to me. Before me are faces radiant with the glad tidings of God, hearts aglow with the fire of the love of God, ears attuned to the melodies of the Kingdom and eyes illumined by the signs and evidences of Divinity.

All created things have their degree, or stage, of maturity. 2
The period of maturity in the life of a tree is the time of its
fruit bearing. The maturity of a plant is the time of its blos-
soming and flower. The animal attains a stage of full growth
and completeness, and in the human kingdom man reaches
his maturity when the lights of intelligence have their greatest
power and development.

From the beginning to the end of his life man passes through 3
certain periods, or stages, each of which is marked by certain
conditions peculiar to itself. For instance, during the period of
childhood his conditions and requirements are characteristic of
that degree of intelligence and capacity. After a time he enters
the period of youth, in which his former conditions and needs
are superseded by new requirements applicable to the advance
in his degree. His faculties of observation are broadened and
deepened; his intelligent capacities are trained and awakened;
the limitations and environment of childhood no longer restrict
his energies and accomplishments. At last he passes out of the
period of youth and enters the stage, or station, of maturity,
which necessitates another transformation and corresponding
advance in his sphere of life activity. New powers and perceptions clothe him, teaching and training commensurate with his
progression occupy his mind, special bounties and bestowals
descend in proportion to his increased capacities, and his former period of youth and its conditions will no longer satisfy his
matured view and vision.

Similarly, there are periods and stages in the life of the aggre- 4
gate world of humanity, which at one time was passing through
its degree of childhood, at another its time of youth but now
has entered its long presaged period of maturity, the evidences
of which are everywhere visible and apparent. Therefore, the requirements and conditions of former periods have changed and

merged into exigencies which distinctly characterize the present age of the world of mankind. That which was applicable to human needs during the early history of the race could neither meet nor satisfy the demands of this day and period of newness and consummation. Humanity has emerged from its former degrees of limitation and preliminary training. Man must now become imbued with new virtues and powers, new moralities, new capacities. New bounties, bestowals and perfections are awaiting and already descending upon him. The gifts and graces of the period of youth, although timely and sufficient during the adolescence of the world of mankind, are now incapable of meeting the requirements of its maturity. The playthings of childhood and infancy no longer satisfy or interest the adult mind.

5   From every standpoint the world of humanity is undergoing a reformation. The laws of former governments and civilizations are in process of revision; scientific ideas and theories are developing and advancing to meet a new range of phenomena; invention and discovery are penetrating hitherto unknown fields, revealing new wonders and hidden secrets of the material universe; industries have vastly wider scope and production; everywhere the world of mankind is in the throes of evolutionary activity indicating the passing of the old conditions and advent of the new age of reformation. Old trees yield no fruitage; old ideas and methods are obsolete and worthless now. Old standards of ethics, moral codes and methods of living in the past will not suffice for the present age of advancement and progress.

6   This is the cycle of maturity and reformation in religion as well. Dogmatic imitations of ancestral beliefs are passing. They have been the axis around which religion revolved but now are no longer fruitful; on the contrary, in this day they have become the cause of human degradation and hindrance. Bigotry and

dogmatic adherence to ancient beliefs have become the central and fundamental source of animosity among men, the obstacle to human progress, the cause of warfare and strife, the destroyer of peace, composure and welfare in the world. Consider conditions in the Balkans today: fathers, mothers, children in grief and lamentation, the foundations of life overturned, cities laid waste and fertile lands made desolate by the ravages of war. These conditions are the outcome of hostility and hatred between nations and peoples of religion who imitate and adhere to the forms and violate the spirit and reality of the divine teachings.

While this is true and apparent, it is, likewise, evident that 7 the Lord of mankind has bestowed infinite bounties upon the world in this century of maturity and consummation. The ocean of divine mercy is surging, the vernal showers are descending, the Sun of Reality is shining gloriously. Heavenly teachings applicable to the advancement in human conditions have been revealed in this merciful age. This reformation and renewal of the fundamental reality of religion constitute the true and outworking spirit of modernism, the unmistakable light of the world, the manifest effulgence of the Word of God, the divine remedy for all human ailment and the bounty of eternal life to all mankind.

Bahá'u'lláh, the Sun of Truth, has dawned from the horizon 8 of the Orient, flooding all regions with the light and life which will never pass away. His teachings, which embody the divine spirit of the age and are applicable to this period of maturity in the life of the human world, are:

The oneness of the world of humanity 9
The protection and guidance of the Holy Spirit 10
The foundation of all religion is one 11
Religion must be the cause of unity 12

13   Religion must accord with science and reason
14   Independent investigation of truth
15   Equality between men and women
16   The abandoning of all prejudices among mankind
17   Universal peace
18   Universal education
19   A universal language
20   Solution of the economic problem
21   An international tribunal.

22   Everyone who truly seeks and justly reflects will admit that the teachings of the present day emanating from mere human sources and authority are the cause of difficulty and disagreement amongst mankind, the very destroyers of humanity, whereas the teachings of Bahá'u'lláh are the very healing of the sick world, the remedy for every need and condition. In them may be found the realization of every desire and aspiration, the cause of the happiness of the world of humanity, the stimulus and illumination of mentality, the impulse for advancement and uplift, the basis of unity for all nations, the fountain source of love amongst mankind, the center of agreement, the means of peace and harmony, the one bond which will unite the East and the West.

23   After every night there is a morn. In the supreme wisdom of God it is decreed that when the gross darkness of religious hatred and hostility, the obscurity of religious ignorance, superstition and blind imitations cover the world, the Sun of Truth shall arise and the spirit of reality become manifest and reflected in human hearts. At such a time as this Bahá'u'lláh appeared upon the horizon of the Orient. For fifty years He endured the greatest hardships and ordeals, ever striving to dispel the darkness of religious conditions, to remove the cause of enmity and rancor, to awaken the world of humanity from the beds of negligence

and heedlessness by the flashing light of the glorious glad tidings and trumpet tone of the heavenly call and summons. For the spread of this message He offered His life and bore every vicissitude. . . . He was always under the threat and menace of the sword, yet He uplifted the standard of divine teachings and flooded the world of the East with illumination. In the Orient today the light of the heavenly glad tidings is visible everywhere, the divine call is heard, the effulgence of the Sun of Reality is shining, the precious rain is pouring down from the clouds of mercy, and the breaths of the Holy Spirit are bestowing fresh life upon the hearts of men. Erelong the darkness will pass away entirely, and the regions of the East will become completely illumined; enmity, hatred, ignorance and bigotry will no longer remain; the satanic powers which destroy human equality and religious unity will be dethroned, and the nations will dwell in peace and harmony under the overspreading banner of the oneness of humanity. Therefore, we supplicate the Lord our God with sincere and contrite hearts, asking aid and assistance in the accomplishment of this mighty end: that the nations shall be unified in the Word of God; that war, enmity and hatred between races, religions, native lands and denominations shall disappear and be forever unknown; and that peoples and nations shall spiritually embrace each other in the indissoluble bond and power of the love of God. Then will the world of humanity become radiant and the human race enjoy to the fullest capacity the graces of divine bestowal. So long as religious discord and enmity continue among mankind, the world of humanity will find neither happiness, rest nor composure.

Pray that God may assist in this heavenly undertaking, that the world of mankind shall be saved from the ordeals of ignorance, blindness and spiritual death. Then will you behold light upon light, joy upon joy, absolute happiness reigning everywhere, the people of the religions consorting together in fragrance and 24 felicity, this world in its maturity becoming the reflection of the eternal Kingdom and this terrestrial abode of man the very paradise of God. Pray for this! Pray for this!

25   O my God! O my God! Verily, Thou dost perceive those who are present here turning unto Thee, relying upon Thee. O my Lord! O my Lord! Illumine their eyes by the light of love, and enkindle their hearts by the rays streaming from the heaven of the Supreme Concourse. Suffer them to become the signs of Thy bestowal amongst the people and the standards of Thy grace amongst mankind. O Lord! Make those who are here the hosts of heaven, and through their service and instrumentality subdue the hearts of humanity. Cause Thy great mercy to descend upon them, and render all Thy friends victorious. Direct them that they may turn toward Thy Kingdom of mercy and proclaim Thy name among the people. May they lead the people to the bounty of Thy most great guidance.

26   O Lord! O Lord! Cast the glance of Thy mercy upon them all.

27   O Lord! O Lord! Ordain for them the beauty of Thy holiness in Thy Kingdom of eternity.

28   O Lord! O Lord! Protect them in every test, make every foot firm in the pathway of Thy love, and help them to be as mighty mountains in Thy Cause so that their faith shall not be wavering, their sight shall not be dimmed nor hindered from witnessing the lights emanating from Thy supreme Kingdom. Verily, Thou art the Generous. Thou art the Almighty. Verily, Thou art the Clement, the Merciful.

4

18 November 1912

Talk at Home of Mr. and Mrs. Frank K. Moxey
575 Riverside Drive, New York

<small>NOTES BY ESTHER FOSTER</small>

I OFFER thanks to God for this meeting with you. From the outer   1
standpoint such meetings are inconceivable, for we are orientals
whereas you are occidentals. Between us there is no patriotic,
linguistic, racial, commercial nor political relation. No worldly
bond nor connection of any kind exists between us that would
justify such a gathering as this. The love of God has brought us
together, and this is the best of means and motive. Every other
bond of friendship is limited in effectiveness, but fellowship
based upon the love of God is unlimited, everlasting, divine
and radiant. Therefore, we must be thankful to God for uniting
us in love and agreement, praise Him for creating such affinity
between us that those from the faraway Orient may associate
with the beloved ones of the West in the utmost fragrance.

Surely for everything there is an all-comprehending wisdom,   2
especially for the great and important affairs of life. The supreme
and most important happening in the human world is the Manifestation of God and the descent of the law of God. The holy,
divine Manifestations did not reveal themselves for the purpose
of founding a nation, sect or faction. They did not appear in
order that a certain number might acknowledge Their Prophethood. They did not declare Their heavenly mission and message
in order to lay the foundation for a religious belief. Even Christ
did not become manifest that we should merely believe in Him

as the Christ, follow Him and adore His mention. All these are limited in scope and requirement, whereas the reality of Christ is an unlimited essence. The infinite and unlimited Reality cannot be bounded by any limitation. Nay, rather, Christ appeared in order to illumine the world of humanity, to render the earthly world celestial, to make the human kingdom a realm of angels, to unite the hearts, to enkindle the light of love in human souls, so that such souls might become independent, attaining complete unity and fellowship, turning to God, entering into the divine Kingdom, receiving the bounties and bestowals of God and partaking of the manna from heaven. Through Christ they were intended to be baptized by the Holy Spirit, attain a new spirit and realize the everlasting life. All the holy precepts and the announcements of prophetic laws were for these various and heavenly purposes. Therefore, we offer thanks to God that although no earthly relation obtains among us, yet—praise be to God!—ideal and divine bonds blend us together. We have gathered here in this meeting, eagerly anticipating the showing forth of the divine bestowals.

3   In past centuries the nations of the world have imagined that the law of God demanded blind imitation of ancestral forms of belief and worship. For example, the Jews were captives of hereditary racial religious observances. The Muslims, likewise, have been held in the bondage of traditionary forms and ceremonials. The Christians also have been implicit followers of ancient tradition and hereditary teaching. At the same time the basic foundation of the religion of God, which was ever the principle of love, unity and the fellowship of humanity, has been forsaken and cast aside, each religious system holding tenaciously to imitations of ancestral forms as the supreme essential. Therefore, hatred and hostility have appeared in the world instead of the divine fruitage of unity and love. By reason of this it has

been impossible for the followers of religion to meet together in fellowship and agreement. Even contact and communication have been considered contaminating, and the outcome has been a condition of complete alienation and mutual bigotry. There has been no investigation of the essential underlying basis of reality. One whose father was a Jew invariably proved to be a Jew, a Muslim was born of a Muslim, a Buddhist was a Buddhist because of the faith of his father before him, and so on. In brief, religion was a heritage descending from father to son, ancestry to posterity, without investigation of the fundamental reality; consequently, all religionists were veiled, obscured and at variance.

Praise be to God! We are living in this most radiant century 4 wherein human perceptions have developed and investigations of real foundations characterize mankind. Individually and collectively man is proving and penetrating into the reality of outer and inner conditions. Therefore, it has come to pass that we are renouncing all that savors of blind imitation, and impartially and independently investigating truth. Let us understand what constitutes the reality of the divine religions. If a Christian sets aside traditionary forms and blind imitation of ceremonials and investigates the reality of the Gospels, he will discover that the foundation principles of the teachings of Christ were mercy, love, fellowship, benevolence, altruism, the resplendence or radiance of divine bestowals, acquisition of the breaths of the Holy Spirit and oneness with God. Furthermore, he will learn that Christ declared that the Father "maketh his sun to rise on the evil and on the good, and sendeth rain on the just and on the unjust." The meaning of this declaration is that the mercy of God encircles all mankind, that not a single individual is deprived of the mercy of God, and no soul is denied the resplendent bestowals of God. The whole human race is submerged in the sea of the mercy of the Lord, and we are all the sheep of the one divine Shepherd. Whatever shortcomings exist among us must be remedied. For example, those who are ignorant must be educated so that they may become wise; the sick must be treated until they recover; those who are immature must be trained in order to reach maturity; those asleep must be awakened. All this must be accomplished through love and not through hatred and hostility. Furthermore, Jesus Christ, referring to the prophecy of Isaiah, spoke of those who having eyes, see not, having ears, hear not, having hearts, understand not; yet they were to be healed. Therefore, it is evident that the bounties of Christ transformed the eye which was blind into a seeing one, rendered the ear which was formerly deaf, attentive, and made the hard, callous heart tender and sensitive. In other words, the meaning is that although the people possess external eyes, yet the insight, or perception, of the soul is blind; although the outer ear hears, the spiritual hearing is deaf; although they possess conscious hearts, they are without illumination; and the bounties of Christ save souls from these conditions. It is evident, then, that the manifestation of the Messiah was synonymous with universal mercy. His providence was universal, and His teachings were for all. His lights were not restricted to a few. Every Christ came to the world of mankind. Therefore, we must investigate the foundation of divine religion, discover its reality, reestablish it and spread its message throughout the world so that it may become the source of illumination and enlightenment to mankind, the spiritually dead become alive, the spiritually blind receive sight and those who are inattentive to God become awakened.

5   The teachings and ordinances of the divine religions are of two kinds. The first are spiritual and essential in nature—such as faith in God, faith in Christ, faith in Moses, faith in Abraham, faith in Muḥammad, the love of God and the oneness of the world of humanity. These divine principles shall be spread

throughout the world. Strife and enmity shall disappear, ignorance, hatred and hostility cease and all the human race be bound together. The second kind of ordinances and teachings concern the outer conditions and transactions of the world of mankind. They are the nonessential, accidental or temporary laws of human affairs which are subject to change and transformation according to the exigencies of time and place. For instance, during the time of Moses divorce was permitted, but in the time of Christ it was made unlawful. In the Torah there are ten commandments concerning retribution for murder, which would not be possible to enforce at the present time and under existing conditions of the world. Therefore, these nonessential, temporary laws are superseded and abrogated to suit the exigencies and requirements of successive periods.

But the followers of the divine religions have turned away 6 from the principles and ordinances which are essential and unchanging in the Word of God, forsaking those fundamental realities which have to do with the life of the human world, the eternal life—such as the love of God, faith in God, philanthropy, knowledge, spiritual perception, divine guidance—holding these to be contingent and nonessential while wrangling and disagreeing over such questions as whether divorce is lawful or unlawful, or whether this or that observance of a minor law is orthodox and true. The Jews consider divorce lawful; the Catholic Christians deem it unlawful; the outcome is discord and hostility between them. If they would investigate the one fundamental reality underlying the laws revealed by Moses and Christ, this condition of hatred and misunderstanding would be dispelled and divine unity prevail.

Christ commanded that if we are smitten upon the right 7 cheek, we should turn the other cheek also. Consider what is happening now in the Balkans. What conformity with the teachings of Christ do we witness in that deplorable picture? Has not man absolutely forgotten and forsaken the divine command of Christ? In fact, such discord and warfare are evidences of disagreement upon the non-essential precepts and laws of religious belief. Investigation of the one fundamental reality and allegiance to the essential unchanging principles of the Word of God can alone establish unity and love in human hearts.

8   Throughout the Orient in the nineteenth century spiritual darkness prevailed, and the religions were submerged in the ocean of blind imitations and adherence to hereditary forms. There was no trace of the essential foundation of divine revelation. Because of this, hostility and hatred surrounded mankind; discord, rancor and warfare afflicted humanity; blood overspread the horizons of the eastern world. Instead of fellowship and agreement, religion had become the cause of hatred; instead of unity, it produced discord, enmity and strife. The conditions were similar to those existing in the Balkans today, where it might appear as if the basis of divine religion were war and conflict, the adherents of one religion seeking to extirpate and destroy another, and the adherents of both imbued with the fanatical impulse to kill. They consider the pathway to the good pleasure of God a pathway of blood, and the more a religionist kills, the nearer he draws to God. These are the results of blind imitations. How gloomy and destructive to humanity is such an outcome! If this be the foundation of divine religion, its absence is preferable; for even the infidels do not shed blood in this way, nor are they hostile toward each other. The forces of hostility and strife are the religions of the present day, and that which should have contributed to the illumination and betterment of the world has become productive of gross darkness and degradation.

9   To resume: Consider how similar blind imitations had made the darkness in the Orient all-encircling. At such a time

Bahá'u'lláh dawned from the eastern horizon like the glory of the sun. He renewed the basis of the religions of God, destroyed blind adherence to ancestral forms and established in their stead love and spiritual fellowship so that no strife, discord or hostility remained. This reconciliation of divergent sects is visible and evident. They now live together in love and unity. If you should enter one of their meetings, you would realize that they have become as one race, one native land, one religion; that they associate together in brotherhood and agreement. Praise be to God! These blind imitations and this darkness have ceased to exist, and the reality of the oneness of humanity has been practically proven.

I consider the American people a highly civilized and intelligent nation, a nation investigating truth and reality. It is my hope that through the efforts of this noble nation the solidarity of humanity may be continually advanced, that the illumination of the human world may become widespread, that the banner of universal peace may be held aloft, the lamp of the oneness of the human world be ignited and the hearts of the East and West be conjoined. Then the reality of the divine religions shall become resplendent and refulgent, indicating that they were meant to be the cause of unity and love and that through them heavenly bestowals have ever been conferring light upon the human world.

5

23 November 1912

Talk at Banquet
Great Northern Hotel
118 West Fifty-seventh Street, New York

NOTES BY EDNA MCKINNEY

1 THROUGHOUT the world there are innumerable meetings and assemblages, more or less important according to their measure of contribution to human betterment, yet limited in their purpose and object to material questions and outcomes. They are political, commercial or educational in character; they seek to promote economic advancement, further agricultural purposes, encourage scientific research and assist discoveries; they provide for the establishment of new institutions, plan financial measures and agree upon laws of civic and social control. Such meetings are useful, but their influence and intention do not extend beyond the material welfare and government of mankind—that is to say, they serve material civilization.

2 This meeting of yours tonight is very different in character. It is a universal gathering; it is heavenly and divine in purpose because it serves the oneness of the world of humanity and promotes international peace. It is devoted to the solidarity and brotherhood of the human race, the spiritual welfare of mankind, unity of religious belief through knowledge of God and the reconciliation of religious teaching with the principles of science and reason. It promotes love and fraternity among all humankind, seeks to abolish and destroy barriers which separate the human family, proclaims the equality of man

and woman, instills divine precepts and morals, illumines and quickens minds with heavenly perception, attracts the infinite bestowals of God, removes racial, national and religious prejudices and establishes the foundation of the heavenly Kingdom in the hearts of all nations and peoples. The effect of such an assembly as this is conducive to divine fellowship and strengthening of the bond which cements and unifies hearts. This is the indestructible bond of spirit which conjoins the East and West. By it the very foundations of race prejudice are uprooted and destroyed, the banner of spiritual democracy is hoisted aloft, the world of religion is purified from superannuated beliefs and hereditary imitations of forms, and the oneness of the reality underlying all religions is revealed and disclosed. For such a meeting is established upon the very foundation of the laws of God. Therefore, in its constraining spiritual bond it unites all religions and reconciles all sects, denominations and factions in kindliness and love toward each other. In this way and by the instrumentality of such a gathering the causes of animosity, hatred and bigotry are removed, and enmity and discord pass away entirely. Every limiting and restricting movement or meeting of mere personal interest is human in nature. Every universal movement unlimited in scope and purpose is divine. The Cause of God is advanced whenever and wherever a universal meeting is established among mankind.

Therefore, endeavor that your attitudes and intentions here 3 tonight be universal and altruistic in nature. Consecrate and devote yourselves to the betterment and service of all the human race. Let no barrier of ill feeling or personal prejudice exist between these souls, for when your motives are universal and your intentions heavenly in character, when your aspirations are centered in the Kingdom, there is no doubt whatever that you will become the recipients of the bounty and good pleasure of God.

4   This meeting is, verily, the noblest and most worthy of all meetings in the world because of these underlying spiritual and universal purposes. Such a banquet and assemblage command the sincere devotion of all present and invite the downpouring of the blessings of God. Therefore, be ye assured and confident that the confirmations of God are descending upon you, the assistance of God will be given unto you, the breaths of the Holy Spirit will quicken you with a new life, the Sun of Reality will shine gloriously upon you, and the fragrant breezes of the rose gardens of divine mercy will waft through the windows of your souls. Be ye confident and steadfast; your services are confirmed by the powers of heaven, for your intentions are lofty, your purposes pure and worthy. God is the helper of those souls whose aim is to serve humanity and whose efforts and endeavors are devoted to the good and betterment of all mankind.

6

29 November 1912

Talk at Home of Mr. and Mrs. Edward B. Kinney
780 West End Avenue, New York

Notes by Esther Foster

1   THIS evening I wish to speak to you concerning the mystery of sacrifice. There are two kinds of sacrifice: the physical and the spiritual. The explanation made by the churches concerning this subject is, in reality, superstition. For instance, it is recorded in the Gospel that Christ said, "I am the living bread which came down from heaven: if any man eat of this bread, he shall

live for ever." He also said, "This [wine] is my blood . . . which is shed for many for the remission of sins." These verses have been interpreted by the churches in such a superstitious way that it is impossible for human reason to understand or accept the explanation.

They say that Adam disobeyed the command of God and par- 2 took of the fruit of the forbidden tree, thereby committing a sin which was transmitted as a heritage to His posterity. They teach that because of Adam's sin all His descendants have, likewise, committed transgression and have become responsible through inheritance; that, consequently, all mankind deserves punishment and must make retribution; and that God sent forth His Son as a sacrifice in order that man might be forgiven and the human race delivered from the consequences of Adam's transgression.

We wish to consider these statements from the standpoint of 3 reason. Could we conceive of the Divinity, Who is Justice itself, inflicting punishment upon the posterity of Adam for Adam's own sin and disobedience? Even if we should see a governor, an earthly ruler punishing a son for the wrongdoing of his father, we would look upon that ruler as an unjust man. Granted the father committed a wrong, what was the wrong committed by the son? There is no connection between the two. Adam's sin was not the sin of His posterity, especially as Adam is a thousand generations back of the man today. If the father of a thousand generations committed a sin, is it just to demand that the present generation should suffer the consequences thereof?

There are other questions and evidences to be considered. 4 Abraham was a Manifestation of God and a descendant of Adam; likewise, Ishmael, Isaac, Jeremiah and the whole line of prophets including David, Solomon and Aaron were among His posterity. Were all these holy men condemned to a realm of punishment because of a deed committed by the first father, because of a mistake said to have been made by their mutual and remotest ancestor Adam? The explanation is made that when Christ came and sacrificed Himself, all the line of holy Prophets who preceded Him became free from sin and punishment. Even a child could not justly make such an assertion. These interpretations and statements are due to a misunderstanding of the meanings of the Bible.

5   In order to understand the reality of sacrifice let us consider the crucifixion and death of Jesus Christ. It is true that He sacrificed Himself for our sake. What is the meaning of this? When Christ appeared, He knew that He must proclaim Himself in opposition to all the nations and peoples of the earth. He knew that mankind would arise against Him and inflict upon Him all manner of tribulations. There is no doubt that one who put forth such a claim as Christ announced would arouse the hostility of the world and be subjected to personal abuse. He realized that His blood would be shed and His body rent by violence. Notwithstanding His knowledge of what would befall Him, He arose to proclaim His message, suffered all tribulation and hardships from the people and finally offered His life as a sacrifice in order to illumine humanity—gave His blood in order to guide the world of mankind. He accepted every calamity and suffering in order to guide men to the truth. Had He desired to save His own life, and were He without wish to offer Himself in sacrifice, He would not have been able to guide a single soul. There was no doubt that His blessed blood would be shed and His body broken. Nevertheless, that Holy Soul accepted calamity and death in His love for mankind. This is one of the meanings of sacrifice.

6   As to the second meaning: He said, "I am the living bread which came down from heaven." It was not the body of Christ which came from heaven. His body came from the womb of

634

Mary, but the Christly perfections descended from heaven; the reality of Christ came down from heaven. The Spirit of Christ and not the body descended from heaven. The body of Christ was but human. There could be no question that the physical body was born from the womb of Mary. But the reality of Christ, the Spirit of Christ, the perfections of Christ all came from heaven. Consequently, by saying He was the bread which came from heaven He meant that the perfections which He showed forth were divine perfections, that the blessings within Him were heavenly gifts and bestowals, that His light was the light of Reality. He said, "If any man eat of this bread, he shall live for ever." That is to say, whosoever assimilates these divine perfections which are within me will never die; whosoever has a share and partakes of these heavenly bounties I embody will find eternal life; he who takes unto himself these divine lights shall find everlasting life. How manifest the meaning is! How evident! For the soul which acquires divine perfections and seeks heavenly illumination from the teachings of Christ will undoubtedly live eternally. This is also one of the mysteries of sacrifice.

In reality, Abraham sacrificed Himself, for He brought heavenly teachings to the world and conferred heavenly food upon mankind. 7

As to the third meaning of sacrifice, it is this: If you plant a seed in the ground, a tree will become manifest from that seed. The seed sacrifices itself to the tree that will come from it. The seed is outwardly lost, destroyed; but the same seed which is sacrificed will be absorbed and embodied in the tree, its blossoms, fruit and branches. If the identity of that seed had not been sacrificed to the tree which became manifest from it, no branches, blossoms or fruits would have been forthcoming. Christ outwardly disappeared. His personal identity became hidden from the eyes, even as the identity of the seed disappeared; 8

635

but the bounties, divine qualities and perfections of Christ became manifest in the Christian community which Christ founded through sacrificing Himself. When you look at the tree, you will realize that the perfections, blessings, properties and beauty of the seed have become manifest in the branches, twigs, blossoms and fruit; consequently, the seed has sacrificed itself to the tree. Had it not done so, the tree would not have come into existence. Christ, like unto the seed, sacrificed Himself for the tree of Christianity. Therefore, His perfections, bounties, favors, lights and graces became manifest in the Christian community, for the coming of which He sacrificed Himself.

9   As to the fourth significance of sacrifice: It is the principle that a reality sacrifices its own characteristics. Man must sever himself from the influences of the world of matter, from the world of nature and its laws; for the material world is the world of corruption and death. It is the world of evil and darkness, of animalism and ferocity, bloodthirstiness, ambition and avarice, of self-worship, egotism and passion; it is the world of nature. Man must strip himself of all these imperfections, must sacrifice these tendencies which are peculiar to the outer and material world of existence.

10   On the other hand, man must acquire heavenly qualities and attain divine attributes. He must become the image and likeness of God. He must seek the bounty of the eternal, become the manifestor of the love of God, the light of guidance, the tree of life and the depository of the bounties of God. That is to say, man must sacrifice the qualities and attributes of the world of nature for the qualities and attributes of the world of God. For instance, consider the substance we call iron. Observe its qualities; it is solid, black, cold. These are the characteristics of iron. When the same iron absorbs heat from the fire, it sacrifices its attribute of solidity for the attribute of fluidity. It sacrifices

its attribute of darkness for the attribute of light, which is a quality of the fire. It sacrifices its attribute of coldness to the quality of heat which the fire possesses so that in the iron there remains no solidity, darkness or cold. It becomes illumined and transformed, having sacrificed its qualities to the qualities and attributes of the fire.

Likewise, man, when separated and severed from the attri- 11 butes of the world of nature, sacrifices the qualities and exigencies of that mortal realm and manifests the perfections of the Kingdom, just as the qualities of the iron disappeared and the qualities of the fire appeared in their place.

Every man trained through the teachings of God and il- 12 lumined by the light of His guidance, who becomes a believer in God and His signs and is enkindled with the fire of the love of God, sacrifices the imperfections of nature for the sake of divine perfections. Consequently, every perfect person, every illumined, heavenly individual stands in the station of sacrifice. It is my hope that through the assistance and providence of God and through the bounties of the Kingdom of Abhá you may be entirely severed from the imperfections of the world of nature, purified from selfish, human desires, receiving life from the Kingdom of Abhá and attaining heavenly graces. May the divine light become manifest upon your faces, the fragrances of holiness refresh your nostrils and the breath of the Holy Spirit quicken you with eternal life.

7

2 December 1912

Talk at Home of Mr. and Mrs. Edward B. Kinney
780 West End Avenue, New York

NOTES BY EDNA MCKINNEY

1 THESE are the days of my farewell to you, for I am sailing on the fifth of the month. Wherever I went in this country, I returned always to New York City. This is my fourth or fifth visit here, and now I am going away to the Orient. It will be difficult for me to visit this country again except it be the will of God. I must, therefore, give you my instructions and exhortations today, and these are none other than the teachings of Bahá'u'lláh.

2 You must manifest complete love and affection toward all mankind. Do not exalt yourselves above others, but consider all as your equals, recognizing them as the servants of one God. Know that God is compassionate toward all; therefore, love all from the depths of your hearts, prefer all religionists before yourselves, be filled with love for every race, and be kind toward the people of all nationalities. Never speak disparagingly of others, but praise without distinction. Pollute not your tongues by speaking evil of another. Recognize your enemies as friends, and consider those who wish you evil as the wishers of good. You must not see evil as evil and then compromise with your opinion, for to treat in a smooth, kindly way one whom you consider evil or an enemy is hypocrisy, and this is not worthy or allowable. You must consider your enemies as your friends, look upon your evil-wishers as your well-wishers and treat them accordingly. Act in such a way that your heart may be free from hatred. Let

not your heart be offended with anyone. If someone commits an error and wrong toward you, you must instantly forgive him. Do not complain of others. Refrain from reprimanding them, and if you wish to give admonition or advice, let it be offered in such a way that it will not burden the bearer. Turn all your thoughts toward bringing joy to hearts. Beware! Beware! lest ye offend any heart. Assist the world of humanity as much as possible. Be the source of consolation to every sad one, assist every weak one, be helpful to every indigent one, care for every sick one, be the cause of glorification to every lowly one, and shelter those who are overshadowed by fear.

In brief, let each one of you be as a lamp shining forth with 3 the light of the virtues of the world of humanity. Be trustworthy, sincere, affectionate and replete with chastity. Be illumined, be spiritual, be divine, be glorious, be quickened of God, be a Bahá'í.

8

2 December 1912

Talk at Home of Mr. and Mrs. Edward B. Kinney
780 West End Avenue, New York

NOTES BY ESTHER FOSTER

YOU are all welcome. This is a goodly assemblage. Praise be to 1 God! The hearts are directed to the Kingdom of Abhá, and souls are rejoiced by the glad tidings of God.

I will speak to you concerning the special teachings of Bahá'u'lláh. 2 All the divine principles announced by the tongue of the Prophets of the past are to be found in the words of Bahá'u'lláh; but in addition to these He has revealed certain new teachings which are not found in any of the sacred Books of former times. I shall mention some of them; the others, which are many in number, may be found in the Books, Tablets and Epistles written by Bahá'u'lláh—such as the Hidden Words, the Glad Tidings, the Words of Paradise, Tajallíyát, Tarázát and others. Likewise, in the Kitáb-i-Aqdas there are new teachings which cannot be found in any of the past Books or Epistles of the Prophets.

3   A fundamental teaching of Bahá'u'lláh is the oneness of the world of humanity. Addressing mankind, He says, "Ye are all leaves of one tree and the fruits of one branch." By this it is meant that the world of humanity is like a tree, the nations or peoples are the different limbs or branches of that tree, and the individual human creatures are as the fruits and blossoms thereof. In this way Bahá'u'lláh expressed the oneness of humankind, whereas in all religious teachings of the past the human world has been represented as divided into two parts: one known as the people of the Book of God, or the pure tree, and the other the people of infidelity and error, or the evil tree. The former were considered as belonging to the faithful, and the others to the hosts of the irreligious and infidel—one part of humanity the recipients of divine mercy, and the other the object of the wrath of their Creator. Bahá'u'lláh removed this by proclaiming the oneness of the world of humanity, and this principle is specialized in His teachings, for He has submerged all mankind in the sea of divine generosity. Some are asleep; they need to be awakened. Some are ailing; they need to be healed. Some are immature as children; they need to be trained. But all are recipients of the bounty and bestowals of God.

4   Another new principle revealed by Bahá'u'lláh is the injunction to investigate truth—that is to say, no man should blindly follow his ancestors and forefathers. Nay, each must see with his own eyes, hear with his own ears and investigate the truth

himself in order that he may follow the truth instead of blind acquiescence and imitation of ancestral beliefs.

Bahá'u'lláh has announced that the foundation of all the 5 religions of God is one, that oneness is truth and truth is oneness which does not admit of plurality. This teaching is new and specialized to this Manifestation.

He sets forth a new principle for this day in the announcement 6 that religion must be the cause of unity, harmony and agreement among mankind. If it is the cause of discord and hostility, if it leads to separation and creates conflict, the absence of religion would be preferable in the world.

Furthermore, He proclaims that religion must be in harmony 7 with science and reason. If it does not conform to science and reconcile with reason, it is superstition. Down to the present day it has been customary for man to accept a religious teaching, even though it was not in accord with human reason and judgment. The harmony of religious belief with reason is a new vista which Bahá'u'lláh has opened for the soul of man.

He establishes the equality of man and woman. This is peculiar to the teachings of Bahá'u'lláh, for all other religions have 8 placed man above woman.

A new religious principle is that prejudice and fanaticism— 9 whether sectarian, denominational, patriotic or political—are destructive to the foundation of human solidarity; therefore, man should release himself from such bonds in order that the oneness of the world of humanity may become manifest.

Universal peace is assured by Bahá'u'lláh as a fundamental 10 accomplishment of the religion of God—that peace shall prevail among nations, governments and peoples, among religions, races and all conditions of mankind. This is one of the special characteristics of the Word of God revealed in this Manifestation.

Bahá'u'lláh declares that all mankind should attain knowl- 11 edge and acquire an education. This is a necessary principle of religious belief and observance, characteristically new in this dispensation.

12   He has set forth the solution and provided the remedy for the economic question. No religious Books of the past Prophets speak of this important human problem.

13   He has ordained and established the House of Justice, which is endowed with a political as well as a religious function, the consummate union and blending of church and state. This institution is under the protecting power of Bahá'u'lláh Himself. A universal, or international, House of Justice shall also be organized. Its rulings shall be in accordance with the commands and teachings of Bahá'u'lláh, and that which the Universal House of Justice ordains shall be obeyed by all mankind. This international House of Justice shall be appointed and organized from the Houses of Justice of the whole world, and all the world shall come under its administration.

14   As to the most great characteristic of the revelation of Bahá'-u'lláh, a specific teaching not given by any of the Prophets of the past: It is the ordination and appointment of the Center of the Covenant. By this appointment and provision He has safeguarded and protected the religion of God against differences and schisms, making it impossible for anyone to create a new sect or faction of belief. To ensure unity and agreement He has entered into a Covenant with all the people of the world, including the interpreter and explainer of His teachings, so that no one may interpret or explain the religion of God according to his own view or opinion and thus create a sect founded upon his individual understanding of the divine Words. The Book of the Covenant or Testament of Bahá'u'lláh is the means of preventing such a possibility, for whosoever shall speak from the authority of himself alone shall be degraded. Be ye informed and cognizant of this. Beware lest anyone shall secretly ques-

tion or deny this to you. There are some people of self-will and desire who do not communicate their intentions to you in clear language. They envelop their meanings in secret statements and insinuations. For instance, they praise a certain individual, saying he is wise and learned, that he was glorified in the presence of Bahá'u'lláh, conveying this to you in an insidious way or by innuendos. Be ye aware of this! Be awakened and enlightened! For Christ has said that no one hides the lamp under a bushel. The purport of my admonition is that certain people will endeavor to influence you in the direction of their own personal views and opinions. Therefore, be upon your guard in order that none may assail the oneness and integrity of Bahá'u'lláh's Cause. Praise be to God! Bahá'u'lláh left nothing unsaid. He explained everything. He left no room for anything further to be said. Yet there are some who for the sake of personal interest and prestige will attempt to sow the seeds of sedition and disloyalty among you. To protect and safeguard the religion of God from this and all other attack, the Center of the Covenant has been named and appointed by Bahá'u'lláh. Therefore, if anyone should set forth a statement in praise or recognition of another than this appointed Center, you must ask him to produce a written proof of the authority he follows. Let him show you a trace from the pen of the Center of the Covenant Himself, substantiating his praise and support of any other than the rightful one. Inform him that you are not permitted to accept the words of everyone. Say to him, "It is possible to love and praise a person today, to accept and follow another tomorrow and still another next day. Therefore, we cannot afford to listen to this or that individual. Where are your proofs and writings? Where is your authority from the pen of the Center of the Covenant?"

My purpose is to explain to you that it is your duty to guard 15 the religion of God so that none shall be able to assail it outwardly or inwardly. If you find harmful teachings are being set forth by some individual, no matter who that individual be, even though he should be my own son, know, verily, that I am completely severed from him. If anyone speaks against the Covenant, even though he should be my son, know that I am opposed to him. Those who speak falsehoods, who covet worldly things and seek to accumulate the riches of this earth are not of me. But when you find a person living up to the teachings of Bahá'u'lláh, following the precepts of the Hidden Words, know that he belongs to Bahá'u'lláh; and, verily, I proclaim that he is of me. If, on the other hand, you see anyone whose deeds and conduct are contrary to and not in conformity with the good pleasure of the Blessed Perfection and against the spirit of the Hidden Words, let that be your standard and criterion of judgment against him, for know that I am altogether severed from him no matter who he may be. This is the truth.

16   The teachings of Bahá'u'lláh are boundless and illimitable. You have asked me what new principles have been revealed by Him. I have mentioned a few only. There are many others, but time does not permit their mention tonight. I, therefore, pray to God that you may be strengthened in good deeds. I pray that God may confirm you in order that you may live according to the teachings of Bahá'u'lláh.

17   Upon ye be Bahá'u'l-Abhá!

9

3 December 1912

Talk at Home of Dr. and Mrs. Florian Krug
830 Park Avenue, New York

You have assembled here this afternoon in the utmost love, 1
engaged in the commemoration of God. It is my hope that this
gathering may increase in number day by day; that you may become more and more attracted, more spiritual, more illumined,
acquire knowledge of the teachings of Bahá'u'lláh from each
other and be able to spread the message of truth. May your
hearts become so attracted that the instant a question is asked,
you will be able to give the right answer and that the truth of
the Holy Spirit may speak through your tongues. Be ye helpful
through the providence and favor of the Blessed Perfection, for
His favors change a drop into an ocean, cause a seed to become
a tree and make an atom as glorious as the sun. His graces are
boundless. The treasure houses of God are filled with bounties.
God, Who hath shown favors unto others, will certainly bestow
favors upon you. I offer supplication to the Kingdom of Abhá
and seek extraordinary blessings and confirmations in your behalf in order that your tongues may become fluent, your hearts
like clear mirrors flooded with the rays of the Sun of Truth, your
thoughts expanded, your comprehension more vivid and that
you may progress in the plane of human perfections.

Until man acquires perfections himself, he will not be able 2
to teach perfections to others. Unless man attains life himself,
he cannot convey life to others. Unless he finds light, he cannot
reflect light. We must, therefore, endeavor ourselves to attain to
the perfections of the world of humanity, lay hold of everlasting

life and seek the divine spirit in order that we may thereby be enabled to confer life upon others, be enabled to breathe life into others.

3   You must offer supplications unto the Kingdom of Abhá and seek eternal bounties from Him. You must pray that your hearts may become filled with glorious lights, even as a purified mirror; then will the lights of the Sun of Truth shine therein. You must supplicate and pray to God every night and every day, seeking His assistance and help, saying:

4   O Lord! We are weak; strengthen us. O God! We are ignorant; make us knowing. O Lord! We are poor; make us wealthy. O God! We are dead; quicken us. O Lord! We are humiliation itself; glorify us in Thy Kingdom. If Thou dost assist us, O Lord, we shall become as scintillating stars. If Thou dost not assist us, we shall become lower than the earth. O Lord! Strengthen us. O God! Confer victory upon us. O God! Enable us to conquer self and overcome desire. O Lord! Deliver us from the bondage of the material world. O Lord! Quicken us through the breath of the Holy Spirit in order that we may arise to serve Thee, engage in worshiping Thee and exert ourselves in Thy Kingdom with the utmost sincerity. O Lord, Thou art powerful. O God, Thou art forgiving. O Lord, Thou art compassionate.

10

3 December 1912

Talk to Mr. Kinney's Bible Class
780 West End Avenue, New York

NOTES BY EDNA MCKINNEY

I HAVE been informed that the purpose of your class meeting is to [1] study the significances and mysteries of the Holy Scriptures and understand the meaning of the divine Testaments. It is a cause of great happiness to me that you are turning unto the Kingdom of God, that you desire to approach the presence of God and to become informed of the realities and precepts of God. It is my hope that you may put forth your most earnest endeavor to accomplish this end, that you may investigate and study the Holy Scriptures word by word so that you may attain knowledge of the mysteries hidden therein. Be not satisfied with words, but seek to understand the spiritual meanings hidden in the heart of the words. The Jews read the Old Testament night and day, memorizing its words and texts yet without comprehending a single meaning or inner significance, for had they understood the real meanings of the Old Testament, they would have become believers in Christ, inasmuch as the Old Testament was revealed to prepare His coming. As the Jewish doctors and rabbis did not believe in Christ, it is evident that they were ignorant of the real significance of the Old Testament. It is difficult to comprehend even the words of a philosopher; how much more difficult it is to understand the Words of God. The divine Words are not to be taken according to their outer sense. They are symbolical and contain realities of spiritual meaning. For instance, in the book of Solomon's songs you will read about the bride and bridegroom. It is evident that the physical bride and bridegroom are not intended. Obviously, these are symbols conveying a hidden and inner significance. In the same way the Revelations of St. John are not to be taken literally, but spiritually. These are the mysteries of God. It is not the reading of the words that profits you; it is the understanding of their meanings. Therefore, pray God that you may be enabled to comprehend the mysteries of the divine Testaments.

2   Consider the symbolical meanings of the Words and teachings of Christ. He said, "I am the living bread which came down from heaven; if any man eat of this bread, he shall live for ever." When the Jews heard this, they took it literally and failed to understand the significance of His meaning and teaching. The spiritual truth which Christ wished to convey to them was that the reality of Divinity within Him was like a blessing which had come down from heaven and that he who partook of this blessing should never die. That is to say, bread was the symbol of the perfections which had descended upon Him from God, and he who ate of this bread, or endowed himself with the perfections of Christ, would undoubtedly attain to everlasting life. The Jews did not understand Him, and taking the words literally, said, "How can this man give us his flesh to eat?" Had they understood the real meaning of the Holy Book, they would have become believers in Christ.

3   All the texts and teachings of the holy Testaments have intrinsic spiritual meanings. They are not to be taken literally. I, therefore, pray in your behalf that you may be given the power of understanding these inner real meanings of the Holy Scriptures and may become informed of the mysteries deposited in the words of the Bible so that you may attain eternal life and that your hearts may be attracted to the Kingdom of God. May your souls be illumined by the light of the Words of God, and

may you become repositories of the mysteries of God, for no comfort is greater and no happiness is sweeter than spiritual comprehension of the divine teachings. If a man understands the real meaning of a poet's verses such as those of Shakespeare, he is pleased and rejoiced. How much greater his joy and pleasure when he perceives the reality of the Holy Scriptures and becomes informed of the mysteries of the Kingdom!

I pray that the divine blessings may descend upon you day by day, that your hearts may be opened to perceive the inner significances of the Word of God. There is no fruit in knowing the mere letters of the Book. Most of the Jews had memorized the texts of the Old Testament and repeated them night and day, but inasmuch as they were ignorant of the meanings, they were deprived of the bounties of Christ. I pray that you may be quickened by the breaths of the Holy Spirit and illumined by the rays of the Sun of Truth. May you be favored with heavenly blessings in the threshold of God and attain to eternal life. This is my prayer. May God bless and enlighten you.

11

3 December 1912

Talk at Home of Mr. and Mrs. Edward B. Kinney
780 West End Avenue, New York

NOTES BY EDNA MCKINNEY

I HAVE attended more meetings in New York than in all the other cities combined. Day and night, individually and collectively you have listened to the teachings and exhortations of Bahá'u'lláh. I have proclaimed unto you the glad tidings of the Kingdom of

God and explained the wishes of the Blessed Perfection. I have set forth that which is conducive to human progress and shown you the humility of servitude. The teachings of Bahá'u'lláh have been clearly interpreted. The time has now come when I must leave you; therefore, this will be our farewell meeting.

2   I am greatly pleased with you all and rejoice that you have shown me the utmost kindness and affection. It is my desire that Bahá'u'lláh shall be pleased with you, that you may follow His precepts and become worthy of His confirmations. The requirements are that your minds must be illumined, your souls must be rejoiced with the glad tidings of God, you must become imbued with spiritual moralities, your daily life must evidence faith and assurance, your hearts must be sanctified and pure, reflecting a high degree of love and attraction toward the Kingdom of Abhá. You must become the lamps of Bahá'u'lláh so that you may shine with eternal light and be the proofs and evidences of His truth. Then will such signs of purity and chastity be witnessed in your deeds and actions that men will behold the heavenly radiance of your lives and say, "Verily, ye are the proofs of Bahá'u'lláh. Verily, Bahá'u'lláh is the True One, for He has trained such souls as these, each one of which is a proof in himself." They will say to others, "Come and witness the conduct of these souls; come and listen to their words, behold the illumination of their hearts, see the evidences of the love of God in them, consider their praiseworthy morals, and discover the foundations of the oneness of humanity firmly implanted within them. What greater proof can there be than these people that the message of Bahá'u'lláh is truth and reality?" It is my hope that each one of you shall be a herald of God, proclaiming the evidences of His appearance, in words, deeds and thoughts. Let your actions and utterances be a witness that you are of the Kingdom of Bahá'u'lláh. These are the duties enjoined upon you by Bahá'u'lláh.

Bahá'u'lláh endured the greatest hardships. He found neither 3 rest by night nor peace by day. He was constantly under the stress of great calamity—now in prison, now in chains, now threatened by the sword—until finally He broke the cage of captivity, left this mortal world and ascended to the heaven of God. He endured all these tribulations for our sakes and suffered these deprivations that we might attain the bestowals of divine bounty. Therefore, we must be faithful to Him and turn away from our own selfish desires and fancies in order that we may accomplish that which is required of us by our Lord.

It is my wish that you shall arise to live according to these 4 teachings and exhortations; that all of us may be divinely strengthened, enter the paradise of the spiritual Kingdom, diffuse the lights of the Sun of Truth, cause the waves of this Most Great Ocean to reach all human souls so that this world of earth may be transformed into the world of heaven and this devastated ground be changed into the paradise of Abhá.

12

4 December 1912

Talk to Theosophical Society
2228 Broadway, New York

NOTES BY ESTHER FOSTER

THOSE who are uninformed of the world of reality, who do not 1 comprehend existing things, who are without perception of the inner truth of creation, who do not penetrate the real mysteries of material and spiritual phenomena and who possess only a superficial idea of universal life and being are but embodiments of pure ignorance. They believe only that which they have heard from their fathers and ancestors. Of themselves they have no hearing, no sight, no reason, no intellect; they rely solely upon tradition. Such persons imagine that the dominion of God is an accidental dominion, or Kingdom.

2 For instance, they believe that this world of existence was created six or seven thousand years ago, as if God did not reign before that time and had no creation before that period. They think that Divinity is accidental, for to them Divinity is dependent upon existing things, whereas, in reality, as long as there has been a God, there has been a creation. As long as there has been light, there have been recipients of that light, for light cannot become manifest unless those things which perceive and appreciate it exist. The world of Divinity presupposes creation, presupposes recipients of bounty, presupposes the existence of worlds. No Divinity can be conceived as separate from creation, for otherwise it would be like imagining an empire without a people. A king must needs have a kingdom, must needs have an army and subjects. Is it possible to be a king and have no country, no army, no subjects? This is an absurdity. If we say that there was a time when there was no country, no army and no subjects, how then could there have been a king and ruler? For these things are essential to a king.

3 Consequently, just as the reality of Divinity never had a beginning—that is, God has ever been a Creator, God has ever been a Provider, God has ever been a Quickener, God has ever been a Bestower—so there never has been a time when the attributes of God have not had expression. The sun is the sun because of its rays, because of its heat. Were we to conceive of a time when there was a sun without heat and light, it would imply that there had been no sun at all and that it became the

sun afterward. So, likewise, if we say there was a time when God had no creation or created beings, a time when there were no recipients of His bounties and that His names and attributes had not been manifested, this would be equivalent to a complete denial of Divinity, for it would mean that Divinity is accidental. To explain it still more clearly, if we think that fifty thousand years ago or one hundred thousand years ago there was no creation, that there were then no worlds, no human beings, no animals, this thought of ours would mean that previous to that period there was no Divinity. If we should say that there was a time when there was a king but there were no subjects, no army, no country for him to rule over, it would really be asserting that there was a time when no king existed and that the king is accidental. It is, therefore, evident that inasmuch as the reality of Divinity is without a beginning, creation is also without a beginning. This is as clear as the sun. When we contemplate this vast machinery of omnipresent power, perceive this illimitable space and its innumerable worlds, it will become evident to us that the lifetime of this infinite creation is more than six thousand years; nay, it is very, very ancient.

Notwithstanding this, we read in Genesis in the Old Testament that the lifetime of creation is but six thousand years. 4 This has an inner meaning and significance; it is not to be taken literally. For instance, it is said in the Old Testament that certain things were created in the first day. The narrative shows that at that time the sun was not yet created. How could we conceive of a day if no sun existed in the heavens? For the day depends upon the light of the sun. Inasmuch as the sun had not been made, how could the first day be realized? Therefore, these statements have significances other than literal.

To be brief: Our purpose is to show that the divine sovereignty, the Kingdom of God, is an ancient sovereignty, that it 5 is not an accidental sovereignty, just as a kingdom presupposes the existence of subjects, of an army, of a country; for otherwise the state of dominion, authority and kingdom cannot be conceived of. Therefore, if we should imagine that the creation is accidental, we would be forced to admit that the Creator is accidental, whereas the divine bounty is ever flowing, and the rays of the Sun of Truth are continuously shining. No cessation is possible to the divine bounty, just as no cessation is possible to the rays of the sun. This is clear and obvious.

6   Thus there have been many holy Manifestations of God. One thousand years ago, two hundred thousand years ago, one million years ago, the bounty of God was flowing, the radiance of God was shining, the dominion of God was existing.

7   Why do these holy Manifestations of God appear? What is the wisdom and purpose of Their coming? What is the outcome of Their mission? It is evident that human personality appears in two aspects: the image or likeness of God, and the aspect of Satan. The human reality stands between these two: the divine and the satanic. It is manifest that beyond this material body, man is endowed with another reality, which is the world of exemplars constituting the heavenly body of man. In speaking, man says, "I saw," "I spoke," "I went." Who is this *I*? It is obvious that this *I* is different from this body. It is clear that when man is thinking, it is as though he were consulting with some other person. With whom is he consulting? It is evident that it is another reality, or one aside from this body, with whom he enters into consultation when he thinks, "Shall I do this work or not?" "What will be the result of my doing this?" Or when he questions the other reality, "What is the objection to this work if I do it?" And then that reality in man communicates its opinion to him concerning the point at issue. Therefore, that reality in man is clearly and obviously other than his body—an

ego with which man enters into consultation and whose opinion man seeks.

Often a man makes up his mind positively about a matter; for instance, he determines to undertake a journey. Then he thinks it over—that is, he consults his inner reality—and finally concludes that he will give up his journey. What has happened? Why did he abandon his original purpose? It is evident that he has consulted his inner reality, which expresses to him the disadvantages of such a journey; therefore, he defers to that reality and changes his original intention. 8

Furthermore, man sees in the world of dreams. He travels in the East; he travels in the West; although his body is stationary, his body is here. It is that reality in him which makes the journey while the body sleeps. There is no doubt that a reality exists other than the outward, physical reality. Again, for instance, a person is dead, is buried in the ground. Afterward, you see him in the world of dreams and speak with him, although his body is interred in the earth. Who is the person you see in your dreams, talk to and who also speaks with you? This again proves that there is another reality different from the physical one which dies and is buried. Thus it is certain that in man there is a reality which is not the physical body. Sometimes the body becomes weak, but that other reality is in its own normal state. The body goes to sleep, becomes as one dead; but that reality is moving about, comprehending things, expressing them and is even conscious of itself. 9

This other and inner reality is called the heavenly body, the ethereal form which corresponds to this body. This is the conscious reality which discovers the inner meaning of things, for the outer body of man does not discover anything. The inner ethereal reality grasps the mysteries of existence, discovers scientific truths and indicates their technical application. It 10 discovers electricity, produces the telegraph, the telephone and opens the door to the world of arts. If the outer material body did this, the animal would, likewise, be able to make scientific and wonderful discoveries, for the animal shares with man all physical powers and limitations. What, then, is that power which penetrates the realities of existence and which is not to be found in the animal? It is the inner reality which comprehends things, throws light upon the mysteries of life and being, discovers the heavenly Kingdom, unseals the mysteries of God and differentiates man from the brute. Of this there can be no doubt.

11 As we have before indicated, this human reality stands between the higher and the lower in man, between the world of the animal and the world of Divinity. When the animal proclivity in man becomes predominant, he sinks even lower than the brute. When the heavenly powers are triumphant in his nature, he becomes the noblest and most superior being in the world of creation. All the imperfections found in the animal are found in man. In him there is antagonism, hatred and selfish struggle for existence; in his nature lurk jealousy, revenge, ferocity, cunning, hypocrisy, greed, injustice and tyranny. So to speak, the reality of man is clad in the outer garment of the animal, the habiliments of the world of nature, the world of darkness, imperfections and unlimited baseness.

12 On the other hand, we find in him justice, sincerity, faithfulness, knowledge, wisdom, illumination, mercy and pity, coupled with intellect, comprehension, the power to grasp the realities of things and the ability to penetrate the truths of existence. All these great perfections are to be found in man. Therefore, we say that man is a reality which stands between light and darkness. From this standpoint his nature is threefold: animal, human and divine. The animal nature is darkness; the heavenly is light in light.

The holy Manifestations of God come into the world to 13 dispel the darkness of the animal, or physical, nature of man, to purify him from his imperfections in order that his heavenly and spiritual nature may become quickened, his divine qualities awakened, his perfections visible, his potential powers revealed and all the virtues of the world of humanity latent within him may come to life. These holy Manifestations of God are the Educators and Trainers of the world of existence, the Teachers of the world of humanity. They liberate man from the darkness of the world of nature, deliver him from despair, error, ignorance, imperfections and all evil qualities. They clothe him in the garment of perfections and exalted virtues. Men are ignorant; the Manifestations of God make them wise. They are animalistic; the Manifestations make them human. They are savage and cruel; the Manifestations lead them into kingdoms of light and love. They are unjust; the Manifestations cause them to become just. Man is selfish; They sever him from self and desire. Man is haughty; They make him meek, humble and friendly. He is earthly; They make him heavenly. Men are material; the Manifestations transform them into divine semblance. They are immature children; the Manifestations develop them into maturity. Man is poor; They endow him with wealth. Man is base, treacherous and mean; the Manifestations of God uplift him into dignity, nobility and loftiness.

These holy Manifestations liberate the world of humanity 14 from the imperfections which beset it and cause men to appear in the beauty of heavenly perfections. Were it not for the coming of these holy Manifestations of God, all mankind would be found on the plane of the animal. They would remain darkened and ignorant like those who have been denied schooling and who never had a teacher or trainer. Undoubtedly, such unfortunates will continue in their condition of need and deprivation.

15   If the mountains, hills and plains of the material world are left wild and uncultivated under the rule of nature, they will remain an unbroken wilderness, no fruitful tree to be found anywhere upon them. A true cultivator changes this forest and jungle into a garden, training its trees to bring forth fruit and causing flowers to grow in place of thorns and thistles. The holy Manifestations are the ideal Gardeners of human souls, the divine Cultivators of human hearts. The world of existence is but a jungle of disorder and confusion, a state of nature producing nothing but fruitless, useless trees. The ideal Gardeners train these wild, uncultivated human trees, cause them to become fruitful, water and cultivate them day by day so that they adorn the world of existence and continue to flourish in the utmost beauty.

16   Consequently, we cannot say that the divine bounty has ceased, that the glory of Divinity is exhausted or the Sun of Truth sunk into eternal sunset, into that darkness which is not followed by light, into that night which is not followed by a sunrise and dawn, into that death which is not followed by life, into that error which is not followed by truth. Is it conceivable that the Sun of Reality should sink into an eternal darkness? No! The sun was created in order that it may shed light upon the world and train all the kingdoms of existence. How then can the ideal Sun of Truth, the Word of God, set forever? For this would mean the cessation of the divine bounty, and the divine bounty by its very nature is continuous and ceaseless. Its sun is ever shining; its cloud is ever producing rain; its breezes are ever blowing; its bestowals are all-comprehending; its gifts are ever perfect. Consequently, we must always anticipate, always be hopeful and pray to God that He will send unto us His holy Manifestations in Their most perfect might, with the divine penetrative power of His Word, so that these heavenly Ones may be distinguished above all other beings

658

in every respect, in every attribute, just as the glorious sun is distinguished above all stars.

Although the stars are scintillating and brilliant, the sun   17
is superior to them in luminous effulgence. Similarly, these holy, divine Manifestations are and must always be distinguished above all other beings in every attribute of glory and perfection in order that it may be proven that the Manifestation is the true Teacher and real Trainer; that He is the Sun of Truth, endowed with a supreme splendor and reflecting the beauty of God. Otherwise, it is not possible for us to train one human individual and then after training him, believe in him and accept him as the holy Manifestation of Divinity. The real Manifestation of God must be endowed with divine knowledge and not dependent upon learning acquired in schools. He must be the Educator, not the educated; His standard, intuition instead of tuition. He must be perfect and not imperfect, great and glorious instead of being weak and impotent. He must be wealthy in the riches of the spiritual world and not indigent. In a word, the holy, divine Manifestation of God must be distinguished above all others of mankind in every aspect and qualification in order that He may be able to train effectively the human body politic, eliminate the darkness enshrouding the human world, uplift humanity from a lower to a higher kingdom, be able through the penetrative power of His Word to promote and spread broadcast the beneficent message of universal peace among men, bring about the unification of mankind in religious belief through a manifest divine power, harmonize all sects and denominations and convert all native lands and nationalities into one native land and fatherland.

It is our hope that the bounties of God will encompass us all,   18
the gifts of the divine become manifest, the lights of the Sun of

659

Truth illumine our eyes, inspire our hearts, convey to our souls cheerful glad tidings of God, cause our thoughts to become lofty and our efforts to be productive of glorious results. In a word, it is our hope that we may attain to that which is the summit of human aspirations and wishes.

19 I have been in America nine months and have traveled to all the large cities, speaking before various assemblages, proclaiming to them the oneness of the world of humanity, summoning all to union, harmony and oneness. I have indeed received the greatest kindness from the American people. I look upon them as a noble nation, capable of every perfection. Tomorrow I am going away to Europe, and now I bid farewell to you all, seeking for you the divine mercy, the eternal glory and everlasting life; and I pray that you may attain the highest station of humanity. I am greatly pleased with this meeting. My happiness is great. I shall never forget you. You shall always live in my thought. I shall always pray and supplicate before the Kingdom of God and seek heavenly blessings for you.

13

5 December 1912

Talk on Day of Departure
On Board Steamship Celtic, New York

NOTES BY MARIAM HANEY

1 THIS is my last meeting with you, for now I am on the ship ready to sail away. These are my final words of exhortation. I have repeatedly summoned you to the cause of the unity of the world of humanity, announcing that all mankind are the

servants of the same God, that God is the creator of all; He is the Provider and Life-giver; all are equally beloved by Him and are His servants upon whom His mercy and compassion descend. Therefore, you must manifest the greatest kindness and love toward the nations of the world, setting aside fanaticism, abandoning religious, national and racial prejudice.

The earth is one native land, one home; and all mankind are 2 the children of one Father. God has created them, and they are the recipients of His compassion. Therefore, if anyone offends another, he offends God. It is the wish of our heavenly Father that every heart should rejoice and be filled with happiness, that we should live together in felicity and joy. The obstacle to human happiness is racial or religious prejudice, the competitive struggle for existence and inhumanity toward each other.

Your eyes have been illumined, your ears are attentive, your 3 hearts knowing. You must be free from prejudice and fanaticism, beholding no differences between the races and religions. You must look to God, for He is the real Shepherd, and all humanity are His sheep. He loves them and loves them equally. As this is true, should the sheep quarrel among themselves? They should manifest gratitude and thankfulness to God, and the best way to thank God is to love one another.

Beware lest ye offend any heart, lest ye speak against anyone 4 in his absence, lest ye estrange yourselves from the servants of God. You must consider all His servants as your own family and relations. Direct your whole effort toward the happiness of those who are despondent, bestow food upon the hungry, clothe the needy, and glorify the humble. Be a helper to every helpless one, and manifest kindness to your fellow creatures in order that ye may attain the good pleasure of God. This is conducive to the illumination of the world of humanity and eternal felicity for yourselves. I seek from God everlasting glory in your behalf; therefore, this is my prayer and exhortation.

5   Consider what is happening in the Balkans. Human blood is being shed, properties are destroyed, possessions pillaged, cities and villages devastated. A world-enkindling fire is astir in the Balkans. God has created men to love each other; but instead, they kill each other with cruelty and bloodshed. God has created them that they may cooperate and mingle in accord; but instead, they ravage, plunder and destroy in the carnage of battle. God has created them to be the cause of mutual felicity and peace; but instead, discord, lamentation and anguish rise from the hearts of the innocent and afflicted.

6   As to you: Your efforts must be lofty. Exert yourselves with heart and soul so that, perchance, through your efforts the light of universal peace may shine and this darkness of estrangement and enmity may be dispelled from amongst men, that all men may become as one family and consort together in love and kindness, that the East may assist the West and the West give help to the East, for all are the inhabitants of one planet, the people of one original native land and the flocks of one Shepherd.

7   Consider how the Prophets Who have been sent, the great souls who have appeared and the sages who have arisen in the world have exhorted mankind to unity and love. This has been the essence of their mission and teaching. This has been the goal of their guidance and message. The Prophets, saints, seers and philosophers have sacrificed their lives in order to establish these principles and teachings amongst men. Consider the heedlessness of the world, for notwithstanding the efforts and sufferings of the Prophets of God, the nations and peoples are still engaged in hostility and fighting. Notwithstanding the heavenly commandments to love one another, they are still shedding each other's blood. How heedless and ignorant are the people of the world! How gross the darkness which envelops them! Although they are the children of a compassionate God, they continue to live and act in opposition to His will and good pleasure. God is

loving and kind to all men, and yet they show the utmost enmity and hatred toward each other. God is the Giver of life to them, and yet they constantly seek to destroy life. God blesses and protects their homes; they rage, sack and destroy each other's homes. Consider their ignorance and heedlessness!

Your duty is of another kind, for you are informed of the mysteries of God. Your eyes are illumined; your ears are quickened with hearing. You must, therefore, look toward each other and then toward mankind with the utmost love and kindness. You have no excuse to bring before God if you fail to live according to His command, for you are informed of that which constitutes the good pleasure of God. You have heard His commandments and precepts. You must, therefore, be kind to all men; you must even treat your enemies as your friends. You must consider your evil-wishers as your well-wishers. Those who are not agreeable toward you must be regarded as those who are congenial and pleasant so that, perchance, this darkness of disagreement and conflict may disappear from amongst men and the light of the divine may shine forth, so that the Orient may be illumined and the Occident filled with fragrance, nay, so that the East and West may embrace each other in love and deal with one another in sympathy and affection. Until man reaches this high station, the world of humanity shall not find rest, and eternal felicity shall not be attained. But if man lives up to these divine commandments, this world of earth shall be transformed into the world of heaven, and this material sphere shall be converted into a paradise of glory. It is my hope that you may become successful in this high calling so that like brilliant lamps you may cast light upon the world of humanity and quicken and stir the body of existence like unto a spirit of life. This is eternal glory. This is everlasting felicity. This is immortal life. This is heavenly attainment. This is being created in the image and likeness of God. And unto this I call you, praying to God to strengthen and bless you.

Appendix

Chronological List of Talks Given by 'Abdu'l-Bahá in the United States and Canada in 1912

11 April	New York, NY	Home of Mr. and Mrs. Edward B. Kinney 780 West End Avenue
12 April	Brooklyn, NY	Home of Mr. and Mrs. Howard MacNutt 935 Eastern Parkway
12 April	New York, NY	Studio of Miss Phillips 39 West Sixty-seventh Street
13 April	New York, NY	Home of Mr. and Mrs. Alexander Morten 141 East Twenty-first Street
14 April	New York, NY	Church of the Ascension Fifth Avenue and Tenth Street
14 April	New York, NY	Union Meeting of Advanced Thought Centers Carnegie Lyceum, West Fifty-seventh Street
15 April	New York, NY	Home of Mountfort Mills 327 West End Avenue
16 April	New York, NY	Bahá'í Friends of New Jersey Hotel Ansonia Broadway and Seventy-third Street
17 April	New York, NY	Hotel Ansonia Broadway and Seventy-third Street
17 April	New York, NY	Home of Mr. and Mrs. Edward B. Kinney 780 West End Avenue
18 April	New York, NY	Home of Mr. and Mrs. Marshall L. Emery 273 West Ninetieth Street
19 April	New York, NY	Columbia University Earl Hall
19 April	New York, NY	Bowery Mission 227 Bowery

Appendix

20 April	Washington, DC	Orient-Occident-Unity Conference Public Library Hall
21 April	Washington, DC	Studio Hall 1219 Connecticut Avenue
21 April	Washington, DC	Universalist Church Thirteenth and L Streets
22 April	Washington, DC	Home of Mr. and Mrs. Arthur J. Parsons 1700 Eighteenth Street, NW
23 April	Washington, DC	Howard University
23 April	Washington, DC	Home of Mr. and Mrs. Arthur J. Parsons 1700 Eighteenth Street, NW
23 April	Washington, DC	Bethel Literary Society Metropolitan African Methodist Episcopal Church M Street, NW
24 April	Washington, DC	Children's Reception, Studio Hall 1219 Connecticut Avenue
24 April	Washington, DC	Home of Mr. and Mrs. Arthur J. Parsons 1700 Eighteenth Street, NW
24 April	Washington, DC	Home of Mrs. Andrew J. Dyer 1937 Thirteenth Street, NW
25 April	Washington, DC	Theosophical Society Home of Mr. and Mrs. Arthur J. Parsons 1700 Eighteenth Street, NW
25 April	Washington, DC	Message to Esperantists Home of Mr. and Mrs. Arthur J. Parsons 1700 Eighteenth Street, NW
25 April	Washington, DC	Home of Mr. and Mrs. Arthur J. Parsons 1700 Eighteenth Street, NW
30 April	Chicago, IL	Public Meeting Concluding Convention of Bahá'í Temple Unity Drill Hall, Masonic Temple
30 April	Chicago, IL	Hull House
30 April	Chicago, IL	Fourth Annual Conference of the National Association for the Advancement of Colored People Handel Hall
1 May	Wilmette, IL	Dedication of the Mashriqu'l-Adhkár Grounds

Appendix

2 May	Chicago, IL	Hotel Plaza
2 May	Chicago, IL	Federation of Women's Clubs Hotel La Salle
2 May	Chicago, IL	Bahá'í Women's Reception Hotel La Salle
2 May	Chicago, IL	Hotel Plaza
2 May	Chicago, IL	Hotel Plaza
3 May	Chicago, IL	Hotel Plaza
3 May	Chicago, IL	Hotel Plaza
4 May	Evanston, IL	Theosophical Society Northwestern University Hall
5 May	Chicago, IL	Children's Meeting, Hotel Plaza
5 May	Chicago, IL	Plymouth Congregational Church 935 East Fiftieth Street
5 May	Chicago, IL	All-Souls Church, Lincoln Center
6 May	Cleveland, OH	Euclid Hall
6 May	Cleveland, OH	Sanatorium of Dr. C. M. Swingle
7 May	Pittsburgh, PA	Hotel Schenley
11 May	New York, NY	227 Riverside Drive
12 May	Montclair, NJ	Unity Church
12 May	New York, NY	Meeting of International Peace Forum Grace Methodist Episcopal Church West 104th Street
13 May	New York, NY	Reception by New York Peace Society Hotel Astor
19 May	New York, NY	Church of the Divine Paternity Central Park West
19 May	Jersey City, NJ	Brotherhood Church Bergen and Fairview Avenues
20 May	New York, NY	Woman's Suffrage Meeting Metropolitan Temple Seventh Avenue and Fourteenth Street
23 May	Cambridge, MA	Home of Mr. and Mrs. Francis W. Breed 367 Harvard Street

24 May	Boston, MA	Free Religious Association, or Unitarian Conference
25 May	Boston, MA	Huntington Chambers
26 May	New York, NY	Mount Morris Baptist Church Fifth Avenue and 126th Street
28 May	New York, NY	Reception at Metropolitan Temple Seventh Avenue and Fourteenth Street
29 May	New York, NY	Home of Mr. and Mrs. Edward B. Kinney 780 West End Avenue
30 May	New York, NY	Theosophical Lodge Broadway and Seventy-ninth Street
31 May	Fanwood, NJ	Town Hall
2 June	New York, NY	Church of the Ascension Fifth Avenue and Tenth Street
8 June	New York, NY	309 West Seventy-eighth Street
9 June	Philadelphia, PA	Unitarian Church Fifteenth Street and Girard Avenue
9 June	Philadelphia, PA	Baptist Temple Broad and Berks Streets
11 June	New York, NY	Open Committee Meeting Home of Mr. and Mrs. Edward B. Kinney 780 West End Avenue
11 June	New York, NY	309 West Seventy-eighth Street
11 June	New York, NY	309 West Seventy-eighth Street
12 June	New York, NY	309 West Seventy-eighth Street
15 June	New York, NY	309 West Seventy-eighth Street
16 June	Brooklyn, NY	Fourth Unitarian Church Beverly Road, Flatbush
16 June	Brooklyn, NY	Home of Mr. and Mrs. Howard MacNutt 935 Eastern Parkway
16 June	Brooklyn, NY	Central Congregational Church Hancock Street

Appendix

17 June	New York, NY	309 West Seventy-eighth Street
18 June	New York, NY	309 West Seventy-eighth Street
20 June	New York, NY	309 West Seventy-eighth Street
23 June	Montclair, NJ	
29 June	West Englewood, NJ	Unity Feast, Outdoors
1 July	New York, NY	309 West Seventy-eighth Street
1 July	New York, NY	309 West Seventy-eighth Street
5 July	New York, NY	309 West Seventy-eighth Street
5 July	New York, NY	309 West Seventy-eighth Street
6 July	New York, NY	309 West Seventy-eighth Street
14 July	New York, NY	All Souls Unitarian Church Fourth Avenue and Twentieth Street
15 July	New York, NY	Home of Dr. and Mrs. Florian Krug 830 Park Avenue
23 July	Boston, MA	Hotel Victoria
24 July	Boston, MA	Theosophical Society The Kensington, Exeter and Boylston Streets
25 July	Boston, MA	Hotel Victoria
5 August	Dublin, NH	Dublin Inn
6 August	Dublin, NH	Home of Mr. and Mrs. Arthur J. Parsons
16 August	Eliot, ME	Green Acre
17 August	Eliot, ME	Green Acre
17 August	Eliot, ME	Green Acre
17 August	Eliot, ME	Green Acre
17 August	Eliot, ME	Green Acre
25 August	Boston, MA	New Thought Forum Metaphysical Club
26 August	Boston, MA	Franklin Square House
27 August	Boston, MA	Metaphysical Club
29 August	Malden, MA	Home of Madame Morey 34 Hillside Avenue
1 September	Montreal, Canada	Church of the Messiah

1 September	Montreal, Canada	Home of Mr. and Mrs. William Sutherland Maxwell 716 Pine Avenue West
1 September	Montreal, Canada	Home of Mr. and Mrs. William Sutherland Maxwell 716 Pine Avenue West
2 September	Montreal, Canada	Home of Mr. and Mrs. William Sutherland Maxwell 716 Pine Avenue West
3 September	Montreal, Canada	Coronation Hall
5 September	Montreal, Canada	St. James Methodist Church
16 September	Chicago, IL	Home of Mrs. Corinne True 5338 Kenmore Avenue
20 September	Minneapolis, MN	Home of Mr. Albert L. Hall 2030 Queen Avenue South
20 September	St. Paul, MN	Home of Dr. and Mrs. Clement Woolson 870 Laurel Avenue
24 September	Denver, CO	Home of Mrs. Sidney E. Roberts
25 September	Denver, CO	Second Divine Science Church 3929 West Thirty-eighth Avenue
7 October	Oakland, CA	Japanese Young Men's Christian Association Japanese Independent Church
8 October	Palo Alto, CA	Leland Stanford Junior University
10 October	San Francisco, CA	Open Forum
12 October	San Francisco, CA	Temple Emmanu-El 450 Sutter Street
25 October	Sacramento, CA	Hotel Sacramento
26 October	Sacramento, CA	Assembly Hall, Hotel Sacramento
31 October	Chicago, IL	Hotel Plaza
1 November	Chicago, IL	Home of Mrs. Corinne True 5338 Kenmore Avenue
5 November	Cincinnati, OH	Grand Hotel
6 November	Washington, DC	Universalist Church Thirteenth and L Streets, NW

Appendix

7 November	Washington, DC	Home of Mr. and Mrs. Arthur J. Parsons 1700 Eighteenth Street, NW
7 November	Washington, DC	Home of Mr. and Mrs. Arthur J. Parsons 1700 Eighteenth Street, NW
8 November	Washington, DC	Eighth Street Temple, Synagogue
9 November	Washington, DC	Home of Mr. and Mrs. Arthur J. Parsons 1700 Eighteenth Street, NW
9 November	Washington, DC	Home of Mr. and Mrs. Arthur J. Parsons 1700 Eighteenth Street, NW
9 November	Washington, DC	Bahá'í Banquet Rauscher's Hall
10 November	Washington, DC	Home of Mr. and Mrs. Arthur J. Parsons 1700 Eighteenth Street, NW
10 November	Washington, DC	Home of Mr. and Mrs. Joseph H. Hannen 1252 Eighth Street, NW
10 November	Washington, DC	1901 Eighteenth Street, NW
15 November	New York, NY	Home of Miss Juliet Thompson 48 West Tenth Street
16 November	New York, NY	309 West Seventy-eighth Street
17 November	New York, NY	Genealogical Hall 252 West Fifty-eighth Street
18 November	New York, NY	Home of Mr. and Mrs. Frank K. Moxey 575 Riverside Drive
23 November	New York, NY	Banquet, Great Northern Hotel 118 West Fifty-seventh Street
29 November	New York, NY	Home of Mr. and Mrs. Edward B. Kinney 780 West End Avenue
2 December	New York, NY	Home of Mr. and Mrs. Edward B. Kinney 780 West End Avenue
2 December	New York, NY	Home of Mr. and Mrs. Edward B. Kinney 780 West End Avenue
3 December	New York, NY	Home of Dr. and Mrs. Florian Krug 830 Park Avenue
3 December	New York, NY	Mr. Kinney's Bible Class 780 West End Avenue

671

3 December	New York, NY	Home of Mr. and Mrs. Edward B. Kinney 780 West End Avenue
4 December	New York, NY	Theosophical Society 2228 Broadway
5 December	New York, NY	On Board Steamship *Celtic,* Day of departure

Index

action(s), 167–68, 330, 517, 598
    following Teachings of Bahá'u'lláh, 11, 330, 335, 476–77
    goodly, 185, 304, 417, 602
    purity of, 149, 391, 395
    unity of, 216, 218–19
    See also intentions; service; volition; work as worship
Adam, 61, 172, 305, 307, 516, 633–34
    descendants of, 137, 320, 416, 449, 501, 600, 633
Adrianople (Turkey, Land of Mystery), 37, 38, 173, 525, 561
advancement, 81, 153, 178
    See also civilization, material, advancement of; mankind,
      advancement of; progress and progressions
affinity
    in animal kingdom, 290–91, 356–57, 375–76
    atomic, 5, 397, 425–26
    limitations on, 550–51
    power of, 336, 597, 598
    religion as source of, 172, 521
    See also cohesion
Afnán, 98
Africa, 313, 582
    lack of education in, 107, 116, 411, 467, 468, 563
    tribes in, 43, 61–62, 155, 265, 430, 433
aggression. *See* hatred; war(s)
agreement, 66, 92–93, 375
    in Bahá'í community, 298–300, 419, 556–57
    Bahá'u'lláh brought, 160, 167, 173, 460, 547
    establishment of, 18, 43, 55, 134, 141, 321, 456, 522
    international, 171, 195, 451
    Manifestations of God bring, 78, 161, 178, 193, 478
    obstacles to, 170, 193
    religion as source of, 90, 135, 137–38, 169, 251, 327–28, 415,
      481, 486–87, 574, 629, 641
    See also consultation; harmony
agriculture, 14, 302, 303, 437, 438, 439
airplanes, 23, 41, 139, 247, 338, 361, 508
altruism, 168, 237, 551, 625

America
  Bahá'u'lláh's Epistle to president of, 311, 608
  character of, 44, 202, 657, 660
  Christianity in, 347–48
  education in, 42, 107, 116, 467, 468
  freedom in, 62, 70, 143, 351, 549, 578
  government of, 66, 152, 231, 419, 452, 547, 548
  Persia's relations with, 47–48, 49, 484
  prayers for, 92, 133
  progress in, 14, 153, 478, 629
  race unity in, 93–94
  spiritual enlightenment in, 26, 31
  See also Bahá'í communities, American; Columbus,
    Christopher; peace, America's role in establishing
amity. See agreement; harmony; love; unity
Ancient Beauty. See Bahá'u'lláh
angels, 27, 31
animal kingdom, 39–40, 51–52, 257–58, 378, 617
  affinity in, 290–91, 356–57, 375–76
  atoms traversing, 121, 122, 315, 397, 398, 427, 493–94
  as captives of nature, 22, 55, 68, 79, 246–48, 337–38, 361,
    423, 433–34, 496, 505, 508
  cohesion in, 77, 290–91, 356–57, 360, 375–76
  colors in, 61, 156, 600
  components of, 92, 95, 426, 596–97
  distinctions in, 93, 265
  equality in, 104, 149, 163, 253, 391, 401, 416, 529, 555, 612
  ferocity in, 77, 141–42, 164, 290–91, 376, 433, 468, 497–
    98, 557
  happiness in, 229, 475
  human kingdom superior to, 67, 84, 95, 337, 360–61, 421,
    450, 471–72, 504–5, 507–8, 656
  lacks knowledge, 157, 240, 360–61, 365–66, 397, 433–34,
    498
  sense perception in, 79, 337, 338, 360, 587–88, 589
  solitariness in, 48, 435, 441–42
  training of, 106–7

Bible
> creation story in, 307, 348
> meanings of, 277, 278–79, 296–97, 634
> *See also* New Testament; Old Testament; prophecies; *and individual books*

bigotry, religious, 56, 146, 193, 416, 446, 625
> wars caused by, 147, 165, 478, 618–19
> *See also* prejudice(s), religious

birds, 257–58
birth, second. *See* Holy Spirit, baptism of; Jesus Christ, second birth taught by; renewal
blacks, gratitude toward whites, 61–62, 155, 156
> *See also* colors, oneness of; races

Blessed Beauty. *See* Bahá'u'lláh
Blessed Perfection. *See* Bahá'u'lláh
blindness, spiritual. *See* beliefs, ancestral; bigotry, religious; imitations, religious
bloodshed. *See* strife; war(s)
bodies, human
> as captives of nature, 112, 655–56
> changes in, 426–27, 585–87
> composition of, 290, 585
> disintegration of, 81, 82–83, 290
> growth of, 93, 464, 468
> spirit's relationship to, 143–44, 287, 335–36, 361–62, 367–69, 386, 428

body politic, 19–20, 136, 534
> advancement of, 388, 435–44, 488, 517, 570
> cohesion in, 77, 237, 486
> educational responsibility of, 417, 450
> *See also* mankind; nations

Bolshevism, 444
Book of the Covenant. *See under* Bahá'u'lláh, Writings of
Books of God. *See* Holy Books
Bowery Mission (New York City), 44–46
brain, 269, 394–95, 409
> *See also* mind

Index

bread of life. *See* Jesus Christ, as bread of life
brotherhood, 171, 179–83, 194–95, 550–52, 602–3
    in Bahá'í community, 556–57
    spiritual, 200, 208, 235, 629
    See also fellowship; races, oneness of
Browne, Edward Granville, 560
Buddha and Buddhists, 308, 310, 489

Cain, 516
California, Bahá'í, 531, 537, 541
Canada, government of, 452
capacities, 140, 143–44, 420
    development of, 32, 48, 272–74, 315
    differences in, 33, 303, 596
    of women, 102, 187–89, 392–96, 556
capitalism and capitalists, 442, 443
capital punishment, 142, 516
Catherine I (wife of Peter the Great), 188, 392, 393
Catholics, 297, 371, 538, 627
    See also Christianity and Christians; Jesus Christ; law(s),
      Christian
cause and effect, 428, 597–98
Cause of Bahá'u'lláh, 197, 318, 333, 539
    distinctive characteristics of, 260–61, 607–15
    growth of, 36–38, 60, 304, 313, 606, 610, 631
    persecution of, 6, 36, 217, 349, 557, 562, 614, 643
    service to, 8, 9–10, 75, 149, 202, 304, 351, 541, 545, 604
    teaching, 75, 101, 109, 295, 296, 537, 543
    See also Bahá'í communities; Bahá'í Faith; Bahá'u'lláh
cells (biological), 77, 357, 374–75, 493–94
Center of the Covenant. *See* 'Abdu'l-Bahá
century of light (Twentieth Century), 10, 299, 328
    equality of women and men in, 102, 184, 395
    God's bestowals in, 51, 173–74, 298, 474
    progress in, 139–40, 180, 198–200, 534
    renewal during, 53, 191–92, 387–88, 535–36
    spiritual progress in, 90, 167–68, 182–83, 401

century of light (Twentieth Century) *(continued)*
    truth in, 56, 160, 262–63, 625–27
    unity in, 195, 212, 230, 319, 321, 521–22
Chaldeans, 573
    unified through Christ, 178, 489, 518–19, 523, 575–76,
        581
change. *See* transformation
character, 44, 60, 62, 97, 602, 607, 612
    See also action(s), goodly; morality; virtues
charity. *See* action(s), goodly; altruism
Chicago, Illinois, 154, 537
    Bahá'í community in, 128–29, 539, 541, 545
    Mashriqu'l-Adhkár in, 97, 98
children
    education of, 71–73, 86, 126–27, 149–50, 185, 186, 243,
        270–71, 297
    growth of, 64, 422, 617, 618
    See also families, unity in; fathers; mothers; orphans, care of
Christianity and Christians, 119, 347–48, 470, 551–52, 605
    Bahá'í Faith's relationship to, 346–47
    foundation of, 8, 214, 279, 403–4
    Jews' relationship to, 283, 311, 371
    literal interpretations by, 343, 624
    Moses' relationship to, 310, 517–18, 520
    Muslims' relationship to, 280, 282, 283, 370–71, 490, 520
    schisms in, 277, 538, 544
    See also Bible; Catholics; Jesus Christ; law(s), Christian;
        Protestants
Christian Science, healing treatments of, 345
churches. *See* temples and churches
cities, 37, 439
    in America, 143, 365, 541
    war's effects on, 414, 513, 567, 619, 662
    See also specific cities
citizenship, 93–94
civilization
    material, 16, 143–44, 534

advancement of, 14–15, 22, 51, 135, 139–40, 151, 179–
80, 287, 402, 462
incompleteness of, 420, 530
warfare in, 132–33, 141–42
in the West, 93–94, 229, 432–33
religion as foundation of, 7, 118, 146–47, 151–52, 200, 452,
517, 551
spiritual, 52, 143–44, 194, 548
advancement of, 51, 180
establishment of, 16, 26, 143–44, 229
need for, 3, 14–15, 22, 133, 140–42, 235, 287, 309, 402,
420, 530
Cleopatra (queen, Egypt), 393
Cleveland, Ohio, 143
cohesion, 77, 136, 170, 289, 290, 374
See also affinity; animal kingdom, cohesion in; composition
collective centers, 89, 219, 226–28, 335, 421–22
colors, oneness of, 60–63, 69–70, 77, 93–94, 96, 155–56, 600–603
See also races
Columbia University (New York City), 42
Columbus, Christopher, 79, 188, 337, 432, 588
combination. *See* composition
commandments. *See* law(s)
Committee of Union and Progress, 49, 284, 314
communications. *See* language; phonographs; telephones
Communion (sacrament). *See* Jesus Christ, as bread of life
composition, 76–77, 121, 136, 289–90, 398, 425–27, 589, 596–97
See also cohesion; creation
comprehension. *See* perception; understanding
conciliation, 15, 308, 532, 547
See also agreement; reconciliation
concord. *See* agreement; harmony; unity
conduct. *See* character; morality
conflicts. *See* discord; war(s)
Confucius, 489
conscience, 146, 149, 268, 276, 330
See also morality

Europe, 469, 518, 584
    education in, 116, 468
    philosophers in, 27–28
    wars in, 7, 115–16, 164, 169, 405, 451
    See also Balkans, war in; *and specific European countries*
Eve, 61
evil, 142, 210, 273, 430, 625, 636, 638, 640, 657
    good and, 55, 56, 119, 151, 412
    See also Satan and satanic qualities
evolution. *See* mankind, evolution of
existence, 110, 170, 308, 412
    causes of, 289–90, 356
    human, 83, 130, 157–58, 289–90, 320, 357, 410, 430
    kingdoms of, 95–96, 101, 104, 106–7, 109–10, 396–400, 494–95, 585
    material, 76–78, 92–93
    phenomenal, 339, 594, 596–97, 598–99
    sources of, 129, 356
    worlds of, 90, 120–25, 170–71, 264, 335–36, 358, 360, 534, 636, 658
    See also creation; life; nature; world(s), phenomenal
eyes. *See* sight, sense of
Ezekiel, 31

faith, 69, 160, 252, 263, 264, 434, 457, 477, 517, 568, 626–27, 650
    of disciples, 101, 185, 394, 556
    firmness of, 38, 65, 286, 316, 464, 537–38, 602
    of Peter, 89, 226, 544, 613
    prayers for, 622
    sacrifices for, 2, 19, 103, 172, 284
    unity through, 18, 101, 483–84
    See also Bahá'í Faith; beliefs, ancestral; religion(s)
families, unity in, 217, 232–33, 311, 321, 502, 600
    limitations to, 456, 479, 550, 551
fanaticism. *See* bigotry, religious; prejudice(s), religious
Farmer, Miss (Sarah), 364

heart(s) *(continued)*
    mirrors of, 19, 72, 204, 341–42
    promptings of, 30, 258, 355–56, 357
    purity of, 60, 95, 97, 128, 149, 155, 185, 273, 409, 417, 555,
      600, 612
    renewal of, 358, 386
heat. *See* energy
Heaven, Kingdom of. *See* Abhá Kingdom; Kingdom of God;
    world(s), spiritual
Hidden Words of Bahá'u'lláh. *See under* Bahá'u'lláh, Writings of
higher criticism, the, 296–97
Him Whom God Shall Make Manifest. *See* Bahá'u'lláh
Hinduism and Hindus, 231–32
Hippocrates, 513, 572
holiness. *See* sanctity
Holy Books, 89, 308, 433, 449, 580
    Bahá'í teachings new to, 607–15, 640–44
    criterion of, 353, 355, 357
    interpretations of, 29, 275, 282, 297, 307, 343–45, 447
    oneness of, 43–44, 311, 347
    proofs in, 257, 324, 355
    prophecies in, 31, 51, 183, 308–9
    revelation of, 81, 413, 551
    symbolism of, 647–49
    See also Bible; Qur'án; teachings, divine
Holy Land. *See* Israel and Israelites; Jerusalem
Holy Spirit, 85, 214, 450
    baptism of, 56, 79–81, 203, 387, 423
    bestowals of, 239, 402–3, 421, 422–23, 445–46, 450
    breaths of, 27, 221, 345, 351, 431, 530
      brotherhood through, 208, 235
      Christ manifested, 6, 15, 348, 349
      education through, 30, 56–57, 235, 287–88, 297, 468,
        470–71
      peace through, 151–52, 457–58
      quickened through, 78, 180–81, 194, 253–54, 331, 431

unity brought by, 5–8, 25, 54, 57, 115, 134, 146, 177–78,
205–6, 215–16, 219, 227–28, 505–6, 518–19, 523–24,
551, 580–81
as Word of God, 159, 214–15, 280–81, 296, 297
See also Christianity and Christians; disciples, of Christ;
law(s), Christian
Jews, 224, 310, 470
adhering to ancestral forms, 371, 624
Christians' relationship to, 283, 311, 371
Muslims' relationship with, 371, 520
persecution of, 312, 584
philosophers among, 512–13
See also Israel and Israelites; Jesus Christ, Jews' rejection of;
law(s), Mosaic
John, Saint (disciple), 213–14, 648
John the Baptist, 232, 358
Joseph, 31, 511
Judaism
Bahá'u'lláh reaffirmed teachings of, 521
Christ reaffirmed teachings of, 517–18, 574–76, 582
Muḥammad reaffirmed teachings of, 577
See also Moses; Old Testament; Talmud
Judas Iscariot (disciple), 185, 275, 539
judgment, 489, 498, 515, 520, 572, 574, 582, 641
standards of, 55, 96, 353–57, 409, 502–4, 644
See also intellect and intelligence; reason
justice, 10, 408, 441, 442, 567, 577
divine, 182, 183, 567
establishment of, 167, 195
religion as source of, 43, 137, 486
See also courts; law(s)

kindness, 86, 375–76, 413, 437, 522, 552, 555
See also God, kindness of; loving kindness
Kingdom of God, 71, 80, 222, 298, 366, 473, 653–54
attainment of, 3, 64–65, 316, 317–18, 403, 450, 472, 475
effulgences of, 21, 33, 221, 422, 589

reality of, 109, 141, 193, 212, 416, 487
revelations by, 177, 192–93, 431–32, 486–91
as Shepherds, 224–25, 228
teachings of all identical, 15–16, 132, 144, 175, 210–12, 213,
    232, 234, 276, 296, 310–11, 327, 411, 413–14, 446, 481,
    491, 499, 517, 639
See also religion(s); revelation; unity, Manifestations bring;
    and individual Manifestations
mankind
advancement of, 40, 179, 229, 252, 253–54, 402–3, 510,
    517, 532
attributes of, 67, 69, 475–76
as collective centers, 421–22
creation of, 5, 54, 113, 258, 413–15, 416, 447–48, 498,
    526–27, 567, 661
    in image and likeness of God, 10, 95–96, 104, 131, 156,
        173, 328, 348, 361, 366–67, 391, 475, 527, 550, 555,
        568–69, 636, 654
dual nature of, 55–56, 111–12, 135
education's effects on, 116–17, 467–72, 579
evolution of, 308, 427, 494, 505–8
honor of, 434, 441–42, 471, 475, 513
love among, 86, 92, 148, 291–92, 323, 405–6, 522, 577–78,
    661
lower nature of, 256–59, 401–2, 403, 411–12, 423, 430, 433,
    493, 499
maturity of, 51, 253–54, 422, 617–22
nature controlled by, 22–23, 24, 41, 68–69, 111–12, 247–48,
    337–38, 368–69, 421, 496–97, 499, 508–9
pathways for, 246–49
progress of, 51, 402–3, 411–12
reality of, 80, 339, 358, 363, 367, 585, 589, 654–55
renewal of, 51–52, 56, 192, 193, 194, 386–91, 423–24, 618
service to, 10, 148
station of, 66–67, 366–67, 530
unification of, 134, 194, 218–19, 225, 235, 239, 251, 266,
    267–68, 282–83, 522
welfare of, 171, 334, 435–44

mankind *(continued)*
  See also body politic; existence, human; human kingdom;
    oneness of mankind; power, of mankind; spirit, of man
manna, 281, 590, 624
marriage laws. *See* divorce, laws regarding; polygamy, laws
    regarding
martyrs
  Bábí, 172, 196
  Bahá'í, 204, 284, 349, 541–42, 557
  Protestant, 371
Mary (mother of Jesus), 243, 281, 491
Mary Magdalene, 185, 243, 394, 556, 593
Mashriqu'l-Adhkárs, 90, 91, 97–98
materialism and materialists, 246-48, 309, 422–23, 474, 530, 597
  advancement of, 131, 222–23
  conditions of, 133, 135
  European, 22, 27–28
  nature and, 110–13, 467
  philosophers of, 69, 92–93, 249–50, 336, 353, 365–66,
    433–34, 467, 504, 530
  See also civilization, material
matrix. *See* mothers, matrix of
matter, 297, 374, 377
maturity. *See* mankind, maturity of
meat, eating of, 236, 346
meetings
  Bahá'í, 255–56, 298–99, 473, 590–93, 630–32
  prayers for, 364, 452–53, 590–91
  See also assembly, international
memory, 111, 330, 461, 498
  nature lacks, 23, 41, 69, 248, 337, 509
  See also mind
men. *See* equality, of women and men
mercy, 262, 379, 387, 441
  See also God, mercy of
Messengers. *See* Manifestations of God
Messiah, 227, 382

philosophers in, 354, 503, 504
religious disunity in, 165–66, 250
unity brought by Bahá'u'lláh, 25–26, 134–35, 167, 172, 176, 178, 326–27, 489–90, 491, 547–58
women in, 230, 236, 351–52
See also Bahá'í community, Persian; Shah of Persia
Peter (disciple)
Christ denied by, 394, 556
education of, 470, 482
faith of, 89, 226, 544, 613
transformation of, 6, 593
philosophers and philosophy, 40, 191, 297, 442, 502–10
Arabian, 493
divine, 42, 81, 336, 353–54, 396, 463–64, 467, 493, 530
Greek, 464, 512–13, 571–72, 580
Illuminati, 336, 355
Jewish, 512–13
natural, 363, 430–31, 463–64
persecution of Christians by, 605, 613
Persian, 102–3, 354, 503, 504
as teachers, 117, 150, 235, 287–88, 564
See also materialism and materialists, philosophers of; *and individual philosophers*
Phoenicians, Christ unified, 178, 523, 575–76, 581
phonographs, 23, 247, 338, 497, 508
physicians. *See* healing and health; Manifestations of God, as Physicians
planets, 354, 496, 503, 588
plants, 80, 110, 374–75, 397, 528–29, 555, 595–96
See also flowers; tree(s); vegetable kingdom
Plato, 297, 464, 493, 504
politics, 267, 275, 333
discord caused by, 54, 324–25, 334
limitations to, 15, 150, 218, 456, 468
prejudice based on, 401, 414, 415, 449, 485
reformation of, 195, 388
See also body politic; government(s)
polygamy, laws regarding, 408, 480, 554

reality *(continued)*
    human, 95, 123, 159, 367, 589
    ideal, 505, 509
    indestructibility of, 277, 585
    intellectual, 337–38, 421
    investigation of, 54, 103, 129, 164, 211, 234, 244, 250, 280,
        309–11, 324, 326–27, 382, 406–11, 447, 481, 483, 487–
        89, 502–10, 515, 526, 610
        through inner vision, 102, 175, 367, 409–10, 465
    light of, 17, 99, 143, 174
    oneness of, 119, 132, 147, 163, 169, 174, 193, 244, 250, 276,
        311, 413, 415–16, 446, 456, 610
    perceptions of, 177, 588
    phenomenal, 120, 290, 461, 594
    of religion, 137–38, 174–76, 192–93, 209, 219, 487, 517,
        526, 569
    revelation of, 53, 139, 463, 464
    See also mankind, reality of; Sun of Reality; truth,
        investigation of
reason
    animals lack, 61, 360, 587–88
    criterion of, 28, 29–30, 55, 353, 354–55, 356, 357, 462,
        503–5, 509
    human, 68, 86, 163, 177, 441
    investigation through, 109, 406, 409, 421, 464
    power of, 72, 444
    religion must agree with, 235, 251, 323, 400, 415, 448–49,
        527–28, 555, 611, 641
    science and, 67, 148, 177
    See also intellect and intelligence; mind
reciprocity, 435–36, 478–79, 552
reconciliation, 115, 169
    establishment of, 142–43, 419
    through Manifestations, 487–88
    of religions, 201–2, 210
    religious, 326, 500, 629
    See also agreement; conciliation

sun *(continued)*
  oneness of, 109, 159, 174, 211, 268–69, 347, 382–83
  perception of, 28–29
  rays of, 80, 123, 399, 445, 532–33, 652–54
  reflection of, 95, 127–28
  See also solar system
Sun of Reality, 118, 347, 383
  appearance of, 18–19, 74, 75, 131–33, 139, 144, 297, 309,
    379, 403–4, 491–92
  as Educator, 367, 378
  effulgences of, 67, 81–82, 103, 158–59, 173, 298, 410, 463,
    468
  light of, 182, 204, 387, 388
  love from, 358, 359
  oneness of, 19, 130–31, 175, 241, 270, 381–82
  rays of, 16, 17, 359
  See also Bahá'u'lláh; reality
Sun of Truth, 102
  appearance of, 21, 31–32, 51, 84, 212, 658
  effulgences of, 80, 431, 433, 463
  illumination from, 158, 160, 659–60
  oneness of, 109, 567
  rays of, 341, 342, 654
  veils obscuring, 108, 132, 206, 223
  See also Bahá'u'lláh; truth
superstitions, 416, 463, 632–33
  elimination of, 108–9, 132, 212, 288, 610
  regarding numbers, 274–75
  religion and science disagreeing, 86–87, 148, 177, 223–24,
    244, 251–52, 400, 415, 528, 555, 641
  truth obscured by, 84–85, 118–19, 147, 249, 448
  wars caused by, 163, 553, 557–58
  See also beliefs, ancestral; imitations, religious
Supreme Concourse, 5, 6, 7, 205, 206, 255, 260, 272, 298, 473,
    590
Súratu'l-Haykal. *See under* Bahá'u'lláh, Writings of
survival of the fittest, 498, 563, 564

unity *(continued)*
    unification of; races, unification of; religion(s), unification
      of
unity feasts, 289, 298–300
universal auxiliary language. *See* language, universal auxiliary
Universal House of Justice, 642
Universalist Church, 53
universe, 307, 397–400
    infinity of, 95, 113, 377, 383
      phenomena in, 77, 109–10, 374

vegetable kingdom, 32, 39, 40, 51, 79, 338, 378, 479
    atoms traversing, 121, 122, 315, 397, 427, 494
    as captive of nature, 110, 496
    cohesion in, 356, 360, 374–75
    colors in, 61, 156
    components of, 92, 95, 426
    comprehension of higher kingdoms impossible, 157–58, 240,
      595–96
    distinctions in, 93, 265
    equality in, 104, 149, 253, 391, 528–29, 555, 612
    growth in, 95, 336–37, 360, 397, 495, 617
    See also flowers; gardens; plants; tree(s)
vegetarianism, 236
veils
    on Persian women, 352
    spiritual, 85, 124, 192–93, 280, 409–10, 478
    See also imitations, religious, truth obscured by
Victoria (queen of England), 393
    Bahá'u'lláh's Epistle to, 283
violence. *See* animal kingdom, ferocity in; human kingdom,
    ferocity in; strife; war(s)
virtues, 15, 43, 52, 122, 131, 342, 564
    attainment of, 5, 7, 9, 24, 123–25, 229, 258, 260–61, 298,
      316–18, 476, 499, 534, 568–69, 636
    development of, 232, 233
    divine, 95–96, 114, 287, 402, 403, 410, 533

PUBLISHING

Bahá'í Publishing and the Bahá'í Faith

Bahá'í Publishing produces books based on the teachings of the Bahá'í Faith. Founded over 160 years ago, the Bahá'í Faith has spread to some 235 nations and territories and is now accepted by more than five million people. The word "Bahá'í" means "follower of Bahá'u'lláh." Bahá'u'lláh, the founder of the Bahá'í Faith, asserted that He is the Messenger of God for all of humanity in this day. The cornerstone of His teachings is the establishment of the spiritual unity of humankind, which will be achieved by personal transformation and the application of clearly identified spiritual principles. Bahá'ís also believe that there is but one religion and that all the Messengers of God—among them Abraham, Zoroaster, Moses, Krishna, Buddha, Jesus, and Muḥammad—have progressively revealed its nature. Together, the world's great religions are expressions of a single, unfolding divine plan. Human beings, not God's Messengers, are the source of religious divisions, prejudices, and hatreds.

The Bahá'í Faith is not a sect or denomination of another religion, nor is it a cult or a social movement. Rather, it is a globally recognized independent world religion founded on new books of scripture revealed by Bahá'u'lláh.

Bahá'í Publishing is an imprint of the National Spiritual Assembly of the Bahá'ís of the United States.

For more information about the Bahá'í Faith,
or to contact Bahá'ís near you,
visit http://www.bahai.us/
or call
1-800-22-UNITE

Other Books Available from Bahá'í Publishing

'ABDU'L-BAHÁ IN AMERICA
Robert H. Stockman
$18.00 US / $20.00 CAN
Trade Paper
ISBN: 978-1-931847-97-1

The amazing account of the journey of 'Abdu'l-Bahá across much of the United States to share the message of the oneness of humanity and the principles of universal peace.

'Abdu'l-Bahá in America is the account of the journey of 'Abdu'l-Bahá, eldest son of Bahá'u'lláh and appointed head of the Bahá'í Faith after his father's passing, across much of the United States in 1912. His exhausting yet exhilarating 239-day trek from coast to coast took him to fifty cities and towns, where he delivered up to four talks a day—about four hundred total—to approximately ninety-three thousand people about Bahá'u'lláh's message of the oneness of humanity and the principles of universal peace. This historic visit to the United States planted the seeds that would take root and germinate into the present-day American Bahá'í community.

The author has meticulously researched the journey of 'Abdu'l-Bahá by combing through discourses as well as the diary of his traveling companion, which describes almost every major event during the journey as well as many private scenes and frank comments by 'Abdu'l-Bahá. The extensive research includes the examination of newspaper and magazine articles published at the time of this historic visit, as well as hundreds of pages of unpublished telegrams, letters, diaries, and memoirs.

PORTALS TO FREEDOM
Howard Colby Ives
$16.00 US / $18.00 CAN
Trade Paper
ISBN: 978-1-931847-99-5

A personal memoir that deals with spiritual transformation, and brings to life in warm and intimate detail the historical figure of 'Abdu'l-Bahá.

Portals to Freedom is an intimate portrait of one of the most significant religious figures in recent history, 'Abdu'l-Bahá—the son and appointed successor of the Prophet of the Bahá'í Faith. Author Howard Colby Ives offers us a remarkably candid and honest description of his own personal spiritual search as a Unitarian minister struggling with questions of faith and spirituality. His search ultimately led him to a discovery of the Bahá'í Faith just a short time before 'Abdu'l-Bahá arrived in North America in 1912 on a quest to share the teachings and vision of his father with the people of the West. In *Portals* we get not only Ives's personal reflections and inner struggles, but a fascinating eyewitness account of the words and actions of one who has been described by his Prophet-father as "the Mystery of God," is considered by Bahá'ís to be the perfect exemplar of the Faith's teachings, and who emerged from a lifetime of exile at the hands of the Ottoman Empire to travel tirelessly and share the Faith's message of unity in a profound and loving manner that touched the hearts of all with whom he came in contact.

SPIRIT OF FAITH
THE HUMAN SOUL
Bahá'í Publishing
$12.00 US / $14.00 CAN
Hardcover
ISBN: 978-1-61851-000-6

A collection of uplifting prayers and writings that focuses on the human soul for spiritual seekers of all faiths.

Spirit of Faith: The Human Soul is a compilation of writings and prayers that focus on the human soul and the qualities of this remarkable and unique aspect of our existence. Spiritual seekers of all faiths will relish these uplifting passages that offer a great deal of insight into the nature and significance of the human soul—a subject that has never been so extensively explored in the religious texts of the past. This collection contains writings from Bahá'u'lláh, the Báb, and 'Abdu'l-Bahá.

   The Spirit of Faith series explores a range of topics—such as the unity of humanity, the eternal covenant of God, the promise of world peace, and much more—by taking an in-depth look at how the writings of the Bahá'í Faith view these issues. The series is designed to encourage readers of all faiths to think about spirituality, and to take time to pray and meditate on these important topics.

TALKS BY 'ABDU'L-BAHÁ
THE EXISTENCE OF GOD
Bahá'í Publishing
$14.00 US / $16.00 CAN
Hardcover
ISBN: 978-1-61851-001-3

A spiritually uplifting and thought-provoking collection of talks that offers insight into the ability to know and worship God.

Talks by 'Abdu'l-Bahá: The Existence of God is a collection of talks given by 'Abdu'l-Bahá—the son and appointed successor of Bahá'u'lláh, the Prophet and Founder of the Bahá'í Faith—during his historic journey to Europe and North America in 1911 and 1912. Speaking in front of multiple audiences, 'Abdu'l-Bahá offered simple yet profound and logical proofs for the existence of God, and discussed humankind's relationship with its Creator. The talks included here present convincing and thought-provoking explanations for some of the weightiest and most complex theological questions we face when trying to untangle the mysteries of life.